# PSYCHOLOGY IN USE
An Introduction to Applied Psychology

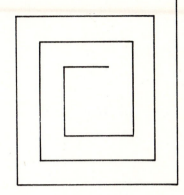

# PSYCHOLOGY IN USE
## An Introduction to Applied Psychology

## Duane P. Schultz
**American University**

**MACMILLAN PUBLISHING CO., INC.**
New York
**COLLIER MACMILLAN PUBLISHERS**
London

Macmillan Publishing Co., Inc.
866 Third Avenue, New York, New York 10022

Collier Macmillan Canada, Ltd.

**Library of Congress Cataloging in Publication Data**

Schultz, Duane P.          (date)
    Psychology in use : an introduction to applied
psychology.

    Includes bibliographies and index.
    1.  Psychology, Applied.  2.  Psychology.  I.  Title.
BF636.S376          158          78–5006
ISBN 0–02–408060–8

Printing:      4 5 6 7 8          Year:      1 2 3 4 5

**To my father**

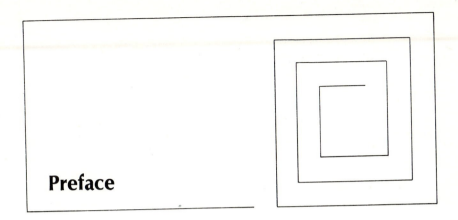

# Preface

The purposes of *Psychology in Use: An Introduction to Applied Psychology* are to introduce students to the many exciting real-world uses and applications of psychology and to demonstrate how psychology affects their personal life and the quality of life for all of us. In my experience, few students seem to develop an appreciation of the practical value of psychology. They learn in great detail the research studies psychologists conduct, but not how the findings are applied to everyday life.

The focus in this book is on psychology in action in areas such as mental and physical health, education, the world of work, the natural and built environments, consumer and voter behavior, the consciousness revolution, and crime and law enforcement. By learning how psychology has an impact on such issues of daily importance, students will be helped to make the difficult adjustments required in their adult lives and careers, and to achieve greater self-understanding.

In addition to learning how psychology is applied to common problems, students will find out how psychologists conduct their work. The methods used by different psychological specialties are presented in the context of solving real problems rather than as academic exercises. Psychological research procedures and techniques are shown to be as practical and necessary as the research results themselves.

The traditional topics presented to beginning students in psychology are discussed in *Psychology in Use* in a manner that offers an immediate awareness of what psychologists do and how the application of findings in areas such as perception, learning, and emotion affect our lives. For example, perception is illustrated through the application of perceptual research findings to the credibility of eyewitness testimony in the courtroom. Learning is presented in terms of actual teaching-learning situations in classrooms, factories, and offices. Emotion is discussed in the

context of its impact on physical health. By understanding how psychological research is applied to practical problems, students may become
motivated to learn more about our field.

*Psychology in Use* is written for the beginning student who has little
or no background in psychology; technical jargon is kept to a minimum.
Each chapter begins with a case study of an application of psychology to
a common situation, and ends with a summary of major issues and a list
of suggested readings. An appendix on the use of standard library tools
in psychology shows the student how to search the literature on psychological research and applications. For the instructor, a manual of
multiple-choice and essay questions is provided.

I wish to thank Gail Jackson, Bob Greives, and Robert Savannah of
Illustrations Unlimited, who prepared the imaginative drawings, and Hurd
Hutchins of Macmillan, who supervised the book's production with extraordinary patience and skill. It is a pleasure to record my gratitude to
my wife, Sydney Ellen, whose bibliographic and editorial abilities are
reflected on every page.

Duane P. Schultz

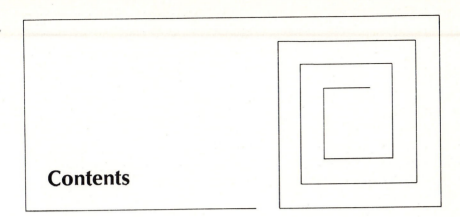

# Contents

# Applications of Psychology to Everyday Life

The woman is seated in a comfortable chair opposite the psychologist. He places a push button in her hand, then speaks in a quiet, calming manner.

"You will have to press this button every twenty seconds," he says. "When you do it right, you will hear the sound of a buzzer. If you are too early or too late, you will hear nothing. Now, go ahead and try."

The woman concentrates, mentally counting the passage of twenty seconds, and then presses the button. Nothing happens; she pressed it too soon. She tries again and this time waits too long.

After eight trials, the psychologist places a 100-watt light bulb directly in front of her that flashes every twenty seconds. All the woman has to do now is wait for the light to come on and then press the button.

But the woman cannot see the light. She can see nothing. She has been blind for five years, having lost her sight during a period of intense emotional and physical problems. At first, it was thought that a physical illness had caused the loss of vision, but repeated examinations revealed no physical reason for her blindness. She was then referred to a psychologist for a radical form of treatment known as *behavior therapy*, to see if it could cure psychologically caused blindness.

The light flashes on and off for eight trials and the patient's button-pressing performance improves slightly. Then the psychologist says he is going to give her a clue to help her. He guides her hand to the light and tells her that it will come on every twenty seconds, whenever it is time to press the button.

"I want you to look toward the light and concentrate on it very hard," the psychologist says.

The patient tries but does worse than before. She grows worried because she cannot see the light. The treatment continues for ten more minutes. Suddenly the woman stops pressing the button and sits absolutely still.

"What's wrong?" the psychologist asks.

Tears are forming in the woman's eyes and she becomes very excited.

"I can see the light," she cries. "I never believed this could happen!"

The treatment continues for several minutes more and she presses the button every time the light flashes. Then the psychologist secretly begins to dim the light, reducing it gradually to 30 watts. The patient continues to press the button every time the light comes on and says nothing about it growing dimmer. In fact, she says that she sees the light more clearly than before.

Next, the psychologist places paper cutouts of various shapes—circles, triangles, and stars—over the light and asks the patient to press the button whenever the light flashes and to tell what she sees. At first she sees only the light but, in a matter of minutes, she is able to identify the shapes.

Other visual symbols are used—simple drawings, letters and numbers, then complex pictures and print of varying sizes. Gradually, the patient is able to distinguish them all. Her blindness has disappeared.

The job is agonizingly dull and monotonous. The workers sit at their desks all day long doing the same thing over and over. It is an assembly line for words. Their task is to answer letters from the company's stockholders. Each morning employees are given a pile of letters to deal with, but they are not allowed to write the replies themselves. Instead, they must construct the letters from a file of form paragraphs designed to handle all situations. They simply combine paragraphs that seem appropriate and pass them on to a supervisor who examines each letter to make sure it is correct. Day in and day out, that is all these workers do.

This is an orderly system developed by management to ensure that no incorrect information is provided to stockholders. There is only one problem: it is an awful job. Worker absences are frequent, turnover is very high, productivity is low, many mistakes are made, and morale is terrible.

Alarmed by this situation, the company brings in a psychologist to see if morale and performance can be improved. After examining the structure and requirements of the job, the psychologist offers a radical recommendation. She totally redesigns the jobs to give each employee increased job duties and responsibility, the opposite of what management believes employees are capable of.

"If they don't work well when the job is simple," an executive asks, "what's going to happen if we make the job harder?"

Using a technique called *job enrichment*, the psychologist plans to give each employee more autonomy and authority. First, each worker is trained to become an expert in a particular area, such as the transfer of stock ownership. When a letter arrives with a question on that topic, it is automatically given to the employee–expert to answer. Next, the form paragraphs are discarded. The employees are allowed to write the replies in their own words.

In addition, letters are signed and mailed by those who wrote them, instead of being signed and verified by the supervisor. That way, if a mistake is made, the responsibility belongs to the individual employee and not the supervisor. Finally, employees are allowed to work at their own pace. No daily quotas are set for them. They decide for themselves how many letters to answer each day.

The results of this enlargement of job duties astound both employees and management. Employees work harder, faster, and better than ever before. Absenteeism drops to its lowest point, very few people quit, mistakes are rare, and morale is quite high. For the first time, the employees like their work. They are happier on the job and in their home life as well.

All this progress has been achieved without any increase in salary, or vacation time, or fringe benefits. The age-old philosophy of management and labor unions—that the only way to get people to work better is to pay them more—has been challenged. These employees are working more efficiently for psychological, not financial reasons.

Nationwide attention is focused on the trial. Reporters crowd the tiny courtroom. Outside, television camera crews wait for glimpses of the accused. Supporters shout and cheer as the defendants are led into the building. They seem unlikely people to be charged with conspiring to kidnap the U.S. Secretary of State and to blow up underground electrical conduits in Washington, D.C. Three of the defendants are Catholic priests, one is a nun, and two others are former clergy members.

This is a time of great national discord and unrest. The nation is involved in an unpopular war in Vietnam, and all across the country demonstrators are voicing their opposition. The defense attorneys are worried because the trial will take place in a small town noted for political conservatism. Is it possible, they ask, to find jury members who will not be hostile to a group of antiwar activists? The attorneys decide to enlist the help of psychologists to select scientifically a jury that might be sympathetic to the defendants' aims.

The psychologists begin their task by conducting a telephone survey of registered voters in the community and comparing the results with the characteristics of those persons on the jury panel (from among whom the jury will be chosen). They find that the registered voters are, on the average, younger than the persons on the jury panel, which means that the panel is not truly representative of the community. Believing that younger people will be more sympathetic to the accused, the defense attorneys show the survey results to the judge. He agrees to select a new panel that contains more young people.

Next the psychologists conduct an in-depth survey of the registered voters, questioning them about their attitudes and personal characteristics. Voters are asked what magazines and newspapers they read, what television programs they watch, how much they know about the case, what churches and other organizations they belong to, how much trust they have in the federal government, and how tolerant they are of protests against the government.

From an analysis of these data, the psychologists determine what kind of juror the defense attorneys should seek (and what kind they should avoid) when they question potential jury members in the courtroom. A profile is established of a person likely to be sympathetic to the defendants' antiwar activities. The results of the in-depth survey show that members of certain religious groups should be avoided (Episcopalians, Presbyterians, Methodists, and Fundamentalists), and others preferred (Catholics and Lutherans). College-educated Republicans over the age of thirty should be avoided, along with those who have a high trust in the federal government.

The characteristics of the ideal juror emerge: a woman who belongs to the Democratic party and has no strong religious affiliation, and who works at a white-collar or skilled blue-collar job.

Following these guidelines, the defense attorneys question prospective jurors carefully, challenging those persons whose characteristics and attitudes diverge widely from the profile. The jury selection process takes weeks, but finally the trial begins.

For two months, the prosecuting attorneys argue their case, presenting sixty-four witnesses. When it is the turn of the defense, the only response is, "The defense rests." The courtroom is stunned into silence.

The jury begins its deliberations. Seven days later the trial is over. The jury, with ten members voting for acquittal and two voting for conviction, is deadlocked. The federal government's $2 million attempt to convict the accused of conspiracy is declared a mistrial.

These three incidents are true. They serve to demonstrate the wide-ranging and often dramatic impact of psychology on our everyday lives. And that is the purpose of this book: to show how psychology is being used to promote human welfare and to improve the quality of life. Psychological research findings are being applied constantly, in countless ways, to make our lives more meaningful, effective, and productive.

Whatever your age, wherever you work, or however you spend your time, your life is influenced in some way by psychology. The work of no other discipline has such a direct and frequent bearing on your life. Let us briefly note some of the ways in which psychology influences us.

In school, you may have met the *school psychologist* responsible for the psychological testing and emotional and vocational counseling that influenced your progress from grade to grade and your choice of a career. Other psychologists are concerned with curriculum development and with increasing our ability to learn by applying psychological knowledge about learning and motivation to the classroom situation. Psychologists are also working on techniques and devices to facilitate learning, such as teaching machines, which have been very successful in helping students learn better and faster.

If you work for some sort of organization—a private company, the federal or state government, the military, a hospital, or a university—the contributions of *industrial psychologists* will determine how far you rise in rank and responsibility and how much satisfaction you derive from your job.

No matter what type of organization you work for, or what kind of work you do, your entire career—from the day you apply for the job until your retirement dinner—is influenced by psychologists.

How well you perform on the tests and selection devices they develop determines whether or not you are hired, the kind of work you are believed capable of doing, and the rank at which you begin. Once on the job your superiors periodically evaluate your performance—just as teachers do in the classroom—to determine your rate of progress and whether you deserve a pay raise, a promotion, or dismissal. These rating techniques are the products of psychological research and have an obvious bearing on your future.

Many organizations send their most promising employees to periodic training sessions on everything from advances in electronics to courses on motivating oneself and one's subordinates. These programs, which are usually steppingstones for promotion, are designed and may be conducted by psychologists.

Whether you work at a machine or a desk, it is likely that psychologists helped design the place in which you work. The layout of an assembly line, the design of complex manufacturing equipment, the arrangement of offices, and even the location of the plant itself are all concerns of industrial psychologists.

Although you may work for forty years and never meet an industrial psychologist in person, the quality of your working life is nevertheless influenced strongly by what industrial psychologists do.

Many of us experience emotional problems at some time in our lives. Some problems are of long duration and others are of a temporary nature in response to a particularly stressful event such as the loss of a loved one. Should you find yourself in these situations, you may desire the assistance of a *clinical psychologist* or a *counselor* to help you resolve your difficulties.

Many different psychological therapies and counseling techniques are in use today. They vary according to the therapist's training and theoretical orientation, and the emotional problem being dealt with. Psychotic or insane persons require extensive and long-term therapy. Persons suffering other problems, such as a temporary period of depression, can often be helped with more modest techniques of counseling in a few sessions.

Whatever the nature of your psychological problem—adjustment to normal periods of development such as adolescence or middle age, a marital crisis, a problem with children, or a crippling, long-term emotional disorder—there is psychological therapy available to help you cope with it.

Many people today seek psychological help even though they are not experiencing any emotional crisis or psychological problem. These people function normally and effectively, but nevertheless would like to function at a higher and healthier level. They are concerned with raising their consciousness levels, increasing their human potential, and actualizing or fulfilling all of their capabilities.

The *human potential movement* has attracted hundreds of thousands of people who have participated in sensitivity sessions, encounter groups, nude marathons, and other forms of growth therapy. Many of these people have apparently found dimensions or potentials in themselves that they never before realized they possessed.

Organizations as well as individuals are eagerly seeking human potential programs. Businesses, government agencies, school systems, employers of all sorts are sending their employees to consciousness-raising groups in the hope that they will develop greater awareness of and sensitivity to themselves and others. This "consciousness revolution" has already influenced the lives of many of us, and it is growing rapidly in popularity.

We are all consumers—of automobiles, toothpastes, deodorants, breakfast cereals, television programs, or political candidates. Each day we make decisions to change from one brand to another, to buy a new product, or to watch a particular program. The work of *consumer psychologists* is a major influence on these commonplace decisions.

You may well be attracted to one kind of mouthwash or one brand of beer because of the psychological image created for the product, the way in which it is packaged, or the emotional need it satisfies in you. These aspects of advertising and marketing emerge from psychological research on the reactions of persons like yourself to new products, new packages for existing products, and new advertising campaigns.

Consumer psychology is a controversial branch of psychology in use. Many people argue (with good reason) that these activities detract from, not contribute to our overall quality of life. However, whether consumer psychology is a force for good or for ill, there is no denying its tremendous impact on our everyday lives and on the nation's economy.

Techniques similar to those designed to help us deal with heartburn and bad breath are also used to sell political candidates. *Marketing methods* are used to create images and to package the personalities of candidates running for elective offices. Indeed, so successful are these activities that some elections are won or lost today not on the candidates' stands on specific issues or on their records of performance, but on how attractive they appear and how well their image comes across in the media.

*Public opinion polling,* a technique developed and refined for use in consumer psychology, affects our lives in areas outside the traditional marketplace. In politics, for example, candidates are alerted to the stand they should take on a particular issue with different constituent groups by the results of opinion polls conducted on those constituents.

Polling techniques are also used to determine television programming. The ratings that indicate whether a program will be canceled after only one month or allowed to run for three years are based on scientifically conducted polls of samples of television viewers.

The design of many consumer products is influenced by *engineering psychologists.* As these goods and gadgets for human use become more complicated, they also grow more difficult to operate efficiently, quickly, and with a minimum of error. In order to design products to take maximum advantage of human capabilities and compensate for human weaknesses, engineering psychologists work in conjunction with engineers.

For example, many of us travel in jet airplanes where our safety depends upon the pilot's ability to react instantly to emergencies and to control the plane safely. The physical and psychological demands on pilots have increased as planes have become faster and more complex. Engineering psychologists have helped pilots to function better in their demanding job by designing aircraft instruments and controls that can be operated quickly and efficiently.

On a different level, engineering psychologists have contributed to the design of automobile instrument panels and to the layout of controls on household items such as kitchen ranges and ovens. Psychologists were also responsible for the redesign of the modern telephone. By changing the motions involved in making a telephone call from dialing to pushing buttons, the time and effort required and the chance of error have been reduced.

We are all concerned about the quality of our natural environment. Considerable national attention has been focused on environmental pollution and the efforts to purify the water we drink and the air we breathe. Noise pollution in the major cities is also a vital concern.

*Environmental psychologists* are active in the efforts to reclaim and restore the environment. Pollution is not only an engineering and technical problem, it is also a psychological problem. There are many behavioral and emotional consequences of living in a polluted world.

Psychologists have conducted much research on the effects on humans of high noise levels, airborne chemical agents, extremes of weather and solar activity, and the overuse of pesticides. In addition, attitudes toward pollutants and other environmental hazards, and toward the organizations responsible for them, are continually being studied. This information yields valuable guidelines for government regulatory agencies about what must be done to alleviate the harmful effects of pollution.

*Environmental psychologists* are also active in studying the effects on our lives of artificial environments. For example, psychologists have investigated the effects on human behavior of the buildings in which we live and work, and they cooperate with architects and designers in the planning of these environments.

Environmental psychologists are concerned with such problems as the effects of crowding; of living and working in high-rise buildings and offices that lack windows; of various colors of walls and furnishings; of various designs and layouts for offices, homes, and apartments; and even of the design of bedrooms and bathrooms. They have developed guidelines for the design of public places to improve convenience, accessibility, physical security, appearance, and frequency of use. They are involved in the design of parks, central plazas and shopping malls, museums, public transportation systems, and even entire communities.

Most of us have been or will be ill at some time in our lives, falling victim to some sickness or disease and spending a great deal of time and money on physicians and hospitals in an effort to be cured. Although medical personnel are easily recognized as a vital part of the modern health care system, it is not generally known that *medical psychologists* also play an important role in maintaining our physical well-being.

Psychologists are active in pinpointing the relationship that seems to exist between personality and disease. Certain personality patterns may predispose some people to illnesses such as heart attacks, ulcers, and cancer. It has long been known that psychological stress can lead to psychosomatic diseases such as high blood pressure, rheumatoid arthritis, asthma, and some skin conditions. Knowledge of the psychological factors associated with disease can be extremely helpful in early identification and treatment, sometimes even before physical symptoms of a disease have appeared.

Medical psychologists also study the effects of emotional characteristics on patient recovery. They have found that patient attitudes toward a personal illness and toward the physician can actually affect the speed of recovery. In fact, these attitudes even bear on whether a patient will recover at all.

Psychologists also help patients who have terminal illnesses to better adapt to the certainty of death. This allows the patients to improve the quality of their remaining lives and their relationships with their families.

As discussed in the case of the blind woman at the beginning of the chapter, psychologists are able to cure certain physical disorders, and in other cases can relieve disturbing symptoms. Using the technique of biofeedback, psychologists teach people to control irregularities in their heartbeat, to lower their blood pressure, to relieve migraine headaches, to prevent epileptic attacks, and to reduce the level of stomach acid. Patients learn to control their own bodies and so are able to reduce the likelihood of acquiring certain diseases or disabilities.

Environmental psychologists have influenced our physical health care system through the design of medical facilities. Waiting and examination rooms are being made more attractive, comfortable, and inviting, thus helping to lessen patient anxiety. Clinics and hospitals are being redesigned to alter their institutional appearance.

The design of medical facilities not only influences patient attitudes, but it can also directly affect the amount and kind of care patients receive. For example, environmental psychologists have shown that hospital corridors that are radial or circular in design (instead of straight-line corridors) cause the nursing staff to pay significantly more attention to their patients; this certainly contributes to patient recovery.

Crime and violence are problems that affect us all. Even though you may never be the victim of a mugger or a burglar, you are still affected by the rising crime rate. Your taxes are high partly because of the cost of crime, and in certain sections of the city, perhaps even in your own neighborhood, you may not feel safe being out after dark. You may no longer go to a favorite restaurant or theater because you have read of increasing crime in the vicinity.

*Forensic psychologists* are directly concerned with problems of crime and are actively involved in all phases of crime prevention, criminal justice, and the penal and rehabilitation systems. Many police departments employ psychologists (full-time or consulting) to provide a variety of services.

These psychologists are developing appropriate selection techniques to eliminate those applicants for the police force who are psychologically or temperamentally unfit to be police officers. The psychologists also work daily with members of the police force. Police work is difficult and demanding; it places heavy burdens on the individuals and their families. Police department psychologists are involved in counseling police officers and families and in dealing with job-related stresses and crises.

Forensic psychologists may work to solve crimes, particularly murders. Through analysis of the crime itself, and clues the murderer may have left, psychologists may be able to develop a personality profile of the killer. With knowledge of personality characteristics, attitudes, background, and habits or mannerisms of the suspect, the search for the killer can often be narrowed considerably.

Psychologists employed in prison facilities are concerned with providing emotional counseling and with devising and conducting rehabilitation programs. Parole boards consider the recommendations of the prison psychologist when evaluating prisoners for parole.

In addition, both forensic and environmental psychologists are active in the design of penal institutions. They are concerned with the effects of crowding and of the design of cells, recreation, and work areas on prisoner behavior.

The findings of environmental psychologists influence the design of communities, homes, and apartment buildings to make them safer from crime. Dealing with what they call "defensible space," environmental psychologists work with architects to design crimeproof living environments. Some considerations are corridor design in high-rise buildings and the optimum distance between the street and the front door of a single-family dwelling.

As you can see, it is no exaggeration to state that psychology is everywhere and anywhere. Its influence is pervasive in our daily lives, affecting how we live and work and play. Because the various fields of psychology influence us so strongly, it is in your own best interest to know something about them. Psychology is personally important, timely, and relevant, and it is fascinating in its own right. What could be more interesting than learning about ourselves? As the study of human nature—human wants, needs, strengths, weaknesses, and capabilities—psychology is the only discipline that tries to understand who and what we are as human beings.

You may want to take additional courses in psychology. You may even want to major in the field and become a psychologist. If so, you will have to work hard, but you will also have the opportunity to contribute to the quality of life, both your own (through challenging and gratifying work) and that of others (through the effect your work will have on them). But that is for the future. For now, let us learn about psychology in use.

SUMMARY

Psychology influences our daily lives in many ways. No matter what we do or where we do it, the chances are great that we are affected, sometimes dramatically, by the contributions of psychologists.

*School psychologists* influence students through programs of psychological testing and emotional and vocational counseling, applications that affect students' personal well-being, their progress through school, and their future careers. School psychologists help determine curriculum content and develop ways of presenting material in the classroom to facilitate the learning process.

*Industrial psychologists* affect every aspect of our careers at work, no matter where we are employed or what kind of work we do. Industrial psychologists determine techniques of selection and training for nearly all jobs, as well as the specific procedures by which the progress of employees is periodically evaluated. Offices and factories are designed, in part, by psychologists, as are the procedures and processes by which much work is performed.

*Clinical psychologists* use a variety of techniques of therapy and counseling to deal with persons who have emotional problems. Whether the problems are mild or crippling, of short or long duration, clinical psychologists are equipped to help resolve them. Psychologists are also involved in the human potential movement, helping thousands of well-adjusted people find and release new and greater levels of potential creativity and personal fulfillment.

*Consumer psychologists* are concerned with the everyday decisions we make in shops and supermarkets, in front of our television sets, and in voting booths. The products we buy, the programs we watch, even the candidates we elect to public office are designed, packaged, and advertised using psychological techniques to increase their attractiveness and their potential to satisfy human needs.

*Engineering psychologists* help design many of the products we buy and use, from automobiles to airplanes, to make them easier and more efficient to operate. Various items of equipment in the factory, on the highway, and in the home are designed to make the best use of human capabilities and to compensate for human weaknesses.

*Environmental psychologists* are concerned with the quality of natural and artificial environments. By investigating the effects of different environments on human behavior, psychologists contribute to the design of more pleasant, safer, and more efficient homes, workplaces, and even entire communities.

*Medical psychologists* play an important role in the physical health care system through research on the psychological aspects of disease and the personality patterns linked to various illnesses. Psychologists influence the recovery rate of patients and their ability to cope with terminal illness, and the nature of the doctor–patient relationship. In addition, psychological techniques have been devised by which we can learn to control the functioning of our own bodies—slowing the heart rate, for example. These can be of immense value in relieving and combating certain diseases.

*Forensic psychologists* are involved with all aspects of crime and law enforcement, from detecting and apprehending criminals to rehabilitating them. They work with police departments, courts, and prisons in their efforts to help those who fight crime and those who commit crimes. In the process, they aid all of us, the potential victims of crimes.

## SUGGESTED READINGS

*American Psychologist*, a monthly journal published by the American Psychological Association, contains general articles on various topics in psychology.

*Annual Review of Psychology*, a yearly publication of Annual Reviews, Inc. (Palo Alto, California), contains chapters reviewing research, theory, and applications of psychology to current problems.

*APA Monitor*, a monthly newsletter published by the American Psychological Association, contains news about psychologists and their current interests.

McKeachie, Wilbert J. Psychology in America's bicentennial year. *American Psychologist*, 1976, **31**, 819–833.

McKinney, Fred. Fifty years of psychology. *American Psychologist*, 1976, **31**, 834–842.

# Psychology: What, How, Who, and Where

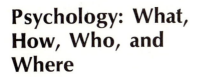

**2**

We live in the age of psychology. No other field of study has captured the imagination of so many people in the twentieth century as has psychology. We use the word "psychology" frequently in our everyday conversation, we read about psychology in our newspapers and magazines, and we hear about it on radio and television. It has become a passion, an obsession, even a religion for millions of people.

Not only do we use the term "psychology" in our daily lives, but a great many people also imagine that they are psychologists, and even act as though they were. In no other field are there so many practicing amateurs. People talk about using "psychology" to get someone to do something, or to get a job or a good grade.

"I used a little psychology on her," the young man says, describing how he talked the boss out of firing him.

The football coach tells reporters about the psychology of getting a winning football team.

The college student describes to her roommate her boyfriend's psychological condition. "I analyzed him," she reports, and proceeds to detail all the problems she thinks he has.

"I have to be part psychologist in my job," the sales manager says. "I have to know the right psychological moment to push for a sale."

A business executive says, "All I need to know about people I can find out by looking them in the eye and talking to them for a few minutes. All it takes is a little psychology."

"I'm really psyched up for this exam," the student says.

Most of these people who talk about psychology have one thing in common: they are usually wrong. Most people who think they are "psychologists" do not really know what psychology is or how psychologists work. They believe that psychology is easy, that a talent for psychology develops naturally from interacting with or liking other people, or that they are "born psychologists." They confuse psychology with psychiatry or think that all psychology came from Sigmund Freud. They believe that psychologists are "shrinks," that psychologists can read a person's mind, and that psychologists are a little weird.

Having met many weird psychologists, I will not argue that point too strongly, but I have also met many weird engineers, historians, salespersons, television repairmen, and students. All the other commonplace assumptions, however, are incorrect, and they demonstrate a general confusion about the nature of psychology. We shall deal with these points in the remainder of this chapter and discuss what psychology is, how it works, who psychologists are, and where they perform the many services that affect the lives of us all.

## WHAT IS PSYCHOLOGY?

Like physics, chemistry, or medicine, psychology is a highly professional and serious field of study that requires years of solid preparation to master. Human nature is probably the most difficult of all subjects because it is elusive, complex, and often perverse. Unlike chemicals in a test tube, which may remain stable and unchanging from one day to the next, human beings do not always act in the same way. They change from day to day, even minute to minute, and will not stay still under the microscope of observation. Consequently, great skill and patience are required to try to understand who and what we are.

Despite the difficulties, we know that the study of human nature has fascinated and perplexed scholars from the beginning of recorded history—and probably also did so even before that time. And why not? We are, after all, an intriguing subject for study. The writings of early philosophers contain speculations, intuitions, and some perceptive observations about human nature.

The word "psychology" comes from the Greeks, who combined two words, "psyche," meaning mind, soul, or spirit, and "logos," meaning knowledge of or study of. This definition of psychology—the study of the mind—lasted until the latter years of the nineteenth century.

Around 1879, psychology was given a new definition and status. It became a totally separate and independent discipline, no longer a part of philosophy. The new definition expressed a radical change in the way in which human nature was to be studied. Psychology was no longer defined as the study of the mind but rather as the *science* of the mind. Modeling itself after the older sciences, particularly physics, the new science of psychology rejected all approaches that were not based on observation and hence were not objective. Meditation, intuition, and inference were discarded as methods and the more rigorous techniques of observation and experimentation were adopted. Thus, the new psychology—now a science—was developing.

In the approximately 100 years since psychology became a science, the field has grown and broadened in many ways. Considerable discussion and controversy about the proper subject matter and methods of psychology have marked this century of history. The issues remain unresolved because psychology is different things to different people.

There is not a single psychology in existence today. Instead, there are several forms of psychology, each geared to a specific purpose. Some psychologists are interested solely in *behavior*, in what people do and say in response to certain stimuli. Other psychologists are concerned with how people feel, with what their *conscious* experiences are. Still others are trying to understand the deep, powerful, *unconscious* forces that motivate human beings.

Each of these approaches to psychology is legitimate and valuable, and each is influential in improving our quality of life. They are all concerned with understanding who and what we are, although they deal with different aspects of that question. Behavior, conscious experience, and unconscious experience are all the subjects of psychology today.

Although psychologists differ in terms of the aspect of human nature they study, they generally agree on what approach to take. Psychology is still a science; that has remained unchanged over the past one hundred years. As we shall see, different kinds of psychologists use different methods. For example, psychologists who try to cure neurotics work differently from those who try to determine the conditions that help people learn better. But the overall approach taken by all psychologists is the scientific one. A science is a body of facts that are organized systematically so as to illustrate the operation of general laws. This characterizes the way in which psychologists work and remains the central core of all psychological research.

Psychology, then, is the science of behavior and of mental phenomena and processes, and is a profession that is dedicated to the promotion of human welfare.

## HOW DO PSYCHOLOGISTS WORK?

Because different kinds of psychologists study different aspects of human nature, they have to use different techniques. These techniques include the experimental method, the method of systematic or naturalistic observation, the correlational method, the clinical methods, and the survey methods. But regardless of the specific technique used, all require the scientific, objective observation of facts.

## The Experimental Method

Imagine that you are an industrial psychologist working for a clothing manufacturer, and you are faced with the following problem. The management of the company is disturbed about the low production levels of its sewing machine operators and calls on you, the company psychologist, to find a way of increasing employee productivity.

From your experience and training in industrial psychology, you know that many factors could account for low productivity; for example, low pay, insufficient job training, a disagreeable supervisor, or poor equipment. However, after examining all aspects of the work process and the workplace, you suspect that the problem is inadequate lighting. You believe that productivity will increase if the lighting is improved.

In scientific terminology, we would say that you have formed a *hypothesis*. In everyday terms, we would say that you have formed a hunch or an educated guess, educated because you inferred it on the basis of your own observation and experience.

Armed with a hypothesis, you are now ready to test it, to see if the prediction that improved lighting will lead to improved productivity is correct. How do you do that? The most precise way to test the hypothesis is to conduct an experiment; increase the lighting and see if the sewing machine operators work faster.

In essence, conducting an experiment is like saying, "Let's try it and see what happens." But there is one important qualification. In an experiment, trying something must be done under well-controlled and systematic conditions. Let us discuss in detail what an experiment involves before dealing with the sewing machine operator problem.

An *experiment* can be defined as a technique for determining the effect of a single variable or event on the behavior of a group of people. The people being studied in an experiment are called *subjects*. We are constantly exposed to stimuli in the world around us—lights, noises, sounds, sights, smells, tastes, instructions, orders, trivial conversation, requests, and so on. If a psychologist wants to find out the effect of just one of these *stimuli* or *variables* (for example, the effect of increased lighting), a situation must be arranged in which only that single variable is allowed to operate. The other variables must be eliminated or kept at constant levels during the experiment. If the subjects' behavior changes (for example, if they work faster) while only the experimental variable has been in operation, then we can be quite certain that the variable alone was responsible for the change in behavior. The change could not have been caused by any other variable because no other variable was allowed to operate during the experiment.

There are two kinds of variables in a psychological experiment. One is the stimulus or *independent variable*, which we can manipulate, and the other is the *dependent variable,* the subjects' behavior in response to our manipulations.

How does all this apply to your problem as the industrial psychologist for the clothing manufacturer? The two variables in your sewing machine operator experiment are easy to identify. The independent variable is the level of illumination. You want to find out what effect increasing the lighting will have on the workers' production rate. Therefore, the resulting production rate (the workers' behavior) is the dependent variable.

Both variables can be observed and measured accurately. With a light meter you can measure the brightness level in the sewing room, and you can count the number of units of work accomplished per hour or per day. The precise *measurement* of both variables is necessary in an experiment; indeed, this is a basic requirement of the experimental method.

So you begin your experiment. First, you must measure the present lighting level and the rate of production under the existing brightness conditions so that the current production rate can be compared with the rate of production after the lighting has been increased. If the hypothesis is correct, production will rise after you increase the brightness of the room. Company records indicate that the current average rate of production is eight units per work hour.

You arrange for the plant electrician to install brighter lights in the sewing room. You wait a certain period of time—say, two weeks—and then measure the rate of production.

Production has increased from eight units to fourteen units per work hour, a large difference. It seems that your hunch was correct and your hypothesis has been confirmed. You have proved that increasing the level of illumination leads to an increase in production, haven't you?

No! You have not proved anything, except that you have not yet learned how to conduct a proper experiment. A vital ingredient of the experimental method was omitted. Reexamine the lighting experiment you conducted. How do you know that some factor other than the increased lighting did not cause the increase in production, some factor of which you were unaware?

Perhaps during the two weeks of the experiment the usually disagreeable supervisor was very pleasant to the workers because he or she knew that you, the company psychologist, would be around. Maybe the workers produced more because they saw you and thought that their jobs were in jeopardy. Or perhaps it was simply that the weather was pleasant during the experimental period, improving worker morale. Many factors, in addition to better lighting, could have led to a production increase. An industrial psychologist must control all these possible influencing variables.

In order to properly control for the operation of factors other than the one you are interested in studying, an experiment must involve two groups of subjects, the *experimental group* and the *control group,* both chosen at random from the same population of subjects.

The experimental group is the one on which the experiment is conducted. In your case, the experimental group consists of the workers who get the increased lighting. The control group does not receive any experimental treatment. In your study, the control group continues to work under the lighting conditions that it has always had.

Measures of the production rates are taken from both the control and experimental groups before and after the experimental period. That way, it is possible to tell if any factors other than the one you are studying have influenced the production rate. If they have, then both groups would show the same results. If they have not—if only the increased lighting influenced the subjects' behavior—then only the experimental group should show a difference in production rate at the end of the experiment. The production rate of the control group would not be affected.

Now, using both experimental and control groups, you conduct the lighting experiment and obtain the following results: the control group's production level remains the same (eight units per work hour before the experimental period and eight after). The experimental group shows an increase in production from eight units per work hour to fourteen (see Table 2–1). You can conclude with certainty that your hunch was correct; increasing the illumination level brought about an increase in production. This increased production could only have been caused by the increased lighting, because all other possible influencing variables had been controlled.

The experimental method is the most precise of all the methods used in psychology and, as a general rule, it should be used whenever and wherever it can. However, the experimental method has certain weak-

**Table 2–1.** Experimental Design

|  | Experimental Group | Control Group |
|---|---|---|
| Average Individual Pre-Experiment Production (units per hour) | 8 | 8 |
|  | Experimental Treatment (brighter lights) | No Treatment |
| Average Individual Post-Experiment Production (units per hour) | 14 | 8 |

nesses and limitations, and there are some situations in which it cannot be used.

Several important aspects of human behavior cannot be studied under the rigorous control and manipulation required by the experimental method: for example, the behavior of people caught up in a panic or a riot. Civil defense organizations and police departments would like to know more about how people behave in those situations. Information from experimental studies could easily lead to methods of preventing panics and riots or stopping them once they have begun. But it cannot be done. It is too dangerous to expose human beings to these situations in the name of science. Psychologists cannot assemble different groups of people in theaters, for example, and then observe how they react when the buildings are set on fire.

Mental health experts would be better able to help people if they had information resulting from controlled experiments on different techniques of child rearing or on the effects of different marital situations. However, ethical considerations prevent such manipulations of human lives.

Another limitation of the experimental method is that circumstances often dictate that an experiment be conducted in an artificial setting, one that attempts to duplicate the conditions of the real world, although subjects recognize that the conditions are not the same as those in the real world. In industry, for example, psychologists often conduct research on new procedures for job performance, new equipment, or new ways of training workers. In many cases the companies support the research because they want to know the results, but they will not let the psychologists conduct the research in the actual job situation.

Carrying out an experiment on the job could greatly disrupt production, reducing the quantity and quality of the goods produced or the efficiency of the office. Consequently, psychologists have to establish a simulated job environment—a duplicate work area—in which to conduct an experiment. This means that the research results are based on how the subjects behave in a situation that may be similar to but is actually not the same as the job setting to which the research findings will be applied. How relevant the findings are depends on how closely the simulated environment resembles the real-world environment.

Another problem with the experimental method is that people may behave differently not because of the manipulation of the independent variable, but simply because they know they are being observed. This is especially true when the subjects are employees of an organization. They may think that their jobs depend on how well they perform in the experiment, so they may work extra hard to please the psychologist and their employer. Obviously, this behavior is not normal job behavior.

People can also react to an experiment in the opposite way. They may resent being part of an experiment and express this resentment by deliberately trying to ruin the study. They may behave in ways opposite to how they think the psychologist wants them to behave.

Reacting in either manner defeats the purpose of the experiment because these behaviors are influenced by the subjects' attitudes toward being in an experiment, a variable quite different from the one the psychologist is studying.

Despite these recognized limitations, the experimental method remains the most accurate and desirable way to study how human beings behave. Experimental research is difficult to conduct properly, but when it is well controlled and systematic it provides the best information available on behavior in different conditions and situations.

## The Systematic Observation Method

When or where it is impractical or undesirable to study human beings by the experimental method, it is often possible to study them by observing them in the real world. The systematic observation method is used frequently by psychologists and it offers certain advantages.

All of us observe other people every day. It is a fascinating pastime and we often learn interesting things about people by watching them. We observe children, students, professors, strangers at airports, and friends in restaurants. And while we are observing others, they are observing us.

Psychologists observe people also but they do it in a more systematic and objective manner. As with the experimental method, psychologists try to exert some control over variables that may affect the behavior of the persons being observed. An element of *control* over the variables is the most important requirement of the method of systematic observation.

There is a fundamental difference between the method of systematic observation and the experimental method. In systematic observation, psychologists do not intrude into the situation to manipulate or change the independent variable. In the experimental method, psychologists change the conditions of the situation, as did the psychologist who increased the lighting level in our last example. In systematic observation, psychologists must work with the actual conditions as they find them, and they cannot alter those conditions.

Suppose that you are the director of the Department of Motor Vehicles in a large city. You are concerned about traffic accidents at intersections where drivers fail to stop. You want to install either stop signs or blinking red lights at the most dangerous corners, but you do not know which signal will be more effective.

You ask the help of Dr. Jackson, a psychologist at the local university, and she tells you that she will study the problem by the method of systematic observation. You are surprised at this; you took a couple of psychology courses in college and know about the advantages of the experimental method.

"Why don't you conduct an experiment?" you ask. "In your laboratory at the university I know you have automobile simulators. I even drove one once. It was almost like driving a real car." [1]

"Yes," Dr. Jackson says, "and those simulators are valuable for studying conditions that would be too dangerous to set up on the highway. But they also have a disadvantage. You said it yourself. 'It was *almost* like driving a real car.' It's not the same as actually being out on the road.

"Also, when you bring subjects into the laboratory, they know they're being studied. They might drive quite differently from when they are in their own cars and don't think anyone is watching them."

Then the psychologist describes to you how the systematic observation will be conducted and you agree to try it because it sounds almost as rigorous as an experiment, without the disadvantages of using the simulators.

The psychologist selects two intersections in the city at which to observe driver behavior. One has a stop sign and the other has a blinking red light. The independent variables are the signals (the stop sign and the blinking red light) and the dependent variable is driver behavior in response to the signals (whether the drivers slowed, came to a complete stop, or drove through the intersection without slowing or stopping).

The independent variables cannot be manipulated; they cannot be presented in different sequences or at different frequencies as they could in a laboratory. However, other variables likely to affect driver behavior can be controlled.

First, by positioning the observers in doorways, the psychologist makes sure that the drivers do not know they are being observed. Second, both intersections chosen are in the same neighborhood. Had intersections in different neighborhoods been used, one set of drivers might have differed radically from the other, for example, in socioeconomic status or ethnic background. These variables could be related to respect for the law or to general obedience to rules. Third, drivers who stop or slow down at the intersections because of a car in front of them are not counted. As you can see, it is possible to control variables that could influence driver behavior and to make totally objective observations using this method.

The results of the systematic observation did not present clear-cut findings that could help you as director of the Department of Motor

---

[1] In automobile simulators, the road ahead is presented on film and the subject manipulates the controls of a stationary car in reaction to turns, curves, stop signs, other cars, and other driving situations on the film.

Vehicles to decide which signal to use. (Sometimes this happens with research, no matter what method is used, and it reflects no failing on the part of the psychologist.) No more than half of the drivers came to a full stop for either signal. In other words, the stop sign and the blinking red light were equally effective or equally ineffective, depending on your point of view.

The study was worthwhile, however, because it could have shown that one signal was much more effective than the other. As it is, at least you can be certain that this is *not* the case; it has been so demonstrated. Sometimes there are no easy solutions.

So what do you do about these dangerous intersections? Which signal do you install? The psychologist reports that the perceptive observers noted something of interest that could help you make your decision. Many drivers confronted by the stop sign did not stop until they were past the intersection line. This was not the case with drivers who faced the blinking red light. On the basis of this information, the psychologist concluded that the light could be seen from a greater distance, something in its favor.[2]

However, as is often the case with such practical decisions, the choice has to be made not only in terms of research findings but also in terms of costs. Blinking red lights may offer an advantage, but they cost considerably more than stop signs.

Which signal will you choose?

## The Correlational Method

Dr. Phillips is a psychologist working for a metropolitan police department that has a serious problem. More than 30 per cent of the department's rookie police quit during their first year on the job. This high turnover costs the city a great deal of money. It is expensive to train new police officers and this investment is quickly lost when they quit. The fact that so many have resigned has also damaged the department's morale.

Something must be done. Some way must be found to identify those who are likely to quit the job before they are hired and sent to the police academy for training.

The police commissioner calls for Dr. Phillips and dumps the problem in his lap.

"And I want the answer soon!" the commissioner snaps.

For a psychologist, this is a very straightforward problem and a com-

[2] The example of the systematic observation method was suggested by C. F. Hummel and G. R. Schmeidler, "Driver Behavior At Dangerous Intersections Marked By Stop Signs Or By Red Blinker Lights," *Journal of Applied Psychology*, **39** (1955), 17–19.

mon one in many areas of psychology. What is needed is an investigation of how the police officers who quit differ from the police officers who remain on the job. Are there differences in intelligence, personality, attitudes, grades in school, family background, or some other variable that can distinguish between these two groups? If so, if those who quit have, for example, measurably different personalities or levels of intelligence from those who stay, that information can be used to predict, before hiring, the candidates most likely to stay on the job.

What Dr. Phillips must find, then, is the degree or strength of the relationship between two variables—for example, between scores on a personality test and remaining on the job. Scientists call this relationship the *correlation.*

Fortunately, when the police department hires police cadets, it gives them a number of psychological tests. If this were not the case, Dr. Phillips would have to give these tests himself; this is not an impossible task, but it would take considerable time. With the test results available, however, the investigation is a simple one.

First, Dr. Phillips collects the test scores and background information on all the men and women who entered the police academy over a period of three years. He examines the information for two items, the test scores of those who are still on the job and the test scores of those who quit during their first year.

For each person, the scores are correlated with longevity on the job by using a statistical formula. The results show the precise degree of relationship between these two variables (test scores and time on the job). In this case, Dr. Phillips found that those persons who quit the police force scored consistently lower on certain personality characteristics than those who stayed. These characteristics, then, clearly distinguish between the two groups of police officers.

Armed with his findings, Dr. Phillips persuades the police department not to hire anyone who scores below a certain level on these personality characteristics. At the end of one year it was found that the turnover rate had dropped from 30 per cent to only 6 per cent, a tremendous difference that reduced the department's expenses and raised morale. The research also benefited those who might have been hired for a job for which they were temperamentally unsuited.

The correlational method is used in those situations in which a prediction must be made about whether a person is likely to succeed, for example, in school, on a job, or in specialized work such as pilot training. College entrance examinations and aptitude and interest tests are based on correlational studies that have demonstrated the degree of relationship between the test scores and success or failure in the classroom or on the job. Whether you are admitted to college or graduate school or are hired for a certain job depends on this kind of correlational study.

## The Clinical Methods

John W. is a twenty-year-old man with a serious problem: he keeps failing at everything he tries. He had a very difficult time throughout his school years but only with his male teachers. With female teachers, John W. was a different person. He was pleasant, obedient, polite, and he made high grades. When he graduated from high school, John W. enrolled at a nearby community college but stayed only one semester. All the teachers there were men.

John W. tried a series of jobs but the result was always the same; he was fired from each one for insolence and insubordination. Whenever a boss (and they were all men) told John to do something, he rebelled. A similar experience occurred in the army, but in that situation it was much worse. John got into a fight with a sergeant during the first week of basic training and was badly beaten. The army gave him a dishonorable discharge.

John's girl friend, Marianne, finally persuaded him to see a psychologist.

"But I'm not crazy," John said. "I don't need to see a shrink."

"Nobody said you're crazy, John," Marianne replied, "but look at what you've done with your life. You need help."

Reluctantly, John went to the county mental health center and was assigned to a clinical psychologist, Dr. Rowe. Luckily for John, the psychologist was a woman.

Clinical psychologists treat people of all ages—from children to retired persons—who have all types of problems. The psychologists use a variety of clinical methods to try to understand these people so that they can help relieve them of their emotional burdens.

A major technique used by most clinical psychologists involves taking a detailed *life history* of the patient, looking for clues in their background that might indicate the source of the problem. Not all clinical psychologists believe, however, that emotional problems originate in childhood. Some psychologists prefer to deal with the patient's present interpersonal relationships or with their future goals. However, most clinicians do believe that background factors are of importance in understanding their patients.

Dr. Rowe questioned John W. carefully about his childhood, particularly his relationship with his parents. In the first meeting, John told Dr. Rowe of his problem getting along with older men, so she was especially interested in how John, as a child, had gotten along with his father.

Thus, the psychologist formed a hypothesis on the basis of her initial observation of John. It appeared likely to her that for some reason John harbored considerable hostility toward his father, which he was acting out in his relationships with all other older men in positions of authority—teachers, bosses, and the army sergeant.

Because the basic approach is a scientific one, the psychologist proceeded to test the hypothesis against the facts of John's background. By inquiring into his childhood relationship with his father, Dr. Rowe will uncover data that will confirm or fail to confirm the hypothesis about the source of John's problem.

Probing into John's childhood was a difficult task, one that John fought almost every session, particularly when the questions related to his father. He talked openly and lovingly of his mother but when the conversation turned to his father, John's face grew bitter and angry and his voice became loud and harsh.

Finally, after many weeks, the psychologist was able to get John to discuss his father in detail, and once he began, the words poured out almost nonstop. In an emotional voice, John described how his father beat him, usually for no reason except that his father was drunk. John's mother was beaten, too; John remembered how, at age four, he had tried to defend his mother. This only caused his father to beat them both more severely.

After reliving these awful childhood experiences, John felt somewhat better, and under the psychologist's guidance he began to see how he had generalized his hatred of his father to all older men in positions of power.

John was not cured overnight. It has been a long and continuing struggle, but because of his sessions with Dr. Rowe, he has held the same job for three years, is happily married, and has a child of his own.

There are other methods used by clinical psychologists, depending upon the nature of a patient's difficulties. *Psychological tests* are frequently given to help diagnose an emotional problem and to reveal aspects of the personality that a patient might be unaware of or unable to talk about openly. *Dream analysis* is also used for the same purpose.

Although the clinical methods are, in general, scientific in their basic approach, they do not offer the same degree of precision found in the experimental method or the correlational method. The data obtained by the clinical methods are much more subjective and deal with largely unconscious phenomena. Such data cannot be measured precisely and are open to the personal biases and interpretations of the clinical psychologist.

Nevertheless, clinical methods are valuable in dealing with disturbed and troubled personalities, unconscious conflicts, and the lingering effects of childhood traumas. No other techniques in psychology are appropriate for such phenomena. Although not as objective as other methods, the clinical methods do provide us with a window through which to view the inner depths of the human personality.

## The Survey Methods

The audience in the movie theater watches the film intently. As each scene flickers on the screen, they react to it internally, as we all do when we see a movie or a television program. Some people like certain scenes, others dislike them; some like the movie as a whole, others do not.

But there is something different about this audience. Every few seconds they are communicating their reactions to the movie producer and those reactions are being permanently recorded, to be studied and analyzed in detail at a later time. The film that the audience is seeing is the pilot for a new television series.

Each member of the audience holds a small plastic box that contains two push buttons. When the people see something they like, they press the top button; when they see something they do not like, they press the bottom button. When they feel neutral or indifferent toward a scene, they press neither button. By analyzing the record of the button presses and the scenes during which they occurred, the producer of the series can tell how much the audience liked the various parts of the program as well as the film as a whole. Then, specific scenes that most of the audience disliked can be omitted or rewritten.

In the conference room of a large office building, a group of people are shown a series of advertisements and then questioned about specific parts of the ads in order to see how much they remembered. In a supermarket an interviewer questions shoppers about their buying habits and which of several brands of peanut butter they prefer. From a noisy room filled with banks of telephones, interviewers call people at their homes to find out which candidate they plan to vote for in the coming election.

All these activities, which occur every day, have one thing in common. They are attempts to measure people's attitudes or feelings about something—a product, an advertisement, or a television program. Whereas the experimental and systematic observation methods deal with actual behavior—what people do in certain situations—the survey methods deal with what people *say* they do or will do. These methods are called survey methods because they survey or sample our attitudes, opinions, or feelings.

The survey methods of research have become big business and have a tremendous impact on many aspects of our lives. They have led to the development of highly accurate, scientific measuring instruments that attempt to make objective and systematic observations. However, because of the subject matter with which they deal, survey methods cannot be as precise or objective as techniques that observe actual human behavior.

The major difficulty with survey methods is that people often say they are going to do one thing and then do something totally different. Sometimes they simply change their minds, for example telling an interviewer on Friday that they plan to vote Republican and then voting Democratic on Tuesday. Sometimes people say they prefer a certain product or brand because they think it will make them look better to the interviewer. For example, they may say they always drink expensive imported beer, but if the interviewer could look in their refrigerators (or check their trash cans) it would be found that they actually drink a cheap local brand. They may not have wanted to appear cheap or unsophisticated to the interviewer.

This source of error can defeat the many hours of work that went into constructing the survey, and it also accounts for lost elections and bankrupt companies. The fault lies not in the methods themselves but in the complex, vague, and often perverse nature of what is being studied—our attitudes, preferences, and opinions. However, you have only to look at elections that were predicted accurately, and products or television programs that have succeeded, to see how valuable survey methods of research can be. They succeed more often than they fail.

There are three basic interviewing situations: in person, by mail, or by telephone. The *face-to-face interview* provides the greatest amount of information but it is also the most expensive and time-consuming technique, and cost must be considered. It takes a great deal of time to question, say, 200 people for an hour each, and to pay trained interviewers for that time. However, when time and money allow, personal interviews can provide very accurate results.

*Mail surveys* are much less expensive and time consuming but they have one serious problem: many people do not return questionnaires they receive in the mail. Thus, it is difficult to obtain responses from all the people selected for the sample. *Telephone surveys* may be the cheapest of all to conduct, and interviewers can keep calling until they talk with all the persons on their list.

The most important aspect of any survey is determining which people to question. If you are interviewing people about a forthcoming presidential election, for example, it is impractical (and probably impossible) to question every eligible voter in the country. Instead, you must construct a *representative sample* of all eligible voters, a population in miniature that reflects in the proper proportions all the characteristics of the larger population. If done correctly, a survey of a sample of only a few thousand persons can provide an accurate prediction of how a population of several million would have responded had they all been questioned. Thus, surveys can provide extremely valuable information on many aspects of our lives.

There is nothing mysterious about psychology's research methods. They all involve some sort of observation of behavior, of conscious feelings, or of unconscious motivations. They are all beneficial to society because they provide psychologists with data that can be used to influence our lives in many ways.

A general understanding of research methods is important for anyone studying the applications of psychology to everyday life. Should you want to become a psychologist, you will have to learn much more about these basic tools, but for now you have learned the essence of what they are and how psychologists use them in their work.

## WHO ARE PSYCHOLOGISTS?

The first step in defining who psychologists are is to specify who and what they are not. Psychologists are not psychiatrists, even though many people believe them to be the same. Although it is true that psychiatrists and one type of psychologist (the clinical psychologist) both work with emotionally disturbed persons and use some of the same clinical methods, they differ in terms of their training and basic professional orientation.

Psychiatrists receive medical training, have the M.D. degree, and become physicians first. They then spend several years specializing in the diagnosis and treatment of emotional illness. Clinical psychologists are trained solely in psychology, hold the Ph.D. degree, and undergo supervised internship in diagnosis and therapy. Because they do not have medical training, clinical psychologists cannot conduct physical examinations, prescribe drugs, or administer certain kinds of physical therapy, such as electric shock therapy. Clinical psychologists can recommend these courses of action but cannot prescribe them or carry them out.

### Becoming a Psychologist

If you are interested in becoming a psychologist you have already made a modest beginning by enrolling in this course, but there are many additional courses you must take. Psychology is a demanding field of study that requires a high degree of motivation, discipline, and sheer hard work. In that respect, psychology does not differ from any other professional or scientific field. Medicine, law, biology, history, indeed most other fields require a serious and long-term commitment if one is to succeed.

As a college undergraduate you should take as many courses in psychology as possible without neglecting related fields or courses that are of general interest to you. You will be a better psychologist, and a more interesting person, if your knowledge extends beyond psychology. Therefore, you may want to take advantage of some elective courses as an undergraduate and save the total immersion in psychology for graduate school.

If you want to become a psychologist, you must go to graduate school. Just as a B.A. or B.S. degree in chemistry or biology will not make you a professional chemist or biologist, so a B.A. or B.S. in psychology will not make you a professional psychologist. The undergraduate major in psychology is a preparation for advanced study. In practical terms, you cannot get a job as a psychologist with only an undergraduate degree.

Graduate schools are selective and competition is keen. Your grades as an undergraduate should be mostly A's and B's, particularly in the junior/senior years and in psychology courses.

Graduate schools offer two advanced-degree programs in psychology, the M.A. or M.S. and the Ph.D. The master's degree is the minimum degree required to work as a psychologist, and it usually involves one or two years of full-time study. In many applied areas of psychology, particularly industrial psychology, employment opportunities are quite good for persons who have a master's degree, but opportunities are better for persons who have earned doctoral degrees.

A Ph.D. requires from three to five years of work, but once obtained, many more positions are open than to persons who have a master's degree. This is especially true for college teaching, in which nearly half of all psychologists in the United States are engaged. In all areas of employment, persons with the Ph.D. will generally rise faster to higher levels of rank and responsibility than persons with the master's degree.

## Types of Psychologists

As discussed in Chapter 1, there are different types of psychologists today working on various aspects of human nature in many settings. What type of psychologist you are interested in becoming depends on what aspect of human nature interests you most. Do you want to work with persons who are disturbed, with architects in designing communities, or with engineers in designing equipment? Do you want to develop new methods for selecting and training the right employees for the best jobs, or to work with the police force, or to work with physicians in helping to cure physical illnesses? Or do you want to understand human nature simply to satisfy your own curiosity, and not to apply psychological knowledge and techniques to improve human lives?

In general, there are two kinds of psychologists: those interested in basic or *pure research* and those interested in *applied research*. Psychologists interested in pure research are concerned with the search for knowledge and understanding for its own sake, independent of any practical application such knowledge might have. This does not mean that basic research never has any practical value; such an assumption is untrue. What it means is that pure research is not designed to satisfy some immediate, practical need. It is carried out to satisfy the curiosity of the scientist. The results of pure research will often have practical value. Indeed, much pure research has had eventual real-world application.

Many psychologists find that pure research offers an immensely satisfying and exciting career. Working mostly in universities, psychologists conducting pure research are free to investigate whatever their own interests and curiosities dictate. They are not constrained by real-world problems or by deadlines imposed by management, a school board, or a suicidal patient.

Applied psychologists, on the other hand, conduct research on problems that directly affect our lives. However, applied psychologists often spend more time applying psychological findings to practical problems than in conducting research. Also, applied psychologists are often under great time pressure in their work. The real world does not always allow sufficient time to conduct adequate research. Contracts and deadlines must be met, and people must be helped, so applied psychologists are frequently required to provide answers or solutions more quickly than psychologists engaged in pure research. Applied psychologists do have the satisfaction of being able to see directly and immediately how their efforts lead to a betterment of the human condition.

Our focus in this book is on applied psychology, but this does not suggest that applied psychologists are more valuable than their colleagues who conduct pure research. Both types are vital to understanding and improving human nature, and in many cases applied psychologists would not have sufficient information to apply to pressing problems without the data supplied by pure researchers.

Once you have decided on pure or applied psychological research for your career, the choices are not yet over. There are a variety of specialities within psychology today, and each speciality deals with a different aspect of human behavior.

The American Psychological Association, the professional organization to which most psychologists belong, has thirty-five affiliated divisions. Each division represents a scientific, professional, or applied speciality (Table 2–2). Each of these divisions represents a different area in which psychologists contribute to human betterment.

You can see from the variety of specialities that all psychologists are not of identical persuasion, training, or temperament. So when you label someone a psychologist, that is not a sufficient description. You must also know what type of psychologist the person is.

**Table 2–2.** Divisions of the American Psychological Association

| | |
|---|---|
| Adult Development and Aging | Philosophical Psychology |
| Child and Youth Services | Physiological and Comparative Psychology |
| Clinical Psychology | |
| Community Psychology | Population and Environmental Psychology |
| Consulting Psychology | |
| Consumer Psychology | Psychologists in Public Service |
| Counseling Psychology | Psychologists Interested in Religious Issues |
| Developmental Psychology | |
| Educational Psychology | Psychology and the Arts |
| Evaluation and Measurement | Psychology of Women |
| Experimental Analysis of Behavior | Psychopharmacology |
| Experimental Psychology | Psychotherapy |
| General Psychology | Rehabilitation Psychology |
| History of Psychology | School Psychology |
| Humanistic Psychology | Society for the Psychological Study of Social Issues |
| Hypnosis | |
| Industrial and Organizational Psychology | Society of Engineering Psychologists |
| | State Psychological Association Affairs |
| Mental Retardation | |
| Military Psychology | Teaching of Psychology |
| Personality and Social Psychology | |

In addition, psychologists change specialities as their personal interests grow. Developmental psychologists may become social psychologists, experimental psychologists may become clinical psychologists, and educational psychologists may become consumer psychologists. They are not permanently committed to their initial career choice. Indeed, it is not at all unusual for psychologists to change their major areas of research interest several times during their careers. This may represent another reason why psychology is such an exciting career choice. Psychologists study the most fascinating subject matter (human nature), they have a wide selection of specialities to choose from, and they can continue their personal growth and development by changing their specialities.

## WHERE DO PSYCHOLOGISTS WORK?

At one time, psychologists worked only in universities, mental hospitals, and private practice. Before World War II, it would have been difficult to find a psychologist who worked elsewhere. Today, reflecting the ever-widening scope of the field, psychologists work in many different settings, including some unlikely ones.

Universities and mental health institutions still constitute the major places of employment; 47 per cent of American psychologists are at universities, and 18 per cent are at clinics, hospitals, and medical schools. Some 12 per cent of psychologists work in public school systems and school districts, 9 per cent in government and private research organizations, 5 per cent in business and industry, 6 per cent in private practice, and the remaining 3 per cent in other settings.[3]

To present more specific information on where applied psychologists work, and to show the kinds of employment opportunities available, Table 2–3 lists actual job titles and places of employment. It indicates what psychologists in applied settings do and where they do it. (The list does not include psychologists in universities whose work may also have real-world application.)

As you can see, not only is psychology anywhere and everywhere, but so are psychologists! Each year finds them making more significant contributions to many areas of human welfare. As we approach the end of the twentieth century, we find psychologists in greater numbers and positions of influence. Their contributions are of immense importance today in shaping how we live and work, and the future offers an unlimited horizon and an ever-growing need for psychological services.


## SUMMARY

Psychology was originally defined as the study of the mind. As such, the discipline goes back many centuries to the time of the Greeks. About 100 years ago psychology was redefined as the *science* of the mind, reflecting a new intent to become an objective and experimental field of inquiry.

In the years of its development, psychology has expanded in many ways. Today there is not one psychology but several different forms of psychology, each devoted to the study of a different aspect of human nature. One aspect is behavior—what people actually do. Another is conscious experience—how people feel. A third is the unconscious forces that motivate each of us.

Each area is a legitimate type of psychology and each is concerned with improving the quality of human life. Each approaches its study of human nature in a scientific way.

Thus, psychology can be defined as a science of behavior and of mental processes and phenomena, and as a profession dedicated to the promotion of human welfare.

Five research techniques are discussed. In the *experimental method*

---

[3] Data from survey of APA–member psychologists in the United States and Canada, 1972 (*Careers in Psychology*, Washington, D.C.: American Psychological Association, 1975, p. 17).

**Table 2–3.** Places of Employment and Job Titles of Selected Applied Psychologists

Continental Oil Company
   Director of Advertising
International Harvester Corporation
   Manager, Corporate Marketing Research
Columbia Broadcasting System
   Director of Compensation
Sears, Roebuck and Company
   National Director of Training and Development
U.S. Naval Personnel Research and Development Center
   Research Engineering Psychologist
Xerox Corporation
   Manager, Information and Planning Services
Port Authority of New York and New Jersey
   Supervisor of Test Development and Evaluation
Reynolds Metals Corporation
   Manager, Personnel Research
U.S. Senate
   Legislative Assistant
U.S. Department of Health, Education, and Welfare
   Social–Urban Planner
State Department of Human Resources
   Director, Psychological Services
City Juvenile Court System
   Assistant Chief Probation Officer
American Bankers Association
   Director, Education and Training
County Public School System
   Program Research Specialist
State Department of Corrections
   Senior Psychologist

City Public School System
   School Psychologist
State Hospital
   Staff Psychologist
City Public School System
   Director of Child Study
U.S. Department of Agriculture
   Principal Research Scientist
U.S. Naval Submarine Base
   Associate Psychologist
Harcourt Brace Jovanovich, Inc.
   Executive Editor
University of Chicago, Drug Abuse Rehabilitation Program
   Director, Treatment Research
National Council of Community Mental Health Centers
   Executive Director
City Police Department
   Research Director
Court Psychiatric Programs, Hospital Center
   Clinical Administrator
City Police Department, Medical Section
   Director, Psychological Services Unit
Center for Population Research, National Institute for Child Health and Human Development
   Psychologist
Television Programming Organization
   Childhood Development Specialist
Environmental Research and Development Foundation
   Ecological Psychologist
U.S. Government Agency
   Researcher on Highway Safety

psychologists study the effect on human behavior of a single variable while holding all other variables constant. The variable being studied is the *independent variable;* the resulting behavior of the subjects is the *dependent variable.* There are two groups of subjects in a psychological experiment: the *experimental group* and the *control group*. Although it is the most precise of all research methods, the experimental method does have weaknesses: (1) some aspects of behavior cannot be studied by the experimental method, (2) experiments must sometimes be performed in artificial settings, and (3) people may not behave in their usual manner when they know they are taking part in an experiment.

The *method of systematic observation* involves the objective observation of human behavior, not under the controlled conditions of the laboratory but in the real world. Although this method offers some degree of control over possible influencing variables, it does not allow for manipulation of the independent variable as does the experimental method.

In the *correlational method* two variables are statistically compared to see how one variable is related to the other. It is useful in cases in which a prediction must be made about how well a person is likely to succeed, for example, in college or on a job.

The *clinical methods* are used to diagnose and treat emotionally disturbed persons. Specific methods include taking a life history, psychological testing, and dream analysis. Although not as objective as other methods, the clinical methods are nevertheless of great value in dealing with problems of the unconscious mind.

The *survey methods* attempt to determine our attitudes and opinions about matters such as consumer products, television programs, or political candidates so that predictions can be made about decisions people are likely to make. Survey methods can be highly accurate but they are sometimes limited by the human tendency to say one thing and then do another. Three basic survey techniques are personal interviews, telephone interviews, and mail interviews.

To become a psychologist one must earn either a master's degree or a doctoral degree. Some psychologists are engaged in *pure research,* in which the search for knowledge is undertaken for its own sake. Other psychologists favor *applied research,* dealing with practical problems for which a solution must be found, often under the pressure of a deadline. Within the pure and applied areas of psychology are a number of specialities, represented by the thirty-five divisions of the American Psychological Association. Applied psychologists perform their services in a variety of settings, ranging from federal and state governments to private industry.

## SUGGESTED READINGS

American Psychological Association. *Careers in Psychology.* Washington, D.C.: American Psychological Association, 1975. (Single copies free to students; write APA, 1200 17th St., N.W., Washington, D.C. 20036).

American Psychological Association. *Graduate Study in Psychology.* Washington, D.C.: American Psychological Association. (An annual publication providing detailed information on graduate programs in the U.S. and Canada.)

Atkinson, Richard C. Reflections on psychology's past and concerns about its future. *American Psychologist,* 1977, **32,** 205–210.

Doherty, Michael E., and Kenneth M. Shemberg. *Asking Questions About Behavior: An Introduction To What Psychologists Do,* 2nd ed. Glenview, Ill.: Scott, Foresman, 1978.

Evans, Richard I. *The Making of Psychology: Discussions With Creative Contributors.* New York: Alfred A. Knopf, 1976.

Hebb, D. O. What psychology is about. *American Psychologist, 1974,* **29,** 71–79.

Hess, Harrie F. Entry requirements for professional practice of psychology. *American Psychologist,* 1977, **32,** 365–368.

Lipsey, Mark W. Research and relevance: A survey of graduate students and faculty in psychology. *American Psychologist,* 1974, **29,** 541–553.

Moskowitz, Merle J. Hugo Münsterberg: A study in the history of applied psychology. *American Psychologist,* 1977, **32,** 824–842.

Peterson, Donald R. Is psychology a profession? *American Psychologist,* 1976, **31,** 572–581.

*Professional Psychology.* (A quarterly journal of the American Psychological Association publishing articles on the work of applied psychologists in many fields.)

Woods, Paul J., Ed. *Career Opportunities for Psychologists: Expanding and Emerging Areas.* Washington, D.C.: American Psychological Association, 1976.

# Psychology Applied to Mental Health: I. The Nature of Mental Illness

**3**

Mary W. is a twenty-seven-year-old housewife and mother whose behavior is unusual, even bizarre. You do not have to be around her for long to suspect that something is very wrong with her. She is not like most people. She is different, she behaves abnormally, she seems to be emotionally disturbed.

It all started a little more than six months ago, after the birth of her first child, a boy who is hearty and healthy in all respects. After Mary and the baby came home from the hospital, her husband Paul began to notice that she was doing some odd things. Mary had always been an extraordinarily neat housekeeper. Her friends used to comment on how clean she kept everything, and her husband marveled at his good fortune in having such a wife. But after she came home from the hospital this desire for cleanliness turned into an all-consuming passion. She attacked dirt—real or imagined—with a vengeance, and seemed to spend every minute of the day dusting and scrubbing, polishing and scouring.

It started with the baby's room. Mary disinfected every inch of that room and tried to sterilize every toy or piece of furniture the baby might touch.

She began to talk about germs and diseases. "We can't be too careful," she would say every morning as she began the daily ritual of disinfecting the baby's room. "Germs," she muttered to herself over and over again.

One night when Paul came home from work he found a pile of white gauze surgical masks on a table outside the baby's room. A sign on the door read: Remove Shoes Before Entering.

"From now on," Mary told him, "nobody goes in that room unless they're wearing a mask. You can't be too careful. There are germs everywhere."

Paul tried to reason with her but she became hysterical. She barred the door of the baby's room and screamed at Paul about germs and bacteria and about the baby getting sick and dying. Paul put on a surgical mask and Mary calmed down.

"OK," he said to himself. "It's just a little quirk. Probably all new mothers go through something like this. She'll get over it."

But Mary didn't get over it; she got worse. From defending only the nursery against germs, she turned to the entire house. Every room and every item of furniture had to be cleaned each day. Some days she didn't finish her work until very late at night. "There's so much to do," she would say. Then early the next morning she would begin again, duplicating the cleaning schedule of the day before.

She refused to do any shopping because she could not bear to touch money. "You never know who has handled it before," she said. So Paul bought the groceries and when he brought the food home Mary would wash the cans and packages before putting them away.

Anyone who entered the house was made to wear a surgical mask and to leave their shoes on the porch outside. Mary would indicate the chairs guests could sit in, the ones draped with white sheets. As soon as the visitors would leave, Mary would grab the sheets and dump them in the washing machine. If a guest coughed or sneezed, Mary promptly told them to leave. "It's for the baby," she would say. "You can't be too careful."

After a while, nobody came to visit them anymore, which made Mary very happy. Nor did she visit anyone because other people didn't keep their houses as germ-free as hers. For the same reason, Mary eventually stopped going anywhere; she even refused to go out into the yard of her own house. She stays indoors all the time now, cleaning, waging her endless battle against germs.

What is amazing about all this is that Mary seems very happy, although somewhat tired from all the work. Her friends are alienated, her husband is confused and worried, but Mary herself is content with the life she has made. The only time she gets upset is when Paul suggests that she see a doctor.

"There's nothing wrong with me," she will shout. "Just because I try to keep the house clean and protect the baby from germs you act as though I were crazy or something!"


It seems very clear to Paul and to Mary's friends—and to those of us who now know about Mary's behavior—that she is indeed "crazy or something," but obviously no one has persuaded Mary of that yet.

There are millions of people like Mary W., handicapped in some way by emotional problems. Many of them continue to function, at least to some degree, in their everyday lives, holding jobs, raising families, and interacting socially, although not as well or as fully as the rest of us. These people may remain disturbed all their lives, or they may seek psychological help, or they may be driven to it by concerned parents, spouses, or friends. More severely disturbed persons have to be institutionalized, admitted to a mental hospital for some period of time because they can no longer function in society at all.

Mental illness is not an isolated problem, a rare occurrence, or something that happens only infrequently. Mental illness is an epidemic.

Think of any ten people you know. Make a list of their names and think of the personality that goes with each name. And then think of this: chances are excellent that at least one of those ten persons will have to be treated at some time in life for some form of mental illness. Ten to 15 per cent of the population in the United States will, at some time in their lives, require treatment for an emotional problem.

That is why mental illness is called an epidemic. It is the nation's chief health problem in terms of frequency of occurrence. More people are hospitalized with some form of mental illness each year than with all the physical diseases combined. And, once hospitalized, mental patients tend to be kept for longer periods than those hospitalized with physical illnesses. On any given day, at least half of all hospital beds in the United States are occupied by persons suffering from mental disturbances.

These frightening statistics tell only a small part of the story; they include only those patients recorded officially by hospitals, mental health clinics, or private practitioners. There are no records of the many more who suffer intense mental anguish and despair but who do not seek treatment. Somehow these people manage to pass their pain-filled days, but at a great price. They may take large doses of tranquilizers as millions of persons do, or consume a great deal of alcohol to drown their misery as more millions do, or be on their way to drug addiction as growing numbers are. In whatever way they manage to survive, it is not without cost to themselves and to those who live and work with them. These people suffer, their loved ones suffer, and, in the long run, society suffers.

Thus, it is vital that psychology understand the nature of mental illness. Untold human misery has been relieved by psychologists' efforts but much more must be done. More research is needed on the causes and cures of mental illness and better application of this knowledge to specific cases is required.

## WHAT IS ABNORMAL BEHAVIOR?

When is a person considered to be mentally ill? At first, this may seem like a naive, even foolish question. Surely we can tell whether a person is behaving normally or abnormally. Isn't it obvious when a person is mentally ill? Clearly, Mary W. is emotionally disturbed, isn't she? Yes, based on what we know about her, she certainly seems to be. But suppose there is something we don't know, something not even Mary's husband knows.

Suppose that shortly after the birth of her baby, Mary's doctor told her that the infant had a rare disorder that would make it extremely susceptible to infection for the first year of life. "You will have to be very careful," the doctor said. "Even a mild cold could be fatal. You must make every effort to protect the child." Mary told no one about the baby's problem because she felt guilty, as though the baby's illness were her fault.

Do you still think Mary is emotionally disturbed? Her behavior is just as bizarre, just as abnormal, but now we have a reason for her behavior. It is true that she may be overreacting to the situation, but it is equally true that a real threat to her baby exists, one which she must protect against. Is she "crazy or something" because of the way she behaves?

Tom B. is a nineteen-year-old college student who suddenly becomes extremely depressed. He can no longer concentrate on his studies, his grades are falling, he has trouble sleeping, and he often breaks into uncontrollable fits of crying. Until two weeks ago Tom was energetic, alert, hard-working, fun to be with, and seemed not to have a care in the world. What happened to him? Why has his behavior changed so drastically?

One explanation is that some deep-seated childhood conflict has surfaced and, as a result, Tom has become emotionally disturbed, perhaps to the point where he will need psychological help or even hospitalization. But maybe there is another explanation. Perhaps two weeks ago Tom learned that his younger brother, whom he loves very much, has leukemia and is going to die. Tom's behavior is the same in both cases. In the first case he would probably be diagnosed as emotionally ill and treated as such. In the second case he would be considered to be undergoing a temporary reaction to an acute stress, one to which, to judge from his history of emotional stability, he will probably adapt in time.

The point is that not all abnormal behavior indicates emotional illness; there may be reasonable causes for abnormal behavior. What seems to be abnormal in one situation may be quite normal in another.

There are other problems in defining abnormal behavior. The word "abnormal" means not average or not typical, something that deviates from the norm or standard. Any characteristic—intelligence, height, weight, or behavior—that deviates from the norm is "abnormal." Thus, abnormality can be defined in statistical terms as any behavior or characteristic that occurs rarely. A person who is 6 feet, 8 inches tall is abnormal; most people are not so tall. Put that 6-foot 8-inch person on a college basketball team, however, and he or she is no longer abnormal; everyone on the basketball team is likely to be unusually tall.

Another way of interpreting this statistical definition of abnormality is to say that what is normal is simply that which occurs most often. Normal or sane behavior is defined as the way in which most people in a given culture behave. If your behavior deviates too greatly, you will be considered abnormal.

Normality and abnormality of behavior, then, do not represent absolutes. They are defined with reference to how most people behave, and this behavior is considered to be the desired norm or standard. Such standards of normality change within a culture over time. Fifty years ago a person who appeared nude on a public beach was considered abnormal. Today hundreds of people appear nude on public beaches every day and most of us don't think anything of it. The standard of normality in this instance has changed. Two centuries ago physicians routinely practiced bloodletting as a method of curing certain physical diseases. If physicians suggested bloodletting today, their sanity would be questioned.

Not only do standards of normal and abnormal behavior change over time, but they also vary from one culture to another. There are some societies in which female babies are put to death if too many are born, and other societies in which adolescents participate in initiation rites that seem cruel and barbaric to us. To one culture, this behavior is normal; to another it is abnormal.

To decide whether a person is emotionally disturbed, it is not enough to know that his or her behavior is abnormal, that is, deviates from average or standard behavior. Although it is true that abnormal behavior may indicate mental illness, it does not automatically do so. To make such a determination, we have to know much more about the person and the behavior.

How harmful is the behavior to the individual and to society? Does the deviant behavior prevent the person from adapting successfully to the demands of everyday life? A person who is extremely depressed or fearful every waking moment will be unable to cope with the problems of daily living. So much time and emotional energy are consumed by the depression that little is left for interpersonal relationships, activities, or jobs. At a more serious level are people who are driven to suicide or murder by the intensity of their emotional distress. Some idea of the degree of harm involved in a person's behavior or emotional state provides a firmer basis for judging whether a person is emotionally ill.

Another criterion is the person's internal suffering. Sometimes people can be emotionally disturbed without displaying any abnormal behavior; they know that something is wrong with them, but it may not be visible to anyone else. These persons may function normally in their daily social interactions or perform reasonably well in classes or jobs.

Internally, however, they may be filled with worry, dread, fear, anxiety, or depression. They typify the expression, "Laughing on the outside and crying on the inside."

Therefore, the question with which we began—When is a person considered mentally ill?—is not so farfetched. In all but the most extreme cases, the determination of mental illness is a difficult one to make. The problem is greatly complicated by the fact that in all but the most bizarre cases, mentally ill persons are very much like you and me!

In terms of the behaviors displayed and the internal feelings experienced, mentally ill persons do not differ greatly from the rest of us. We all occasionally show behaviors and experience feelings similar to those of emotionally disturbed persons, although not at the same level of intensity. The difference between the normal and the emotionally ill is in degree, not kind. In other words, mentally ill persons do not behave or feel differently than others, but their behaviors and feelings are more intense or exaggerated. For example, we may be temporarily depressed about something, but we are still able to function reasonably well. In contrast, the mentally ill can be so overwhelmed by depression that they are literally unable to do anything. Their depression is not of a different nature, but it is significantly more intense.

There is no distinct dividing line between mental health and mental illness, no barrier that one suddenly crosses to find oneself on the other side. There is no "other side," merely a different degree of mental health. This can be demonstrated graphically by a concept that is widely used in psychology, the normal curve of distribution (Figure 3–1).

The normal curve shows the distribution of psychological health in any large group of people, such as the population of the United States. As you can see, most people cluster around the center of the distribution, indicating that they show an average level of adjustment. A small number of persons are above average in mental health and a smaller number are extremely healthy. A small number of persons are below average in mental health and a smaller number are mentally disturbed, probably to the point of requiring institutionalization. In this chapter we discuss those persons who exhibit a less-than-average level of mental health.

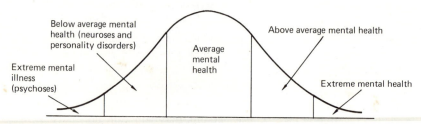

Figure 3–1.   Normal curve of psychological health.

As Figure 3–1 indicates, there are no sharp breaks in these degrees of psychological health. Each level merges into the next and it is difficult (except in extreme cases) to differentiate one level of psychological health from the next. An analogy can be made with height. If we measured the height of every person in the United States, the results would approximate a normal curve of distribution. Most people are of average height and so would fall in the center of the distribution. Because few of us are extremely tall or extremely short, few would fall at the two ends of the distribution.

If you were judging height, you would have no difficulty with these extreme cases; persons who are unusually tall or short would be easy to pick out in a large group of people. But what about all those people who deviate only slightly from the average, those who are only a couple of inches taller or shorter than the average? Observing them in school, in shops, or on the job, in the company of many other people, it would be very difficult for you to judge their height accurately. So it is with judgments of mental health. Because the differences can be small (and again, they are a matter of degree not of kind), mental health is difficult to assess, except for those persons whose behavior is extreme.

To carry the analogy to its logical conclusion, you could use a tape measure or ruler to determine precisely how tall each person is. It follows that through precise measurement, we can make accurate judgments of mental health also. That is nice in theory but it does not work in practice. We do not have infallible yardsticks of the mind. There are no objective indicators that can be used to measure a person's amount of mental health. Nor are there counterparts to measurements of physical health. An x-ray or a blood test can provide objective indication of the condition of various organs or processes within the body, but there are no such techniques for measuring the conditions within the mind.

It is true that we have many psychological tests that attempt to measure various aspects of the personality, and we have the diagnostic skills of psychiatrists and clinical psychologists, but in both cases these assessments are subjective processes. The evaluations of mental health that derive from psychological tests and clinical diagnoses are human judgments and, as such, can be faulty.

In brief, our methods of assessing or measuring mental health are not very accurate. This was demonstrated dramatically in a study by psychologist David Rosenhan, who sent normal persons, including himself, to twelve different mental hospitals to see if hospital staff members would be able to detect the presence of these sane people among the insane.[1]

---

[1] D. L. Rosenhan, "On Being Sane in Insane Places," *Science*, **179** (January 19, 1973), 250–258. This article also contains a fascinating description of life in a mental hospital.

In order to gain admittance to the mental hospitals, Rosenhan and his confederates (psychologists, a pediatrician, a psychiatrist, a painter, a housewife, and a graduate student in psychology) all told of the same complaint; they had been hearing voices. These voices, they reported, were unclear but seemed to be saying, "empty," "hollow," and "thud." Except for the voices, all the pseudopatients were truthful about their past and present circumstances (although real names and occupations were not given).

Almost all the pseudopatients were diagnosed as schizophrenic and all were admitted to the hospitals. Once inside, they acted perfectly normally and stopped any semblance of abnormal behavior. Presumably, sane persons should be easily and quickly detected among a population of insane persons. In fact, they worried initially that they would be immediately exposed as frauds. Shortly after admission, however, that worry turned to concern about getting out, so they were highly motivated to behave as normally as possible and were extremely cooperative with the hospital staff.

How long did it take for their normality to be detected? How well did their sanity stand out in the midst of insanity? They were never detected! Some were in the hospital as long as fifty-two days and were discharged only because of the intervention of someone outside the hospital, not because the staff realized that they had made an incorrect diagnosis. All pseudopatients were released with a diagnosis of "schizophrenia in remission," meaning that they were still considered to be insane but that their symptoms had temporarily abated.

It is interesting that although the mental hospital staff never detected the sanity of these people, some of the real patients did. Of 118 patients on one ward, 35 of them were suspicious of the pseudopatients. "You're not crazy," they said. "You're a journalist or a professor. . . . You're checking up on the hospital." [2]

Rosenhan conducted another study to determine if hospital staff members who expected to admit pseudopatients could separate the sane from the insane. [3] The staff members at the hospital being studied knew of the results of Rosenhan's first study and refused to believe that such mistakes could occur in their hospital. Rosenhan told the staff that at some time during the following three-month period, one or more pseudopatients would try to gain admission to the hospital.

How accurate were the judgments of the mental hospital staff? A total of 193 persons were admitted during the three-month period. Of these, 41 were judged with a high level of confidence to be pseudopatients, that

[2] Ibid., p. 252.

[3] D. L. Rosenhan, "Letters," Science, **180** (April 27, 1973), 356–365; Rosenhan's reply, 365–369.

is, to be perfectly sane. Another 23 of those admitted were suspected to be sane by at least one psychiatrist, and 19 others were suspected to be sane by one psychiatrist and one other staff member. How did these judgments compare with the number of pseudopatients Rosenhan had sent? Very poorly. Rosenhan had not sent *any* pseudopatients to the hospital!

Thus, we can conclude that even professionals in the mental health field have great difficulty distinguishing the normal and the abnormal, the mentally healthy and the mentally ill. Rosenhan noted: "The fact is that the unreliability of psychiatric diagnoses as they are commonly made has been known for a long time, so long that it is remarkable that the impression of sturdiness could have been sustained in the face of such an overwhelmingly contrary literature." [4]

This does not mean that it is not possible to determine who is normal and who is not. Psychologists and psychiatrists make such judgments every day and their experience suggests that they are correct in a great many cases. The important point is that any human judgment is subject to error; psychologists and psychiatrists are not infallible. Also, the judgments themselves are exceedingly complex and focus on an area of human nature that we do not fully understand. Much more research is needed on the nature of both abnormality and normality. Until we know precisely what constitutes mental health, we cannot be certain about what constitutes mental illness; they are, in a sense, two sides of the same coin. (In Chapter 5 we discuss what is known about mental health.)

In summary, any judgment or description of mental illness must consider (1) all possible underlying causes of the behaviors or feelings in question, (2) how much these behaviors deviate from the norm in a given situation, time period, or culture, and (3) how harmful these behaviors are likely to be to the individual (externally and internally) and to society.

## TYPES OF MENTAL ILLNESS

There are many types of emotional disorders, more than most people realize. Emotional disorders can be organized in several ways, but the problem with any classification is that there is often overlap, confusion, or similarity among various diagnostic categories. For example, patients with different sets of symptoms are sometimes given the same diagnosis, and it may well be correct in all cases. Similarly, some patients given different diagnoses may exhibit the same symptoms, and again the diagnoses may be correct. Despite these recognized weaknesses of classifica-

[4] Ibid., p. 368.

**Table 3–1.** Classification of Mental Disorders *

1. *Neuroses:* Moderately severe maladaptive disorders.
2. *Organic Brain Syndromes (Psychoses):* Psychotic disorders in which there is some form of organic brain damage.
3. *Psychoses:* Psychoses not caused by any physical condition.
4. *Personality Disorders:* Disorders that are socially maladaptive, such as psychopathic, sexual, alcoholic, and drug problems.
5. *Psychophysiologic Disorders:* Psychosomatic problems in which emotional factors are associated with physical illness.
6. *Mental Retardation:* Disorders associated with low IQ.
7. *Behavior Disorders of Childhood and Adolescence:* Disorders unique to these stages of development.
8. *Transient Situational Disturbances:* Disorders caused by specific situational stresses, such as adjustment problems at various stages of life.
9. *Conditions Without Manifest Psychiatric Disorder and Nonspecific Conditions:* Problems of marital, social, and career adjustment.
10. *Special Symptoms:* Disorders of sleep, speech, learning, eating, and other psychomotor functions.

* Suggested by the *Diagnostic and Statistical Manual of Mental Disorders* (2nd ed.; Washington, D.C.: American Psychiatric Association, 1968).

tions, however, there is general agreement among psychologists and psychiatrists about meaningful categories of mental illness.

Probably the most useful and accepted classification scheme is provided by the American Psychiatric Association in its *Diagnostic and Statistical Manual of Mental Disorders.*[5] This system groups mental disorders in ten categories (Table 3–1).

Categories 1–4 are discussed in this chapter. Category 5 is discussed in Chapter 6 ("Psychology Applied to Physical Health"), and Category 6 is treated in Chapter 10 ("Psychology Applied to the Classroom"). Categories 7–10 deal with adjustment problems related to family, career, social, age, or other specific situations. These problems are not popularly considered to be forms of "mental illness" as such, and there are many sources of counseling readily available to help people deal with these temporary difficulties in adjusting to daily life. In this chapter we shall deal with the major forms of mental illness: neuroses, psychoses, and personality disorders.

[5] *Diagnostic and Statistical Manual of Mental Disorders* (2nd ed.; Washington, D.C.: American Psychiatric Association, 1968). A major revision, *DSM–III*, is in preparation. See Thomas Schacht and Peter E. Nathan, "But Is It Good For the Psychologists? Appraisal and Status of DSM–III," *American Psychologist,* **32** (1977), 1017–1025; Daniel Goleman, "Who's Mentally Ill?" *Psychology Today,* **11** (January 1978), 34–41.

## NEUROSES

The word "neurosis" is frequently used and heard in everyday conversation, and we often use it erroneously to describe any behavior that is out of the ordinary. A *neurosis* is a moderate-to-severe form of illness that can interfere with a person's functioning. Often the person requires some form of professional help, although usually not institutionalization. On the normal curve of distribution (Figure 3–1), neuroses would appear in the area designated "below-average mental health."

There are several specific forms of neuroses, but they all have two things in common: (1) neuroses are maladaptive in terms of coping with life, and (2) neuroses center around anxiety. *Anxiety* is a kind of fear—a powerful, sometimes crippling fear. In normal persons fear is of something specific (for example, fear of failing an examination, fear of snakes, fear of heights), but neurotic persons cannot point to the source of their fear. They know they are afraid, apprehensive, worried, and they may feel that way all the time, but they do not know what they are afraid of. When you do not know what you are afraid of, how can you protect yourself against it? This is the essence of the problem: neurotics are constantly fighting their anxiety through the use of the neurotic mechanisms. The anxiety never leaves these persons, which is why they cannot function in life at full capacity.

In addition, neurotics are unhappy and tense persons. They believe they are basically inferior and inadequate in coping with life. They are constantly threatened by situations that seem perfectly normal to other people, such as a party or a job promotion. Neurotics try, in a sense, to withdraw from life, to avoid coping with it. They feel dissatisfied with themselves, guilty, threatened, and in emotional pain much of the time. One of the simplest and most descriptive statements made about neurotics is that they are characterized by a "loss of joy in living." [6]

This is the general clinical picture of the emotional state of neurotic persons. However, as we noted, neuroses take several specific forms that focus on different symptoms. We discuss six common neurotic conditions: anxiety neurosis, phobias, obsessions and compulsions, hysteria, hypochondria, and depressive neurosis.

### Anxiety Neurosis

As we noted, anxiety underlies all neurotic behavior and is a symptom common to all neuroses. In *anxiety neurosis*, however, the feeling of anxiety is much more pronounced and pervasive. Anxiety neurotics ex-

---

[6] Philip G. Zimbardo and Floyd L. Ruch, *Psychology and Life* (9th ed.; Glenview, Ill.: Scott, Foresman, 1975), p. 476.

perience a high degree of fear every waking moment. So intense is the fear that it can become panic. Anxiety neurotics are extremely sensitive, even defensive about the reactions of other people toward them. They find it hard to concentrate on their work, or on anything, and have great difficulty making decisions, even about the simplest matters. In addition, they may experience physical symptoms associated with fear: rapid heartbeat, sweating, dizziness, and diarrhea. Even at night they are not free of their fears. They often have trouble sleeping; when they do get to sleep, they may be plagued by nightmares. Anxiety neurotics are truly tortured people, insecure, depressed, feeling unworthy, always tense and worried, always expecting a calamity to befall them.

It has been suggested that anxiety neurotics have extremely high standards of what they should be and do, so high as to be unrealistic. Usually, these expectations were developed in childhood, from parents who expected a great deal and threatened to withhold their love if the children did not live up to those expectations. Such children, it seems, often grow up with considerable apprehension and fear about their ability to meet what life demands, and, more important, what they demand of themselves. Although not the only possible cause of anxiety neurosis, this childhood situation does seem to be a dominant one.[7]

Coleman described the case of a thirty-four-year-old dentist whose anxiety attacks started shortly after his practice began to decline slightly.[8]

[He] complained of continual worry, difficulty in sleeping, and a vague dread that he was "failing." As a result, he increased his hours of practice during the evenings from one to five nights and began driving himself beyond all reason in a desperate effort to "insure the success of his practice." Although his dental practice now increased beyond what it had been previously, he found himself still haunted by the vague fears and apprehensions of failure. These, in turn, became further augmented by frequent heart palpitations and pains which he erroneously diagnosed as at least an incapacitating if not a fatal heart ailment. At this point his anxiety became so great that he voluntarily came to a clinic for assistance.

In the course of assessment and treatment, a somewhat typical pattern was revealed. The patient had a history of early and chronic emotional insecurity. No matter what his accomplishments, his parents continued to reject and belittle him, which led him to feel inferior and to anticipate failure. When he once proudly told his parents that the school counselor informed him he had a very high IQ, they demanded to know why he didn't make better grades. He remembered occasionally receiving presents,

[7] R. L. Jenkins, cited in James C. Coleman, *Abnormal Psychology and Modern Life* (4th ed.; Glenview, Ill.: Scott, Foresman, 1972), p. 223.

[8] Coleman, op. cit., p. 223. Copyright © 1972 by Scott, Foresman and Company. Reprinted by permission.

such as a model airplane set, which were always beyond his age level so that his father would have to help him assemble the kit. Linked to his continual failure and inferiority was a very high level of aspiration—reflecting the expectations of his parents and his desire to accomplish something that would win their approval and support.

As a result of this early background, the dentist was unable to enjoy the successes he did achieve, for he always felt he could be accomplishing more. Even the mere suggestion of failure in his professional work as an adult was met by exaggerated fear and anxiety and a frantic redoubling of effort. . . .

This case illustrates how anxiety neurosis arises from unrealistic expectations developed in childhood.

## Phobias

A *phobia* is an all-consuming fear that is totally out of proportion to reality. The fear in this case differs from the generalized fear felt in anxiety; a phobic fear is of something specific. There are almost as many possible phobias as there are objects in the world to be afraid of, but some phobias are more common than others, for example, fear of heights (acrophobia), fear of small closed tight places (claustrophobia), fear of darkness (nyctophobia), and fear of germs (mysophobia).

Many of us fear certain objects in the environment, such as snakes or high places, but our fears are usually mild and do not interfere with our daily activities. Phobias, however, are much more intense and do interfere with normal functioning. A person with a phobia about snakes may never be able to go outdoors for fear of meeting a snake. Someone with a phobia about heights may never be able to drive across a bridge, so strong is the fear of falling off.

> Mildred K. had an intense fear of eyes. Her friends noticed that she never looked at anyone directly but always glanced away while talking. Her reason, the young woman explained to a psychologist, was that the sight of an eyeball caused her to feel an uncontrollable emotional panic. She was unable to remember when the phobia started, for it seemed to her that she had been afraid of eyes all her life. Recently the phobia had become intensified and some related symptoms had appeared. Mildred had frequent nightmares of persons whose eyes were horrible and staring and whom she took to be insane. . . . Because of her concern about her phobia and because of the accompanying state of more general anxiety, Mildred's efficiency was seriously impaired. She found it increasingly difficult to study and could not concentrate on what she was reading. Her phobia also made her avoid her friends. As a result, her academic standing was affected and her social relationships were approaching ruin.[9]

[9] Laurance F. Shaffer and Edward J. Shoben, Jr., *The Psychology of Adjustment*, 2nd ed. (Boston: Houghton Mifflin, 1956), pp. 217–218. Copyright © 1956 by L. F. Shaffer and E. J. Shoben. Reprinted by permission of Houghton Mifflin Company.

You can understand how intrusive such an irrational fear can be. Recall Mary W., the case that opened this chapter. Her problem might have been mysophobia (fear of germs); she no longer had time or energy for any semblance of a normal life, so busy was her continuing fight against germs.

Most phobics know that their fears are totally irrational, that they have no basis in reality. The person who lives in the heart of New York City and won't go outdoors because of a fear of snakes really knows that there is virtually no chance of a snake appearing on a crowded sidewalk. Yet, while recognizing the absurdity of the fear, phobics are prisoners of them.

In a great many cases these irrational fears were learned in childhood when the object of the fear came to be associated with some particularly painful or emotionally disturbing situation. Mildred's fear of eyes, for example, was finally traced to an incident that occurred when she was seven years old, visiting an aunt who was blind.

> Little Mildred set out to explore the house and, with considerable excitement and some guilty fear of being caught in the act, she was peeping in the bureau drawers. As she opened one drawer, out of it stared two horrible eyes, eyes perfectly real but without a face. They were glass eyes belonging to the blind aunt. Mildred fled in terror. Even in telling the story to the psychologist years later she showed evidence of strong emotion and wept.[10]

Sometimes phobias develop unconsciously in order to protect the individual against doing something that he or she will feel guilty or shameful about. For example, a boy who feels guilty about sex may develop such a strong fear of girls that he will avoid ever coming into contact with them. Avoiding girls prevents the anxiety that would appear if he socialized with girls.

## Obsessions and Compulsions

When we say that people are *obsessed* with something, we mean that it preys on their mind a lot. We have all had the experience of a tune running through our mind that we cannot stop thinking about. The neurotic obsession is similar but very much stronger. The obsession—an idea or thought—is constantly in the mind, and we cannot get rid of it. Also, persons obsessed with such a thought are not free to think about anything else. This is why the neurotic obsession is so disturbing and intrusive.

Neurotics can be obsessed with almost anything: for example, the idea that they left the water running at home, that they have cancer,

[10] Ibid., p. 219.

that they will kill themselves or someone else, or that they will commit an obscene act. Not uncommon neurotic obsessions are those of parents obsessed with the idea of murdering their child, or of a husband or wife obsessed with the idea of stabbing or shooting a spouse.

Whereas obsessions are ideas that intrude into the mind, *compulsions are actual behaviors that a person is compelled to perform.* The behaviors or rituals must be performed repeatedly, and this leaves the person little time for normal activities. A common compulsion is hand washing; the hands may be washed dozens of times each day. In extreme cases, compulsive persons may wash their hands so often that the skin becomes raw.

Some neurotics are compulsive in a more general way, that is, in the order, neatness, and precision with which they regulate their lives and possessions. Everything must be undertaken or maintained in a certain order—pencils arranged just so on the desk, clothes hung in a definite way in the closet, the meat eaten before the vegetables at dinner. No deviation from this orderly routine is allowed.

These established patterns and routines provide emotional comfort to neurotics. The compulsions bring order out of what neurotics see as a chaotic world, and protect neurotics from anxiety by preventing them from thinking or doing something that they associate with shame or guilt.

Neurotics are disturbed by troublesome impulses that make them feel anxious. By constantly thinking certain thoughts or performing certain acts, they leave no time for such anxiety-provoking impulses. Therefore, the only way neurotics can avoid the pain of anxiety is through their obsessions and compulsions, which are themselves disturbing and unproductive.

## Hysteria

The common usage of the word "hysteria" does not coincide with the way it is used in psychology. We tend to think of hysteria as a state in which a person is screaming, crying, or wailing, and behaving in a frenzied manner. This does not describe the person suffering from a hysterical neurosis.

There are two kinds of hysterical neuroses: conversion reactions and dissociative reactions. In the *conversion reaction* a psychological disturbance is converted into a physical disturbance, producing an actual physical malfunction of the body such as blindness, deafness, or paralysis of the limbs for which no physical cause can be found. Hysterical persons are not deliberately faking the physical symptoms, but there is no physical cause for them. No matter how hard they try, hysterical persons cannot overcome what has become a very real physical disturbance.

The physical disability provides some benefits; it may protect the person from some conflict and the anxiety associated with it, or prevent the person from doing something that is fear-laden or repulsive, or it may secure for the person love and attention not otherwise obtainable.

John R. was an infantryman in Vietnam and the sole survivor of an ambush of his patrol. He saw his close friends killed and he feigned death for hours while enemy soldiers looted the corpses all around him. Two days after that action John awoke to find both legs paralyzed. He was sent from one hospital to another and many doctors examined him for physical damage to his legs. No damage could be found. Finally, he was treated by a psychiatrist who found the real cause of the paralysis. John was terrified of returning to combat after his close call with death, but he knew no honorable way out. He knew he was scheduled for a patrol the evening of the day his paralysis began. The paralysis, dictated by his unconscious mind, prevented him from returning to combat.

It is interesting that hysterical conversions usually disappear when the person is under hypnosis; this is additional evidence for the lack of a physical cause for the bodily ailment. Also, the symptoms are not always consistent; they may shift from one part of the body to another. For example, a patient with a paralyzed right hand may awaken one morning to find that the paralysis has shifted to the left hand.

As a rule, hysterics are not greatly upset by their physical condition, not nearly as disturbed as those persons who find themselves with a genuine physical disability such as blindness or paralysis.

The other type of hysterical neurosis, the *dissociative reaction*, refers to the situation in which some parts of the personality become separated from other parts. In this way, hysterical persons defend themselves against threatening thoughts or inner conflicts. There are several ways in which this dissociation can take place: for example, amnesia, somnambulism, and multiple personality.

*Amnesia*—in case you have forgotten—refers to a loss of memory, usually for a specific incident or period of time. It is an attempt on the part of the unconscious to blot from memory some painful experience. If a person has done something he or she considers shameful, and the memory of it is too painful to bear, the incident may be erased from the memory as a protective device.

In extreme cases, amnesiacs forget everything about themselves, including their names, addresses, families, and occupations. They are unable to recognize anyone or anything connected with their past life. They are repressing their entire former life, not merely a single incident.

Sometimes amnesiacs escape their past identity even more completely by disappearing, turning up one day in another part of the country. In this "fugue" state (derived from the Latin word for flight), amnesiacs may wander for weeks having no idea of who they are or where they live.

Susan J. is a twenty-four-year-old nurse who wanted to go back to work three months after the birth of her first child. Her husband argued violently against it, saying that a mother's place was with her baby. Then, Susan's mother died and her father, partially crippled by a stroke, came to live with Susan and her husband. She felt increasingly frustrated and tense about being unable to return to her job and having to care for both a new baby and an aged parent who, in addition to requiring constant attention, was irritable and difficult to get along with.

One morning, Susan left her home to go to the supermarket, leaving a neighbor in charge of her two "patients," and disappeared. She was found by the police three weeks later wandering in a city approximately 2000 miles from her home. She had no idea who she was. Gradually she recovered her memory, but when questioned about her three weeks away found that she could recall nothing about that time. It was as though the incident had never happened.

*Somnambulism* or sleepwalking is a dissociative state in which people move about during sleep and often perform acts that they could not perform while awake. For example, a woman who harbors hostility toward her husband may express it unconsciously during sleep by physically attacking him. When awakened, she would be unable to remember anything she had done while asleep.

The most severe and dramatic form of dissociation involves *multiple personality*, the development of two or more totally different personalities that alternately dominate the person. In other words, the person becomes two or more people, sometimes acting as one and sometimes as another. One personality does not know of the existence of the other.

Also, there is amnesia for the alternate personality; these persons cannot remember what they did while they were the other person.

This is a rare condition but certainly one of the most sensational of all the neuroses. The well-known Dr. Jekyll and Mr. Hyde story describes such a condition, in which the person is alternately good and evil.

The differences among the multiple personalities can be remarkable; they may dress and speak differently, have different facial expressions, and even different postures and gestures. This alternation of personality usually derives from conflicting motivations, each of which the person unconsciously acts out at different times.[11]

## Hypochondria

*Hypochondria* involves an intense and exaggerated concern for one's health and physical condition. Hypochondriacs are constantly alert for any sign of abnormality and are ready (even eager) to pronounce a headache a brain tumor, a gas pain a heart attack, or a stomachache a cancer. It has been said that hypochondriacs enjoy suffering and poor health; they seem almost happy when a new symptom appears particularly if they believe that it indicates a terminal illness.

Hypochondria is a perfect defense against participating fully in life and easily allows these persons to avoid situations they would find stressful. "I'd love to go out more and meet people and be sociable," a hypochondriac says, "but I can't because I'm so sick all the time." It could well be that the person is terribly afraid of social situations, fearful of meeting new people or of being in groups. The "illness" prevents one from having to do such things.

## Depressive Neurosis

*Depressive neurotics* are characterized by an intense, compelling, pervasive, and continuous feeling of depression. These persons are enveloped in gloom and experience strong feelings of rejection. Any experience that is even the least bit negative is magnified out of proportion to reality. When a catastrophe does occur, such as the loss of a loved one, depressive neurotics are more despondent and stricken than normal persons would be, and are likely to be affected for a much longer period of time.

Each day in the lives of depressive neurotics is filled with sadness. It is not uncommon for them to resort to alcohol or drugs in an effort to

---

[11] See, for example, C. H. Thigpen and H. Cleckley, *The Three Faces of Eve* (New York: McGraw-Hill, 1957); C. C. Sizemore and E. S. Pittillo, *I'm Eve* (New York: Doubleday, 1977); F. R. Schreiber, *Sybil* (New York: Warner, 1974).

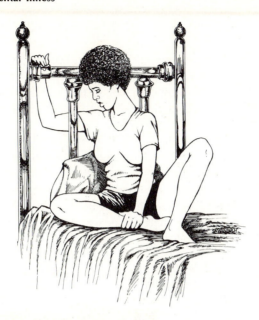

contain the emotional pain they constantly live with. They often have trouble sleeping, concentrating on work, making decisions, or even getting out of bed in the morning to face a new day. In turn, these difficulties may cause them to feel inadequate, amplifying the problem.

This intense depression is often precipitated by a real loss, for example of a job or a spouse. But it can also originate in childhood from a feeling of being unloved or unwanted. Such persons often grow up doubting that anyone can love them. This feeling may be confirmed by the loss of a friend or the divorce of a spouse as an adult, or by the accumulation of small losses and disappointments over a period of time. Usually, the severe depression moderates after some weeks or months, but a mild depression may remain for a longer period.

You may have noticed that all these neurotic reactions, in one way or another, help a person adapt to a high level of anxiety, usually by avoiding it. It may seem strange to describe such bizarre, disturbing, and painful reactions as useful and helpful, but that is what they are. Without these neurotic reactions, a person might be literally overcome by anxiety. Of course, it is preferable not to be neurotic at all, but it is better to be neurotic than to be totally engulfed by anxiety.

Neurotics can at least function in the real world, however limited their functioning may be. They maintain contact with reality, and this is a more satisfactory adjustment than that made by persons with a more severe form of mental illness: psychosis.

## PSYCHOSES

Psychoses are the most extreme and debilitating form of mental illness, the lowest level of mental health. On the normal curve of distribution (Figure 3–1), they would appear at the far left end. In popular terminology, we call people with psychoses "crazy"; in legal terminology we call them "insane."

Psychotic persons have lost all contact with reality and have withdrawn into a fantasy world of their own construction, in which they live amid hallucinations, delusions, and visions. Obviously, they cannot behave in a normal way, as can neurotics, and they usually have to be institutionalized, sometimes for life. Extremely psychotic persons have absolutely no control over their actions and may be violent, both to themselves and to others.

There are two general types of psychoses, differing in terms of origin. *Organic* psychoses are caused by actual physical brain damage and can be induced by tumors, diseases of the brain and central nervous system such as syphilis, the long-term use of alcohol, and circulation disturbances common to old age. In *functional* psychoses there is no brain damage; the cause of the psychosis seems to be psychological in nature.

Recent research has blurred what was once a clear-cut distinction between these two types of psychoses. Biochemical imbalances or brain malfunctions may exist in functional psychotics that can be triggered by psychological stress, causing a psychotic reaction. In general, however, the differing causal factors still hold: physical damage to the brain in organic psychoses and psychological background factors in functional psychoses. We shall discuss here the two primary types of psychologically induced functional psychoses: schizophrenia and manic depressive.

### Schizophrenia

Schizophrenia does not mean "split" personality (in the sense of multiple personalities), although this is how many people incorrectly use the term. *Schizophrenia* means that the personality of the individual is split off from reality, and that within the personality the thought processes are split off from the emotions. It is the most frequent form of psychosis and accounts for the majority of mental hospital admissions and readmissions. The cure rate for schizophrenia is not very high.

There are different varieties of schizophrenia characterized by different symptoms, but there are some general symptoms that seem to describe most schizophrenics. Their behavior is unusual, even bizarre, and often inappropriate to the situation in which they find themselves. They may, for example, laugh at what would be a time of sadness and grief for a more normal person. Their thought processes are convoluted and greatly disordered, often containing hallucinations (seeing and hearing things that are not really there). Emotionally, they may seem dull and spiritless.

There are many forms of schizophrenia; we shall limit our discussion to the four major types: simple schizophrenia, hebephrenic schizophrenia, catatonic schizophrenia, and paranoid schizophrenia.

Persons suffering from *simple schizophrenia* are severely withdrawn from all reality, show no interest in and little awareness of the world around them, and display a decline in intellectual ability. It is not that these persons have a low IQ, but rather that they are totally indifferent to their environment and, consequently, have difficulty performing even the simplest task.

Their behavior is less extreme or bizarre than the other varieties of schizophrenia, and so they do not always require hospitalization. They sometimes survive on the fringes of society, becoming tramps or prostitutes or working sporadically at low-level jobs. They may seem dull-witted, slow, silent, and apathetic, and their appearance is often dirty and unkempt. Occasionally, they may exhibit aggressive outbursts and it is that behavior, or running afoul of the law, that can lead to hospitalization.

A. J. was seventeen years old when he was admitted to a mental hospital. He had always been shy and somewhat reclusive, and he did so poorly in high school that he quit at the end of his sophomore year.

> After leaving school, A. J. worked at a number of odd jobs but was irregular in performing his duties and never held any one job longer than a few weeks. He finally became unemployable and stayed home, becoming more and more seclusive and withdrawn from community and family life. He would sit with his head bowed most of the time, refused to eat with the family, and when visitors came would hide under the bed. He further neglected his appearance, refusing to bathe or get a haircut. He occasionally made "strange" remarks and frequently covered his face with his hands because he felt he looked "funny." [12]

In most cases of simple schizophrenia, the retirement or withdrawal from life develops slowly, in childhood or in adolescence.

*Hebephrenic schizophrenia* presents a different set of symptoms. Hebephrenics often become childish in speech and behavior: giggling and acting silly; relieving themselves wherever they choose; eating with their hands instead of with a knife, fork, or spoon; and making grotesque faces. Their thought processes are disorganized and totally illogical, a

---

[12] Albert I. Rabin, cited in Ernest R. Hilgard, Richard C. Atkinson, and Rita L. Atkinson, *Introduction to Psychology* (6th ed.; New York: Harcourt Brace Jovanovich, 1975), p. 476.

jumble of ideas and images that lack connection or meaning. Their emotions are quick to change and are inappropriate to the situation, and they have frequent bizarre delusions and hallucinations.

Robert A. is a twenty-four-year-old hebephrenic schizophrenic who had this conversation with the ward doctor.

> Patient: I've been lured. I've been lured time and time again. I've been lured by mobs and lured by money to build space. They talk about pleasure principle, pleasure purpose, it's merely false sex.
>
> Doctor: What do you mean?
>
> Pt.: I know what I'm doing. I'm living out my grandfather's life. They had to tell me, my mother went. America sees its own heirs. . . .
>
> Dr.: Have you ever seen any visions?
>
> Pt.: I don't see visions. I see God in word and deed. My mother couldn't stand any such program.
>
> Dr.: What does that chair look like to you?
>
> Pt.: Sex. It's immaterial. The legs are like the moon, sexy to a point. They tell me that the clothes were divided. I want to see who's lying. They've got the greater part of the money. They live out lies. When I meet God I can live out a clean conscience. . . .
>
> Pt. (reading a magazine): These are stepping stones. They are prunes on a piano. They go ding, dong, a good piano thrill.
>
> Dr.: Are you getting along all right here?
>
> Pt.: Yes, it's a wash on the tub.
>
> Dr.: What do you mean by that?
>
> Pt.: Ding dong on the piano.[13]

Robert's unusual behavior began in childhood, as is usually the case with the hebephrenic reaction, and grew more bizarre over the years. Finally, after he had mutilated his penis (so that, as he put it, he could get his girl friend "pregnant at a distance") and said that he had been stuck with green needles by dwarfs, he was committed to an institution.

*Catatonic schizophrenics* present a more dramatic symptom picture than any other type because of their tendency to assume rigid poses and maintain them for hours or even days. They are able to remain stiff, in unchanging positions that normal people would be physically unable to hold for more than several minutes. In these fixed states catatonics are completely withdrawn and isolated; they do not talk or respond to others and often have to be tube-fed.

Catatonic schizophrenics may move on their own when so directed, but they move like robots or mechanical figures. Some allow their bodies to be contorted into uncomfortable positions by the doctor, positions which they will then hold for a period of time. Sometimes they behave in belligerent and hostile ways or become physically violent.

[13] Melvin Zax and George Stricker, *Patterns of Psychopathology* (New York: Macmillan, 1963), pp. 65–66.

They also have intense hallucinations and delusions. When not holding a rigid pose, catatonics may perform certain acts or gestures repeatedly in a mechanical way.

In *paranoid schizophrenia,* the most common of the schizophrenic disorders, persons suffer from the delusion that they are being persecuted. They believe that friends, relatives, or such organizations as the CIA or the FBI are out to get them. They think that they are being spied upon, followed, x-rayed, and that people are reading their thoughts, implanting thoughts in their heads, or elaborately trying to deceive them in some way.

Because they believe that some person or group is spending considerable time and effort to persecute them, paranoid schizophrenics come to develop delusions of grandeur. After all, they reason, they must be very important people if they are spied upon and followed in such an elaborate manner. And so they often imagine themselves to be God, or the President of the United States, or a famous military leader such as Napoleon, or a millionaire, or the inventor of some marvelous device or scheme to cure cancer or end war for all time. Paranoid schizophrenics are prone to hallucinations, and they frequently hear voices telling them what to do.

Coleman reported the following conversation between a paranoid schizophrenic patient and a psychiatrist.[14]

Doctor: What's your name?
Patient: Who are you?
Dr.: I'm a doctor. Who are you?
Pt.: I can't tell you who I am.
Dr.: Why can't you tell me?
Pt.: You wouldn't believe me.
Dr.: What are you doing here?
Pt.: Well, I've been sent here to thwart the Russians. I'm the only one in the world who knows how to deal with them. They got their spies all around here though to get me, but I'm smarter than any of them.
Dr.: What are you going to do to thwart the Russians?
Pt.: I'm organizing.
Dr.: Whom are you going to organize?
Pt.: Everybody. I'm the only man in the world who can do that, but they're trying to get me. But I'm going to use my atomic bomb media to blow them up.
Dr.: You must be a terribly important person then.
Pt.: Well, of course.
Dr.: What do you call yourself?
Pt.: You used to know me as Franklin D. Roosevelt.
Dr.: Isn't he dead?

[14] Coleman, op. cit., p. 276. Copyright © 1972 by Scott, Foresman and Company. Reprinted by permission.

Pt.: Sure he's dead, but I'm alive.

Dr.: But you're Franklin D. Roosevelt?

Pt.: His spirit. He, God, and I figured this out. And now I'm going to make a race of healthy people. My agents are lining them up. Say, who are you?

Dr.: I'm a doctor here.

Pt.: You don't look like a doctor. You look like a Russian to me.

In this case, both types of delusions are present, delusions of persecution and delusions of grandeur. The patient believed that the Russians had been after him for some time prior to his admittance to the hospital. He said they surrounded him in his neighborhood and tried to drop a bomb on him.

## Manic-Depressive Psychosis

In the *manic-depressive psychosis*, sometimes called *affective psychosis*, the person is characterized by extremes of mood or feeling. All of us have ups and downs, periods of depression and periods of joy. Such mood swings seem to be a normal part of daily living. Manic-depressive psychosis, however, is much more intense. The manic periods are often characterized by violent outbursts of frenetic activity and the depressed periods are often marked by thoughts of suicide.

In general, most manic-depressive psychotics display only one of these extremes. They are either depressed or manic. Some manic depressives, however, alternate between the two extremes.

J. M., a forty-four-year-old housewife, is typical of the latter type. Her mood swings became so intense that she had to be hospitalized.

During the depressed periods she is sad, dejected, engages in no activity and speaks almost entirely in monosyllables. She frequently takes a minute or two to answer a simple question and then replies in a dismal tone with a single word. She gives the appearance of one who has the weight of the world on her shoulders. Usually she sits with head bowed, brow wrinkled and hands clasped in her lap. Even the simplest request appears to require too much activity and when she does speak it is only to say that she is very sick. She complains that her bowels won't move, that her head is heavy and that she would be better off dead. . . .

In the manic phase we would not recognize her as the same individual. It appears to be impossible for her to remain still for an instant. She is all over the ward, dancing, singing, slapping patients and nurses on the back, pulling off her clothes and throwing things about with absolute abandon. She writes poetry and insists on reciting it to everyone near her, monopolizes the conversation and has a flippant reply for every remark that is made by anyone else. In these phases she becomes unusually demanding, and when repulsed is abusive both in language and activity. She hurls, not only remarks, but anything she can lay her hands on at those who refuse her requests. Her ideas are grandiose and she has plans that can't fail to solve the situation. A good bit of her behavior at this time is erotic. She tears off all of her clothing, talks of her sex appeal and of men trying to seduce her and throws her arms about any man who happens to appear.[15]

Usually, these psychotic episodes appear and disappear, alternating with generally normal behavior that shows little sign of either extreme of mood. When the psychotic episodes do appear, however, they can last as long as several months, and the person must almost always be hospitalized during these times. The periods of institutionalization are usually shorter for manic depressives than for the other psychotic patients and seldom last longer than a year at a time.

Psychologists are uncertain about the specific causes of psychoses, although there are several theories about their origin. Some theorists believe that the causes are psychological, related primarily to conflicts originating in early childhood. Other theorists cite physiological causes, such as biochemical imbalances, that may predispose a person to psychosis. A related suggestion is that psychotic behavior, or the predisposition to psychotic behavior, may be inherited. The advocates of each position can claim empirical support for their respective points of view, but the issue is far from settled. Much more research is needed to answer the question of why some persons become psychotic.

## PERSONALITY DISORDERS

The group of abnormalities known collectively as personality disorders certainly qualifies as mental illness and, as such, falls to the left of the average mental health category in the normal distribution of mental health (Figure 3–1).

Personality disorders differ, however, from neuroses and psychoses in two important respects. First, personality disorders are behavioral or acting-out disorders rather than illnesses characterized by excessive emotional torment. There is usually little inner pain involved in personality disorders; the pathology is often less disturbing to the individual than to society, which is often the real victim of such disorders.

Second, persons suffering from personality disorders are not hounded by the intense feelings of anxiety that plague neurotics, nor have they lost contact with reality as have psychotics. For these reasons, personality disorders are sometimes considered to be less serious than neuroses

---

[15] R. M. Dorcus and G. W. Shaffer, *Textbook of Abnormal Psychology* (4th ed; Baltimore: Williams & Wilkins, 1950), pp. 454–455.

and psychoses, but this is not always true. Personality disorders can cripple or ruin lives just as completely as any neurotic or psychotic disorder. Further, personality disorders often cause a person to get in trouble with the law for exhibiting behavior that society usually considers undesirable or immoral.

The three major types of personality disorders are (1) addiction to drugs or alcohol and certain sexual behaviors considered to be deviant, (2) disturbances characterized by a dominant trend within the personality, and (3) the psychopathic personality.

As you know, there are substances and activities to which we can become addicted. Many people are dependent on alcohol and others on drugs, such as cocaine, heroin, or physician-prescribed tranquilizers. Such people have difficulty coping with life without their daily bottle or fix. Drugs or alcohol may become more important to them than food.

Some people are addicted to work (the "workaholic") and others to gambling. They are driven by their addiction to engage in these activities. Regardless of the object of the addiction, these people have great difficulty leading normal lives.

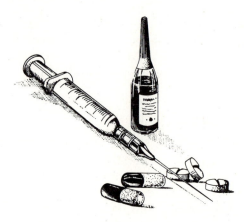

Some of the sexual behaviors considered deviant by society are listed in Table 3–2. These sexual deviations usually derive from an inability to have what are considered normal sexual relations, and often have their origins in childhood or early adolescence.

Although addictions and sexual disturbances are serious problems in our society, we shall concentrate here on more traditional personality disturbances: dominant personality trends and the psychopathic personality.

Disturbances that manifest themselves as dominant trends within the personality are of several kinds.

**Table 3–2.** Deviant Sexual Behaviors

*Agalmatophilia:* Having a sexual attraction to statues.

*Exhibitionism:* Exposing one's genitals in public.

*Fetishism:* Becoming sexually aroused by objects such as items of clothing or by parts of the body not usually associated with sex.

*Forcible Rape:* Forcing another person to have sexual relations.

*Incest:* Engaging in sexual relations with a close relative.

*Masochism:* Deriving sexual pleasure from having pain inflicted on oneself.

*Necrophilia:* Having an erotic attraction to corpses.

*Pedophilia:* Taking a sexual interest in young children of the same or other sex.

*Sadism:* Deriving sexual pleasure from inflicting pain on another person.

*Transvestism:* Deriving sexual pleasure from dressing in the clothing of the other sex.

*Voyeurism:* Observing other people engaging in sexual activities.

*Zoophilia:* Having sexual relations with animals.

*The paranoid personality.* These persons are usually very suspicious of other people, are likely to blame others for their own shortcomings, and may be envious or jealous of others.

*The schizoid personality.* Schizoids have very shallow emotional lives and tend to be reclusive, shy, sensitive, and aloof from others.

*The inadequate personality.* These persons do not react well to the demands and stresses of life. They tend to be unstable socially, inept in their dealings with others, and lacking in stamina.

*The explosive personality.* These persons are prone to uncontrollable outbursts of temper and become excitable and aggressive during these fits, quite unlike their normal behavior.

*The passive personality.* There are two variations of the passive personality: passive dependent and passive aggressive. Passive dependent persons are extremely dependent on other people. Quite helpless on their own, they rely on others for all satisfactions. Passive aggressive persons are also dependent on others, but they combine this dependency with feelings of hostility toward those upon whom they depend.

*The compulsive personality.* Compulsives are likely to be very conforming to standards of propriety and to their own conscience. They work extremely hard and find it difficult to relax.

These personality disturbances are not sufficiently severe to be considered neurotic, but they are nonetheless capable of interfering with normal life adjustment.

The third type of personality disorders, and the most dangerous to society, is the *psychopathic personality* (also called sociopathic). Psychopaths have no consideration for other people and no feelings of guilt about any act they may commit. They are totally lacking in conscience or in normal feelings of responsibility toward others. They may lie, cheat, rob, and murder without hesitation or remorse. They are emotionally immature, following the impulse of the moment no matter where it leads or what effects their behavior may have on others. Easily frustrated, psychopaths may act out their rage in violent behavior.

These persons show no concern about breaking laws or behaving in unethical or immoral ways. Some psychopaths are successful in business, in part because of their ruthless practices, but also because they are often very bright and even charming. Most psychopaths, however, are not successful at anything they undertake, and they spend their lives on the fringes of society, often living out one jail sentence after another.[16]

Roger H., a twenty-seven-year-old inmate of a state prison, is a psychopath. He is serving a five- to fifteen-year sentence for breaking and entering, the latest in a long string of arrests and convictions. Roger's unruly behavior was evident by the time he was in the second grade. He threw things at teachers, disobeyed them, and was aggressive toward the other children. By the time he was twelve he had been expelled from three schools.

He injured his Sunday-school teacher, assaulted his eighth-grade teacher, and was frequently truant from school. At the age of fourteen he was expelled from the city school system altogether, whereupon his parents placed him in a private school; he lasted only two weeks. During those two weeks he beat the housemother and behaved so aggressively that the other boys refused to allow him in their rooms.

After one more failure in a private school, Roger became involved in criminal activities until, at sixteen, he was sent to a state institution for delinquents. Paroled after seven months, he spent the next seven years going from one encounter with the police to another. He worked at a series of odd jobs, but never kept any of them more than two months. His crimes include larceny, assaulting a police officer, assault and battery, parole violation, drunk and disorderly conduct, and resisting arrest.

---

[16] Truman Capote wrote a vivid and true account of two psychopaths, *In Cold Blood* (New York: Random House, 1966), which was later made into a movie. He describes the lives of two men who brutally murdered a family of four.

While he was being sentenced to the state prison for his latest term, the presiding judge had this to say about him.

> There are very few individuals who, in my opinion, do not have any good qualities whatsoever, but if this man has anything good about him I have never discovered it. I do not believe, therefore, that there is any chance of rehabilitating him by any appeal to his better nature. I would strongly recommend that his confinement be made as rugged as possible. . . . In my opinion there is an excellent chance that this man will end up murdering someone or being killed by a policeman's bullet.[17]

Roger was diagnosed as psychopathic by the prison psychiatrist shortly before his appearance before the parole board. The psychiatrist described Roger in these terms.

> He is entirely without insight, feels that the law-enforcing agencies have persecuted him. . . . This man presents a *sociopathic personality disturbance*, is a chronically antisocial person who does not profit from experience and who still shows marked emotional immaturity, lack of judgment, and a tendency to rationalize. In my book, he is a very unpre-dictable type of person. While he is not psychotic, he is the same unstable individual as at the time of admission; he is merely doing time, day by day, and has no goals for the future. He is very apt to return to his former pattern of behavior upon release.[18]

Despite the psychiatrist's report and Roger's long history of offenses, he was paroled after four years. Four months later he was returned to prison, having violated his parole by severely assaulting a man in a tavern. Asked why he broke his parole, Roger shrugged, showing a total lack of concern, and said, "It was just one of those things." [19]

We have discussed a large number and variety of abnormal behaviors. However, identifying the nature and characteristics of mental illnesses is only one facet of psychology's continuing concern. Of possibly greater importance is the attempt to reduce this staggering emotional toll and to treat those who are disturbed. This is a pressing and vital application of psychology to the well-being of us all.

## SUMMARY

Mental illness is an epidemic affecting at least one out of every ten people in the United States, who, at some time in their lives, will have

---

[17] Albert I. Rabin, "Psychopathic (Sociopathic) Personalities," *Legal and Criminal Psychology*, ed. Hans Toch (New York: Holt, Rinehart and Winston, 1961), p. 274.
[18] Ibid., p. 271.
[19] Ibid., p. 274.

to be treated for abnormal behavior. Millions more turn to tranquilizers, alcohol, drugs, or suffer in silence because of emotional problems.

Determining whether someone is mentally ill is difficult in all but the most extreme and obvious cases because what is abnormal in one situation may be normal and adaptive in another situation. Abnormality is defined in statistical terms, that is, by the relative frequency of occurrence of such behavior. But that is not sufficient to judge a person mentally ill. One must also consider how harmful the behavior is to the individual and to others, and the person's degree of internal suffering.

The behavior of mentally ill persons differs only in degree and not in kind from the behavior of normal persons; there are usually no sharp distinctions between normal and abnormal behavior. As a result, even psychiatrists and psychologists often have difficulty distinguishing sane from insane persons, except in extreme cases.

The specific types of mental illnesses discussed include neuroses, psychoses, and personality disorders.

In *neurosis,* a moderate-to-severe form of mental illness, the person retains contact with reality but has difficulty coping with life. The condition is characterized by strong feelings of anxiety. Specific neuroses include *anxiety neurosis,* characterized by an intense level of anxiety that interferes with all activities; *phobias,* an intense, constant, and irrational fear of some object or situation; *obsessions and compulsions,* persistent ideas (obsessions) or behaviors (compulsions) that the person must think about or act out constantly; *hysteria,* manifested as *conversion reactions* (the conversion of some psychological disturbance into a physical disturbance such as blindness or paralysis) or *dissociative reactions* (the dissociation of parts of the personality in the form of amnesia, somnambulism, or multiple personality); *hypochondria,* excessive and exaggerated concern for one's health and physical condition; and *depressive neurosis,* powerful, persistent, and compelling feelings of depression, gloom, discouragement, and rejection.

*Psychoses* are more severe forms of mental illness than neuroses. Psychotic persons, legally labeled "insane," maintain no contact with reality, live in a personal fantasy world, and usually have to be hospitalized. Two major categories of psychoses are *organic psychoses,* caused by physical damage to the brain, and *functional psychoses,* caused by psychological factors. Two major functional psychoses are *schizophrenia,* the splitting of the personality from reality and of the thought processes from the emotions, and *manic-depressive psychosis,* extreme fluctuations of moods and feelings from the depths of depression to the heights of euphoria.

*Personality disorders* differ from neuroses in that they are not characterized by intense feelings of anxiety, and from psychoses in that contact with reality is not lost. Three forms of personality disorders are *addictions* to drugs or alcohol and the practice of *deviant sexual behaviors; dominant personality trends* such as the paranoid, schizoid, inadequate, explosive, passive, and compulsive personalities; and the *psychopathic personality*, distinguished by an absence of consideration for others and a total lack of guilt or remorse about antisocial and often violent behavior.

## SUGGESTED READINGS

Barclay, Martin. *Abnormal Psychology: Clinical and Scientific Perspectives.* New York: Holt, Rinehart and Winston, 1977.

Calhoun, James F. *Abnormal Psychology: Current Perspectives,* 2nd ed. New York: Random House, 1976.

Coleman, James C. *Abnormal Psychology and Modern Life,* 5th ed. Glenview, Ill.: Scott, Foresman, 1976.

Costin, Frank. *Abnormal Psychology: Programmed Learning Aid Series.* Homewood, Ill.: Learning Systems, 1976.

Davison, Gerald C., and John M. Neale. *Abnormal Psychology: An Experimental Clinical Approach.* New York: Wiley, 1974.

Goleman, Daniel. Who's mentally ill? *Psychology Today,* 1978 (January), **11,** 34–41.

Milt, Harry. *Alcoholism: Its Causes and Cure.* New York: Scribner's, 1976.

Rosenhan, D. L. On being sane in insane places. *Science,* 1973 (January 19), **179,** 250–258.

Sarason, Irwin G. *Abnormal Psychology: The Problem of Maladaptive Behavior,* 2nd ed. Englewood Cliffs, N.J.: Prentice-Hall, 1976.

# Psychology Applied to Mental Health: II. The Treatment of Mental Illness

**4**

The patient was twenty-eight years old and single, and he lived with his mother, to whom he was a devoted and attentive son. He worked as an accountant and was, in all ways, a quiet, kind, and gentle person. He was troubled, however, by strong feelings of anxiety; he was afraid but he did not know why. He was also unhappy in his work, which he thought was increasingly futile. His sleep was restless and fitful, plagued by nightmares. One recurring dream particularly frightened him, a dream in which a truck that he was driving ran over and killed a woman.

On his fortieth visit to the psychologist, he talked about that dream.

Patient: I had another of those dreams last night. I woke up in a sweat and was frightened almost to death.

Doctor: Tell me about it.

Pt.: It's pretty much the same thing. I was driving a big truck along a dark country road at night. I saw a woman walking along it ahead of me, and I could have avoided her easily. But (great agitation) I didn't seem to want to! I just held the truck to the curve of the road on the right side, and I hit her! I hit her! And it was awful! I stopped and went around to her, and she was still alive but dying fast, and she was terribly battered!

Dr.: Tell me about the woman. Just say whatever comes to mind now. Think about the woman and just say whatever occurs to you.

Pt.: Well, she was nobody I've ever known. She seemed small and sort of helpless. She was just walking along the road. It's not always the same woman in these dreams, but they're usually little old ladies like this one. She had dark hair and was terribly, terribly disfigured after the truck hit her. Mother's hair is almost snow white now, but this woman was dark. I've never known anybody like her. (pause)

Dr.: It seems important to you not to know who this woman was. Go on.

Pt.: But I don't know who she was! She was just a little old woman on a dark country road. It was horrible! The accident messed her up so dreadfully! I felt nauseated and revolted by all the mess as well as by the horror of what I had done. But—and this is very strange—I didn't feel any real remorse in the dream, I don't think. I was terrified and sick at the sight but not really sorry. I think that's what wakes me up. I'm not really sorry.

Dr.: Almost as if you were glad to have got rid of this little old lady. Go on. Just say whatever comes to mind.

Pt.: (after a long pause) I guess the horror of the sight is that she was so messy and bloody. Mother, the only older woman that I know really well, is always so neat and clean and well taken care of. This woman in the dream seemed, I don't know, evil somehow in spite of her being so helpless.

Dr.: Your mother is quite a burden on you at times, isn't she?

Pt.: Why no! How can you say that? She's a wonderful person, and I'm glad to do what I can for her. She means more to me than anybody else.

Dr.: These things are pretty painful to think about at times, but I'm pretty impressed by your knowing only your mother as a helpless little old lady and your dreaming so repeatedly about killing just such a person. And *you* are the one who dreams it.*

You have no doubt guessed what the psychologist is suggesting in these comments to the patient. From what the patient has related of his anxieties, his life, and his dreams, the psychologist suspects that the patient harbors unconscious resentment and hostility toward his mother, and these feelings are undermining his mental health. Because he cannot openly admit this resentment to himself, it is manifested in dreams. By helping the patient recognize and accept these feelings toward his mother, the psychologist hopes to help the patient deal with them in a realistic manner.

This patient has been undergoing one form of treatment or therapy for his emotional problems, a therapy that is based on probing a person's unconscious feelings and motivations. Although this approach is widely used today, it is not the only form of therapy available. There are many therapies for mental illness, and each focuses on a different aspect of psychological functioning or is appropriate treatment for illnesses of different kinds and severities.

Some therapies concentrate on conscious feelings of the moment and ignore unconscious conflicts that may have their origins in a person's past. Other therapies focus only on the overt symptoms the person displays and attempt to change behavior rather than any internal aspect of the personality, conscious or unconscious. Other treatments rely more

---

*Laurance F. Shaffer and Edward J. Shoben, Jr., *The Psychology of Adjustment*, 2nd ed. (Boston: Houghton Mifflin, 1956), pp. 516–517. Copyright © 1956 by L. F. Shaffer and E. J. Shoben. Reprinted by permission of Houghton Mifflin Company.

on a medical than a psychological approach and include drugs, electric shock, and surgery on the brain.

In addition, some therapies are conducted on an individual basis; the patient and therapist meet alone for an hour or so perhaps one or more times a week. Other therapies are based on a group approach, in which as many as ten or twelve patients meet to discuss their mutual problems with a single therapist. Some therapies are designed for use with children; others are for adults. Some allow the patient to physically act out his or her problems; others favor only a verbal release. Some therapies are conducted only by trained, experienced, professional psychiatrists and psychologists; others are carried out by persons with minimal training under the supervision of skilled professionals.

Thus, whatever emotional or behavioral problem an individual faces, there is a form of therapy that claims to be capable of resolving the problem.

We do not know how many people in the United States are undergoing therapy at any one time because many people are treated by private practitioners who do not ordinarily make their records available. However, we do know that the number is very large, certainly larger than the number of persons confined in mental institutions. Whether for neuroses, psychoses, or temporary adjustment problems, millions of emotionally troubled persons seek psychological help. (Indeed, in some circles it has become fashionable to do so.) It seems true today that there is much less social stigma attached to being treated by a psychologist or a psychiatrist than there once was.

But untold millions of persons are not treated by professionals for their emotional problems. Some of them visit their family physicians, who usually prescribe tranquilizers or sleeping pills because they are rarely trained to give psychological therapy or counseling. Other persons talk with their pastors, priests, or rabbis, only some of whom are trained to deal with emotional problems (although the number is increasing rapidly). Still others talk to their family or friends. Unfortunately, however, many people still suffer in silence with their problems because they are ashamed, or believe they are too poor to seek professional help. The number of people who do not receive any help is sizable.

We will discuss seven forms or approaches to the treatment of mental illness: physical therapy, individual psychotherapy, group psychotherapy, behavior therapy, play therapy, psychodrama, and community-based therapy (which includes the use of paraprofessional personnel).

## PHYSICAL THERAPY

The various types of physical treatment for mental illness are usually reserved for the most severely disturbed patients, those whose contact with reality is minimal. Persons who suffer from extremes of depression, anxiety, and disorientation usually cannot be treated by therapies that require a person to communicate with a therapist and to understand what the therapist is saying. It is difficult to treat such a person by psychotherapy (to treat the mind), so treatment is directed instead toward the body, in the hope of making the person more aware of and responsive to the real world and thus potentially responsive to psychotherapy.

Because the physical therapies are designed to treat the most severe mental illnesses, those most likely to require hospitalization, physical treatments are used in mental hospitals more than any other form of therapy. Usually, persons who can benefit from other forms of therapy do not need hospitalization and can be treated on an outpatient basis.

The major types of physical therapy are shock therapy, drug therapy, and psychosurgery.

## Shock Therapy

In *shock therapy*, an electric or drug-induced shock is delivered to the patient, producing strong bodily convulsions followed by a period of unconsciousness. This is an extreme and potentially dangerous form of therapy, but it seems to be effective in some cases, often when no other treatment has been satisfactory.

Originally, shocks were induced through large doses of insulin, but that has been largely replaced by a drug called metrazol. However, the convulsions produced by metrazol are so extremely violent that patients often break bones. Also, the drug produces a fear of repeated treatments in patients. Nonetheless, it is still in use and is often successful.

Since the late 1930s, the primary form of shock therapy has been electric shock therapy, also called electroshock therapy, electroconvulsive therapy, and ECT. Patients are usually given a muscle relaxant before the electric shock to reduce the danger of broken bones. Then they are strapped to padded treatment tables, electrodes are clamped to the head, and a shock as large as 130 volts is administered for a fraction of a second. Convulsions follow (some as severe as epileptic fits) and the patients immediately lose consciousness, sometimes for as long as several hours. The standard course of treatment with electroshock therapy is twenty or thirty shocks administered over several weeks.

Patients apparently do not suffer pain with this treatment and, when they regain consciousness, they usually have no memory of the treatment or of the preparation for it. Nevertheless, many patients become frightened of repeated treatments.

Electroshock seems to be very effective in cases of intense depression.

It can sometimes alleviate the depression without any additional kinds of treatment. At the least, shock treatments often bring patients out of their depression to the point where they become communicative. Then they can be treated by other, less drastic therapies. No one knows how electroshock therapy works or why it is successful with depressives. It is suspected that the shock produces some internal physiological changes as well as psychological changes.

## Drug Therapy

The development of a host of new drugs since the 1950s has brought about a revolution in the treatment of mental illness. Of all the forms of therapy developed in the twentieth century, none has produced so profound a change in dealing with emotional disturbances as these chemical forms of treatment.

Millions of people are better able to cope with their depressions and anxieties because of such drugs. They have noticeably altered the behavior of patients in mental hospitals as well. Before the "chemical revolution," psychotic patients frequently had to be forcibly restrained (by straitjackets, for example), and mental wards were characterized by bedlam—patients running amok, cursing, screaming, and physically attacking one another and the staff. Nowadays mental wards are quieter and considerably easier to manage, and patients are much less violent because of the use of drug therapy.

Three general types of drugs are useful in treating mentally ill persons: antipsychotic drugs, antianxiety drugs, and antidepressant drugs. The first two types are popularly known as tranquilizers or "downers," which act to calm a person, and the latter are known as "uppers," which act to restore vitality.

*Antipsychotic drugs* are very strong tranquilizers capable of calming the intense and often violent psychotic behaviors. They can produce startling behavior changes, sometimes in less than forty-eight hours, in patients who had been highly resistant to other forms of therapy. Long-term delusions and hallucinations usually disappear and most patients seem to regain at least partial contact with the environment. These results have been found even with long-term schizophrenics.

Although antipsychotic drugs are extremely valuable in reducing or relieving symptoms of psychoses, they do not by themselves cure the patients' emotional problems. What they can do, aside from symptom relief, is to make patients more responsive and communicative so that treatment by psychotherapy, previously impossible, can be conducted.

With some patients the use of antipsychotic drugs brings about such dramatic behavioral changes that they can be discharged from the hospital. They have not been cured, but their behavior has become less bizarre and violent. As long as they continue to take the antipsychotic drug, they can return to society, without harm to themselves or to others. In recent years there has been a marked increase in the number of persons discharged from mental hospitals, a phenomenon related less to the clinical skills and training of the hospital staff than to the daily intake of drugs.

More than sixty million Americans are familiar with *antianxiety drugs.* These are the mild tranquilizers, for which family physicians write prescriptions every day for persons who are worried, tense, or agitated. The most popular ones are valium and librium, and many people are on a daily diet of such antianxiety drugs. These drugs allow persons who are governed by neuroses or are faced with critical stresses of job or marriage to function in their everyday lives without having to seek counseling or psychotherapy. Many people take these drugs habitually, to help them cope with the ordinary tensions of daily life, which, unfortunately, they are unable to handle on their own.

As is the case with antipsychotic drugs, antianxiety drugs calm us and make us feel better by freeing us from worry and tension. Also, antianxiety drugs do not cure emotional problems or attack the causes of the problems. They relieve the symptoms caused by the emotional problems, and this is important in itself. These drugs are not without side effects, however; they often make people drowsy and weak and may interfere with intellectual activities.

*Antidepressant drugs* work in the opposite way from the tranquilizers. Whereas tranquilizers calm us, antidepressant drugs pick us up. Antidepressant drugs are particularly effective in combating intense depression. Severely depressed persons need something to restore vitality, energy, and interest in life and in their surroundings.

Occasionally, these drugs will bring a depressed person so far up that he or she becomes nervous and agitated. In general, however, antidepressant drugs have been remarkably successful in dealing with depressives, both by enabling them to benefit from psychotherapy, to which they are unresponsive while in the severely depressed state, and by shortening their stay in a mental hospital.

It should be noted that not much is known about possible long-range consequences of taking daily doses of any of these drugs. In addition, there is the danger of harmful interaction effects if people are taking any of these drugs along with pain-killers or sleeping pills. Many people in our society have become too dependent on drugs of all types, particularly tranquilizers and sleeping pills, and this overmedication may eventually prove to be another unfortunate example of the cure being worse than the illness.

## Psychosurgery

A dramatic form of treatment for mental illness is surgery on the brain, *psychosurgery*, to sever the frontal lobes of the brain from other brain structures that control emotion. This technique has been used since the late 1930s as a last-resort measure for patients with a long history of suffering, for whom nothing else has worked.

Psychosurgery is used for a number of disabling conditions: severe depression, obsessive-compulsive and anxiety neuroses, and some types of schizophrenia.

Consider the case of T. M., a thirty-seven-year-old woman who had her first psychotic episode during her early twenties. She experienced a long period of hallucinations and schizophrenic tendencies and later became an alcoholic. Her treatment included nearly thirty electric shocks and sixty insulin coma shocks, none of which seemed to help. Finally, after three psychosurgical operations, she improved. When asked if she would recommend psychosurgery, she said, "It's a godsend, it is, I cannot say enough about them (the operations). I don't know why they work or how they work, but they are a true godsend. They gave me back my life." [1]

Despite such successes, the technique has remained highly controversial. The U.S. Congress has tried several times to outlaw it. What are the problems with psychosurgery? First, it does not always work. Some patients showed no improvement and a few patients became worse after the surgery. Second, those who are helped apparently pay a price for their relief in terms of a flattening or dulling of their personalities. Many patients become apathetic and emotionless following surgery.

Nevertheless, the technique continues to be used; approximately four hundred psychosurgical operations are performed each year in the United States. In 1976 the National Commission for Protection of Human Subjects of Biomedical and Behavioral Research endorsed the continued use of psychosurgery, noting that the technique has "potential merit" and that it is not excessively risky. [2]

## INDIVIDUAL PSYCHOTHERAPY

None of the physical therapies is capable of curing mental illness in any complete sense, that is, restoring the patient to a pre-illness state of normality by eliminating the cause of the problem. Physical therapies

[1] Sharland Trotter, "Federal Commission OK's Psychosurgery," *APA Monitor*, 7 (November 1976), 4–5.

[2] Ibid., p. 4.

are quite good for their purpose—to relieve symptoms and emotional pain—and they have helped millions of persons to cope better with their emotional problems. However, they do not attempt to treat a person's feelings or emotional state in a psychological manner. Physical therapies deal with a person's physiological aspects and alter physiological functioning (in ways not fully understood); this results in symptom relief.

*Psychotherapy*, obviously a more psychological kind of therapy, attempts to deal directly with a person's psychological condition. Through the use of psychological techniques, psychotherapy tries to deal with the reasons or causes of a person's suffering in an effort to eliminate those causes or to help the person adapt realistically to them.

In the discussion of clinical research methods (Chapter 2), some of the specific techniques used in psychotherapy were noted: taking a patient's life history, psychological tests to define aspects of the individual's personality, and dream analysis. (An example of the use of dream analysis is presented in the case at the beginning of this chapter.) The differences between these clinical research methods, which are psychological in nature, and the physical therapy techniques, which are physiologically oriented, should be apparent.

The primary aim of psychotherapy is to achieve insight into the patient's problem. Patients are led to an awareness of their innermost fears and feelings in order to achieve an understanding of who and what they are. It is an attempt to follow one of our oldest maxims, "know thyself," an extremely difficult, time-consuming, and even painful process. Through psychotherapy, patients are helped to gain insight into the cause (or causes) of their problem, how their neurotic defenses hinder their adjustment to life, and how to deal more realistically with their emotional ills.

Some approaches to psychotherapy are based on the idea that the root causes of all emotional disorders can be found in childhood traumas and conflicts kept hidden in the dark recesses of the unconscious mind. Patients must, in a sense, be led back into these previously invisible areas of the mind in order to uncover and to face whatever past conflicts are buried there. The theory of psychoanalysis, the work of Sigmund Freud, is the most prominent example of this approach.

Other forms of psychotherapy do not probe the unconscious or try to seek explanations in childhood experiences. They focus more on present conscious feelings, how people feel about themselves at the moment. This approach is represented by client-centered therapy, the work of Carl Rogers.

Both of these types of psychotherapy are conducted on an individual basis; the patient and the therapist, together, talk through the patient's problem. A different form of psychotherapy—group psychotherapy—is conducted with six to twelve persons who have similar problems; they have an opportunity to share their feelings and their pain with one another and with the therapist.


## Psychoanalysis

Sigmund Freud's method of *psychoanalysis* is the original form of psychotherapy, and the one with which most people are familiar. It is no longer the only technique of psychotherapy, although it continues to be a popular one.

The primary assumption behind Freud's approach to therapy is that mental illness results from the repression into the unconscious of traumas and conflicts that occurred in childhood. These traumatic childhood events, usually centering around sex or aggression, are too painful for the individual to remember consciously. Therefore, the conflict and everything associated with it is pushed deep into the unconscious, where it serves as a powerful motivating force and a source of internal conflict and anxiety.

Freud believed that it was this anxiety, and the constant attempts to deal with it, that led to neurosis. To free the individual of the burden of the anxiety, it is necessary to bring the material repressed in the unconscious back into consciousness so that the person is made aware of the source of the problem. Once the individual thus gains insight into the source of the problem, it becomes possible to face the conflict and the anxiety and to deal rationally with them.

Bringing to the surface repressed conflicts from childhood experiences is a very difficult task, which patients often unconsciously resist because they are afraid to face these experiences. As a result, psychoanalysis is a time-consuming, laborious, and sometimes emotionally painful process. Rarely is a psychoanalytic procedure completed in less than one year. It is more common for treatment to continue for two to three years or even longer.

Each psychoanalytic session lasts approximately one hour, and sessions may be scheduled from once to five times per week. Undergoing psychoanalysis requires a serious investment of time, emotional energy, and money (minimum treatment costs are $25 per hour).

Freud developed four techniques for bringing unconscious material into conscious awareness: free association, dream analysis, analysis of resistance, and analysis of transference.

*Free association* is the most basic technique of psychoanalysis. Patients must tell the analyst everything that comes to mind during a therapy session. To encourage this, patients recline on a couch so that they may feel as comfortable as possible. The therapist sits behind the couch, out of sight of the patient.[3]

In free association, patients daydream, in a sense, out loud; they let their minds wander freely, saying anything that comes to them. They are instructed to tell everything they are thinking about, no matter how trivial, silly, or embarrassing it may seem. They are also cautioned not to rearrange or distort the material in any way, simply to relate whatever appears in the "stream of consciousness," as it appears.

Freud believed that there was nothing random about free associations, nor were they subject to the patient's conscious choice. Instead, they are predetermined, forced on the individual by the nature of the conflict that is the cause of the problem. Free association is not an easy process. Throughout our lives we consciously control what we say to other people, fearful of how much we may reveal of ourselves. It is difficult to suddenly permit everything to pass through the filter of consciousness, and this difficulty is a major part of the psychoanalytic process.

*Dream analysis*, another technique of psychoanalysis developed by Freud, is another way of reaching into the unconscious and bringing repressed incidents and conflicts to the surface. Freud considered dreams to be so important that he called them the "royal road" to the unconscious, and he used them for his personal analysis.

When he was forty-one, and suffering from a number of neurotic difficulties that seem to fit the category of anxiety neurosis, Freud decided that he needed psychoanalyzing. He had to psychoanalyze himself because at that time he was the only psychoanalyst in the world. For the next several years he investigated his own dreams, free associating to them every morning. In the process, he apparently freed himself of his neurosis.

Freud reasoned that when people are asleep, their conscious mind is less on guard against material in the unconscious. Thus, events and conflicts repressed in the unconscious can surface during sleep in the form of dreams. However, some repressed material is so abhorrent and repulsive that even in sleep it cannot surface openly. It appears instead in disguised or symbolic form in the dreams.

In the first case in this chapter, the son's hostility toward his mother was disguised in the dream. The woman he repeatedly killed in his dream was not at all like his mother—her hair color was different, for example. The therapist told him: "It seems important to you not to know who this woman was." And it *was* important to him; he could not admit to himself the existence of feelings of hostility toward his mother.

---

[3] Freud chose to sit behind his patients because he said he could not bear to be stared at all day.

But these feelings were there all along, causing his emotional problems and appearing at night in the form of nightmares.

The task of the therapist is to interpret the symbols of the dream, to uncover their hidden meaning. There are two aspects or contents of dreams, according to Freud: the manifest content and the latent content. The *manifest content* is the actual dream story as the person remembers and tells it. The *latent content* is the hidden or symbolic meaning, what the story of the dream signifies. The analyst must proceed from the manifest content to the latent content in order to find the unconscious motives and conflicts that are being symbolically expressed in the dream.

Dream interpretation is a difficult task, one that cannot be accomplished on the basis of a single dream. A number of dreams from the same patient must be analyzed in order to determine if similar themes appear. Freud believed that dreams should be interpreted as symbolic fulfillments of wishes or desires that the person cannot consciously express.

A third technique of psychoanalysis, *analysis of resistance,* attempts to deal with the inability or unwillingness of patients to talk about certain aspects of their past lives. In free association, and sometimes in reporting dreams, patients often resist revealing to the therapist emotional or anxiety-filled incidents.

As noted, free association is difficult for most people and their conversation during this period is frequently marked by long silences and outward signs of embarrassment or agitation. These indications of resistance tell the therapist that the analysis is getting close to highly sensitive material, which may be suggestive of the basis of a person's problem.

Freud believed that what people do not talk about—what they cannot admit to themselves or to others—may be more personally revealing than what they do talk about. The therapist must break down these resistances and bring the repressed material to the surface so that the patient can be taught to live with and accept it. The hidden conflicts must be made visible; there is no other way for the patient to come to grips with them in a realistic way.

Breaking down resistance is a long and usually painful process. The barriers preventing the surfacing of the unconscious material are very strong and the patient usually tries to keep these barriers intact as long as possible.

A fourth technique of psychoanalysis is the *analysis of transference.* Freud recognized that the relationship between therapist and patient is an intimate one. Patients reveal thoughts, memories, and desires to their therapist that they may never have revealed to anyone else, not to parents, spouses, or close friends. The relationship involves more than an intellectual exchange or dialogue; there is a strong emotional component as well. Once this intimate, emotional bond has been established, patients usually transfer to the therapist the feelings and attitudes they once held toward some other significant person in their life, usually a parent. Patients reenact that earlier relationship and may look upon the therapist as, for example, a father figure, idolizing the therapist as they once did their father.

Of course, children do not always love their father; sometimes they hate him. And this is true for the transference to the analyst. When the feelings toward the analyst are those of love or admiration, the process is called a positive transference. When the feelings consist of hatred or hostility, it is a negative transference. Usually, patients vacillate between these two kinds of transference, depending upon their attitude toward the father figure at the moment.

By expressing these feelings, and allowing the analyst to interpret them, patients can develop insight into early personal relationships and into their own functioning. For example, by means of transference patients are able to express and to work through possible conflicts they may have with respect to their father, or anyone else who played a significant role in their life.

The development of transference can work in the opposite direction as well. Therapists often develop countertransference to a patient, which they then have to work through.

These principles and techniques of psychoanalysis constitute the traditional Freudian version, the initial approach to psychotherapy. Although many therapists continue to use the methods prescribed by Freud, others prefer to apply modifications of these techniques. In the years since Freud first formulated his system of therapy, psychologists and psychiatrists have developed other approaches to psychotherapy that differ from orthodox Freudian psychoanalysis.

In general, these neo-Freudian analysts do not focus on past events in the life of a patient, but stress instead the person's current situation. They disagree with Freud's view that all mental illness is rooted in childhood traumas and conflicts relating to sex or aggression. As a result, they do not dwell on the development of a patient's life and how the patient coped with adjustment problems in the childhood years. The focus is on the person's present situation and conscious feelings, not on hidden, unconscious motivations from the past.

Despite these modifications, critics of psychoanalysis argue that the process is too time consuming and expensive. Many feel that its usefulness is limited to affluent and well-educated persons who are able to articulate their feelings, hopes, and fears. Thus, Freudian psychoanalysis and its derivatives, although widely used in the treatment of neurotics, do not enjoy universal acceptance. Also, psychoanalysis cannot be used with all forms of mental illness; it is not very successful with psychotics, for example.

## Client-Centered Therapy

Another current form of psychotherapy is the work of Carl Rogers and his *client-centered therapy*. The major difference between client-centered therapy and psychoanalysis is indicated in Rogers' choice of a label for his therapy. It is centered on the client. Freud's approach is therapist-centered, in that the ultimate responsibility and authority for the cure lies in the guidance, interpretation, and direction given by the therapist. Freud believed that it was the task of the analyst to direct the course of free association, to interpret the patient's words and dreams, and to actively lead the patient to the understanding and resolution of the conflict.

Rogers places all that responsibility directly on the patient or client; Rogers prefers the latter term. The therapist does not ask the client leading questions, offer advice or guidance, or interpret what the client says. Instead, the client must learn how to solve the problem in his or her own way. The treatment or counseling sessions are structured by the client, not by the therapist, and the client talks about anything he or she wishes. (Indeed, a client may not talk at all if he or she does not feel like doing so.) The insight into the client's problem is arrived at solely by the client; it is not dictated to the client by the therapist.

What do counselors do during the treatment sessions? They listen to what the clients tell them, but it is a highly skilled and specialized kind of listening. Counselors provide an atmosphere of warmth, acceptance, and trust, an environment considered totally permissive for clients. Clients can say and do anything they desire without fear of reproof or punishment.

Client-centered or nondirective counselors are careful not to show in any way—by words, gestures, or facial expressions—that they may disapprove of anything their clients say. Not the slightest sign of criticism must be given. Clients are accepted fully, for who and what they are, whether good or bad, weak or strong. As a result of this warm and permissive attitude, clients are able to express and to accept their own feelings, particularly those they previously kept hidden because of fear of eliciting displeasure or rejection from others.

In this therapeutic environment clients come to feel valued and worthy as persons, often for the first time in their lives. They are able to achieve a higher level of self-understanding and self-acceptance and to see their emotions, fears, and longings in more positive ways. Out of these self-derived personal insights they are ultimately able to direct the course of their own growth; they do not need the doctor to tell them what to do. This means that they do not have to depend on an expert, an authority to guide their lives. They are capable of making decisions for themselves, and this further strengthens their newly acquired feelings of self-worth.

The counselors provide the therapeutic atmosphere that makes these changes possible, but they do not simply sit quietly and passively during the treatment sessions. Nondirective counselors interact verbally with clients much of the time, particularly when clients pause in their own commentary. The counselors supply a special type of verbal feedback, reflecting what the clients say and elaborating upon it.

Counselors rephrase in their own words what clients tell them. In this way they try to clarify their clients' feelings. By restating the clients' thoughts and feelings the counselors indicate to the clients that they (the counselors) constantly recognize and understand the clients' views of themselves and of their world. Counselors try to see their clients' problems through the clients' eyes, adopting the clients' frame of reference or viewpoint. This further enables the clients to feel worthy and valued as individuals and encourages them to talk about deep, intimate feelings. Clients believe that the counselors are genuinely interested in them, agree with them, share their viewpoints, and, most important, do not judge them.

As an example of this nondirective, client-centered procedure, the words of a client and a therapist in their thirteenth counseling session follow. The client is Robert S., an unusually handsome eighteen-year-old boy plagued by doubts and insecurities. He has been talking about his strong desire not to be inferior in anything he does, and about how he tries to conceal his inferiorities.

Client: Yes, but you can never destroy the things you're inferior in. They always remain where everybody can see 'em, right on the surface. No matter how well you can talk, no matter how well you can dance, no matter how good a time you are to the persons who are with you, you certainly can't wear a veil.

Therapist: M-hm. It's *looks* again, isn't it? . . .

Cl.: That's it, all of it. (Pause.) Isn't one thing about me I like. Can't even like my own fingernails. They're not smooth like yours. They've got ridges running all down them. My fingers are long and yet they're— they're long and they're—yet look stubby, gnarled, and cut. My skin's all fluked up. That's just my hands alone. My knuckles look screwy. . . . I can wear a hat to cover up this crumpled hair. It won't look nice when it's combed and it won't look nice when it's mussed. . . . I'm too darn light. I don't like my face. I don't like my eyebrows and my eyes. Blood-shot, little cow-eyes. I hate my pimple chin and I detest the way my face is lopsided. One side is so much different from the other. One side, the chin bones stick out further and the jaw bones are more pronounced.

My mouth isn't right. Even when I smile, I don't smile the way other people do. . . . I'm clumsy as the devil.[4]

Th.: You feel sort of sorry for yourself, isn't that right?

Cl.: Yes, self-pity, that's me. Sure, I know I pity myself, but I got something to pity. If there were two of me I would punch myself right in the nose just for the fun of it.

Th.: M-hm.

Cl.: Sometimes I get so disgusted with myself!

Th.: Sometimes you feel somewhat ashamed of yourself for pointing out all of those physical inadequacies, right?

Cl.: Yes, I know I should forget them—yeah, forget them—I should think of something else. And that's—I hate myself because I'm not sure. That's just another thing I can hate myself for.

Th.: You're sort of in a dilemma because you can't like yourself, and yet you dislike the fact that you don't like yourself.

Cl.: M-hm. I know it isn't natural for a person not to like himself. In fact, most people are in love with themselves. They don't know quite so much of themselves. I've known people like that.

Th.: M-hm.

Cl.: But not me. (Pause.) I don't see how anybody loves me, even Mom. Maybe it's just maternal love. They can't help it, poor things. (Pause.)

Th.: You feel so worthless you wonder how anyone would think much of you.

Cl.: Yeah. But I'm not gonna worry about it. I've just gotta make up for it, that's all. I've just gotta forget it. And try to compensate for it.

Th.: M-hm. (Pause.)

Cl.: I've always tried to compensate for it. Everything I did in high school was to compensate for it.

Th.: M-hm. You've never had much reason to think that people really cared about you, is that right?

Cl.: That's right. Oh, if you only knew how they—

Th.: M-hm.

Cl.: Everything anyone ever said or ever did they were just trying to get something out of me. Or else they were—

Th.: It sort of made you feel inadequate not having the security of having people show that they cared a lot for you.

Cl.: That's right.

Th.: M-hm.

Cl.: No one ever did. . . .[5]

You can see how accepting and supporting the therapist is of the client's view of himself and of the world. In spite of the fact that others

---

[4] Remember that the client is considered to be very good-looking.

[5] William U. Snyder, *Casebook of Non-directive Counseling* (Boston: Houghton Mifflin, 1947), pp. 83–85. Copyright © 1947 by William U. Snyder. Reprinted by permission of Houghton Mifflin Company.

see Robert as very attractive, he does not. Indeed, he is unhappy about his appearance. The therapist does not try to point out that Robert is wrong in this regard. Instead, the therapist accepts Robert's view of reality as being real to Robert, and his view of himself as the core of his negative feelings of self-worth. The therapist neither approves nor disapproves but reflects and amplifies Robert's feelings.

The beginning of some self-insight on Robert's part is also apparent, a way in which he can live with and adapt to his own feelings. Toward the end of the session he spoke of not worrying about his feelings of worthlessness, of forgetting them and compensating for them. Perhaps, in time, he will understand that his feelings about himself, whether correct or incorrect, are not as important as he once thought.

A form of therapy such as client-centered therapy, which presupposes the ability to develop personal insight and to arrive at one's own resolution of life problems, can be used only with persons who maintain good contact with reality, are reasonably intelligent, and are introspective. It works well with moderately severe neuroses and mild adjustment problems, but not with psychoses or severe neuroses.

## GROUP PSYCHOTHERAPY

Psychoanalysis and client-centered therapy are undertaken on a one-to-one basis; therapists using these techniques can treat only one patient at a time. Given the large number of persons who need treatment, and the relatively small number of therapists, the individual approach may seem uneconomical and inefficient. Also, many people cannot afford the high fees charged for individual treatment. These considerations created the climate in which the *group psychotherapy* technique was developed.

But it is not economy and efficiency alone that have made group psychotherapy so popular. It offers other advantages over the individual approach. Because one of the major problems of mental illness is difficulty in relating to others, and feelings of isolation and rejection from others, psychologists believe that the group therapeutic setting can help people learn how to achieve more satisfactory interpersonal relationships. Therapists are able to observe directly how patients relate to one another instead of relying on what the patients tell them of their relations with other people.

The group setting also enables patients to work through their problems in the company of others, to learn directly that others have similar problems, and to get feedback on their feelings and behavior not only from the therapist, but also from persons of diverse backgrounds and perspectives. Hearing how others perceive and react to us is often illuminating, particularly if we have not known such open and honest relationships before.

Psychotherapy groups typically consist of six to twelve persons, who have similar or related problems, and a therapist. The meetings, usually one hour at a time, take place in comfortable surroundings with the members seated in a circle. The therapist plays a *nondirective* role in the sessions, remaining in the background as much as possible and serving more as a moderator or facilitator than as a leader. Thus, the therapist does not take an authoritative role; he or she does not give advice or tell patients what to do about their problems. Often the therapist will not even answer questions but will redirect the questions to the group members for them to answer. "What do you think of that?" the therapist may say to the group in response to a person's question. Thus, the therapist gradually turns authority over to the group members.

After a while, the members begin to talk more among themselves than to the therapist. They question one another about motives and feelings, although some prompting from the therapist may be required.

"Jim, what makes you think other people don't like you?" a member may ask. "Mary, why are you so hostile toward Ann?" another may say. When they discuss such questions group members often offer new insights or interpretations that the object of the question may never have thought of before. The group becomes its own authority and source of advice and support.

The therapist may offer additional insights and interpretations but will do so gently and subtly, not in an authoritarian or direct manner. Also, the therapist will guide the group on to a new topic or a different person if too much focus is placed on one topic or person.

Once a climate of openness and trust has been established, the group members do not hesitate to reveal their fears and anxieties, and they can be quite perceptive in their reactions to another person's self-disclosures. Group members also spend considerable time discussing the dynamics of the group, the interactions among themselves and with the therapist.

Group psychotherapy has been used in hospitals and mental health clinics and in private practice with both neurotic and psychotic patients (when the psychotic behavior allows some contact with reality and the ability to communicate). Sometimes group psychotherapy is used as the sole form of treatment; at other times it is used in combination with some type of individual psychotherapy.

A different kind of group psychotherapy is the approach promoted by *Gestalt therapy* under the leadership of Frederick (Fritz) Perls, once a Freudian psychoanalyst. Although the sessions are conducted in a group setting, the therapist focuses on only one person at a time. The other group members do not participate; they watch and listen as an audience. The sessions or seminars last several hours and a number of persons can be treated; an individual may receive attention only for a matter of minutes.

The German word *Gestalt* means pattern or whole, and this indicates the purpose of Gestalt therapy. It attempts to unite or make whole all aspects of an individual's personality. Using a directive approach, Perls tried to make persons aware of those aspects of their being that they had been avoiding, and to have them work through the "unfinished situations" we all carry around with us. These situations are the source of anxiety and tension. In order to be made whole, we must be aware of all parts of our personality, and we must finish or complete our unfinished situations.

Perls used a number of techniques, including dream analysis, acting out both sides of a conversation with someone significant in the patient's life, and getting in touch with the "here and now" (compelling the person to function fully in the present instead of in the past or the future). There are no fixed rules for Gestalt therapy and Perls's approach to treatment was flexible, spontaneous, and experimental. He employed whatever techniques he thought would work with a particular person.

The following exchange between Fritz Perls and a female patient deals with the patient's dream.

Patient: I dreamed that I watch . . . a lake . . . drying up, and there is a small island in the middle of the lake, and a circle of . . . porpoises—they're like porpoises except that they can stand up, so they're like porpoises that are people, and they're in a circle, sort of like a religious ceremony . . . I feel very sad because they can breathe, they are sort of dancing around the circle, but the water, their element, is drying up. So it's like a dying—like watching a race of people, or a race of creatures, dying. . . . And I think that there's one good point about the water drying up, I think—well, at least at the bottom, when all the water dries up, there will probably be some sort of treasure there, because at the bottom of the lake there should be things that have fallen in, like coins or something, but I look carefully and all that I can find is an old license plate. . . .
Fritz: Will you please play the license plate.
Pt.: I'm an old license plate, thrown in the bottom of a lake. I have no use because I'm no value—although I'm not rusted—I'm outdated, so I can't be used as a license plate . . . and I'm just thrown on the rubbish heap. . . .
F.: Well, how do you feel about this?
Pt.: (quietly) . . . I don't like being a license plate—useless.
F.: Could you talk about this. That was such a long dream until you came to find the license plate, I'm sure this must be of great importance.
Pt.: (sighs) Useless. Outdated. . . . The use of a license plate is to allow

—give a car permission to go . . . and I can't give anyone permission to do anything because I'm outdated. . . . In California, they just paste a little—you buy a sticker—and stick it on the car, on the old license plate. So maybe someone could put me on their car and stick this sticker on, I I don't know . . . .

F.: Okeh, now play the lake.

Pt.: I'm a lake. . . . I'm drying up, and disappearing, soaking in to the earth, I become a part of the earth—so maybe I water the surrounding area, so . . . even in the lake, even in my bed, flowers can grow (sighs) . . . New life can grow . . . from me (cries). . . .

F.: You see the existential message?

Pt.: (sadly, but with conviction) I can paint . . . I can create beauty. . . . I'm like the porpoise . . . but I . . . keep wanting to say I'm food. . . . I . . . I water the earth, and give life-growing things, the water— they need both the earth and the water, and the . . . and the air and the sun, but as the water from the lake, I can play a part in something. . . .

F.: You see the contrast: On the surface, you find something, some artifact—the license plate, the artificial you—but then when you go deeper, you find the apparent death of the lake is actually fertility.

Pt.: And I don't need a license plate, or a permission, a license in order to . . .

F.: (gently) Nature doesn't need a license plate to grow. You don't have to be useless, if you are organismically creative, which means if you are involved.

Pt.: And I don't need permission to be creative.[6]

It is apparent from this example that the Gestalt therapist is actively involved in the treatment, directing and interpreting the person's thoughts. Patients develop insight under the guidance of the therapist.

Gestalt therapy has been carried on by Perls's followers since his death in 1970 and it is widely used in the United States today. It seems to work well with mildly neurotic persons and with those who have adjustment problems and are reasonably bright and well educated.

One of the newer approaches to therapy in groups is *family therapy*, in which the therapist treats the family as a unit. By observing how family members communicate and interact, the sources of family tensions and strains can often be uncovered. In addition, behavior or personality problems of one member of a family may be traceable to the person's role in the family complex. Because such problems may arise from the family structure, they are best treated within that context by having all family members participate in the therapy.

In recent years, group therapies have become increasingly popular and have been extended and modified for use with normal persons. Millions

[6] F. S. Perls, *Gestalt Therapy Verbatim* (Moab, Utah: Real People Press, 1969), pp. 85–87. Reprinted by permission of the publisher.

of Americans, not suffering from any neurosis or psychosis, have chosen to participate in various kinds of encounter groups and sensitivity sessions designed to enhance interpersonal skills, increase awareness, and raise consciousness levels. As primary tools of the human potential movement, these derivatives of group psychotherapy have become an important part of American culture (see Chapter 5).

## BEHAVIOR THERAPY

In the 1960s a radical form of therapy became prominent. The "psycho" or mind therapies, whether individual or group, share an emphasis on unconscious or conscious functioning. They are concerned with inner conflicts, traumas, and anxieties, with patients' feelings about themselves and about others. The psychotherapeutic approach to the treatment of mental illness probes inside the person because that is where the problems are believed to lie.

What is so radical about *behavior therapy* (or *behavior modification*) is that it ignores completely a person's mental processes. It makes no attempt to deal with conscious or unconscious functioning.

We described in Chapter 2 the three major forces in modern psychology: the focus on consciousness, the focus on the unconscious, and the focus on overt behavior. Psychotherapy represents the first two approaches; behavior therapy represents the third.

Behavior therapy derives from behaviorism, the experimental approach to psychology that evolved from the early research on conditioning conducted by the Russian physiologist Ivan Pavlov, and from the elaborations of Pavlov's work by the American psychologists John B. Watson in the 1910–1920 period and B. F. Skinner since the 1940s.

In studying human nature behaviorists are not interested in anything inside the person. In dealing with abnormal behavior they focus solely on behavior, not on any presumed conflict or anxiety such as that psychotherapists believe to be the cause of abnormal behavior. Thus, behaviorists are not concerned with mental illness. Instead, they focus on undesirable or maladaptive behaviors that people have learned by being rewarded or reinforced for behaving in that way. For example, hypochondriacs are rewarded with attention and care when they are sick. Hence, they learn to be sick because it brings those rewards.

If all abnormal behavior is the result of learning, the best way to change or eliminate the behavior is to unlearn or relearn it. Thus, behavior therapy is a learning process in which the emphasis is on changing *behavior* and not on changing *personality*. Behavior therapists believe that the maladaptive behavior itself is the real problem the person faces; such behavior is not simply the symptom of a deeper problem. It is the person's behavior that causes difficulties in adjustment. If behavior therapists can cure that behavior, the person will become better able to function in the real world. For example, the person who fears crowds will, once relieved of this behavior problem, be able to go out among large groups of people without fear.

Specific techniques of behavior therapy derive from the extensive psychological research on human learning carried out since the early years of the twentieth century. Research techniques from the laboratory have been applied to the real world of mental health clinics and hospitals, and provide an excellent example of how pure research is often of immense practical value. The techniques are based on the use of reward or punishment as a means of compelling people to alter their behavior.

We discuss five behavior therapy techniques: positive reinforcement, extinction, aversive conditioning, systematic desensitization, and modeling.

## Positive Reinforcement

The basic principle behind the *positive reinforcement* approach to behavior therapy is that behavior can be changed from abnormal to normal by rewarding or reinforcing patients whenever they behave normally and ignoring them (not rewarding them) when they behave abnormally. This is a fundamental technique of learning that you have probably applied yourself, for example, if you have ever trained a dog to perform tricks. Each time the dog does the trick correctly, you give it a dog biscuit or pet it. The dog receives nothing when it does not perform the trick correctly. If you have watched trained animals perform (such as seals, dolphins, or lions), you may have noticed that the trainer rewards the animals after each correct behavior. This is positive reinforcement at work.

A similar approach is taken to change abnormal human behavior, even of the intense psychotic type. If, for example, a hospital staff is trained to ignore schizophrenic patients when they behave in a bizarre manner and to reward them with attention when they behave in a more normal way, the behavior of the psychotics usually improves noticeably in a very short time. The patients are not suddenly cured, but their behavior has been modified to the extent that they are not as troublesome to themselves or to others as they once were. The patients learn these normal behaviors because they receive something for them, a reward that is of value to them.

The positive reinforcement technique has proved to be successful in dealing with a wide range of abnormal behaviors. Children who have violent behavior problems have learned to speak intelligently and to interact with others in a calm, quiet manner. Mute schizophrenics have learned to speak again (including one case of a patient who had not spoken for nineteen years), and wards of previously helpless, hopeless psychotics have learned to take care of themselves and to assist other patients and the hospital staff. In all these cases, positive reinforcement changed the patients' behavior to such an extent that they were no longer management problems, no longer violent to themselves or to others, and were capable of being helped by other forms of therapy.

## Extinction

If behaviors can be taught by reinforcing them, then perhaps they can be eliminated if they no longer bring reinforcement. This principle, known as the *extinction* of learned responses, was first demonstrated by Pavlov. Since that time, numerous research studies, on organisms from rats to human beings, have shown how effective this process can be in eliminating undesirable behaviors. In the discussion of positive reinforcement, we noted that part of that approach involved extinction, ignoring all forms of bizarre or abnormal behavior, not reinforcing such behavior in any way, not even by recognition.

For example, a two-year-old boy made life miserable for his parents by having tantrums whenever they left his room at night after putting him to bed. The child resisted falling asleep for as long as he could. As a result, his parents had to stay with him for as long as two hours every night. Of course, the child was being rewarded for the tantrums with the company and attention of his parents.

The solution was to stop reinforcing the undesirable behavior by ignoring it. The parents put the boy to bed, talked pleasantly and calmly with him for a moment, then left the room. The first night this happened the child screamed for forty-five minutes. By the tenth evening the tantrums had ceased; the behavior had been extinguished. The case was followed for two years and the child did not exhibit any more tantrums.[7]

## Aversive Conditioning

The positive reinforcement and extinction techniques attempt to modify behavior by administering or withholding a reward. *Aversive conditioning* involves actually punishing the individual for displaying undesirable or abnormal behavior. In general, psychological research on learning has shown that positive reinforcement is more effective than punishment, but punishment is not without value.

Aversive conditioning has been used to treat a wide range of behavior disorders, including alcoholism, smoking, stuttering, and homosexuality, by presenting a noxious stimulus (such as an electric shock or a nausea-

[7] Suggested by Carl D. Williams, "The Elimination of Tantrum Behavior by Extinction Procedures," *Journal of Abnormal and Social Psychology*, **59** (1959), 269.

inducing drug) every time the person displays the undesirable behavior. For example, persons suffering from alcoholism are given an alcoholic drink along with a drug that produces instantaneous and violent vomiting. Homosexuals are given an electric shock each time they are shown a picture of a nude person of the same sex. Before long, discomfort or pain, and its anticipation, become linked to the undesirable behavior and the behavior disappears. Obsessions, compulsions, and fetishes have also been successfully treated by aversive conditioning.

## Systematic Desensitization

In the *systematic desensitization* technique, patients are methodically desensitized to anxiety-producing situations or objects until the anxiety ceases to exist. First, the therapist finds out from the patient the objects or situations that are anxiety producing. Second, a list of all stimuli associated with the anxiety-producing situations is compiled and arranged in a hierarchy from "least feared" to "most feared" item.

Third, the patient is trained to relax, on the assumption that relaxation is the opposite of anxiety and will indeed inhibit or reduce anxiety. One cannot be both relaxed and fearful at the same time. The goal is to pair this relaxed state with the anxiety-producing situation in small steps, working up the hierarchy from least feared to most feared anxiety-producing stimulus.

Several procedures are used to teach patients to relax, including hypnosis, drugs, and a conscious effort to relax individual body muscles.

Fourth, the relaxation response is matched with the patient's image or visualization of each anxiety-producing stimulus in the hierarchy in turn. Initially, the patient visualizes the weakest stimulus. If he or she remains relaxed, the next stimulus may be visualized, and so on, proceeding up the hierarchy to the most feared stimulus. If the imagining of any item induces anxiety, this step is repeated until the patient can remain completely relaxed while visualizing the stimulus. Finally, when the full hierarchy of stimuli have been covered, the patient has learned to respond with relaxation instead of with anxiety to all the stimuli that had previously produced the anxiety.

As an example of systematic desensitization in practice, the case of a seventeen-year-old boy who became tense and anxious after an automobile accident follows.[8] He was irritable, lost his appetite, had trouble sleeping and concentrating, and could not force himself to drive a car again. After learning to relax completely, he was instructed to visualize

[8] Malcolm Kushner, "Desensitization of a Post-Traumatic Phobia," *Case Studies in Behavior Modification*, eds. L. Ullmann and L. Krasner (New York: Holt, Rinehart and Winston, 1965), pp. 193–196.

himself in each of the following situations in turn: looking at his car as it appeared before the accident, leaning against the car, sitting in the car, sitting in the car with the motor running, turning the engine on himself, backing the car out of the driveway into the street, and driving around the block from his house. The sequence continued over several sessions and each additional scene brought the patient closer to a reconstruction of the scene of his accident. The treatment took two and one-half weeks, at the end of which the patient could drive a car again with no anxiety, sleep and eat well, and show no trace of his previous difficulties.

A variation of the systematic desensitization approach involves the actual physical stimuli or situations instead of imagining or visualizing them. This approach has been particularly successful in treating sexual problems such as impotence and frigidity. By having patients proceed slowly through a number of preliminary sexual situations with their partner (lying together in bed clothed, then partially clothed, for example), and relaxing with each step, their behavior has been successfully modified so that they are capable of completing intercourse, an act that was previously too terrifying for them to perform.

### Modeling

Much of what we learn in life, from behaviors to attitudes, is learned by observing other people and imitating them. This is particularly characteristic of learning in childhood. Infants model their behavior after their parents and learn to speak, act, and think in similar ways. If behavior (normal or abnormal) is learned initially by imitating models, it should be possible to change or relearn behavior in the same manner.

*Modeling* is a successful technique of behavior therapy used to eliminate phobic and other intense emotional reactions. One classic study [9] showed that adults were able to free themselves of their strong fear of snakes. They were shown a film of people making progressively closer and bolder contact with a snake, first a plastic snake and later a real snake. The subjects could stop the film whenever it became too threatening and restart it from a less frightening scene.

A more effective technique is for a person to watch a live model (another person) handle a snake. Then, guided by the model, the person makes increasingly closer contact with the snake. The person might first wear gloves to touch the snake, then touch the snake without gloves. The person might touch just the middle of the snake while it is held securely by the model, then hold the snake, then handle it alone. This

[9] A. Bandura, *Principles of Behavior Modification* (New York: Holt, Rinehart and Winston, 1969).

modeling approach has been successful with more than 90 per cent of the snake phobias on which it has been tried.

In general, behavior therapy is a popular means of changing a wide range of abnormal behaviors. The reported cure rates are high, around 75 to 90 per cent. A major advantage is that behavior therapy is quicker and cheaper than psychotherapy, and requires far fewer treatment sessions. A major criticism is that behavior therapy does not relieve the conflict or anxiety that is the presumed underlying cause of the abnormal behavior, but behavior therapists do not believe this is necessary. In their view, the problem is with external behavior alone, not with any internal emotional condition.

## PLAY THERAPY

Conducting therapy with emotionally disturbed children is difficult for several reasons. Their attention span is limited, they are easily bored, their vocabulary and ability to express themselves are restricted, and they lack the introspective ability needed for insight therapy. For these reasons, then, play therapy was developed for use with children. Using toys, dolls, modeling clay, punching bags, and paints, an emotionally disturbed child is allowed to play naturally and spontaneously under the observant eyes of a therapist.

Advocates of play therapy believe that children reveal their inner feelings, fears, and conflicts in their play, feelings they cannot express verbally. The therapist watches the child's play to see how spontaneous

or inhibited it may be, and whether it is purposeful or aimless, constructive or destructive.

Jenny W. was a four-year-old girl brought to the therapist by her concerned parents. She was sullen, moody, and withdrawn, and she seldom spoke. She showed little of the animation or vitality one expects in a four-year-old child. At first she was suspicious of the therapist, but soon she began to play with the toys in the office, frequently looking over her shoulder to see what the therapist was doing. By the third session Jenny seemed more relaxed and her play was more spontaneous. From a collection of dolls she selected five, the number of people in her family, and arranged four of them in a row. She explained that two were "Mommy and Daddy," one was her brother Jeff (a two-year-old), and one was Tommy (the baby in the family). "This is me," she said sadly, pointing to the fifth doll she had placed apart from the others.

"Why aren't you with the rest of the family?" the therapist asked.

Jenny started to cry, then reached down and picked up the Mommy and Daddy dolls and threw them against the wall. " 'Cause they only like boys," she said. "They don't like me 'cause I'm a girl. They don't want me!"

Talking to Jenny might not have uncovered the cause of her problem. Allowing her to express herself by playing with the dolls not only revealed the problem but was also of some therapeutic value in itself. Jenny was able, perhaps for the first time, to give vent to her feelings without fear of being punished for them.

Play therapy of a different sort is being used increasingly with adults. Many disturbed persons react positively to various kinds of activity therapy, such as arts and crafts, music, dance, poetry writing, and sports. Often, such activities provide an emotional release for the patients, allowing them to express feelings that they could not express verbally. The use of sports as a form of therapy is discussed in Chapter 15.

## PSYCHODRAMA

*Psychodrama* is an approach to therapy that permits emotionally disturbed persons to act out their feelings and conflicts. Conducted in a group setting, psychodrama allows for the active expression of one's feelings within a social situation rather than in a one-to-one interaction with a therapist.

The method is to stage a play, skit, or drama in which patients play roles, either themselves or someone significant in their lives such as a spouse or a parent. In this setting, patients express fears and fantasies of which they might be unaware, or which they might be unable to admit in a more straightforward psychotherapeutic situation.

The dramas take place on stage with props and lights, usually before an audience of other patients. The dramas are spontaneous and unrehearsed; there are no scripts. Trained psychodrama actors begin the play, portraying persons who are important in the patients' lives, thus preparing the way for a patient to act out some important event or feeling.

Although many patients seem reluctant or shy initially about publicly acting out a role, eventually they become quite involved in the process. They are soon actively and enthusiastically participating in the portrayal of the drama of their lives. Not only can this acting out reveal to patient and therapist previously hidden conflicts and anxieties, but it can also provide a therapeutic release of emotion. In addition, members of the audience may benefit by seeing problems similar to their own acted out.

## COMMUNITY–BASED THERAPY

Since the early 1960s there has been a concerted effort to treat mentally ill persons as outpatients in local mental health centers instead of committing them to large, isolated mental hospitals or institutions. Not only does this approach do away with the stigma of being "put away" in a mental hospital, but it also eliminates the often difficult problem of reentry (readjusting to home and community upon release from a mental hospital). In addition, community-based therapy allows for faster and more individualized treatment than can usually be provided in the crowded wards of mental hospitals.

Some types of mentally ill persons require institutionalization for their own safety and that of their families and society. But providing treatment facilities in most communities or neighborhoods means that a great many people who would otherwise be hospitalized (because there was no other place for them to be treated) no longer have to be. These people can, as long as their behavior is not overly disruptive, remain at home and on the job while being treated on an outpatient basis.

Another type of community mental health facility is the halfway house, in which emotionally disturbed persons can live with other patients and staff, an arrangement that also minimizes the trauma associated with confinement in the often dehumanizing environment of a mental hospital.

Unfortunately, this idea, although noble in purpose, seems to have been a failure. However, it is not the concept that has failed, but rather its implementation. Since the first community mental health centers opened some twenty years ago, the number of patients confined in mental hospitals has decreased by approximately two-thirds. The problem is that not nearly enough community mental health centers have been built to provide care for the newly-released patients.

It was planned to build 1,500 such centers, but only about 600 exist today. Thus, only 40 per cent of those who have been in institutions are receiving adequate care on the outside. The plight of the remainder of these former patients is a national tragedy and disgrace. Most of them live in inner-city ghettos, squalid nursing homes, or rundown hotels. Left on their own, these people spend their days wandering aimlessly around the city streets, living in fear, and receiving inadequate care, food, and shelter. Not surprisingly, about half of these former patients are readmitted to hospitals, at least temporarily, within a year of their release.

The idea of halfway houses, in which people can be treated without the stigma of institutionalization, is an excellent one, but unless it is sufficiently funded, it will continue to be a failure.

Through local *crisis intervention centers,* which stress immediate, practical help, people with drug, marital, or other adjustment problems; suicidal urges; anxiety; depression; or grief following the loss of a loved one can be helped at once, with no waiting for an appointment and little or no financial expense. Often such help can be obtained in a few seconds by means of a *telephone hotline.* These efforts are staffed twenty-four hours a day by trained personnel and can provide instant comfort and support for anyone who calls. This prompt access to help can be very important. In the time it may take to get an appointment with a psychologist or psychiatrist, a person's mental condition can deteriorate severely.

A significant aspect of the community mental health center approach to therapy is the increasing use of *paraprofessionals* as therapists. The nationwide shortage of clinical psychologists and psychiatrists is keenly felt by local treatment centers. For that reason, many persons who lack the credentials thought necessary to provide therapy (the Ph.D. or M.D. degrees) are being trained to supplement the professional mental health staff.

High school and college students, clergy, retired persons, part-time workers, former patients, ex-alcoholics, and ex-drug addicts have all been trained to perform certain therapies, with a high rate of success. For example, treatment programs for drug addicts staffed by former addicts, and programs for alcoholics staffed by ex-alcoholics (such as Alcoholics Anonymous), report a higher cure rate than some programs administered by psychologists or psychiatrists.

Many paraprofessionals have little formal education (such as the hard-core unemployed in our cities' ghettos), and most have had no prior experience in dealing with the mentally ill. Paraprofessionals have been trained in a few weeks' time to conduct behavior modification therapies and group counseling sessions, and have dealt successfully with neurotics and psychotics. As a rule, paraprofessionals work under the supervision of more professionally trained therapists.

The inclusion of paraprofessionals on the mental health care team allows for the treatment of many more patients and provides rewarding and challenging work for the paraprofessionals themselves.

Perhaps a more important function of community mental health centers in the long run is the attempt to prevent mental illness. By applying the results of research on sources of personal and community stress, people can be educated in ways to minimize the stress. Also, children with potential emotional problems can be identified and helped before their problems become very serious.

As we have seen, there are many approaches to treating abnormal behavior. From physical therapies to psychological therapies, from work with individuals to groups, from drugs to acting out, the therapies practiced today are making considerable progress in alleviating human misery and suffering. Improving these techniques and devising new and better ones is a major challenge facing those who apply psychology to this facet of everyday life.

Psychologists are also interested in improving the quality of life of those who are free of emotional problems, seeking to foster the healthy personality.

## SUMMARY

There are several approaches to the treatment of the mentally ill. Some focus on unconscious motivations, some on conscious feelings, and others on the behavioral symptoms rather than on any possible underlying cause. Some therapies take a medical rather than a psychological approach, some are conducted on a group rather than on an individual basis, and others are designed for children rather than for adults. Finally, some therapies can be conducted only by psychologists or psychiatrists, and others are performed by persons who have had only a small amount of professional training. Seven forms of therapy are discussed.

1. *Physical therapies* are used for the most severe cases of mental illness, in which patients are uncommunicative and unresponsive to the psychological therapies. Three forms of physical therapy are shock therapy, drug therapy, and psychosurgery. *Shock therapy,* in which a patient is rendered unconscious following a brief period of severe convulsions, is administered by drugs or by electric shock. *Drug therapy*

has been useful in changing patient behavior and has led to rapid release from mental institutions. It has also allowed the treatment of many emotionally disturbed persons as outpatients. *Antipsychotic drugs* calm intense and violent psychotic behaviors, *antianxiety drugs* provide relief from worry and tension, and *antidepressant drugs* relieve depression and help restore energy and vitality. *Psychosurgery* involves severing the frontal lobes of the brain from other brain structures that control emotion. It is used as a last-resort form of treatment when no other therapies have worked. Physical therapies do not by themselves cure mental illness. They are useful for behavior change, symptom relief, and for rendering patients more amenable to psychological forms of therapy.

2. *Individual psychotherapy* tries to uncover the underlying reason for an emotional disturbance and to achieve self-insight into personal fears and feelings. *Psychoanalysis,* developed by Sigmund Freud, explores a person's childhood experiences in order to bring to the surface the trauma or conflict that has been repressed in the unconscious. Once the person is made aware of the repressed material, he or she can be taught to cope with it. Four basic techniques in psychoanalysis are: *free association,* a sort of daydreaming out loud in which a patient says everything that comes to mind; *dream analysis,* in which the analyst interprets the symbols in dreams; *analysis of resistance,* in which the patient is persuaded to talk about events, persons, or situations they have resisted revealing; and *analysis of transference,* in which the patient transfers to the analyst feelings held toward other persons. *Client-centered therapy,* developed by Carl Rogers, places the responsibility for achieving self-insight and for resolving the emotional problem on the patient rather than on the therapist. The therapist provides a permissive and accepting atmosphere and rephrases and elaborates on the client's revelations in such a way that the client develops self-understanding and acceptance.

3. *Group psychotherapy* involves six to twelve patients meeting with a therapist. It provides for improving interpersonal relations skills, learning how others handle similar problems, and finding out how others react to one's own feelings and thoughts. Group members discuss their problems openly, question the motivations of other group members, and offer insights and interpretations supplemented by those of the therapist. *Gestalt therapy,* developed by Fritz Perls, is a type of group psychotherapy in which treatment focuses on one person at a time in a group setting. The goal is to make patients aware of all aspects of their personalities and to help them work through their unfinished situations.

4. *Behavior therapy* attempts to change abnormal behavior without trying to uncover potential unconscious causes of the behavior. Based on psychological research on learning, behavior therapy alters behavior

by having the person unlearn or relearn undesirable behaviors. Five techniques are available: *positive reinforcement*, rewarding a person for displaying normal behavior; *extinction*, ignoring a person for displaying abnormal behavior; *aversive conditioning*, punishing a person for displaying abnormal behavior; *systematic desensitization*, teaching a person to respond with relaxation instead of with anxiety to previously anxiety-inducing stimuli; and *modeling*, teaching new behavior by having a person watch and imitate a model who displays the desired behavior.

5. *Play therapy* is used with children to induce them to reveal and to act out, through their play activities, their inner feelings and conflicts.

6. *Psychodrama* involves the acting out of inner feelings in a play in which patients portray themselves or significant persons in their lives.

7. *Community-based therapy* is an effort to provide treatment at the community level rather than in mental hospitals. Faster treatment can be provided and many people can be spared the indignity of institutionalization. Community mental health centers are concerned with prevention as well as treatment of mental illness, and are making increasing use of *paraprofessional* mental health personnel.

## SUGGESTED READINGS

Brammer, Lawrence M., and Everett L. Shostrom. *Therapeutic Psychology: Fundamentals of Counseling and Psychotherapy*, 3rd ed. Englewood Cliffs, N.J.: Prentice-Hall, 1977.

Craighead, W. Edward, Alan E. Kazdin, and Michael J. Mahoney. *Behavior Modification: Principles, Issues, and Applications*. Boston: Houghton Mifflin, 1976.

Gaylin, J. You are cordially invited to help save a life. *Psychology Today*, 1977 (March), **10**, 108–119, 122–123. (On community crisis intervention networks involving friends, relatives, and neighbors.)

Goleman, Daniel. Meditation without mystery. *Psychology Today*, 1977 (March), **10**, 54–67, 88.

Guerin, Philip J., Jr., Ed. *Family Therapy: Theory and Practice*. New York: Gardner Press, 1976.

Haley, Jay. *Problem-Solving Therapy: New Strategies for Effective Family Therapy*. San Francisco: Jossey-Bass, 1976.

Hansen, James C., Richard W. Warner, and Elsie M. Smith. *Group Counseling: Theory and Process*. Chicago: Rand McNally, 1976.

Kovel, Joel A. *A Complete Guide to Therapy: From Psychoanalysis To Behavior Modification*. New York: Pantheon Books, 1976.

Krumboltz, John D., and Carl E. Thoresen, Eds. *Counseling Methods*. New York: Holt, Rinehart and Winston, 1976.

Lazarus, Richard S. *Patterns of Adjustment*, 3rd ed. New York: McGraw-Hill, 1976.

Lewis, Judith A., and Michael D. Lewis. *Community Counseling: A Human Services Approach*. New York: Wiley, 1977.

Lindgren, Henry Clay, and Leonard W. Fisk. *Psychology of Personal Development*, 3rd ed. New York: Wiley, 1976.

Mahoney, M. J., and K. Mahoney. Fight fat with behavior control. *Psychology Today*, 1976 (May), **12**, 39–43, 92–94.

Miller, Milton H. *If the Patient Is You (Or Someone You Love): Psychiatry Inside-Out*. New York: Scribner's, 1977.

Moos, Rudolf H., Ed. *Human Adaptation: Coping with Life Crises*. Lexington, Mass.: Heath, 1976.

Perls, Frederick S. (Fritz). *Gestalt Therapy Verbatim*. Moab, Utah: Real People Press, 1969.

Rogers, Carl. Personal power at work. *Psychology Today*, 1977 (April), **10**, 60–62, 93–94.

Sansweet, Stephen J. *The Punishment Cure: How Aversion Therapy Is Being Used To Eliminate Smoking, Drinking, Obesity, Homosexuality . . . and Practically Anything Else*. New York: Mason/Charter, 1976.

Sarason, Seymour B. Community psychology, networks, and Mr. Everyman. *American Psychologist*, 1976, **31**, 317–328.

Shectman, Fred. Conventional and contemporary approaches to psychotherapy: Freud meets Skinner, Janov, and others. *American Psychologist*, 1977, **32**, 197–204.

Spitzer, Robert L., and Donald F. Klein, Eds. *Evaluation of Psychological Therapies: Psychotherapies, Behavior Therapies, Drug Therapies, and Their Interactions*. Baltimore: Johns Hopkins University Press, 1976.

Stumphauzer, Jerome S. *Behavior Modification Principles: An Introduction and Training Manual*. Kalamazoo, Mich.: Behaviordelia, 1977.

Valenstein, Elliot S. *Brain Control*. New York: Wiley, 1974.

Wilson, G. Terence, and Gerald C. Davison. Behavior therapy: A road to self-control. *Psychology Today*, 1975 (October), **9**, 54–60.

# Psychology Applied to Mental Health: III. The Healthy Personality

There were twenty people in the room and most of them were nervous and apprehensive about what they expected to happen. It was a diverse group—five housewives, three engineers, two schoolteachers, two social workers, two magazine editors, four clinical psychologists, a pharmacist, and an artist—evenly divided by sex, ten men and ten women. There was one married couple, and the rest were single or were attending without their marriage partners.

They met for the first time on a Friday evening at a large private resort, Deer Park Nudist Camp near Escondido, California, which had been closed for the weekend to the public. The extensive grounds, approximately 400 acres, offered great natural beauty and all the usual amenities of a luxury resort. The people would remain until Sunday afternoon, a marathon of togetherness broken only for six hours' sleep on Friday and Saturday nights. During the weekend they would learn more about one another than most of them knew about their closest friends.

They introduced themselves, joked, made light–hearted conversation, and formed those silent first impressions we all form when meeting new people. Then Dr. Paul Bindrim, a psychologist and leader of the group, explained some of the six major rules. Everyone was required to participate in all group activities. They must remain together for the entire time as a group; no cliques could be formed. Drinking and drug taking were not allowed. Kissing and hugging was permitted but not the fondling of genitals or sexual intercourse.

Dr. Bindrim then invited everyone to talk about their feelings and expectations about the experience. Everything said was tape-recorded.

Ken: This is entirely new to me . . . I'm scared to death . . . scared of my reaction to other people, and of course scared to death of having an erection.

Greg: I've never tried it before, and I'll say that I have some inhibitions about it, mild to moderate.

Ted: As I mentioned to Vicky earlier, I wasn't going to be the first, but I wasn't going to be the last one, either.

The group moved into a room containing a large Jacuzzi whirlpool bath with the water heated to a temperature of 102°F. Hesitantly at first, then more willingly, the group members took off all their clothes and plunged into the water. Later, still nude, they went into another room where moving colored lights made patterns on their bodies. Some people sat quietly and watched others who posed in front of a full-length mirror, admiring the effects of the designs and colors on their skin.

The next morning, the group members talked about their experiences.

Lee: I enjoyed looking at the lovely female bodies last night.

Jack: It was like one of my fantasies come into reality—all these girls . . . .

Vicky: The thought crossed my mind last night—what a shame it is that this wonderful structure, this human body, created by Nature, has to be covered up for a whole lifetime.

Ted: I was constantly thinking about just this idea of wanting to touch . . . .

Kathleen: There seemed to be such a change in personality as the people got into the water.

The members talked about how much they enjoyed the freedom to look at other nude bodies and to have others look at theirs, and how comfortable, exhilarated, and close to the others they felt. They mentioned feeling guilty about their own bodies, as well as a feeling of euphoria that prevented many of them from sleeping.

They remained together for the rest of the weekend, always nude, taking long walks around the grounds, more whirlpool baths, dance, movement, and sensory awareness experiences, and periods of meditation. Although there was no overt sexual activity, the members engaged in frequent body contact with little hesitation, and they felt less concern about the appearance of their own bodies.

Most of the participants were greatly affected by the meditation, reporting experiences not unlike drug-induced highs; "tripping out" was how one member described it.

Murray: I found it to be a very tranquil experience. I got out somewhere on the stream of the universe.

Evelyn: (after a period of time on the floor, going through labor pains and the movements of giving birth) I feel as though I'm in labor . . . I feel like I created something . . . I guess God is always right here . . . I gave birth but I feel purged at the same time . . . I'm shook up but boy, do I feel good . . . I feel like laughing and crying and everything all over.

Five weeks later, after they had time to reflect on it, fifteen members of the group got together to talk about the experience and what it meant to them. They all felt that they had been changed for the better, and spoke of increased feelings of inner worth and value, of being better able to relate to other people, of feeling less hostility toward members of the opposite sex, and of a better understanding of their spouses (which, in one case, led to a friendly divorce).*

These people were engaging in an unusual approach to therapy, one that has become increasingly popular in the United States and abroad. It is known by various names—growth therapy, encounter therapy, sensitivity sessions, T- or training-groups. Millions of people are exploring and exposing their inner selves through these therapies and are finding personal dimensions and potentials they never before realized they possessed. They are expanding their consciousness level, learning how to relate and respond to other people better, releasing new talents and abilities, and growing more deeply in touch with themselves and their world.

There are more than eight thousand types of growth therapies according to *Newsweek* magazine,[1] and they share the same goal: to awaken, liberate, expand, and enrich the human personality. They are a part of the *human potential movement*, oriented toward improving our psychological health.

There are two important differences between growth therapies and mental illness therapies (discussed in Chapter 4). One difference has to do with the kinds of people treated by these therapies. Growth therapies are designed for people of average or normal mental health. Mental illness therapies are designed for people who are suffering from neuroses, psychoses, or other kinds of emotional or behavioral problems.

The second difference has to do with the goal or purpose of the treatment. Mental illness therapies are oriented toward healing conflicts, anxieties, and emotional scars, or eliminating abnormal behavior. Growth therapies attempt to release previously hidden reservoirs of talent, creativity, energy, and motivation. Growth therapies focus on what people can become rather than on what they have been or are at the moment. They attempt to make people stronger, more creative, more fully alive and in use.

* Paul Bindrim, "A Report on a Nude Marathon: The Effects of Physical Nudity Upon the Practice of Interaction in the Marathon Group," *Psychotherapy: Theory, Research and Practice,* 5 (September 1968), 180–188.

[1]"Getting Your Head Together," *Newsweek,* September 6, 1976, p. 56.

## GROWTH PSYCHOLOGY

The focus on human potential has brought about a quiet revolution in psychology since the late 1950s. For most of its history, psychology has been primarily concerned with the unhealthy aspects of personality (mental illness) and has ignored conditions of psychological health. Although psychology is still deeply interested in understanding and treating emotional disturbances, there has been increasing concern with understanding the healthy personality and finding ways of reaching this desirable mental state.

In terms of the normal curve of distribution of psychological health (Figure 5–1), modern psychology covers the full range of personality from the lowest or poorest level of human functioning to the highest.

*Growth psychologists,* sometimes called *humanistic psychologists,* have been critical of Freud and others who dealt with the human personality by focusing on the sick or crippled side of humanity instead of the normal side, the emotionally disturbed instead of the healthy personality, the worst of human nature instead of the best.

Abraham Maslow, a leading American growth psychologist, argued persuasively that psychology must study the best, healthiest, and most mature human beings it could find. Only in that way can we learn what humans are capable of being and becoming. Maslow and other growth psychologists believed that all people possess an innate tendency toward a healthy personality, an inborn predisposition to psychological health. The potential for psychological health exists in each of us, and it is the task of growth psychologists to help us realize or fulfill that potential.

It has long been suspected by those who study human nature that most people do not use more than a fraction of their abilities and talents, perhaps no more than 10 per cent. How can we tap these immense reserves, the remaining 90 per cent of our potential, for full development? How can we become more alive, zestful, and fully in use? These are the questions to which growth psychologists seek answers. If we are able to unleash even half of our unused potential, the significance of this action in terms of human health, happiness, and the betterment of society is staggering.

How can an expansion of the human personality be brought about? There are two related approaches to the problem. First, there is the attempt, through research on psychologically healthy people, to try to understand their characteristics to determine how they differ from psychologically unhealthy people. Second, there are the various techniques of growth therapy designed to enhance those healthy characteristics, to raise levels of consciousness in order to release unused human potential.

## CHARACTERISTICS OF PSYCHOLOGICAL HEALTH

It may appear obvious what psychologically healthy people are like. If mental illness is characterized by the psychological and behavioral disturbances discussed in Chapter 3—neuroses, psychoses, and personality disorders—then mental health must be characterized by an absence of such disturbances. The distinction seems clear-cut and is generally correct, but it does not define adequately the nature of the healthy personality.

Growth psychologists emphasize a fundamental difference between normal or average mental health and superior mental health (the level of functioning we deal with in this chapter). In this view, the truly healthy, superior personality has achieved a level of development considerably greater than average. Growth psychologists believe that it is not sufficient to be free of neurosis or psychosis. The absence of mental illness in a person does not qualify him or her as a healthy personality. The absence of emotional disturbance is no more than a first step on the path to true psychological health. The person must reach and grow beyond this minimum condition of psychological health.

This distinction can be seen clearly on the normal curve of distribution (Figure 5–1). At the center or peak of the curve, where most people are represented, is average mental health, an emotional state relatively free of mental illness. The truly healthy personality is represented by the extreme right part of the curve, the highest point on the mental health continuum.

But what is wrong with being average or normal? Isn't it possible to have a rich, happy, meaningful life without working to advance to some higher level of personal development? Isn't it enough to be free of neuroses and psychoses? No, not according to the growth psychologists. They believe that even if we satisfy all our needs and drives and are unimpaired by mental illness, we can still feel unhappy and unfulfilled.

This, the growth psychologists assert, is verified in their own clinical practice and in the daily lives of millions of people who may be function-

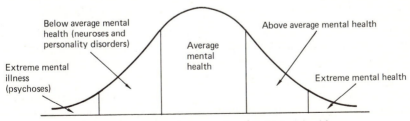

Figure 5–1. Normal curve of psychological health.

ing satisfactorily in all aspects of their daily lives and yet suffer agonizing boredom, stagnation, hopelessness, and meaninglessness. You probably know people who live comfortably, have secure jobs, warm and loving families, and lives that seem free of major problems and worries, yet who never seem to experience any great joy, overwhelming enthusiasm, or feeling of intense dedication or commitment. Obviously, all is not well; their lives are not so rich as they could be. Their human potential is undeveloped and under-utilized; they are not functioning at the level at which they are capable of functioning, similar to an automobile running on only a few of its eight cylinders. The car may still move, but not so smoothly, powerfully, or rapidly as it could. Most of its potential is not being used.

That is another reason why it is so important to understand the nature and characteristics of psychologically healthy people. It is the only way we can determine the capacity for human fulfillment, the only way to learn how far the human personality can stretch and develop. Further, by understanding the nature of psychologically healthy people we may be able to discover environmental conditions capable of fostering their development. For example, if we know that psychological health requires childhood feelings of autonomy and independence, then parents and schools could be urged to provide opportunities for the development and expression of those conditions. Similarly, in adulthood, jobs could be designed to allow for the maximum expression of these characteristics.

There have been many attempts to define the nature of the healthy personality. Some psychologists have offered models of a healthy personality based on their clinical experiences treating the mentally ill. Other psychologists have conducted research on people judged to have a high level of psychological health, using interviews, psychological tests, and clinical techniques of assessment.

Using data from both approaches, psychologists have developed several descriptions of a psychologically healthy person. However, there is one problem with these descriptions; they do not always agree. Some points are identical, some overlapping, and others contradictory. We cannot say with certainty what the healthy personality is like, but this may simply mean that there is no universal prescription for psychological health. In other words, there may not be a single definition or standard of psychological health that is appropriate for everyone. Different people may manifest psychological health in different ways.

What we can say with certainty about human nature is that people differ from one another; each person is a unique pattern of needs, fears, values, goals, and attributes. People are not duplicates of one another in their behavior, their expressions of mental illness, their normal functioning, or, it seems, in their form of psychological health.

As you read the descriptions of and prescriptions for the healthy personality, remember not only the principle of individual differences, but also that characteristics of psychological health differ in the same person at different ages. We know that human values, wants, needs, fears, and hopes change as people move from one stage of development to the next. Important aspects of our personality change from childhood to adolescence, young adulthood to middle age and old age. What we are and desire to become may be different at age forty from what it was at age twenty, and by age sixty our ideas will probably have altered again. For most of us, the personality does not remain static; we expand and enrich ourselves (or diminish or regress) as we grow older. Therefore, what is considered to be superior psychological health at one age may be poor psychological health at another.

What do psychologists know about the characteristics and nature of the healthy personality? We will present several experimental research studies and theoretical models of the healthy personality derived from clinical experience, then discuss some consistencies in these findings.

## Studies of Adolescents

The period of transition from high school to college is often difficult, requiring adjustments to new experiences, pressures, and expectations. It is reasonable to assume that people who have a high degree of psychological health will have fewer adjustment problems than those whose mental health is not as good. Two studies have investigated how psychologically healthy high school seniors coped with the stresses of college.

In one study,[2] high school seniors in the top half of their class, rated by their teachers as being high in traits such as motivation, initiative, concern for others, and emotional stability, and who had no neurotic symptoms, were interviewed weekly toward the end of the school year. The students all expected to go to college and looked forward to the experiences, challenges, and uncertainties facing them. The challenges were seen as exciting, not threatening, and the students were not at all anxious about their ability to perform college-level work.

They were self-reliant and determined in making their preparations for college and had realistic aspirations about grades, financial responsibilities, and social adjustments. The students all had a strong self-image and a realistic perception of their strengths and weaknesses. They were clearly future-oriented.

[2] E. Silber, D. A. Hamburg, G. V. Coelho, E. B. Murphy, M. Rosenberg, and L. F. Perlin, "Adaptive Behavior in Competent Adolescents," *Archives of General Psychiatry*, **5** (1961), 354–365.

Another study [3] examined a group of psychologically healthy adolescents to determine how they handled the experiences involved in actually beginning college life. Their personality characteristics were similar to those of the high school seniors in the first study. The college freshmen were oriented toward the future and were adept at planning and organizing their time to meet the deadlines of examinations and term papers. They were good at establishing priorities of work to be done and distinguishing what was important from a list of demands on their time.

They set personal standards of performance, in terms of grades, that were higher for more important courses (those in their major field) than for less important courses. Disappointments, such as receiving a low grade in an important subject, were handled rationally in ways that preserved their self-image. They were able to study well despite noisy dormitory environments, and they did not succumb to the distractions or temptations common to college life. In addition to these intellectual and emotional adjustments, their social adjustments were effective.

## A Study of Graduate Students

Eighty male graduate students, rated high by their professors in "personal soundness," were studied intently for six months. [4] On weekends they lived with the psychologists who were conducting the study, and were observed informally during meals and formally during interviews, group discussions and exercises, and while taking psychological tests. Psychologically healthy graduate students were found to be unusually efficient in their work, adaptable, persistent, resourceful, friendly, and stable. Other adjectives used by the psychologists to describe the psychologically healthy persons included ambitious, confident, dependable, helpful, realistic, considerate, good-natured, sincere, sociable, tolerant, and trusting.

Those subjects considered to be lower in psychological health were found to be anxious, emotional, moody, immature, and unstable. The psychologists also described them as inhibited, dissatisfied, defensive, egotistical, undependable, and withdrawn. The differences in overall personality patterns between more healthy and less healthy students are apparent from these descriptions.

Of particular interest in this study is the investigation of life history or personal background factors associated with psychological health.

[3] G. V. Coelho, D. A. Hamburg, and E. B. Murphy, "Coping Strategies in a New Learning Environment: A Study of American College Freshmen," *Archives of General Psychiatry*, 9 (1963), 433–443.

[4] F. Barron, "Personal Soundness in University Graduate Students," *Creativity and Personal Freedom* (New York: D. Van Nostrand, 1968), pp. 37–65.

The subjects were divided into two groups, those higher in personal soundness and those lower in personal soundness. The background factors closely related to psychological health were a stable home life with both parents and a high degree of economic security, a father who was respected and successful and a model valued by the son, early independence from the family, and early establishment of lasting heterosexual relations. The background factors of those lower in psychological health were considerable parental conflict in the home with the mother dominant, being the focus of racial or religious prejudice, and maternal emphasis on intellectual achievement.

## A Study of Astronauts

The selection and training of the U.S. astronauts in the early 1960s for the Project Mercury space flights provided an opportunity to study men of exceptionally high intelligence and physical and mental health.[5] The seven astronauts, selected from a field of sixty-nine candidates, were interviewed and tested in three phases during the selection and training programs for the space missions. The astronauts had similar backgrounds: affluent, middle-class parents, upbringing in small towns or on farms, and enjoyment of outdoor living and sports. Also, they were all engineers by training.

Their childhoods were free of major crises, their families and communities were stable, and they strongly identified with their father, whom they viewed as being very competent. (This corresponds to the background of the psychologically healthy graduate students discussed above.) The astronauts were not given to introspection, meditation, or fantasy life; their focus of attention was the external world rather than the internal, subjective world.

They were effective in their interpersonal relationships, sensitive to the feelings of others, and, although they preferred to work independently, they were not resentful when their work required dependence on others. They had a strong need to be in charge of their own destiny and great confidence in their ability to direct that destiny. The astronauts also possessed a high need to achieve, to strive toward success effectively and competently. Because they did achieve success in their chosen field, their feelings of self-esteem and self-worth, already high, were reinforced.

Their high level of ambition caused them to be bothered by work-related disappointments, but they were never defeated by these. They reacted constructively to disappointments with renewed vitality and energy. They were capable of feeling all emotions deeply but were able

[5] S. J. Korchin and G. E. Ruff, "Personality Characteristics of the Mercury Astronauts," *The Threat of Impending Disaster*, eds. G. H. Grosser, H. Wechsler, and M. Greenblatt (Cambridge, Mass.: MIT Press, 1964), pp. 197–207.

to control their emotions, particularly the negative and disturbing ones. For example, fear did not diminish their effectiveness because they could control it, and they felt confident that they could overcome fear.

## ALLPORT'S STUDIES OF MATURE PERSONALITIES [6]

Gordon Allport (1897–1967) was a prominent psychologist who devoted his career at Harvard University to the study of what he called the "mature person" who possesses a high degree of psychological health. His studies of healthy adults led him to conclude that healthy personalities are not controlled by unconscious forces or by childhood traumas and conflicts. Instead, he believed that psychologically healthy people function on a rational and conscious level. This means that they are in control of the forces that affect their lives. Also, they are guided by the present and by their intentions for the future.

Allport proposed seven characteristics of the healthy personality.

*Extension of the sense of self.*   Psychologically healthy people actively and directly extend themselves into interests and activities beyond their own being. This extension includes a genuine involvement with someone or something (a job, an ideal, a cause) that is meaningful to the individual. The more a person is involved with activities, people, or ideas, the more psychologically healthy he or she will be.

*Warm relating of self to others.*   Healthy personalities have the capacity for displaying compassion and intimacy or love for other people. This means that they can genuinely interact with others and that they have a sense of warmth, understanding, and kinship for all people. This makes them tolerant of other people's weaknesses and failings.

*Emotional security.*   Psychologically healthy people are secure within themselves. They can accept all facets of their being, both good and bad. They are not dominated by their emotions (as neurotics are) and are able to tolerate frustration as well as fear and insecurity.

*Realistic perception.*   A symptom of severe mental illness is a distorted view of reality and sometimes even a lack of contact with reality. Healthy personalities view the world accurately and objectively and accept reality for what it is.

---

[6] The theories of Allport, Maslow, Rogers, Fromm, Frankl, and Perls are also discussed in Duane Schultz, *Growth Psychology: Models of the Healthy Personality* (New York: D. Van Nostrand, 1977).

*Skills and assignments.*   A wholehearted commitment to work of some kind is important for psychological health. Healthy persons have developed their skills and abilities so as to achieve a high level of competence in their work. This absorption in and commitment to work is considered by many psychologists to be a requisite for psychological health, a point confirmed in the studies of adolescents, graduate students, and astronauts.

*Self-objectification.*   Allport believed that psychologically healthy people have realistic, objective pictures of themselves; they know who and what they are.

*A unifying philosophy of life.*   Healthy personalities are forward-looking, motivated by long-range goals and plans. They have a sense of purpose, a mission to work toward, as the cornerstone of their life. A person's system of values supplies the framework for specific goals and a unifying philosophy of life. Psychologically healthy people hold these values consistently and apply them to all aspects of their lives.


## MASLOW'S STUDY OF SELF–ACTUALIZING PEOPLE

Abraham Maslow (1908–1970) was a pioneer in the human potential movement. Growth psychology owes a great debt to his work, which was one of the first attempts to determine how much potential human beings have for full human development and expression, that is, for psychological health. Maslow studied forty-nine people who seemed to him to be models of psychological health. He used a variety of techniques, including interviews, free association, psychological tests, biographies, and autobiographies. Some subjects were studied directly; others, such as Thomas Jefferson, Abraham Lincoln, Albert Einstein, Eleanor Roosevelt, Jane Addams, and George Washington Carver, were studied retrospectively.

On the basis of this research Maslow developed both a list of characteristics of psychologically healthy people and a theory of human motivation (see Chapter 13).

Maslow described psychologically healthy people as "self-actualizing" because they have satisfied what he believed to be the highest human need, the need for self-actualization. This refers to the supreme development and use of all our abilities, the fulfillment of all our potentials.

Self-actualizing people are, in Maslow's view, middle-aged or older. It is difficult for younger people to become self-actualizing (although they can be heading toward it) because they usually have not developed a strong sense of identity and autonomy. Nor have they developed lasting values, patience, courage, wisdom, an enduring love relationship, or a calling to which to devote themselves.

Maslow discussed several specific characteristics of self-actualizers.

*An efficient perception of reality.* In agreement with Allport, Maslow found that psychologically healthy people perceive the world objectively. They see reality as it is and not as they might want or need it to be. Mentally ill persons, on the other hand, perceive the world in their own subjective terms, forcing it to fit the shape of their fears, anxieties, and needs.

*An acceptance of nature, others, and themselves.* Self-actualizing people are able to accept weaknesses and imperfections in other people, in themselves, and in nature, without being upset or disturbed by them. They accept these conditions as the natural order of things and are comfortable with all aspects of human nature. They do not feel shame or guilt about their shortcomings or failures.

*Spontaneity, simplicity, and naturalness.* Healthy people are totally devoid of pretense. They behave naturally and openly and do not try to hide or falsify their feelings and emotions, except where the display of such feelings might hurt others. In general, they are confident and secure enough to simply be themselves.

*A focus on problems outside themselves.* Without exception, the psychologically healthy people studied by Maslow were committed to some absorbing work; Maslow believed that psychological health was impossible without this dedication to work. Self-actualizing people truly love their work. It is more than just a way of making a living; it is something they genuinely want to do. They work harder than people of average mental health, but it is not really work to self-actualizers; it is their play as well.

*A need for privacy and independence.* Psychologically healthy people do not need other people; they are not dependent on other people for their security and satisfaction. They depend on themselves and prefer detachment and solitude. They do not fear other people or deliberately avoid them; they simply do not need them.

*Autonomous functioning.* Related to self-actualizers' need for privacy and independence is the need and ability to function autonomously of the social and physical environment. The satisfactions of psychologically healthy people come from within themselves, from their own resources and potential; they are self-contained.

*A continued freshness of appreciation.* Self-actualizing people have the ability to continually appreciate certain experiences—a sunset, a symphony, a favorite food, or a child's laughter—with a great amount of pleasure and wonder. A particular grove of trees on the way to work, for example, will be experienced with as much pleasure after five years as it was on the first day. Self-actualizers do not become bored by repeated experiences and are thankful for what they feel and possess.

*Mystical or peak experiences.* Healthy personalities frequently undergo what Maslow called "peak" experiences, which involve intense feelings of ecstasy, bliss, and awe, not unlike deep religious experiences. During these moments the person feels an intense sense of power, confidence, and decisiveness; there is nothing he or she could not do or become. The activity being engaged in at that moment—work, music, art, sex, or even watching a sunset—is magnified to overwhelming and exhilarating proportions.

*Social interest.* The psychologically healthy people Maslow studied possessed a strong and deep affection for all humanity, a sense of communion with all members of the human race.

*Interpersonal relations.* Self-actualizers are capable of stronger and deeper friendships, and greater love for other individuals, than people of average mental health. However, although their friendships are more intense, they are fewer in number; their circle of companions is small. Their love of another person is totally unselfish, and giving love is at least as important as receiving it. Healthy people care for the growth and development of the loved one as much as they do for their own.

*A democratic character structure.* Psychologically healthy people are totally free of prejudice. Differences of social class, educational level, religion, race, or color are of no importance to them.

*Creativeness.* Self-actualizing people are original, inventive, and innovative. However, they are not all artists or writers; they do not all produce artistic creations. Maslow defined creativeness as an attitude, similar to the naive imagination of children, with which healthy people perceive and react to the world around them.

*Resistance to conformity.* People who are self-contained and autonomous are guided by themselves, not by others. They do not deliberately flout social conventions and rules, but they are nonetheless capable of going their own way, resisting pressure to conform to the ideas, behaviors, and values of others.

Maslow's study of self-actualizing people is one of the most complete attempts to date to determine the criteria of psychological health. However, as is true of all the descriptions of psychological health in this chapter, Maslow's views may apply only to those people he studied and to the way in which he interpreted their behavior. The extent to which Maslow's views, or the views of any other researcher, apply to all people has yet to be determined. Given our present state of knowledge, we must consider these models of psychological health with open minds.

We have examined the results of research studies that have investigated people designated by various criteria as psychologically healthy. Another approach to the study of the healthy personality is derived not from specific research studies but rather from the clinical experiences of psychologists working primarily with disturbed people. In their attempts to determine the causes of mental illness, these psychologists have developed profiles of superior psychological health. These clinical pictures are based on the behavior of patients once they have been cured of their emotional disturbances and have achieved a new level of psychological health.

## ROGERS'S MODEL OF THE FULLY FUNCTIONING PERSON

In discussing Carl Rogers's client-centered counseling (Chapter 4), we noted the emphasis on the client's view of the world as the framework within which he or she functions. Rogers (1902–  ) believes that all people must rely on their own experience of the world because this is the only reality they can know. He argues that this is true not only for the mentally ill but also for the psychologically healthy, and it is a characteristic of the healthy personality.

Becoming psychologically healthy (what Rogers calls "fully functioning") is a difficult and painful process involving the continuous testing and stretching of a person's abilities. Like Maslow, Rogers believes that psychologically healthy people are truly themselves. They do not pretend to be someone they are not or hide behind a social role. They are nonconforming people who follow the path they choose for themselves.

Rogers lists five specific characteristics of the fully functioning person.

*They are open to all experiences.*   Healthy people are able to experience all feelings and attitudes as they occur, without having to distort them or hide from them. Unlike the mentally ill, fully functioning persons do not believe that any experience is threatening. Because they can experience the full range of emotions, their personalities are broader, fuller, and more flexible.

*They live fully in every moment of existence.* Because fully functioning people are open to all experiences, they do not have to defend themselves against any kind of experience. As a result, they are consistently influenced by each new experience and their personality is open to everything that happens to them.

*They trust their own organism.* Psychologically healthy people place more reliance on the "feel" of a situation than on rational or intellectual factors. They are capable of acting on momentary and intuitive impulses, and this gives them great spontaneity and freedom in their behavior. However, acting on impulse does not mean behaving irrationally or irresponsibly. Rational factors guide their behavior but so do unconscious and emotional factors. Thus, all elements of the personality are involved.

*They have a sense of freedom.* Because they are open to experience, live fully, and trust their own organism, fully functioning persons have a great deal of freedom of choice and action. They are not constrained or inhibited by a need to conform to the desires of others. This also gives them a sense of power and control over their own lives. They believe that their destiny is in their own hands, and is not determined by other people or by past events. As a result, they see many options in their life and are capable of doing and becoming anything they would like.

*They are highly creative.* Fully functioning persons express themselves creatively in everything they do, that is, with inventiveness, originality, and spontaneity.

## FROMM'S THEORY OF THE PRODUCTIVE PERSON

Along with most writers on psychological health, Erich Fromm (1900–  ) believes that everyone possesses an inherent striving or tendency to grow and develop to the full utilization of their potential. That more people do not achieve a state of psychological health is because of repressive and irrational societies, according to Fromm. Sick societies produce sick people. Fromm argues that societal reform is the only way to produce large numbers of healthy or "productive" people.

Productive people use all their powers, potentials, and abilities. The productive orientation is a general attitude that encompasses all aspects of life, including the intellectual and emotional. Fromm defines productive people in terms of their ability to love and to think, and in terms of happiness and conscience.

*Productive love.* Productive love is a free and equal relationship in which both partners are able to maintain their individuality. One person's self is not lost in the love of another but is expanded. Achieving productive love is difficult because it involves four challenges: to care, to be responsible for, to respect, and to know. A person must care for the loved one, being concerned with his or her well-being and furthering growth and development. Responsibility means being responsive to the loved one's needs. Also, a person must respect the loved one for who and what he or she is and have a full and objective knowledge of their nature.

*Productive thinking.* Productive love involves a genuine sense of participating with and caring for the loved one, and productive thinking involves the same degree of participating with and caring for the object of thought. Productive thinkers are motivated by a strong interest in and concern about the object of their thought. There is an intimate relationship between the thinker and what he or she is thinking about and the person examines the object in an objective, respectful, and caring manner.

*Happiness.* Productive people are happy because happiness is a natural outcome of living in accordance with the productive orientation. The happiness of which Fromm writes is more than a feeling of pleasantness. It is a condition of vigor and vitality, physical health, and the fulfillment of one's potentials.

*Conscience.* Productive people have a special kind of conscience; Fromm calls it a "humanistic" conscience. Nonhealthy people, on the other hand, have an "authoritarian" conscience that represents the strict moral code learned from their parents. The behaviors and thoughts of these people are dictated by the authoritarian conscience, which produces guilt whenever the moral code is violated. Thus, nonhealthy persons are guided by forces outside themselves, forces that prevent their full functioning and development.

The humanistic conscience that guides the healthy personality is the voice of the self. It leads the person to behave in ways that bring internal approval, the full development and expression of the personality, and a feeling of happiness. The healthy personality is self-directed and self-regulated.

Although Fromm believes that some people approach the psychologically healthy state of productivity, this condition nevertheless remains an ideal or goal, one rarely achieved in any society. Fromm has stated that the only way to bring about the productive orientation is to live in a sane, healthy society, and to this end, he has frequently argued for social reforms.

## FRANKL'S MODEL OF THE SELF–TRANSCENDENT PERSON

Viktor Frankl (1905–   ) returned from his years in the Nazi concentration camps during World War II convinced that people have a conscious choice over their actions in all situations, even those as terrifying as the death camps. We are always free to choose an attitude or way of reacting to our fate, to decide the outcome of our existence, and to find a meaning in life, even in the face of death.

Frankl's view of psychological health stresses what he calls "the will to meaning," finding a meaning, reason, or purpose to life. The meaning for which we must search is an essence or quality beyond our selves. It is not sufficient, he argues, to be self-actualizing or fully functioning, or productive. We must transcend the self; we must relate to a person, an ideal, or a form of work beyond the focus on the self.

Psychologically healthy people have found a meaning in life and have reached the state of self-transcendence. They can consciously choose and direct the course of their own life and are personally responsible for it. They do not blame others, such as parents or society, for their misfortunes. In addition to these general points, Frankl noted specific characteristics of healthy personalities.

*They are oriented toward the future.*   Psychologically healthy people are motivated to reach specific goals. Life can have no meaning without goals for which to strive.

*They are committed to work.*   As did Maslow, Frankl stresses that a feeling of dedication to work is vital for psychological health and is a fundamental way of finding meaning in life. It is not the nature or content of the work that is so important but rather the way in which we perform the work—what we bring to the job with our unique personality.

*They are able to give and receive love.*   One way to realize our uniqueness and find meaning in life is through work. Another way is through love. Frankl considers love to be the ultimate human goal. He believes that our salvation is through love. Both partners in a love relationship are enhanced, and each helps the other to realize untapped potentials by making the partner aware of what he or she can become. This is similar to Fromm's definition of productive love.

## PERLS'S MODEL OF THE "HERE AND NOW" PERSON

In Chapter 4 we discussed Perls's approach to the treatment of the mentally ill. His Gestalt therapy centers on uniting the personality or making it whole, and completing unfinished situations from the person's past. Out of his work with patients Perls (1893–1970) developed a model of the healthy personality, which includes the following characteristics.

*They function in the "here and now," the present.* Psychologically healthy people do not dwell on events in the past or live exclusively in anticipation (or dread) of the future. Their full awareness and satisfaction derive from their moment-to-moment existence in the real world.

*They understand and accept who and what they are.* Healthy personalities know their strengths and weaknesses. They know what they have the potential to be and what they do not have the potential to be. Therefore, they do not strive for goals they know they cannot reach, or try to be something they are not.

*They express their impulses and yearnings.* "Here and now" persons can express all aspects of their being without inhibition or guilt. They are secure enough to let everyone know what they are feeling, thinking, or desiring at the moment.

*They take responsibility for their own lives.* In agreement with Frankl, Perls believed that psychologically healthy people recognize that they alone are responsible for what they make of their lives. They do not shift this responsibility to parents, spouses, bad luck, or an impoverished childhood.

*They shun responsibility for anyone else.* Expressing a controversial view, Perls argued that healthy people are no more responsible for other people than others are for them. He believed that if we take responsibility for another person we interfere with that person's life, causing him or her to become dependent on us. As a result, that person may feel no sense of responsibility for his or her own life.

*They are completely in touch with self and world.* Healthy people are in touch with their senses and feelings and are fully aware of everything that goes on around them.

*They express resentments openly.* Whereas unhealthy people suppress their resentments, in Perls's view healthy people do not hesitate to express resentments without inhibition.

*They are free of external regulation of their life.* They are not guided or dictated to by anyone else's conception of proper behavior, nor do they try to live up to anyone else's image of what they should be. They rely instead on their own standards and, as a result, their behavior is spontaneous and natural, reflecting who and what they are.

*They are not actively seeking happiness.* Perls believed that people who make happiness a goal dwell in the future. This takes attention and energy away from the present. Psychologically healthy people do not pursue happiness, but nevertheless they experience happy moments. However, Perls thought that happiness was transitory and occurred simply by being who and what we are.

We have read several descriptions of psychological health and can note points of agreement and disagreement. Probably the major point of agreement is that psychologically healthy persons are in conscious control of their life. They are capable of directing their behavior and being in charge of their own destiny. They are not motivated by unconscious forces or by the dictates of other people.

The theorists also seem to agree that psychologically healthy people know who and what they are. They are aware of and accept their strengths and weaknesses, virtues and vices. They do not pretend to be anything other than what they really are.

Another characteristic of these theories of psychological health is an anchoring in the present, the experiences of the moment. Healthy people do not dwell on past injustices or traumas, nor do they live in their yearnings for the future. However, they are concerned with future goals and missions, and they actively work to achieve them.

Other common characteristics are the ability to give and receive love, dedication and commitment to work, care and responsibility for others (except in Perls's view), good interpersonal relations, and a need for independence and autonomy.

## GROWTH THERAPIES: TECHNIQUES FOR INCREASING HUMAN POTENTIAL

Research findings on the nature of psychological health have been applied to the development of the growth therapies, and these therapies have affected the lives of thousands of people. The widespread proliferation of growth therapies since the mid-1960s is the most significant aspect of the human potential movement, in terms of its practical impact on our culture. Deriving, in part, from group therapies used with the mentally ill, growth therapies are used with people of normal or average mental health who want to raise their consciousness level, learn how to relate better to themselves and to others, and release hidden potentials for creativity and development. In other words, growth therapies are designed to make people better than they are, to make them more productive, more fully functioning, more self-actualizing, and more psychologically healthy.

Growth therapies have many names—encounter groups, T-groups, sensitivity sessions—and there are many variations on the basic procedure. We began this chapter with an example of a nude encounter session, one of the more controversial approaches. Some groups meet only for a few hours; others use the marathon approach involving a weekend or longer of group encounter.

Some growth therapies emphasize verbal interaction, others stress physical activity, in which members may scream at each other, crawl on the floor, hug, dance, beat pillows, or engage in other forms of physical expression and interpersonal contact.

The growth therapies have spread to many segments of society. Encounter groups are conducted in schools (from kindergarten to graduate school), in industry (where thousands of employees are given growth training each year), at all levels of government, in church groups, and in prisons. In addition, private growth therapy centers have been established in almost every city in the United States. People in all walks of life—from criminals to ambassadors—have enrolled in sensitivity sessions.

In the modern age, when many of us suffer anxiety and loneliness, when it is difficult to establish intimate relationships with other people, and when we feel so anonymous in the complexities of daily living, encounter groups offer an intense feeling of participation, involvement, and community. The group sessions focus on the emotional and behavioral interactions of group members and encourage openness and honesty of expression. Members are given the opportunity to talk about how they feel—in a situation quite different from their job, home life, or ordinary social relationships—without fear of punishment for being candid.

Not only can group members be honest with one another, but they will also receive sincere feedback about what they say and do. They can learn how others react to them; it may be the first time in their life

they have received such an honest appraisal. Sometimes these can be painful revelations but, according to the growth therapists, they are a vital part of the process of coming to know oneself.

All this takes place in an atmosphere of love and support—verbal and physical—from the other group members. Although it may appear that persons are being criticized brutally, and having their facades stripped from them, the other group members will still accept them, give them encouragement to grow and, if necessary, let them cry in their arms.

## ENCOUNTER GROUP PROCEDURES

Carl Rogers, a leading proponent of encounter groups, analyzed the complex interactions that take place during group sessions and specified a number of events. We present them in the sequence in which they usually occur, although the order can vary from one group to another.[7]

*"Milling around."* Because the groups are free of a structure and lack direction from a group leader or facilitator, there is initially a feeling of awkwardness and confusion about what people should say and do. The members look to the leader to tell them what to do but they soon realize that the structure and direction must come from them.

*"Resistance to personal expression or exploration."* Not surprisingly, at first group members resist revealing much about themselves to strangers. They are inhibited by the social roles and pretenses from everyday life. Only with difficulty do most people begin to break down these facades. Consider how difficult it would be for you to reveal, to a group of strangers, things about yourself that you may never have told your closest friend, and perhaps even have difficulty admitting to yourself.

*"Description of past feelings."* Although hesitantly and uncertainly, group members do begin to reveal aspects of their life that they find troublesome or worrying. A young person may speak of personal indecision about marriage, a manager may reveal anxiety about the threat from younger people at work, and another may talk about problems with aging parents.

*"Expression of negative feelings."* This represents the first expression of the members' feelings toward the others in the group and it is almost always negative. They attack one another, and often the leader as well,

[7] Excerpts from *Carl Rogers on Encounter Groups* by Carl R. Rogers, pp. 14–36. Copyright © 1970 by Carl R. Rogers. By permission of Harper and Row, Publishers, Inc.

for not providing a structure and direction. Rogers believes that these first expressions are negative because the group members want to test the others, to find out if it is "safe" to express their true feelings and to see what kind of response they will get from the others.

*"Expression and exploration of personally meaningful material."* The event most likely to occur next is the expression of personal feelings by some members of the group. Apparently realizing that there will be acceptance by the group, a sense of trust is established, and, as a result, members begin to feel free to talk about themselves. They offer deeper revelations than the past feelings described earlier. These are more intimate recollections and thus are more difficult to express. This process marks the beginning of the "journey to the center of the self," the painful process of learning to understand one's feelings and motivations.

*"The expression of immediate interpersonal feelings in the group."* Here the members begin to react in both positive and negative ways toward one another, expressing their present feelings toward what others say and do. For example: "I feel threatened by your silence," "You remind me of my mother, with whom I had a tough time," "I took an instant dislike to you the first moment I saw you," and "I dislike you more every time you speak up." These feelings must then be explored by the group to determine what they reveal about the person and about the dynamics of the group.

*"The development of a healing capacity in the group."* In this process, some of the group members reveal an apparently natural and spontaneous capacity for responding with sensitivity to the pain and suffering of the others. Along with the facilitator, these members respond with sympathy, support, and insightful interpretations of a member's problems, together with guidance on how to cope with the problem. They form a "helping relationship" with the person, which usually leads to self-acceptance.

*"Self-acceptance and the beginning of change."* Through the healing capacity of the group—the helping relationship—members often come to accept the existence of some troubling aspect of themselves and to begin to change it, usually for the first time in their life. For example, a business executive came to see how he had been a cold and unloving person even to those he dearly loved. In less than a week this self-acceptance led to a change for the better in his relationships with his wife and child. In another case, a young man, Art, talked about the "shell" he had encased himself in.

Art: When that shell's on, it's, uh . . . .

Lois: It's on!

Art: Yeah, it's on tight.

Susan: Are you always so closed in when you're in your shell?

Art: No, I'm so darn used to living with the shell, it doesn't even bother me. I don't even know the real me. I think I've, well, I've pushed the shell away more here. When I'm out of my shell—only twice—once just a few minutes ago—I'm really me, I guess. But then I just sort of pull in a cord after me when I'm in my shell, and that's almost all the time. And I leave the front standing outside when I'm back in the shell.

Facilitator: And nobody's back in there with you?

Art: (Crying) Nobody else is in there with me, just me. I just pull everything into the shell and roll the shell up and shove it in my pocket. I take the shell, and the real me, and put it in my pocket where it's safe. I guess that's really the way I do it—I go into my shell and turn off the real world. And here—that's what I want to do here in this group, y'know —come out of my shell and actually throw it away.

Lois: You're making progress already. At least you can talk about it.

Facilitator: Yeah. The thing that's going to be hardest is to stay out of the shell.

Art: (Still crying) Well, yeah, if I can keep talking about it I can come out and stay out, but I'm gonna have to, y'know, protect me. It hurts. It's actually hurting to talk about it.[8]

As a result of the sensitivity and support of the facilitator and some of the group members, Art began to accept himself and to undergo the painful process of change.

*"The cracking of facades."*   As the group session progresses, the members become increasingly impatient with and intolerant of anyone who persists in hiding behind a mask or social role and refuses to reveal his or her true self. The group can become harsh in its insistence that all members be honest, open, and revealing. Group members persist until all pretenses are stripped away.

*"The individual receives feedback."*   Throughout the group experience, the members are receiving feedback on how others perceive them. It is often a surprise to learn that other people do not see them as they see themselves. For example, a person who actively tries to show concern for other group members may be told that he or she seems to be trying to dominate the group by acting as a parent to them all. A person who pauses before speaking because he or she takes pride in talking clearly and precisely may be told that this seems reserved and stuffy. Usually,

[8] Ibid., p. 26.

people have not received such blunt feedback before and it helps them analyze their picture of who and what they are.

*"Confrontation."* Throughout the sessions, members confront each other, sometimes positively, but usually negatively, displaying anger and even violence. For example, one member of a group, Alice, had made contemptuous remarks to another member, John, who had told of going into religious service. At the next group meeting, Norma, who had been very quiet at previous sessions, confronted Alice.

> Norma: (Loud sigh) Well, I don't have *any* respect for you, Alice. *None!* (Pause) There's about a hundred things going through my mind I want to say to you, and *by God* I hope I get through 'em all! First of all, if you wanted us to respect you, then why couldn't you respect *John's* feelings last night? *Why have you been on him today?* H'mm? Last night—*couldn't you—couldn't you* accept—*couldn't you* comprehend in any way at all that—that *he felt* his unworthiness in the service of God? *Couldn't you accept this* or did you have to dig into it today to find something *else* there? H'mm? I personally don't think John has any problems that are *any* of *your damn business!* . . . Any real woman that I know wouldn't have acted as you have this week, and particularly what you said this afternoon. That was so *crass!* It just made me want to puke, right there! ! ! And—I'm just *shaking* I'm so mad at you—I don't think you've been real once this week! . . . I'm so infuriated that *I want to come over and beat the hell out of you! I want to slap you across the mouth so hard and*—oh, and you're so, you're many years above me—and I respect age, and I respect people who are older than me, *but I don't respect you, Alice. At all!* (A startled pause.) [9]

Growth therapists believe that such confrontations are a vital part of the therapy for all members of the group. Parties directly involved learn something about themselves, and others may experience vicarious emotional releases or be inspired to provoke their own confrontations.

An additional aspect of encounter groups is the finding that the helping relationships established during the sessions often continue outside the group situation. Rogers and others have written about the extent of the support and care that some group members have given to others in everyday life.

These group experiences facilitate more intimate and intense relationships than many people otherwise experience. Group members often feel closer to one another than they do to relatives and friends. The closeness and intimacy, and the sense of openness and trust provided by the group, seem to allow people to feel safe enough to explore their deepest feelings, to shed pretenses and facades, and to relate fully to one another. By honestly and directly displaying their feelings, members become capable of expressing and utilizing all aspects of their personality. They

[9] Ibid., pp. 31–32.

uncover new dimensions and potentials and grow more fully human. That is what the human potential movement and the growth therapies are all about.

## Dangers of Encounter Groups

Not all people benefit from encounter groups. Not all people grow and become more fully human. Some are unaffected by group experiences but others are harmed by their participation.

Some people become disturbed when they try to carry over the new-found sense of openness, honesty, and caring from the encounter group to the real world of job and family. It is upsetting when they realize that colleagues and spouses seem threatened by such honesty, or grow angry because they too are expected to become as revealing and candid as the encounter group members. The open expression of one's feelings, or telling others what one really thinks of them, is usually poorly received on the job or over the breakfast table by people who have not experienced the group sessions. People may become depressed by this situation and may join group after group, finding that they need the sense of openness and sharing that cannot be found anywhere else. They become encounter group junkies.

Much more serious is the problem of people who cannot withstand the pressure of this intensely emotional group experience. Some members of encounter groups reveal problems and conflicts of which they had been unaware. In psychoanalytic treatment, that kind of revelation is good, assuming that the conflict is then worked through with a therapist. Unfortunately, these problems may not be sufficiently worked through in an encounter group, and the person who, encouraged by the trust and openness of a group session, reveals a repressed conflict may require psychotherapy to resolve it.

Occasionally, someone in a group has a psychotic episode, apparently as a result of the encounter group pressures. Some people are overwhelmed by the failure to relate to or be accepted by a group, and this damages their self-esteem. Studies of the aftereffects of participation in encounter groups reveal psychological casualty rates of less than 1 per cent to almost 50 per cent.[10] Whatever the actual incidence of harm, it is clear that encounter group sessions are potentially damaging.

## OTHER APPROACHES TO INCREASING HUMAN POTENTIAL

Although the encounter group experience is a popular form of growth therapy, it is not the only one. There are several other approaches.

[10] Dianna Hartley, Howard B. Roback, and Stephen I. Abramowitz, "Deterioration Effects in Encounter Groups," *American Psychologist*, **31** (1976), 247–255.

A widely used technique for increasing human potential is *meditation,* which is usually practiced individually. It has been estimated that as many as one million people, representing many occupational groups, practice this silent exercise for two twenty-minute periods each day. The basic approach is that promoted by the Maharishi Mahesh Yogi, known as *Transcendental Meditation* or *TM.* This easily learned technique involves sitting quietly and silently repeating the *mantra,* a single word chosen for each individual by a TM leader.

Designed to combat the effects of stress, TM is described as a path to perfect consciousness, a means of raising one's ordinary level of consciousness. The person's everyday conscious contents are reduced or stopped altogether during meditation, and are replaced by new and higher levels of consciousness. These new levels of consciousness result in total relaxation of the mind and body and in greater creativity and healthier personalities.

Physiological changes have been reported to take place during meditation. Studies have shown that the electrical activity of the brain in the form of brain waves, as measured by the electroencephalograph (EEG), changes to a state of consciousness not found in waking, sleeping, or dreaming. Apparently, meditators exhibit a fourth state of consciousness in which they are deeply relaxed yet able to respond to physical stimuli. Also, during meditation oxygen consumption decreases by as much as 20 per cent, respiration rate falls, and the body's metabolic rate slows.

Some form of meditation has been practiced by Eastern religions for centuries. Whether it will benefit people of Western cultures, by increasing human potential and producing healthier personalities, is undetermined, but one cannot deny that a large number of people find it of great help in reducing the tensions of everyday living.

Another frequently used technique designed to increase human potential is *sensory awareness training,* the purpose of which is to increase our contact with the physical environment, thus enhancing our sensory awareness of the world around us. Through a series of exercises, people are trained to regain the intimate sensory contacts of childhood that have become suppressed in the process of growing up. According to proponents of sensory awareness training, we must reestablish our childlike sense of wonder and awe in reacting to stimuli, to sights, sounds, smells, touches, and tastes.

The exercises are also designed to make people aware of what is happening in their own bodies. They include such activities as lying quietly on the floor while concentrating on every physical sensation; sensory contact with other people, such as sitting back to back or dancing spontaneously to music; experiencing pleasant and foul aromas; breathing exercises; and body massages. Some sensory awareness training activities are performed individually; others take place in groups.

Another technique for actualizing human potential is inducing *peak experiences*. Peak experiences are the intense experiences felt by self-actualizing persons when they are fully expanding their potentials. To induce a peak experience as a form of growth therapy, a person is asked to recall any peak experiences he or she may have had. Then, with a therapist, the stimuli or activities that can help bring about peak experiences are explored. Finally, the person is encouraged to relax and enter his or her inner fantasy world in the presence of stimuli that induce peak experiences, for example, listening to a favorite piece of music. The result, according to proponents of this approach, is a new-found strength with which to deal with anxiety and a higher level of personal growth and development.

An unusual growth therapy, dealing with the body instead of the mind, is *structural integration* or *rolfing*, named after its originator, Dr. Ida Rolf. The technique is based on the assumption that the body reflects past experiences that have thrown it out of alignment. For example, repeated fear in childhood will, Dr. Rolf explains, collapse the diaphragm and shorten the upper chest muscles. A body thus damaged by emotional experiences must be restructured.

In rolfing the therapist uses the elbow and hands to dig deeply into the patient's muscles, manipulating them so as to unlock supporting tissue. In the process of relaxing and realigning the muscles, the harmful emotional memories are assumed to be released. This is often painful but the pain is believed to be part of the therapy. Once the body's muscles have been realigned, the person is able to experience enhanced awareness of both body and mind.

These are only a few of the growth therapy techniques. Some approaches undoubtedly are fads and will decline in popularity. Others, such as encounter group sessions, are long-lasting and have helped many people unleash their full human potentials and become healthier personalities.

## SUMMARY

Growth therapy is oriented toward expanding and enriching the human personality, improving psychological health, and tapping previously unused human potential. Growth therapy techniques are used with people of average or normal mental health, people who are not suffering from neurosis, psychosis, or other emotional or behavioral problems.

Growth or humanistic psychologists study the positive side of personality (psychological health) instead of the negative side (mental illness). This interest in psychological health is being expressed in two ways: in research that attempts to understand the characteristics of psychologically healthy people, and in specific techniques designed to foster the development of those characteristics.

Growth psychologists have identified a number of characteristics of psychological health. In addition to being free of neuroses and psychoses, psychologically healthy people have achieved a level of growth and a utilization of human potential considerably higher than persons of average mental health. However, there is no universal description of a healthy personality. Different types of psychological health are appropriate for different people or for the same person at different ages.

Research studies of psychologically healthy adolescents, graduate students, and astronauts showed them to be, in general, self-reliant, competent, hard-working, future-oriented, emotionally stable, realistic, and from stable homes and communities.

Models of psychological health proposed by Gordon Allport, Abraham Maslow, Carl Rogers, Erich Fromm, Viktor Frankl, and Fritz Perls are discussed.

*Allport* proposed seven criteria of the *mature personality:* extension of the sense of self, warm relating of self to others, emotional security, realistic perception, skills and assignments, self-objectification, and a unifying philosophy of life.

*Maslow's* study of *self-actualizing people* showed them to have an efficient perception of reality; an acceptance of nature, others, and themselves; spontaneity, simplicity, and naturalness; a focus on problems outside themselves; a need for privacy and independence; autonomous functioning; a continued freshness of appreciation; mystical or peak experiences; social interest; deep interpersonal relations; a democratic character structure; creativeness; and a resistance to conformity.

*Rogers* found that *fully functioning persons* can be described as open to all experiences, living fully in every moment, trusting their own organism, enjoying a sense of freedom, and highly creative.

*Fromm* described psychologically healthy people as *productive* and defined them in terms of their ability to love productively, think productively, experience genuine happiness, and be guided by their own conscience.

In *Frankl's* view the *self-transcendent person* is oriented toward the future, committed to work, able to give and receive love, and possessed of a meaning and purpose in life.

*Perls's* model of psychological health, the *"here and now"* person, has the following characteristics: such persons function in the present, they understand and accept who and what they are, they express their impulses and yearnings, they take responsibility for their own lives, they shed responsibility for others, they are completely in touch with self and world, they express resentments openly, they are free of external regulation, and they are not engaged in the pursuit of happiness.

There are general similarities among these models of psychological health. Healthy people are in conscious control of their life, they know who and what they are, they are anchored in the present, they can give and receive love, they are committed to work, they care for and feel responsible for others, they have positive interpersonal relations, and they need independence and autonomy.

*Growth therapy,* designed to promote psychological health, has several forms; the *group encounter approach* is probably the most popular. Through intense and intimate emotional interactions, encounter group members learn how to relate better to themselves and to others, and how others respond to them. In the process, they raise their consciousness levels to new heights and uncover hidden potentials.

According to Rogers, encounter groups proceed through a sequence of complex interactions: milling around, resistance to personal expression or exploration, description of past feelings, expression of negative feelings, expression and exploration of personally meaningful material, expression of immediate interpersonal feelings in the group, development of a healing capacity in the group, self-acceptance and the beginning of change, the cracking of facades, receipt of feedback, and confrontation.

Some people are harmed by encounter group experiences because they find that they cannot relate as openly and honestly to the rest of the world as they can to members of their group. Persons who reveal problems or conflicts that the group does not resolve, or who fail to relate to or be accepted by the group, are also damaged by group experiences.

Another popular technique of growth therapy is *meditation,* a way to reduce stress, relax totally, and increase one's level of consciousness in order to release new creativity.

Other approaches to increasing psychological health include *sensory awareness training,* in which people establish closer contact with the physical world, *induced peak experiences,* in which one undergoes a voyage into an inner fantasy world in order to enhance personal growth, and *rolfing,* in which the body muscles are relaxed and realigned in order to release harmful emotional memories.

## SUGGESTED READINGS

Allport, Gordon. *Pattern and Growth in Personality.* New York: Holt, Rinehart and Winston, 1961.

Allport, Gordon. Autobiography. In *A History of Psychology in Autobiography,* vol. 5. New York: Appleton-Century-Crofts, 1967.

Back, K. *Beyond Words: The Story of Sensitivity Training and the Encounter Movement.* New York: Russell Sage Foundation, 1972.

Evans, Richard I. *Dialogue With Erich Fromm.* New York: Harper and Row, 1966.

Frankl, Viktor. *The Will To Meaning: Foundations and Applications of Logotherapy.* Cleveland: World, 1969.

Fromm, Erich. *Escape From Freedom.* New York: Holt, Rinehart and Winston, 1941.

Goldberg, Carl. *Encounter: Group Sensitivity Training Experience.* New York: Science House, 1970.

Hall, Mary Harrington. A conversation with Carl Rogers. *Psychology Today,* 1967 (December), **1**, 18–21, 62–66.

Hall, Mary Harrington. A conversation with Viktor Frankl of Vienna. *Psychology Today,* 1968 (February), **2**, 57–63.

Hall, Mary Harrington. A conversation with Abraham H. Maslow. *Psychology Today,* 1968 (July), **2**, 34–37, 54–57.

Jourard, Sidney M. *Healthy Personality: An Approach From the Viewpoint of Humanistic Psychology.* New York: Macmillan, 1974.

Libo, Lester. *Is There Life After Group?* New York: Anchor Books, 1977.

Lieberman, M., I. Yalom, and M. Miles. *Encounter Groups: First Facts.* New York: Basic Books, 1973.

Maslow, Abraham H. *Motivation and Personality,* 2nd ed. New York: Harper and Row, 1970.

Otto, Herbert A., Ed. *Human Potentialities: The Challenge and the Promise.* St. Louis: Warren H. Green, 1968.

Perls, Frederick S. (Fritz). *Gestalt Therapy Verbatim.* Moab, Utah: Real People Press, 1969.

Rogers, Carl R. *On Becoming A Person: A Therapist's View of Psychotherapy.* Boston: Houghton Mifflin, 1961.

Rosenbaum, Max, and Alvin Snadowsky. *The Intensive Group Experience.* New York: Free Press, 1976.

Schultz, Duane. *Growth Psychology: Models of the Healthy Personality.* New York: D. Van Nostrand, 1977.

Shepard, M. *Fritz: An Intimate Portrait of Fritz Perls and Gestalt Therapy.* New York: Dutton, 1975.

Vaillant, George E. *Adaptation To Life.* Boston: Little, Brown, 1977.

Vaillant, George E. The climb to maturity. How the best and the brightest came of age. *Psychology Today,* 1977 (September), **11**, 34–41, 107–110.

# Psychology Applied to Physical Health

**6**

Dr. Robert Parker stared at his medical school diploma for what seemed like a long time. Then, with a sigh and a slow shake of his head, he sat down at his desk. He was tired after a full day of seeing patients, but more than that he was confused and disturbed. He reviewed in his mind the patients he had seen during the day, recalling their complaints and symptoms and the treatment he had prescribed for each one. It was the usual collection of ills that any doctor in general practice confronts in the course of a day. He had treated them in the usual way, by the methods he had been taught in medical school.

There were injections for some, prescriptions for drugs for others, advice on diet and rest, and, in a few cases, referrals to specialists for problems he did not feel competent to handle. All of his diagnoses and treatments had one thing in common; they were physical in nature, designed to restore or repair some damaged organ or part of the body. Surgery, drugs, radiation therapy, special diets—the same kinds of treatments he had been giving for fifteen years. "That's what doctors do," he said aloud. "We heal the body."

Although he spoke these words with conviction, lately he was finding it increasingly difficult to believe them, and that was why he was so upset again today (as he had been for the past few months).

Dr. Parker remembered when it began, right here in his office when he had to tell a patient that he had throat cancer. The tests from the hospital and the specialists confirmed it. There was nothing to be done, no cure. The patient might live six months, perhaps a year, but certainly no longer; that was beyond question, a medical certainty.

Dr. Parker smiled to himself as he remembered the patient's reaction. The man was a cantankerous sort, a self-made businessman who, through shrewd common sense and a lot of hard work, had become very wealthy. He slammed his fist on the doctor's desk and said, "Goddamn it, Doc, I'm not ready to die yet. I've got too much to live for. I'm gonna fight this thing and beat it."

That had been six months ago. Last week the man came in smiling broadly, apparently in perfect health. "Check me out, Doc," he said. "Cancer's gone. I told you I was gonna beat it." And sure enough, to Dr. Parker's amazement, not a trace of the disease could be found. He sent the patient back to the specialists and they confirmed it.

"Spontaneous remission," Dr. Parker told the patient, repeating the stock answer for cases like this one, an answer that meant that doctors could not explain how it had happened.

"Spontaneous hell!" the patient roared. "I did it myself," and he went on to tell the doctor how he had achieved his cure. The story was incredible, even bizarre, and Dr. Parker did not know whether to explode in anger or to laugh.

The patient had gone to a clinic in New York City where he was treated by a psychologist and a radiologist. He was given radiation treatments, which the specialists had said were worthless because the cancer was too far advanced, and also was taught how to meditate and to actively visualize the destruction of his cancer. Three times a day the patient relaxed deeply, going into a state of meditation, during which he visualized the x-rays in the form of bullets attacking the cancer cells and destroying them one by one. Then he saw, in his mind's eye, great numbers of white blood cells sweeping the now dead cancer cells away through the bloodstream and out of the body altogether.

When the patient finished describing his unorthodox treatment, he stood up and grinned with smug satisfaction. "It's time you people learned there's more to healing than giving pills and cutting people up," he said. He tapped his finger against the side of his head. "The greatest healer of all," he said, "is the mind."

"Ridiculous," Dr. Parker told himself when the man left the office. "It's like voodoo and faith healing. We might as well go back to witch doctors."

But Dr. Parker was no longer sure it was so ridiculous. He had been reading some disturbing books about psychological research on emotional factors that may cause cancer, heart attacks, ulcers, rheumatism, asthma, skin conditions, and other disorders. He talked to colleagues and a few of them, the younger ones, did not scoff at the idea. One told him about a patient who had a severe ulcer. "I told him to quit his job and change his life-style. Six weeks later the ulcer was gone. I had treated him for a year before that with no results." Another told him about a patient who was stricken with a severe respiratory infection every time his mother-in-law came to visit. "You can't tell me there isn't something emotional in that!" the doctor said.

Other physicians mentioned cures they had brought about not with drugs or surgery but by the power of suggestion alone. "We tried everything," one doctor said, "but nothing worked. Finally, in desperation I gave the patient some sugar pills—harmless but worthless—and said it was brand new and the most powerful medicine ever developed for the disease. I said it had worked every time. Two weeks later the pain and the growth were gone." The doctor threw up her hands and finished the story. "You figure it out. I can't. There's something here," the doctor added, tapping the side of her head as Dr. Parker's patient had done, "that sometimes works better than all our medicine."

Parker swiveled around in his office chair and looked at his diploma again, his anger growing apace with his confusion. "It just can't be," he said. "It goes against everything I was taught and ever believed in. Disease is physical not mental, and it needs to be treated physically. The mind cannot influence the body that much!" He pounded his fist on the arm of the chair and stood up. As he did so, he winced. Dr. Parker had a headache, one of many he had gotten during the past few months.

The notion that the human mind can influence the body, to the extent of causing or curing disease, is an old idea that can be traced back to the Greeks. Socrates wrote that there can be no illness of the body separate from the mind. Hippocrates, the father of medicine, wrote, "It is more important to know what kind of person has a disease than to know what kind of disease a person has," thus suggesting the importance of personality and emotional factors in the cause and treatment of disease.

The idea was not popular for most of the twentieth century because this was a time of strong belief in science and technology. And nowhere was this belief more pronounced than in medicine, where the development of new drugs, surgical techniques (for example, organ transplants), and technological advances (such as radiation therapy and lasars) convinced medical authorities that they were on the threshold of permanently conquering disease. In many cases they were correct.

Immunization protects us from polio, which only a few decades ago crippled children by the thousands each year. Through medication we can control diabetes, which used to be fatal. The list of diseases prevented or controlled and the number of lives saved by treating only the body are great. These positive results strengthened our belief in science and technology and confirmed the apparent wisdom of focusing solely on the body. There seemed no need or value to considering the mind as a factor in disease. As a result, medicine generally ignored the influence of the mind, and medical students received only cursory instruction in psychology and psychiatry.

Fortunately, this one-sided emphasis is changing, primarily because of the research findings of a small but growing number of psychologists on the emotional aspects of disease. These psychologists—whom we may call *medical* or *health psychologists*—are concerned with the psychosomatic diseases, which have their origin in emotional factors such as stress. It is thought that as much as 80 per cent of all disease may be psychosomatic.

Medical psychologists, along with psychiatrists, physicians, and sociologists, have studied the influence of stress on disease, how different personality types may be predisposed to different diseases, and how stress can be prevented or reduced. Also, specific physiological functions, such as heart rate and muscle tension, have been studied to determine how deliberate acts of will on the part of a patient can influence them. This work has enormous implications for our health and has the potential for revolutionizing our entire health care system.

## THE NATURE OF STRESS

You already know what stress is and how it affects your body. How do you feel when you are about to take a difficult examination, or when a car runs a stop sign and is speeding toward you, or when a sinister figure follows you down a dark street? You feel anxious, tense, and frightened. Your heart beats faster and your stomach knots. Inside your body, dramatic and potentially harmful physiological changes are taking place in response to the stress. However, these changes are designed to help you cope with stress, particularly with emergencies. If an attacker follows you down a dark street and suddenly lunges at you, you will need extra energy to either run or fight. To help you act, your body responds to meet the crisis.

Adrenalin is released from the adrenal glands; this speeds up body functions by raising blood pressure, increasing heart rate, and releasing extra sugar from the liver into the bloodstream. The increased blood circulation brings greater energy to the brain and muscles, and this makes you stronger and more alert. Blood is taken from the digestive processes, which slow drastically, so that the maximum amount of energy can be concentrated where it is vitally needed, in the muscles and the brain.

In this situation, stress mobilizes, activates, and directs the energy of the body, boosting it to a level far beyond its normal capacity. You have read about people who display amazing strength in emergencies, such as lifting an automobile off someone trapped beneath it, something they could never accomplish under ordinary circumstances. Such feats are possible in times of stress only because of the energizing capacity of the body.

However, the body cannot remain in this state for very long; the body does not have an inexhaustible supply of energy to draw upon. The soldier in combat, for example, must be taken out of the front line periodically to recuperate physically. Rest, which means freedom from stress, allows the body to replenish its supply of energy. But the energy supply is never totally restored to its original level. Each time the energy must be expended, there is slightly less of it available with which to meet the next stressful situation.

Thus, over the course of our lives, the amount of energy we have to draw upon steadily diminishes. How fast it diminishes, and by how much, depends on how much stress we have to cope with. People who work in stressful occupations (for example, air traffic controllers) deplete the body's energy at a much faster rate than others. In any case, the effects of this gradual diminishing of our physical energy contribute to the process we know as *aging*.

## The Stresses of Everyday Life

So far, we have considered emergency situations such as combat or avoiding a mugger in the streets. Most of us do not face such dramatic occurrences, or if we do it is rare. However, stress is not limited to physical threats. It also refers to any mental or emotional strain or tension, anything that produces wear and tear on the body. In our daily lives there are scores of major and minor sources of strain and tension with which we must cope. All produce different levels of stress.

How many stresses did you face on your way to class? Did you oversleep and have to rush through breakfast, have an argument with your parents, roommate, or spouse, get caught in a traffic jam, or find the parking lot full? Each of these events is stressful and each brings about the physiological changes discussed previously. The bodily changes induced by a traffic jam are not so great as those caused by the presence of a mugger, but each low-level stress adds to the previous ones and the effects accumulate.

If, at the same time you must cope with these low-level stresses, you are also worried or tense about something else—perhaps whether you will graduate or get a job—your body is subjected to even greater deterioration. In addition, long-standing emotional problems contribute to the overall level of stress. People who are constantly tense, anxious, fearful, or hostile are wearing down their body's reserves of energy every day.

In these cases, the heart and circulatory rates are always elevated, extra adrenalin is always coursing through the bloodstream, and in time there is physiological damage to organs and tissues. Soon these people become physically ill and the continuing depletion of their energy reserves makes them much more susceptible to infection. Also, the illness caused by prolonged stress itself serves as a new stress, and a vicious cycle is established. Thus, we can see how harmful stress is to health.

Enormous amounts of energy are made available to the body during stress, but what happens to it? If a mugger attacks you, this energy is used up in fighting or fleeing, but everyday stresses do not usually allow us to release all the energy the body has provided. If your parents, boss, or teacher are the sources of your stress you cannot, as a rule, dissipate the extra energy in your body by physically running from them or attacking them. You must suppress it, keeping your anger and hostility within you. This is what happens with ordinary stresses. Outwardly, we must remain calm and civil, but inwardly our rage builds as each stress occurs, and further deterioration takes place.

It is impossible to escape stress altogether. Research has shown that even ordinary events in our lives induce stress. Not all of them are unusual events, nor are they physically threatening. Some are the normal milestones that most of us pass.

Two physicians, Holmes and Rahe, constructed a scale of stress values showing the amount of stress induced by forty-three different experiences, ranging from unhappy events, such as the death of a spouse, to happy occasions, such as marriage or an outstanding personal achievement. All the events involve some kind of change in a person's life, to which adaptation is required. As such, the events induce varying levels of stress (Table 6–1).[1]

Once this scale was developed, the next step was to determine the relationship between the stress represented by an event and subsequent illness. This was done with different groups of people, and the results provide a dramatic indication of the effects of stress on health.

The events listed in Table 6–1 were collected in the *Social Readjustment Rating Scale*, which was administered to eighty-eight young physicians. They were instructed to check the events that had occurred in their lives during the past ten years. Most of the events checked had individual mean values of 18 to 25. The scale was scored by adding the appropriate mean values for each of the previous ten years about which the physicians had been asked. In some cases, the annual totals were quite large.

In relating the onset of illness to the various life stress events it was found that 93 per cent of the illnesses the physicians suffered occurred within two years after they showed a yearly life event value of 150 or more. This is a significant finding; the odds that this high rate of illness could have occurred by chance are less than 1 in 1000.

On the basis of these findings the researchers established 150 and above (the sum of all the stress events in the course of a year) as a "life crisis." You might add up your own score, or that of a relative or friend.

[1] Thomas H. Holmes and R. H. Rahe, "The Social Readjustment Rating Scale," *Journal of Psychosomatic Research,* **11** (1967), 213–218; Thomas H. Holmes and Minoru Masuda, "Psychosomatic Syndrome," *Psychology Today,* **5** (April 1972), 71–72, 106.

**Table 6–1.** Life Stress Events *

| Rank | Life Event | Mean Value † |
|---|---|---|
| 1. | Death of spouse | 100 |
| 2. | Divorce | 73 |
| 3. | Marital separation | 65 |
| 4. | Jail term | 63 |
| 5. | Death of close family member | 63 |
| 6. | Personal injury or illness | 53 |
| 7. | Marriage | 50 |
| 8. | Fired at work | 47 |
| 9. | Marital reconciliation | 45 |
| 10. | Retirement | 45 |
| 11. | Change in health of family member | 44 |
| 12. | Pregnancy | 40 |
| 13. | Sex difficulties | 39 |
| 14. | Gain of new family member | 39 |
| 15. | Business readjustment | 39 |
| 16. | Change in financial state | 38 |
| 17. | Death of close friend | 37 |
| 18. | Change to different line of work | 36 |
| 19. | Change in number of arguments with spouse | 35 |
| 20. | Mortgage over $10,000 | 31 |
| 21. | Foreclosure of mortgage or loan | 30 |
| 22. | Change in responsibilities at work | 29 |
| 23. | Son or daughter leaving home | 29 |
| 24. | Trouble with in-laws | 29 |
| 25. | Outstanding personal achievement | 28 |
| 26. | Wife begin or stop work | 26 |
| 27. | Begin or end school | 26 |
| 28. | Change in living conditions | 25 |
| 29. | Revision of personal habits | 24 |
| 30. | Trouble with boss | 23 |
| 31. | Change in work hours or conditions | 20 |
| 32. | Change in residence | 20 |
| 33. | Change in schools | 20 |
| 34. | Change in recreation | 19 |
| 35. | Change in church activities | 19 |
| 36. | Change in social activities | 18 |
| 37. | Mortgage or loan less than $10,000 | 17 |
| 38. | Change in sleeping habits | 16 |
| 39. | Change in number of family get-togethers | 15 |
| 40. | Change in eating habits | 15 |
| 41. | Vacation | 13 |
| 42. | Christmas | 12 |
| 43. | Minor violations of the law | 11 |

* From Thomas H. Holmes and R. H. Rahe, "The Social Readjustment Rating Scale," *Journal of Psychosomatic Research*, **11** (1967), 216. Reprinted by permission of Pergamon Press, Ltd.

† Numerical value assigned reflecting the amount of life change brought about by the event.

If you know someone who has recently been ill, you might question him or her about the life events that occurred in the year before the onset of the illness. Chances are good that these events will yield a score of at least 150.

Once you have added the yearly life events of yourself or someone else, you can predict the chances of an illness occurring within a year's time. For example, if the sum of the yearly life events is between 150 and 199, there is a 37 per cent chance of becoming ill in the next year, and the possibility of becoming sick increases markedly when life event scores are higher. With a score of 200 to 299, the chance of getting ill during the next year climbs to 51 per cent. With a score in excess of 300, the chance of illness jumps to 79 per cent. The evidence is clear: the greater the stress, the higher the likelihood of developing some illness.

Another test of the predictive value of the Social Readjustment Rating Scale involved 2500 officers and enlisted personnel of the U.S. Navy. Two groups were compared, the 30 per cent with the highest life change scores and the 30 per cent with the lowest scores. The high-scoring group developed almost 90 per cent more illnesses than the low-scoring group.

Additional research has also shown that those people who experience the more severe life crises (and accumulate higher life event scores) not only develop more illnesses but also more serious illnesses. Those who are under the greatest stress are much more likely to develop chronic diseases, such as leukemia, cancer, and heart trouble.

The most stressful life event on the Social Readjustment Rating Scale, the death of a spouse, is the one most likely to bring on a serious illness. The chances of illness and death increase markedly in the first six months following the loss. One study of widows showed that their illness rate was sixteen times higher than a control group of women of the same age and background who had not lost their husbands.

Research evidence shows unmistakably that the health of children is also affected by stress. In a study comparing sick and healthy children between the ages of six and twelve it was found that all the sick children had experienced at least one major life change in the six months prior to their illness. The illnesses ranged from infections such as pneumonia to rheumatic fever and kidney disorders. Most of the healthy children had also undergone life changes in the previous six months, but they were of a minor nature.

Research has also shown that the health of college students is affected by stressful events. In one study, researchers developed a modified form of the Social Readjustment Rating Scale called the *College Schedule of Recent Experience,* which added items representing stressful situations for college students. For example: "entered college," "change in major field of study," "experienced or fathered pregnancy," "change in use of drugs," "broke or had broken a steady relationship." Those students who later became physically ill had experienced major life events prior to their illness.[2]

One life change that affects a great many people in our mobile society is change of residence. When we move from one community or city to another we disrupt many aspects of our lives. Although this factor of change of residence receives a mean value of only 20 on the Social Readjustment Rating Scale, it brings about life changes in personal habits, social activities, schools, working conditions, and perhaps even a new kind of work. Adding all the events that can be affected by moving yields a score of 287, clearly in the danger zone of life change events. When you add all the other life change events that can occur in the course of a year, it is not surprising that many people become ill within a year after moving.

We noted earlier that there is a limited amount of physical energy available to us. If we use up a considerable portion of that energy in coping with ordinary life change events, there is less energy available for more serious events. The more we are required to cope with in a given period of time, the more likely we are to suffer some form of illness.

## The General Adaptation Syndrome

We know that stress produces major and potentially harmful physiological changes in the body. If the stress is severe enough, some sort of disease or illness is the likely result. What intervenes between the body's initial reaction to stress and the appearance of illness? In other words, what converts physiological change into disease?

The most useful explanation of what takes place is the General Adaptation Syndrome proposed by Hans Selye.[3] Through years of experimentation with animals, Selye observed the presence of three distinct stages in the body's reaction to stress: alarm, resistance, and exhaustion. These stages appear in the same sequence, no matter whether the stress being faced is of a physical or an emotional nature.

The *alarm* reaction is the initial response to stress and it involves all the physiological changes discussed: increased heart and respiration rates, release of adrenalin into the bloodstream, and so on. As noted, these changes energize the body in order to cope with the stress, but the price to be paid for this mobilization of the body's defenses is in terms of physical symptoms or complaints. During the alarm stage it is not

[2] Martin B. Marx, Thomas F. Garrity, and Frank R. Bowers, "The Influence of Recent Life Experience on the Health of College Freshmen," *Journal of Psychosomatic Research*, **19** (1975), 87–98.

[3] Hans Selye, *The Stress of Life*, 2nd ed. (New York: McGraw-Hill, 1976); "The Evolution of the Stress Concept," *American Scientist*, **61** (1973), 692–699.

unusual for people to be afflicted with headaches, tiredness, a general rundown feeling, muscle aches, and loss of appetite.

*Resistance* is the second stage in the General Adaptation Syndrome and it is reached only if the situation producing the stress has continued for a sufficient period of time. This is sometimes called the adaptation stage because the individual seems to be adapting to the stress. The symptoms that appeared during the alarm stage are reduced, or disappear altogether, and the individual seems to be coping with the situation better than during the alarm stage.

However, the adaptation to continuing stress has debilitating physical effects. Too much adrenalin is being produced; if this situation continues too long, physiological damage, particularly increased blood pressure and heart disease, will result.

The final stage, *exhaustion*, is reached if exposure to stress is prolonged. By this time, the reserves of body energy (notably adrenalin) are depleted, and the individual can no longer adapt to or resist the stress. The person is extremely susceptible to infection and to the diseases of stress, particularly arthritis and rheumatism (both of which may be relieved by drugs that stimulate the adrenal glands).

Thus, research has established clearly that the mind affects the body and can cause actual physical disorders known as the psychosomatic diseases. The word "psychosomatic" is very descriptive of these conditions because the "psyche" or mind is strongly influencing the "soma" or body.

## PSYCHOSOMATICS: THE DISEASES OF STRESS

The first point to note about psychosomatic diseases is that they are definitely not imaginary. People who have such diseases are not hypochondriacs; they are not worried about illnesses that have no actual physical counterpart. Psychosomatic diseases are real; there is definite tissue and organ damage. Although they are caused by emotional and psychological factors, they do involve very real damage to the body.

Second, psychosomatic diseases are very prevalent. They are not isolated or rare phenomena that affect only a few unfortunate people. On the contrary, psychosomatic diseases affect millions of people. As many as 80 per cent of the people who feel sick enough to consult a physician may have illnesses that originate in emotional problems; the minimum estimate is 50 per cent. Some researchers even suggest that all disease is somehow related to the emotional life of the patient. The incidence of psychosomatic illness is of epidemic proportions.

Third, disorders that are widely believed to be psychosomatic, such as asthma, can also be caused by physical factors. Therefore, we cannot conclude that every case of asthma, for example, has resulted from emotional factors alone. Keep in mind as the various psychosomatic diseases are discussed that not everyone who suffers from asthma or ulcers or headaches does so because of emotional problems or other forms of stress. There are diseases that are transmitted genetically, such as hemophilia, and others caused by environmental pollutants. On the other hand, although some diseases may have no emotional roots, it is nevertheless possible that emotional factors may aggravate them or add to their severity.

There is no question that stress and other emotional factors do contribute to disease; stress makes us ill in a great many ways. The list of psychosomatic disorders is a long one and includes skin disorders (for example, eczema, acne, and hives), backaches, headaches, arthritis, asthma, recurring bronchitis, hypertension and other cardiovascular disorders, cancer, ulcers and colitis, genitourinary disorders, obesity, and hyperthyroidism.

With such a variety of diseases resulting from stress, what determines why a person develops one disease instead of another in response to emotional factors? One answer involves a genetic predisposition toward a disease, which makes a person more vulnerable or susceptible to it than to others. Another answer lies in childhood experiences, which may cause a person to learn to react to difficulties by experiencing symptoms in a particular organ or part of the body.

Suppose that as a child you had, for whatever reason, a fear of going to school. In response to this fear (a stress), you developed physical symptoms such as headaches, stomach upsets, and a general feeling of weakness. Suppose that your mother was particularly disturbed by the stomach upsets and let you stay home from school whenever you displayed these symptoms. By her actions, she reinforced or rewarded your behavior. In other words, because she kept you home from school whenever you had an upset stomach, your stomach worked for you by keeping you out of a situation you feared. As an adult, you may continue, unconsciously, to develop stomach problems in any situation of stress because of the reinforcement for this response in your childhood.

Another reason for contracting one disease instead of another may have to do with personality. It has been established that certain personality types are predisposed or more susceptible to certain diseases. This is an old idea that enjoys a great deal of research support. For some diseases, as many as 80 per cent of the sufferers possess the same personality characteristics.

A persuasive test of the relationship between personality and disease was carried out by a psychiatrist, Dr. Floyd Ring.[4] He wanted to deter-

[4] Floyd O. Ring, "Testing the Validity of Personality Profiles in Psychosomatic Illnesses," *American Journal of Psychiatry*, **113** (1957), 1075–1080.

mine how accurately a person's illness could be diagnosed on the basis of personality factors alone. He asked physicians to refer to him more than 400 patients whom they had diagnosed as suffering from any of fourteen specific ailments, including asthma, backache, arthritis, diabetes, hypertension, and ulcers.

It was vital that Ring be provided with no clues about the patients' illnesses, so he interviewed them under very stringent conditions. Patients were told to say nothing about their symptoms, disabilities, or treatments. They were to reveal nothing about their bodies, only about their personalities. As a further control, the patients' bodies were covered during the interviews to prevent Ring and the other examiners from seeing any physical signs of disease. Two observers were present during the interviews to make sure that the patients did not inadvertently reveal something of their physical condition to the examiners. Those who did were not included in the results of the study.

How accurate were the diagnoses of physical disease when the examinations were strictly psychological in nature and not physical? They were very accurate indeed for certain illnesses. For example, 100 per cent of the hyperthyroid patients were correctly diagnosed on the basis of personality alone, as were 83 per cent of those with peptic ulcers and rheumatoid arthritis, 71 per cent of those with coronary occlusion (an obstruction of a coronary artery), and 60 to 67 per cent of those with asthma, diabetes, hypertension, and ulcerative colitis.

Recall that no physical examinations were conducted, and that the psychiatric interviews lasted only fifteen to twenty-five minutes. Under these conditions, the diagnoses may be considered to be extremely accurate. In one case, Ring's diagnosis differed from that made by the referring physician who performed a physical examination; it turned out that Ring's diagnosis, made on the basis of personality alone, was the correct one.

On the basis of this extensive research, Ring concluded that there are three broad categories of personality, each of which is related to different psychosomatic diseases. One technique used to differentiate among personality types was to ask patients questions relating to aggressiveness, personal ambition, fears, pleasures, and kind of people liked and disliked. For example:

> If you were sitting on a park bench on a nice warm spring day, very well relaxed and enjoying the sunshine, watching the birds flit around on the grass in front of you, and someone just your size, age, and sex, whom you had never seen, walked up, said nothing, and kicked you in the shins, what would you do? [5]

[5] F. O. Ring, op. cit., p. 1078.

Most people felt that they would respond aggressively, saying, "I'd beat the hell out of him," or something equally strong. Ring called these people *excessive reactors*, and he found that they were prone to coronary occlusion, degenerative arthritis, and peptic ulcers.

Some people reported that they would do nothing in this situation. Ring described them as being unaware of their fear and anger and inhibiting their thoughts and behavior. These people, called *deficient reactors*, tend to develop dermatitis, rheumatoid arthritis, and ulcerative colitis.

*Restrained reactors* are the third personality type. They are aware of their fear and anger but rarely express them. Their typical reaction is, "I might hit him." These people tend to develop asthma, diabetes, hypertension, hyperthyroidism, and migraine headaches.

Let us examine in greater detail the personality correlates of six physical disorders: ulcers, asthma, headaches, rheumatoid arthritis, heart disease, and cancer.

## Ulcers

Ulcers are a common affliction in the United States today. It is estimated that at least 10 per cent of the population will develop an ulcer at some time in their life. Ulcers are present in both sexes but are two to three times more likely to occur in men. They develop from excess acid in the stomach's digestive juices that causes an open sore on the inner lining of the stomach or on the duodenum (part of the small intestine connected to the stomach).

A popular stereotype depicts ulcer sufferers as hard-driving, aggressive people who work frantically in a high-pressure job such as that of a business executive. As far as it goes, this stereotype is true. The stress of work, and being aggressively involved in it, is a potent factor in the development of ulcers. However, there is another factor in the personality of the ulcer victim: a strong conflict between being dependent and being independent.

Ulcer victims have strong dependency needs that are carried over from childhood. They want to be protected, loved, and cared for. Yet, at the same time, they want to be independent of other people because they feel guilty and inferior about their dependency needs. As a result, these people tend to overcompensate by exaggerating their independence, aggressiveness, and ambition. But no matter how much they overcompensate, no matter how often they refuse help from others and assume all the burdens of the job themselves, the conflict remains. Unconsciously, they still long for the security and protection they knew as children.

Extended vacations and rest cures are often effective in relieving ulcers because they remove the sufferers from the work situation in which they feel compelled to display aggressiveness and ambition. Away from work they can shed responsibilities and give in to their deep desires to be passive and dependent. Of course, the ulcers usually reappear when these people return to work.

## Asthma

Asthma is the leading cause of chronic illness among children and adolescents, and is an extremely distressing disorder to have. During an asthmatic attack, the bronchial tubes become restricted, making breathing difficult. The victim wheezes as he or she tries to force air into the lungs. In severe attacks there is coughing and a desperate fight to get air with every breath. Asthmatic attacks can be mild or severe and can last as long as several hours.

Asthma can originate in allergies to various substances in the air, or in infections, and may be aggravated by emotional factors. Indeed, a person's momentary emotional state may bring on an attack. In addition, asthma can be caused solely by emotional conditions, independent of allergies or infections.

A major personality characteristic of most people who suffer from asthma is a strong dependence on their mother. An attack occurs whenever that dependence is threatened, for example, when a child does something that brings disapproval from the mother or is faced with the prospect of leaving the mother (such as going away to summer camp). This kind of reaction may be learned through reinforcement on the part of the mother. Some children believe that the only time they are loved is when they are sick. Their mother may reject them when they are healthy and show signs of independence, but shower them with attention and protection when they are sick and dependent.

Another interesting emotional component of asthma is the difficulty asthmatics have in crying; this problem is psychological rather than physical. Some researchers believe that asthmatic attacks are a substitute for crying. They have found that some people are able to learn to stop asthmatic attacks, and even to prevent them, by forcing themselves to cry.

## Headaches

There is no need to explain what headaches are like. Most likely, there is no one who has not suffered from a headache at some time. Some headaches are caused by physical conditions—brain tumors, indigestion, constipation, and hypertension—but at least 90 per cent of all headaches are emotional in origin.

Tension headaches are caused by a tightening of the muscles in the back of the neck and head. One effect of the increased muscle tension is the constriction of the arteries that supply blood to the scalp and brain. Tension headaches can be brought on by any kind of stress or worry, such as an argument with a close friend or the fear of failing an examination.

More serious are migraine headaches, which can incapacitate the sufferer. The pain is intense and can last several days, and may be accompanied by chills and nausea. The physiological cause of migraines is the dilation or enlargement of the cranial arteries, but there is an emotional factor that causes the enlargement in the first place.

A consistent personality pattern has been identified for migraine sufferers. Typically, a migraine begins after a period of repressed rage or anger, and it often disappears when the person is able to express this inhibited anger. The migraine sufferer usually harbors a great deal of resentment and frustration about not being able to accomplish personal goals, which are usually set too high. These people often feel unworthy and inferior, and try to compensate for their feelings by taking on more responsibility than they can handle. Because of their basic sense of inferiority, they desperately need the love and approval of other people, and they work very hard for this admiration. In fact, they work so hard to be loved that they tend to be perfectionists in everything they do.

## Rheumatoid Arthritis

Arthritis is an inflammation of the joints. Osteoarthritis, which occurs as a result of the normal aging process, is distinct from rheumatoid arthritis, which is strongly related to emotional factors. The latter begins around the age of thirty-five and is more likely to affect women than men. It is a very painful disorder and often leads to crippling and irreversible damage.

There seems to be a genetic component to rheumatoid arthritis, an inherited susceptibility to the disease. But the factor that determines whether this predisposition becomes an actuality is the emotional life of the individual.

Victims of rheumatoid arthritis have a recognizable personality pattern; this is particularly consistent for female sufferers. Female rheumatoid arthritis sufferers tend to be shy, somewhat inhibited, and self-conscious. At the same time, they are perfectionists in everything they do and compulsive in all aspects of their behavior. They are often nervous, but this may not be apparent because they are capable of hiding their emotions.

A particularly strong characteristic is the female arthritic's need to sacrifice for and to serve others. This is not entirely for altruistic reasons; quite the opposite. By serving others, arthritics are attempting to control them. Typically, they are demanding of their children, yet always ready to do things for them. A parent who sacrifices everything for the children is in a good position to control them by expecting a great deal in return.

## Heart Disease

Heart disease is a major cause of death in the United States, responsible for the loss of more than seven hundred thousand lives every year. Men are more prone to heart disease than women, although the percentage of female sufferers is rising, and growing numbers of people are suffering from heart disease at comparatively young ages (forties and fifties).

Much research has been conducted on physical causes of heart disease, and we have been warned about the dangers of smoking, high cholesterol levels, and lack of exercise. However, these factors may account for no more than 25 per cent of all heart disease; the rest is believed to be caused by the stress related to a distinct personality pattern. The relationship between this personality pattern and heart disease is very strong. People who do not display this personality pattern almost never suffer heart attacks before the age of seventy, no matter how much fatty food they eat, how many cigarettes they smoke, or how little exercise they get. Those people who do have this kind of personality are two to three times more likely to develop heart disease in middle age.

Research on the psychological factors involved in heart disease was conducted by two cardiologists, Drs. Friedman and Rosenman.[6] On the basis of their long-term study of 3500 men between the ages of thirty-five and fifty-nine, Friedman and Rosenman uncovered the personality types they call *Type A* (those most likely to have heart attacks) and *Type B* (those least likely to have heart attacks).

Two fundamental characteristics of the Type A personality are an extremely high competitive drive and a constant sense of time urgency (labeled "hurry sickness"). Type A people are intensely ambitious and aggressive and are constantly working to achieve something. These striving, driving individuals are always racing against the clock, pressured by their time urgency, rushing through life from one self-imposed deadline to the next. It is not enough for them merely to strive and achieve; the goal must be reached today. Tomorrow is too late.

Type A personalities are also hostile, but they successfully hide this

[6] Meyer Friedman and Ray H. Rosenman, *Type A Behavior and Your Heart* (New York: Alfred A. Knopf, 1974).

hostility from other people and from themselves. Their hostility and aggressiveness are expressed indirectly in their continuing competition with others, whether on the job or in leisure activities such as a card game. Type A people are impatient and quick to anger if other people are working too slowly. They will interfere with others to speed them up. This applies even to a friendly conversation if the other person seems to be speaking too slowly; Type A people will finish another person's sentences in an effort to hurry him or her along.

As a result of these characteristics, Type A people are chronically in a state of tension and stress, and this, of course, leads to the physiological changes discussed previously.

Type B people, although they may be just as ambitious, do not exhibit the other characteristics shown by Type A people, and, consequently, are far less likely to become victims of heart disease.

Drs. Friedman and Rosenman believe that it is relatively easy to spot a Type A person, and some of the typical Type A behaviors are listed in Table 6–2. If a majority of the items describe you, you may well be a Type A personality.

Friedman and Rosenman note that the Type A personality can be changed significantly to reduce the amount of stress on the individual. Their book contains specific advice on how to bring about such changes.

## Cancer

A recent exploration into the relationship between personality and disease involves cancer. The extensive research conducted to date reveals the existence of a cancer personality, a consistent personality pattern found in a majority of cancer patients. The presence of cancer, like the presence of asthma, arthritis, or heart disease, may indicate that something is wrong in the emotional life of the affected individual. One of the most persistent researchers in this field is the psychologist Lawrence LeShan, who has uncovered a common background in cancer patients as well as a common personality pattern.[7]

Dr. LeShan found that cancer personalities felt lonely and isolated during their childhood and adolescence. This resulted from disturbed relations with their parents, from the disruption of the family unit through death or divorce, or from marital discord between the parents. Whatever the cause, the child felt anxious, insecure, and rejected.

Driven by the need to be accepted, secure, and loved, the potential cancer personalities try to please others so that they will be liked and accepted by them. As a result, their behavior is seen by other people as very thoughtful and considerate. Friends describe them as "too good to

[7] Lawrence LeShan, *You Can Fight for Your Life: Emotional Factors in the Causation of Cancer* (New York: M. Evans, 1977).

**Table 6–2.** Are You a Type A Person? *

*Do you:*

———  *always do everything very rapidly?* Type A people eat, move, walk, and talk at a brisk pace. They speak with emphasis on certain words, and the ends of their sentences are spoken much faster than the beginnings.

———  *become extremely impatient with the speed at which things are accomplished?* Type A people continually say "yes, yes" or "uh huh" to whoever is talking to them, and even finish other persons' sentences for them. They become outraged by a slow car ahead of them or a slow-moving line in a restaurant or theater. When they read, they skim the material quickly and prefer summaries or condensations of books.

———  *always think about or try to do two or more things at the same time?* For example, Type A people may think about one thing while talking to someone about something else, or they may try to eat and drive at the same time, in an effort to get more accomplished in a given period of time.

———  *feel guilty when you are on vacation or trying to relax for a few hours?*

———  *fail to be aware of interesting or beautiful things?* Type A people do not notice a lovely sunset or the new flowers of spring. If asked, they cannot recall the furnishings or details of an office or home they just visited.

———  *always try to schedule more events and activities than you can properly attend to?* This is another manifestation of the sense of time urgency Type A people feel.

———  *have nervous gestures or tics such as clenching your fists or banging on a desk to emphasize a point you are making?* These gestures point to the continuing tension at the root of the Type A personality.

———  *consistently evaluate your worth in quantitative terms?* For Type A persons, numbers alone define their sense of accomplishment and importance. Type A executives boast about their salary or their company's profits, Type A surgeons tell how many operations they have performed, and Type A students report how many *As* they have received in school. These people focus on the quantitative rather than the qualitative aspects of life.

* For a more detailed discussion of Type A characteristics, see Meyer Friedman and Ray H. Rosenman, *Type A Behavior and Your Heart* (New York: Alfred A. Knopf, 1974), pp. 82–85.

be true." Beneath this facade, however, cancer-prone persons still feel unloved and unworthy.

In adulthood, cancer personalities usually find meaningful relationships in which they have the love and security they so desperately need.

Through their spouse and children, and sometimes through their jobs, they find genuine happiness for the first time in their life. This means, however, that their continued happiness depends on having these people and situations remain constant.

But life is full of change; children leave home, spouses die or obtain a divorce, or a person may be fired or retired from a job. When these emotional props are no longer available, cancer personalities find themselves reliving their childhood experiences of rejection, loneliness, and insecurity. Within six months to one year, according to Dr. LeShan, cancer develops, causing these persons to feel even more helpless and pessimistic, a vicious cycle that usually ends in death.

According to LeShan, this is the background of the cancer personality. Let us now examine the common personality pattern.

The primary factor in the emotional lives of these people is the loss of what LeShan calls their "reason for being," that relationship to family or job on which their security depended. For the first time since childhood, they feel isolated, having lost the only meaningful role they had ever established. Of course, many people lose what is central to their lives and not all or even most of them will develop cancer. There are other factors in the personality of cancer victims.

A second characteristic is an inability to express anger, resentment, and hostility. These feelings are suppressed beneath a facade of pleasing and considerate behaviors. Cancer personalities are also characterized by a high degree of self-distrust and self-hatred. They do not think highly of themselves, nor do they respect their achievements and accomplishments. Other people usually think more highly of them than they do of themselves.

Perhaps the dominant element in the emotional lives of cancer personalities is despair. This despair does not appear for the first time after the discovery of the cancer (when it would seem understandable), but rather before they become ill. Indeed, they have felt this despair for most of their lives. So overwhelming is the despair that they feel no hope of overcoming it. Nothing can help—not other people or possessions or even themselves. They see no possibility of change or growth and have nothing to look forward to but the continuing pain of isolation and loneliness.

Other studies of cancer patients tend to support the personality portrait developed by LeShan, particularly the influence of the childhood conflict with parents and the adult losses in work or marriage.

Thus, personality factors seem definitely related to the development of cancer. Evidence also suggests that personality factors are related to the rate of growth of the cancer. For example, patients whose disease progressed rapidly were found to be more defensive, depressed, and anxious than those whose illness progressed more slowly. (These personality characteristics were determined *before* the rates of growth were established.) Patients whose chances of survival were high tended to be above average in intelligence, have good emotional control, and have strong hostility drives. Also, they did not feel as helpless or pessimistic about their illness as did those patients who had a poorer prognosis. Those who possess a strong will to live, who are angered by their illness, and who fight against it have a better chance of recovery.

## REDUCING STRESS AND ITS EFFECTS

We have discussed how harmful stress is to human health and how it is related to the development of specific diseases. No matter whether the source of the stress is external, such as a high-pressure job, or internal, such as long-standing insecurity or anxiety, or a combination of the two, stress does affect physiological functioning.

In other words, the mind is capable of inducing illness in the body. Some researchers have asked: If the mind can make the body sick, can it also cure the body? If the mind can cause illness, why can't it cure illness? Even more important, can the mind prevent illness? These questions, and the positive research they have stimulated, are bringing about a major change in the treatment of certain diseases. A new form of therapy is being developed that cures not through drugs or surgery but through the mental control of internal bodily states and conditions. This idea may revolutionize the present system of health care and maintenance, and allow each of us to become our own healer.

We shall deal with three techniques for reducing stress and its effects: biofeedback, meditation, and visualization.

### Biofeedback

Have you ever practiced shooting an arrow at a target, or throwing a snowball, football, or baseball at a specific spot, or learned to hit a tennis ball to different parts of your opponent's side of the court? If so, then you already know something about the nature of *feedback*. When you aim at a target your eyes and muscles supply information to the brain as you make each shot. That information, which is feedback, includes your knowledge of where the arrow or ball hit in relation to where you were aiming, and allows you to correct your stance or form to make your next shot better. And so it goes with each successive shot. You improve with practice; as more information about your performance is fed back to you, you become more skillful. If you tried to learn to hit the target while blindfolded, you would never improve; you would receive no feedback from your performance on how well or poorly you were doing.

*Biofeedback* operates in a similar manner. What you are trying to change or improve are physiological functions of the body. How do you get feedback on how your muscles or your heart or your other body processes are performing? The answer has become simple in this amazing technological age. Many of our internal bodily processes and functions can be measured by electronic instruments such as the electrocardiograph. Anything that can be measured can also be amplified and converted into easily observable signals such as a flashing light or a tone. Thus, we are provided with biofeedback, information about the performance of our internal physiology. Once we have that information, we can use it to control the inner workings of the body.

For example, if a light flashes on whenever our heart is beating at a relaxed rate, we can learn to keep the light on by keeping our heart beating at that rate. Exactly how we learn this control is not yet known, but the fact that such control is possible and effective is beyond question. Further, after sufficient practice with a biofeedback machine, a person may control physiological functioning without the machine. The benefits will be enormous if people learn to control, consciously, their heart rate, muscle tension, body temperature, brain waves, stomach acidity, blood pressure, and other functions. Through our own efforts we could prevent the harmful effects of stress on the body. Indeed, this is happening in clinics all over the United States today.

We will discuss examples of biofeedback training with tension headaches and with blood pressure. In one clinic, headache victims listened to a tone that amplified the contractions of their forehead muscles. Every time the muscles contracted, the tone sounded. The more the muscles contracted, the higher the pitch of the tone; the more the muscles relaxed, the lower the pitch. The subjects were instructed to keep the tone low as much as possible. In twenty minutes, they had reduced muscle tension by as much as 50 per cent. Before too long, they learned to relax their muscles whenever they felt a headache coming on and soon they could prevent headaches altogether. Within two weeks of daily training sessions, people who had been plagued by tension headaches for years were completely free of them. In addition, they experienced profound relaxation of the entire body, which was beneficial to other physiological functions. After sufficient training they were able to relax their muscles on their own command, without the biofeedback machine.

Patients with high blood pressure received feedback on their blood pressure level from a flashing light and tone. The better the patients were able to control their blood pressure, the more the light and tone were on. Poor control or no control were indicated by sporadic light and sound or none at all. In a short time patients learned to keep the signals on, thus lowering their blood pressure. High blood pressure is a dangerous condition that predisposes a person to strokes and heart attacks. Certain drugs can lower blood pressure, but they have possible harmful side effects. It seems much safer to be able to control blood pressure by oneself, without relying on medicine.

There are no known side effects of biofeedback except the total relaxation of the body and mind. This may be the greatest overall value of biofeedback: to reduce the impact of daily stress on the body's systems, thus preventing the occurrence of stress-related disease. There is also the satisfaction of being in control of your own body and regulating its functioning instead of being a slave to pills or other medical treatment administered by a physician.

## Meditation

In Chapter 5 we discussed *meditation* as a way of increasing human potential and raising the level of consciousness. The most popular form of meditation is TM (transcendental meditation), which involves sitting quietly for two 20-minute periods each day and silently repeating a *mantra*, a single word chosen for each person by a TM leader.

Meditation results in total relaxation of the mind and body, and thus serves to reduce the effects of stress. Many studies have been conducted on people while they were meditating and the results show consistent and important changes in physiological functioning. Oxygen consumption is decreased during meditation, and blood pressure, respiration, and heart rates are reduced considerably. The normal heart rate is seventy-two beats per minute. Under meditation, this has decreased to as few as twenty-four beats per minute. Respiration rate has slowed to six breaths per minute, oxygen consumption reduced by as much as 20 per cent (a reduction greater than that which occurs during sleep), and cardiac output reduced as much as 30 per cent. These are highly significant and beneficial changes and are the opposite of the highly active state of these functions during stress.

A direct measure of the amount of stress a person is experiencing is the galvanic skin response (GSR), which measures the amount of skin resistance to electrical current. When people are anxious and tense they perspire, and the moisture on the skin increases the rate of conductance of electricity from one point on the skin to another. Thus, resistance to current decreases. The resistance of dry skin is much higher. The GSR is the basic component of the lie detector, which, although not infallible, can indicate how much a person is experiencing stress when questions are being asked about his or her involvement in a crime. Under meditation, skin resistance has been found to increase by as much as 400 per cent, indicating a tremendous decrease in tension and anxiety.

There are other medically beneficial effects of meditation. Meditators often find that they need less sleep. This suggests that much bodily energy is being renewed or restored during periods of meditation. It is believed that meditation is more refreshing to both body and mind than deep sleep.

Meditation is helpful in combating the ravaging effects of stress and preventing damage to physiological functioning. People who meditate regularly report generally better health than those who do not meditate consistently. A study comparing experienced meditators with a control group of nonmeditators found a marked reduction in psychosomatic disorders such as headaches and colds among the meditators.

Those who meditate regularly, particularly in times of stress, seem to have a health advantage over those who are not able to exercise this control over the workings of their body.

## Visualization

Of the three techniques for reducing stress discussed here, visualization is the least known, although it has a long history as an Eastern technique of meditation. *Visualization* involves focusing awareness on a real or imaginary object. This concentration screens out all other thoughts, feelings, and sensations. In ancient Japan, some people spent a portion of each day looking at a favorite rock in their garden. By concentrating on the rock, "watching it grow," all psychological energy was drawn to the task and taken away from other mental and physiological activities. Presumably, visualization has a soothing effect on mind and body that results in a slowing of all bodily processes.

Visualization, in combination with meditation, has been applied not only to the prevention of physiological damage from stress but also to healing that damage after it has taken place. The most spectacular work with visualization has been its application to cancer by an oncologist (a physician specializing in the treatment of cancer), O. Carl Simonton, and a psychotherapist, Stephanie M. Simonton.[8]

One of their cases was the man with the throat cancer mentioned at the beginning of the chapter. The man was treated by radiation therapy and by relaxing three times a day while visualizing the actual destruction of his cancer cells by the x-rays. The man visualized his white blood cells sweeping away the dead cancer cells through the bloodstream and out of his body. The patient recovered after three months of this unusual treatment. An examination eighteen months later showed no sign of the cancer.

In another case, visualization plus radiation treatments cured a patient

---

[8] O. Carl Simonton and Stephanie M. Simonton, "Belief Systems and Management of the Emotional Aspects of Malignancy," *Journal of Transpersonal Psychology*, 7 (1975), 29–47; see also the discussion of the Simontons' work in Kenneth R. Pelletier, *Mind as Healer, Mind as Slayer* (New York: Dell, 1977), pp. 252–262.

who had a tumor in the throat and cancer of the mouth. Chances of recovery had been rated by physicians as no better than 10 per cent, yet the patient was cured after ten weeks of visualization treatment.

Central to the visualization treatment is a positive attitude on the part of patients, a belief that they are going to be cured. They must believe in the technique for it to be effective. This is additional evidence of the tremendous power the mind has over the body, power sufficient to kill and cure. Biofeedback, meditation, and visualization draw on the healing capacity of the mind. Cure rates for these techniques are, in many cases, more impressive than those for traditional medical procedures.

## PSYCHOLOGICAL APPROACHES TO PAIN

An inevitable accompaniment of many diseases and bodily disorders is pain. Sometimes it is relatively short-lived—when we hit our shins, for example—and in other cases it can last for years, as in arthritis, chronic back trouble, or headaches. Sometimes pain can be relieved medically by pain-killing drugs, or surgically such as when a ruptured appendix is removed. And sometimes no organic cause can be found for the pain and a person may suffer in agony with no way to find relief.

In recent years, psychologists and medical researchers have recognized that there is a large psychological component to pain, that pain is not totally a physical problem. Pain is a combination of physical sensations and our psychological reaction to those sensations, which can either magnify or reduce the intensity of the pain. During World War II, a doctor at an army field hospital noticed that soldiers who had suffered severe wounds did not plead for pain medication, as he had expected, considering the amount of pain they must have been feeling. They even refused pain medication when it was offered. It turned out that there was a psychological reason why the soldiers were not feeling much pain. The pain had been suppressed by their happiness at having survived the combat and receiving a wound serious enough to require extensive treatment. This would keep them out of combat for a long time, perhaps permanently. In contrast, most patients in civilian hospitals demand pain-killing drugs following operations that are much less severe than the wounds received by the soldiers.

The fact that placebos [9] often relieve pain also attests to its psychological component. Even intense pain suffered by people who have incurable illnesses has been relieved by placebos. These pills work effectively with as many as 42 per cent of those suffering from cancer and 39 per cent of those experiencing severe postsurgical pain. There are

---

[9] A placebo is a substance administered as a drug but which has no medical effect, such as a sugar pill; pronounced "pla-see-bow."

Psychology Applied to Physical Health

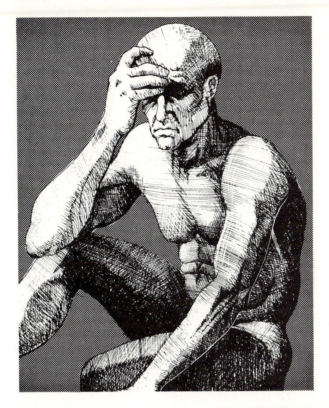

personality differences between persons who react favorably to placebos and those who do not. Those whose pain is relieved by placebos tend to be anxious and dependent; those who do not react to placebos are more withdrawn and rigid.

Psychologists have found that some people are more susceptible to pain than others. They have identified a chronic pain personality characterized by hypochondria, depression, and hysteria. Such people also show a greater-than-average number of stress-induced disorders and emotional problems than those who are less susceptible to pain.

If pain is partly psychological, can it be treated by psychological procedures? In other words, if the mind can cause or magnify pain, can it also reduce pain, or at least help us become more tolerant of it?

These questions are being considered by the medical-psychological speciality known as dolorology—the study of the treatment of pain—and have led to the establishment of approximately one hundred pain clinics in the United States in the 1970s. These clinics use psychological approaches to relieve pain instead of traditional medical techniques, and they hold the view that pain is primarily a learned behavior. The purpose of the clinics is to change patients' attitudes toward their pain, and to eliminate all "pain behaviors," such as complaining, moaning, wincing, and inactivity. These behaviors may have been reinforced in the past by well-meaning relatives and friends.

Most people who seek help at a pain clinic have been suffering from pain for at least six months and have tried drugs and even surgical procedures without success. According to dolorologists, these people have been reinforced for their behavior with regard to their pain. The reinforcement has been the attention, sympathy, and support of friends, relatives, and perhaps health care personnel. They also receive reinforcement by being excused from what, to them, are disagreeable activities such as work, social commitments, and even sex. People have been tolerant of the pain patients and expected less from them because of their condition. Thus, pain has not been without benefits for these people.

Pain clinics use a number of psychological techniques to provide pain relief, including biofeedback, meditation, and hypnosis, but their major approach uses behavior modification (discussed in Chapter 4). While they are being treated at a pain clinic, patients never receive reinforcement or any psychological benefit from their pain. The first rule for patients in pain clinics is that they must not talk to staff members about their pain. The medical staff is instructed to walk away from any patient who complains about pain. The only time patients may talk of their pain is during a consultation with a physician, and then they are only allowed to say if the pain is the same, worse, or better.

Although pain behaviors are never rewarded, "well" behaviors are. Staff members lavish attention on patients who demonstrate their lack of preoccupation with pain. A vital part of this treatment involves teaching the patient's family the principles of behavior modification, and warning them against reinforcing the patient's pain behaviors at home.

Another approach used in pain clinics is to keep patients busy so they have little time to think about their pain. This is contrary to the usual advice given by physicians to rest, take it easy, and not overdo. It seems that taking it easy can make pain worse. By withdrawing from normal sources of stimulation, pain sufferers experience feelings of boredom and isolation, which have been found to increase their sensitivity to pain. Also, with nothing else to do, they dwell on their pain. They become much more aware of and anxious about the pain than if they were engrossed in some activity. In pain clinics patients have little time to focus on their pain. The days are structured and include callisthenics, long walks, body massages, biofeedback and meditation training, and rigorous drill in a variety of mental exercises designed to help them cope more constructively with their pain.

Pain clinics are too recent an innovation for their effectiveness to be fully evaluated, but preliminary research indicates a success rate of as high as 60 per cent in reducing the severity of pain or in helping people adjust to pain so that they can return to normal lives. Also, it should be remembered that these patients had tried all the traditional medical procedures and found no relief from pain.

## PSYCHOLOGICAL ASPECTS OF DEATH AND DYING

We have discussed how psychological factors can predispose people to certain kinds of illnesses, some of which are fatal, and influence the amount of pain they feel. Therefore, it should be no surprise that our emotional state also influences when and how we die. The mind has the capacity to determine the disease we die from, how long we live with a terminal illness, and, of course, the attitude with which we face death.

Psychologists have been studying psychological reactions to the imminence of death, counseling dying patients, and trying to determine why some people who have fatal illnesses live longer than others who have the same diseases of the same severity.

### Hope and Hopelessness

Feelings of hope, spirit, meaning, and purpose can prolong life even in the face of terminal illness. There have been many cases of people who were told they had only a short time to live, who have exceeded that time because of their determination to be present at an important life event such as a child's college graduation or a grandchild's birth. No one knows how this happens; it cannot be explained medically. It is clear that a sense of purpose somehow affects the body to the point of "miraculously" extending the person's life. Once the anticipated event has taken place, death often follows quickly.

Hope can extend life, and lack of hope can shorten it. Physicians have often observed that some patients die following surgery or illness when, from a medical standpoint, they should have lived. "They don't seem to have the will to live," doctors say. These patients have nothing to live for; they feel helpless and hopeless, isolated and worthless, and lack goals or meaning or purpose in their lives. When faced with an illness, they do not mobilize the mental and physical resources needed to combat it, and they die sooner than they should. They have simply given up.

This phenomenon has also occurred among prisoners-of-war and concentration camp inmates. Those who are without hope for the future withdraw into themselves, shutting off the outside world. They literally pull the bedcovers over their heads and refuse all social contact, communication, assistance, or food. During the Korean War, some prisoners gave up and died. Their friends had tried to force them out of bed, wash, dress, and feed them, and even insult and hit them to make them angry; they tried everything to restore the spirit. Sometimes these tactics worked, but most of the time they failed to arouse a sufficient reason for living.

### Stages of Terminal Illness

Beginning in the 1970s, psychologists have shown considerable interest in the emotional reactions of people who have been told that they have a terminal illness. Thousands of patients have been interviewed to determine how they react to and cope with the dreaded news. Patients experience five distinct stages: denial and isolation, anger, bargaining, depression, and acceptance.[10]

The *denial and isolation* stage occurs immediately after being told of a terminal illness. "It isn't true! It can't be true," patients say. Often they go to elaborate lengths to straighten out what is "obviously a mistake." Some go to other doctors (sometimes to many other doctors), some want the records checked to make sure their charts were not mixed up with those of someone else, and some demand that the tests be repeated. Usually, the denial stage does not last long and is replaced by partial acceptance.

The isolation part of this stage occurs once the diagnosis of a terminal illness has been confirmed. Prior to that time, hospital staff members are attentive to a patient as they conduct test after test. Once the condition is known, however, the staff tends to leave the patient alone, believing that there is nothing more to be done for the patient. (Perhaps staff members are also uncomfortable being around hopelessly ill persons.) It is at this time that psychological counseling, and supportive family and friends, are necessary to counter the patient's loneliness.

The second stage is marked by *anger* at having a terminal illness. "Why me, God, why me?" they ask. Their anger is directed at the doctors, the staff, and even at family and friends. Terminally ill patients become hostile, demanding, and difficult. If other people react to a patient with anger, it only increases the patient's hostility. Counseling and understanding on the part of staff and family are required during this stage.

The *bargaining* stage follows, in which the patient hopes to be rewarded for being good. "If I survive this, God, I'll be a much better person and I'll go to church every week," a patient may say. Patients at this stage are hoping for freedom from pain or an extension of their lives, and are apparently trying to relive experiences from childhood when they were rewarded for good behavior.

[10] The five stages are discussed more fully in the pioneering work by Elisabeth Kübler–Ross, *On Death and Dying* (New York: Macmillan, 1969).

As the pain and the treatments become worse, and patients grow weaker and obviously closer to death, they enter into the fourth stage, *depression*. There are ample reasons to feel depressed; these persons will soon lose everything and everyone they know and love. Patients at this stage are encouraged to express their sorrow to sympathetic listeners. The depression is also believed to be a necessary preparation for death; grief must be worked through.

Finally, the stage of *acceptance* is reached. Patients are no longer angry or depressed. Acceptance is a much more positive feeling than the earlier hopelessness. This is a time of peace and quiet expectation. Patients usually wish to be left alone and seem almost empty of feelings. "It is as if the pain had gone, the struggle is over, and there comes a time for 'the final rest before the long journey' as one patient phrased it." [11] In the final stage, the family needs much more counseling and support than the patient needs.

## Counseling Terminally Ill Patients

For many years, counseling for terminally ill persons was rare. They were not believed to be neurotic or psychotic in the traditional sense, and it was felt that they had nothing to gain; they might even die before the counseling was completed. Fortunately, these attitudes have changed and growing numbers of terminally ill patients are helped to cope through psychological counseling. From the discussion of the five stages of terminal illness, it is easy to understand how valuable psychological help could be to both patient and family. The quality of life that remains for these people can be improved considerably as a result of counseling. Psychological therapy has also enabled some patients to live longer and respond better to medical treatment.

The goal of therapy with terminally ill patients is to help them make the best of however long they have to live, to find a sense of personal fulfillment and hope in the face of a seemingly hopeless situation, and to die with a sense of dignity and full acceptance of the worth of their lives. As one terminally ill patient said, "Death is nothing. It is inevitable. Everyone has to die. What matters is *how* you live and die." [12]

Through psychological counseling, it is possible for patients and their families to find meaning and fulfillment even in the experience of dying.

The human mind, and the stresses to which modern living subjects it, exerts an enormous influence on physical health. Negative emotions, such as tension and anger, debilitate our bodies and cause a variety of diseases and illnesses. Psychological research on the impact of the mind

[11] Ibid., p. 100.
[12] LeShan, op. cit., p. 98.

on the body is revealing ways to heal illnesses and to prevent their occurrence, offering enormous benefits to us all.

## SUMMARY

The idea that the mind can affect the body and cause or cure disease was first recognized by the ancient Greeks. It was out of favor during the twentieth century because of our strong belief in science and technology. Fortunately, the idea is again gaining prominence, primarily because of research findings of *medical psychologists* on emotional aspects of disease. Their work has important implications for the total health care system.

*Stress* produces physiological changes that are designed to help the individual cope with the stressful experience. These bodily changes include the release of adrenalin, extra sugar from the liver, and increased circulation and heart rate. Energy is directed to the brain and muscles, where it is needed to deal with the stress. However, we cannot remain in such a highly active condition for very long, because we have only a limited amount of energy on which to draw. If the stress continues, it depletes the body's reserves of energy.

Stress is any kind of emotional strain or tension. It produces wear and tear on the body and encompasses situations from annoyances, such as getting caught in a traffic jam, to crises, such as being attacked by a mugger. Each stress adds to the ones before, so the effects of stress are cumulative. Worry, anxiety, and long-standing emotional problems are also sources of stress. People who are constantly tense, worried, fearful, or hostile are continually wearing down their bodily reserves of energy. This, in time, leads to actual physiological damage to organs and tissues, and makes us more susceptible to infections. Thus, stress can lead directly to illness and disease.

It is impossible to escape stress altogether. Even the normal milestones of life such as marriage, moving, retirement, changing jobs or schools, and taking vacations are stresses because they involve a change in a person's life, to which he or she must adapt. The *Social Readjustment Rating Scale*, composed of common life stress events, has been useful in predicting the onset of illness. Persons who experience a certain number of life change events in the course of a year are much more likely to get sick during the following year than those who have fewer life changes. The most stressful change is the death of a spouse. The chances of illness and death increase dramatically in the six months following such a loss.

The *General Adaptation Syndrome* provides an explanation of what takes place between the initial appearance of stress and the subsequent development of an illness. Three stages in the body's reaction to stress are *alarm,* in which the physiological changes in response to stress serve to mobilize the body's defenses; *resistance,* in which the person seems to be adapting to the stress; and *exhaustion,* in which the bodily reserves of energy are depleted such that the person can no longer resist the stress and becomes susceptible to disease and infection.

*Psychosomatic diseases* involve real physical damage caused by stress and by other emotional and psychological factors. It is estimated that 50 to 80 per cent of all illness is psychosomatic. Psychosomatic disorders include eczema, acne, hives, backaches, headaches, arthritis, asthma, bronchitis, hypertension and other cardiovascular disorders, cancer, ulcers, colitis, genitourinary disorders, obesity, and hyperthyroidism.

Three possible reasons why a person under stress contracts one psychosomatic illness instead of another are *genetic predisposition, learning* (in which a particular set of symptoms has been reinforced), and *personality factors.*

Psychologists have determined that certain illnesses can be accurately diagnosed on the basis of personality characteristics alone, without conducting a physical examination. Three personality categories, each related to different psychosomatic diseases, are *excessive reactors,* who are prone to coronary occlusion, degenerative arthritis, and ulcers; *deficient reactors,* who are prone to dermatitis, rheumatoid arthritis, and colitis; and *restrained reactors,* who are prone to asthma, diabetes, hypertension, hyperthyroidism, and migraine headaches.

Personality correlates of six disorders are discussed. *Ulcer* victims are hard-driving, aggressive people who have strong conflicts between being dependent and being independent. People with *asthma* usually have a strong dependence on their mother. An asthmatic attack occurs when that dependency is threatened. *Migraine headache* sufferers feel unworthy and inferior and harbor resentment and frustration at not being able to accomplish their goals, which they usually set too high. People who have *rheumatoid arthritis* tend to be shy, inhibited, self-conscious, nervous, and compulsive and perfectionistic about everything they do. They also have strong needs to sacrifice for and serve others. Victims of *heart disease* have a recognizable personality pattern known as *Type A.* This includes a high competitive drive, a constant sense of time urgency, and high levels of ambition, aggressiveness, and hostility. They are impatient with other people and are always under tension and stress. The background and personality characteristics of *cancer* patients include the loss of a close relationship on which their security depended, causing them to feel lonely and isolated; an inability to express anger, resentment, and hostility; a high degree of self-hatred and self-distrust; and overwhelming despair.

Three techniques for reducing stress and its effects are biofeedback, meditation, and visualization. *Biofeedback* involves learning to control bodily processes such as heart rate and muscle tension in order to slow them during times of stress. *Meditation* decreases rates of mental and physical functioning, thus reducing the effects of stress and improving general health. *Visualization* involves focusing the mind's eye on a real or imaginary object. It has been used with cancer patients who focus on the actual destruction of their cancerous cells.

Psychological approaches to *pain reduction* have been successful in reducing the severity of the pain and in helping people adjust to the pain and thus lead normal lives. In pain clinics, *dolorologists* (persons who specialize in treating pain) use a variety of psychological techniques, including biofeedback, meditation, hypnosis, and behavior modification. Through behavior modification, dolorologists eliminate pain behaviors such as complaining, which may have been rewarded in the past.

Psychologists studying *death and dying* are concerned with the reactions of the terminally ill and counseling them so that they may be able to find meaning and purpose in the final days of their lives. How strongly a person wants to live can influence how long he or she does live in the face of terminal illness, or in a highly stressful situation such as a prisoner-of-war camp. Patients who have terminal illnesses pass through five psychological stages: denial and isolation, anger, bargaining, depression, and acceptance.

## SUGGESTED READINGS

APA Task Force on Health Research. Contributions of psychology to health research: Patterns, problems, and potentials. *American Psychologist,* 1976, **31,** 263–274.

Brown, Barbara B. *Stress and the Art of Biofeedback.* New York: Harper and Row, 1977.

Cherry, Laurence. Solving the mysteries of pain. *New York Times Magazine,* January 30, 1977, 12–13, 50–53.

Cullen, J. W., B. H. Fox, and R. N. Isom, Eds. *Cancer: The Behavioral Dimensions.* New York: Raven Press, 1976.

Engel, G. Emotional stress and sudden death. *Psychology Today,* 1977 (November), **11,** 114, 118, 153–154.

Fordyce, Wilbert E. *Behavioral Methods For Chronic Pain and Illness.* St. Louis: Mosby, 1976.

Friedman, Meyer, and Ray H. Rosenman. *Type A Behavior and Your Heart.* New York: Alfred A. Knopf, 1974.

Glass, D. C. Stress, competition and heart attacks. *Psychology Today,* 1976 (December), **10,** 54–57, 134.

Goleman, Daniel. Meditation helps break the stress spiral. *Psychology Today,* 1976 (February), **9,** 82–86, 93.

Goleman, Daniel. Migraine and tension headaches: Why your temples pound. *Psychology Today,* 1976 (August), **10,** 41–42, 76–78.

Goleman, Daniel. We are breaking the silence about death. *Psychology Today,* 1976 (September), **10**, 44–47, 103.

Gunderson, E. K. Eric, and Richard H. Rahe, Eds. *Life Stress and Illness.* Springfield, Ill.: Charles C Thomas, 1974.

Hilgard, E. R., and J. R. Hilgard. *Hypnosis in the Relief of Pain.* Los Altos, Cal.: William Kaufmann, 1975.

Howard, Jan, and Anselm Strauss, Eds. *Humanizing Health Care.* New York: Wiley, 1975.

Kastenbaum, Robert, and Paul Costa, Jr. Psychological perspectives on death. *Annual Review of Psychology,* 1977, **28**, 225–250.

Kübler-Ross, Elisabeth. *On Death and Dying.* New York: Macmillan, 1969.

LeShan, Lawrence. *You Can Fight For Your Life: Emotional Factors in the Causation of Cancer.* New York: M. Evans, 1977.

Lewis, Howard R., and Martha E. Lewis. *Psychosomatics: How Your Emotions Can Damage Your Health.* New York: Viking Press, 1972.

Liebeskind, John C., and Linda Paul. Psychological and physiological mechanisms of pain. *Annual Review of Psychology,* 1977, **28**, 41–60.

Marcus, M. G. Cancer and character. *Psychology Today,* 1976 (June), **10**, 52–59, 85.

Pelletier, Kenneth R. *Mind As Healer, Mind As Slayer.* New York: Dell, 1977.

Rushmer, R. F. *Humanizing Health Care: Alternative Futures In Medicine.* Cambridge, Mass.: MIT Press, 1976.

Schneidman, Edwin S., Ed. *Death: Current Perspectives.* Palo Alto, Cal.: Mayfield, 1976.

Selye, Hans. *The Stress of Life,* 2nd ed. New York: McGraw-Hill, 1976.

Slobogin, Kathy. Stress. *New York Times Magazine,* November 20, 1977, 48–50, 96–106.

Sternbach, Richard A. *Pain Patients: Traits and Treatments.* New York: Academic Press, 1974.

Suinn, R. M. How to break the vicious cycle of stress. *Psychology Today,* 1976 (December), **10**, 59–60.

Wallace, Robert Keith, and Herbert Benson. The physiology of meditation. *Scientific American,* 1972 (February), **226**, 84–90.

Wexler, Murray. The behavioral sciences in medical education: A view from psychology. *American Psychologist,* 1976, **31**, 275–283.

# Psychology Applied to the Environment

**7**

It had been planned as a utopian community, a paradise, but before long it turned into a nightmare world of cruelty and perversion marked by bizarre and abnormal behavior. As the designer of the community put it, "Utopia had become hell." The population grew and grew until all the normal rules and roles of social behavior disintegrated. The perfect community became a jungle fit for no one, not even the most cunning and sadistic.

Eventually, two thousand individuals lived there, about twice the optimum number. Conditions became crowded and chaotic, living space was jammed, and privacy no longer existed. Nature took its own course under these unnatural conditions of overcrowding and the population began an irreversible decline. Finally, there was no one left in the utopia; the adults all died and not enough infants survived to replace them.

The male members of the community were the most severely affected by the living conditions, and several deviant types developed. They no longer participated in their normal social roles. For some reason, they had been ejected from the high-rise apartment units the community inhabited. They did not live in the normal family groups but spent all of their time in the open, living in gangs with others of their own kind. They slept and ate in the public places, never venturing far from their cohorts. They stopped engaging in heterosexual behavior and became very aggressive, much more so than they had been before the community became so crowded. They were given to sudden sporadic and intense outbursts of violence, seemingly for no purpose, which resulted in severe injuries to their victims.

Other deviant males behaved in different ways. Some, instead of forming gangs, became solitary and withdrawn, hiding quietly anywhere they could find room. A third type of deviant male withdrew from the community in another way. These were called the "beautiful ones" because they looked so well groomed and attractive, but they avoided becoming involved in the community, even more so than the other deviant males. The beautiful ones lived together in the apartment units but never with females. Like the other deviant males, they had no sex lives at all. They behaved like adolescents whose development had stopped. Immature, withdrawn, and isolated, their behavior was described in these terms: "Don't go out, don't get involved, you can't win. Stay where you are; stay out of it."

There were female deviants also. Some of them became aggressive and physically attacked others of either sex who got too close to them. Those who had sexual relations with the few males still interested in sex did so in abnormal and disoriented fashion. Few of them became pregnant and many of those who did, spontaneously aborted their pregnancies. Those who gave birth were extremely poor mothers and took such sloppy care of their babies that most died shortly after birth.

The decline of this community is a horrifying story, and a true one. The community had been planned to provide ample living space in sixteen high-rise units and enough overall space to support one thousand individuals in comfort. And as long as the population remained below that number, everything was fine. No deviant or abnormal behavior of any kind was ever observed. What went wrong was overcrowding, the stress of which totally disrupted the social order and the lives of every member of the community.

There is one more thing to report about the community; the inhabitants were mice, and the planner was a psychologist studying the effects of crowding and population density on animal behavior.*

The results of this study, and a number of other similar studies, confirm what psychologists, social planners, urban policy makers, and common sense have been telling us for many years: our environment affects our behavior in many ways. All of us work and play in a variety of environments and all of them influence how we feel and behave, sometimes in obvious and direct ways and sometimes in subtle and indirect ways.

The noise, traffic, and other high-level stimuli of a downtown city street make some people nervous and tense and excite others and make them more alert. A quiet, peaceful setting by a country stream can relax one person and make another restless and bored.

We cannot escape environmental influences. Even a hermit living in a cave moves in an environment that shapes daily behavior and emotions. Most of us live in private homes, garden or high-rise apartment buildings, or dormitories, and each environment offers different stimuli that affect our attitudes and behavior. We work in factories, stores, offices, or classrooms; we ride on city streets in cars or buses or under them in

* Halsey M. Marsden, "Crowding and Animal Behavior," *Environment and the Social Sciences: Perspectives and Applications,* eds. J. F. Wohlwill and D. H. Carson (Washington, D.C.: American Psychological Association, 1972), pp. 5–14.

subways. We shop in large shopping centers or in tiny neighborhood stores, eat in quaint restaurants or in fast-food-carryout establishments. We socialize in bars, country clubs, student unions, or on beaches and in parks. When you think about it, you can easily realize that you are exposed to scores of different environments every day.

Something that has such a pervasive and powerful impact on human behavior deserves to be the object of serious scientific study. This is what the field of *environmental psychology* is all about. Combining the talents of psychologists, sociologists, architects, urban planners, and anthropologists, environmental psychology investigates the relationships between human behavior and every kind of environment in which human beings operate.

Environmental psychologists are concerned with three major aspects of the relationship between people and the environment in which they live and work: environmental planning (urban and architectural planning, personal space, and overcrowding); stressful environments (pollution, noise, extreme heat and cold, and radiation); and special environments (submarines, ships, airplanes, space vehicles, and oil-drilling rigs, for example).

Although the field is concerned primarily with the influence or impact of environment on behavior, it recognizes that this is not always a one-way effect. Our environment undoubtedly influences our behavior, but it is also true that we affect the environment. Thus, there is an interrelationship; each one influences the other.

It is easy to find examples of how we affect the environment. The building or house in which you are sitting while reading this chapter changed the environment on which it stands. Our cities and towns, shopping centers and highways, and even our natural parks and forests all bear the imprint of human design, sometimes for the better but often for the worse. Thus, the ultimate relationship between environment and behavior is circular. The environment influences our behavior, but we design the environment.

To study these influences, environmental psychologists and their colleagues from other disciplines use many of the standard research methods discussed in Chapter 2. Experimental research in laboratories, systematic observation in natural settings, and survey research methods are used to study actual behavior, feelings, and attitudes about various aspects of the environment. In addition, projective techniques, such as the Rorschach Inkblot Test, the Thematic Apperception Test, and word-association and sentence-completion techniques, are used to investigate our reactions to and feelings about our environment. The topics studied range from the design of entire communities to the desk at which you sit, from the use of recreational facilities and natural environments to attitudes toward environmental stresses such as air pollution.

We shall discuss some of this research as it relates to several visible aspects of our environment, such as homes, schools, and workplaces. First, however, we consider three larger issues that affect our behavior in all kinds of environments: two human needs that are satisfied or frustrated by the environment (privacy and territoriality), and the effects of overcrowding (what can happen when these two needs are not met).

## HUMAN ENVIRONMENTAL NEEDS

Imagine that you live in a huge single room like an army barracks with ninety-nine other people. The room is entirely open; there are no partitions or other barriers separating the rows of cots from one another. There is one large open bathroom serving all the residents. Next door is the dining hall with just enough tables and chairs to serve the one thousand people who live in the ten barracks that surround it. There is a swimming pool, small and always crowded, and other recreational facilities, all jammed together in a small area. There are no private nooks, corners, or hideaways of any kind. All day long and all night as well you are in constant and close contact with other people.

Most people in our culture would find such an environment to be highly stressful, and their behavior would certainly be influenced by living under these conditions. Many people would become tense and anxious, short-tempered, and hostile and aggressive toward the others crowded around them. If they lived in such a place long enough, the changes could become permanent and they might begin to behave in ways similar to the mice in the example at the beginning of the chapter, or to behave like prisoners in overcrowded jails. Two human needs —the needs for privacy and for space (territoriality)—are being violated in such a crowded environment.

### Privacy

We all know, in general, what we mean by privacy. We may speak of having private thoughts and feelings, meaning that they are personal and that we don't want to share them with anyone else. We speak of a private place, or of enjoying our privacy, meaning that we want to be alone and undisturbed in a place free of intrusions. Some of us want or need more privacy than others, and the need for privacy varies also from one culture to another. The privacy needs of Italians and South Americans are not the same as those of Swedes and Germans. The latter peoples desire more privacy and they build their homes and public places accordingly.

Privacy needs can vary from time to time. After a particularly hectic and stressful week at school or work, we may wish to spend the weekend removed from other people. After a few days of solitude, we may then seek out other people and prefer their company to being alone.

Privacy relates primarily to interpersonal interactions, that is, to the presence or absence of other people. However, the frequency and intensity of these interpersonal interactions can be hindered or facilitated by certain aspects of the physical environment. If on a sunny day you want to sit quietly and privately in your back yard undisturbed by other people, it might be nice to have a 6-foot-high wooden fence surrounding your yard. Without a fence, you might be driven indoors by a gregarious neighbor who insists on sitting down and talking to you for an hour.

In our homes, hospitals, prisons, schools—indeed, in all our built environments—privacy can be provided by architectural features such as walls and fences. Even in a public place such as a garden, privacy can be facilitated by the sound of a fountain to drown out the voices of passersby, or by tall hedges to screen people on adjoining paths from view.

Perhaps the most important aspect of privacy is the individual's freedom of choice to find privacy whenever he or she wants it. We do not need or even want to live behind high fences all the time, but neither do most of us want to live in the barracks described previously. We want the option of being in contact with other people, or being away from them, on our own terms.

What gives us the choice are the design features of our environment. A simple example are the doors in the rooms of our houses, which enable us to close off or open up our rooms to other people. Without doors, we would have no such choice. Many design features in homes, workplaces, and recreational spaces contribute to freedom of choice for privacy.

## Territoriality and Space

Closely related to the need for privacy is the need for territoriality, a space that is our very own, into which no one else may intrude. We all need such personal territory and we become upset and angry when it is violated. We speak of being "on our own turf," perhaps the neighborhood or street on which we live. In this case, the territory we define as ours is shared with other, usually similar, people. It gives us a sense of security and belonging, and we may fight to defend our turf from outsiders, that is, anyone who does not live there. This phenomenon is evident in ethnic neighborhoods in which adults may organize and protest, and teenagers fight, to keep out members of a different ethnic group. We may feel that anyone who is not "one of us" does not belong in our neighborhood, our territory.

Territoriality extends to the personal level as well. We defend our

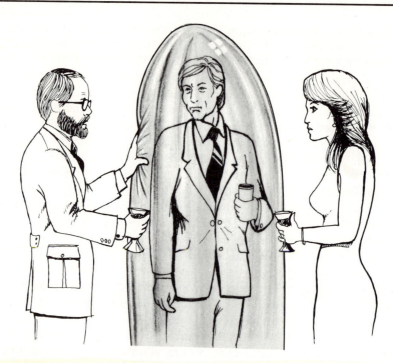

houses from intruders and we are possessive about our locker in school or our desk at work. Many people become uncomfortable if they see someone else using their desk, or even sitting on it while engaging in conversation, or leaning on their car in a parking lot. They feel that the desk or the car is "mine," and you are not to use it. Many people are attached to a favorite chair or toy; it is their possession, part of their territory.

Territoriality includes not only possessions but also the space around our bodies. In a very real sense we go through life encased in an invisible and flexible bubble. This bubble encloses our private space, into which others may not intrude. If someone gets too close to us, thereby piercing our bubble, we become uneasy and try to back away quickly.

You can test this proposition yourself with a simple experiment. Look for someone who is sitting alone at one end of a bench in a park or at a bus stop. Walk up to the bench and sit down. Your natural inclination would probably be to sit at the opposite end of the bench, as far from the other person as possible. To sit too close would violate your personal space. But this time, force yourself to sit in the middle of the bench, close to the other person, and watch what happens. Chances are excellent that in less than one minute the person will show signs of uneasiness, perhaps even anger. He or she may turn away from you, fidget uncomfortably, edge away, or get up and walk away, casting a withering glance at you.

Environmental psychologists have conducted many similar studies in naturalistic settings. One study was conducted in a university library, in which the personal space of female subjects sitting alone at large tables was invaded by another person. The closer the intruder sat to the subject, the greater was the subject's visible discomfort. The greatest disturbance was produced when the intruder moved her chair to within 3 inches of the subject's chair. Faced with that situation, 70 per cent of the subjects got up and left.

As with privacy, there are individual and cultural differences in the amount of personal space desired. Some of us are less bothered by intrusions than others, and can allow people to get closer without being disturbed by it. So it is with different cultures. Observe two English people talking to each other and note the amount of separation they maintain. Observe two Spaniards or Arabs talking and note how close they get to each other. Mediterranean, South American, and Middle Eastern peoples are better able to tolerate such proximity; indeed, they seem to prefer it. If an Arab and a German were talking, you might see the German backing away to protect his or her personal space from the unwanted intrusion.

In addition to individual and cultural differences in space needs, the size of one's personal space changes with the situation. Specifically, it changes with the nature of the relationship one person has with another. We noted that the invisible bubble that defines our personal space is flexible; it expands or contracts depending on who is approaching it. We allow someone we love to be physically closer to us than a drunken stranger we encounter on a dark and deserted street.

Between the extremes of these examples, our personal space bubble assumes a number of different sizes. Edward Hall,[1] an anthropologist, has defined four distance zones that he believes apply to middle-class adults in the United States. These four zones define our space needs with respect to other people and social situations: intimate distance, personal distance, social distance, and public distance. Within each of these zones there are two additional distances, a close phase and a far phase.

The *intimate distance* involves a minimal or no distance between people. In this distance zone, people are so close that their facial features may appear blurred and the heat and smell of their bodies detected. Sharp vision is distorted in part because the eyes focus inward, giving the uncomfortable sensation of being crosseyed. The close phase of intimate distance involves actual body contact as in lovemaking, caressing, and comforting. The far phase of intimate distance ranges from 6 to 18 inches. Physical contact is more likely to be with hands rather than

[1] Edward T. Hall, *The Hidden Dimension* (New York: Doubleday, 1966), pp. 110–120.

portions of the whole body. As with the close phase, it may be difficult to focus the eyes sharply.

The use of intimate distance by most of us is restricted to private situations and avoided in public, particularly among strangers. In situations that force intimacy, such as a crowded subway car or elevator, people try to avoid intimate contact by backing away from each other, keeping their hands at their sides or in their pockets, and staring at the walls or at some point in space to avoid even eye contact at this intimate distance.

In *personal distance*, the amount of separation between people is greater than in intimate distance; there is less physical contact. The close phase is from 1½ to 2½ feet, close enough to touch, as in shaking hands, but not so close as to produce visual distortion. This distance is usually reserved for friends. Strangers at this distance would be intruding. The far phase is from 2½ to 4 feet, just beyond touching distance. Acquaintances and even strangers may be allowed this near, depending on the situation.

*Social distance* marks the end of intimate contact and is likely to characterize social and formal situations rather than private and informal ones. The close phase ranges from 4 to 7 feet and is found in working relationships and social gatherings such as cocktail parties. The far phase is from 7 to 12 feet and characterizes even more formal business and social situations. Desks of high-status people such as business executives are usually large enough to keep people that distance away. Because of the greater distance involved, eye contact is very important, as is raising the volume of one's voice. In situations in which physical privacy is not allowed, this far phase of social distance affords a psychological sense of privacy by screening people from one another. For example, in a large workroom, people may work together without feeling the need to speak. Because of the distance from one another, they may remain uninvolved without seeming to be rude. At shorter distances, it is more difficult to remain uncommunicative.

*Public distance* further reduces both the actuality and the possibility of being involved with other people. The close phase ranges from 12 to 25 feet, too far for physical contact or for conversation in a normal tone of voice. The far phase refers to distances greater than 25 feet.

These distance zones can be augmented or destroyed by design features of the environment. Design in relation to personal space has become critical as our population increases and more of us live and work in congested cities. Poor design features can pierce our personal space bubbles and force us into unwanted relationships with others, thus contributing to stress. As stress increases, we become more sensitive to the people around us and, consequently, we feel the need for greater space, although there is actually less of it available. In other words, as we become more affected by overcrowding, it destroys our privacy and frustrates our needs for space and territoriality.

## THE EFFECTS OF OVERCROWDING

In the example at the beginning of the chapter we presented the disastrous effects of overcrowding on mice. It destroyed normal behavior by violating territoriality and space needs, which animals display as keenly as human beings. Other animal studies, conducted in laboratories and in the real world, have confirmed the harmful effects of overcrowding. Autopsies of animals that have lived under such conditions show unmistakable signs of physiological damage as a result of the stress of overcrowding.

Although we must be cautious in generalizing from animals to human beings, it is nevertheless possible to suggest that overcrowding may disrupt normal human behavior and serve as a form of stress in our everyday lives. This hypothesis has been supported by both observational and research studies of human beings in crowded situations.

Before we discuss the effects of overcrowding, let us define the concept. When does crowding become overcrowding? At what point does a city or a room become a source of stress because there are too many people in it?

Not surprisingly, this is a difficult concept to define objectively. Two environmental psychologists, Heimstra and McFarling, noted that the term *population density* is often used along with the term *overcrowding*, and that they represent two different attempts at definition.[2] Population density attempts to be an objective way of measuring overcrowding; it refers to the number of people who occupy a particular unit of space, such as a room or a neighborhood. According to this approach, overcrowding occurs when the population density reaches a certain level or number.

Despite attempts to measure overcrowding with precision, it remains a highly personal and subjective matter. A population density that is stressful for one person may be stimulating and enjoyable for another. Also, a population density that is stressful for a person today may not be stressful for that same person tomorrow or next week. Our level of tolerance is subject to change. A particular population density may be stressful in one situation and not stressful in another situation for the same person. For example, a crowded dormitory may be stressful for a student studying for a final examination, but that student may not be bothered by the same population density at the beach.

[2] N. W. Heimstra and L. H. McFarling, *Environmental Psychology* (Monterey, Calif.: Brooks /Cole, 1974), pp. 154–155.

Because overcrowding does not mean the same thing for everyone and does not produce the same effects in all situations, it is extremely difficult to generalize about the phenomenon. Nevertheless, it seems to be true that there is a level of population density for each of us that may be defined as overcrowded.

That specific density depends on several factors: (1) the actual *situation* (the size of the facility, the number of people in it, the arrangement of space, and the length of time a person must stay there); (2) the *past experience* of the individual (whether the person has developed a tolerance for crowds, as may be the case with someone raised in New York City but not someone raised on a Kansas farm); (3) *personality* factors (some people have a higher tolerance than others for any kind of stress); and (4) the nature of the *interactions* that take place in the situation (the same number of people may be more stressful in a work environment such as a laboratory than in a play environment such as a football stadium).

Although we cannot define overcrowding with the precision desired in science, we can conclude with some degree of certainty that each individual defines a situation as overcrowded when its density reaches the point at which his or her privacy and space needs are violated over a long enough period of time.

What are the effects of crowding on human behavior? We noted that there have been a number of studies to investigate the effects of overcrowding on animals, and many of our speculations about overcrowding and human behavior come from these studies. Few laboratory studies have dealt directly with human behavior; scientists cannot put people in long-term, highly stressful situations because of obvious ethical considerations.

Some short-term studies have been conducted with human beings. These produce less stress than caused by real world overcrowded conditions, but nevertheless they provide us with some indication of the effects on people of overcrowding. It has been shown under laboratory conditions that subjects exposed to overcrowding for short periods of time (1) show hostility toward a stranger who enters a room that has high density and high temperature; (2) demonstrate more signs of aggressiveness (true for males but not females); (3) give stiffer sentences in a simulated trial (true for males but not females); (4) interact less with others; and (5) demonstrate evidence of increased anxiety.

Much more impressive are data from observational and correlational studies of people who live in cities of high population density. American cities are living laboratories for the study of overcrowding. We know from our own experience that people who live in large cities tend to be more rude and lacking in consideration and politeness than those who live in small towns. City dwellers also tend to be more withdrawn and uncommunicative. They don't smile at or speak to strangers as readily as those who live in smaller communities, nor do they usually get involved helping others in distress. Sensational murders committed in large cities have been reported in which passersby and neighbors were so uninvolved that they did not even telephone the police from the distance and safety of their own apartment. High population densities seem to cause people to insulate themselves from others, perhaps as a means of ensuring psychological privacy and personal space.

Correlational studies, relating high population densities to deviant behavior, also suggest unfortunate effects of overcrowding. Studies conducted recently, as well as others dating back fifty years, show a high correlation between crime and population density. Crime rates are consistently higher in inner-city areas than in suburbs. Similarly, vandalism and juvenile delinquency occur more frequently in areas of high population density.

A similar relationship holds for mental illness and population density. The incidence of mental illness is highest in the centers of cities, and it progressively decreases as we move toward the less heavily populated suburban areas.

Overcrowding is also highly correlated with death rates. One study, investigating a state prison system and psychiatric hospital, showed that death rates increased as the population increased and declined as the population fell.

It has also been found that people tend to be more isolated in high-population-density areas. The number and nature of interpersonal contacts is much greater in suburban areas than in inner cities.

Finally, evidence suggests that women do not live as long in high-population-density areas. In rural and suburban communities, women tend to live about seven years longer than men. In inner-city areas, that difference in average life span is reduced dramatically.

There is no denying the increased incidence of these undesirable behaviors in high population areas; many studies confirm the findings. The problem lies in interpreting what these findings mean. They suggest that high density is the causal factor but do not prove it. When we compare inner city areas with suburbs, we can find points of difference other than the density of the population.

For example, there are usually wide differences in socioeconomic levels between city and suburb. In the city, people with marginal incomes may be under greater emotional stress and thus more tempted by the alleged rewards of crime. Less income means poorer health care, fewer educational opportunities, and a restricted choice of recreation and leisure activities. Although inner cities may be less healthy places in which to live, population density may not be the sole contributing factor. It may serve to aggravate other conditions, or perhaps have no influence at all; we do not know for sure. It is clear that population density affects behavior, but exactly how or in what way is less clear. The answers to these questions are among the most crucial facing environmental psychologists.

## HUMAN BEHAVIOR AND THE DESIGN OF SPECIFIC ENVIRONMENTS

While we wait for an answer to the problems created by large-scale environments such as cities, we can deal with smaller, more specific environments that are easier to study. To illustrate the work environmental psychologists are doing, we shall examine six situations and discuss how their design features influence human behavior. These examples include single- and multiple-family homes, workplaces, schools, hospitals, and prisons.

### Single-Family Homes

A major component of the "American dream" has long been the ownership of a single-family detached house in the suburbs, separated from other houses by a small plot of land. In the years since the end of World War II, this aspiration has significantly altered the landscape as well as our living habits. Inner cities have decayed as more affluent people have fled to the suburbs and beyond, leaving a lower tax base with which to maintain the attractiveness and livability of cities.

Hundreds of thousands of square miles of once-open countryside have been scarred by highways, shopping centers, and millions of tract homes, which has made us more dependent on the automobile. People who live in the suburbs are faced with longer commuting times to work, reducing the amount of time they can spend with their families. Schools and other services take longer to reach. As a result, the family as a whole spends less time together.

Shopping is done in identical shopping centers, which lack the diversity of downtown shopping areas, and suburbanites often live in identical, sterile surroundings, in which they are exposed to a blandness that makes one suburb look like any other. Most suburbs no longer have the physical, cultural, and ethnic diversity that makes cities stimulating places in which to live. Thus, you can see that the suburbanization of the United States has had a profound impact on how we live and provides an excellent example of how the environment can influence human behavior. Let us examine the houses in which suburbanites live, considering both exterior and interior features.

The location of a house relative to other houses is important because it can determine the number and frequency of interpersonal contacts. It has been shown, for example, that the distance between houses influences friendship patterns. More friendships are formed with persons in directly neighboring houses than with those in more distant houses.

Friendship patterns are also influenced by the way in which the houses are laid out in a neighborhood. People who live on deadend streets or culs-de-sac seem to develop more friendships with their neighbors than do those who live on through streets. Even the location of doors can influence social interaction. People are much more likely to develop friendships if their doors open onto a common sidewalk.

Another external feature of importance is where the house is placed on the lot. This influences both privacy and safety. Placing the house closer to the street decreases privacy, particularly if there are a lot of windows in the front rooms of the house. Putting the house as far from the street as possible, and screening it with thick bushes, can cut down on traffic noise and provide a greater sense of privacy.

Unfortunately, what provides the greatest amount of privacy tends to provide the least amount of safety from burglars. The best house location for minimizing break-ins is as close to the street as possible, with no shrubs or trees hiding doors and windows (they can also hide a burglar from public view). As additional protection from robbery in single-family houses, side and back yards should be enclosed by fences. However, the fences should not be high enough to hide a thief from being seen by neighbors once inside the fence.

A topic of major importance in the interior of homes is the amount of space available relative to the number of people occupying the house. Obviously, this has a direct effect on satisfaction of the privacy and space needs of individual family members. A ghetto family of six living in two rooms in a tenement has virtually no personal space or privacy compared to a suburban family of six living in a four-bedroom house.

A standard way to measure available space is to calculate the number of square feet per person in a house. The larger the area available per person, the more space or living room each member of the family has. Less than about 130 square feet per person characterizes poor and crowded housing conditions.

Other aspects of housing interiors studied by environmental psychologists include features that may make housekeeping tasks easier, and the ways in which rooms are used by different members of a family. By studying the kinds of activities performed in different rooms, as well as which rooms people use for privacy and which for the company of others, environmental psychologists contribute to the design of more functional housing.

## Multiple-Family Housing

For many reasons, ranging from insufficient income to a dislike of mowing lawns, many people live in apartments, either low-rise garden apartments or multistory high-rise buildings. Apartment residents have fewer opportunities to satisfy their privacy and personal space needs than do single-family home dwellers, and they are more subject to the pressures of overcrowding. The interior dimensions of apartments are often smaller than those of private homes, and there is greater proximity to other people.

The residents of an apartment may be almost totally surrounded by other people—above, below, and on at least two sides. Apartments are separated by common walls which, unless soundproofed, allow noises from one apartment to enter another. Surveys reveal that lack of privacy is a major complaint of apartment dwellers.

Garden apartments (usually two or three stories tall) are preferred over high-rise units, although the difference in preference is not very great. People with young children seem to prefer low-rise apartments because it is easier to watch children from the first or second floor than from the tenth or twelfth floor.

Residents of apartment units are greatly concerned with the attractiveness of the lobby and other public areas, and with the design of the building as a whole. People prefer buildings of unique design instead of simple squares and rectangles. With regard to interior layout, most people prefer a separate dining room or dining area to the combination living–dining room.

A problem often faced by apartment dwellers is isolation, a feeling of having too little interpersonal contact with neighbors. It is much easier to have a casual conversation and to socialize in a neighborhood of single-family homes than it is in an apartment building. Isolation is especially common in high-rise buildings, in which it is not unusual for people to have no interaction with neighbors of several years beyond a nod while passing in the corridor. High-rise units do not provide common places for socializing that encourage conversation. Isolation is less of a problem in garden apartments. Research has shown that residents of garden apartments have as many as three times more friends in their immediate neighborhood than do high-rise dwellers.

We know that overcrowding produces stress in people; and the opposite condition, isolation, can also be stressful. One study of families of British military personnel stationed in Germany after World War II compared those who lived in high-rise apartment buildings with those who lived in private homes. The differences in stress produced by the two environments were dramatic. The incidence of physical and mental illness was more than 50 per cent greater among those who lived in the apartments. Within high-rise apartment buildings, those who lived on the higher floors showed a higher rate of mental illness than those who lived on lower floors.

Another kind of stress produced by living in high-rise apartments is an increased fear for personal safety. The incidence of crime is much higher in high-rise apartments than in garden apartments or private homes. The taller the building, the higher is its crime rate. This finding is particularly evident in public housing projects.

Why does crime increase with building height? Most of the reasons have to do with the physical design and layout of high-rise apartments. First, there are more people living in a high-rise building than in a garden apartment project. However, it is not the sheer number of people that is the problem but rather that increased numbers mean that fewer of the residents know or recognize other residents. Thus, it is harder to spot strangers, people who do not belong in the building and who may be there to engage in some criminal activity. By contrast, a low-rise garden apartment building may have only six or eight apartments, making it much easier to notice strangers.

A second reason why crime is greater in high-rise apartments is that there are more vulnerable and indefensible places in which crimes may occur. Elevators, laundry rooms, stairways, and deadend corridors all provide excellent places for criminals to attack residents. Fire escapes and rear doors provide quick escape routes. Luxury high-rise units are safer than public housing because they usually provide twenty-four-hour protection in the form of doorkeepers, security guards, or closed circuit television. Also, fewer teenagers live in luxury high-rise buildings; adolescents commit a major share of today's crimes.

Design features of buildings can greatly reduce crime. The places of greatest vulnerability may be made more open and visible. Visual surveillance of entrance doors and lobbies can be enhanced by having apartment windows overlook the entrance. In that way, residents might notice strangers or suspicious persons before they enter the building.

Another design feature that has been shown to reduce crime is shorter hallways. The incidence of crime is higher in long corridors, which may contain fifty or more apartment doors, and lower in short corridors, which serve only a few apartments.

Environmental psychologists are making significant contributions to the quality of life by designing buildings in which people may live with less fear of being victimized by crime.

One kind of multiple-family housing with which you may be familiar is the college dormitory. As you probably know, most dormitory rooms are small and tend to feel and appear crowded when two or three people are living in them. One way to reduce this feeling is to place the dormitory so that the rooms receive full sunlight, especially in late afternoons when most students are in their rooms. Rooms flooded with natural light give the appearance of being larger and less crowded.

Many students personalize their rooms with pictures, posters, plants, calendars, and the like. Environmental psychologists have found that this personal decoration correlated highly with the decision to remain in college. Those students who decorated their rooms more, particularly with items of a personal nature, were much less likely to drop out of college than those who did little or no decorating. Presumably, decorating one's room is a manifestation of territoriality and signifies a stronger commitment to the room, hence to the university of which the room is a part.[3]

## The Workplace

An environment in which we spend almost as much time as in our homes is the place in which we work. Whether it is a classroom, factory, office, or store, its design and appearance contribute to our level of productivity (how well we work), our job satisfaction (how we feel about our work), and our general emotional well-being.

Industrial psychologists have been concerned for many years with the physical aspects of workplaces—lighting, wall colors, temperature, arrangement of the furniture and tools of work—and they have made significant improvements in our work environments to make them more comfortable, efficient, and safe (Chapter 14). Environmental psychologists have come to share that concern and have also done considerable work in this area, particularly in the design of offices.

As with factories, the physical design and appearance of offices influence the quality and quantity of work produced and the satisfaction that work brings to employees. The efforts of environmental psychologists range from the design of office furniture to the total rearrangement of an office, changing the work flow, communication patterns, and social groupings.

One thing that most people in offices do a lot is sit down. Industrial and engineering psychologists have devoted considerable time to studying the optimum design of chairs for waiting rooms and offices, as well as automobile and aircraft passenger seats and seating arrangements for astronauts on space flights. They have taken thousands of measurements of the human body to determine average body size.[4] From these measurements, they have been able to present guidelines on various aspects of chair design, such as the height of the seat from the floor, seat depth, backrest height, and size and position of armrests.

Environmental psychologists have made extensive use of these data and have also conducted research on the comfort of different types of chairs. Studies have shown that an improved office chair can increase

---

[3] William B. Hansen and Irwin Altman, "Decorating Personal Places: A Descriptive Analysis," *Environment and Behavior*, **8** (December 1976), 491–504.

[4] This is called the science of anthropometry.

worker efficiency as well as health; poor posture is related to several medical problems.

On a larger scale, environmental psychologists are concerned with the effects of office size on employee behavior. Some offices are small, containing only a few people, whereas others may contain hundreds of workers. The latter, known as "bull pens," often house clerical workers in private and government organizations. Desks are arranged in neat military-style formation with narrow aisles separating each row. Some bull pens are as large as football fields.

When office workers have been surveyed about their preference in office size, little difference has been found between small and large offices, although men voiced a somewhat greater preference for larger offices than women. The greatest disadvantage of large open offices is the difficulty in concentrating on one's work because of the constant noise and other distractions. The major advantage of large offices is that they facilitate communication among working groups.

Small offices have a positive effect on social relations among employees. Friendships and social cohesiveness are much more readily established in a small office than in a large one, although there are fewer opportunities in a small office to meet employees beyond one's immediate work group.

A modern approach to office design, the *landscaped office,* attempts to combine the best features of large and small offices. The landscaped office is open in the sense that there are no floor-to-ceiling walls or partitions, but it is not like the bull-pen type of office. Each working unit is set apart from the others by low barriers (none over 4 feet high) such as bookcases, divider screens, and plants. No employee is isolated or separated visually from any other, including high-level managers. Their offices are like all the others, separated only by landscaping from the other work areas. The physical and psychological distance that traditionally separates management from employees in separate closed offices does not exist in landscaped office designs.

Many financial, social, and psychological advantages are claimed for landscaped offices. They are cheaper to build than traditional offices with walls and doors. They cost less to clean and maintain and are more flexible than ordinary offices. If working units need to be shifted to a new location, it is quicker and easier to do so with desks and low partitions than when walls must be torn down and replaced elsewhere.

Another advantage of landscaped offices is an improvement in work flow and communication, attributable to the lack of walls that formerly separated one work group from another. It is also alleged that landscaped offices maintain the friendship that develops among people who work in small offices while allowing for cohesiveness to develop on a larger scale with members of neighboring groups.

The landscaped office is popular in the United States and in Europe, and it appears to be an improvement over traditional approaches to office design. However, appearances may be misleading. There has been little sound research comparing the traditional with the landscaped office, and the few studies that have been conducted are not in agreement. If you were trying to decide whether your company should change to landscaped offices, the current research would not settle the matter for you.

Some studies have shown that employees think landscaped offices are more attractive places in which to work, and that their social interactions are improved by the openness of the design. However, these positive aspects did not translate into increased work efficiency; employees believed that their efficiency declined in the landscaped office. They perceived the landscaped office to be noisier and less private, offering many distractions (the sights and sounds of so many other people).

Other research has found that communication between working units and between employees and managers improved in the landscaped office. Some employees felt that their work was easier to accomplish. At least one study found that workers and managers became more of a cohesive community where the physical and psychological barriers imposed by walls were removed.

Additional research is required before the issue is resolved. For the present, perhaps all we can conclude is that not every environmental change that looks nice leads to positive changes in behavior.

## Schools

All of us have spent many years of our lives in schools and classrooms. We know from our own experiences that the difficult work of being a student can be helped or hindered by physical features of the learning environment. Poor lighting, glare on blackboards, outside noise, uncomfortable chairs, and overcrowded classrooms are just a few of the physical characteristics that may interfere with our performance as students.

The traditional classroom design is a square or rectangular room with a desk and chair at one end for the teacher, and rows of student desks and chairs facing the teacher. Is this the most effective design? Does it encourage people to learn, to become involved in discussion, and to find enjoyment and satisfaction in the process?

The traditional classroom design may provide all of these benefits for highly motivated students, but not necessarily for other students.

Consider the psychological barrier created between the teacher and the students by the distance separating them, the different style of furniture each uses, and the fact that the teacher's desk may be raised on a platform or stage. These physical features create a visible impression of dominance or superiority on the part of the teacher, which may inhibit student participation.

The rows of student chairs or desks may create other problems. Pupils who sit at the back of the room may have difficulty seeing the blackboard or hearing the teacher, problems severely aggravated for students who have visual or hearing impairments. Also, students seated in a corner or at the rear may feel isolated from the class and have no sense of membership or affiliation with the other students.

Within the limitations of the traditional classroom, certain changes can be made to increase student participation and eliminate feelings of isolation. Chairs may be arranged in a semicircle so that all students are at the same distance from the teacher. Large tables, at which several students can sit, may be used instead of individual desks. The tables can be arranged in a square so that students face one another, an arrangement frequently used in college seminar rooms.

One environmental change in schools is the *open classroom,* not unlike the landscaped office, in which an entire floor of a school building may lack traditional floor-to-ceiling walls. There may be low barriers such as bookcases or cabinets, but usually the space is not structured or defined by furnishings. The open classroom was popular in elementary schools; more than half of the new schools built in the late 1960s and early 1970s incorporated this design.

How well does the open classroom work? This is not the place to evaluate the educational philosophy behind open classrooms. Our concern is the influence of the altered physical environment. As with landscaped offices, there are both advantages and disadvantages to open classrooms.[5]

Surprisingly, studies do not show that open classrooms are noisier or more distracting than separate classrooms. Indeed, open classrooms may be quieter than regular classrooms.

Student behavior is affected by the open classroom arrangement. Students have many more opportunities to satisfy personal space needs by separating themselves from others; they are not forced to remain in the same place or the same seat. They may work alone or with small groups of their own choosing. They are much more active over the course of the day, engaging in more activities with a variety of tools, toys, and equipment.

Relations with teachers are more personal and informal. No artificial barriers separate teacher and student as in the traditional classroom. When students work with a teacher as a group in an open classroom they tend to draw closer together; this can enhance feelings of membership and participation.

[5] Many educators no longer believe that the open classroom concept is desirable.

## Hospitals

Many of us will spend time in a hospital at some point in our life. Supposedly, hospitals are designed to treat illnesses and injuries and to facilitate patient recovery. As such, it is reasonable to assume that they are designed with the patient in mind, that patient safety and comfort are the major design criteria. This is usually not the case. Most of our hospitals are designed primarily for the comfort and convenience of the hospital staff rather than for the people they are treating. Patient needs, such as the need for privacy, are often ignored.

The hospital environment presents many opportunities for environmental psychologists to improve the quality of life (and the quality of dying) for millions of people. We will consider two kinds of hospitals in this section: general hospitals for the treatment of physical illness, and mental hospitals. Each type offers unique problems.

If you have ever been a patient in a *general hospital* or have visited someone who was a patient, you probably noticed the lack of privacy. For a daily room rate higher than that of most luxury hotels, a patient is housed with a stranger in a semiprivate room, or with several strangers in a ward. Thus, privacy is hard to find when the patient wants to read, sleep, or have an intimate conversation with his or her physician or family. Therefore, in most hospitals, the stress induced by the violation of privacy and space needs is added to the stress of illness.

Other sources of stress in hospitals come from the physical and psychological environments. Because of space limitations, some patients are not allowed to move around, either in their room or in the corridors, even though movement may facilitate recovery and allow the patient to feel less like an invalid. Even when movement is encouraged, where is a patient to go? Hospital corridors are usually unpleasant, noisy, and drab, and patients can often be seen shuffling along, trying to avoid those who move faster, and keeping their eyes straight ahead to avoid violating the privacy of other patients, whose doors are usually kept open.

One design aspect of hospitals that strongly influences patient behavior is the layout and arrangement of patients' rooms relative to the nursing station on the floor. Nurses are usually overworked; the optimum design would ease their work by allowing them to monitor their patients and attend to their needs as quickly as possible. A layout that reduces the amount of time nurses must spend walking back and forth between their station and the patients' rooms would increase efficiency and result in better patient care.

For example, one study compared a circular unit, in which the patients' rooms radiated from the central nursing station like the spokes of a wheel, with the traditional, rectangular, long hallway arrangement. In the latter, the nurses' station was in the middle or at the end of the corridor, and the nurses were required to leave their station and walk up and down the corridors in order to see the patients. Patients in rooms farthest from the station had to wait longer for a nurse to respond to a call than those whose rooms were closer to the station.

The circular arrangement eliminated both of those problems. All patient rooms were the same distance from the nursing station, and the nurses could look into every room without leaving the station. The psychologists concluded that this was a superior arrangement from the standpoint of nursing efficiency. However, because the patients were visible at all times, many of them complained of a lack of privacy. They believed that they were never left alone, that they were always under observation.

Hospitals or hospital wards for children present different design problems than facilities for adults; hospitalized children have different emotional needs and problems. Environmental psychologists have found that children much prefer to see other people than a view of the grounds outside the hospital. Therefore, children's rooms should be centered around or open onto a common activity or play area instead of a corridor, which is drab and empty much of the time, and a window that reveals an equally unchanging view.[6]

*Mental hospitals* offer special design problems because of the potential behaviors of the patients. Rehabilitative work with mentally ill persons usually emphasizes social activities and group interactions. Remaining alone, avoiding contact with others, is considered by the hospital staff to be detrimental to patient recovery. Of course, the design of the physical environment can facilitate or inhibit social interaction. For example, attractive meeting rooms, in which patients can gather to talk, read, play cards, or watch television, can encourage group activities.

Another physical feature that can aid or hinder social interaction is the size of patients' rooms. It seems reasonable to assume that the more patients there are living in a room, the more socially active they will be. However, research has shown that this assumption is not true. Studies indicate that patients in larger rooms are much more likely to be passive and isolated than patients in smaller rooms that contain fewer people. Patients in small or in private rooms interact more with patients from other rooms. Therefore, to increase social involvement among mental patients, the environment should be designed so that smaller rooms are provided.

The physical environment of mental hospitals is definitely a factor that influences recovery. In addition to the specific design features mentioned, the overall size of the treatment facility is important. Recovery

[6] Hermann H. Field, "Environmental Design Implications of a Changing Health Care System," *Environment and Cognition*, ed. William H. Ittelson (New York: Seminar Press, 1973), pp. 127–156.

rates for patients in large hospitals are slower than for patients in small ones. Also, reducing the institutional appearance of a mental hospital can enhance recovery by minimizing its separateness from the real world.

## Prisons

Design features also influence the behavior of prisoners. There are at least two similarities between prisons and hospitals. First, most patients, and all prisoners, are not in these institutions voluntarily; these people would certainly prefer to be elsewhere. Second, because crowded conditions are common to both institutions, the satisfaction of privacy and personal space needs is difficult.

Prisons differ from hospitals, and from all other institutions, in the absolute control exerted over every aspect of a prisoner's life, and in the restrictions on social interaction. Authority is exercised at two levels: to keep prisoners isolated from society, and to limit opportunities for prisoners to socialize with one another. Both are accomplished by means of design, the former by the exterior features of prisons such as walls and fences, and the latter by cells, bolted doors, and interior partitions.

Prisoners who may be dangerous to other inmates must be isolated. Young prisoners, jailed for their first offense, should be kept from contact with hardened, long-term prisoners. Those who are responding well to rehabilitative efforts should be kept away from those who are resisting attempts at rehabilitation.

With regard to the basic living arrangements for prisoners, single cells are preferred over dormitories. A prisoner who lives alone in a cell is much better able to satisfy privacy and space needs than a prisoner who lives with several others in a large room. Research has found that the size of the cell is not nearly so important as the amount of time a prisoner must remain in it each day. Prisoners voice few complaints about cell size when they are allowed to move about in other parts of the prison during the day.

In most institutions, most prisoners are given the opportunity to use certain areas of the prison compound. They may visit other cells, the exercise yard, or dayrooms. In addition, many prisoners attend classes, use the library, or work in prison shops. Some activities are structured and all inmates are required to participate in them. However, some parts of the day are unstructured; psychologists believe that it is important that the design of the prison allow inmates to find places of privacy and quiet outside their cells during these "free" periods of time.

The vital aspect of prison design is the same as for any other facility in which people live and work: the individual should have some freedom of choice to find privacy whenever he or she wants it. In prisons, satisfying privacy and personal space needs is an important factor in re-habilitation. (Also important to rehabilitation is, as noted, isolating those prisoners who are negative influences on other prisoners.) These features can be brought about by proper design of the institution.

## ENVIRONMENTAL QUALITY

In discussing the influences of environmental psychology, we have so far dealt only with built environments—the structures and communities in which we live and work. These constitute a major portion of the environment in which we function (particularly for the majority of us who live in cities), but they do not make up the total environment. Our behavior can also be influenced by various aspects of the natural environment—the air we breathe; the parks and recreation areas we relax in; the mountain trails we hike; and the trees, streams, rivers, and lawns we may notice on our way to work. Because we can be soothed and rested by vacations at the beach, the mountains, or in other outdoor environments, environmental psychologists are conducting research on our use of recreational facilities, such as national parks and wilderness areas. Psychologists have surveyed attitudes toward littering, paper recycling, conservation of electricity, and obeying "Keep Off the Grass" signs in public parks.

Some aspects of the natural environment can also be stressful and harmful. Earthquakes, tornadoes, hurricanes, and tidal waves are physical and psychological hazards, to which people in some parts of the world are exposed repeatedly. Destruction or degradation of natural beauty can also be stressful, whether it is the thoughtless littering and vandalizing of a public park or the strip mining of a mountainside forest. In the twentieth century, human beings have spoiled and polluted much of the natural environment, the land, the water, and the air we breathe. Because the resulting negative aspects of the environment affect our behavior, they have been the subject of study by environmental psychologists.

To demonstrate the kinds of research being conducted by psychologists on environmental quality, let us consider the problem of air pollution. This condition has made many of our large cities unhealthy places in which to live. Air pollution irritates the eyes and the respiratory system and has been linked to lung cancer. Elderly people are particularly vulnerable to high levels of air pollution; their sickness and death rates increase under conditions of high pollution.

I live on the outskirts of Washington, D.C. On clear days, I enjoy a magnificent view of trees and sky from my eighth-floor apartment. But in the spring and summer the city has become increasingly afflicted with high pollution; "air pollution alerts" and "air stagnation advisories" sometimes last for several days. Elderly people, and those with respiratory illnesses, are warned to stay indoors, and everyone is advised not to exercise or jog. The view from my window turns to a dirty haze. Thus, our behavior is affected by the polluted air. People who enjoy being outdoors (joggers, picnickers, even those who like to walk to work or to shopping) are less likely to go outside. Many complain of being tired, listless, and less mentally alert.

National surveys have shown consistently that a large percentage of Americans express alarm over air and water pollution. Yet this concern does not translate into a compelling need to take action, or even to an awareness that there is a problem in the area in which many people live. For example, when people in cities with air pollution problems are asked if their community is a healthy place in which to live, most of them answer "yes." However, when people in these same cities are asked directly if they are personally bothered by air pollution, most of them also answer "yes."

We know from our discussion of the survey research methods (Chapter 2) that the answer one gets is often markedly influenced by the way in which the question is worded. When people are asked directly about air pollution they express alarm, but they do not spontaneously indicate concern about air pollution even if they live in a heavily polluted area. At best we can say that this is a paradox, one of many exhibited by human beings.

Environmental psychologists cannot change the air quality as they can change the design of a home or a school, but they do try to measure attitudes toward pollution. They can determine, through surveys, what sacrifices people are willing to make in exchange for cleaner air, and what action people want the government to take. Through advertising and other promotional techniques (see Chapter 8), environmental psychologists try to change our attitudes and behaviors so that we may become more willing to act to improve the quality of our natural environment.

## SUMMARY

*Environmental psychologists* investigate the relationships between human behavior and the various environments in which we live and work. The field combines the talents of psychologists, sociologists, architects, urban planners, and anthropologists. We build and shape our environments, and these in turn influence our behavior. To study these mutual effects, environmental psychologists use standard methods of psychological research: experimental research in laboratories, systematic observation in natural settings, and survey research methods.

**Psychology Applied to the Environment**

Two fundamental human needs that are strongly influenced by our environment are the needs for privacy and for personal space.

The need for *privacy* (to be alone and undisturbed by other people) varies from one person or culture to another. Some people need more privacy than others. The privacy need also varies within the same person from one situation to another. Sometimes we need to be alone and at other times we need the company of other people. Satisfaction of privacy needs can be hindered or helped by certain aspects of the physical environment. Privacy can be provided by architectural features such as walls, fences, and shrubbery. The most important aspect of privacy is an individual's free choice to find it whenever he or she desires. Our environment should give us the option of when and under what conditions we want to be with other people or to be alone.

*Personal space* (territoriality) is the need for a space that is our own, into which no one else may intrude. The phenomenon of territoriality includes personal possessions as well as the space around our body. If someone gets too close to us they may violate our personal space and make us feel uncomfortable. As with privacy, there are individual and cultural differences in personal space needs. Some of us need more space than others. Space needs also vary with the nature of the person with whom we are interacting. A loved one is allowed to get much closer than a stranger.

The anthropologist Edward Hall has defined four distance zones that characterize our space needs with respect to other people: *intimate distance* (the close phase involves actual body contact and the far phase ranges from 6 to 18 inches); *personal distance* (the close phase is 1½ to 2½ feet and the far phase is 2½ to 4 feet); *social distance* (the close phase is from 4 to 7 feet and the far phase is 7 to 12 feet); and *public distance* (the close phase is 12 to 25 feet and the far phase is beyond 25 feet).

When privacy and personal space needs are frustrated, we may find ourselves in a situation of *overcrowding*. Animal studies show that overcrowding is stressful and produces harmful behavioral and physiological effects. Overcrowding is also stressful to human beings. An objective way to measure overcrowding is to calculate *population density*, the number of people who occupy a particular unit of space. However, overcrowding remains a personal and subjective matter and depends on the actual situation, the past experience of the individual, personality factors, and the nature of the interaction. Each person defines a situation as overcrowded when his or her privacy and personal space needs are violated over a long period of time. Correlational studies show that high population densities are related to high rates of crime and mental illness, to reduced interpersonal contact, and to a shorter life span for women.

Environmental psychologists study large-scale environments such as cities as well as specific small-scale environments such as the following.

*Single-family homes* have significantly changed the landscape of the United States as well as our life-style and behavior. The location of a house relative to other houses, and where it is situated on a lot, influences friendship patterns, privacy, and safety. The size of a house and its interior arrangement of rooms affect the privacy of those who live in it. The amount of space available to each person determines how crowded the living conditions seem.

People who live in *multiple-family housing* may find it more difficult to satisfy privacy and space needs. They are more subject to the pressures of overcrowding and, at the same time, are more isolated from their neighbors than people who live in single-family homes. These problems are more severe in high-rise apartments than in low-rise garden apartments. Crime is a greater problem in high-rise units because there are more residents and more vulnerable and indefensible places in which crimes may occur. Designing shorter hallways, and installing closed-circuit television and other safety features can reduce the incidence of crime.

The *workplace* most frequently studied by environmental psychologists is the office. Their efforts range from the design of chairs to the layout of the office as a whole. The *landscaped office* contains no floor-to-ceiling walls and is more attractive than traditional offices. Landscaped offices may improve communication, work flow, and social interaction, but may also offer less privacy.

Traditional *schools* present environmental and psychological barriers between teacher and student through the size of the room and the type and arrangement of the furniture. *Open classrooms* reduce those barriers by doing away with walls. They result in greater satisfaction of personal space needs and they increase students' informal relations with teachers.

*Hospitals* are often designed for the convenience of the staff rather than for the comfort of the patients. They offer very little patient privacy. The way in which a hospital floor or wing is laid out can significantly influence nursing care by affecting the amount of time required for nurses to attend to patient needs. In mental hospitals, smaller patient rooms can influence recovery by facilitating greater social interaction.

Inmates of *prisons* are strongly controlled by features of the physical environment. Certain prisoners must be isolated from others by walls and other barriers. Single cells are superior to dormitories for the satisfaction of privacy and personal space needs, important factors in rehabilitation.

Environmental psychologists are concerned with the *quality of the natural environment*, whether wilderness areas or air and water pollution conditions. They study attitudes toward environmental quality and try to find ways to change these attitudes. In studying air pollution, environmental psychologists have found that although many people are alarmed about it, they are not willing to do much about it.

## SUGGESTED READINGS

Altman, Irwin. *The Environment and Social Behavior: Privacy, Personal Space, Territory and Crowding.* Monterey, Cal.: Brooks/Cole, 1975.

Ashcraft, Norman, and Albert E. Scheflen. *People Space: The Making and Breaking of Human Boundaries.* New York: Anchor Books, 1976.

Bass, Bernard M., and Ruth Bass. Concern for the environment: Implications for industrial and organizational psychology. *American Psychologist,* 1976, **31,** 158–166.

Baum, Andrew, and Stuart Valins. *Architecture and Social Behavior.* Hillsdale, N.J.: Lawrence Erlbaum, 1977.

Bennett, Corwin. *Spaces For People: Human Factors in Design.* Englewood Cliffs, N.J.: Prentice-Hall, 1977.

Bowman, J. S. Public opinion and the environment. *Environment and Behavior,* 1977 (September), **9,** 385–416.

Driver, B. L., and R. C. Knopf. Personality, outdoor recreation, and expected consequences. *Environment and Behavior,* 1977 (June), **9,** 169–194.

Evans, Gary W., and Daniel Stokols, Eds. Special issue on privacy, territoriality, personal space, and crowding. *Environment and Behavior,* 1976 (March), **8.**

Hansen, William B., and Irwin Altman. Decorating personal places: A descriptive analysis. *Environment and Behavior,* 1976 (December), **8,** 491–504.

Heimsath, C. *Behavioral Architecture: Toward An Accountable Design Process.* New York: McGraw-Hill, 1977.

High, T., and E. Sundstrom. Room flexibility and space use in a dormitory. *Environment and Behavior,* 1977 (March), **9,** 81–90.

Insel, P. M., and Henry Clay Lindgren. Too close for comfort. *Psychology Today,* 1977 (December), **11,** 100–106.

Jobes, P. C. Problems facing social scientists participating in environmental impact research. *Human Factors,* 1977, **19,** 47–54.

Kaplan, R. Patterns of environmental preference. *Environment and Behavior,* 1977 (June), **9,** 195–216.

Lounsbury, J. W., and L. G. Tornatzky. A scale for assessing attitudes toward environmental quality. *Journal of Social Psychology,* 1977 (April), **101,** 299–305.

McKechnie, George E. The Environmental Response Inventory in application. *Environment and Behavior,* 1977 (June), **9,** 255–276.

Mehrabian, Albert. *Public Places and Private Spaces: The Psychology of Work, Play, and Living Environments.* New York: Basic Books, 1976.

Michelson, William. *Environmental Choice, Human Behavior, and Residential Satisfaction.* New York: Oxford University Press, 1977.

Newman, Oscar. *Defensible Space: Crime Prevention Through Urban Design.* New York: Macmillan, 1972.

Proshansky, Harold M. Environmental psychology and the real world. *American Psychologist*, 1976, **31**, 303–310.

Proshansky, Harold M., William H. Ittelson, and Leanne G. Rivlin. *Environmental Psychology: People and Their Physical Settings*, 2nd ed. New York: Holt, Rinehart and Winston, 1976.

Rappaport, M. Human factors applications in medicine. *Human Factors*, 1970, **12**, 25–35.

Robinson, Stuart N. Littering behavior in public places. *Environment and Behavior*, 1976 (September), **8**, 363–384.

Ronco, P. C. Human factors applied to hospital patient care. *Human Factors*, 1972, **14**, 461–470.

Schiffenbauer, A. I. The relationship between density and crowding: Some architectural modifiers. *Environment and Behavior*, 1977 (March), **9**, 3–14.

Stokols, Daniel. Environmental psychology. *Annual Review of Psychology*, 1978, **29**, 253–295.

Tognacci, L. Environmental quality: How real is public concern. *Environment and Behavior*, 1972 (March), **4**, 73–86.

Wohlwill, J. F., and D. H. Carson, Eds. *Environment and the Social Sciences: Perspectives and Applications*. Washington, D.C.: American Psychological Association, 1972.

# Psychology Applied to Consumer Behavior

**8**

When it first appeared on the market it was considered a revolutionary product that would completely change American drinking habits and bring its manufacturer enormous profits. It was certain to be popular because it was quick and easy for anyone to prepare, no skill or patience was required, and there was virtually no possibility of making a mistake. Also, it cost less than the traditional drink it was designed to replace. Great amounts of money and creative talent were devoted to extensive nationwide advertising campaigns, using every known means of persuasion.

With such a product and such widespread marketing efforts, surely it would be an immediate success. But to everyone's surprise, the drink was not doing well at all. It captured no more than a small share of the market, even though the manufacturers of the traditional product spent considerably less money on advertising than the maker of the new product. Clearly, something was wrong. The manufacturer of the new product was convinced that it was a superior product in terms of cost and ease of preparation, so why were consumers buying so little of it? The survival of a fledgling industry was at stake, careers were on the line, and much money seemed certain to be lost if sales did not improve. Somehow, people had to be persuaded to buy and use this revolutionary drink.

The product was instant coffee, something that today is such a common part of our lives that we wonder how we ever lived without it. In our modern fast-paced age, laboriously preparing fresh coffee several times a day using complex and time-consuming methods and cumbersome pieces of apparatus seems, to most of us, like a chore out of the last century. Instant coffee came on the market in the 1940s but for a time it appeared that the product would fail.

Consumer psychologists were asked to find out what the problem was, to determine why consumers were resisting this new miracle time saver. First the psychologists conducted a direct survey of attitudes toward Nescafé, one of the earlier instant coffee products. Through the use of questionnaires, a representative sample of people were asked if they used instant coffee. Those who did not were asked what they disliked about the product. Most people gave one answer; they did not like the flavor.

The company management did not believe that flavor was the real reason. They were sure that most people could not tell the difference between their product and freshly brewed coffee. They suspected that there were underlying motives behind consumer rejection of instant coffee that had nothing to do with flavor. Accordingly, a psychological study was conducted, using an indirect approach, to investigate deeper consumer attitudes toward instant coffee.

Instead of asking people what they disliked about instant coffee, the psychologist compiled two shopping lists, showed them to two groups of women, and asked the women to describe the personality and character of the person who had allegedly drawn up each list. The lists were identical except for one item on each; one list included instant coffee and the other included fresh coffee (Table 8–1).*

The resulting personality portraits of the two fictitious shoppers were radically different. People described the shopper who bought instant coffee as lazy, a poor planner, sloppy, and probably not a good wife. The shopper who bought fresh coffee was described as practical, frugal, sensible, interested in the family, and one who enjoyed cooking.

Thus, the results of the study showed that the instant coffee user was perceived in very negative terms. The new, miracle time-saving product had an unpleasant image in the minds of consumers. The advertised advantages of instant coffee—efficiency, speed, and ease of preparation—were emotional liabilities rather than assets. The self-image of persons who bought instant coffee was negative; they believed themselves to be lazy and sloppy, and did

**Table 8–1.** Shopping Lists in Instant-Coffee Study

| List 1 | List 2 |
| --- | --- |
| 1 can Rumford's baking powder | 1 can Rumford's baking powder |
| 2 loaves Wonder bread | 2 loaves Wonder bread |
| bunch of carrots | bunch of carrots |
| Nescafé instant coffee | 1 lb Maxwell House coffee (drip ground) |
| 1½ lb hamburger | 1½ lb hamburger |
| 2 cans Del Monte peaches | 2 cans Del Monte peaches |
| 5 lb potatoes | 5 lb potatoes |

*M. Haire, "Projective Techniques in Marketing Research," *Journal of Marketing*, **14** (April 1950), 649–656.

not display the proper concern for the family, otherwise they would have labored over the brewing of fresh coffee. No wonder so few people bought the product!

A new image for instant coffee was required, and so the advertising themes were altered. Instead of stressing the speed and convenience of instant coffee, the new advertisements focused on the idea that the flavor, aroma, and "rich full body" of fresh coffee could be found in instant coffee. Full-page advertisements in magazines showed large brown coffee beans piled high behind a cup of coffee. Slogans such as "100 per cent pure coffee" were placed on instant-coffee jar labels. Soon, the negative images were overcome and instant coffee has since become the largest selling form of coffee in the Western world. People who brew fresh coffee today constitute a minority of coffee drinkers. Apparently, consumers have been persuaded that buying instant coffee no longer means that they are lazy and inefficient. In similar fashion, we as consumers have been convinced almost daily of the value of other new products.

Consumer psychology affects all of us because we are all consumers. Advertising urges us to purchase a particular breakfast cereal, toothpaste, perfume, automobile, or deodorant, to choose a certain vacation spot or political candidate, or to donate to a college or charity. Every day we are influenced, consciously or unconsciously, by advertising appeals of various kinds.

The average American is bombarded by as many as fifteen hundred advertisements every day through magazines, newspapers, radio, television, and billboards. Of course, we are not consciously aware of all of these; we do not actually see or hear that many advertisements. We may notice no more than one hundred of them, and consciously attend to as few as a dozen. But those few influence our lives in significant ways because the products they persuade us to buy convey to ourselves and to others a sense of who and what we think we are or hope to be. Thus, advertising influences our sense of self-esteem and self-worth, and defines the personal image we present to other people.

Not only do we constantly see and hear the results of the work of consumer psychologists in advertising, but we also contribute, in increasing numbers, to their research. We respond to surveys, clip coupons, and are observed as shoppers in supermarkets. Our buying, television viewing, credit, and travel habits are all studied by consumer psychologists. They call us on the telephone, stop us in shopping centers and airports, and mail us questionnaires to inquire about the products we use, the purchases we plan to make, or the programs we watch. They send us samples of new products to see if we will buy them when the samples run out. They are continually probing and peeking at us to determine our likes and dislikes, and then prodding and persuading us with advertising messages developed on the basis of this research.

It is true that some advertisements are obnoxious and deliberately deceitful, but others can be interesting and enjoyable as well as informative. Advertising in the local newspaper can save us money in our shopping by directing us to stores that are having sales on items we want. Advertising about complex items such as automobiles and stereo equipment can instruct us about the differences among brands.

Also, advertising is a vital part of the economy of the United States, stimulating the demand for products, which, in turn, can lead to the creation of more jobs. The economy, and the companies for which many of you will work, depend heavily on advertising. Manufacturers must be able to reach consumers with information about their products. To do that effectively, they rely on the services of consumer psychologists who develop appropriate advertising appeals and determine which medium provides the best means for reaching potential customers.

There is more to consumer psychology than one-way communication from producer to consumer. The optimum matching of product and customer can only be accomplished by finding out what the customer wants. Therefore, consumer psychologists are interested in the opinions and behaviors of consumers so that producers of goods may respond to changes in the market by modifying advertising appeals, package designs, or the product itself.

This is why consumer psychologists study consumers in so many ways and places. By investigating our needs and desires, and how they are influenced by age, education, race, socioeconomic level, interests, or personality factors, the potential markets for various kinds of products can be determined. On the basis of this market information, decisions are made not only about advertising but also about packaging, displaying, and distributing the product, and about production schedules. Companies prosper by continuing to produce what people want to buy, or, as was the case with instant coffee, by persuading people that they should buy a product.

## HOW PSYCHOLOGISTS STUDY CONSUMER BEHAVIOR

Most research in consumer psychology uses some form of *survey* or *public opinion poll*. (These research methods are discussed in Chapter 2.) These deal with what people say they do or will do in various situations, but not with their actual behavior. Thus, survey or polling techniques deal with attitudes, opinions, and feelings. These are more subjective variables than the behavior studied by the experimental method.

As we noted with the initial instant coffee survey, people often report an attitude toward a product (or toward a political candidate or anything else that is being sold) that does not accurately reflect their feelings. There are several reasons for this behavior: a desire to impress an interviewer, an attempt to conceal some personal characteristic, or a lack of awareness of one's true feelings. This is the major difficulty with the survey methods. Frequently, people say one thing and do another. This misleads those who try to predict the vote for a candidate or the degree of acceptance of a new product.

Because people may misrepresent themselves to interviewers, some consumer psychologists do not use survey methods. Instead, they choose to study consumer behavior by an indirect approach known as the *in-depth* method. This procedure attempts to probe unconscious human motivations and feelings through the use of *projective techniques*. The two shopping lists in the second instant coffee study (Table 8–1) are projective techniques, as is the well-known *Rorschach Inkblot Test*. The theory behind projective techniques is that when people are presented with an ambiguous stimulus such as an inkblot or picture, which may be interpreted in more than one way, they will project their own hidden needs, fears, and longings onto that stimulus when they voice their reactions to it. Thus, in the shopping-list study, the shoppers were really describing their own deep feelings about instant coffee in the guise of describing the imaginary shopper. They were not reluctant to do so because they did not believe that they were directly revealing themselves to the psychologist.

Another in–depth technique for studying consumer behavior is the *focus group*, in which eight to ten consumers discuss various aspects of a product and its advertising with a representative of the manufacturer or advertising agency.

Projective techniques are used in clinical settings to diagnose emotional disturbances, and in industrial settings to select executives for high-level jobs; they have been found to have doubtful validity in both situations. Even the most highly trained and experienced psychologists often disagree in their interpretations of a person's responses on a projective technique. From a scientific standpoint, projective techniques are not very accurate instruments for measuring human feelings.[1]

Thus, both survey and in-depth methods have drawbacks in trying to deal with consumer attitudes and feelings. Because of these problems, some consumer psychologists focus on the measurement of actual *consumer behavior* rather than attitudes. Instead of asking people what they like or what they are going to buy, the consumer behavior ap-

---

[1] Later studies have cast doubt on the methodology and results of the instant-coffee study. See Conrad R. Hill, "Haire's Classic Instant Coffee Study—18 Years Later," *Journalism Quarterly*, **45** (1968), 466–472.

proach investigates what people actually do when purchasing a product or expressing a preference for one brand over another, either in a laboratory or in a real-world setting such as a shopping center.

Objective methods for studying consumer behavior include sales records, observation of purchasing behavior, brand identification and preference, and coupon returns.

On the basis of common sense, it may seem that *sales figures* for a new product or advertising campaign would provide the best test of how well consumers are accepting that product or advertisement. If, for example, sales of a deodorant increase by 10 per cent after a new advertising campaign has been implemented, surely the new campaign was responsible for the increased sales. Unfortunately, this is not always an accurate conclusion. Sales figures alone may provide misleading data because all the other factors that could have influenced sales have not been controlled.

Perhaps the company's sales representatives arranged prominent and eye-catching displays of the deodorant during the time of the advertising campaign. Perhaps the leading competitor was publicly accused of using a dangerous chemical in their deodorant. Both factors could account for an increase in sales, independent of the advertising campaign itself. Sales figures can only be used as a measure of consumer behavior if all other possible influencing variables are controlled.

*Observing actual buying behavior* in stores, although expensive and time consuming, can provide a great deal of useful information. In addition to showing actual purchases, observations can reveal which family members buy what products, how many people compare prices, and how many purchases seem to be habitual rather than decided at the time of purchase. As with all observational studies, these must be well controlled. Stores in different geographic locations, and shoppers from different socioeconomic levels, must be sampled.

Studies of *brand identification and preference* are usually conducted in laboratories. Consumers are asked if they can distinguish among various brands of a product when all labels and identifying characteristics have been removed. For example, two brands of beer are served in identical containers and people are asked which they prefer. Often, this approach is used to test consumer reaction to a new product before it is released to the public. Brand preference studies have been conducted on the texture or feel of different clothing fabrics, the crispness of breakfast cereals, and the taste of different soft drinks.

*Coupon returns* are used to test the effectiveness of newspaper and magazine advertisements. Coupons are primarily used to entice the consumer to send for a free sample or a brochure, or to enter a contest. The rate of coupon return may indicate the attention-getting value of the advertisement, or the attractiveness of whatever is being offered in return for the coupon, but it does not indicate how effective the advertisement may be in increasing sales for the product.

Through these and other techniques, consumer psychologists measure important aspects of the relationship between buyer and seller. We shall discuss the results of some of this extensive research as we explore the three essential components of consumer psychology: the consumer, the product, and the advertising message.

## THE CONSUMER

Not all purchases are made because we are influenced by advertising. Although advertising has a considerable effect on our consuming behavior, other factors provide an equally powerful impetus in determining what we buy. These factors include buying habits and brand loyalties; personality characteristics; and the social, ethnic, and age groups to which we belong.

*Buying habits and brand loyalty.* Many people, having chosen a particular brand (perhaps through the influence of advertising), persist in buying only that brand, sometimes for life. Buying the same brand habitually is much simpler than continually deciding among competing brands. Loyalty to one brand makes it difficult for promoters of competing brands to reach these consumers. They are relatively impervious to advertisements for brands other than those to which they are loyal.

*Personality characteristics.* Consumer psychologists have conducted a great deal of research on the personality characteristics of people who use particular brands of products. Obviously, this information is valuable to manufacturers. For example, if an advertiser knows how the people who prefer one brand of shampoo differ from those who prefer another brand, an advertising campaign that focuses on these distinctive characteristics can be designed.

One psychological study investigated the personality characteristics of nine thousand people, and correlated their scores on a personality test with cigarette smoking behavior. Smokers scored higher than nonsmokers on needs for sex, aggression, and achievement. Among smokers, those who preferred filter cigarettes were higher on dominance and achievement needs and lower on aggression and independence needs than those who preferred nonfilter cigarettes. If a manufacturer planned to introduce a new brand of filter cigarette, an effective advertising appeal could be based on the personality characteristics of the filter cigarette smoker.

Another study measured three personality factors in a group of male subjects: compliance, aggressiveness, and detachment. These factors were correlated with product preferences. Compliant people were found to be much more likely to use mouthwash, Dial soap, and Bayer aspirin. Aggressive people preferred Van Heusen shirts, Old Spice deodorant, and manual instead of electric razors. Detached people preferred tea much more than the other two types.

Not all studies of personality characteristics have found significant differences. Some studies reveal no personality differences in preferences for different products or brands. It may be the case that no personality differences exist in the preference for certain products.

*Social class.* Many studies from sociology and psychology have revealed that members of different social classes often behave in different ways. People of different social classes have different values and goals, religious and political philosophies, prejudices and attitudes. They live, think, and act differently, and thus it would be surprising if their consumer behavior did not also differ.

People in the upper classes, secure in their wealth and social position, often think it vulgar to display their affluence. They may drive old cars and wear traditional clothing that does not reflect the latest fashion trends. Striving, middle-class people often go deeply in debt in order to display, through automobiles, homes, and clothing, the affluence they really do not have but wish other people to think they have.

One study compared the shopping behavior of more than one thousand female department store customers and found striking differences between upper-class and lower-class shoppers. Upper-class shoppers relied on newspaper advertising to help with shopping to a much greater degree than did lower-class shoppers. More than 90 per cent of the upper-class shoppers used advertisements as compared to 39 per cent of the lower-class shoppers.

Another difference was the frequency of shopping. Upper-class shoppers made many more shopping trips during a year. Also, upper-class shoppers preferred department stores and rarely patronized discount stores. Most lower-class shoppers used discount stores as well as department stores.

Social class differences in consumer behavior today are not so obvious as they once were. The incomes of those in the lower classes have been steadily rising. This relatively greater affluence, and the widespread acceptance of installment or credit buying, has given lower- and middle-class consumers more opportunities to emulate the upper classes in buying behavior (or in buying what they believe the upper classes are buying).

*Ethnic group membership.* Consumer psychologists have found significant differences in the buying behavior of people of different ethnic backgrounds. Blacks, Puerto Ricans, Orientals, Mexican Americans, Italian Americans, Jews, and other groups display consistent and distinct preferences for certain brands and products. Many products are designed and marketed specifically for different ethnic groups. Because some of these groups represent large numbers of potential customers, advertisers are keenly interested in identifying their preferences.

For example, blacks constitute approximately 12 per cent of the population of the United States. In many large cities, they are more than 90 per cent of the inhabitants. This is a very large market with a lot of purchasing power. Since the 1960s, when advertisers recognized the size of the market, many studies have been conducted to determine product preferences of black consumers.

It has been found that blacks purchase more than half of all the Scotch whiskey sold in the United States, nearly half of all the grape soda, and substantially more cooked cereals, cream, rice, frozen vegetables, and syrup than nonblack consumers. Blacks also tend to purchase higher-priced automobiles than whites with comparable incomes.

Black women purchase more household cleaning products than do white women, and they are a stronger market for "keep-in-touch" products, such as greeting cards, stationery, cameras, and film.

Ethnic group differences are particularly evident in food purchases. Italian and Jewish women strongly prefer fresh foods over processed and packaged foods; black women, however, buy more convenience foods. Differences have also been found with frozen food dinners. Jewish and Italian women rarely use them, black women use them to a moderate degree, and the greatest sales are to Puerto Rican women. Knowledge of such preferences is important to food producers and distributors and to supermarkets, for it determines what products should be stocked in different neighborhood stores.

*Age.* Common sense and experience tell us that people are interested in different kinds of products at different ages. Our clothing, entertainment, food preferences, and leisure activities change as we grow older. Advertisers are aware of this and they know that people at different ages respond to different advertising appeals. A sixty-year-old may not be as concerned as an eighteen-year-old with personal attractiveness to the opposite sex, for example. Thus, older people may not be persuaded to buy grooming products by advertisements that feature youthful music and life-styles. You can easily pick out magazine advertisements or television commercials that are oriented toward different age groups.

A large portion of the advertising in the United States is directed at the youth market, particularly the teenage audience, which spends a lot of money each year for certain kinds of products. Advertisers spend millions of dollars trying to reach these consumers. Today's youth are not only more affluent than those of past generations, but they are also better educated and more sophisticated with regard to advertising practices. These factors influence the kinds of advertising appeals that will persuade them to buy a product.

Young people are more demanding consumers today than their parents were at that age, placing greater emphasis on the value, quality, and durability of the products they buy. They do not respond well to advertising appeals that emphasize prestige and status. They prefer ads characterized by humor, simplicity, and candor. Presenting products in a straightforward, clever manner, and admitting to imperfections, seems to be an effective way of reaching the youth market.

Considerable advertising is aimed at children. Even though young children buy little on their own, they can strongly influence the purchases their parents make. Modern society teaches children to be consumers from a very early age. Studies show that children display evidence of consumer behavior as early as the age of seven. At first, as with all other behaviors, children imitate the buying behavior of their parents. Once they begin school, the behavior of their peers provides another powerful model for them to follow. Adultlike consumer behavior patterns are solidly formed around the age of eleven.

Marketing products to children takes a number of approaches. Many young children accompany parents to the supermarket, and there they find manufacturers ready for them. Products that appeal to children are deliberately placed on lower shelves, where they can be readily seen and picked up. Pencils, book covers, and T-shirts with a product name boldly displayed on it are often given away to children.

Most advertising for children appears on television, usually on programs produced directly for children. The United States population includes approximately 48 million persons age thirteen and under, and they spend more time watching television than attending school or doing anything else. The average American child sees more than 25,000 television commercials each year, and it is estimated that $400 million is spent annually to produce these advertisements. Although there is controversy over the ethics of advertising for children, there is no denying its effectiveness in selling products. Studies of the effects of television commercials show that they definitely increase a child's desire for many of the products advertised.

The immediate effect of television advertising is positive for the advertisers, but the long-range effects may not be. Because of their early and massive exposure to commercials, children learn quickly to distrust advertising and, consequently, to be skeptical of other segments of society as well. Negative attitudes toward commercials develop by the age of five and become even more negative as children get older.

At first, children are merely annoyed by commercials, but this attitude soon changes to distrust and suspicion. By the time they are seven, children have begun to reject advertisements that are misleading; they have learned that many advertising claims and promises are not true and they feel cheated. However, children also begin to realize that society, usually represented by their parents, does not believe that there is anything wrong with misleading advertising. Thus, they learn that hypocrisy, deception, and outright lying may often be sanctioned by society. This conclusion conflicts with the moral principles they are being taught at home, in church, and at school. Children perceive that society is teaching them one code of conduct and living by another one.

Of course, children see many forms of hypocrisy in addition to television commercials. Their parents may cheat on income tax returns or break traffic laws, and then brag about getting away with it. Politicians may lie and teachers may turn out to be less than perfect. All of these examples reinforce a child's growing cynicism. Thus, advertising plays a potentially harmful part in determining the values children learn.[2]

It must be noted that despite the negative attitudes children develop toward commercials, the advertisements still accomplish their intended task; children buy or urge their parents to buy many of the products they see in the television commercials they neither like nor trust.

## THE PRODUCT

The second major component of consumer psychology concerns the product itself, the ways in which it is packaged and promoted. Our concern is not with the quality of the product's ingredients or construction, but with external factors that can be manipulated by advertisers in order to increase sales. These include the package in which the product is contained, the trademark, the product's image, and the price.

*The package.* Many products appear in boxes or other kinds of packaging. Therefore, it is the package and not the product itself that the customer sees at the time of decision. The attractiveness of the package may be the key factor in the decision to purchase. A consumer looking for cookies in a supermarket faced with a dizzying display of several dozen kinds may not remember the television commercial seen the previous night for a particular brand. In this case, the package—perhaps a

---

[2] See T. G. Bever, M. L. Smith, B. Bengen, and T. C. Johnson, "Young Viewers' Troubling Response to TV Ads," *Harvard Business Review,* **53**(6) (1975), 109–120.

mouth-watering picture of a mound of chocolate chips—may well make up the customer's mind.

The saying that we cannot judge a book by its cover may be true, but nevertheless we all tend to make decisions on the basis of a cover, an external appearance, or a package. In dealing with other people we evaluate them on the basis of superficial features such as their clothing or make of automobile.

We evaluate many of the products we buy on the same basis. Consumer psychologists have found many instances of people judging a product by the wrapping or package in which it appears, not by its quality. For example, two groups of people were asked to judge the taste of coffee. One group was served coffee from a modern electric coffee maker while the other group was served from an antique coffee urn. The coffee was the same for both groups; the only difference was the container. The group that had its coffee poured from the antique urn judged it to be much better tasting than the group that had coffee poured from the electric coffee maker.

Even the size of a product (which, like a package, can be manipulated independently of the ingredients or components) can affect perceived quality. Groups of physicians and patients were shown pills of two different sizes and asked to rate their potency. On the basis of size alone, both groups judged the larger pills to be the more powerful. In fact, the smaller pills were the more powerful.

A well-known consumer psychologist, Ernest Dichter, noted that a properly designed package must satisfy six criteria [3]: (1) convenience: a package should never be too bulky or heavy but should hold just enough of the product to satisfy the average user's needs; (2) adaptability: the package must be of a shape and size that fits the space normally available for it (for example, medicine bottles should not be too tall for medicine cabinets, the place in which they are usually kept); (3) security: the package must assure the consumer that the product is of high quality; (4) status or prestige: packages must allow consumers to feel that their sense of worth and esteem (in the eyes of others) is enhanced; (5) dependability: packages must assure consumers that they can depend on the product and its manufacturer; and (6) aesthetic satisfaction: the design, shape, and color of the package must be pleasing to consumers.

The proper design of a package can be determined through research on consumer reactions to existing and new packages. Subjects may be asked to examine a package and to report the images and feelings they associate with it. Survey and in-depth methods are also used to determine package preferences. Products sometimes fail in the marketplace not because they are of poor quality, but because of poor packaging.

[3] E. Dichter, "The Man in the Package," *Consumer Behavior in Theory and in Action*, ed. S. H. Britt (New York: John Wiley, 1970), pp. 356–360.

Psychology Applied to Consumer Behavior

*The trademark.* A trademark that is widely known to the consuming public will greatly facilitate sales because it serves as a symbol of all the feelings and images that have come to be associated with the product. An easily recognized trademark stimulates people to recall the product and its image, without any additional advertising message.

Most trademarks are simply the name of the product—such as Coca-Cola, Kleenex, or Xerox—but it sometimes happens that a trademark is so effective that it comes to stand for all brands of the same kind of product. For example, to many people "xerox" means any kind of photocopier, and "levis" means any kind of jeans. When this happens, the company loses its unique status, along with a share of the market.

Sometimes a distinctive slogan, such as "I'd walk a mile for a Camel," becomes so strongly associated with a product that it too becomes a trademark. Also, an unusual advertising format or jingle can take on the characteristics of a trademark.

Because trademarks can be so effective in increasing the sales of a product, consumer psychologists devote considerable time to studying their effectiveness. They are concerned with two aspects of trademarks: ease of identification and psychological meaning.

Studies dealing with the ease and speed of trademark identification use a piece of laboratory apparatus known as a *tachistoscope*. This device flashes trademarks (or any other stimulus psychologists wish to study) to the subject very briefly, as fast as a fraction of a second. Various designs and labels can be studied in this way to determine which can be recognized by consumers in the shortest possible time.

Figure 8–1. Trademarks. (Courtesy of Levi Strauss & Co., and U.S. Pioneer Electronics Corp.)

The psychological meaning of a trademark is studied by having people free-associate to it; they are asked to say the first word that comes to mind when they see a trademark or hear a jingle. The psychological meaning of a trademark can be a potent factor in sales and is closely related to the concept of product image.

*The product's image.* By the image of a product we mean the collection of ideas, thoughts, and feelings that are associated with the product; what we might call the product's personality. Different products, or different brands of the same product, project different images to consumers. The "personality" of a Porsche Carrera is different from that of a Ford station wagon. Each represents a different life-style and is designed to appeal to a different consumer group.

Advertisers spend a great deal of money to develop product images with which people will want to identify. So important is the image of the product that a successful image has brought companies from obscurity to prosperity almost overnight. In fact, the image can be more important than the characteristics of the product itself.

A well-known example of the effects of a product's image is the case of Hathaway shirts. A relatively unknown shirt manufacturer became an instant and continuing success because of the new image for its product. Through a series of advertisements, in which the shirts were modeled by a distinguished-looking man wearing a black eye patch, the company projected an image of sophistication.

It is not difficult to transmit an image to the public through various advertising channels. What is much more difficult is the determination of what the image should be. What personality should be stressed? Only proper research can determine this.

One way to study product images is to interview consumers, questioning them in detail about their thoughts about various products. The purpose is to uncover hidden feelings, both positive and negative, that may exist toward the products.

A more objective way to investigate product images uses a checklist composed of a number of descriptive adjectives. Consumers are shown or told about a particular product and asked to select the adjectives that best describe their feelings toward the product.

*The price.* Although the ingredients or components of a product and the cost of manufacturing it dictate the minimum price at which the company will make a profit, manufacturers do have some flexibility in deciding how much to charge. The price may determine whether or not consumers buy the product, regardless of the product's quality or the advertising messages used to promote it.

Consumers frequently use price as a measure of quality. Many people believe that the more a product costs, the better it must be; they automatically select the highest-priced brands. Knowing this, many manufacturers deliberately charge a price for their product that is higher than their competitors' prices. Consumer psychologists have discovered that when people are shown identical products, which differ only in price, they will often judge the more expensive product to be higher in quality.

Another way in which manufacturers manipulate prices is to charge a price lower than the competition when they introduce their brand of a product. The theory behind this introductory-offer technique is that shoppers will continue to buy the product out of habit when the price is later raised. This may sound clever, but it does not work. Sales of new items are high during introductory-offer periods, but they drop sharply when the price is raised to the level of competing brands. However, if the prevailing market price is charged from the outset (no low-price introductory-offer period), sales for the new brand are usually higher than those of competing brands.

Many shoppers do not consider price at all when they buy certain items, especially in grocery stores. Most people do not examine prices of breakfast cereals and are unaware of current prices of other food items when questioned about them. For products such as Coca-Cola and coffee, however, most shoppers can report current prices accurately.

## THE ADVERTISING MESSAGE

The third component of consumer psychology is the advertising message. This is the link between product and consumer. The function of the advertising message is to persuade or seduce people to decide to buy a particular product. On a larger scale, advertising attempts to manipulate people by persuading them that they need a new product or gadget that they had not needed or wanted before.

Advertising is a big business; more than four thousand advertising agencies serve more than four million firms in the United States. Most of the money spent by these firms on advertising is on six major media or outlets. These are, in the order of their frequency of use, newspapers, television, direct mail, magazines, radio, and outdoor advertising (such as billboards).

It is important to remember that the money spent on advertising supports much of our mass entertainment and information industries. Television and radio programs are funded almost entirely by advertising. Newspapers and magazines rely primarily on advertising revenues. Without this financial base we would have to pay exorbitant prices for reading and viewing materials.

Advertising messages may be grouped in three categories: direct sell, awareness, and image.

Most advertising is of the *direct sell* type. This includes appeals made directly to consumers to get them to buy a product. The majority of the advertisements we see in the newspaper or hear on the radio are of this type.

Some advertising is designed to create consumer *awareness* of a new or improved product, or of a new package or price change. Awareness advertising tries to establish and reinforce the product's brand name, to maintain the name of the product or the company in the public's awareness.

A third type of advertising is designed to establish an *image* for a product, a service, or an organization. We discussed previously the importance of the image of a product in terms of increasing sales. For example, an automobile is rarely advertised as merely a means of transportation. Instead, the advertising focuses on the image of the product, how the model will make its owner feel younger, sportier, or higher in status than people who drive other kinds of cars.

A significant portion of image advertising is devoted not to consumer products but to companies and institutions. The goal of this institutional advertising is to persuade the public that a business firm is truly a benefactor to the community or the nation. For example, advertisements sponsored by major oil companies may stress safe driving habits, or try to show how the companies are improving the environment. Institutional advertising attempts to generate goodwill for the organization, which may later be translated into higher sales for its products or services, but these advertisements are not for the purpose of selling products directly.

Different *advertising appeals* may be used for advertisements in each of these three categories. The appeal of an advertisement refers to what the product promises to do for the purchaser, what needs or motivations it will satisfy.

There are a great many human needs, which psychologists consider to be of two general types: the primary or innate needs, and the secondary or learned needs. The primary needs, because they are inborn, are found in everyone. They include the needs for food, water, air, safety, and sexual satisfaction.

The secondary needs are learned; therefore, not everyone has the same secondary needs. They differ from one person to another and from one culture or subculture to another. Some examples of secondary needs are the needs for achievement, social approval, affiliation, status, and prestige.

Secondary needs depend a great deal on a person's past experiences. A girl who grows up in Beverly Hills, California, will develop a different set of adult needs from a boy who grows up in Harlem in New York City. Advertisers try to develop messages that will satisfy the right secondary needs, but with such diversity among them, this may be

Steam helping to recover trapped oil in old wells. At a cost, to date, of $45 million in this one field alone.

Maurice F. Granville,
Chairman, Texaco Inc.

We're going all out to get you the energy you need. That includes more than exploring. More than drilling. And more than developing alternate sources of energy.

We're going back to reopen old oil wells. They're wells that were no longer productive and we had no practical way to recover the oil we knew remained. But today, we are able to recover some of that oil.

At one field here in the U.S., we are using steam as a recovery method. We're forcing steam down 44 wells there. The heat and pressure of the steam work to help loosen the oil and aid recovery.

It's an enormously difficult and expensive operation. So far, we've spent $45 million and we estimate we'll have to spend about another $147 million before the field is depleted. And it's just one of the many ways we're working hard to meet your energy needs for the future.

**TEXACO**

### We're working to keep your trust.

Figure 8–2. Company image advertising. (Courtesy of Texaco Inc.)

difficult. However, the needs that will be satisfied by a particular product help determine the kind of appeal the advertisement should use.

In many advertisements, it is easy to uncover the need the product is intended to satisfy. A toothpaste ad asks about your love life, a mouthwash or shampoo guarantees that the opposite sex won't be able to leave you alone, and an after-dinner drink consumed in a penthouse apartment assures you of sophistication. A product endorsed by celebrities invites your identification with their personal attributes or achievements. These advertisements are direct, even blatant, about the needs they promise to satisfy.

Consumer psychologists continually study consumer needs in order to define those that may emerge from changing social values, and to make certain that their advertising campaigns are oriented toward the correct needs. Sometimes research can lead to a drastic change in an advertising appeal. For example, the theme expressed in advertisements for a well-known household cleaner stressed its cleaning speed. It got the job done so quickly, said the ads, that the homemaker had time for more enjoyable and rewarding pursuits.

The product was not selling well and a consumer study was undertaken. People who used the cleaner were questioned about their feelings and attitudes toward the product. Few of them reported that they used the product because of its cleaning speed. More than half of the people interviewed liked the product because it was gentle to their hands. Obviously, the wrong appeal was being used and a new advertising campaign was prepared to emphasize the beauty of a person's hands as a result of using the product. Sales increased substantially.

Once the nature of the advertising appeal has been determined, a choice must be made about the manner in which the appeal can best be presented or expressed. Two general types of presentation are the positive appeal and the negative appeal.

A *positive appeal* shows that something pleasant or desirable happens to the consumer who uses the product. In marketing a new bath soap, for example, a commercial might depict a person who has lots of dates or is the center of attention at parties because he or she uses the product. A *negative appeal* shows that something unpleasant or undesirable happens to the person who does not use the product. In the case of the new bath soap, a negative advertisement might depict someone who sits home alone on Saturday night because he or she failed to use the product.

Negative appeals are useful with many products, unless the unpleasant consequences are extreme. For example, in a campaign to promote safe driving, graphic pictures of gruesome automobile accidents were not effective. The pictures distracted people from the theme and appeal of the advertising message.

# REGGIE JACKSON DRIVES A RABBIT??

Reggie appreciates the finer things in life.

He has a collection of fine cars, including a Rolls-Royce, but the car he really depends on is his VW Rabbit. Why?

"Because it holds everything I want it to hold. And it does everything I want it to do."

That's high praise, coming from a man who re-wrote baseball history. And who can clearly afford to drive any car (or cars) he pleases.

It's also high praise coming from a man who's 6'2," weighs 210 pounds and doesn't like his style cramped. By any body or any thing.

We understand exactly why he's so impressed: Rabbit has more trunk space and glass area than a Cadillac Seville. And more people room than 40 other cars on the market.

Reggie knows enough about cars to appreciate Rabbit's front-wheel drive for better tracking, especially in bad weather. To say nothing of front disc brakes, an independent stabilizer rear axle and rack-and-pinion steering.

He also knows magic when he sees it; his Rabbit "L" is the only car he could buy that has seat belts that actually put themselves on.

It's an impressive list, to say the least. But Reggie, in his own way, says it most:

"The only one I have to impress —is me."

## VOLKSWAGEN DOES IT AGAIN

©VOLKSWAGEN OF AMERICA, INC.

Figure 8–3. Celebrity advertising. (Courtesy of Volkswagen of America, Inc., 1978.)

A simple but effective approach is to combine positive and negative appeals in the same advertisement, first showing the negative consequences of not using the product followed by the positive consequences of using it. For example, a television commercial may begin with a teenager complaining to a friend about how he never has any dates. The

I was flat

till I went fluffy with Prell Concentrate.

Say these fingers are hairs.

Dirt and oil deposit in here between them

and make hair go flat like this.

Prell Concentrate® leaves no deposits, nothing to flatten hair. So your hair fluffs full. No shampoo leaves your hair fuller.

Go from flat to fluffy with Prell Concentrate.

© 1977 The Procter & Gamble Company

Figure 8–4. Negative appeal/positive appeal advertising. (Reprinted by permission of The Procter & Gamble Company.)

friend, who apparently never goes anywhere without carrying a bottle of mouthwash, recommends the product. The commercial ends with the previously dateless person grinning as he returns home from a successful date. His whole life has been changed, just by using the product.

Sex in advertising, featuring attractive men and women in seductive poses and sensuous surroundings, is used to sell a variety of products. However, this type of appeal does not seem to be effective. The value of sexy images in advertising is accepted on faith; there is little research support for it.

Research has shown that sex in advertising has a high attention-getting value for both men and women. Consumers were studied as they looked at magazine advertisements. When there were several ads on the same page, most people looked first at the ads that contained a hint of sex. So far, this sounds positive; sex in advertising obviously gets our attention. However, its usefulness apparently ends at that point because it turns out that the wrong audience reads the advertising message that accompanies a sexy picture. Provocative pictures of women, designed to attract men to an advertisement, do so, but many more women than men actually read the advertising message. Similarly, women look at the ads containing pictures of handsome men, but more men than women read the message.

More discouraging research showed a very low rate of recall for advertising messages with sexy pictures. In one study, two groups of men were shown several ads, some with sexy illustrations and some without. Later, they were shown the same ads with the brand names deleted and asked to name the product. After twenty-four hours there was no difference in recall between those who had seen the sexy ads and those who had seen the nonsexy ones. A week later they were questioned again and it was found that those who had seen the sexy ads had forgotten much more than those who had seen the nonsexy ones.

Despite its widespread use, sex in advertising does not seem to be very effective as an advertising appeal. The wrong audience reads the message and, although many people enjoy looking at the ads, they do not remember the message.

## TELEVISION PROGRAMMING

Consumer psychologists devote much effort to studying the effectiveness of television as a vehicle for presenting advertisements. The stakes are high because television advertising time is very expensive. Advertisers want to push their products on the most popular programs, the ones with the larger audiences, and so they are continually concerned about two aspects of television viewing: reactions to new programs, and audience size and reactions to current programs.

*Predicting reactions to new programs.* Often, before a new television series is aired, it is pretested to determine the reactions of a representative sample of television viewers. While the people watch the pilot film of the series, they indicate their feelings about every aspect of the program.

Viewers are given control devices that usually contain two push buttons. Every time they see a scene they like, they press one button; when they see something they do not like, they press the other button. When neither button is pressed, it means that the viewers are neutral or indifferent to what is being shown. Each control device is linked to a recorder and a permanent record of individual responses is made. Analysis is conducted on two levels: the minute-by-minute or scene-by-scene reaction and the reaction to the program as a whole.

Based on this information, television producers can alter or delete scenes and incidents that were disliked and add more desirable material. The effectiveness of the results, however, depends on how representative the sample is of the general viewing audience. Assuming a high degree of representativeness, this technique is excellent for predicting audience reaction to new television programs.

*Determining audience size and reactions to current programs.* Consumer psychologists survey audience reactions daily to the programs shown on television. The results of these interviews and polls determine not only which programs will remain on the air and which will be canceled, but they also influence the cost of television advertising. Programs that receive higher ratings are considerably more expensive to sponsor than those that receive lower ratings.

Several techniques are used to determine audience size and reactions. The simplest and most direct way is to question television viewers by mail or by telephone. Mail surveys are not often used because few mailed questionnaires are returned. Telephone surveys are used very frequently. Viewers may be asked to name the program they are watching at the moment of the telephone call, or asked what program(s) they watched recently, such as on the previous night.

Some television viewing research uses a mechanical device to record television viewing automatically. This eliminates the need to question the viewers directly. The device is attached to the television sets of a representative sample of viewers and it records the times the sets are on and off and the channels to which they are tuned. This technique is basic to the Nielsen television ratings, which have a powerful influence on decisions to cancel programs. The Nielsen device is called an "audimeter," and it is attached to television sets in 1170 homes.

There are several problems with the mechanical approach. A recorder tells the researchers which channels were selected at what times, but it does not tell which family members were watching television. In fact, it cannot tell if *anyone* was watching television. Some people leave a television set on because they like some sound in the house, or use it as a baby-sitter for infants and children. Therefore, the information provided by mechanical recorders can be misleading because it is not known with certainty how many people in the sample actually watched a particular program.

Another technique for measuring audience size and reactions assesses attitudes toward various programs rather than actual viewing behavior. In this approach, a representative sample of viewers complete questionnaires at the end of every month. The questionnaires deal with all network programs shown during the month, including those the viewer did not see. Each program is rated by each viewer on a six-point scale, ranging from "one of my favorites" to "never seen." A television quotient (TVQ) is calculated for each program by dividing the number of people in the sample who said the program was one of their favorites by the number of people who did not see the program. TVQs may be computed for the total viewing audience and for different segments of an audience such as children, adults, males, and females.

The results of these calculations are often used to determine program schedules. It often happens that a program people say they like does not draw many viewers because it is shown at the same time as a more popular program. In such a case, moving the program to a different time slot usually increases the size of the viewing audience.

## HOW EFFECTIVE IS ADVERTISING?

A basic question must be asked about advertising: Does it work? In other words, is all the effort, money, and time devoted to advertising truly worthwhile? Does advertising cause sales to increase?

This is difficult to answer for two reasons. First, many advertising agencies and the companies for which they work do not know if their advertising campaigns were successful. Surprisingly, little research is conducted to investigate the success of an advertising campaign, despite the availability of appropriate research methods. Most advertising agencies do not even establish objective criteria against which the success of a campaign can be evaluated. Most advertising agencies make extravagant claims of success, but rarely are these claims supported by research.

Second, most companies maintain secrecy about the success or failure of their advertising campaigns. They do not want competitors to learn of advertising successes that have resulted from a new technique or appeal, and they do not want to publicize failures.

One of the few attempts to measure the effects of advertising did not produce encouraging or positive results. An analysis was made over a ten-year period of 108 products that had been advertised in eight countries. The criterion used to evaluate the campaigns' success was whether they led to an increase in sales.

The results of the study showed that a 1 per cent increase in the amount of money spent on advertising yielded no more than a 0.25 per cent increase in sales, not a high rate of return. Additional increases in the amount of money spent on advertising yielded diminishing returns. Thus, doubling the advertising budget never caused a doubling of sales. The companies studied did increase their sales through advertising, but it is questionable whether the amount of increase in sales warranted the greater advertising expenditures.

Other research to measure advertising success dealt with individual promotions or different styles of advertisements. In one study, thirteen different advertisements were mailed to two groups of women, randomly selected from the general population. One group received an ad every week for thirteen weeks; the other group received an ad every four weeks for one year. The purpose of the study was to determine if the different rates of exposure to the ads affected the ability to remember them. Through telephone interviews, subjects were questioned about an ad to see how much of it they could recall. Those who had received the ads every week remembered much more of the content than those who had received the ads every four weeks.

We might have predicted, on the basis of common sense, that the more often we see something, the better we will remember it. However, as we have noted in several instances, common sense may be unfounded. Only when commonsense beliefs are verified by sound psychological research, such as this study on advertisement recall, can we truly have confidence in them.

Another study investigated the effects of advertising on the shopping behavior of more than five hundred women. We discuss this study in order to demonstrate how such research can be performed and how advertising affects our behavior. The women had made at least one shopping trip during the month preceding the study, and they were interviewed in detail about them.

One finding dealt with the low overall influence of advertising on shopping behavior. Only 24 per cent of the purchases had been made on the basis of information supplied through some form of advertising. However, the influence of advertising was high for certain products, such as appliances, toys, furniture, and automobile accessories. These items were purchased relatively infrequently and so shoppers had little current information about different brands and prices. Hence they relied on advertising for information.

For other items, such as shoes and personal accessories, advertising use was as low as 10 per cent. These items are purchased more frequently than appliances or furniture, and shoppers knew much more about them from their own experience. Thus, they did not feel the need to rely on advertising.

Another factor related to the use of advertising was product price. The more expensive the product, the greater was the use of advertising information. However, even for the most expensive items, advertising was used no more than 50 per cent of the time.

A comparison was made between shoppers who relied heavily on advertising and those who did not. It was found that people who used advertising more frequently were better informed about the products they bought, shopped at more than one store, and were much more concerned about price than people who used advertising less frequently.

What can we conclude about the effectiveness of advertising? In general, advertising may not return the investment made in it, but it can be effective for certain products under certain conditions. For other products and situations it is of limited value. We know that advertising is a visible and vital part of our society and our economy. It touches our lives in many ways, and consumer psychologists continue to play an important role in its development and application.

## SUMMARY

The activities of consumer psychologists affect our daily lives as consumers, and we are all exposed to the advertisements developed to promote the products society offers. We are bombarded by as many as fifteen hundred advertisements every day, although we may attend to no more than a dozen of them. Consumer psychologists are interested in the communications link between the producers and the consumers of goods, and continually study human needs, desires, and reactions to advertisements and products.

*Research methods* in consumer psychology include surveys and public opinion polls, in-depth methods, and studies of behavior. *Surveys* deal with what people say they will do—attitudes, opinions, and feelings—rather than with actual behavior. They are subject to error because people may say one thing and do another. Through projective devices, *in-depth methods* attempt to probe unconscious motivations and feelings. Instead of asking people what they like or plan to buy, the *behavioral* approach observes what people actually do. Four methods are used: *sales records*, although sales figures do not allow for the control of other factors that could influence sales; *observation of purchases*, in which shopping behavior is observed; *brand identification and preference*, which attempts to determine if consumers can distinguish among various brands of a product; and *coupon returns,* to test the effectiveness of newspaper and magazine advertisements.

Three components of consumer psychology are the consumer, the product, and the advertising message. Studies of *consumers* deal with personal factors that influence buying behavior: buying habits and brand loyalty, personality characteristics, social class, ethnic-group membership, and age. Many consumers develop a *loyalty* to one brand. This means that their shopping preferences are determined by habit. They are relatively uninfluenced by advertising for brands other than those to which they are loyal. *Personality characteristics* are sometimes associated with preferences for certain products or for certain brands of the same product. These can be determined by correlating scores on personality tests with product preferences. People in different *social classes* and *ethnic groups* buy different products, shop in different stores, and respond to different kinds of advertising appeals. *Age* influences shopping preferences and much advertising is oriented toward children and youth. Evidence shows that children begin to distrust television commercials by the time they are seven years old, yet they still desire to have the products advertised.

The *product* is subject to much manipulation by advertisers to boost sales. Aspects of the product of interest to consumer psychologists include the package, the trademark, the image, and the price. The *package* in which a product appears can influence sales because a product's quality is often judged on the basis of the package. Packages should meet the following criteria: convenience, adaptability, security, status, dependability, and aesthetic satisfaction. The *trademark* serves as a symbol for the image of the product. That *image* (the product's personality) encompasses the ideas, thoughts, and feelings that people associate with the product. The problem facing advertisers is to determine the image that best fits a particular product. *Price* is often used by consumers as an index of quality; many people believe that the more a product costs, the better it must be. For some items, however, price is not considered in purchasing decisions.

The *advertising message* is the third component of consumer psychology. Three categories of advertising are *direct sell,* in which a direct appeal is made to consumers to buy a product; *awareness,* to make consumers aware of a new or improved product or a new package or price; and *image,* to establish a personality for a product, service, or organization. Much image advertising is devoted to enhancing the goodwill of companies and institutions.

*Advertising appeals* should be based on the human needs or motivations the product promises to satisfy. There are two kinds of needs: *primary or innate needs* (physiological needs shared by everyone) and *secondary or learned needs* (social-psychological needs that vary from one person or culture to another, depending on past experiences). Consumer psychologists study human needs to define them and to ensure that their advertising appeals are oriented toward the appropriate needs.

Advertising appeals may be positive or negative. *Positive* appeals show that something pleasant happens as a result of using a certain product; *negative* appeals show that something unpleasant happens as a result of not using the product. An effective approach is to combine both appeals in the same advertisement, with the positive appeal following the negative one. *Sex in advertising* is frequently used, but it attracts the wrong audience. Also, many people do not remember the content of the ads that accompany sexy illustrations.

Research is conducted on *television programming* to predict reactions to new programs and to determine audience size and reactions to current programs. Television viewing research uses mail and telephone surveys, mechanical devices to record television viewing automatically, and measures of attitudes toward various programs.

Advertising campaigns do not always result in greater sales; nevertheless, they can influence consumer behavior with regard to certain products and in certain situations.

## SUGGESTED READINGS

Baker, Michael J., and Gilbert A. Churchill, Jr. The impact of physically attractive models on advertising evaluations. *Journal of Marketing Research*, 1977, **14**, 538–555.

Blackwell, R. D. *Contemporary Cases in Consumer Behavior*. New York: Holt, Rinehart and Winston, 1976.

Bloch, C. E., and K. J. Roering. *Essentials of Consumer Behavior*. New York: Holt, Rinehart and Winston, 1976.

Blum, M. L. *Psychology and Consumer Affairs*. New York: Harper and Row, 1977.

Cadbury, N. When, where, and how to test market. *Harvard Business Review*, 1975, **53**, 96–105.

Davidson, J. H. Why most new consumer brands fail. *Harvard Business Review*, 1976, **54**, 117–122.

Dichter, E. *Packaging: The Sixth Sense*. Boston: Cahners, 1975.

Donohue, T. Effect of commercials on black children. *Journal of Advertising Research*, 1975, **15**, 41–47.

Farley, J. U., J. A. Howard, and L. W. Ring, Eds. *Consumer Behavior: Theory and Application*. Boston: Allyn and Bacon, 1974.

Jacoby, J. Consumer psychology: An octennium. *Annual Review of Psychology*, 1976, **27**, 331–358.

Kizilbash, A. H., and E. T. Garman. Grocery retailing in Spanish neighborhoods. *Journal of Retailing*, 1975–1976 (Winter), **51**, 15–21, 86.

Lambin, J. What is the real impact of advertising? *Harvard Business Review*, 1975, **53**, 139–147.

Lesser, Gerald S. Applications of psychology to television programming: Formulation of program objectives. *American Psychologist*, 1976, **31**, 135–136.

Nuckols, R. C. On the reproduction of consumer psychologists. *Professional Psychology*, 1976, **7**, 609–617.

Palmer, Edward L. Applications of psychology to television programming: Program execution. *American Psychologist*, 1976, **31**, 137–138.

Peretti, P., and C. Lucas. Newspaper advertising influences on consumers' behavior by socioeconomic status of customers. *Psychological Reports*, 1975, **37**, 693–694.

Reynolds, F. D., and W. D. Wells. *Consumer Behavior*. New York: McGraw-Hill, 1977.

Scitovsky, T. *The Joyless Economy: An Inquiry into Human Satisfaction and Consumer Dissatisfaction*. New York: Oxford University Press, 1976.

Scott, R. *The Female Consumer*. New York: Halsted Press, 1976.

Sexton, Donald E., Jr. Differences in food shopping habits by area of residence, race, and income. *Journal of Retailing*, 1974 (Spring), **50**, 37–48, 91.

Venkatesan, M., and J. Losco. Women in magazine ads: 1959–1971. *Journal of Advertising Research*, 1975, **15**, 49–54.

Villani, K. Personality/life style and television viewing behavior. *Journal of Marketing Research*, 1975, **12**, 432–439.

# Psychology Applied to Crime and Law Enforcement

**9**

The surprise raids were carried out in the early morning hours. All ten of the Stanford University students were arrested without difficulty. They were charged with felonies, advised of their rights, searched, handcuffed, and taken to the Palo Alto, California, police station. There they were fingerprinted and placed in separate detention cells.

Shortly thereafter, they were blindfolded and transferred to the Stanford County Prison. They were stripped, searched, and deloused. Each prisoner was given a uniform, bedding, soap, and a towel. In a menacing tone, the prison warden read them a list of sixteen rules and made it very clear that any infraction of the rules would lead to punishment. The students found themselves in a situation in which they had no rights; the guards had absolute power over them twenty-four hours a day. None of the students had ever been arrested before, and they felt bewildered and apprehensive about what was happening. But the worst was yet to come.

They were placed in individual, small, barren cells and chains were bolted around their ankles. The cells had no windows. Poor ventilation in the cell block allowed the odor of unwashed bodies to become very strong. The guards walked up and down past the rows of cells. Each guard seemed to be a carbon copy of every other. They wore khaki uniforms without name tags and silver reflector sunglasses to hide their eyes. The prisoners were required to call the guards "Mr. Correctional Officer," and they could never address one another by name, only by the identification number stenciled on their uniforms.

A few hours after the prisoners fell asleep, the guards woke them with shrill blasts of their whistles. They had to remain awake for a prisoner count and for questions to find out how well they had learned the rules. These counts were carried out by each shift of guards. Sometimes they lasted several hours as the bored guards amused themselves at the prisoners' expense.

The treatment was so harsh that the prisoners revolted on the morning of the second day, but there was no chance that they would succeed. Skin-chilling carbon dioxide gas was sprayed on them and the ringleaders were placed in solitary confinement. After this incident the guards became even more abusive. They never beat the prisoners, but they crushed their spirit.

Petty, meaningless rules were enforced. Prisoners were made to do push-ups (sometimes while another prisoner was sitting on them), ordered to curse one another, and their blankets were dragged through bushes laden with thorns and the prisoners were ordered to pick the thorns out.

Soon the prisoners changed. They became passive, dependent, and deferential to the guards, trying to ingratiate themselves with the guards in order to obtain privileges. They came to accept the guards' low opinion of them. They made negative and deprecating comments about one another, just as the guards were doing.

On the third day a prisoner broke down. He had periods of uncontrollable crying alternating with fits of rage. His thinking became disorganized and incoherent, and he was extremely depressed. He had to be removed from the cell block. Over the next three days, three more prisoners were removed for similar behavior. Another prisoner developed a psychosomatic rash over his entire body. At the end of six days, all of the prisoners were taken away because they were developing pathological symptoms. The Stanford County Prison had to be closed down.

When the prisoners and the guards were gone, the cell block reverted to what it had been just a few weeks earlier, the basement of the psychology building at Stanford University. The prison had been a psychological experiment designed to study the psychology of prison life.* It was planned to continue for two weeks but the prisoners—college students chosen for their high degree of maturity and emotional stability—could not tolerate the conditions. They knew what they were volunteering for, received $15 a day, and believed that they would have no problem lasting two weeks. But they had not been told that they would be arrested by actual police officers and put through all the normal arrest procedures. That unexpected stress gave the experience a highly realistic beginning.

Who were the guards who acted with such hostility and cruelty toward the prisoners? They were also college student volunteers. They, too, had been selected because of their high degree of emotional stability. When the study began, there had been no measurable differences between them and the students who served as prisoners. The choice of who would be a prisoner and who a guard was made by tossing a coin.

Not only the prisoners had changed in the experiment, but the guards had changed as well. They had been warned about the potential dangers of the

---

* P. G. Zimbardo, C. Haney, W. C. Banks, and D. Jaffe, "The Mind Is a Formidable Jailer: A Pirandellian Prison," *New York Times Magazine* (April 8, 1973), 38–60.

situation, but beyond that they received no instructions or training of any kind in how to behave toward the prisoners. All they were told was that they had to maintain order in the prison. How they accomplished that was left up to them. Every one of them behaved abusively toward the prisoners at some time during the six days, and many of them seemed to enjoy their position of superiority and control over the prisoners. Normal, bright, stable young men became bullies and sadists. They knew it was an experiment, an artificial setting, yet they behaved as though it were real.

Read what the guards had to say about their own behavior.†

> I was surprised at myself . . . I made them call each other names and clean the toilets out with their bare hands. I practically considered the prisoners cattle, and I kept thinking: "I have to watch out for them in case they try something."
>
> . . . . . . . . . . . . . . . . . . . . . . . . . . . . . . . . . . . . . . . . . . . . .
>
> I am very angry at this prisoner for causing discomfort and trouble for the others. [The prisoner had refused to eat and the guards decided to punish all the prisoners if he continued to refuse.] I decided to force-feed him, but he wouldn't eat. I let the food slide down his face. I didn't believe it was me doing it. I hated myself for making him eat but I hated him more for not eating.

Recall that these were emotionally stable college students. It was the situation, the environment, that produced their behavior, not some personal abnormality or pathology. The students were radically changed by the psychology of the prison environment. If such drastic personality and behavior changes can be induced in six days, in a situation that did not permit the excesses that routinely occur in a real prison, imagine what must happen to real guards and prisoners locked up together for years at a time. Even if few of these people were neurotics or psychopaths at the beginning of their prison experience, the situation would quickly bring about such behaviors.

Many people in the United States and other countries are locked up in prisons. Many more are victims of the crimes these people commit, or live in fear of becoming victims. Therefore, criminal behavior has a strong and direct effect on the quality of our lives, particularly for those of us who live in big cities, where crime is most prevalent. Crimes occur at the rate of more than one every minute, and the number of crimes, particularly violent ones, increases every year. Crime is higher in inner-city areas but is not confined to them; it is rapidly spreading to suburban and rural communities. The cost of a high crime rate is staggering, perhaps as high as $60 billion a year in the United States.

As many as 12 million people each year have some contact with law

† Ibid., pp. 42, 53, 56.

enforcement agencies, either because they have committed a crime or they are suspected of committing one. The majority of these people are male and at least half are juveniles. In addition, approximately 700,000 people are in prisons in the United States and nearly 2 million are on probation.

Psychologists have been interested in criminal behavior and problems of law enforcement for many years. In 1906, Sigmund Freud pointed out the value of psychology to judges. In 1908, a German psychologist at Harvard University, Hugo Münsterberg, demonstrated the value of experimental psychology for the problem of the credibility of eyewitness testimony in a book entitled *On The Witness Stand*.[1]

However, despite this early recognition of the contributions psychology could make if applied to crime and law enforcement problems, it was not until the 1970s that the effort drew sizable support from psychologists and from those actively engaged in law enforcement efforts. Increasing numbers of research studies and books in the area have appeared, and universities are offering courses as well as degree programs in the field. In 1976, the *Annual Review of Psychology*, which publishes definitive articles on topics of current interest to psychologists, contained "Psychology and the Law," the first article on the topic to be published in this source.[2]

Thus, *forensic psychology*—the application of psychology to the criminal justice system—has finally been recognized as an important area of application of psychology. Many psychologists are working full-time or as part-time consultants to police departments, courts, and prisons. University-based psychologists are conducting valuable research on a variety of aspects of criminal behavior, such as the personality and behavior patterns of murderers, sex offenders, and drug addicts; how best to treat criminal behavior; and the psychology of prison life (as exemplified by the study at the beginning of the chapter).

## PSYCHOLOGY IN POLICE DEPARTMENTS

The job of police officer is extremely stressful and requires skills, abilities, and physical and psychological courage demanded by few other occupations today. It is also one of the most important jobs for maintaining the fragile fabric of civilized society. Psychologists are making major contributions to police departments throughout the United States, primarily in four areas: selecting police officers, training police officers, counseling police officers, and preventing and detecting crime.

[1] Published by Doubleday, Page of New York.

[2] June L. Tapp, "Psychology and the Law: An Overture," *Annual Review of Psychology*, **27** (1976), 359–404.

## Selecting Police Officers

For many years, psychologists have been concerned about the problems of selecting the right person for a particular job. They have developed several selection techniques for use with nearly every kind of contemporary job (see Chapter 11). When you begin your working career you will be exposed to these selection techniques, and the kind and level of job you are offered will be determined by how well you perform on them. Selection techniques such as psychological tests, interviews, application forms, and assessment centers are used in industry, the military, and government.

Recently, these techniques have been applied to the selection of the best candidates for the job of police officer. Tests of personality, intelligence, interest, and aptitude are used, as well as interview techniques, which attempt to determine how well candidates react under stress. Proper selection is crucial for police departments not only for hiring the most qualified personnel, but also for ensuring that persons who are psychologically unfit are not hired. Those whose personalities show pathological conditions—such as sadists or psychopaths—must not be allowed to become police officers. Only through proper psychological selection procedures can such people be identified before they might be hired.

## Training Police Officers

After qualified candidates have been selected, they must be trained in the police procedures necessary for them to carry out their jobs. However, in addition to this type of training, it has been recognized that police officers should receive psychological training in such areas as personality, motivation, mental illness, race relations, and techniques of interrogation. Many police departments offer formal courses in psychology taught by university professors, and encourage enrollment in other psychology courses at nearby community or four-year colleges.

Special training for police in human relations skills is also provided. Through sensitivity training (discussed in Chapter 5), police officers receive a greater understanding of themselves and of the kinds of people they will come in contact with on the street. This increased insight into the problems of minority-group members, drug addicts, alcoholics, young people, and others may radically alter for the better the way in which police officers respond to them.

## Counseling Police Officers

Police work offers many stresses and strains not found in other occupations. Also, the effects of pressures or emotional disturbances may be more dangerous to police officers (and to those with whom they deal) than to business executives or other workers. For these reasons, many police departments employ psychologists to provide counseling and psychotherapy, for both police officers and their spouses. The responsibility of the psychologist in this situation is very serious because police officers carry weapons and have tremendous power over other people. An incorrect diagnosis by the psychologist, or an inadequate course of therapy, can have harmful consequences not only to the police officer but also to those he or she may confront on the job.

That psychological counseling is necessary for police officers is made clear by these statistics. At least half of all policemen get divorced or have serious problems with their wives or girl friends. One of every five police officers is likely to become an alcoholic by the time he or she is in the late thirties or early forties. The suicide rate among police is as much as six times higher than the national average. From 10 to 35 per cent of all police officers become unfit for their jobs because of excessive aggressiveness, brutality, or severe emotional problems. Clearly, this is one group that could benefit from psychological counseling.

Often, police officers are referred to psychologists by their commanding officer, who may have noticed personality or behavioral changes or signs of deteriorating job performance. Some police officers refer themselves for the same reasons. Through psychological testing and interviewing, the psychologist must decide if the police officer can be allowed to continue on the job. Should the officer be transferred to a less stressful job, for example, from vice to traffic? Should the officer be allowed to continue to carry firearms? Is the officer capable of handling the added stress of a higher rank? Police psychologists are required to make such decisions every day. How well they do their job strongly affects the safety of our streets and neighborhoods.

## Preventing and Detecting Crime

Psychologists are continually demonstrating their ability to help police in dealing with criminal behavior. You may have seen examples of this on television; the detectives ask a psychologist for help in identifying the kind of person who has committed a particular crime. Often, psychologists are able to construct a personality profile of a criminal based on clues left at the scene of a crime or on the nature of the crime itself. This effort is especially valuable when dealing with a mentally disturbed killer or sex offender, who acts out an emotional problem through a series of identical crimes.

Psychologists are helpful to police in controlling riots and preventing their occurrence. The principles of social psychology dealing with group functioning and behavior have been applied to the prevention and control of riots in college campuses, inner-city ghettos, and prisons. Psychologists have assisted in improving communications between rioters and police and in providing effective means of handling grievances before they may be expressed in violent behavior.

The recent phenomenon of taking hostages, either for political reasons or because a person caught committing a crime uses hostages in an attempt to flee, has also become a concern of psychologists. (This situation is discussed later in the chapter.)

Another example of psychologists' contributions to crime prevention involves one of the most common crises with which police are required to deal—family disturbances. The family disturbance call, usually the result of a fight between husband and wife, is dreaded by police officers. The situation often results in both parties assaulting the police officer, leading to serious injury or death; more police officers are killed answering domestic violence calls than in any other aspect of their work.

In an attempt to reduce this type of violence, the New York City police department trained eighteen officers in one precinct in psychological techniques of handling family disputes. The month-long training, conducted at the City College of New York, included individual meetings with advanced graduate students in clinical psychology and weekly group sessions with psychologists about the procedures and skills of family crisis intervention.

The officers worked in pairs, providing round-the-clock coverage for the precinct. Whenever a family disturbance call was received, it was handled by the specially trained pairs of officers. Their police cars contained a card index file of past cases, so that the officers could quickly determine if a particular family had a history of crisis calls.

The results of the special psychological training have been dramatic. Over a twenty-two-month period, dealing with more than 1300 family disturbances, there was not a single injury to any of the officers. Also, there were no homicides in the families involved and a significant drop in the number of arrests. Intervening in family crises by skillfully applying psychological techniques of mediation rather than force was thus beneficial to both sides and also reduced crime.

## PSYCHOLOGY IN THE COURTS

Once the police have solved a crime and arrested a suspect, the drama of law enforcement moves into the courtroom, where guilt or innocence is decided. Psychologists play important roles in courtroom deliberations. Four areas of their involvement are in family courts, as expert witnesses, in determining the credibility of eyewitness testimony, and in conducting research on jury behavior.

## Psychologists in Family Courts

Family courts deal primarily with two kinds of problems: juvenile offenders, and matters arising from divorce cases such as support payments, child custody, and visitation rights. Psychologists are usually involved with the first kind of problem. Even though juveniles may (and often do) commit the same types of crimes as adults commit, they are not tried in the same courts or judged by the same standards.

Juveniles are tried separately for two reasons. First, it is assumed that children and adolescents should not be held as responsible for their actions as adults because they are immature and have not developed sufficient understanding of the consequences of their behavior. Second, it is assumed that because the personality of a juvenile is not fully developed, he or she has a better chance of being helped or rehabilitated than an adult.

Psychologists are primarily interested in diagnosing the level of intellectual and emotional functioning of the juvenile offender. Judges routinely refer youthful criminals to a psychologist for testing and evaluation, and take the psychologist's diagnosis into consideration when pronouncing sentence or ordering treatment.

The diagnostic tests used with juvenile offenders include intelligence tests (to determine the amount and kind of additional education that might benefit the offender), tests that indicate the possibility of brain damage, and personality tests.

Another kind of family court case in which psychologists are involved concerns adolescents who have not yet broken the law but whose parents are unable to control them. This is a growing problem because many children are left unsupervised for long periods of time when both parents are working. Such children may run away from home, fail to attend school, take drugs, engage in frequent sexual activities, steal from their parents or from shops, or take the family car without permission. From inner-city areas as well as affluent suburbs, many parents are bringing their uncontrollable children to court to ask that they be placed elsewhere. Psychological evaluation of these children can assist judges in determining the appropriate environment for the children, such as a foster home or a state institution.

## Psychologists as Expert Witnesses

Not all activities of psychologists in the courts take place behind the scenes. Often they are called to the witness stand to provide testimony in a trial. The number of psychologists serving as expert witnesses is growing, but some courts still question their testimony on the grounds that only a psychiatrist (who holds an M.D. degree) is qualified to testify on problems involving mental health. This controversy about the competence of psychologists to serve as expert witnesses was decided in the U.S. Court of Appeals in 1962. The judge ruled that the lack of a medical degree should not automatically disqualify psychologists from testifying in court, provided that they are properly trained and experienced.

Most psychologists who testify as expert witnesses are clinical psychologists, reporting on their evaluations of defendants based on interviews and diagnostic tests. With adult criminals, psychologists often testify about the degree of legal responsibility a person is capable of feeling for a criminal act. Psychologists have also been called to testify in automobile accident cases on the extent and nature of brain damage resulting from an accident.

Experimental psychologists also serve as expert witnesses, demonstrating the value of their research and laboratory skills in the determination of guilt or innocence. One case, which took place in England, involved an accusation of homosexuality.[3] Two police officers, hidden in a closet in a public rest room, arrested two men for engaging in a homosexual act. The defense argued that the police had mistakenly identified a pink scarf held by one of the accused as the man's penis.

The psychologist working with the defense photographed a reconstruction of the incident as it had been described by the defendants. The photographs were made under experimental conditions of different lighting and exposure times, rendering them more or less distinct. They were shown to a number of adults. The photographs made under the conditions of illumination and exposure time closest to that which existed at the time of the incident were identified as depicting indecent behavior only 12 per cent of the time. Based on this demonstration that the arresting officers could easily have been mistaken in what they saw, the case was dismissed.

Another example of the value of experimental psychology in determining what did or did not happen at the scene of a crime involved a murder case, in which a police officer testified that he had seen the defendant shoot the victim.[4] It was virtually certain that the defendant would be convicted, but the defense attorneys called upon a psychologist to provide evidence that the police officer could not possibly have seen what he said he saw.

The psychologist examined the scene of the crime at the same time of night that the murder had occurred. He found that the doorway in which it had taken place was so dimly lit that it was impossible to

[3] L. R. C. Haward, "The Psychologist in English Criminal Law," *Journal of Forensic Psychology,* **1** (1969), 11–22.

[4] R. Buckhout, "Eyewitness Testimony," *Scientific American,* **231** (December, 1974), 23–31.

identify anyone from 120 feet away, the distance at which the police officer was standing at the time of the crime.

Photographs were taken of the scene, along with measurements of the brightness in the doorway relative to other parts of the street. These figures showed that the brightness level in the doorway was less than one-fifth the light that would be provided by a candle, certainly not enough light to allow a person to be identified from a distance of 120 feet. After the psychologist's evidence was presented in court, the jury was taken to the scene of the crime. A black member of the jury stood where the black defendant had allegedly stood; the rest of the jury stood where the police officer had been. No one on the jury could identify the features of their fellow jury member. The defendant was acquitted.

In both these examples, the psychologist's testimony was based on demonstrated fact, experimental re-creations of the crimes under laboratory conditions. This is quite different from the testimony of clinical psychologists, which often contains more opinion than irrefutable fact. Clinical testimony is often challenged by the equally competent psychologist testifying for the opposing side in a trial, and the jury is left to ponder which of the expert witnesses to believe. It is much more difficult to challenge a thoroughly researched demonstration in which only the facts are at issue, not the psychologist's opinion, however expert it may be.

## Credibility of Eyewitness Testimony

In the murder case discussed previously, the defendant could easily have been convicted and imprisoned on the basis of the eyewitness testimony of a skilled, trained observer, a police officer. In this case the eyewitness was incorrect; it was physically impossible for him to have seen what he thought he saw. Yet, he was convinced of the accuracy of his testimony.

Unfortunately, this is a common phenomenon in the courtroom. Eyewitness testimony is often a key factor in a prosecutor's case. The witness's comment, "But I saw it with my own eyes," usually carries a great deal of weight with a jury. However, as psychologists have known for years, and as lawyers, judges, and police officers are slowly coming to realize, eyewitness testimony is frequently wrong. Even when two or three, or as many as five eyewitnesses agree on what they saw, they can all be mistaken. More often than the legal profession would like to admit, people have been convicted on the basis of mistaken identity and the real culprit is found some time later. Miscarriages of justice have been committed on the basis of what a witness was convinced that he or she saw.

How can mistakes occur in what seems like a straightforward process, seeing an event and reporting on it later? How can we so often be in error in interpreting what we have seen with our own eyes? The answer lies in two aspects of human functioning that psychologists have studied for at least a century: perception and memory.

Psychologists have long known that we do not perceive the world around us exactly as it is, in totally objective terms. The picture or image we have of something we see does not precisely mirror what we are looking at. Our *perception* is inaccurate and incomplete and may be distorted by our needs, fears, values, attitudes, and prejudices. An old adage states that "we see what we want to see," and psychologists have found much truth to that bit of folk wisdom.

Consider a classic study on perception, devised by Gordon Allport of Harvard University, in which a group of observers were shown, briefly, a drawing of people in a subway car. Clearly highlighted were two men who were standing and facing each other. One man was white and the other was black. The white man was holding a straight razor and was gesturing with his finger at the black man. When asked to describe the scene, half of the people who had seen it said that the black man was holding the razor. What these people had seen (what was depicted in the actual drawing) had been distorted in their perception to fit their prejudices and the stereotype that blacks, not whites, carry straight razors.

Many studies on the psychology of perception have yielded similar results, showing that many people are poor observers of the world around them.

The other aspect of human functioning that influences eyewitness credibility is *memory*. What we recall or remember of an event we have witnessed is as strongly subject to error as what we perceived in the first place. Psychological research has shown that not only do we see what we want to see, but we also remember what we want to remember. Our memories are subjective and selective, influenced by our needs, fears, values, and prejudices. The accuracy of memory is also affected by the length of time that has elapsed between witnessing an event and the attempt to recall it. In general, the longer this period of time is, the less accurate is our memory. With eyewitness testimony in a courtroom, months or even years may elapse before a witness is asked to recall at a trial what he or she had seen.

Thus, both critical processes in eyewitness testimony—perception and memory—are likely to be inaccurate. They do not provide a strong base on which to make the crucial decisions that are required in a trial.

Let us consider some of the research findings of forensic psychologists on eyewitness testimony. This type of research has a long history, dating from Hugo Münsterberg's 1908 book, *On the Witness Stand*, mentioned earlier. In a series of experiments and demonstrations in his class-room, Münsterberg found that even highly trained observers, who had been given advance warning, could not agree on what they had seen. Such disagreements occurred not only with complex scenes and events but also with simple matters such as the number of squares on a board or the amount of time elapsed between two clicking sounds. On the basis of this research, Münsterberg argued that psychologists should be allowed to test the perception and memory abilities of eyewitnesses.

These kinds of experiments have been repeated many times since Münsterberg's work, yielding similar results. For example, an incident was staged on a college campus in which a professor was attacked by a man in front of 141 witnesses.[5] The scene was filmed so that eyewitness statements could be compared with what had actually occurred.

Immediately after the assault, all eyewitnesses were questioned and asked to describe the attacker (clothing, age, weight, height) and any-thing else they could remember about the incident. The descriptions were scored for accuracy; the maximum score represented perfect per-ception and recall. The total accuracy score for the group, questioned immediately after the event and not some weeks or months later, was only 25 per cent of the maximum. These descriptions would have been of little help to the police in finding the guilty person!

Another factor that influences eyewitness testimony is the manner in which the witnesses are questioned by attorneys in the courtroom. Subtle differences in the wording of a question, leading a witness in the direction desired by the attorney, can produce dramatically different answers. For example, just substituting the word "the" for the word "a" can distort testimony. A group of observers were shown a film of a multicar accident and then questioned about what they had seen. Half of them were asked, "Did you see *a* broken headlight?" The other half were asked, "Did you see *the* broken headlight?" Twice as many who were asked about *the* headlight answered "yes" as compared to those who were asked about *a* headlight. There was no broken headlight in the film. Both questions led the observers to believe that they were being asked about something that actually existed. Using the word "the," however, implied more strongly that there had been a broken headlight.[6]

In another experiment, a group of people were shown films of traffic accidents and asked how fast the cars involved were going. However, the question was worded in different ways. Some people were asked how fast the cars were going when they *hit* each other. Other observers were asked questions that implied varying speeds; how fast the cars were going when they smashed, collided, bumped, or contacted. The

[5] Buckhout, op. cit., p. 29.

[6] E. F. Loftus, "Reconstructing Memory: The Incredible Eyewitness," *Psychology Today*, **8** (December 1974), 116–119.

eyewitness accounts of the speeds varied with the wording of the question. The highest speed was associated with the word "smashed" and the lowest speed with the word "contacted." [7] The speed had been the same in all cases; all observers had seen the same films.

Many specific factors may account for inaccuracies in eyewitness testimony. The witnesses' ages and physical conditions are important variables. Eyesight—whether a person is nearsighted, farsighted, or colorblind, for example—can affect accuracy, as can illness or fatigue at the time of the observation. Research suggests that the level of intelligence of the witness also affects accuracy; the more intelligent person is likely to produce the more reliable report.

If the eyewitness is involved in the crime or accident, rather than observing from a safe distance, the stress of being in physical danger will affect the accuracy of perception and recall. Even people who are used to stress, such as police officers or combat pilots, become poor observers when under the stress of a personal threat.

The research of forensic psychologists on eyewitness testimony has considerable practical value. If it serves no other purpose than to remind juries to be suspicious of the witness who resolutely states, "I saw it with my own eyes," then it indeed serves a worthwhile cause.

## Research on Jury Behavior

In the examples of psychology in use presented in Chapter 1, we discussed how psychologists have been able to select a jury scientifically that will be sympathetic to the defendant. However, scientific jury selection is expensive and therefore it is used in only a minority of cases today. Most defendants are tried before juries that have been selected in an unscientific manner through the challenges available to defense and prosecuting attorneys. Also, the jury pool, from which individual jury members are selected, is usually not representative of the population of a given city or community.

Psychologists study how juries behave, how they consider the evidence presented to them and the forces that influence their deliberations. Two types of psychological research relate to these questions: research by social psychologists on how small groups function, and research by forensic psychologists on how juries function.

*Research by social psychologists on how small groups function.* Social psychology is one of the largest and most active areas in the field of psychology, and many social psychologists are interested in the dynamics of small groups, that is, what happens in a group of strangers who meet to solve a specific problem. This describes a jury precisely; it is a group

[7] Ibid., p. 119

of people who have not met before and who must deal with and resolve a particular problem. Therefore, the findings of small group research conducted by social psychologists are relevant to the question of jury behavior.

There is a vast research literature dealing with the powerful effect of group pressure in changing the opinions and the behavior of individual members of a group. These studies show that when one or two members of a group hold an opinion that is opposed by all the other members of a group, these members will most likely be pressured into changing their viewpoint to agree with the majority position. It is difficult to be the only one in a group who feels or thinks a certain way, whether in an experiment, a classroom, an office, or a jury.

Social-psychological research has found that some people are more easily pressured or persuaded than others; that is, some people will more readily conform to the majority opinion. In a jury, these people would be unlikely to maintain their position if most of the other members take the opposite view. These easily persuaded people tend to feel inadequate socially, to inhibit actively their aggressive feelings, and to be frequently depressed. There are also people who are highly resistant to pressure to conform to the opinions of others. In a jury, these people may obstinately cling to their minority position, and it may become impossible for the jury to reach a unanimous verdict. These resistant people tend to show neuroticism, social withdrawal, and aggressiveness.

Another social-psychological factor that influences jury behavior is the relative social status of the jury members. Juries are often composed of people from all socioeconomic levels, from laborers who have had little formal education to highly educated professionals. Studies have found that low-status people in a group will participate much less than high-status people. Therefore, high-status people may more easily direct or lead the discussion in a jury room and be elected as jury leader. Low-status people may be reluctant to offer their own views. Therefore, all members of the jury may not have an equal voice or an equal chance of having their vote reflect their true opinion.

*Research by forensic psychologists on how juries function.* The large number of studies in forensic psychology on the behavior of juries date from the 1920s to the present. It is not possible to interfere with actual juries in their work in order to conduct psychological experiments, so most research studies take place in simulated courtroom situations. The composition of the juries and the problems with which they must deal are made as realistic as possible.

In general, it has been found that jury members cannot follow and evaluate the facts of a case as well as a trained individual such as a judge. Within a jury, women are more careful in considering evidence than men, and written evidence has been found to be more persuasive than evidence given orally.

One depressing finding is that many jury members do not understand the legal aspects of cases they are trying. In questioning actual jurors after their courtroom service had ended, it was found that 40 per cent of them said that they had not understood the instructions given them by the judges prior to their deliberations.

Jury members tend to base their decisions more on the behavior of the attorneys than on the facts of the case. They also tend to ignore a judge's admonition to disregard an item of testimony, and they are automatically suspicious of defendants simply because they are on trial. In other words, jury members may presume the defendant to be guilty until proven innocent, the reverse of what our legal system intends (that a person is innocent until proven guilty).

Confirming the social-psychological research discussed previously, studies by forensic psychologists of simulated juries and interviews with real jurors show that high-status people are almost always elected as jury leaders. High-status people tend to participate more in the deliberations and are better able to understand the judge's instructions. However, there is no forensic research evidence that one or two jury members, regardless of status, ever dominate a jury to the point where all the other members give in to them. It has also been found that virtually all those who serve as jurors take the responsibility seriously.

## PSYCHOLOGY IN PRISONS

People who are convicted of crimes in courtrooms are usually sentenced to spend time in some form of penal institution. Prisons remove offenders from society for a period of time, punish them by depriving them of their freedom, and attempt to rehabilitate them so that they may become more responsible members of the community.

Rehabilitation efforts, however, seem to be a dismal failure. Despite the best intentions and actions of many people (psychologists included), approximately 65 per cent of the people who are released from prison will return there, convicted of committing another crime. This high rate of recidivism (a repeated relapse into criminal activity) is the same regardless of the kind of rehabilitative effort made, or even if there is no attempt at rehabilitation. Because the idea of rehabilitation is noble in purpose and humanitarian in intent, it is still attempted in many prisons, despite growing evidence of its lack of success.

Psychologists are involved not only in rehabilitation but also in other aspects of prison life. For example, environmental psychologists assist in prison design in an effort to satisfy the prisoners' needs for space and privacy (see Chapter 7). Satisfaction of these needs in prison can help prevent disturbances such as riots by providing for greater physical separation among prisoners. Other psychologists, called *correctional psychologists,* work within the prison walls in daily contact with staff and inmates. They are concerned primarily with four activities: evaluating new prisoners, counseling prisoners, training the prison staff, and advising on paroles.

### Evaluating New Prisoners

One of the major tasks of correctional psychologists is to evaluate new prisoners to determine their level of intelligence, personality, and vocational aptitudes and interests. Usually, this evaluation includes a personal interview and the administration of psychological tests. The information is used by the prison staff in making decisions about where a prisoner should be housed (for example, in maximum or minimum security), whether the prisoner would benefit from psychological counseling, and what kind of prison work, vocational training, and educational opportunities are appropriate for the prisoner.

Intelligence tests and high school achievement tests are used to determine a prisoner's potential to benefit from educational programs. Many prisons offer the opportunity to obtain high school and college degrees. First, however, the staff must know how much each prisoner is likely to benefit from academic instruction so that an individual is not pushed beyond his or her capabilities.

Vocational aptitude and interest tests help to determine the trade or skill in which a prisoner should be trained, and how far he or she might progress in such training.

This kind of testing to predict behavior (such as in a vocational training program) is similar to that performed by psychologists in industry (see Chapter 11). The goal in both cases is to place the individual in the job for which he or she is best qualified.

Personality tests on incoming prisoners provide important information that can help prevent the outbreak of serious disturbances. For example, prisoners found to have suicidal or homosexual tendencies or who are unusually hostile, sadistic, or aggressive can be isolated from other prisoners so that their behavior can be monitored more effectively. Also, once identified, these prisoners can be referred to psychologists for counseling.

### Counseling Prisoners

It is estimated that at least 10 per cent of all prison inmates are actually or potentially psychotic, and that half of all prisoners have other emotional and behavioral disorders, ranging from mild to severe neuroses. If not properly treated, these disorders may intensify under the stresses and restrictions of prison life.

The methods used to deal with emotional problems of prisoners are the same as those used in any other clinical setting. They include psychoanalysis and other individual psychotherapies as well as group techniques that focus on raising consciousness and increasing personal potential. The progress of a prisoner through a program of therapy will influence any decision made about parole. Therefore, there are benefits for prisoners who demonstrate evidence of positive personality and behavior change (or who persuade the psychologist that such changes have taken place).

## Training the Prison Staff

Correctional psychologists must ensure that the staff members of a prison are aware of what the psychologists are trying to do, and of the educational, vocational, and therapy programs the psychologists are involved in. The staff should also be informed about each prisoner's progress in these programs. Prison guards should be advised about a prisoner who has a psychological problem that could be aggravated by bullying, or about a prisoner who has suicidal tendencies.

Correctional psychologists frequently offer formal courses for the prison staff on human behavior, particularly on the nature of mental illness, the psychology of crime, race relations, and sensitivity training. These courses can significantly affect the everyday behavior of the staff members and teach the guards some degree of understanding of the prisoners. Equipped with a more enlightened attitude, guards can often facilitate the therapeutic aims of the psychologists because the guards are in more regular contact with the prisoners.

Correctional psychologists can assist the prison warden in selecting people for the prison guard staff. They recommend those persons who demonstrate potential for promotion and weed out those who relate poorly to prisoners. Also, they suggest the specific prison locations in which the abilities of individual guards may be used to best advantage.

## Advising on Paroles

Providing recommendations about prisoners for the consideration of parole boards is a major responsibility of correctional psychologists. Not only do these recommendations affect the life of the prisoner, but they also may affect potential victims, should the prisoner be released and resume a life of crime. The advice of correctional psychologists is so important that few parole boards will act in the absence of a recommendation. The psychologists must decide, on the basis of a prisoner's history of offenses, behavior and adjustment during imprisonment, performance on psychological tests, and progress in therapy (if the prisoner was a candidate for therapy) how good a risk he or she is if returned to the outside world.

The recommendations of correctional psychologists also enter into decisions about furloughs or work-release programs for prisoners. Growing numbers of inmates are allowed to leave prison during the day to attend school or hold a job, returning to prison at night. In order to allow this part-time interaction with society, the correctional psychologist must have a thorough knowledge of the prisoner's emotional state and potential, information obtained from psychological tests and interviews.

## PSYCHOLOGY AND SPECIFIC CRIMES

Let us consider what psychologists have learned about specific criminal offenses: murder, rape, juvenile crime, and terrorism and hostage taking.

### Murder

Although our chances of being murdered are not as high as our chances of being killed in a traffic accident, more of us live in fear of murder. Most of us drive our cars day or night in snow or sunshine on icy roads or in heavy traffic, and we may take unnecessary chances by driving recklessly, at excessive speed, and without wearing safety belts. We seem to be indifferent to the possibility of death on the road, but many of us live in fear of being killed in the streets.

We avoid certain sections of town. If we are old or poor and live in high-crime neighborhoods, we may rarely venture outside our home. The fear of violence keeps many people prisoners in their homes and apartments, barricaded behind locks, latches, and alarm systems.

Are these fears justified? On the average, someone is murdered in the United States every half hour. In the borough of Manhattan in New York City, more people are murdered every year than in all of England, where the population is much larger. In some inner-city areas in the United States, one person out of every 500 is murdered each year. If we include the number of attempted murders, the statistics are more frightening; there are eight to nine times as many murder attempts as there are actual murders.

Most murders occur on weekends, and the most dangerous time is Saturday night. In fact, most murders take place at night. Men are more likely to be killed outside the home; women are more likely to be killed in the home, usually in the bedroom. In at least 80 per cent of all murder cases, the murderer and the victim are of the same race and are much more likely to be black than white. The majority of murder victims are black males in their twenties. Murderers are likely to have a record of previous arrests, particularly for crimes involving bodily assault and injury. Surprisingly, more than half of all murder victims also have prior arrest records. Drinking plays a role in more than 60 per cent of all murders, either on the part of the victim, the killer, or both.

Guns are used in two-thirds of all killings. The lack of gun control laws in the United States may help to explain the high murder rate. In countries such as England, which have strict gun control laws, there are many fewer murders. Knives are used in approximately 20 per cent of the murders in the United States. The remainder are carried out with weapons such as clubs, poisons, and hands or fists.

In more than half of the cases, the murderer and the victim knew each other before the crime was committed; in 25 per cent of the cases they are members of the same family. Most other victims are killed by friends and acquaintances. Statistically speaking, then, friends and relatives are much more dangerous than strangers on the street! Most murders result from an argument between friends (usually about something trivial), a fight between husband and wife, or out of jealousy. Relatively few murders occur during a robbery or the commission of another crime.

As an example of the psychological research conducted on the nature of murder, consider the case of adolescents who have committed this crime. One study of twenty teenagers found several common events in their lives prior to the killings.[8]

1. Loss of a significant relationship. Some of the teenage killers had suffered the loss of someone very close to them, on whom they had depended, shortly before they committed murder. Usually, these losses did not involve the death of the other person, but rather the "death" of a close relationship, for a variety of reasons. The person to whom the adolescent had clung for emotional support was no longer available.

2. Rapidly rising emotion. These adolescent murderers became increasingly agitated, restless, and disturbed in the days prior to their crime. Their sleeping and eating patterns were upset, and some talked to themselves in an incoherent manner. Others demonstrated acute anxiety and panic attacks with periods of uncontrollable crying and sobbing.

3. Noticeable mood changes. Within the forty-eight hours before the murders, the teenagers became overly pessimistic about themselves and about all aspects of their lives. They brooded intensely and their self-criticism turned to self-hatred.

4. The call for help unanswered. Close friends and relatives failed to

[8] C. P. Malmquist, "Premonitory Signs of Homocidal Aggression in Juveniles," *American Journal of Psychiatry,* **128** (1971), 461–465.

notice the dramatic behavioral and mood changes of the teenagers during this period, or if they did notice, they believed them to be temporary problems that would soon be dispelled. A few of the teenagers had sought psychiatric help during this depressed period, but the psychiatrists apparently had not taken their problems seriously.

5. Use of drugs. Half of the adolescents studied were taking either "downers" (barbiturates and tranquilizers) or "uppers" (amphetamines). Those who were taking downers had significantly increased the use of the drugs immediately prior to the killings, apparently in an effort to try to control their feelings of distress. In one case, the murderer was under the influence of a psychedelic drug.

6. A persistent medical problem, apparently of psychosomatic origin. Half of the adolescents complained of headaches and other physical pains. Two believed that a particular organ was diseased for a period of time prior to the act of murder. These complaints had been evident for some time, but they intensified shortly before the murder.

7. Sexual difficulties. Two events in some of the teenagers' backgrounds related to sexual matters. The first involved threats from teenage girls to the boys' manhood, usually goading the boys into fights among themselves. The other threat was homosexual; one member of a homosexual pair murdered the other because of fear for his physical safety or because he saw no other way out of the relationship.

The more we learn about the psychological and behavioral characteristics of persons who commit murder, the more readily we may be able to prevent the act by providing appropriate psychological help.

### Rape

Rape is a particularly distasteful crime for three reasons: it involves physical brutality, the psychological effects on the victims are severe and long lasting, and the victims are frequently treated as though they were somehow responsible for the attack.

The incidence of reported rape has increased alarmingly. In addition, many rapes are not reported to the police for reasons of shame or guilt, fear of the rapist, concern about a husband's or boyfriend's reaction, or the lack of sensitivity known to be widespread on the part of police officers, attorneys, and judges. Fortunately, police officers are being trained to display greater sympathy and understanding of rape victims, and many police departments assign female officers to deal with rape cases, on the assumption that the victims will be more comfortable with them than with male officers.

Police investigations show that in as many as two-thirds of the rape cases, the attacker and the victim knew each other prior to the crime.

Most rapists are relatively young men; more than two-thirds are in their twenties or younger. As many as 50 per cent of rapists are married men. Most continue to commit rape until they are caught. Approximately half of the rapists who are caught either have their cases dismissed in court or are acquitted.

Sexual motivations are, of course, involved in rape, but aggression and hostility are also important factors in many cases. Rape may be an outlet for aggressive needs, and the intent of the act is not sexual satisfaction as much as the need to harm or defile the victim. Rape for aggressive reasons often occurs after an argument or some other disturbance between the rapist and an important woman in his life, such as his wife or mother. The argument leads to an uncontrollable impulse to assault another woman, who need not be attractive, sexually desirable, or even particularly young; many rape victims are elderly women. In cases in which aggression and hostility are the major motivations, the rapist frequently does not have an orgasm.

Not all rapists are driven by the need to express their aggression and hostility. Some are quiet, passive people who have no antisocial impulses. However, they are obsessed with their sexual adequacy and seem to be almost always sexually excited. Their motivation for rape is purely sexual and they may have an orgasm while stalking or pursuing a victim. Their motivation and behavior differ greatly from those of the aggression-driven rapists. For example, those men who are driven by the sexual motive are likely to run away if the victim fights, and they usually feel guilty after committing a rape. Sometimes they will apologize to the victim, express concern about her feelings, and offer to drive her home.

A third kind of rapist is motivated neither by aggressive nor by sexual desires. In this case the rape is a spontaneous act, determined by opportunity and the impulse of the moment. For example, during the commission of a robbery, the thief might also become a rapist if the situation allows sufficient privacy and time, and if the woman available is at all appealing to him.

Most rapists evidence strong emotional disturbances, and many of them are psychopaths. Except for the latter, there has been a modest amount of success in treating rapists through psychotherapy, particularly group therapy, and with behavior modification techniques.

## Juvenile Crime

Crimes committed by juveniles (persons under age eighteen) continually show staggering increases in all categories, particularly in crimes of violence. Juveniles commit approximately 10 per cent of all murders, 20 per cent of all rapes, more than 30 per cent of all robberies, and up to 80 per cent of all acts of vandalism. Most juvenile offenders are male, but the number of females arrested for law violations is growing.

In addition to these crimes, juveniles are frequently arrested for breaking and entering, auto theft, drug and liquor law violations, disorderly conduct, aggravated assault, prostitution, and the carrying of weapons. So rampant is juvenile crime that in general it is the young criminal who makes our city streets unsafe by night or day. Juvenile courts tend to be lenient with youthful offenders, and many juveniles are out on the streets shortly after being arrested for committing a crime for which an adult offender would have been imprisoned.

There are several explanations for juvenile crime, but the primary one focuses on the family, the major source of attitudes, values, and behaviors for all young people. In most cases, delinquency can be traced to negative features of the relationship between the delinquent and his or her parents. Several family relationship patterns have been found to be related to delinquent behavior.

One pattern centers on extremes of parental behavior, either excessively protecting or rejecting the child. Overprotection can be manifested in too much support, which can smother the child and foster the development of dependence and hostility. This sort of parental behavior includes unusual punishment, denial, and discipline in the absence of genuine love. Rejecting a child can also lead to the development of hostility, as well as anxiety and insecurity.

An especially harmful form of rejection for male children involves the common situation in which the father rejects the child and provides neither affection and support nor a model with which to identify. At the same time, the mother is very protective and domineering. Several studies of delinquents confirm this family pattern in the background of as many as 90 per cent of delinquent boys. The boys felt hostility toward their father and were close to their mother.

Because rejection by the father has been shown to be a major cause of delinquency, it is not surprising to learn that many youthful male offenders have divorced parents. In a great many cases, the sons are raised by the mother, grandmother, or some other relative. This is particularly characteristic of black juvenile delinquents. The most critical time for a divorce, in terms of the emotional effects on male children, is when they are around the age of five or six.

Another family background characteristic of male delinquents is when the father is present in the house but provides a poor example for the boys to follow. Fathers who are brutal to their wives and children, who drink a lot, and who frequently get into fights or trouble with the law may be teaching delinquent behaviors to their sons as a way of life.

Female delinquents are strongly affected by parental behaviors, including poor examples to follow and divorce. In addition, these girls frequently have a history of parental abuse, harsh and inconsistent discipline, and rejection by the mother. In many homes the mothers have paid little attention to their daughters, who turn instead to their father for affection. At the time of puberty, they begin to look outside the home for affection because their need has become mingled with sexual desires that cannot be satisfied by their father (except in rare cases of incest).

Because of the lack of attention in childhood, delinquent girls have a poor sense of self-esteem and self-worth. They received little praise when they were growing up, no matter what they did or how well they did it, and so they have rarely felt successful at anything. Delinquent girls believe that because they are not considered important by their parents, particularly by the mother, they are unwanted, unloved, and unworthy of love. As a result they feel vulnerable, worthless, and anxious.

Drugs play a causal role in the delinquent behavior of both sexes. The rapid rise in two juvenile offenses—prostitution and theft—seems to be directly related to drug use. Adolescents who are hooked on hard drugs such as heroin find themselves with an increasingly expensive addiction because ever-larger doses are required to produce the same effects.

The young addict may require $100 or more a day to support the addiction, and by this time there is no longer a choice about doing so. Failure to get the drug is very painful. There are few legitimate ways in which adolescents can get that kind of money, so they often turn to crime, some by becoming pushers and making other teenagers drug dependent. A male pusher may force female customers into prostitution to support the drug habit. Burglary is also a source of money. Teenage addicts frequently break into suburban homes during the day and cart off expensive stereo and television sets.

Juveniles under the influence of amphetamines engage in more violent crimes. These drugs, taken in sufficient quantity, produce a powerful surge of energy that causes a person to become highly excitable. At the same time, the addicts become confused, incoherent, and paranoid in their thinking. They are no longer in rational control of themselves, and it is not uncommon for such users to commit suicide or to violently assault others. Because of the heightened energy levels of these drug users, the beatings they inflict often result in death.

Although many juvenile crimes are committed by individuals, many more are committed by gangs. As many as 90 per cent of all crimes committed by teenagers are carried out by two or more together. Adolescence is ordinarily a time of strong peer-group identification; the individual needs to be accepted by his or her peers. Belonging to a group and being accepted by the group members satisfies an intense drive in most adolescents. This is true of emotionally healthy teenagers as well as those who have emotional problems (parental rejection, failure in school, or feelings of being unloved and unworthy).

Emotionally unstable adolescents, believing themselves to be outside the mainstream of normal community and social activities, find what they so desperately seek—acceptance, security, belonging, and love—by joining a gang. Gang membership provides status, recognition, and identification that the individual was previously unable to find.

Gangs of adolescent boys are a familiar phenomenon in large cities, staking out their territory or "turf," defending it from rival gangs, mugging children and adults, and even terrorizing entire neighborhoods. Periodically, large-scale violence erupts in brutal gang wars marked by ambushes of solitary rival gang members, vicious battles, and a number of serious injuries and deaths.

A recent phenomenon is the appearance of gangs of adolescent girls, sometimes operating alone and sometimes in conjunction with boys' gangs. The levels of aggression and violence shown by these female gangs are as vicious as those of their male counterparts. In some large cities, female gangs are responsible for up to 30 per cent of all juvenile crime. They, too, engage in gang wars, robberies, muggings, and assaults, and apparently find similar emotional satisfaction in gang membership.

There are several ways of treating juvenile offenders, including behavior modification, which has been effective with delinquents in institutions, and traditional techniques of counseling and psychotherapy. A major problem with juveniles in correctional institutions is that those jailed for minor offenses—such as persistent truancy or promiscuity, which are not crimes against persons or property—may be placed with those jailed for more serious offenses such as murder, rape, or armed robbery. Those who have been convicted of less serious offenses may be induced to become hardened criminals by the example and instruction of those with whom they are confined.

## Terrorism and Hostage Taking

A difficult situation with which police forces throughout the world are being forced to cope is the seizure of hostages. Sometimes the act is committed for political reasons (calling attention to a cause or trying to get other terrorists released from prison), and sometimes for personal reasons (trying to redress a real or imagined grievance or to escape from a thwarted robbery attempt).

For example, in the spring of 1977 there were two large-scale terrorist acts of a political nature. In Washington, D.C., a group of Hanafi Muslims held 134 hostages in two downtown locations for thirty-nine hours before a settlement was reached and the hostages released, although several had been seriously wounded. In The Netherlands, a band of South Moluccan terrorists held more than 150 hostages in a school building and aboard a train for almost twenty days. There, negotiations were not successful (as they had been with previous South Moluccan terrorist acts), and Royal Dutch Marines released the hostages by force; several hostages and terrorists were killed or wounded in the process.

These acts of terrorism must be handled delicately because the lives of innocent victims are at stake and the terrorists are in complete control. The policy in the United States and in Western European countries that have experienced acts of terrorism is to negotiate and delay as long as possible to try to end the siege peacefully. In the incident in The Netherlands mentioned previously, the military forces stormed the train and the school because they feared that after twenty days of captivity the hostages were reaching the limits of their physical and psychological endurance. Israel, often the target of hostage-taking incidents, does not favor negotiation and delaying tactics, preferring instead to overwhelm the terrorists as quickly as possible in the hope that potential terrorists might see that they cannot get away with such acts. The Israelis have had some spectacular successes in releasing hostages by force.

In countries that favor negotiation, a psychology of terrorism has been developed and applied effectively to bring about the peaceful resolution of most crises. Psychologists and psychiatrists have been active in negotiating directly with terrorists and in teaching police officers how best to cope with the situation. The FBI offers psychological training in dealing with terrorists and has trained agents at each of the fifty-nine field divisions in the United States. Since 1974, the San Francisco, California, police department has trained officers in negotiating with terrorists. In fifteen hostage-taking incidents, they have been able to save all the hostages without firing a shot. Other police departments offer similar training and candidates for the training are psychologically screened. Those who show signs of being unable to handle high levels of stress are turned down.

Police are taught to treat terrorists with respect because of the life-threatening situation for the hostages. A hostile or threatening attitude toward the terrorists is unproductive. Channels of communication must be kept open and the negotiator must encourage terrorist leaders to keep talking about their demands or grievances. Meanwhile, the police attempt to develop a psychological profile of the terrorist leaders to establish their basic motivations and weaknesses. They try to learn everything they can by talking to relatives and friends, monitoring telephone calls, and assessing reports of past behavior.

In one case, the psychological profile of a lone hostage taker revealed that he suffered from claustrophobia. To play on that fear, the FBI agent in charge had the lights and heat turned off in the room in which the gunman was holding the hostage. The telephone number was changed so that there could be no incoming calls. Then the FBI agent sat back to wait, predicting that the terrorist would give up within three days. Sixty-two hours later, the gunman surrendered.

Usually, the negotiator talks continually with the terrorists, trying to establish rapport and making concessions on small matters, though always getting something in return. For example, a gunman who held several hostages in a bank agreed to a series of exchanges; one hostage for a six-pack of beer, another for a submarine sandwich, and a third for a bullhorn. In this way, a relationship of mutual trust can be established, leading to an easing of a tense situation.

While the negotiations continue, a subtle change usually takes place between the terrorists and their hostages. At first, hostages are generally treated callously, even brutally, because they are the "enemy." But after hours or days of being confined together, the terrorists and the hostages being to talk to one another, sometimes becoming friendly. This works well for the hostages; then they are usually treated better and there is less danger to their lives. It is easier for a terrorist to kill a stranger (as hostages are at the beginning of such an incident) than to kill someone who has become known. The relationship may become one of comradeship; terrorist and hostage may find themselves in a difficult situation together, and both may now view the police as the "enemy." From this point on, negotiations become easier.

All of us are potential victims of criminal acts, but through the efforts of forensic psychologists the high cost of crime may eventually be reduced. From research into the causes of criminal behavior, the training of police officers, and the counseling of criminals, this important field of psychology attempts to make our cities and homes safer places in which to live and work.

## SUMMARY

Criminal behavior has a direct and forceful impact on the quality of our lives and has long been an interest of psychologists. The application of psychology to crime and law enforcement—*forensic psychology*—began in the early years of the twentieth century, but in the 1970s the effort began to receive sizable support from psychologists and those engaged in law enforcement. Psychologists work in police departments, courts, and prisons, or conduct research on aspects of criminal behavior.

Psychologists in police departments are concerned with: (1) *Selecting police officers:* using selection techniques such as psychological tests, interviews, and application blanks (the same kinds of techniques used for selection in industry and government), psychologists assist police departments in choosing the most qualified applicants. (2) *Training police officers:* police officers are trained by psychologists in such areas as personality, motivation, mental illness, race relations, and human relations skills, to enable them to better understand the people with whom they deal on the streets. (3) *Counseling police officers:* to cope with the unusual stresses of police work, counseling and psychotherapy are provided by psychologists and may determine the kind of work a police officer is allowed to do. (4) *Preventing and detecting crime:* police psychologists help to solve crimes by constructing a personality profile of the type of person the police should be looking for in a particular crime. Psychological knowledge is applied in controlling and preventing riots, and in dealing with potentially explosive situations such as family disturbances.

Psychologists are active in four aspects of courtroom procedure: (1) *Psychologists in family courts:* in dealing with juvenile offenders, psychologists diagnose their levels of intellectual and emotional functioning, and make recommendations about appropriate treatment. Psychologists evaluate children and adolescents who are considered by their parents to be uncontrollable. These evaluations are used by judges in deciding on the proper environment in which to place the child. (2) *Psychologists as expert witnesses:* both clinical and experimental psychologists testify at trials. Clinicians testify about the diagnosis of a defendant's intellectual and emotional characteristics. Experimental psychologists testify about their experimental re-creations of the scene of a crime to show that what actually happened differed from the investigating officer's testimony. (3) *Credibility of eyewitness testimony:* psychological research on human perception confirms that what people see is distorted by needs, fears, values, and prejudices. Psychological research on memory shows that what we recall of an event is also subject to error. Research dealing directly with the accuracy of eyewitness testimony reports a high rate of error in such testimony. The accuracy of eyewitness testimony can be influenced by the wording of an attorney's questions in the courtroom. (4) *Jury behavior:* psychologists are involved in scientifically selecting juries so that the members will be sympathetic to the defendant. Psychologists also conduct research on how juries function. Research findings of social psychologists on the dynamics of small groups and of forensic psychologists on simulated juries indicate that jury members are affected by group pressure and by the status of the other jury members. Also, jurors have difficulty understanding the legal aspects of a case as well as the judge's instructions.

Psychology in prisons involves the physical design of prisons as well as the following activities: (1) *Evaluating new prisoners:* psychologists evaluate new prisoners to determine their level of intelligence, personality, and vocational aptitudes and interests. This information is valuable to the prison staff in order to determine where a prisoner should be housed and what kind of work, vocational training, or educational opportunities would be appropriate. (2) *Counseling prisoners:* many prisoners have emotional problems and can benefit from the same kinds of psychological counseling and psychotherapy used in other clinical settings. (3) *Training the prison staff:* psychologists offer formal courses to prison guards on the nature of mental illness, the psychology of crime, race relations, and sensitivity training. (4) *Advising on parole:* correctional psychologists advise parole boards on the suitability of a prisoner for parole or furlough programs.

The crime of *murder* occurs mostly on weekends; Saturday night is the most dangerous time. In most cases, the victim and the killer know each other and are of the same race. Guns are used in two-thirds of all murders, and drinking plays a prominent role. Studies of adolescent murderers show that they experienced noticeable mood changes which were ignored, lost a significant relationship, had a persistent medical problem, and experienced rapidly rising emotion shortly before committing the murder. Drugs, a threat to manhood, and homosexuality played a role in some of these murders.

*Rape* involves brutality and long-lasting psychological effects for the victim. Two-thirds of all rapists are in their twenties or younger. In two-thirds of the cases, the rapist and the victim knew each other before the assault. Motivations for rape include sexual needs, aggression and hostility, and a spontaneous impulse. Most rapists are emotionally disturbed.

The primary cause of *juvenile crime* is a negative family relationship that involves extremes of parental behavior, either excessively protecting or rejecting the child. For young males, the family background usually includes a protective, domineering mother, a rejecting father who provides a poor example, and divorced parents. Female delinquents are also affected by parental behavior and they often have a history of parental abuse, harsh and inconsistent discipline, and rejection by the mother. Delinquent girls feel unwanted and unloved, vulnerable, worthless, and anxious. Drugs play a role in juvenile crime because of the large amount of money needed to support an addiction to hard drugs, and the excitability and lack of rational control caused by the use of amphetamines. As much as 90 per cent of all juvenile crime is committed by gangs. These groups provide a sense of acceptance, security, and belonging to their members. In treating juvenile delinquents, if those who are jailed for minor offenses are placed with those who have committed more serious offenses, then correctional institutions become training grounds in criminal behavior.

*Terrorism and hostage taking* for political or personal reasons is difficult to deal with because the lives of innocent hostages are at stake. The psychology of terrorism is being taught to police officers throughout the United States. This involves treating the terrorists with respect, keeping channels of communication open, developing a psychological profile of the terrorists, trying to establish rapport with them, and making concessions on small matters and receiving something in return. After a period of confinement, the initial hostility felt by terrorists toward their hostages changes to a feeling that they are all in a difficult situation together.

## SUGGESTED READINGS

Bard, Morton, and Robert Shellow. *Issues in Law Enforcement: Essays and Case Studies*. Reston, Va.: Reston, 1976.

Bard, Morton, and J. Zacker. How police handle explosive squabbles. *Psychology Today*, 1976 (November), **10**, 71–74, 113.

Belz, M., et al. Is there a treatment for terror: Six therapists report on their work with hostages held by the Hanafis. *Psychology Today*, 1977 (October), **11**, 54–56, 108, 111–112.

Bermant, Gordon, Charlan Nemeth, and Neil Vidmar, Eds. *Psychology and the Law: Research Frontiers*. Lexington, Mass.: Lexington Books, 1976.

Brodsky, S. L. *Psychologists in the Criminal Justice System*. Urbana: University of Illinois Press, 1972.

Brodsky, S. L. Psychology and criminal justice. In Paul J. Woods, Ed., *Career Opportunities for Psychologists: Expanding and Emerging Areas*. Washington, D.C.: American Psychological Association, 1976. Pp. 152–156.

Buckhout, R., and K. W. Ellison. The line–up: A critical look. *Psychology Today*, 1977 (June), **11**, 82–84, 88.

Chubb, G. P. Human factors and the law. *Human Factors*, 1972, **14**, 1–40.

Darley, John T., and Evan W. Pickrel. Some psychological contributions to defenses against hijackers. *American Psychologist*, 1975, **30**, 161–165.

Dudycha, George J. *Psychology For Law Enforcement Officers*. Springfield, Ill.: Charles C Thomas, 1976.

Eysenck, H. J. *Crime and Personality*, rev. ed. London: Routledge and Kegan Paul, 1977.

Fenster, C. A., et al. Careers in forensic psychology. In Paul J. Woods, Ed., *Career Opportunities for Psychologists: Expanding and Emerging Areas*. Washington, D.C.: American Psychological Association, 1976. Pp. 123–151.

Fenyvesti, C. Six months later: Living with a fearful memory. *Psychology Today*, 1977 (October), **11**, 61, 115–116 [about hostages]

Gormally, J., and S. L. Brodsky. Utilization and training of psychologists in the criminal system. *American Psychologist*, 1973, **28**, 926–928.

Hardy, R. E., and J. G. Cull. *Applied Psychology in Law Enforcement and Corrections*. Springfield, Ill.: Charles C Thomas, 1973.

Hardy, R. E., and J. G. Cull. *Fundamentals of Juvenile Criminal Behavior and Drug Abuse*. Springfield, Ill.: Charles C Thomas, 1975.

James, Pat, and Martha Nelson. *Police Wife: How To Live with the Law and Like It*. Springfield, Ill.: Charles C Thomas, 1975.

Kolasa, B. J. Psychology and the law. *American Psychologist,* 1972, **27,** 499–503.

Lee, M., P. Zimbardo, and M. Bertholf. Shy murderers. *Psychology Today,* 1977 (November), **11,** 69-70, 76, 148.

Lefkowitz, Joel. Industrial-organizational psychology and the police. *American Psychologist,* 1977, **32,** 346-364.

Lester, David, and Gene Lester. *Crime of Passion: Murder and the Murderer.* Chicago: Nelson-Hall, 1975.

Loftus, E. F. Reconstructing memory: The incredible eyewitness. *Psychology Today,* 1974 (December), **8,** 116-119.

Miller, W. The rumble this time. *Psychology Today,* 1977 (May), **10,** 52-59, 88. [about youth gangs]

Newcomb, Theodore M. Youth in college and in corrections: Institutional influences. *American Psychologist,* 1978, **33,** 114-124.

Nietzel, M. T., and C. S. Moss. The psychologist in the criminal justice system. *Professional Psychology,* 1972, **3,** 259–269.

Robitscher, J., and R. Williams. Should psychiatrists get out of the courtroom? *Psychology Today,* 1977 (December), **11,** 85-86, 91-92, 138-140.

Russell, Harold E., and Allan Beigel. *Understanding Human Behavior for Effective Police Work.* New York: Basic Books, 1976.

Tapp, June L. Psychology and the law: An overture. *Annual Review of Psychology,* 1976, **27,** 359-404.

Toch, Hans. *Men In Crisis: Human Breakdowns in Prison.* Chicago: Aldine, 1975.

Walker, Marcia J., and S. L. Brodsky, Eds. *Sexual Assault: The Victim and the Rapist.* Lexington, Mass.: Lexington Books, 1976.

Wicks, Robert. *Applied Psychology for Law Enforcement and Correctional Officers.* New York: McGraw-Hill, 1974.

# Psychology Applied to the Classroom

**10**

Mary Cosgrove was in her first year of teaching and, on the whole, she was enjoying it very much. Her class of second-graders consisted mostly of bright, energetic, and attractive children who seemed to respond well to her. They laughed when she said something funny, joined enthusiastically in the games in which she led them, and seemed to be learning the lessons she tried to teach them.

But there were problems. Some of her lessons were not so successful as others, and not all of the children were happy and content in her class. A few were withdrawn and sullen, or hostile and disruptive, and one or two did not seem to be learning anything, no matter how hard they, and she, tried. These problems baffled her until she received advice from some of the older teachers. Prompted by their suggestions, Ms. Cosgrove got out the textbooks and class notes from her college psychology courses. She recalled that one of the psychology professors had said that the findings of psychology would prove valuable to those who were going into the teaching profession. As she reviewed the books and notes, she realized the truth of that statement, and she resolved to apply psychological principles to her students.

She tried first with Bobby, the most disruptive child in the class. No matter what the other students were doing, Bobby always did something different to draw attention to himself—yelling while Ms. Cosgrove was talking, tearing up the pictures the other children were drawing, and throwing the ball over the fence during recess. Previously, she had scolded Bobby and punished him in various ways, but none of these was successful.

As Ms. Cosgrove reviewed what she had learned about psychology, she found that by punishing Bobby she was reacting exactly the way in which he wanted her to. His disruptive behavior was a way of saying, "Hey, pay attention to me," and when Ms. Cosgrove stopped her lessons to scold him, she was doing just that. She was rewarding or reinforcing his disruptive behavior.

She read again about psychological reinforcement and about how to eliminate unwanted behavior that previously had been reinforced. The answer was simple: through the process of extinction, undesirable behavior is no longer reinforced and, soon, it will stop.

In class the next morning, Ms. Cosgrove completely ignored Bobby's unruly behavior; she continued with her teaching every time he misbehaved. Of course, Bobby reacted to being ignored by becoming even more rowdy, and she found it difficult not to scold him. But she knew that if she gave in just once to that impulse she would be rewarding Bobby again for his aggressive behavior. The other pupils saw that Ms. Cosgrove was ignoring Bobby and they began to follow her example. After a few days, no one paid any attention to Bobby.

Confused and angry, Bobby did not know what to do. Once he cried out, "Hey, look at me," but no one did.

Although Ms. Cosgrove studiously ignored his destructive behavior, she was careful to notice any constructive behavior on his part. Whenever Bobby did anything remotely resembling what the class was supposed to be doing, she reinforced him. When he attempted to draw a picture of a house, as the rest of the class was doing, she praised his effort, even though the few lines he had drawn looked nothing like a house. "That's very interesting, Bobby," she said. "That's a good beginning."

Within two weeks, Bobby's behavior had changed dramatically. He learned that the only time Ms. Cosgrove would pay any attention to him was when he behaved in constructive and desirable ways. Behavior modification had accomplished in two weeks what the previous two months of scolding and punishing had failed to accomplish. In addition, the success of this application of psychological techniques and principles reinforced Ms. Cosgrove's belief in them, and she looked around the class to see where else they could be applied.

There was Jeff. He belonged to a minority race. Although never a behavior problem, Jeff was listless and uninterested in everything the class did. He did not pay attention, never volunteered an answer, and never knew the answer when he was called upon. He didn't seem to care. Ms. Cosgrove believed that Jeff was as bright as any of the other students and she decided that he needed extra praise and encouragement. Talking to him after class one day she had learned that he received little attention at home. Within a month, Jeff was an active participant in the class and was learning faster than many of the other students.

Anne sat quietly in class and tried very hard to please. She was the first to raise her hand whenever Ms. Cosgrove asked for volunteers and the first to ask the teacher to look at her work. She was continually seeking approval, asking, "Did I do this right?" She would cry at any suggestion that her work was not the best in the class. Whenever the students formed into play groups, Anne always sat next to Ms. Cosgrove, clinging to her hand and resisting all efforts to get her to play with the others. On the playground, Anne sat apart from the other pupils, talking to herself and watching her classmates with a look of sadness.

Ms. Cosgrove suspected that Anne's behavior indicated some emotional problem. She knew this much from her psychology courses and she also knew that she was not trained to deal with the situation. She realized that she might do more harm than good if she tried to offer guidance or therapy. She asked the school psychologist to observe Anne's behavior for a few days and to talk with her. The psychologist agreed that Anne needed counseling and she congratulated Ms. Cosgrove for recognizing the problem. If Anne had gone untreated, her emotional problems would probably have worsened. After two months of therapy, Anne's behavior showed a noticeable improvement.

All of us spend a portion of our lives in school. How well we function there—intellectually, socially, and emotionally—influences our lives and our careers. School represents our first interaction with the world beyond our parents, and is, therefore, a vital part of the socialization process by which we become mature, competent, responsible adults.

The work of psychologists concerned with education affects each of us. It determines what and how we are taught, how our rate of learning is evaluated, and how well we learn to get along with others. The application of psychology to the classroom involves the emotional and behavioral development of children (as in the previous example), and also their intellectual development, which is the primary mission of education. Principles of group behavior, classroom management, and behavior modification are applied daily by knowledgeable teachers. Research on principles of learning and motivation determines the best kinds of teaching materials and the most effective teacher behavior to facilitate learning.

The field of *educational psychology* is a central part of all teacher education. Its research efforts are concerned primarily with ways of fostering intellectual development through studies on learning, teaching methods, special education programs,[1] and testing (for intelligence, aptitudes, achievement levels, and occupational interests). The field of *school psychology* is concerned with testing and counseling (both behavioral and vocational) in the school situation and with school administration and curriculum development for all grade levels (preschool, elementary, junior high, high school, college, graduate and professional, and adult). Most school systems employ school psychologists to work

[1] Special education programs are designed for various types of pupils: gifted, mentally retarded, socially and emotionally disturbed, physically handicapped, and learning disabled.

with children, parents, and teachers in an effort to treat emotional and learning problems of pupils.

## INDIVIDUAL DIFFERENCES IN LEARNING ABILITY

There is a great deal of inequality to be found in any group of people—a nation, a city, a neighborhood, a factory, or a classroom. Each of us is an individual possessing characteristics and abilities not duplicated in any other person.

The most obvious individual differences are in physical features. Look around your classroom and you notice how the students differ in height, weight, length of hair, color of eyes, and general attractiveness. If you know the people, you may recognize other differences, for example, in sociability, humor, aggressiveness, hostility, ambition, nervousness, and other social and personal characteristics. Also, you may observe that some of them seem smarter than others, or at least they perform better. Some students always know the correct answers and get the best grades, others coast along with passing grades, and still others fail.

Part of the difference in class performance can be attributed to *personality factors*. If a student is hostile toward all authority figures, for example, including teachers, he or she will do poorly in class and resist everything the teacher says or tries to do.

*Motivational factors* also influence the ability to learn. Some people perform well in school because of sheer determination, persistence, and a lot of hard work. These highly motivated people often do better than those who are more intelligent but lazy.

A third factor that accounts for individual differences in classroom performance is *intelligence*. This may be the most important factor. Although motivational and personality characteristics do influence our scholastic performance, how much we may learn and how far we are able to advance are limited by our level of intelligence.

### What Is Intelligence?

This seems like a simple, straightforward question, but psychologists cannot offer a simple, straightforward answer. There are many definitions of intelligence, but not one with which all psychologists agree. Some psychologists define intelligence as the ability to learn and to profit by experience, others speak of it as the capacity to make judgments and to reason effectively, and still others believe it is the ability to think in abstract terms.

Whichever definition you accept, however, there is no denying the importance of intelligence in influencing what we are able to do with our lives. The concept of intelligence is also important to psychologists and educators who must make predictions about how people will behave in certain situations. Whether you are admitted to college, medical or law school, pilot training, or management training programs in industry, for example, will be determined, in large part, by the assessment made of your intelligence. Thus, although we cannot precisely define intelligence, we can use it to predict with a high degree of accuracy many aspects of life, from elementary school onward.

## Measuring Intelligence

It is virtually impossible to go through life without having your intelligence measured at least once, and usually more than once. Public and private schools, colleges and universities, the military services, business and industry all give intelligence tests (popularly known as IQ tests, for "intelligence quotient") to people who are in, or who would like to join, their organizations or institutions. For example, an admissions director at a medical school uses intelligence test results in the following way. Because the applicant who possesses an IQ of 130 has a greater chance of succeeding in medical school than an applicant with an IQ of 105, the first applicant will be admitted and the second will not.

How can intelligence be measured if we do not know for sure what it is? Psychologists measure intelligence in terms of its effects on behavior, by concluding that the person who answers correctly more of the standard questions on an IQ test is more intelligent than the person who cannot answer as many of the items correctly. Intelligence, then, is manifested by or expressed in terms of level of performance on an IQ test. This is similar to the way in which psychologists measure personality or aptitude or any other internal characteristic, by observing its differential effects on behavior as shown by psychological tests.

Intelligence tests have been in use for many years. In 1905, a French psychologist, Alfred Binet, developed a test in response to a request from the Paris, France, public school system. Educators realized that some children lacked the capacity to learn as well or as rapidly as other children. The educators asked Binet to devise a test that would identify slow learners so that they could be sent to special schools.

Binet's test was a great success. Not only did it identify children who possessed low levels of intelligence, but it also detected children who possessed average and above-average levels of intelligence. This was the first objective measure of the wide range of human intelligence.

In 1916, an American psychologist, Lewis M. Terman of Stanford University, substantially revised Binet's test for use with school children in the United States. The Stanford-Binet test, through several revisions, remains a popular intelligence test for use with children.

Terman also developed the concept of IQ as a precise means of measuring intelligence. The Binet test was scored in terms of mental age. For example, if a six-year-old child scored at the same level as the average six-year-old child, his or her mental age would be six. But if a six-year-old child scored only as high as the average five-year-old child, then the mental age would only be five. Terman's IQ score offers a more direct indication of intelligence because it shows the relationship between mental age and chronological age. The formula for calculating IQ is

$$\frac{\text{mental age}}{\text{chronological age}} \times 100 = IQ$$

For example, a six-year-old child with a mental age of six has an IQ of 100 (6/6 × 100 = 100). A six-year-old child with a mental age of five has an IQ of 83 (5/6 × 100 = 83). Because later research showed that mental age stops increasing after the age of eighteen, the chronological age of eighteen is always used to calculate the IQ of someone over that age, regardless of their true chronological age.

In 1939, David Wechsler, a psychologist at Bellevue Hospital in New York City, developed an intelligence test for adults. Called the *Wechsler Adult Intelligence Scale,* the test consists of two parts: *verbal* skills, such as vocabulary and memory, and *performance* skills, such as puzzles and picture arrangement. A separate IQ score is calculated for each part. The performance scale is particularly useful in testing people who have language difficulties, such as those for whom English is not the primary language, or those who have poorly developed verbal skills because of inadequate schooling. Wechsler also developed an IQ test for children (the *Wechsler Intelligence Scale for Children*) that contains both verbal and performance scales.

The Wechsler tests are widely used tests of intelligence, but they are not the only ones. Many other intelligence tests are used in schools and in other situations where large numbers of people have to be tested.

The Wechsler and the Stanford-Binet tests are time-consuming and can be given to only one person at a time. In addition, the person giving the test must be trained in the proper methods of test administration. Other tests are designed to be given to a large number of people at the same time, so they are more economical to use. However, group intelligence tests do not measure IQ as precisely as individual tests. Nevertheless, group tests are useful for providing satisfactory approximations of IQ.

## The Meaning of IQ Scores

What do IQ scores tell us about a person's level of intelligence? How do they help educators in the classroom? What will it mean in terms of

**Psychology Applied to the Classroom**

learning ability that Johnny has an IQ of 100 and Susan has an IQ of 130?

The first point to remember about IQ scores is that, like every other human characteristic, they are found in the population in accordance with the normal curve of distribution. Most people score around the average level (an IQ of 100), and many fewer score significantly higher or lower than that. The distribution of IQ scores in the United States is shown in Figure 10–1. Few people obtain the IQ scores at the extreme high and low ends of the distribution. Thus, extremely bright and extremely dull people are rare. Figure 10–1 also gives the percentages of people in the various IQ ranges, and the labels usually applied to each category.

What do these scores mean in terms of ability to perform in school? Consider people with average IQs, the 50 per cent of the population that scores between 90 and 109. What sort of academic achievement can we expect of them? Those persons who score in the top half of the average range (100–109) have the ability to finish high school but would experience some difficulty getting through college. Those persons who score in the bottom half of the average range (90–99) have the ability to finish the eighth grade but would have some difficulty completing high school. Note that this average range of IQ scores characterizes half the people in the United States. A person's level of motivation is also a factor in scholastic performance, however. It is possible for a person who pos-

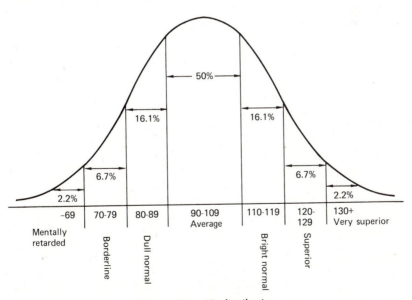

Figure 10–1. IQ distribution.

sesses an IQ of 105 and a very high drive to succeed to finish college with better grades than a classmate who has an IQ of 115.

The prospects for persons with IQs below average are not so good. Those in the 80–89 range would have problems getting as far as the seventh or eighth grades, and those in the 70–79 range rarely go beyond the fifth grade. Persons whose IQs are below 70 usually do not advance beyond the third-grade level of development; even as adults these people have the intellectual ability of a third-grader, an eight-year-old child.

Thus, IQ scores are useful to educators, enabling them to provide for the kind and level of instruction appropriate to each person's ability and potential. Measures of intelligence allow teachers to predict the level of performance to be expected of a child with a particular IQ; this is beneficial to the child in that no more will be demanded than he or she could achieve. However, IQ scores can be misused, resulting in harm to a child's development.

### Abuses of IQ Scores

There are two potential abuses of intelligence tests. The first relates to the interpretations made of individual IQ scores, and the second deals with possible discriminatory aspects of intelligence testing.

We noted that IQ scores may be used by teachers as a basis for deciding the kind of instruction most appropriate to a child, and for judging the level of performance or achievement to be expected. However, a teacher may also decide, on the basis of an IQ score, that no amount of attention would help a particular child. For example, the teacher may believe that it is not worthwhile to devote extra effort to helping the child whose IQ is 85 when other children in the class who have higher IQ scores and thus greater potential could benefit more from additional instruction.

It could well be the case that the unfortunate child's IQ is really higher than 85 and that the score is unrealistically low because he or she was not feeling well on the day of the testing. But unless the child is retested, he or she will be characterized for life as not being very bright, and teachers are likely to believe that academic progress is hopeless. The label "dull normal" could remain permanently in the child's school record, and all who see it will expect little from the child and, consequently, offer little help. Similar harmful consequences could result even if the child's IQ were really 85; the child would not be encouraged to develop to full potential, however limited it may be. Thus, an IQ score can become a dangerous label.

A second possible abuse of intelligence testing is that it may discriminate against disadvantaged children. Most intelligence tests rely on verbal ability. Oral directions must be understood, and most of the items require the use of words to answer. Therefore, the tests may favor those who attend better schools and discriminate against those who attend poorer schools or live in culturally deprived environments.

Because IQ tests do not measure inherent intellectual capacity (there is no known way to measure this) but rather one's current level of achievement or ability, it follows that persons who have greater opportunities to achieve and develop their abilities—through better schools and supportive parents—score higher on IQ tests than those who lack these opportunities. As a general rule, IQ scores reflect a person's socioeconomic level in society, and the corresponding opportunities for development.

Teachers and counselors must examine and interpret students' intelligence test scores with caution, taking into consideration the home and school environments and cultural opportunities available to each child because these influence the level of intellectual potential. Several cities in the United States, including New York, Los Angeles, and Washington, D.C., have outlawed the use of group IQ tests with children because of the suggested capacity to discriminate against those from disadvantaged backgrounds. These school systems use achievement tests—such as tests of reading and arithmetic level—as a means of assessing student ability.

## Are There Racial Differences in Intelligence?

We noted previously that IQ scores may reflect social and academic background. It follows that in the United States blacks from lower-income families would have lower IQ scores than whites from higher-income families because of the difference in educational and cultural opportunities. In general, black children as a group do not score as high on IQ tests as white children. Is this difference, found consistently in psychological research studies, attributable to socioeconomic causes or to inherent racial differences in intelligence?

The question revolves around the basic nature of intelligence. Is intelligence determined largely by environmental factors such as schooling, or is it determined by genetic factors? If it is determined by environmental factors, then all society need do is improve the educational opportunities for those who are deprived and IQ scores will rise, erasing these differences. If, on the other hand, intelligence is determined by our genes, our inheritance, then no amount of environmental improvement will have an appreciable effect.

Scientists who favor the genetic view of intelligence cite the consistent finding that the IQ scores of blacks average fifteen points below the IQ scores for whites, and that these differences hold even for blacks in the upper socioeconomic classes. They also note that IQ scores for American Indians, who suffer at least as much discrimination and poverty as blacks, are, nevertheless, higher than those for blacks. It should be pointed out that these statistics refer to average scores; when one examines individual scores one finds that many blacks have scores far above the average white IQ score.

Obviously, the suggestion of racial inferiority or superiority is controversial and emotional, and the problem is unresolved. Opponents of the genetic view present equally impressive evidence to support their position that the lower average IQ scores of blacks are the result of generations of poverty and discrimination that have denied blacks equal educational and cultural opportunities with whites.

Research has shown that environmental factors do affect IQ scores. For example, blacks who have migrated from the rural south to the urban north (from a deprived to a more enriched environment) show an increase in average IQ scores. These scores continue to increase with each year of residence in the north. Further, studies show that average IQs of northern blacks are often higher than those of southern whites. Also, black children adopted by white families achieve IQ test scores significantly higher than those of other black children.

Until all children have equal educational, social, and cultural opportunities, it may be unrealistic to expect them to perform at the same level on tests that depend so greatly on these opportunities.

## EFFECTS OF INDIVIDUAL DIFFERENCES ON EDUCATION

The individual differences that exist in intelligence profoundly affect the organization and structure of teaching. Every school system serves children at all levels of ability, from IQs of 70 to those of 140. Certainly, all students cannot be taught in the same way, or even in the same classroom, nor can the school system or the teachers hold the same expectations of pupils of such varying abilities. These differences in intellectual competence must be accommodated. Let us consider the two extremes of intelligence: the mentally retarded and the gifted.

### Mentally Retarded Children

Persons whose IQs are below 70 make up approximately 2.2 per cent of the population, nearly 5 million people. As children, they are educated in special schools or in special classes in public schools. With IQ tests, they can be identified at an early age and kept out of regular classrooms, where they would meet with failure and probably social rejection.

There are different levels of mental retardation. Some children cannot benefit from any kind of education and require custodial care, and others can be trained to function reasonably well in society and to hold a job. It is imperative that once a mentally retarded child is identified, the pre-

261

cise level of retardation be measured so that the education most likely to benefit the child can be provided. Most mentally retarded people are in mild-to-moderately severe categories, which means that they can benefit from some education or training.

In general, school systems devote considerable effort to teaching retarded children, and the results of these programs seem to justify the time and expense. By placing retarded children in special classes and providing them with teachers trained to deal with their unique problems, the full potential of retarded children can be achieved. Although some schools place retarded children in regular classes (and some research shows that this produces greater achievement than special classes), the social and personal adjustments are superior when retarded children are taught in a group.

Mentally retarded children require assistance in reading and basic arithmetic skills, and frequent changes in learning tasks because their attention span is limited. Teaching retarded children is often tedious, but with patience and appropriate instruction, many can be taught to care for themselves and to practice occupational skills.

## Gifted Children

At the other end of the IQ distribution are children of superior ability, with IQs above 130. There are approximately the same number of gifted children as retarded children, and they, too, place unique demands on the school system and on individual teachers. If they are provided with stimulating educational opportunities, gifted children are capable of making enormous contributions to society. If, however, their education is not sufficiently challenging, their tremendous potential may remain undeveloped and unfulfilled.

Gifted children require special training and sensitive teachers as much as do retarded children. It is also important that their superior level of ability be recognized at an early age. Because most teachers are not trained to recognize truly superior intellectual functioning, this is best accomplished with intelligence tests. Unfortunately, most school systems lack educational programs for gifted children, even though research clearly shows that their level of achievement improves considerably when they are grouped in special classes.

A partially satisfactory alternative to special classes for gifted children is to allow them to skip grades and be placed in more advanced classes, in which the work may be more challenging. However, skipping grades may cause social and personal adjustment problems because the gifted child's classmates are older.

In regular classes, where no provisions have been made to meet their needs, gifted children may become problem children. They are likely to be bored and, as a result, may become lazy and lose interest in school altogether. For this reason, it is not unusual for gifted children to receive failing grades. They also face problems with teachers in regular classes. Few teachers (indeed, few people in any occupation) are of superior intelligence, and so they are often unable to answer the questions of gifted children or keep up with their problem-solving abilities. They are likely to consider these children arrogant or pretentious and to punish them instead of helping or encouraging them. As a result, gifted children are often believed to be a nuisance to teachers, who treat them accordingly and further alienate them from school.

Psychologist Lewis Terman and his colleagues at Stanford University, mentioned previously, conducted a long-term investigation of children who showed very superior IQs, following their progress for more than forty years. As children they were superior not only in intelligence but also in other physical and psychological characteristics. They were taller, heavier, and more physically attractive than children of average ability, and were better adjusted socially and emotionally. The research refuted the popular belief that bright people are somehow peculiar, maladjusted, and social misfits.

In adult life, Terman's gifted people were, in general, very successful, both in an occupational and an emotional sense. They made important contributions in their chosen fields, were well adjusted psychologically, and had better marriages than those of lesser intelligence. Not all of them were successful, however. Some dropped out of school and held routine jobs, a few became drifters and some turned to crime, although these were the exceptions and were fewer in number than one would find in a group of individuals with average IQs.

## Children of Average Ability

If we exclude the extremes of intelligence, we are left with the large middle range of intellectual ability that characterizes approximately 90 per cent of the pupils in a public school classroom. However, this is not a homogeneous group, but includes a wide range of differences in intelligence and hence in ability to learn. Such a group contains children whose IQs may range from the 80s to the 120s, from dull normal to superior. Some of these children lack the ability to complete public school, and others will experience no difficulty finishing college and even graduate school.

Obviously, they are not equal in potential and should not be treated as though they were. To teach this group at one level of expectation would frustrate the slow learners and bore the fast learners. To maximize the potential of all groups, their special needs must be recognized and dealt with appropriately. How can this be accomplished?

First, each child's level of intellectual ability must be measured objectively so that a teacher knows what to expect of each child. Next, the best way to fulfill these expectations must be determined. Two popular approaches to accommodating individual differences in the classroom are homogeneous grouping and nongraded programs.

*Homogeneous grouping,* sometimes known as the track system, places students together in terms of their level of ability. For example, the brightest children (with IQs above 115 or 120) may be placed in one class, those of average IQ in another, and those of below-average IQ in a third (assuming that gifted and retarded children have their own special classes).

Superficially, this approach appears to be sensible, but the research conducted to date does not show conclusively that it is particularly good or poor. It seems, however, that instruction most appropriate to the students' learning abilities is achieved when a teacher is dealing with a narrow instead of a wide range of abilities. For this reason, many teachers prefer homogeneous grouping, except for those who are assigned to teach the lower-ability groups.

The major complaint about homogeneous grouping is that it may be undemocratic and discriminatory, segregating lower-class children from those of the middle and upper classes. Critics charge that, as a result, lower-class children receive inferior educational opportunities. Studies show that the higher the social class of the pupils, the more likely they are to be assigned to the higher tracks. Conversely, lower-class children are much more likely to be assigned to the lower tracks.

Often, the grouping into tracks has been determined not by scores on intelligence or achievement tests but on the basis of the social class to which a child belongs. Because more blacks than whites come from lower-class backgrounds, especially in large cities, more blacks are assigned to the lower scholastic tracks.

Consider the tracking system used in Washington, D.C., until 1967. There were four tracks or levels to which pupils were assigned: honors, regular, general, and basic. It was found that poor blacks were routinely assigned to the basic track and most whites were assigned to the honors and regular tracks. Many predominantly white schools did not have a basic track and many black schools had no honors track.

The system was declared unconstitutional on the grounds that it did not grant blacks equal educational opportunities. No matter how intelligent a black child from a poor family might have been, he or she was assigned to the basic track, the level of which would not provide an adequate background for college.

Not only do educational opportunities vary with the level of the group to which children are assigned, but teachers' expectations do also. Teachers of honors students expect high performance from their pupils and work harder to get it. Also, they help increase the pupils' self-esteem and confidence by reminding them that they are the brightest students in the school. The reverse is frequently true for teachers of the lower groups. They expect little and often remind pupils of their inferior status. This decreases self-confidence and causes the students to feel unworthy. This situation cannot bring out the best in the students and their potential remains undeveloped.

*Nongraded programs,* another approach to dealing with individual differences in the classroom, are used chiefly at the elementary school level, although some high schools have recently begun to use them. Nongraded programs do away with grouping by grade levels—such as first, second, and third—through which children pass each school year if their classroom performance is satisfactory. Instead, the pupils proceed through individual units of work from one to the next, whenever they demonstrate their competence in the present unit. Each student proceeds at his or her own pace, in accordance with individual levels of ability and motivation.

Nongraded programs offer flexibility. A child advances from one group or classroom to another whenever he or she is ready. There is no promotion from one grade to the next at the end of each year, and there are no failures, although some children will take longer than others to complete a unit of work. Because there is no threat of failure, there is less anxiety. The brighter students generally move rapidly to succeeding units of work and therefore are continually stimulated and challenged by new, more demanding material. They are not held back by slower students, nor are slower students constantly competing with brighter students for the reward of being promoted to the next grade. There is no pressure to complete a certain amount of work in a definite period of time.

Psychological research on nongraded programs has yielded no clear-cut evidence either for or against them. However, current educational practice favors the nongraded approach because it allows for individualized instruction and seems more democratic and less discriminatory than homogeneous grouping.

## PSYCHOLOGICAL PRINCIPLES OF LEARNING

Although there are social, emotional, and political considerations involved in the classroom, the ultimate function of the classroom situation is learning. Psychologists have conducted an enormous amount of research on the learning process, whether memorizing lines of poetry or learning a skill such as playing the violin. A variety of organisms have been studied, from flatworms to human beings. Many of the research findings have been applied by educational psychologists to alter the ways in which we are taught. We shall discuss several psychological learning principles that have significance for the classroom situation.

## Reinforcement

In our discussions of behavior modification, we noted the importance of reinforcement in changing human behavior. In these cases, all that is necessary to induce people to change their behavior (that is, to learn to behave in a different way) is to reward or reinforce them every time they display the desired behavior. Reinforcement is a simple concept, and its origin is usually associated with the Russian physiologist, Ivan Pavlov, who developed his *law of reinforcement* in the early years of the twentieth century. In research with dogs, Pavlov found that they could be taught (or conditioned) to respond to such stimuli as bells and flashing lights by presenting food (a reinforcement) immediately after the stimulus was presented. The dogs learned quickly to respond to the stimulus because they received the reward for doing so.

This kind of learning is called *respondent conditioning* because the organism is conditioned or trained to respond to a specific stimulus in the environment. The concept explains how animals and human beings learn many basic behaviors, but it does not adequately account for more complex behaviors such as those learned in the classroom.

To explain higher-level learning, the American psychologist B. F. Skinner introduced the concept of *operant* or *instrumental conditioning,* which, though different from respondent conditioning, nevertheless relies on reinforcement. The behavioral changes or new learning brought about through behavior modification techniques are based on Skinner's operant conditioning. In operant conditioning, the organism's response is not made to a concrete stimulus such as a bell. Instead, the organism must first display the correct behavior, the one that will produce the reinforcement. Then, having seen that a particular behavior is followed by reinforcement, the organism is likely to display that behavior again, in anticipation of further reinforcement.

In previous examples of behavior modification we discussed how the person being treated was reinforced only when he or she behaved in the way considered desirable by the therapist, and was never reinforced when behaving in an undesirable way. If you have ever trained a dog to perform a trick, you have engaged in behavior modification using reinforcement. You reward the dog by petting it or giving it a dog biscuit when it does what you want it to do. The dog gets nothing when it fails to do what you want it to do.

Two types of reinforcement are useful in learning: positive reinforcement and negative reinforcement. *Positive reinforcement* is what we have discussed, rewarding behavior with something desirable, pleasant, or positive. Positive reinforcement is, in essence, a payoff, and it can be a powerful device in the classroom because teachers have the power to use many positive rewards to alter student behavior. All students need some amount of positive reinforcement if they are to behave appropriately in the classroom and to learn. Grades are a constant classroom reward for performance at all levels of education. In elementary school, teachers use such rewards as gold stars on a chart next to a student's name for exemplary performance or behavior. Other positive reinforcements in the classroom are smiling at or praising students and expressing interest in and approval of their work.

In *negative reinforcement,* a person is rewarded for behaving in a certain way by removing something that is undesirable or unpleasant. If a child is doing poorly in school, the parents may scold and withhold privileges such as watching television. By changing his or her behavior (studying harder), the child may get better grades, and this leads to the removal of the restriction on television viewing.

Often, positive and negative reinforcements operate simultaneously in the classroom. Children study to get good grades and the praise and other rewards good grades bring from their parents, and also to avoid negative situations.

The greater or stronger is the reinforcement for a certain behavior, the more readily and rapidly that behavior is learned. If a teacher tells a class that A's are never given, the students probably will not work so hard, knowing that the highest grade or reward they can receive is a B. If it were possible to earn an A, they would probably work harder for the greater reward.

To be maximally effective, reinforcement must be given immediately after the desired behavior takes place. The longer the delay between behavior and reinforcement, the less effective the reinforcement will be because the connection between proper behavior and the reward it brings will be less clear. If you wait ten minutes after your dog has performed a trick before rewarding it, the dog is not likely to learn the trick. If a teacher waits a half-hour after a student has displayed some desirable behavior before offering praise, the child will be less likely to repeat the behavior than if the praise had come seconds after the behavior was displayed.

When applying conditioning principles initially, the reinforcement should be given every time the behavior occurs. However, once the behavior has been learned, *continuous reinforcement* is no longer necessary to maintain the behavior. Learned behavior can be maintained and even strengthened by *partial reinforcement.* The reward could be presented only every third or fourth time the behavior is displayed, instead of every time.

Psychologists have determined the relative effectiveness of various schedules of reinforcement, such as the fixed interval schedule, in which the reinforcement is presented at fixed intervals of time, and the fixed ratio schedule, in which the reinforcement is presented only after a certain number of responses have been made. If a teacher gives a test every two weeks, he or she is operating on a fixed interval schedule. If you must complete five reports for a course before receiving a grade, you are working on a fixed ratio schedule of reinforcement.

Another aspect of reinforcement is extinction, which involves the cessation of reinforcement for a particular behavior. As typified by the case of Bobby in the example at the beginning of the chapter, undesirable behavior can be eliminated (extinguished) by the simple expedient of no longer rewarding it. Some behaviors are more difficult to extinguish than others, particularly those that are complex, have been partially reinforced, and very strongly conditioned.

## Punishment

It is popularly believed, by parents, teachers, and society in general, that punishment is an effective means of changing behavior. The threat of punishment is with us all of our lives and takes many forms—being scolded by our parents, kept after school by our teachers, or detained by the police. However, we all know from our own experience that punishment does not always work.

Punishment can be effective in training infants and very young children, but only if it is applied immediately and consistently every time the undesirable behavior is displayed. Also, stronger punishment may be more effective with young children than weaker punishment.

With older children and adults, punishment may be effective only for a short period of time, particularly if the undesirable behavior has been strongly rewarded in the past and if there are no alternative behaviors available to the individual. Punishment is more effective if it is combined with positive reinforcement for more desirable behaviors. For example, if a child is scolded for disrupting a class and praised when cooperating with the class, his or her behavior is much more likely to change for the better than if punishment alone is used.

## Active Practice of the Material

Learning is greatly facilitated when students are actively involved in the learning process rather than passively receiving information from a teacher or a textbook. Actively participating by taking notes, outlining material from a book, discussing the information with others, or reciting it will result in greater learning than hearing the same material presented in a lecture. Studies have shown that the more time students spend actively reciting material (instead of passively reading it), the greater is their learning. This finding holds for all kinds of material, from specific items such as foreign language vocabulary to abstract philosophical concepts.

## Massed Versus Distributed Practice

What is the best way of scheduling study sessions? How long should they be? Should students study for relatively long periods of time without interruption (called *massed practice*), or should they study during a large number of short sessions (*distributed practice*)?

Psychological research on learning has shown that distributed practice is, in general, superior to massed practice because students may easily become fatigued by a lengthy, uninterrupted study session. This does not mean that massed practice should never be used. Short and simple material can be learned effectively by massed practice because the study session would not have to be very long.

## Whole Versus Part Learning

Should material to be learned be divided into small parts, each of which is studied separately, or should it be learned as a whole? The relative effectiveness of whole or part learning depends on the level of intelligence of the student and the nature of the material. Brighter students are capable of learning larger units of material; thus the whole method is better for them. Students who are less bright learn material better if it is divided into parts. Some material may lend itself readily to part learning, whereas other material may be meaningless if it is not learned as a whole. For example, it would be inappropriate to apply part learning to driving a car, breaking down driving skill into components such as learning to turn on the ignition and learning to shift from neutral into first gear. Driving is a continuous series of movements and actions and can be more efficiently learned as a whole.

## Transfer

Transfer refers to how the learning of one kind of material affects the learning of another kind of material. There are two kinds of transfer: positive and negative.

In *positive* transfer, the skills or information learned in one task facilitate the learning of another task. For example, learning the alphabet makes it easier for us to learn to read words and sentences; there is positive transfer from one learning situation to the other. In *negative* transfer, material learned in one situation makes it harder to learn a different kind of material. For example, knowledge of the Spanish language makes later learning of the French language more difficult because the two languages have dissimilar pronunciations of similar words. Certainly, education should be oriented toward positive transfer as much as possible.

## Knowledge of Results

We noted the importance of knowledge of results in Chapter 6 in the discussion of biofeedback as a means of controlling internal bodily processes. The application to the classroom is similar, in principle. We are able to learn more easily when we have a clear idea of how we are progressing. When teachers supply continuous feedback or knowledge of results to students, the students are always aware of their level of achievement and can maintain or improve their study habits accordingly.

Several standard ways of providing knowledge of results in the classroom are end-of-term grades, teacher comments on papers and reports, and examinations. The feedback enables students to know what they are doing well or what kinds of errors they are making.

For feedback to be maximally effective, it should be given as soon as possible. Examinations and papers should be returned promptly to students so that mistakes can be determined immediately. Feedback should also be specific. The more detailed is a student's knowledge of his or her results, the more useful this information will be as a learning device. Knowledge of results should be given in a way that stresses what students have done correctly rather than what they have done incorrectly. In other words, right answers should be emphasized or praised more heavily than wrong answers are criticized. This reinforces the students' good work, which serves to motivate them to perform better.

## MECHANICAL AIDS TO LEARNING

Machines play an important part in the learning process at all levels of education. Through films, closed-circuit television, cassettes, slides, charts, and transparencies, classes can be considerably enlivened and students exposed to information in ways more exciting than the traditional teacher–textbook–lecture approach.

However, these audiovisual and mechanical aids are adjuncts to the lecture system; they supplement the material supplied by the teacher. Also, they merely present information to the student. However exciting and dramatic they may be, the student remains passive, receiving information and not actively participating in the learning process.

Two types of mechanical aids to learning differ from the familiar audiovisual materials in that they engage the students' active participation. These are programmed instruction and computer-assisted instruction.

## Programmed Instruction

Programmed instruction involves self-paced instruction in which the students with their "teaching machines" or programmed textbooks function as their own teachers and proceed at their own speed to learn the material, which gradually increases in difficulty. This is a radical departure from the traditional classroom situation in which all students must keep pace with the level of instruction set by the teacher. Programmed instruction is applied to many segments of society, from teaching in kindergartens through colleges to job training in industry and the military.

In programmed instruction, the subject matter to be learned is presented to the students in a highly detailed format (called a *program*). The students respond to questions at frequent intervals, giving the precise answers based on the material previously presented to them. The material begins at an easy level and becomes more complex in very small steps. In this way, slow learners can proceed at a comfortable pace and faster learners can proceed more rapidly. Therefore, programmed instruction is more suitable for dealing with individual levels of ability than a teacher dealing with a group of students.

Programmed instruction techniques include paper-and-pencil book formats as well as expensive electronic equipment, but the concept of individualized instruction is the same.

Table 10–1 shows several steps in a programmed instruction course dealing with the topic of programmed instruction. This example of programmed learning is of the paper-and-pencil variety, in which students use a card to cover the answers on one side of the page. As soon as they write their answers in the blanks, they move the card down the page and compare their answer with the correct one. Thus, they learn immediately if their answer is right or wrong.

In terms of the psychological principles of learning, programmed instruction offers several advantages over traditional instructional methods. Programmed instruction provides for continuous and *active participation* on the part of the students; they must record their answers to one item before moving on to the next one. In some machine versions, it is physically impossible to proceed to the next item unless the current one has been answered. Programmed instruction provides constant and immediate *feedback* or knowledge of results because students are informed after each item whether their answer is correct or incorrect. Programmed instruction provides *positive reinforcement*. The items are

**Table 10–1.** Sample Programmed Instruction Material *

| programmed | One of the methods of organizing material to be learned, based on the psychological principles of learning, is called *programmed learning.* Much of this study guide is presented in the form of _____ learning. |
| --- | --- |
| frame | In programmed learning, the material is arranged so that you can learn it on your own with a minimum number of errors. Each item, called a *frame,* builds on the preceding _____ in such a way that there is little conceptual distance between them. |
| step | In other words, each frame tries to convey to you only a small amount of new information. The *steps* between frames are very small. The size of a _____ is important. The smaller the step size, the fewer *errors* you are likely to make. |
| errors<br>incorrect | Small steps are necessary to ensure that you make a minimum number of _____. The idea is for you to make a correct response to each frame and rarely, if ever, make an _____ response. |

* Adapted from Rita Atkinson and Richard Atkinson, *Study Guide to Introduction to Psychology* (6th ed.; New York: Harcourt Brace Jovanovich, 1975), pp. 125–126.

purposely constructed so that students should easily be able to learn the correct response.

Programmed instruction offers several other advantages. By eliminating the need for a teacher, students can learn whenever and wherever they choose (particularly with the book format), and they do not all have to be assembled at one time and place. Because programmed instruction is oriented toward individual differences, each student is able to proceed at his or her own pace. Finally, the course of study is so standardized that all students are exposed to the same material. This is not the case if different sections of a course are taught by different teachers, each of whom may emphasize, change, or omit parts of the material to be learned.

There are also disadvantages to programmed instruction. Some students find the technique boring after a while and become restless as the small steps continue in robotlike fashion. Some material cannot be taught so effectively with programmed instruction, which is more suited to concrete, factual material such as biology or a foreign language than to abstract material such as philosophy. Programmed instruction is also expensive; the equipment and the programs are very costly to develop.

Studies that have compared programmed instruction with the traditional teacher–textbook approach have shown that the level of learning achieved by the students is the same with both methods. However, teaching machines allow for the learning of the same amount of material in a much shorter period of time.

## Computer-Assisted Instruction

Computer-assisted instruction (CAI) is a derivative of programmed instruction. It has been tried at all levels of education, with reports of great success. In this approach, a computer stores an entire program of instruction and serves as a teacher, interacting on an individual basis with the students. Each student has a separate terminal and the computer can teach several thousand students at the same time.

The computer transmits lessons to the display screens (CRTs) of each terminal. Students also receive aural messages over earphones. To answer each question, students enter their response on a typewriter keyboard or touch the appropriate spot on the visual display with an electronic pencil. Each answer is instantly analyzed and recorded. If the answer is correct, the computer presents the next item. If the answer is incorrect, the computer analyzes the kind of mistake made and presents remedial material designed to overcome that kind of error.

Students who make rapid progress on a unit of material may skip to more advanced sections of the course. Students who have difficulty learning the material may be given review material. In this manner, CAI offers more individualized instruction than the programmed instruction technique discussed previously. In essence, each student has a private teacher in the form of the computer, who responds instantly and who never gets tired or irritated.

CAI allows students to actively participate in the learning process, and provides positive reinforcement and immediate knowledge of results. Elementary school students, in particular, are fascinated by the

gadgetry of CAI; some have been known to sneak into the classroom after school hours to play with the system. Elementary school pupils and college students both learn material significantly faster with CAI than by the traditional approach to instruction.

## BEHAVIOR DISORDERS IN THE CLASSROOM

Although the primary mission of the classroom is learning, educational and school psychologists as well as teachers must also focus on psychological adjustment. Emotional or behavioral disorders will interfere with a child's ability to learn, and the incidence of behavior disorders in the classroom is alarmingly high. Surveys show that close to one-third of all elementary school children have mild emotional problems; at least one out of every ten needs psychological counseling. In absolute terms, this means that more than 10 million school children could benefit from some kind of psychological help to enable them to deal with their emotional problems. Several million more children suffer from physiologically based learning disabilities that interfere with intellectual development. Thus, there are two kinds of behavior disorders found in the classroom, those that are emotional in nature and those that are neurophysiological in nature and origin.

### Learning Disabilities

Two of the major neurophysiologically based learning disabilities are dyslexia and hyperkinesis.

*Dyslexia* is an impairment of the ability to read as a result of some brain abnormality. Because it afflicts only one aspect of learning, it is not similar to mental retardation, which prevents or inhibits learning of all kinds. A dyslexic child may have a good vocabulary and know the meanings of many words, but be unable to read them or understand the spoken words. There are two kinds of dyslexia: visual and auditory.

A visual dyslexic child cannot translate the printed word into sounds; that is, the child cannot understand the meanings of words and individual letters. The child may also find it hard to discriminate between letters that look similar, such as *b* and *d*, and between words that look similar, such as *hat* and *pat*. An auditory dyslexic child has difficulty differentiating between letters and words that sound similar.

Teachers must be trained to identify dyslexic children and not confuse them with mentally retarded children. Through special education classes, dyslexic children can be taught to discriminate between different letters, beginning with simple differences and proceeding to more complex differences. This can be accomplished most readily by reinforcing the child for selecting the correct symbol from among several similar ones.

*Hyperkinesis* is a very serious disorder which is being found increasingly among children. Hyperkinetic children are unusually active, excitable, and impulsive; easily distracted; and often clumsy. They cannot seem to be still and constantly move around the classroom in a frenzy of activity. Obviously, they tend to be disruptive and have difficulty concentrating on their school work. They are usually rejected by their classmates, which depresses their sense of self-esteem and self-worth.

Hyperkinesis seems to result from brain damage, and it can be aggravated by psychological factors such as stress and anxiety. The most effective treatment for hyperkinesis at this time is the administration of stimulant drugs such as amphetamines. Why these drugs, which stimulate normal children, have a calming effect on hyperactive children is not known, but the drugs do improve the hyperkinetic child's ability to concentrate.

Another approach to treatment, which is currently being tested, involves the administration of massive daily doses of vitamins (thiamine, niacin, and pyridoxine). Preliminary research suggests that vitamin treatment can produce significant behavioral changes within three weeks.

## Emotional and Social Disorders

The failure of many school-age children to learn, to develop normal social relationships, and to mature adequately can often be traced to emotional disorders. In terms of a child's development, one of the teacher's most important activities may be the early detection of signs of emotional abnormality so that the child can be properly treated. Undetected and untreated, emotional problems become more severe as the person grows older. In general, the more severe the disorder is in childhood, the more incapacitating it will be in adulthood, unless treatment is instituted. Therefore, teachers have a great opportunity and responsibility to influence the future emotional lives of their pupils.

It is vital that teachers receive sufficient training in psychology to enable them to recognize the warning signs of emotional disorder. Teachers should be alert for the following behaviors [2]:

1. An unexplained inability to learn. This is probably the most significant indicator of the existence of an emotional problem because it suggests an unwillingness to use one's abilities.

2. An inability to have satisfactory social relationships with other children or with adults. A child who is unable to demonstrate warmth

[2] Robert Craig, William Mehrens, and Harvey Clarizio, *Contemporary Educational Psychology: Concepts, Issues, Applications* (New York: John Wiley, 1975), p. 355.

and compassion for others, to develop close friendships, or to get along with others may have feelings of inadequacy or hostility.

3. An inability to behave at a level appropriate to one's level of development. This refers to the child who behaves in an immature fashion, displaying interests and values of children who are younger.

4. An inability to display confidence and belief in oneself. This may indicate deep feelings of inferiority and inadequacy, which can be manifested in being unusually sensitive to criticism, excessively responsive to flattery, and in constantly discrediting the achievements of others.

5. An inability to overcome feelings of sadness. This reflects a basic unhappiness; excitement and joy are lacking in the child's school activities and social relations. The child is unable to share with classmates in even the most joyous occasions, remaining instead on the sidelines, unsmiling and glum.

6. An inability to cope with stressful personal or school situations. The disturbed child is likely to react to stressful situations by displaying obvious and excessive fear and anxiety, and often by developing physical symptoms such as headaches and stomachaches.

Common emotional problems among school-age children include anxiety, aggression, and dependency. These are possible precursors to the mental illnesses discussed in Chapter 3.

A child's *anxiety* may not disrupt a classroom as a whole, but it certainly disrupts and inhibits the intellectual, emotional, and social growth of the child. Anxiety is a fear of nothing specific but of everything in general. Some children become so anxious about school and everything connected with it that they are always fearful, always expecting some catastrophe to befall them. Obviously, such fear will detract from classroom performance and satisfactory social relations.

Teachers may help overcome a child's anxiety, or at least reduce its effects, in several ways. They can reinforce the child's positive behaviors, set realistic goals that the anxious child has a chance to reach, minimize opportunities for failure (both intellectual and social), and provide a classroom environment that is nonthreatening because it is predictable and routine for the anxious child. The anxious child does not react well to classrooms that are characterized by a high level of stimulation and by unpredictability.

*Aggression* on the part of a child can disrupt the learning and social opportunities of the classroom and the individual. Aggressive behavior is very common in most children; a certain level of it is expected and does not necessarily indicate emotional abnormality. However, even the normal amount of aggressiveness must be controlled or a class may degenerate into anarchy. At the same time, aggressiveness must not be curbed so completely and ruthlessly that its positive aspects—such as assertiveness, self-confidence, and competitiveness—are repressed. Great skill and patience on the part of a teacher are required when dealing with the aggressive child.

Abnormal aggressiveness in children, particularly when it results in hostile attacks on others, cannot be tolerated in the classroom. It is unfair to the rest of a class to have its activities interrupted by one unruly member; teachers must be firm in preventing this. They must set limits on classroom behavior and stick to them, and ensure that overly aggressive pupils are constantly supervised. If necessary, aggressive students may have to work alone or in small groups.

At the same time, however, teachers must display warmth and personal regard for aggressive and nonaggressive students alike. A calm demeanor will serve as a better example or model than reacting to aggressive behavior in kind. Behavior modification is often successful with unusually aggressive children, either providing positive reinforcement for nonaggressive behaviors or extinguishing aggressive behaviors by taking care not to reinforce them.

*Dependency* in school children can inhibit their social and emotional growth and prevent the development of self-confidence. Dependent children are less able to develop the desirable characteristics of autonomy and independence because they lean on or cling to others for emotional and intellectual support. The most noticeable behavioral indicator of dependency in children is constantly asking teachers for help.

Dependent children are unable to take the initiative in dealing with classroom assignments and finding solutions to problems. This applies to easy as well as difficult problems. Dependent children cannot make even minor decisions for themselves and will always seek their teacher's assistance.

Dependency is also indicated by behaviors designed to attract attention. These children frequently call on the teacher with requests to "Look at me," or "Look at what I've done." They constantly bring their work to the teacher for approval because they are sensitive to what the teacher thinks of them. Dependent children may also want physical contact with the teacher. On a school outing, for example, a dependent child will stay close to the teacher and insist on holding the teacher's hand.

Dependency cannot be encouraged in the classroom because it can inhibit a child's growth. Teachers must strive to help these children develop self-confidence and independence, usually through the use of reinforcement. Teachers must not reward dependent behavior by providing recognition or affection for it. Instead, teachers must encourage dependent children to show more initiative in their work, and they must reinforce independent behavior whenever it occurs. Teachers must also ensure that classmates are not reinforcing the dependent student.

Psychology Applied to the Classroom

Providing short assignments is another way to reduce dependency. The student can be encouraged to complete the assignment independently and then be praised for working alone. It is easier for a dependent child to work alone on a five-minute problem than on one that requires thirty minutes to complete. Gradually, the length of the assignments can be increased.

## TEACHER BEHAVIOR

We have described throughout the chapter the important role teachers play in the intellectual, emotional, and social development of their pupils. They may function as adjuncts to the educational and school psychologists, detecting indications of abnormality and trying to change them, or referring children for specialized help. Of course, this role assumes that teachers are well adjusted and emotionally stable, but, like people in any occupation, this is not always the case.

Teachers who have mental health problems can do great harm to the students, particularly to children in elementary school. Authoritarian teachers who are hostile toward their pupils can stifle creativity and independence, foster anxiety, and cause the development of negative attitudes toward school.

Teachers who are insecure may try to satisfy their own security needs by forcing their students to become dependent on them, behaving in ways that are likely to stunt the intellectual and emotional development of the students. For example, insecure teachers may provide a great deal of assistance, perhaps even giving answers on an examination, so that students will grow to depend on them. Also, teachers who are fearful and anxious may induce anxiety among their pupils.

Because teachers have so much power to influence children directly in the classroom and indirectly as examples or models, teacher mental health is an important problem. Teachers can also shape attitudes, sometimes negatively. For example, they may communicate their prejudices and stereotypes to young and impressionable students.

The list of such influences is long, but the point has been made. Teacher behavior may influence children for good or for ill. So pervasive is the influence of teachers, so powerful is their example, that they can determine the nature of their students' development. Therefore, educational and school psychologists, and teachers themselves, must be aware of mental health problems and of the usefulness of psychological counseling or therapy. Some school systems encourage their teachers to take advantage of counseling. One day school psychologists may offer their services as openly to teachers as they do to pupils.

Research indicates that teacher therapy can vastly improve the climate in the classroom. In one study of teachers who underwent psychotherapy, more than 90 per cent believed that the counseling had increased their ability to understand their students and to be able to help them with their own problems. The teachers also believed that they were more capable of working with difficult or withdrawn students and could accept their students' negative behaviors.

Because the quality of the education we receive influences the course of our lives, the application of the findings of educational and school psychology is of major importance to all of us.

## SUMMARY

The application of psychology to the classroom influences our intellectual, emotional, and behavioral development. *Educational* psychology is concerned with research on intellectual development and *school* psychology is concerned with testing and counseling.

*Individual differences* in learning ability arise from differences in personality, motivation, and intelligence. Although personality and motivation influence our performance in school, the most important factor is *intelligence*. There is not complete agreement among psychologists on a definition of intelligence, but this does not prevent the concept from being measured and used to predict behavior in many situations with a high degree of accuracy. Much of your future will be determined by how high you score on an intelligence test.

Intelligence is measured indirectly, in terms of the effect it has on behavior, that is, in terms of levels of performance on an IQ test. The first intelligence test was developed in 1905 by Binet. In 1916, Terman revised Binet's test for use with U.S. children (the *Stanford-Binet* test). Terman also developed the concept of IQ (intelligence quotient), which shows the relationship between mental age and chronological age by the formula

$$\frac{\text{mental age}}{\text{chronological age}} \times 100 = IQ$$

In 1939, Wechsler developed an IQ test for use with adults (the *Wechsler Adult Intelligence Scale*); it has verbal and performance scales. The latter is useful with people who have language difficulties or whose verbal skills are poorly developed. Wechsler also developed an IQ test for children (the *Wechsler Intelligence Scale for Children*).

Intelligence, like all other human characteristics, is distributed in the population in accordance with the normal curve. Most people score around the average level and few score at the extreme high or low ends.

Approximately 50 per cent of the population have IQs between 90 and 109. Knowledge of a person's IQ enables educators to provide the appropriate kind and level of instruction for the person's ability and potential.

There are two possible abuses of intelligence testing. First, a teacher may incorrectly interpret a student's IQ score and so lower the student's opportunities. Second, IQ testing can discriminate against disadvantaged children. Because most intelligence tests depend primarily on verbal ability, they favor those who have access to better schools and discriminate against those from poorer schools. Also, because IQ tests measure one's current level of achievement, people who have had greater educational and cultural opportunities generally score higher than those who lack these opportunities.

The issue of racial differences in intelligence is highly controversial. Primarily because of lesser educational opportunities, blacks have lower average IQ scores than whites. Whether these differences are determined by environmental or genetic factors is unresolved; current thinking favors the environmental explanation.

Individual differences affect education because a classroom contains pupils representing a range of intelligence. Different educational opportunities must be provided for students with different levels of intelligence.

Mentally retarded children, with IQs below 70, require special educational opportunities, particularly in reading and arithmetic skills, and are usually taught in separate classes by specially trained teachers. Some mentally retarded children derive little benefit from education, but others can be trained to hold a job and to function reasonably well in society.

Gifted children, with IQs above 130, also require special educational opportunities to allow them to make the most of their potential. By placing them in special classes or allowing them to skip grades, they can receive the educational challenge and stimulation demanded by their high IQs. Terman's long-term study of the gifted showed them to be superior intellectually, physically, and psychologically to those with lower IQs.

Children in the middle range of ability also represent wide differences in intelligence and require different educational opportunities. Two popular approaches are homogeneous grouping and nongraded programs.

*Homogeneous grouping,* or tracking, groups students in terms of their ability, with the brightest in one track, the average students in another track, and so on. Tracking has been used in a discriminatory manner in which students are grouped not by IQ score but by race or social class.

*Nongraded programs* eliminate the grade levels through which children pass at the end of each school year. Instead, pupils proceed to new work units whenever they have demonstrated competence in the material of the preceding unit. Children advance to the next unit when they are ready, and no child suffers the stigma of failure.

The *psychological principles of learning* have special significance for the classroom. *Reinforcement* is a fundamental way to change human behavior and it involves two kinds of conditioning: *respondent conditioning,* which involves learning a response to a specific stimulus, and *operant conditioning,* which involves being reinforced only for displaying the appropriate behavior.

In *positive reinforcement,* a person is rewarded with something desirable. In *negative reinforcement,* the reward involves the removal of something undesirable. In *continuous reinforcement,* a person is rewarded every time the desired behavior occurs. *Partial reinforcement* rewards the behavior only some of the time. The phenomenon of *extinction* involves the cessation of reinforcement. *Punishment* is not effective in general, but can be useful combined with positive reinforcement.

Learning is facilitated when students can *actively participate* in the learning process, when *distributed* rather than *massed practice* is used, when the learning situation allows for *positive* rather than *negative transfer,* and when *knowledge of results* is supplied. Whether *whole* or *part learning* is more effective depends on the nature of the material and the level of intelligence of the learner.

Two mechanical aids to learning involve *programmed instruction* and *computer-assisted instruction.* Both approaches satisfy the psychological principles of learning and bring about faster learning than traditional approaches to teaching.

*Learning disabilities* include *dyslexia,* an impairment of the ability to read, and *hyperkinesis,* a disorder that causes children to be hyperactive, excitable, and impulsive. Dyslexia requires remedial training in reading; hyperkinesis is usually treated by stimulant drugs.

*Emotional disorders* in children include anxiety, aggression, and dependency. These can be recognized by a child's inability to learn, have satisfactory social relationships, behave at a level appropriate to his or her development, display confidence and belief in himself or herself, overcome feelings of sadness, or cope with stressful personal and school experiences.

*Teacher behavior* may influence the intellectual and emotional development of students for good or for ill. Teachers who receive psychological counseling have been found to be better able to deal with their students, particularly with troubled and withdrawn students.

## SUGGESTED READINGS

Barbe, Walter B., and Joseph S. Renzulli, Eds. *Psychology and Education of the Gifted,* 2nd ed. New York: Irvington, 1975.

Bardon, Jack I. The state of the art (and science) of school psychology. *American Psychologist,* 1976, **31,** 785-791.

Block, N. J., and Gerald Dworkin, Eds. *The IQ Controversy: Critical Readings.* New York: Pantheon, 1976.

Cronbach, Lee J. *Educational Psychology,* 3rd ed. New York: Harcourt Brace Jovanovich, 1977.

Dembo, Myron H. *Teaching for Learning: Applying Educational Psychology in the Classroom.* Pacific Palisades, Calif.: Goodyear, 1977.

Drew, Clifford J., Michael L. Hardman, and Harry P. Bluhm. *Mental Retardation: Social and Educational Perspectives.* St. Louis, Mo.: Mosby, 1977.

Lahey, Benjamin B., and Martha Johnson. *Psychology and Instruction: A Practical Approach to Educational Psychology.* Glenview, Ill.: Scott, Foresman, 1978.

Lindgren, Henry Clay. *Educational Psychology in the Classroom,* 5th ed. New York: John Wiley, 1976.

Robinson, Nancy M., and Halbert B. Robinson. *The Mentally Retarded Child: A Psychological Approach,* 2nd ed. New York: McGraw-Hill, 1976.

Ross, Alan O. *Psychological Aspects of Learning Disabilities and Reading Disorders.* New York: McGraw-Hill, 1976.

Seagoe, May V. *Terman and the Gifted.* Los Altos, Calif.: William Kauffmann, 1975.

Sears, Robert R. Sources of life satisfactions of the Terman gifted men. *American Psychologist,* 1977, **32,** 119-128.

Sprinthall, Richard C., and Norman A. Sprinthall. *Educational Psychology: A Developmental Approach.* Reading, Mass.: Addison-Wesley, 1974.

Strain, Phillip S., Thomas P. Cooke, and Tony Apolloni. *Teaching Exceptional Children: Assessing and Modifying Social Behavior.* New York: Academic Press, 1976.

Stumphauzer, Jerome S. *Behavior Modification Principles: An Introduction and Training Manual.* Kalamazoo, Mich.: Behaviordelia, 1977.

Super, Donald E., and Douglas T. Hall. Career development: Exploration and planning. *Annual Review of Psychology,* 1978, **29,** 333-372.

Wallach, Michael A., and Lisl Wallach. *Teaching All Children to Read.* Chicago: University of Chicago Press, 1976.

Yelon, Stephen L., and Grace W. Weinstein. *A Teacher's World: Psychology in the Classroom.* New York: McGraw-Hill, 1977.

# Psychology Applied to the World of Work: I. Selecting People for Work

**11**

One at a time, the candidates met with the psychologists behind the barn on the large, secluded estate. Some wooden poles and blocks of different shapes and sizes lay on the ground. Like a giant tinker-toy set, the blocks contained holes in which the poles could be placed in order to build various structures. Each candidate was told to assemble a 5-foot cube in ten minutes using, as helpers, two men who happened to be working in the barn.

Because this was partly a test of leadership ability, the candidates were instructed not to do any of the work themselves but to act as supervisors to the two workers, directing them to build the cube. The psychologists summoned the two workers and asked if they would be willing to help out for a few minutes. They agreed. The psychologists sat down a few feet away, looking grim, to observe each candidate at work.

The construction job would not be a difficult one under ordinary conditions but, unknown to the candidates, these were not ordinary conditions. The problem, as each candidate soon learned, was with the two workers. They did not "just happen" to be working in the barn; it was their job to agree to help the candidates. They were actually paid by the psychologists to make it as difficult and frustrating as possible for the candidates to finish the construction task in ten minutes. In fact, the helpers did their work so well that no candidate ever finished in time!

The two helpers did carry out whatever instructions the candidates gave them, but they did so carelessly, sloppily, and stupidly. For example, if the structure were halfway finished, one of the workers would "accidentally" hit it with a wooden pole, knocking it all down. If the candidate began constructing the cube the wrong way, the helpers would follow the orders for a while, and then tell the candidate that he was wrong as they started dismantling the structure on their own.

All the while, of course, the clock was ticking and time was running out. And the psychologists were presumed to be writing negative comments about the candidate's ability to carry out this simple task. The situation was extremely frustrating for the candidates; they very much wanted to be evaluated favorably on their leadership ability and be selected for the position. The task was deliberately arranged so that the psychologists could observe the way in which the candidates reacted to stress.

And there was more stress than just being able to complete the task within ten minutes. The two helpers were also instructed to humiliate and embarrass the candidates, to criticize them no matter what they did. For example:

> What kind of work did you do before you came here? Never did any building, I bet. Jeez, I've seen a lot of guys, but no one as dumb as you. . . .
>
> Well, what kind of boss are you anyway? You haven't told me anything to do. You stand there and say "get to work, get to work," but you don't say what I should do. . . . Why don't you act like a boss? . . .
>
> What kind of man are you anyway? Why in hell don't you make up your mind and stick to it? Be decisive. . . . What are you—man or mouse?*

In addition to these remarks, the helpers made comments to distract the candidates. If there was anything unusual about the candidates—baldness, a foreign accent, or a quiet demeanor—the helpers focused on this characteristic to provoke them. Then, if a candidate became distracted because of these taunts, the helpers accused the candidate of neglecting the job!

> Jeez, they send a boy out here to do a man's job, and when he can't do it he starts blaming his helpers. . . . Cripes, they must really be scraping the bottom of the barrel now.†

You can imagine how difficult this situation was for the candidates. Nothing was working right, they were being harassed, humiliated, and criticized in front of the psychologists, and time was moving on. They were failing at what seemed like such a simple task.

Candidates reacted to this problem in diverse ways. Some began to do the work themselves, telling the helpers to "get lost." Others became authoritarian and tried to discipline the helpers, which only made them work more poorly. Others gave up trying to be leaders and followed the suggestions of the helpers. A few completely lost control of their temper and physically attacked the helpers.

This stress selection situation was repeated many times during World War II, part of a unique and rigorous program of the Office of Strategic

---

*The OSS Assessment Staff, *Assessment of Men: Selection of Personnel for the U.S. Office of Strategic Services* (New York: Rinehart, 1948), pp. 108–109.
†Ibid., p. 110.

Services (OSS) to select people to be secret agents and to parachute behind enemy lines in order to engage in acts of sabotage and organize guerrilla forces. The psychologists charged with selecting people for the OSS tried to devise realistic situations—such as the cube-construction one just described—to see how candidates reacted to stress. The technique, then called *situational testing*, now called *selection by simulation*, is used, with some modifications, to select managers and executives for industry and government. It is part of a large, impressive arsenal of selection techniques that psychologists have developed to enable organizations to choose the right person for each job.

Nearly every person who holds a job will find that it is difficult to go through a working career without taking part in some psychological selection procedure. Whatever your job, rank, or responsibilities, the job you are offered will be determined by how well you perform on these selection procedures. It has been said that one of the most important days of your life is the day you apply for a job and take a battery of psychological tests, submit to an interview, and undertake whatever other tasks the organization asks of its applicants.

Even when you are already working, you are not finished with psychological selection techniques. They can determine how far you rise in your organization. Many companies require that employees who are being considered for promotion take the same kinds of selection tests used for hiring new employees.

These applications of psychology to the selection of people for employment are, of course, directly relevant to your own future. Indeed, you probably had some experience with selection procedures when you applied for admission to college. It is important, therefore, that you know something about them, if only for your own protection. Psychological selection techniques are one of the most visible applications of psychology to your daily life. Let us describe what they are and how they are used.

## STEPS IN THE SELECTION PROCESS

When employee selection is done correctly, it is a sophisticated, complex, and expensive process that draws heavily on the results of psychological research. A great deal of work must be done before the first applicant appears in the personnel office, and research on the selection procedures must continue even after the applicants have been hired and are working on the job. Research must be repeated periodically on the selection procedures to make sure they are still appropriate for a particular job.

The entire selection process is more difficult and time-consuming than would appear at first glance. There is more to selection than putting an advertisement in the newspaper and waiting for people to show up at the employment office. Five steps in an effective selection program are:

1. Conducting job and worker analyses.
2. Setting cutoff scores and minimum levels of abilities.
3. Recruiting applicants.
4. Administering selection techniques.
5. Validating selection procedures.

*Conducting job and worker analyses.* The first thing to be determined when hiring workers for a particular job is what that job is like. The job must be analyzed to find out exactly what tasks the workers are expected to perform. Job analyses typically include the following information: what tools or equipment are used, what operations are performed, and what characteristics distinguish the job (for example, safety hazards, special skills, or extensive training). It is very sensible to conduct a job analysis at the beginning of the selection process; how could we possibly know what kind of people to look for to perform the job unless we know what is involved in performing the job?

On the basis of the job analysis, a worker analysis is undertaken. Once we know what is involved in performing the job, we can determine the workers' skills, abilities, and characteristics that are suitable. For example, does the job require the ability to read blueprints, or a high level of mechanical aptitude, or speed with numerical calculations? Different jobs, of course, have different worker requirements. Work on an assembly line requires more physical stamina and agility than is needed by an office clerk. An accountant may need better vision for close work than a routine factory employee. Many physical and psychological characteristics affect how well workers perform their jobs. It is important to hire only those persons who possess the right characteristics demanded by the job.

Because the worker analysis derives from the job analysis, the job analysis is conducted first. The job analysis is also the more difficult of the two, particularly when the job is new. For many current jobs, analyses have been published in the *Dictionary of Occupational Titles* (DOT), issued by the U.S. Employment Service. The DOT contains brief but detailed descriptions of some 22,000 jobs. A few of these are listed in Table 11–1. The information provided here is usually not as comprehensive as may be required for a job analysis, but the DOT is helpful in learning the general nature of a job. Also, many companies have on file analyses they have conducted on the same or similar jobs.

However, for a comprehensive job analysis, it is usually best to conduct an actual investigation of the job in question. Probably the most frequently used technique is to *interview* those who are directly con-

**Table 11–1.** Sample Job Descriptions from the *Dictionary of Occupational Titles* *

---

*Bowling-Ball Finisher*
Tends buffing machine that removes scratches and polishes surface of bowling balls.

*Clip Coater*
Coats tips of sunglass clips with protective plastic and cures coated clips in oven.

*Dog Bather*
Bathes dogs in preparation for grooming.

*Maturity Checker*
Tends machine that mashes peas and registers force required to crush them to ascertain hardness (maturity) and grades peas.

*Potato-Chip Sorter*
Observes potato chips on conveyor and removes chips that are burned, discolored, or broken.

*Sequins Stringer*
Strings plastic sequins on thread for use as decoration on wearing apparel.

*Squeak, Rattle, and Leak Repairer*
Drives automobiles of service customers to determine origin of noises and leaks, and repairs or adjusts components to eliminate cause of complaint.

*Whizzer*
Tends machine that spins felt hat bodies to remove excess water.

---

* *Dictionary of Occupational Titles*, 4th ed. (Washington, D.C.: U.S. Department of Labor, Employment and Training Administration, 1977).

nected with the job—the workers, their supervisors, and perhaps the persons who train workers for the job. Because questions are asked of those who have the most intimate knowledge of the job, the carefully conducted interview provides a highly detailed job analysis.

Workers are often suspicious when a representative of management questions them, so it is important to secure their full and open cooperation in advance of the interview. Employees must be fully briefed about the purpose of the interview and should be assured that their personal competence on the job is not being investigated. The interview questions also must be thoroughly planned, and this is where the information from published job analyses can be helpful.

A second approach to job analysis involves administering *questionnaires* to the persons connected with the job. This approach is not as satisfactory as interviewing, for two reasons: first, workers may not be motivated to answer impersonal, written questions as thoroughly or accurately as questions asked by an interviewer in person; and second, unless the questionnaire is exceedingly long, it may not provide sufficiently detailed information.

A third way to analyze a job is to *systematically observe* the workers performing the job. The observers must remain as unobtrusive as possible (as in any naturalistic observation situation) because people often behave differently when they know they are being watched.

A fourth approach to job analysis is the *critical incidents technique,* in which workers or their supervisors record specific incidents that are vital to the successful performance of the job. These incidents are specific behaviors that distinguish good workers from poor workers, and often focus on how the workers react to unusual or emergency situations.

Job analyses are important in today's world of work not only in the selection process, but also in establishing training programs (How could we know what the workers have to be trained to do unless we know what the job requires?), redesigning jobs to increase worker efficiency, and uncovering safety hazards in job performance or in the tools and equipment used.

*Setting cutoff scores and minimum levels of abilities.* From the worker analysis we can determine the characteristics necessary to perform the job in question. Specific selection techniques must then be chosen or developed that will reveal the extent to which applicants for the job possess those characteristics. For example, if the job requires a high school education, a better-than-average IQ, and a high level of mechanical aptitude, the selection techniques must be able to tell the personnel office how each applicant ranks on these characteristics.

Some information—for example, if an applicant graduated from high school—can be easily determined from an application blank or a personal interview. Other information—for example, an applicant's degree of mechanical aptitude—can only be determined by a psychological test. After the proper test has been developed or chosen, a decision must be made as to what score on the test is acceptable. Specifically, how much mechanical ability, clerical aptitude, or intelligence must an applicant possess in order to be able to perform the job satisfactorily?

Thus, *cutoff scores* are established. Applicants who score below these levels are not hired. Sometimes it may be necessary to study workers performing the same or similar jobs to determine precisely where to establish the minimum or cutoff scores.

*Recruiting applicants.* Recruiting is an important part of the overall selection process because it directly affects the efficiency of the selection techniques. If too few applicants are recruited, cutoff scores may have to be lowered, thus reducing the minimum standards set for employment. Suppose, for example, that a company has to hire fifty new employees within two weeks. If the recruiting program brings only sixty applicants, the personnel office cannot afford to be as discriminating as if there were 160 applicants to choose among.

Most organizations devote considerable money and effort to the recruiting process, particularly for high-level jobs. For low-level jobs, companies usually rely on the job applicants who routinely visit the employment office, on referrals from present employees, or, if the need is great, on newspaper advertisements and private employment agencies. For more responsible jobs—managers and executives, scientists, engineers, and other professionals—organizations use more intensive recruiting procedures. This is particularly apparent in business's continuing efforts to recruit bright college seniors each year on campuses throughout the United States. As some of you already know, many companies descend on colleges every spring to interview long lines of students.

College recruiting is a costly undertaking and there is some evidence that it does not always produce desirable results. It has been shown that half of all college graduates leave their first job within five years, primarily because of dissatisfaction with the job. One reason for this dissatisfaction lies in the campus recruitment interview, in which both sides—the student and the company—offer false or idealized pictures of themselves in an effort to impress the other party.

Corporations often present a rosy image of the new graduate's job, an image that may not coincide with the job's reality. The obvious solution is for companies to be more honest about what lies in store for new graduates when they begin work. This procedure is now used by a growing number of organizations with great success. Sears, Roebuck and Company, for example, tells applicants about the disadvantages as well as the advantages of working for them. Candidates are told bluntly about long and erratic hours, frequent transfers, and the hectic work pace. As a result, prospective employees know exactly what to expect when they begin work. Those who do not like such conditions do not accept jobs with Sears, and the company has found that people who are hired with this realistic perception are better employees than those hired previously.

Realistic job previews are now provided for all levels of employment, and by organizations as diverse as Prudential Insurance Company and the U.S. Military Academy at West Point. Some companies, such as the Southern New England Telephone Company, show films to all applicants of their telephone operators talking about the good and bad sides of their job. As a result, fewer new operators quit, and job satisfaction is much higher.

Some companies provide an actual job sample to applicants by letting them perform the work for which they are applying. In this way, applicants have a chance to see if they like the work and if they can do it. Being honest about the job and working conditions, and providing previews of the job, are beneficial both to the company and to those persons being recruited. The applicants know what they are getting into. This means that there will be many fewer surprises, frustrations, and disappointments once they have begun work.

Another way in which industrial psychologists have contributed to the recruiting process is through research on recruiter characteristics and on the various job aspects that appeal to different people.

The characteristics of recruiters are very important because recruiters are the first representatives of the company with whom applicants come in contact. Through studies on college seniors, researchers have identified recruiter characteristics that are disliked by students. If the applicants are unfavorably disposed to the recruiter, they will not be favorably disposed to the company the recruiter represents.

In one study,[1] college seniors disliked recruiters who did not show a personal interest in them, who treated them like numbers instead of human beings, who seemed interested only in filling their quotas, and who did not allow the students time to ask questions. If a company is aware of these negative recruiter characteristics, it can train the recruiters not to display them.

Research on job characteristics that appeal to different people can be valuable to a company, enabling it to emphasize in its recruiting efforts those aspects of work that are of greatest interest to the desired applicants. For example, it has been found that college honors students are interested in different aspects of a job than average students are. Honors students are more concerned with interesting work and with opportunities for self-development. Average students are more interested in salary increases.[2] Therefore, recruiters must offer different inducements to different applicants, assuming that the inducements fairly represent the company and the job.

*Administering selection techniques.* When the applicants who have been recruited by the company to apply for a job appear in the personnel office, they are given the selection techniques appropriate for that particular job. (Specific selection techniques are discussed in the following section.)

Most people are understandably nervous when applying for a job, so it is important that the facilities of the personnel office make applicants as comfortable and as relaxed as possible. Simple matters such as a

[1] W. F. Glueck, "How Recruiters Influence Job Choices on Campus," *Personnel*, **48** (1971), 46–52.

[2] F. T. Paine, "What Do Better College Students Want From Their Jobs?" *Personnel Administration*, **32** (1969), 26–29.

courteous receptionist and a pleasant waiting room can help a great deal.

Application forms, used by most organizations, should be clear, easy to read, and not too long. It is discouraging to be asked to provide four or five pages of detailed information; an applicant's patience and interest may wane toward the end of the form.

Most companies conduct personal interviews with all applicants, and these can be particularly stressful. It is vital that interviewers establish rapport quickly with applicants to make them feel at ease. The less nervous and tense the applicants are, the more effectively they will be able to respond to questions and thus present themselves in a favorable light.

When employee selection involves the administering of psychological tests, it is especially important that the conditions be conducive to relaxation. Many people become tense and anxious about taking tests.

If the conditions under which the tests are given are not satisfactory, they may adversely affect the applicants' performance. For example, if the testing room is noisy and full of interruptions, the applicants may not do as well as they are capable of doing.

It is also important that the people who give the tests be trained not only to establish rapport, but also in the proper methods of testing, such as correct and consistent reading of test instructions and allowing proper time for the completion of the test. Everyone who takes a particular test must do so under identical conditions, and any violation of this consistency damages the usefulness of the test.

*Validating selection procedures.*   The final step in establishing a selection program may be the most important of all. It involves determining the usefulness of the selection techniques in predicting which applicants will be successful workers. Prediction of success on the job is the sole reason for using selection techniques, and if the methods do not result in the hiring of good workers, they are useless.

What is involved here is testing the selection techniques; this is called *validation*. To validate something means to substantiate or confirm it. The process of doing this with selection techniques is accomplished by finding out how well those people who are selected by the technique actually perform on the job, and then comparing that measurement of job performance with the earlier performance on the selection technique.

Suppose that a company has hired 200 employees through the use of a new psychological test developed by the company psychologist. Six months after the workers have been on the job, the psychologist secures an objective indication of how well each employee is doing. This information may be obtained from production records—such as the worker's hourly or daily rate of production—or from job performance ratings made by the employee's supervisor.

These two numbers for each worker (production levels or job ratings, for example, and the score on the psychological test) are compared by the statistical procedure known as *correlation,* which, as discussed in Chapter 2, tells the psychologist the strength of the relationship between these two factors. If this comparison shows that all those employees who received high ratings from their supervisors also received high scores on the psychological test, and all those who received low ratings got low scores on the test, then the psychologist has impressive evidence that the test is valid. The test can be used with confidence to select those applicants who are best qualified for the job. Without undertaking such a comparison however, it would be impossible to determine whether or not the test was of any value.

## KINDS OF SELECTION TECHNIQUES

The major selection techniques in use today are application blanks, personal interviews, letters of recommendation, assessment centers, and psychological tests. Most organizations use some or all of these techniques to select people for employment.

### Application Blanks

Most of you have filled out at least one application blank in your career, so you already have some idea of what they are like. Application blanks are in such widespread use that rarely is anyone hired for a job without first completing one. They provide the company with useful information about job candidates, from routine background data (name, address, Social Security number, education, work experience, and marital status) to more personal information (financial situation, criminal conviction record, and hobbies) (see Figure 11–1).

Beyond the routine background data, however, an organization may ask only for information about applicants that has been shown to be related to success on the job. Only in this way is the application blank useful for predicting which applicants are likely to succeed and which are not. Therefore, items on the application form must be correlated with some measure of job success. Any item that does not show a high correlation with job success must be eliminated.

For example, research in one company showed that their successful executives were all college graduates who had achieved a specific grade-point average and engaged in certain extracurricular activities in college. Clearly, it is to the company's advantage to question applicants on those points as soon as possible in the selection process. Those applicants who are not college graduates with these characteristics can be eliminated from consideration right away, sparing the time and expense of administering additional selection techniques.

A successful modification of the standard application blank is the *weighted application blank*. In this more sophisticated instrument, each item can be scored by assigning a numerical weight to it. For example, if research demonstrates that 80 per cent of all married workers in the company are rated by their supervisors as being very good at their jobs, and only 40 per cent of single workers are so rated, then a score of eight can be given to all married job applicants and a score of four to all single applicants.

A similar scoring procedure can be followed for other items of information, such as amount of education, military experience, number of years of employment, and homeowner or renter. The requirement for assigning weights, however, is that research identify the characteristics of the more successful workers. If, for example, there are no differences in job performance between veterans and nonveterans, that information would be of no value in predicting job success. But if 60 per cent of the veterans are rated successful and only 20 per cent of nonveterans are rated successful, then that item of information is useful as a prediction device.

The weighted application blank is scored in the same way as a test, by adding the number of points for each item to obtain a total score.

Another modification of the standard application form is the *biographical information blank*, which asks for information on a candidate's life in great detail. These forms are usually much longer than standard application blanks and are developed on the basis of extensive research correlating each item with a measure of job success. Biographical information blanks are very much like psychological tests in terms of the type of personal information sought.

The following questions are typical biographical information blank items.

With regard to my personal appearance, as compared with the appearance of my friends, I think that
   A. Most of my friends make a better appearance.
   B. I am equal to most of them in appearance.
   C. I am better than most of them in appearance.
   D. I don't feel strongly one way or the other about my appearance.

During my teens, my parents permitted me to make the final decisions concerning
   A. Attending religious services.
   B. Decorating my room.
   C. Drinking.
   D. Selecting my clothes.
   E. Smoking.

# PART A

## PERSONAL DATA:

☐ SINGLE ☐ ENGAGED ☐ WIDOWED | NUMBER OF CHILDREN | AGES | OTHER DEPENDENTS (give relationships)
☐ MARRIED ☐ SEPARATED ☐ DIVORCED

U.S. CITIZEN    IF NO, INDICATE TYPE VISA
☐ YES    ☐ PERMANENT ☐ EXCHANGE ☐ OTHER
☐ NO    ☐ STUDENT ☐ VISITORS      (specify)

HAVE YOU EVER BEEN CONVICTED OF A CRIME:    IF YES, EXPLAIN (Omit minor traffic violations)
☐ YES ☐ NO

NAME RELATIVES WITH THIS COMPANY AND GIVE YOUR RELATIONSHIP

## EDUCATION RECORD:

| SCHOOL NAME AND LOCATION | DATES (MO/YR) | YEAR GRADUATED | DEGREE | MAJOR/MINOR | GRADE AVERAGE | CLASS STANDING |
|---|---|---|---|---|---|---|
| | | | | | EXAMPLE | EXAMPLE |
| | | | | | MY AVG. 3.2/ ALL A's /4.0 | MY STANDING 3/ OUT OF /20 |
| HIGH SCHOOL | FROM | | | | | |
| | TO | | | | | |
| COLLEGE | FROM | | | MAJOR | MAJOR | MAJOR |
| | TO | | | MINOR | OVERALL | OVERALL |
| | FROM | | | MAJOR | MAJOR | MAJOR |
| | TO | | | MINOR | OVERALL | OVERALL |
| | FROM | | | MAJOR | MAJOR | MAJOR |
| | TO | | | MINOR | OVERALL | OVERALL |

EXTRACURRICULAR ACTIVITIES (Indicate offices held, omit those identifying race, religion, creed, color or national origin)

ACADEMIC AWARDS, HONORARY SOCIETIES, DISTINCTIONS (eg. Dean's list, scholarships)

HOW WAS YOUR EDUCATION FINANCED? (% part-time work, % parents, % scholarships, etc.)

PART B

**EXPERIENCE RECORD:** (Please begin with present or most recent employer. Include Graduate Assistantships and pertinent summer jobs)

| EMPLOYER NAME AND ADDRESS | DATES (MO/YR) | | SUPERVISOR'S NAME AND TITLE | YOUR TITLE | | YOUR RESPONSIBILITIES | SALARY (annual) | | REASON(S) FOR LEAVING |
|---|---|---|---|---|---|---|---|---|---|
| | FROM | TO | | STARTING | FINAL | | STARTING | FINAL | |
| | FROM | TO | | STARTING | FINAL | | STARTING | FINAL | |
| | FROM | TO | | STARTING | FINAL | | STARTING | FINAL | |
| | FROM | TO | | STARTING | FINAL | | STARTING | FINAL | |
| | FROM | TO | | STARTING | FINAL | | STARTING | FINAL | |

Figure 11–1. Application blank (Parts A, B, and C).

## PART  C

**CAREER INTERESTS:**

Type of Work Desired Initially (be as specific as possible)

_____

_____

Type of Work Desired Long Range

_____

_____

In Your Work, What Do You Enjoy Most?  Least?

_____

_____

What Literature Do You Read in Your Field?

_____

List Business and Professional Organizations You Are a Member of
(Indicate offices held, if any.)

_____

_____

**OUTSIDE INTERESTS:**

List Social or Community Organizations, etc. (Indicate offices held;
omit those identifying race, religion, creed, color or national origin.)

_____

_____

Leisure Activities, Hobbies

_____

_____

_____

F.  Taking music lessons.
G.  The hour I should come home.
H.  Use of my spare time.
I.  Use of the automobile.

My usual scholastic standing in high school was in the
A.  Top 5 per cent.
B.  Upper third but not the top 5 per cent.
C.  Middle third.
D.  Lower third.
E.  I do not know.[3]

A number of companies have had great success with biographical information blanks for hiring at all levels, from production and sales

[3] Alec D. Schrader and H. G. Osburn, "Biodata Faking," *Personnel Psychology,* **30** (1977), 397–398.

workers to scientists and managers, and for promoting people from one level to another.

## Personal Interviews

It is unlikely that anyone is hired for any kind of job today without first spending at least a few minutes being interviewed. Having a chance to meet and talk in person with an applicant is something every employer seems to want to do. Some interviews are quick and cursory—five minutes of seemingly casual chatter—and others can last for hours, or even a day or two, as the applicant is passed along from one person to another in the corporate hierarchy.

Interviews can be grueling affairs; applicants are constantly on view, in the glare of probing questions about themselves and their backgrounds. Frequently overlooked is the fact that the employment interview may be a two-way street; applicants may interview the organization to see if it appeals to them while the organization interviews the applicants. Information should flow both ways in the interview.

Two approaches to the personal interview are the *structured* approach and the *unstructured* approach. The unstructured interview is not planned and is conducted in a loose, even haphazard, manner. The interviewers have no formal list of topics they wish to pursue with the applicants but will instead follow whatever turns the conversation seems to take. There is no systematization or consistency in this approach. With an application blank, everyone applying for the same job is asked identical questions. This procedure makes it possible to compare directly one applicant with another. With unstructured interviewing, persons applying for the same job may not be asked the same questions (even if they are all interviewed by the same person), so it becomes extremely difficult to make comparative judgments about them.

Research has shown that five different interviewers, each spending a half-hour with the same applicant, can obtain five different impressions of that person. Each interviewer asks different questions about various aspects of the applicant's background and personality. Because of this lack of consistency, the unstructured interview is not a valid technique for predicting success on the job. It is extremely low in predictive accuracy. Unfortunately, many organizations do not believe the massive amount of evidence that psychologists have gathered against the unstructured interview (or, more likely, they do not know about it), and they continue to try to hire employees on the basis of this unsystematic approach.

The structured interview is of much greater value in predicting success on the job. In this approach, the same predetermined set of questions is asked of every applicant applying for the same kind of job. This standardization and consistency makes it possible to compare the interview results of different applicants. Further, there is less opportunity for subjective or personal factors on the part of the interviewers to enter into the interview situation and bias the results. Interviewers cannot make up their own questions.

So standardized is the structured interview that interviewers follow a form on which the questions are printed and the applicant's answers recorded. It is not unlike an application blank that is filled out by the interviewer instead of by the applicant. The following are typical structured interview questions used by a company for interviewing college graduates. The first set of questions refers to prior work experience and the second set to an applicant's early home life. As you read these questions, consider how you would answer them if you were applying for the job. One day you will probably be asked questions very much like these.

*Prior work experience*
1. What was your first job after leaving college?
2. What would you say your major accomplishments were on that job?
3. What were some of the things you might have done less well, things that perhaps pointed to the opportunity for further development?
4. What did you learn about yourself on that job?
5. What aspects of the job did you find most stimulating and satisfying?

*Early home life*
1. How would you describe your father in terms of his temperament or personality?
2. What influence would you say that he had on your development?
3. How would you describe your mother?
4. What influence would you say that she had on your development?
5. Which parent would you say that you resemble the most? In what way?

The structured interview provides a much more valid prediction of ultimate success on a job. Although it does not completely eliminate subjective bias on the part of interviewers that can distort their assessment of a candidate, it does allow for less bias than the unstructured interview.

*Subjectivity* can never be completely eliminated from the interview situation, but interviewers can be trained to reduce the effect of their personal likes and dislikes on their judgments of applicants. Subjectivity can operate either for or against applicants. That is, different interviewers can react either positively or negatively to specific traits and characteristics; this may predispose them to assess a candidate favorably or unfavorably.

A particular interviewer may, for example, believe that all applicants who maintain eye contact, whose shoes are shined and fingernails neatly clipped, and who don't smoke make better employees than those who do not display these characteristics. An applicant who fits this description has a greater chance of being hired than one who does not fit this description.

Also, an interviewer may be so favorably impressed by these characteristics that he or she will tend to rate such an applicant high on all other traits, even when this is not really warranted. This common phenomenon, known as the *halo effect*, involves generalizing from one or a set of traits to all others. The halo effect frequently occurs whenever one human being makes a judgment about another.

Interviewers' judgments can also be biased by the pressure they are under to hire a certain number of people in a fixed period of time, in other words, to meet a quota. Research has shown that interviewers under quota pressures gave much more favorable judgments to a group of candidates than interviewers who were not under such pressure.

Finally, interviewers' judgments can be biased by how good or how poor the preceding candidates have been. For example, if an interviewer has seen three undesirable applicants in a row, he or she will tend to be very favorably impressed with the next candidate even if that candidate is only marginally better than the previous three. Thus, an applicant of only average qualifications may be viewed as considerably above average, depending on who was interviewed before. This effect can work in the opposite way as well. An average candidate can be seen as below average if the previous applicants were all highly qualified.

## Letters of Recommendation

Prospective employers frequently ask for letters of recommendation about applicants from those who have known them well—former teachers, past employers, and coworkers. The purposes of these letters are worthwhile in principle: to verify the nature and extent of an applicant's previous work experience as reported on an application blank, and to examine the impressions that other people have of the applicant. It seems reasonable to expect that how a person performed in a past job will give some indication of how he or she will perform in the job being applied for.

Unfortunately, these goals are not always (or even often) accomplished by letters of recommendation. Frequently, letters of recommendation present a misleading picture of the applicants. Most people are reluctant to give a bad reference to former employees, and most letters tend to be overly lenient or so full of generalities and clichés that they are useless. Sometimes an employer will write a glowing

**UNIVERSITY CAREER DEVELOPMENT CENTER**

Please type a statement in the space provided below concerning the candidate whose name is listed. Employers will be interested in your evaluation of this candidate's competency and potential.

_____
Name of Candidate

Signature _____
Type Name _____          Official Position _____
Date _____          Institution/Business _____
                                                        Address _____

Federal Legislation stipulates that Letters of Recommendation are no longer confidential and may be shown to the candidate upon request.

Figure 11–2. Recommendation form.

letter of recommendation for an employee who has not been a very good worker in the hope that he or she will be hired by the other company.

There are four ways of obtaining letters of recommendation. The most common procedure is to ask a former employer to write a _letter_ describing the characteristics and attributes of the candidate. Another approach is to send the former employer a _questionnaire_ to fill out, in which specific, detailed information is sought. A third way to check references is to _telephone_ them to ask about the applicant. A skillful interviewer can obtain much more useful information in this way than through a questionnaire or letter because people are often more willing to be candid in their appraisals of an applicant when their judgment is not formally committed to paper. A fourth approach is the *field investigation*, in which references are interviewed in person. This is the most expensive and time-consuming approach and is usually used only for high-level jobs.

## Assessment Centers

Selection of employees through the use of assessment centers has become extremely popular in business and industry, despite the substantial investment of time and money required. The assessment center approach involves placing applicants in a simulated real-life situation, such as would be encountered on the job for which they are applying, and observing their behavior. How applicants behave under the stress of this selection situation indicates how well they will be able to perform under the similar stresses of the actual job. This procedure is a direct outgrowth of the situational testing used by the OSS, described at the beginning of the chapter.

Situational testing was first used in industry in the 1950s, and the number of organizations using it has continued to grow. The Ford Motor Company, IBM, AT&T, Kodak, and the U.S. Department of Agriculture are a few of the employers who use assessment centers today, primarily to select managers and executives. The cost is estimated at $500 to $600 per candidate, but these and other organizations believe that the technique is useful in selecting the most qualified candidates.

Candidates are given psychological tests, especially intelligence and personality tests, and are also interviewed, but most of the several days spent at an assessment center are devoted to exercises representing the kinds of problems encountered on the job. Two exercises frequently used in assessment centers are the in-basket exercise and the leaderless group discussion.

An *in-basket* may be found on every executive desk, and it contains memos, requests, problems, and directives that the executive is supposed to be able to deal with as quickly and as efficiently as possible. In an assessment center, the in-basket exercise works in a similar manner. Candidates must examine the material in their in-baskets within a limited period of time and take action on the assorted problems and memos they find there. When they have completed the tasks, they may be asked to explain the actions they took and to justify their decisions.

While they are conducting the in-basket exercise, candidates are closely observed to see how they work in this stressful situation. How systematically does the candidate go through the material? Does he or she establish meaningful priorities? Do the candidates delegate authority or try to do all the work themselves? How nervous and tense does an applicant become? It is interesting that some people who have not functioned as managers before find this first taste of executive life not to their liking, and they refuse the job when it is offered. How much better for them and for the company to find out this incompatibility during the selection process rather than after being hired and spending some time on the job.

In the *leaderless group discussion* exercise, groups of six to twelve candidates meet to resolve an actual business problem. For example, they may be told that their job, as managers of a particular company, is to bring about an increase in profits in a certain period of time. They are given all the necessary information about the company and are left on their own to decide how best to accomplish the task. No one is appointed a leader, and they are given no rules or guidelines about how to proceed. Periodically, they are informed of increased costs for raw materials, or price changes for other commodities, sometimes immediately after they have solved the problem.

Usually, one member of the group emerges as the leader to take charge of the problem, and that person's leadership ability is evaluated. The other group members are evaluated on their cooperation with the leader and their contribution to the solution. The situation is quite stressful, and some candidates show the effects of the stress more visibly than others, becoming tense and angry or disrupting the group's efforts. It soon becomes obvious which candidates function well under this kind of pressure and which do not.

Assessment centers are used for hiring new employees and for selecting people for promotion who already work for the organization. Most research on assessment centers has been favorable with regard to their predictive value. Those people selected by assessment centers have been shown to perform as much as 50 per cent better than those selected by other techniques. Other studies have shown that candidates who did not do well in assessment centers, but who were hired or promoted anyway, were much more likely to be poor managers than those who did well in assessment centers.

## Psychological Tests

Psychological tests are frequently used in personnel selection for jobs ranging from apprentice to corporate president. As with assessment centers, psychological tests are used to hire new employees and to select from among current employees those most eligible for promotion. Organizations today devote considerable time and money to research for the development of psychological tests, and much of the work done by psychologists in business and industry is concerned with the problems of testing.

A good test is much more than a list of questions that may appear to be relevant to the characteristic being measured. To be useful as a selection technique, psychological tests must meet four specific and rigorous criteria: standardization, the availability of norms, reliability, and validity.

We discussed the characteristic of standardization in the previous section on the proper administration of selection techniques. There it was noted that everyone taking a test must do so under identical and consistent conditions. *Standardization* is the term for this consistency or uniformity of procedures for administering a test.

Every psychological test has its own standardized procedure that must be followed with precision. Everyone taking the test must be exposed to the same set of instructions, with no variation. Even the omission of a single word changes the conditions under which the test is given. In addition, everyone must have the same amount of time in which to take the test and must take it in the same or a similar setting. Any change in instructions, time allowed, or physical setting may influence a person's score on the test.

The second criterion that all psychological tests must meet is the availability of adequate test *norms*. Norms are the sets of scores of a large group of people who are similar to the job applicants for whom the test is devised. Norms are accumulated before the test is available for actual use in selection, and they serve as a yardstick or frame of reference, a point of comparison for the score of an individual job applicant who takes the test.

Suppose that a company gives a test of mechanical aptitude to all high school graduates who apply for its apprentice training program. If an applicant scores, say, 82 on the test, how does the company interpret this? What does the score reveal about the applicant's degree of mechanical aptitude? By itself, the score tells the company nothing. However, if the applicant's score can be compared with norms—a set of scores obtained from 600 high school graduates—then there is a basis for interpreting the individual score. If the average score for the 600 high school graduates is 80, we know that the applicant's score of 82 is just about average, not particularly good but not bad either.

Good psychological tests may have several sets of norms for different age levels, sexes, and levels of education so that more complete comparisons can be made. A test without any norms is very difficult to interpret and should not be used.

*Reliability*, the third characteristic of good psychological tests, refers to the consistency of scores on a test. If a group of people are given an intelligence test and the average score is 120, but a month later the same people achieve an average score of only 85, the test would be considered unreliable. The test has something wrong with it, either with the questions or with the way in which it is scored. It is useless for predicting how well people will perform on a job. Several statistical procedures determine precisely how reliable or consistent a test is.

We have already discussed *validity*, the fourth criterion for psychological tests. To reiterate briefly, validity refers to how well a test measures what it purports to measure. A test designed to measure success in a pilot training program can be considered valid if those persons who score high on the test do well in the pilot training, and those who score low on the test do poorly in the training. To establish the validity of a test we must correlate the test scores with a later measure of success on the job. A test with a low validity is useless as a selection device.

There are a great many psychological tests commercially available today for use in personnel selection. They vary in quality from excellent to poor, depending on their levels of reliability and validity, the adequacy of their norms, and how effectively they are standardized. The better tests can be used to predict success in many jobs. Sometimes, however, psychologists must develop a new test specifically for a particular job. This may happen when a job is so new or specialized that no existing test is appropriate for it. Developing a new test is an expensive and time-consuming procedure; the psychologist must conduct research to establish the four criteria discussed previously. In addition, when developing a new test, each item has to be validated as well as the test as a whole. The responses to each question must be correlated with the scores on the test as a whole to see if each question can discriminate between those applicants who score high on the total test and those who score low. This process is known as *item analysis*.

Whether a test is chosen from those already published or is developed specifically for a particular job, it will fall into one of several categories of psychological tests. Tests may be grouped by the way in which they are administered, or by the aspect of behavior they measure. Categories in terms of administration are as follows.

*Individual and group tests.* Individual tests can be given to only one person at a time. They are seldom used for industrial selection purposes, where large numbers of people must be tested, but are used primarily for vocational counseling or diagnostic work in clinical psychology. Group tests can be given to many people at the same time—as many as the size of the testing facility allows. Group tests are frequently used for selection purposes.

*Speed and power tests.* The major difference between speed and power tests is in the amount of time applicants have to complete the test. A speed test has a fixed time limit. When that time has expired, everyone must stop taking the test. A power test has no time limit. A power test usually contains more difficult items than a speed test, but applicants are allowed to take as much time as they need to complete the test. Speed tests are most often used for large-scale selection programs because of their convenience; the testing for a group of applicants can be completed at the same time. Also, for jobs such as those in clerical fields, such as typing, the ability to work fast is an important characteristic to be assessed.

*Paper-and-pencil and performance tests.* All of you have taken paper-and-pencil tests in the classroom. They are the most frequently used kind of psychological test. The questions appear in printed form and the answers are recorded on an answer sheet. Most selection testing uses paper-and-pencil tests. In performance testing, applicants perform some mechanical operation, such as typing, which represents the kind of work for which they are applying. Some performance tests involve the use of complex equipment to evaluate highly developed and sophisticated skills.

The second way in which psychological tests may be grouped is in terms of the area of behavior they measure. Tests are available to measure mental ability or intelligence, interests, aptitudes, motor ability, and personality.

*Mental ability or intelligence.* Most of you have probably taken at least one intelligence test in your school career or applying for a job. It is difficult to get through life today without having your IQ measured several times. Many companies, the military, and other kinds of employing organizations routinely give intelligence tests to all job applicants, not only to find out if they should be hired, but also to determine the kind of work to which they should be assigned.

Most intelligence tests used for selection purposes are group tests that take very little time to administer (one takes only twelve minutes), can be easily and quickly scored, and serve as rough screening devices to indicate an applicant's general level of intelligence. For the most part, tests of mental ability have been more successful in predicting success in training programs than in predicting actual job performance.

A widely used intelligence test is the *Wesman Personnel Classification Test* consisting of an eighteen-minute verbal analogies test and a ten-minute mathematical computation test. The Wesman has been shown to be useful for selecting higher-level personnel.

*Interests.* It is likely that you were given an interest test in high school. Many schools routinely administer them to all students to help them choose the kind of work for which they are best suited. Many employing organizations also give interest tests as part of their general testing program.

Interest inventories include questions about the everyday activities and objects a person prefers. For example, one of the most popular interest inventories, the *Kuder Occupational Interest Survey*, presents the following activities; an applicant must choose the one most preferred and the one least preferred.[4] The items are arranged in groups of threes and applicants must answer every set.

Visit an art gallery.
Browse in a library.
Visit a museum.

What do such preferences indicate about the kind of job for which an applicant is best suited? The theory behind interest inventories is that if a person exhibits the same pattern of interests and preferences as people who are successful in a particular occupation, chances are good that he or she will be satisfied with that occupation.

Norms are very important in interest inventories. The test scores of a large number of people considered successful in a particular occupation are the criteria with which the individual applicant's score is compared.

The *Kuder Occupational Interest Survey* can be scored for seventy-seven occupations for men and fifty-seven occupations for women. Another frequently used interest inventory is the *Strong-Campbell Interest Inventory*, which can be scored for occupations in six areas: realistic, investigative, artistic, social, enterprising, and conventional.

*Aptitudes.* Whereas interest tests measure one's interests in different vocational areas, aptitude tests measure one's talents or abilities for different occupations. Two types of aptitude tests frequently used for industrial selection purposes measure clerical and mechanical aptitudes.

Tests of clerical aptitude are usually speed tests because speed of performance is a requisite for that kind of work. Accuracy is also important in clerical work, and those persons taking clerical aptitude tests must work as fast as possible while making the smallest number of errors.

One type of test item for measuring both speed and accuracy of clerical performance is number comparison. Applicants must compare pairs of numbers to see if they are identical. Working very quickly, which of these pairs of numbers are identical?

| | |
|---|---|
| 729810274 | 728910274 |
| 690743219 | 690743129 |
| 240759139 | 240759139 |

This type of item appears in the two most frequently used clerical aptitude tests, the *Minnesota Clerical Test* and the *Clerical Aptitude*

[4] G. F. Kuder, *General Manual* (Chicago: Science Research Associates, 1966).

When the two numbers or names in a pair are
*exactly the same,* make a check mark on the
line between them.

66273894 _____ 66273984
527384578_____ 527384578
New York World _____ New York World
Cargill Grain Co. _____ Cargil Grain Co.

Figure 11–3. Sample items, Minnesota Clerical Test. (Reproduced by permission. Copyright 1933, renewed 1961 by The Psychological Corporation, New York, N.Y. All rights reserved.)

*Test.* Other items involve name comparison, vocabulary, arithmetic, and general reasoning ability.

Tests of mechanical aptitude focus on the skills of mechanical comprehension and spatial visualization. For example, applicants are shown segments of a figure and asked to indicate what the total figure would look like if the segments were put together. Another kind of item shows pictures along with questions about the mechanical principles depicted in them. One such picture shows a bus with lines indicating three different passenger seat locations in various parts of the bus. Applicants must tell which location provides the smoothest ride.

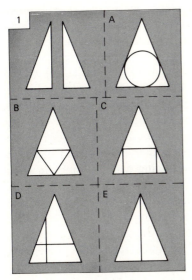
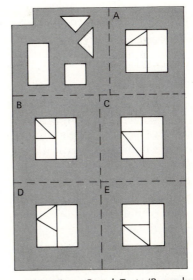

Figure 11–4. Sample items, Revised Minnesota Paper Form Board Test. (Reproduced by permission. Copyright 1941, renewed 1969 by The Psychological Corporation, New York, N.Y. All rights reserved.)

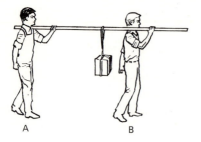

X
Which man carries more weight?
(If equal, mark C.)

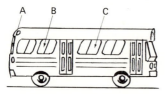

Y
Which letter shows the seat where
a passenger will get the smoothest ride?

Figure 11–5. Sample items, Bennett Mechanical Comprehension Test. Reproduced by permission. Copyright 1940, renewed 1967; 1941, renewed 1969; 1942, renewed 1969; © 1967, 1968 by The Psychological Corporation, New York, N.Y. All rights reserved.

Two popular mechanical aptitude tests are the *Revised Minnesota Paper Form Board Test* and the *Bennett Mechanical Comprehension Test*.

*Motor ability.* Many jobs in industry require a high degree of motor skill such as muscular coordination, finger dexterity, and precise eye–hand coordination. Tests of motor ability measure these skills through a number of paper-and-pencil and performance exercises. The paper-and-pencil tests include such items as drawing a line through tiny openings in a number of vertical lines, making dots on paper as fast as possible, copying simple designs, visually tracing assorted lines in a maze, and determining the number of blocks in a drawing.

Some of the items found in performance tests include placing pins in a series of holes as quickly as possible, placing blocks in holes and then turning them all over as fast as possible, using tweezers to place pins in holes and then placing collars over the pins, and placing small screws in holes using a screwdriver. Such items are useful in predicting success in assembly jobs such as those in the electronics industry.

Standard tests of motor ability are the *Purdue Pegboard* and the *Crawford Small Parts Dexterity Test*.

*Personality.*  Of all the tests used for selection purposes, personality tests are the most controversial. They often contain personal questions that may constitute an invasion of privacy. Also, some research evidence casts doubt on the predictive value of personality tests. Nevertheless, they are often used to select employees, particularly at the managerial and executive levels.

The most frequently used approach to personality testing employs the personality inventory. In this kind of test, applicants are presented with a variety of items that deal with specific situations, symptoms, and personal feelings. They are asked how well each item describes themselves or how much they agree with each item.

The *Guilford-Zimmerman Temperament Survey* contains such items as the following.[5]

1. You start work on a new project with a great deal of enthusiasm  .......................................  YES  ?  NO
2. You are often low in spirits ......................  YES  ?  NO
3. Most people use politeness to cover up what is really "cutthroat" competition  ........................  YES  ?  NO

This test measures ten personality traits, including emotional stability, personal relations, masculinity, restraint, friendliness, thoughtfulness, general activity, ascendance, sociability, and objectivity.

Another popular personality inventory is the *Minnesota Multiphasic Personality Inventory* (MMPI). This test contains 566 items. A high degree of motivation is required to complete the test with proper attention to every item. The MMPI measures clinical conditions or symptoms, including hypochondriasis, depression, hysteria, psychopathic deviate, masculinity–femininity, paranoia, and schizophrenia.

A derivative of the MMPI is the *California Psychological Inventory.* This test contains 480 true–false items, and research has shown its usefulness for several occupational groups.

Personality inventories have rather low predictive validities. One factor that may contribute to this situation is the potential dishonesty of applicants taking such tests. It is usually not difficult for a person to understand what is being sought in many of the test items and to make an accurate guess about what the items are designed to reveal. Therefore, people who want to hide or distort certain aspects of their personality, or who want to appear to be something other than what they really are, can do so with relative ease. And, in an employment situation, the motivation to fake responses is high if a person desperately wants or needs the job being applied for.

[5] *Manual* (Beverly Hills, Calif.: Sheridan Psychological Services).

Suppose that you are applying for a sales job and you are asked to answer the following questions.

I enjoy meeting new people ..................... YES    NO
I get along well with most people ................ YES    NO
I find it easy to talk to people .................... YES    NO

It is easy for you to figure out which way people in sales should answer. They should say that they enjoy meeting people, get along well with most people, and find it easy to talk to people. Most applicants who want or need this sales job would answer in these ways, regardless of whether the answers reflect their true nature.

Of course, in the long run, distorting or faking test responses may work to an applicant's disadvantage. If the person does not enjoy meeting new people and does not get along well with others, he or she will probably not succeed in sales work or, at the least, will be unhappy in it. However, it is hard to convince an eager job seeker of that in advance.

Fortunately, some psychological tests, including the *Guilford-Zimmerman Temperament Survey*, the *MMPI*, and the *Kuder Occupational Interest Survey*, have developed scales to detect deliberate faking. Most tests, however, do not have such provisions.

There are other problems with psychological tests. First, there has been an overacceptance of psychological tests on the part of many personnel managers, who are unable to differentiate between good and poor tests. Many tests have low reliabilities and validities (or no such data at all), no norms, and poor standardization. Personnel managers who lack training in psychology often do not know what characteristics to look for in a test. Frequently, they choose tests that are of no value in predicting success on the job.

A second problem with tests is that many people react to them negatively, with anxiety, fear, suspicion, and hostility. This can easily influence how well they perform on the tests. Most of us do not like to be tested, but often we have no choice in the matter. Refusal to take an organization's psychological test almost always results in not being hired or promoted. Labor unions traditionally have been opposed to psychological testing programs, arguing that the programs serve the interests of the company, not the employee.

A third problem with psychological tests involves the charge that tests constitute an unwarranted invasion of personal privacy. This charge applies almost exclusively to the personality tests, which contain intimate and probing questions.

Finally, it is contended that many psychological tests unfairly discriminate against minority-group applicants, violating their civil rights.

This is a serious problem; we will discuss the problem of discrimination in employment in the following section.

If there are so many problems connected with the use of psychological tests for selection, then why are they used so frequently? There is a simple and practical reason for their widespread use: they can and do improve the selection process. A properly developed testing program, well researched and carefully administered, more than pays for itself in the higher quality of employees hired.

Good tests can provide a great deal of useful information about a job applicant in a relatively short period of time. The information provided by tests is objective, unlike the information provided by interviews and letters of recommendation, which is often distorted by subjective bias.

In general, psychological tests have been more successful with lower-level jobs—such as clerical workers, assembly line operators, general factory workers, and other skilled and unskilled personnel—than with higher-level jobs such as managers and executives.

## FAIR EMPLOYMENT LEGISLATION AND SELECTION

The difficulties involved in personnel selection have increased since the passage of the 1964 Civil Rights Act, which made it illegal to discriminate against job applicants because of race, color, religion, sex, or national origin.[6] There is no denying that discrimination, particularly against minority-group members, was widespread before the passage of that legislation. Also, discrimination continues today, although it has been considerably reduced.

In 1972, the Equal Employment Opportunity Commission (EEOC) was established, which has the power to bring legal action against any employer who discriminates in hiring. Unfortunately, EEOC's staff is small and is inundated with claims. In 1977 they had a backlog of 130,000 complaints and were receiving 1,000 new complaints each month. However, they are attacking the problem of job discrimination with vigor. Some company managements have been convicted of discriminatory practices, and their example is serving to reduce the problem in other organizations.

As a result, most companies are aware of the necessity of ensuring that all people have equal access to job opportunities. Personnel departments have reevaluated their screening and selection techniques to make such that applicants are not discriminated against because they are, for example, female, black, Mexican American, Puerto Rican, or Catholic.

[6] Much support for the passage of the Civil Rights Act came from the research of social psychologists, who documented the harmful effects of discrimination. This is another example of how psychology influences our daily lives.

Suppose that a company decided that only those applicants would be hired who had graduated from high school and scored at a certain level on tests of arithmetic ability and verbal skill. These requirements may automatically disqualify minority-group members who may not have been able to finish high school for reasons having nothing to do with intelligence. Also, perhaps because the schools were inferior, these applicants do not perform well on tests of arithmetic and verbal abilities.

In order to use these selection criteria, the company must demonstrate scientifically, through correlational studies, that the requirements of a high school education and certain arithmetic and verbal skills are related to success on the job. All requirements must be justified today by showing conclusively that applicants who do not meet the requirements will not be able to perform well on the job. If the job requirements show no relationship to job success, they are discriminating unfairly against some members of our society. This is clearly illegal.

It has always been considered desirable to validate selection procedures, but this is costly and time-consuming. Since the passage of civil rights legislation, however, validation is a legal requirement. This has made the services of psychologists to the world of work more important than ever. The burden of proof that a psychological test or any other selection procedure or requirement is definitely job-related is on the employing organization. This job relatedness can be demonstrated only through the correlational method.

In addition to the requirement that validation studies be undertaken, equal employment opportunity regulations have affected personnel selection in another way, influencing the questions that can and cannot be asked of applicants in interviews or on application blanks. Any question that could discriminate against applicants on the basis of race, color, religion, sex, or national origin cannot be asked.

The following questions are considered discriminatory. It is unlawful to ask applicants:

1. If they have ever been arrested.
2. To name their birthplace or the birthplace of their parents, spouse, or other close relatives.
3. For their religious affiliation.
4. For a wife's or mother's maiden name.
5. For the names of the clubs, societies, or lodges to which they belong.
6. To include a photograph with their application.

With regard to item 1, it is known that minority-group members are much more likely to be arrested on suspicion because of possible prejudice among police officers. It is permissible, however, to ask applicants if they have ever been *convicted* of a crime. The other items could reveal the race, creed, color, or national origin of applicants; it is illegal to inquire about these facts.[7]

Considerable progress has been made in meeting the legal requirements of equal employment opportunity. The elimination of discrimination in hiring involves moral, legal, and technical challenges for psychologists and directly influences the lives of millions of people. The actions of psychologists in meeting these challenges provide excellent examples of the influence of the field on the quality of our lives.

## SUMMARY

The initial application of psychology to the world of work began with the employee selection process. Psychological selection techniques are used to screen and hire people at all levels of employment and to identify current employees who are qualified for promotion. Therefore, these psychological techniques are extremely important to your own future.

Employee selection is an expensive and time-consuming process that involves five specific steps or procedures.

1. *Job analysis and worker analysis.* To determine the skills and abilities needed to perform a job, it is necessary to analyze the job in detail and to derive from that the characteristics and abilities required of the workers. Job analysis can be conducted by interviewing persons connected with the job, giving them questionnaires, observing them, or recording critical incidents on the job.

2. *Setting cutoff scores and minimum levels of abilities.* Based on the skills and abilities needed for the job, specific levels of performance on the selection techniques (say, a certain score on an IQ test), and background factors such as number of years of education, must be established. No one is to be hired who does not meet these criteria.

3. *Recruiting of applicants.* This initial contact with the organization must offer candidates realistic previews of what the job will be like. Attention must also be paid to the behavior and manner of the recruiters and to the recruiting appeals that are effective for different kinds of people.

4. *Administration of selection techniques.* Applicants should be made to feel as comfortable and relaxed as possible. All selection techniques must be administered under conditions that render them maximally effective.

5. *Validation of selection procedures.* All selection techniques must be

---

[7] Robert L. Minter, "Human Rights Laws and Pre–Employment Inquiries," *Personnel Journal*, **51** (1972), 431–433.

correlated with some objective measure of job success, to ensure that the techniques are capable of selecting among good and poor workers.

Several techniques are discussed: application blanks, personal interviews, letters of recommendation, assessment centers, and psychological tests.

*Application blanks* must ask only for information that has been shown to relate to job success. Two modifications of the standard application blank are the *weighted application blank,* in which each item is given a numerical weight determined by how strongly the item predicts job success, and the *biographical information blank,* which explores the candidate's life history in great detail.

*Personal interviews* are of two types: *unstructured,* in which interviewers follow their individual line of questioning, and *structured,* in which interviewers ask the same questions in the same order of all applicants. The structured interview is of far greater value in predicting job success. In any interview, subjectivity and personal bias can distort the results. The interviewer's own prejudices can affect results, as can quota pressure and the quality of the preceding job applicants.

*Letters of recommendation,* although frequently used, are not very useful predictors of job success. Four ways of securing recommendations are by letter, questionnaire, telephone, and field investigation.

*Assessment centers* involve placing job applicants in a simulated real-life situation such as they would encounter on the job for which they are applying. Two exercises frequently used in assessment centers are the *in-basket test* and the *leaderless group discussion,* both of which involve actual management problems. Applicants are observed during the performance of these exercises to see how they cope with the stresses involved.

*Psychological tests* as selection devices must meet four criteria: *standardization* (consistent and uniform procedures of administration), availability of test *norms* (sets of scores of similar people against which applicants' scores are compared), *reliability* (the consistency of test scores), and *validity* (how well the test measures what it purports to measure).

Tests can be categorized in terms of the way in which they are administered (individual and group tests, speed and power tests, and paper-and-pencil and performance tests), and the kind of behavior they measure (mental ability or intelligence, interests, aptitudes, motor ability, and personality).

Although tests can be useful aids to the selection process, there are problems involved with their use: deliberate faking of responses, negative attitudes toward tests, invasion of privacy, and discrimination against minority-group applicants.

The passage of the 1964 Civil Rights Act, and the establishment of the Equal Employment Opportunity Commission in 1972, have made it illegal to discriminate against job applicants because of race, color, religion, sex, or national origin. This legislation has had an impact on personnel selection, influencing the kinds of questions that can be asked of applicants in interviews or on application blanks, and requiring that proper validation studies be conducted on all psychological tests used for selection purposes.

## SUGGESTED READINGS

Anastasi, Anne. *Psychological Testing,* 4th ed. New York: Macmillan, 1976.

Asch, P., and L. Kroeker. Personnel selection, classification, and placement. *Annual Review of Psychology,* 1975, **26,** 481-507.

Bem, S., and D. Bem. Does sex-biased job advertising "aid and abet" sex discrimination? *Journal of Applied Social Psychology,* 1973, **3,** 6-18.

Brecher, R. Ten common mistakes in college recruiting—or how to try without really succeeding. *Personnel,* 1975 (March–April), **52,** 19–28.

Clarke, W. Who gains when you cheat on a personality test? *Personnel Journal,* 1974, **53,** 302-303.

Finkle, R. Managerial assessment centers. In M. Dunnette, Ed., *Handbook of Industrial and Organizational Psychology.* Chicago: Rand McNally, 1976. Pp. 861-888.

Foxley, C. *Locating, Recruiting, and Employing Women: An Equal Opportunity Approach.* Garrett Park, Md.: Garrett Park Press, 1976.

Ghiselli, E. The validity of aptitude tests in personnel selection. *Personnel Psychology,* 1973, **26,** 461-477.

Goodale, James G. Tailoring the selection interview to the job. *Personnel Journal,* 1976, **55,** 62-65, 83.

Gough, H. Personality and personality assessment. In M. Dunnette, Ed., *Handbook of Industrial and Organizational Psychology.* Chicago: Rand McNally, 1976. Pp. 571-607.

Guion, R. Recruiting, selection, and job placement. In M. Dunnette, Ed., *Handbook of Industrial and Organizational Psychology.* Chicago: Rand McNally, 1976. Pp. 777-828.

Hall, Douglas T. *Careers in Organizations.* Pacific Palisades, Calif.: Goodyear, 1976.

Jones, A., and P. A. Whittaker. *Testing Industrial Skills.* New York: Halsted Press, 1975.

Kraut, Allen I. New frontiers for assessment centers. *Personnel,* 1976 (July–August), **53,** 30–38.

Lipsett, Laurence. Selecting personnel without tests. *Personnel Journal,* 1972, **51,** 648–654.

Lipsett, Laurence. What rights of privacy should job applicants have? *Supervisory Management,* 1977 (October), **22,** 30–36.

Miller, K. M., Ed. *Psychological Tests in Personnel Assessment.* New York: Halsted Press, 1975.

Owens, W. Background data. In M. Dunnette, Ed., *Handbook of Industrial and Organizational Psychology.* Chicago: Rand McNally, 1976. Pp. 609–644.

Rogers, J., and W. Fortson. *Fair Employment Interviewing.* Reading, Mass.: Addison–Wesley, 1976.

Samuda, R. J. *Psychological Testing of American Minorities: Issues and Consequences.* New York: Harper and Row, 1975.

Schmitt, N., and B. Coyle. Applicant decisions in the employment interview. *Journal of Applied Psychology,* 1976, **61,** 184–192.

Schultz, Duane P. *Psychology and Industry Today,* 2nd ed. New York: Macmillan, 1978.

Wanous, J. Tell it like it is at realistic job previews. *Personnel,* 1975 (July–August), **52,** 50–60.

Ward, L., and A. Athos. *Student Expectations of Corporate Life: Implications for Management Recruiting.* Boston: Harvard University Graduate School of Business Administration, 1972.

Wilson, J., and W. Tatge. Assessment centers—further assessment needed? *Personnel Journal,* 1973, **52,** 172–179.

# Psychology Applied to the World of Work: II. Training and Evaluating People at Work

John Kirby was very excited as he approached the gate of the Lockland Steel Company. This was the day he had looked forward to for a long time, his first day on his new job. He looked down at the shiny new badge pinned on his shirt and smiled with immense satisfaction as he punched his time card; he was fifteen minutes early. John was determined to do well on the new job, to work hard at learning it and to advance himself in the company.

As he walked toward the half-mile-long building where he was to work, he thought back to the day he had spent in the company's personnel office. He had filled out his application blank carefully, paying particular attention to the part-time jobs he had held while he was finishing high school. He wrote down the names of his former bosses as references. He had done well in those earlier jobs and he knew the bosses would recommend him highly.

John had breezed through the psychological tests the company gave him. He was a bright young man and he found the intelligence and aptitude tests to be very easy. On the interest test he had answered every item honestly, not pretending to be anything he was not. He knew the test would tell the personnel people the kind of job for which he was best suited, and he recognized that it was to his advantage not to fake his answers.

In the interview with the personnel manager, John was relaxed, self-assured, and quietly aggressive in asking questions about the company and its policies, particularly with regard to the kind of training he would receive. He knew that he had to learn a lot about whatever job he would get, so he wanted to make sure that adequate training would be provided. John had done well in his studies in school, he was a quick learner, and he enjoyed the challenge of learning.

To the personnel manager, John Kirby was the ideal job candidate—good grades in high school, fast promotions to greater responsibilities in his past part-time jobs, top scores on the selection tests, eager, conscientious, neatly dressed, and highly personable in his manner. John's high school grades in physics and chemistry, together with the results of his aptitude, intelligence, and interest tests, qualified him for a good job in the metallurgical department as a trainee inspector, checking on the quality of the steel the company produced.

The personnel manager shook John's hand at the end of the interview. "You'll start Monday morning, John," he said. "If you're willing to work hard, there's no limit to how far you can go."

After John left, the personnel manager reviewed John's file and silently wished he had more applicants like him. "He'll do well," he said to himself.

Two weeks later, John Kirby quit the Lockland Steel Company in anger, bitterness, and disgust, and began looking for another job elsewhere. The promise and excitement of the new job in the metallurgical department had begun to sour on his first morning at work.

"Oh yeah, you're the new guy," the harassed foreman had said to John. "Follow me." And he led John off at a fast pace past a row of giant rotary shears that cut steel into different lengths, depending on what the customers had ordered. As the steel was cut, it moved along a huge conveyor belt at high speed. Halfway down the length of each conveyor belt, an inspector sat on a stool watching as each piece of steel flashed by at speeds up to 30 miles per hour. The inspector's right hand moved rhythmically as he brought down a large rubber stamp on each sheet, certifying that it had passed inspection. Occasionally, his left hand operated a lever that opened a metal panel on the conveyor belt, feeding rejected sheets of steel into a bin beneath the belt.

It all looked very confusing to John and his mind raced with questions, but before he could ask any of them, the foreman stopped next to one of the inspectors.

"A new kid, Charley," the foreman said, gesturing with his thumb at John. "Break him in," and the foreman turned and walked away without another word.

Charley shot a quick and suspicious glance at John, shook his head and sighed, and turned back to his work. For several minutes he said nothing, and John shifted uncomfortably from one foot to another while he tried to figure out what Charley was doing.

Charley muttered to himself and slammed the stamp on the passing sheets of steel harder than before. If there was anything Charley hated it was breaking in a new man, and for one very good reason; almost every employee he had broken in over the years had been promoted to a better job, either to faster lines where they made more money or to the testing laboratory, where the work was quiet and clean. Charley, the poorest of all the inspectors, stayed on the oldest and slowest line, where he knew he would remain until he retired. Every new employee was brought to Charley precisely because his line was the slowest; a trainee could do less damage there than on the faster lines.

Finally, with another loud sigh, Charley spoke. He gestured to one of the pieces of steel coming down the line. "Scale," he said, pointing to the rough flaking surface. "Can't have scale," and he threw down the lever, guiding the steel into the reject bin.

Slowly, a few words at a time, Charley pointed to various defects that had to be rejected, but this was an unsystematic and unsatisfactory kind of instruction. Sometimes he would let pass pieces of steel that looked as bad as some he had rejected. When John tried to ask why those pieces had been passed, Charley would shrug and say, "It's just something you know after a while."

John stayed with Charley for five days, and in all that time he never had any of his questions answered. Soon he stopped asking. Charley refused to let him operate the reject lever. "It's too tricky. Mess up when you get your own line, not on mine."

Charley did tell John about the red light located next to the reject lever. "It's an x-ray. It tells if the steel's not the right thickness." But he didn't tell John that the machine had to be calibrated every week, and his had not been calibrated for six months. Of course, Charley never used the x-ray anyway, relying instead on his subjective judgment about whether a piece of steel was too thick or too thin. John became confused if Charley rejected some sheets of steel when the red light hadn't come on—"too thick," he'd say—and pass others when the light had come on. "It's just something you know after a while," was the only answer Charley had.

Ordinarily, new workers spent two weeks working alongside an experienced inspector, the first week with Charley and the second week with a better inspector on a faster line. As a result, most people were able to make up for Charley's inadequate instruction and to operate their own lines with a minimum of mistakes. It did not work out that way for John. When he started his second week with the company, he was put to work on one of the faster lines by himself because several inspectors were absent. "Got three men out with the flu today," the foreman said. "You'll have to fill in."

It was a disastrous day for John. Everything that could go wrong did. And no wonder; he had not been properly trained for a job that was very demanding. He passed steel that should have been rejected, rejected steel that should have been passed, and caused a monumental pileup of steel by opening the trapdoor a fraction of a second too late, causing the fast-moving sheets of steel to butt against one another. The conveyor belt had to be closed down for almost an hour while the damaged steel was untangled.

"The new kid doesn't have it," Charley told the foreman with great pleasure, and the foreman, looking at the buckled, misshapen steel piled all around the conveyor belt, agreed. John was taken off the line and put to work as a laborer, sweeping the floor and pulling rejected steel out of the bins whenever the piles got too high. At the end of the week, John quit.

The point of this story is obvious; no matter how sophisticated is a company's selection program, no matter how well qualified are the people hired through that selection program, they will not be able to perform well on the job unless they are thoroughly trained. Without adequate training, both the company and the employee lose, and all the money and time spent in selecting the right people for the job are wasted.

I have seen this happen many times in industry, beginning in college when I worked summers as an inspector in a steel mill doing the same job for which John Kirby was hired. I was lucky; I was assigned to an inspector who knew the job well and, more important, he knew how to teach it to someone else. A friend of mine was not so lucky. He was assigned to a Charley and spent the rest of the summer sweeping floors at a much lower rate of pay.

Psychologists are extensively involved in training people for various kinds of work at all levels, from apprentice to executive. In Chapter 10 we discussed the application of psychology to education in the classroom and noted how psychological research has influenced the way in which students are taught and the way in which they learn academic material. In this chapter we will discuss how learning takes place on the job.

For most of you, learning will not stop when you go from classroom to job. Most jobs require some kind of training, sometimes practiced on the job (as in the previous example) and sometimes practiced in classrooms that are better equipped than many colleges. Many employees, relieved to be out of a classroom when they graduate from high school or college, once again face teachers and textbooks in a company classroom.

## TRAINING IS A BIG BUSINESS

Most employing organizations take training very seriously and spend a great deal of money on it. Why? Because it works. It is not at all unusual for overall job efficiency, as measured by actual production levels, to increase by as much as 40 per cent as a result of properly conducted training programs. In addition, training can greatly improve job satisfaction and morale and reduce employee turnover and accident rates. Training programs are costly for companies, but if they are properly designed and executed, they can more than pay for themselves.

Training can also be of immense value to the employee. For example, adequate job training can greatly increase an employee's feelings of job security and can provide increased opportunities for promotion. This, in turn, enhances a worker's feelings of status and self-worth.

Training can also increase the quality of life of the hard-core unemployed. Without sufficient training opportunities, these people will remain unemployable in a society in which job requirements and skills have become increasingly complex. Many organizations provide training opportunities for previously unemployable people, enabling many of them to become contributing members of society for the first time.

Training also offers hope for those whose previous jobs have been rendered obsolete. Automated procedures, for instance, have often eliminated many jobs, including some that were highly skilled. With opportunity to be trained in new skills, these people can be placed in different jobs at the same or higher levels than before.

So important are training opportunities offered by employing organizations that they can be legitimately looked upon as fringe benefits, as valuable as pension and insurance plans. Indeed, training programs can cost a company a lot more than traditional fringe benefits. Let us examine a few examples of the investment in training made by modern organizations.

The First National City Bank of New York has established a school system larger than those in many small towns. With a teaching staff of sixty-five, and the latest in closed-circuit television and video tape recorders, the bank's school has more than 6000 students a year, all employees being trained to improve their job skills.

On a larger scale, the Western Electric Company has set up its own college on a 190-acre campus. Called the Corporate Education Center, the college offers more than 300 courses in engineering and management to employees who live on campus in dormitories. Newly hired engineers are sent to the college for six weeks of orientation training, engineers already employed can attend month-long courses to keep them up to date in their specialty areas, and managers take courses to improve their leadership skills. In addition, the college offers more than 100 correspondence courses for self-improvement in many areas.

General Motors runs the General Motors Institute, which offers employees a four-year college degree in engineering and management.

The Xerox Corporation has a $55 million training center called the International Center for Training and Management Development. The center, on a 2200-acre site in Virginia, houses as many as 1000 employee-students and trains them in classrooms filled with the latest in audiovisual instructional equipment. The center offers a variety of courses in everything from machine repair to sales and management techniques.

Training is a big business, costing $10 to $12 billion a year, and an exceedingly important one to you and to the organization for which you work.

## ESTABLISHING A TRAINING PROGRAM

Education and training procedures, like selection techniques, are difficult to establish and require careful attention to three factors: what is to be taught, how it is to be taught, and who shall teach it.

### Determining Training Objectives

The first step involved in setting up a selection program is the precise determination of what workers actually do on the job; in other words, how, specifically, do they perform the job? This is also the first step in establishing a training program. We cannot know what skills and abilities must be taught without knowing what skills and abilities are required to successfully perform the job in question.

Thus, the initial step in a training program is to specify the objectives in as much detail as possible. This requires the study of actual job performance. The most frequently used technique for determining training objectives is *job analysis*, discussed in Chapter 11. The job analysis yields a detailed list of the characteristics needed to successfully perform the job, and the precise sequence of the operations or procedures involved.

Another method of determining training objectives is the *critical incidents* technique, also discussed in Chapter 11. By evaluating desirable and undesirable behaviors on the job, much can be learned about how employees cope with critical events that occur. For example, how well do assembly line workers cope with jammed machinery? How well do supervisors handle personal disputes among their subordinates? By examining such critical incidents, training directors can determine the kind of training employees need to cope with them.

A third way to determine training needs is by examining the results of the periodic *performance evaluations* most employees receive. Virtually everyone who works, from the lowest to the highest level, is graded on how well he or she is performing the job. These evaluations focus on weaknesses and strengths and, as a result, often lead to recommendations for training to correct work deficiencies.

There are other sources of information on training needs and objectives. *Production records* can indicate whether workers are performing at maximum levels of productivity. If they are not, additional training may be necessary to improve their productivity. *Accident records* can reveal unsafe working habits or practices that can be corrected through training. An alert management must constantly monitor all aspects of an organization's operational efficiency to determine when and where training might be of value.

By whatever method, it is vital to specify the needs and objectives of a training program. Indeed, this can determine whether or not the entire training program is worth the time and money devoted to it.

## Methods of Instruction

Once it is known in detail what skills and abilities must be taught, the proper method of instruction may be decided upon. As you know from your school experiences, there are a number of ways of teaching. In the traditional lecture method, an instructor imparts the content of the course to the students. Usually, the lecture method is supplemented by a textbook or other material to be read and studied by the students.

In addition, there are audiovisual aids that can be used alone or in conjunction with the teacher–textbook method. Many excellent films are available to teach everything from safe working procedures in a factory to physics or psychology. Video and audio tape cassettes are also used frequently in training, along with slides, recordings, and other forms of visual presentation. Teaching machines (programmed learning) are also popular devices for imparting information to trainees.

Student participation is frequently used in teaching, as you know from your experiences presenting reports in the classroom or carrying out some operation in shop class or biology lab. This learning-by-doing approach is very popular in industrial training.

The kind of training approach taken depends on the skill, ability, or knowledge to be taught. Suppose, for example, that you are a training director for a large trucking firm, and you are told to set up a training program for diesel mechanics. In order to learn the theory of how a diesel engine operates, you may engage a knowledgeable instructor and choose some films and books about diesel engines.

This is adequate for learning about the nature and manner of operation of diesel engines, things mechanics should know, but this approach alone will not satisfactorily teach people how actually to repair diesel engines. For this, trainees need the hands-on experience of working with the engines. A facility must be provided in which students can tear down engines to their component parts and put them back together. We shall discuss several examples of how different skills and kinds of knowledge are taught.

## Training Instructors

The third question to be answered in setting up a training program is: "Who is to do the training?" This is a particularly crucial decision because a poor teacher can exert a harmful influence on a person's ability, motivation, and readiness to learn. This was the case with John Kirby in the steel mill described at the beginning of the chapter, and you have no doubt observed this situation in some of your classes.

The key factor in teaching any subject at any level is not so much the teacher's level of competence or expertise in the subject, but rather the ability to communicate the material clearly to the students and to motivate them to want to learn. Thus, knowledge of subject matter, although important, does not by itself make for a successful trainer or teacher.

Trainers must know something more than the subject matter; they must know the proper methods of teaching. Therefore, a crucial aspect of establishing any training program is the education of those who will do the training. Extensive research clearly shows that instructors trained in teaching methods induce a higher rate of learning in their students than instructors who are not trained in teaching methods.

Unfortunately, despite this strong evidence, training in industry is frequently conducted by persons who may be experienced in the skill or ability to be taught, but who have had no formal training in how to teach that skill to others. For example, it is customary in many kinds of jobs in industry to use foremen or experienced workers to train or break in new employees. These people may know everything about the job, but unless they are skilled and motivated in the art of teaching, they will be no more effective than the Charley in our opening example.

The obvious solution to this problem is to use professional teachers in training programs, people who have been trained both in the skills to be taught and in methods of teaching, and many large organizations do just that. They employ full-time teachers who are equipped to teach several subjects. This provides not only for the most effective instruction, but it also prevents interference with the ongoing activities and operations of the organization, such as can happen when foremen or workers must take time away from their jobs to train new employees.

We have discussed the decisions that must be made in setting up a training program. We now turn to a consideration of the different kinds of training in use today in employing organizations. In general, training methods differ with the level of the job. Although the distinction is not absolute, it is useful to divide training methods into two types: methods used for skilled and semiskilled jobs, which we call nonsupervisory, and methods used for supervisory and management jobs.

## TRAINING METHODS FOR NONSUPERVISORY JOBS

The most frequently used methods of training for nonsupervisory employees are on-the-job training, vestibule training, apprenticeship, programmed instruction, and behavior modification.

## On-the-Job Training

As the name suggests, on-the-job training takes place directly on the job for which workers are being trained. Under the guidance of an experienced worker, a supervisor, or a trained instructor, trainees learn while working. They operate the actual machinery or the assembly process in the production facility.

An apparent advantage of this approach is economy. The company does not have to go to the considerable expense of building a special training facility and duplicating the equipment and machinery used on the job. Also, if workers or foremen serve as trainers, the company saves the cost of professional instructors.

However, there are less visible costs of on-the-job training. The trainers must take time away from their regular jobs, and this may lower their productivity. Also, new and inexperienced trainees may slow production themselves or damage the machinery or the product that is being manufactured. Thus, on-the-job training is not as economical as it seems, although it is probably cheaper to implement than most other training methods.

Another advantage of on-the-job training is that trainees learn the job on the same equipment and in the same facility in which they will actually be working once training has been completed. This provides what psychologists call *positive transfer of training;* everything learned in the training situation carries over or transfers to the actual working situation. Sometimes a training facility is so different from the actual work facility that much of what was learned in training does not transfer positively to the work situation. This is not the problem with on-the-job training.

Although there are definite advantages to on-the-job training, there are disadvantages as well. We mentioned the potential decreases in production and damage to machinery and product that can be caused by trainees. In addition, with some jobs it may be hazardous to allow trainees to operate machinery. Accident rates among trainees are higher than among experienced workers.

The case of John Kirby at the beginning of the chapter highlighted the disadvantage of using current workers as trainers. This problem can be overcome by teaching workers and foremen how to train new employees on the job, and impressing upon them the importance of training. Unfortunately, this is rarely done in industry today.

Despite these disadvantages, on-the-job training is popular for many skilled and semiskilled jobs. With proper safeguards and precautions, it can be a very effective means of training, particularly for clerical, production, and retail sales jobs.

## Vestibule Training

Because on-the-job training can interfere with the ongoing production process, many companies prefer to conduct their training programs in separate, specially constructed facilities designed to duplicate or simulate the actual workplace. In this vestibule training, trainees learn to perform the job under the guidance of skilled instructors, using the same kinds of equipment, machinery, and operating procedures as they will find on the job.

There are several obvious advantages to vestibule training. There is no possibility of trainees committing costly errors that will slow production or damage machinery or the product. For that reason, there is less pressure on the trainees and no possibility of their making embarrassing or stupid mistakes in front of coworkers. This reduced pressure, plus the use of professional trainers, means that more individualized instruction can be given to the trainees.

The major drawback to vestibule training is its expense. The company must set up a facility duplicating the production facility and must maintain a full-time staff of instructors. Unless there is a large number of new employees, requiring frequent training sessions, such expenditures are not justifiable.

Another drawback to vestibule training is related to transfer of training. If the training situation does not closely resemble the actual work situation (if, for example, the machinery is obsolete and no longer the type used on the job), additional training will be needed when the trainees actually begin work. Psychologists call this *negative transfer;* what has been learned in the training situation hampers or interferes with performance on the job.

## Apprenticeship

Apprentice programs are frequently used for skilled crafts and trades. These programs combine classroom learning and on-the-job experience; that is, formal training in the nature and theory of the skill from professional instructors and actual work experience under the guidance of experts in the trade. This combination can provide excellent training in highly complex skills such as those required for plumbers, electricians, masons, and bricklayers.

Some apprentice programs are run jointly by unions and private industry, and they require a trainee to agree to work for a company for a fixed period of time in return for a specified amount of training and a salary about half that of the skilled craftsperson. Unions will usually not allow anyone to join unless they have first completed an apprenticeship. Because union membership is usually required to get a job in a particular trade, apprenticeship programs ensure an adequate supply of trained workers (and also ensure that not too many people are trained, for that may result in lower wages).

## Programmed Instruction

A recent development in employee training is the use of the teaching machine, or programmed instruction technique, discussed in Chapter 10. Programmed instruction offers several advantages. It provides constant and immediate feedback (knowledge of results), continuous and active participation on the part of trainees, and positive reinforcement. In addition, each trainee is able to proceed at his or her own pace.

There are also limitations to the use of programmed instruction in employee training. It is expensive and can only be used efficiently with large numbers of trainees. It is not effective in teaching complex job skills. Also, some trainees are easily bored by the routine and mechanical nature of programmed instruction. However, for organizations that must train large numbers of workers in a short time to perform relatively simple tasks, programmed instruction is an effective training technique.

## Behavior Modification

Behavior modification was discussed in Chapter 4 as an effective means of changing behavior, in the clinical setting, from undesirable to desirable. Behavior modification is used in a similar way, and for the same purpose, in the world of work. Punishment is not used when employees fail to display the desired behavior. Instead, employees are rewarded or reinforced when they do display the desired behavior.

Consider the case of a hardware company that was plagued by high employee absenteeism and tardiness.[1] To change this behavior, the company organized a monthly drawing in which employees were eligible to win a variety of home appliances. To be eligible for the drawing, employees had to come to work on time every day for the preceding month. At the end of six months of the behavior modification program there was another drawing, this time for a color television set. Eligibility required perfect attendance and punctuality for the full six months.

The program was very successful. After one year, absenteeism and tardiness had dropped by 75 per cent. The employees who had mild colds were much more likely to come to work, whereas previously they would have stayed home. Even severe snowstorms did not keep them

[1] W. Nord, "Improving Attendance Through Rewards," *Personnel Administration*, **33** (1970), 37–41.

away from work. Thus, positive reinforcement was effective in changing behavior on the job.

Behavior modification is being used with increasing frequency in industry. It has been successful in changing behavior and significantly improving job performance. In some behavior modification programs, the reinforcement does not consist of prizes, bonuses, or increased pay, but includes instead praise and recognition given the employees by their supervisors. One company developed a handbook for supervisors that details 150 different rewards and recognitions, ranging from a smile to specific praise for a job well done.

## TRAINING METHODS FOR MANAGERS

The need for training, although important at the nonsupervisory level, is even more critical at the supervisory or management level. The cost to the company of an incompetent department head or vice president is far greater than the cost of an incompetent assembly line worker. Managing or supervising others is a difficult and demanding job that requires certain aptitudes, personality traits, and interpersonal skills, characteristics that must be formally developed and exercised before a person can become a competent manager. As a result, most employing organizations devote enormous amounts of time and money to training their managerial personnel. Management training includes a variety of skills, ranging from specific leadership, decision-making, and problem-solving abilities to the broader area of human relations skills.

The primary techniques used for management training include the case study method, business games, in-basket training, role playing, sensitivity training, and university and special institute courses.

### The Case Study Method

In this popular method of management training, a complex problem, of the kind managers face daily on the job, is presented to the trainees prior to their first meeting as a group. They are told to familiarize themselves with every aspect of the problem and to find, on their own, whatever additional information they feel is relevant to a possible solution.

Later, when the trainees meet as a group, each of them must present and discuss his or her interpretation of and solution to the problem. According to proponents of the case study method, the presentation of differing viewpoints causes the trainees to recognize and appreciate the fact that there are various ways of looking at a problem and, consequently, different ways of trying to resolve it. As a rule, there is no single correct solution to the problem, and the group leader does not suggest a particular solution; the solution is up to the group of trainees as a whole.

The purpose of the case study approach is to teach trainees the skills necessary for group problem solving and decision making, the ability to analyze and criticize their own assumptions and interpretations, and the ability to be open and receptive to points of view that may differ from their own.

## Business Games

In this approach to management training, complex, real-life business situations are simulated. Teams of trainees compete to resolve the situations. Each team represents a separate company, and the teams are given detailed information about all aspects of the company's operation, including data on finances, sales, advertising, production, personnel, and inventories.

Each team must organize itself into an efficient management unit; a leader must be selected and the various tasks and responsibilities assigned to the members. As the game proceeds, and each team makes its decisions, instructors evaluate the results and inform the teams of the effects of their decisions on the operation of the company. Often, additional decisions must be made on the basis of these evaluations.

The business problems on which the teams are working are carefully designed to be realistic, and frequently the team members become emotionally involved with their company and its problems. The trainees have the opportunity to exercise their problem-solving and decision-making skills on actual business problems under the pressures of time and competition, but they do so in a situation in which any mistakes they make will not truly harm a real organization.

## In-Basket Training

The in-basket technique as a method of selection was discussed in Chapter 11. The procedure is used in a similar way as a method of training people in the techniques and principles of leadership. In essence, when used for training purposes, the in-basket technique is very much like a business game in that it simulates the tasks and responsibilities of a manager on the job. The difference between in-basket training and the business game is that trainees operate individually in the in-basket technique, not as part of a group.

The trainees are presented with in-baskets filled with the kinds of problems faced by managers daily—letters, memos, complaints from customers, requests from subordinates, and the like. The trainees must

deal with each item within a limited period of time, specifying exactly what action they would take in each case.

After all the items have been acted upon, each trainee reports on the decisions to a group composed of the trainer and other trainees, who discuss and criticize each decision. As with business games and the case study method, the in-basket technique presents a faithful simulation of problems that the trainees would face as managers. Therefore, considerable stress is brought about by the competition with other trainees. This too simulates the stressful conditions managers face on the job in terms of competition with other managers.

## Role Playing

The techniques discussed previously are oriented toward teaching specific management skills, notably decision making, problem solving, and the delegation of authority. Another aspect of a manager's job involves interpersonal skills and sensitivity to the feelings of others. To develop these human relations skills, role playing and sensitivity training are used.

In role playing, trainees are asked to play different roles, to act out the behaviors and feelings they think are appropriate to each situation.

For example, trainees may be asked to play the role of a manager who must fire a subordinate whose work has been inadequate. Another trainee plays the role of the subordinate. Then they may reverse roles and replay the situation.

Most trainees feel self-conscious and somewhat foolish at first about acting in front of other trainees and the trainer. But almost always they soon develop strong feelings for the role they are playing, and they become the people they are pretending to be and act spontaneously and naturally.

As a result of these various role-playing exercises, trainees have a chance to practice and to get a feel for the roles they will have to play as managers. Through discussion and feedback from the trainer and other trainees, they learn how to improve their behavior in these situations.

More valuable may be the heightened sensitivity trainees develop about the feelings of other people, particularly their subordinates. By playing the role of a subordinate, a trainee gains an understanding of the subordinate's feelings, perspectives, and rights as a human being. Assuming positive transfer to the job, role playing can greatly enhance a manager's compassion, insight, and understanding.

## Sensitivity Training

Sensitivity training is a popular means of raising consciousness levels and improving interpersonal skills. The technique has been frequently used by employing organizations as part of their management training programs. The purpose of sensitivity training is to develop in managers a clearer and more accurate picture of themselves by demonstrating to them how other people perceive them. Managers also have the opportunity to learn about the effect their behavior has on others.

Sensitivity sessions for management training are conducted much like those run for the general public. Trainees meet in groups of about twelve for a few hours a day for several weeks, or for marathon sessions lasting two or more days. Often, the training takes place at a comfortable and secluded retreat, away from the pressures, strains, and securities of everyday life and work. Management sensitivity sessions are as intense, emotional, and revealing as those conducted for any group.

Many managers who finish sensitivity training report a greater tolerance and acceptance of others, increased self-insight, greater self-control, and a more cooperative and tactful attitude in dealing with others. However, there is little sound research support for these reported changes.

Whether any results from sensitivity training sessions make a real difference in a manager's productive capacity and decision-making ability has yet to be demonstrated. Regardless, a large number of organizations believe that there is value to sensitivity training for managers and executives, and the technique has become a major part of the overall management training program.

## University Courses and Special Institutes

Many universities and institutes offer special training programs for executives designed to improve their management skills and to broaden their social and cultural backgrounds. The courses are frequently held on a university or institute campus, such as the Aspen Institute of Humanistic Studies and the University of Colorado Center for Management and Technical Programs, and last from a few weeks to several months.

Some of these courses are highly practical and directly related to a manager's job, such as marketing, computer resources, public policy, and product planning. Other courses concentrate on the liberal arts, for example, art, history, music, ethics, logic, foreign policy, and literature.

How do such courses help managers and executives to perform their demanding jobs more effectively? No one has a definite answer to that question, and it may take many years before any impact of such training is felt. Still, corporate leaders believe in the value of special courses and send their most promising executives to participate in them.

## THE EVALUATION OF EMPLOYEE PERFORMANCE

Once employees have been trained to perform their jobs, the level or quality of their performance is periodically and systematically evaluated by means of a number of techniques devised by industrial psychologists. Performance evaluation is something with which you as a student are already familiar. Every time you take an examination, submit a term paper, or give a report in class, the quality of your performance is evaluated by your instructor.

The information provided by these evaluations of your performance is valuable both to you and to your teacher. It enables the instructor to know how well you are mastering the material of the course and the areas in which you may need special help. Performance evaluation tells you whether you are effectively performing your job of studying and allows you to gauge your progress and development as a student.

Periodic evaluation of your performance does not end when you leave school. Performance evaluations continue throughout your working career and provide you and your employer with the same type of information provided by your classroom evaluations.

Properly conducted performance evaluations tell you what your superiors think of you, what you are doing particularly well on the job, what areas of your work need improvement, and what your future in the organization may be. A performance evaluation can be a valuable learning experience, revealing your strengths and weaknesses, assets and liabilities.

Performance evaluations also provide a great deal of information to your employer. The information obtained can be used to motivate good employees to do better and to inspire average performers as well. Employees who have the potential for advancement are identified through performance evaluations, and decisions on promotions and salary can be made on the basis of an objective measure of how well people do on their jobs. If it becomes necessary to reduce the size of the work force, performance evaluations provide an objective record of those who are poor performers.

An important use of performance evaluations is to provide a measure of job success to use in validating selection techniques. The only way of validating a selection technique is to compare performance on it with subsequent performance on the job. Another purpose of performance evaluation is to help determine training needs and the specific skills that must be taught in a training program.

## TECHNIQUES OF PERFORMANCE EVALUATION

The techniques by which job performance can be evaluated vary with the kind of work. Evaluating the work performed in a routine and repetitive assembly line job is different from evaluating the work of an advertising account executive. Different techniques are required for various types of jobs, techniques that adequately reflect the nature and complexity of the work.

Three categories of performance evaluation techniques are those for production jobs, for nonproduction jobs, and for executive jobs.

### Evaluating Performance on Production Jobs

Measuring performance levels on production jobs is relatively simple and usually involves recording the number of units a worker produces in a given period of time. This measurement of the quantity of production is widely used in industry because detailed records of production are available for these kinds of jobs.

However, for some jobs it is not sufficient to assess only the quantity of production as a measure of employee performance; the quality of production must also be considered. For example, consider the case of two secretaries; one types seventy words per minute and the other types fifty-five words per minute. If we use quantity as the only measure of performance, the first secretary would receive the better performance evaluation.

However, let us look at the quality of their work. The first secretary makes an average of twenty mistakes per minute and the second secretary makes no mistakes. Now, considering quality of performance along with quantity, the initial performance ratings must be reversed and the second secretary would receive the higher evaluation.

Additional factors must be taken into account. Certain aspects of the work environment and of the actual work itself may adversely affect performance. Suppose that the first secretary (who makes so many errors) works in a noisy office and is constantly plagued by distractions. The second secretary works in peaceful and quiet surroundings. Obviously, this important difference must be considered if we are to evaluate the job performance of the two employees fairly. Also, there may be significant differences in the nature of the work these secretaries perform. One may type only short, simple business letters and the other may type lengthy, complex engineering reports. Therefore, we must remember that the simple quantitative measure may not provide enough information to use in evaluating a worker's performance objectively.

The more factors that have to be taken into consideration, the less objective is the resulting performance appraisal, but it will more accurately reflect the nature of the work.

## Evaluating Performance on Nonproduction Jobs

A nonproduction job is any job that does not result in the production of anything that can be counted meaningfully. Consider the job of firefighter. How would you evaluate their performance? Certainly not by counting the number of fires they put out each day. What about brain surgeons or business executives? Counting their output—the number of brains operated upon or the number of decisions made per day—does not provide a meaningful way of evaluating their job performance.

The only way to evaluate performance on nonproduction jobs is by observing that performance over a period of time and rendering an opinion about its quality. The people best qualified to make these observations and judgments are those who are most familiar with the employee's work—supervisors and sometimes coworkers.

These judgments are necessarily of a subjective nature because they are not based on objective data such as the number of units produced. However, psychologists have devised techniques for making these judgments of performance, techniques that try to minimize, as much as possible, the role of subjective biasing factors. These techniques are called, collectively, *merit rating techniques,* and that is their purpose, to rate an employee's merit. They include several specific procedures: rating, ranking, paired comparisons, forced distribution, and forced choice.

The *rating* technique is the most frequently used means of evaluating performance. Supervisors rate their employees on a number of specific traits, abilities, or characteristics, indicating how much of the trait or ability each employee possesses. Ratings should be specific and are often given in numerical form. For example, on a rating scale ranging from 1 to 5, where a numerical rating of 1 represents a poor showing on a specific characteristic, a rating of 3 represents an average showing, and a rating of 5 represents excellence, an employee rated 3.2 has received an evaluation indicating that he or she is slightly above average in performance.

Ratings can be made on many traits. One company asks its supervisors to rate subordinates on the following items: knowledge of work, quantity of work, quality of work, ability to learn new duties, initiative, cooperation, judgment, and common sense. On some rating forms, supervisors are also asked to compare the current ratings with the previous ratings for each employee. This comparison indicates whether the employee has improved, become less efficient, or remained the same.

The rating approach to merit rating is popular because it is relatively simple to carry out and to design.

In the *ranking* technique, supervisors list their employees in rank order from best to worst, either in terms of overall job effectiveness or on a number of specific characteristics. In ranking, each employee is compared with all others in the same working unit, whereas in rating, each employee is compared with his or her own past performance or with some company standard of exemplary performance.

In general, ranking is a simple method. No complicated forms or instructions are needed, but it does become difficult to accomplish when a large number of subordinates must be evaluated. A supervisor with only ten subordinates would have little problem in rank ordering them in terms of quality of job performance, but a supervisor with fifty or one hundred subordinates would find ranking an extremely complicated task.

There are other problems with the ranking technique. Because of its simplicity, ranking provides little information about an employee's strengths or weaknesses. Evaluation of workers on a number of specific characteristics, as in rating, provides much more information. Also, the ranking method makes it impossible to indicate that some employees perform at the same level. For example, if two employees show equally superior job performance, this will not be apparent in the ranking; only one person can be at the top of the list.

Thus, ranking is a simple but crude measure of job performance and is only useful in situations where there are a small number of workers to be evaluated and little specific information is desired on personal characteristics and abilities.

The *paired comparisons* technique involves a direct comparison of each worker with every other worker in a department, section, or other work unit. The comparisons are made between two subordinates at a time, and the pair is rank-ordered; that is, a judgment is made as to which of the two is the better worker. If judgments on specific characteristics are required, the comparison must be repeated for each characteristic.

It is easier to judge two subordinates at a time than several, as in the ranking technique. The major drawback to the paired comparisons approach becomes apparent when a large number of people must be evaluated. If a supervisor has sixty subordinates, for example, he or she would be required to make almost 1800 judgments in order to compare each worker with every other worker. Also, if the supervisor has to compare the workers on several separate characteristics, the 1800 comparisons must be repeated several times, not a very inviting task.

You are already familiar with the principle underlying the *forced distribution* technique from the grading system used in some of your courses. In this approach, subordinates are evaluated by a predetermined distribution of ratings. A fixed percentage of the workers must be placed in each of several categories. For example, 10 per cent of the workers must be rated "superior," 20 per cent "better than average," 40 per cent "average," 20 per cent "below average," and 10 per cent "poor."

Thus, if a supervisor has 100 subordinates to rate, ten must be assigned to the superior category, twenty to the better than average category, and so on. This is like giving the top 10 per cent of a class A's, the next 20 per cent B's, and so on. No matter what their level of performance, all students or employees must be placed in these categories. You can see that such a system is sometimes unfair. Suppose that all the workers in a department are very good; none of them deserves to be evaluated as below average or poor. In the forced distribution technique, however, 30 per cent of them must be given low ratings even though the ratings would not accurately describe their abilities.

The *forced choice* approach to performance evaluation is designed to eliminate the effects of personal bias, prejudice, or favoritism on the part of those who make the ratings. In this approach, supervisors have no way of knowing how favorable or unfavorable their ratings are. Therefore, they cannot reward or punish an employee by giving a good or bad rating strictly for some personal reason.

The person doing the rating is given a series of descriptive statements (in pairs or groups of three or four) and must choose the statement that most accurately describes the employee being evaluated. The statements appear to be equally favorable. Consider the following pairs of statements.

1. Is reliable.
2. Is agreeable.

1. Is careful.
2. Is diligent.

The supervisor must select one statement in each pair that best describes a particular worker. As you can see, because the statements seem to be equally favorable, it is extremely difficult for a supervisor to deliberately give a good or poor rating. Often, pairs of equally unfavorable statements are also used from which the supervisor must choose the statement that is the least descriptive of an employee.

These statements only *seem* to be equally favorable or unfavorable; in reality they are not. Each statement has been carefully evaluated by psychologists to determine how well it correlates with some measure of job success. One statement in each pair has been shown to be capable of discriminating between better and poorer workers.

The considerable amount of research necessary to develop these statements may be the major disadvantage of the forced choice technique, making it by far the most expensive method of performance evaluation. Also, many supervisors find the task difficult to understand and to carry out. However, as noted, the forced choice technique does offer the great advantage of eliminating personal bias, always a problem when one person is asked to evaluate another.

## Evaluating Executive Performance

The evaluation techniques discussed previously are used primarily for lower-level employees, such as those in clerical, manufacturing, or retail sales jobs. Evaluating higher-level executive positions requires other appraisal techniques because of the diversity of responsibilities, tasks, and skills in executive jobs. Clerks, factory workers, or salespersons are usually more homogeneous groups than executives in terms of background, abilities, and work duties; thus, they are easier to evaluate than executives.

Techniques to evaluate executive performance include the in-basket technique, evaluation by superiors, peer ratings, and self-evaluation.

We discussed the use of the *in-basket* technique for selection and training. It is used in much the same way for evaluating executive performance. While the person being evaluated is dealing with the letters, memos, and directives in the in-basket, his or her performance is being observed and assessed.

The in-basket procedure does not evaluate how executives perform on the job, but rather in a simulation of the job. The question still unanswered is how well performance on the in-basket exercise reflects performance on the job. Other procedures used in assessment centers, such as group problem-solving tasks, are also beginning to be used to evaluate executive performance.

*Evaluation by superiors* is the most widespread means of executive performance appraisal. These evaluations, unlike the rating techniques, are rarely carried out on formal rating sheets. Instead, an executive's superior writes a general description, in his or her own words and format, of the subordinate's level of performance. Frequently, executives are evaluated not only by their immediate superior, but by those several levels above them as well.

In the *peer rating* approach to executive appraisal, individuals are evaluated by their colleagues, usually those who are at the same corporate level. This approach is used extensively in the military for evaluations of officers as well as in business and industry, where it has been found particularly useful in identifying people with potential for promotion.

You have no doubt recognized the potential problem with peer rating. Colleagues at work may also be close friends, and this can serve to bias the ratings. Also, some colleagues are perceived as rivals; this may tempt one person to give another a low rating.

An unusual approach to executive appraisal is *self-evaluation,* in which each individual assesses his or her own abilities. This has been found to be useful for dealing with an executive's strengths and weaknesses, but it does not provide the kind of information needed for personnel decisions such as pay raises and promotions.

Executives and their superiors begin the process of self-evaluation by mutually agreeing on a set of work objectives for the executive, such as skills to develop or improve. After several months, the executives report on how well they believe they have met these goals. Then a new set of objectives, or a modification of the initial set, are established and the process continues.

Self-appraisals deal mainly with interpersonal and human relations skills; evaluations by superiors focus on technical skills and abilities specific to the job. Not surprisingly, self-evaluations tend to be more favorable than those given by superiors. We often think more highly of ourselves than others do.

## SUMMARY

*Training* people for work is a major activity of industrial psychologists and one that is vital to you and to the organization for which you work. No matter how sophisticated and valid is a company's selection program, no matter how well qualified are individual employees, maximum efficiency on the job cannot be reached without adequate job training. From apprentice to company president, training is a continuing activity to which employing organizations devote a great deal of time and money.

Training is of such importance that it can legitimately be considered a fringe benefit of a job. A good training program increases employees' feelings of job security, status, and self-worth, and their opportunities for promotion. Training also enhances the quality of life of the hard-core unemployed—enabling many of them to become contributing members of society for the first time—and of workers whose jobs have been rendered obsolete by technological changes.

Establishing a training program is a costly and complex undertaking that requires careful attention to three factors. (1) What is to be taught? We cannot know what to teach without first knowing what skills and abilities are needed to successfully perform the job. This information is derived from job analyses, critical incidents, performance evaluations, and examination of production and accident records. (2) How is it to be taught? Once the skills to be taught are known, the best teaching methods must be determined. Methods include the traditional teacher—textbook approach, audiovisual materials, student participation, and on-the-job training. (3) Who shall teach it? Trainers must have competence in the subject matter to be taught, be skilled in the art of communicating, and be able to motivate trainees to learn. Many companies employ professional trainers.

Two types of training methods are those for nonsupervisory employees and those for supervisory or management employees. Training methods for *nonsupervisory* jobs include: (1) *On-the-job training:* training people on the job at which they will be working provides for positive transfer of training. However, it can disrupt the production process. (2) *Vestibule training:* training that takes place in a separate facility designed to simulate the actual workplace eliminates the possibility of trainees interfering with the production process. However, it is an expensive technique and may not always provide positive transfer of training to the actual job. (3) *Apprentice programs:* these involve both classroom learning and on-the-job experience and are used primarily for skilled crafts and trades. (4) *Programmed instruction:* the material to be learned is presented in small steps so that trainees can proceed at their own pace, in line with their individual abilities. The technique provides constant feedback on progress, active participation, and positive reinforcement, but its usefulness is limited to the teaching of relatively simple job skills. (5) *Behavior modification:* employees are rewarded or reinforced only when they display the desired behaviors. Rewards range from tangible prizes or bonuses to less tangible forms of praise and recognition.

Training programs for *managers* include: (1) The *case study method:* groups of trainees discuss their individual solutions to complex business problems. This teaches them the value of recognizing differing ways of looking at a problem. (2) *Business games:* teams of trainees compete to solve business problems. Each team must organize itself effectively in order to present the most efficient solution to the problem under the pressure of time. (3) *In-basket training:* individual trainees must handle the problems found in their in-baskets as effectively and quickly as possible. (4) *Role playing:* through acting out the behaviors and feelings of other people in different roles, trainees develop interpersonal skills and sensitivity to the feelings of others. (5) *Sensitivity training:* through this intense, emotional, and revealing group interaction, trainees develop greater self-understanding and increased tolerance and acceptance of others. (6) *University and special institute courses:* these formal courses include instruction in specific management skills as well as in liberal arts and philosophy. The programs are designed to broaden an executive's cultural and intellectual background.

*Performance evaluation* is an activity that continues throughout an employee's career. It is used as a basis for determining pay raises, promotions, demotions, and dismissals. Performance evaluation attempts to assess workers' strengths and weaknesses so that they can improve their job performance. Three categories of performance evaluation techniques are those for production jobs, for nonproduction jobs, and for executive jobs.

Evaluating performance on *production jobs* involves recording the number of units a worker produces in a given period of time. However, this quantitative measure must be qualified by assessments of the quality of the work, the conditions under which the work is performed, and the nature of the work itself.

Performance evaluations of *nonproduction jobs* involve *merit rating* techniques, by which a supervisor may rate an employee's level of performance. Merit rating techniques include: (1) *Rating:* supervisors assign a numerical rating to subordinates on a number of specific traits. (2) *Ranking:* all subordinates in a working unit are rank ordered from best to worst in terms of overall job effectiveness or on specific traits. The technique is difficult when there are many subordinates to evaluate. (3) *Paired comparisons:* each worker is compared with every other worker and each pair is rank ordered. This technique is unwieldy with large numbers of subordinates. (4) *Forced distribution:* a fixed percentage of the workers must be placed in each of several categories. This is similar to some classroom grading systems. (5) *Forced choice:* supervisors must choose which of several apparently favorable or unfavorable statements best characterizes each subordinate.

*Executive* performance evaluation is carried out by: (1) The *in-basket technique:* this is used in the same way as for selection and training purposes. (2) *Evaluation by superiors:* superiors write general descriptions of their subordinates' level of performance. (3) *Peer rating:* colleagues perform the evaluations. (4) *Self-evaluation:* each executive assesses his or her own abilities, strengths, and weaknesses.

## SUGGESTED READINGS

Broadwell, M. *Supervisor and On the Job Training,* 2nd ed. Reading, Mass.: Addison–Wesley, 1975.

Cummings, L. L., and D. P. Schwab. *Performance in Organizations: Determinants and Appraisal.* Glenview, Ill.: Scott, Foresman, 1973.

Fisher, Delbert W. Educational psychology involved in on–the–job training. *Personnel Journal,* 1977, **56,** 516–519.

Gannon, M. Attitudes of government executives toward management training. *Public Personnel Management,* 1975, **4,** 63–68.

Goldstein, I. *Training: Program Development and Evaluation.* Monterey, Calif.: Brooks/Cole, 1974.

Hague, H. *Executive Self–Development.* New York: Halsted Press, 1974.

Hinrichs, J. R. Personnel training. In M. Dunnette, Ed., *Handbook of Industrial and Organizational Psychology.* Chicago: Rand McNally, 1976. Pp. 829–860.

Kellogg, M. S. *What to Do About Performance Appraisal,* rev. ed. New York: American Management Association, 1976.

Locher, Alan H., and Kenneth S. Teel. Performance appraisal—a survey of current practices. *Personnel Journal,* 1977, **56,** 245–247, 254.

Maier, N. R. F. *The Appraisal Interview: Three Basic Approaches.* San Diego, Calif.: University Associates, 1976.

Newell, G. How to plan a training program. *Personnel Journal,* 1976, **55,** 220–225.

Patz, A. Performance appraisal: Useful but still resisted. *Harvard Business Review,* 1975 (May–June), **53,** 74–80.

Schneier, C. Behavior modification: Training the hard–core unemployed. *Personnel,* 1973 (May–June), **50,** 65–69.

Tracey, W. *Managing Training and Development Systems.* New York: American Management Association, 1974.

Zawacki, Robert A., and Robert L. Taylor. A view of performance appraisal from organizations using it. *Personnel Journal,* 1976, **55,** 290–292, 299.

# Psychology Applied to the World of Work: III. Managing, Motivating, and Satisfying People at Work

**13**

The fifteen employees of Arthur Friedman's appliance store sat in stunned silence when he finished his speech.* No one moved or spoke and the period of silence grew embarrassingly long. Then, with a sign from Friedman that the meeting was over, they filed out of his office and went back to work, uncertain, confused, and perhaps a little frightened by what the man they all worked for had just told them. None of them had ever heard anything like it before. It sounded bizarre, even preposterous, and none of them knew what to make of it.

A few days earlier Friedman had told his brother about the new way he was going to run his store. His brother looked at him, shook his head in disbelief, and muttered, "Oh, my God!" When Friedman's wife found out about his idea she said, "Here he goes again, another dumb stunt."

And on the face of it, what Friedman told his employees that day seemed like a very dumb stunt indeed, contrary to every established rule and belief about how to manage and motivate employees.

"You decide how much money you're worth," he told his employees, "and that's what you'll be paid. Just tell the bookkeeper to put it in your envelope next week. No questions asked."

If that wasn't enough of a shock, Friedman had another surprise or two.

"Work any time, any day, any hours you want. Having a bad day? Go home. Hate working Saturdays? No problem. Want to go to Reno for a week, need a rest? Go, go, no need to ask. If you need some money for the slot machines, take it out of petty cash. Just come back when you feel ready to work again."

For the first month, none of the employees took Arthur Friedman at his word, but then, hesitantly, a few of them went to the payroll clerk and told him how much of a raise they wanted. The clerk checked with Friedman but

* Martin Koughan, "Arthur Friedman's Outrage: Employees Decide Their Pay," *The Washington Post*, February 23, 1975.

**343**

the boss refused to even talk about it. "I finally figured out he was serious," the clerk said.

Soon Friedman's scheme took root as several more employees decided, and demanded, how much more they should be paid. Some asked for $50 a week more and others as high as $60. A delivery truck driver was the most ambitious of all; he demanded and got a $100-a-week raise. And he was not a very good employee, at least not until he received his pay increase. After that he became a model worker, coming to work early and working harder than ever before.

However, contrary to what we might have expected, the average requested wage increase was not very high, and some employees did not ask for a raise at all. Overall, the employees showed amazing restraint and an awareness of the effects that considerable pay increases would have on the business. One man declined to ask for a pay increase because he didn't "want to work that hard," recognizing that increased productivity should accompany increased wages. Another employee said, "You have to use common sense; no one wins if you end up closing the business down. If you want more money, you have to produce more. It can't work any other way." Another employee who did not ask for a raise said, "I figure if everybody asks for more, then inflation will just get worse. I'll hold out as long as I can."

This experience contradicts management's traditional expectation of what workers and their unions want—more money for less work. Indeed, everything about the behavior of Friedman's employees under the new scheme contradicts orthodox management beliefs. The employees did not take advantage of their employer even though it would have been very easy to do so. Attendance and punctuality improved, employees worked harder, and the store's profits increased, although the hours of operation were reduced. The shop was closed evenings and Sundays because the employees decided that they did not want to work those hours. Also, employees took fewer sick days than before.

Another startling development involved the petty cash system. All employees were given keys to the store and to the cash box, and were told that any time they needed extra money they were free to take it, leaving a voucher in return. At one time there was a $10 discrepancy in the amount that should have been in the cash box, but it was $10 over, not under! "We never could figure out where it came from," Friedman said.

Arthur Friedman took a chance on his employees, a big chance (according to his friends it was a stupid chance), when he announced the changes in the work environment. He believed that his employees were mature, responsible, honest, and trustworthy people, capable both of deciding certain aspects of store policy on their own and of behaving rationally in accordance with those decisions. "If you give people what they want, you get what you want," Friedman said. In effect, he believed that if you treat employees with suspicion and hostility, you get suspicion and hostility in return. If you treat them as children, as inferior and dependent beings, you get rebellious behavior in return. If you treat them as incapable of exercising restraint, maturity of judgment, or responsibility, then indeed they will not display these characteristics.

Arthur Friedman's appliance store provides an excellent and all too rare example of how to manage, motivate, and satisfy people at work. Psychologists have conducted a great deal of research on the nature and characteristics of effective employee management, the nature of worker motivation, and the satisfactions people find (or fail to find) in the world of work. This research is helping to bring about dramatic changes in the ways in which people are managed and the kinds of rewards they find in their jobs.

The authoritarian worker-management and motivation philosophy prevalent for many decades is fading as more and more employees are being offered the opportunity to participate in decision making in their organizations, and are finding more personal freedom, challenge, and meaning in the design of their jobs. The idea that managers have to be dictatorial to get anything done, and the notion that employees are idle, lazy, shiftless, and wanting something for nothing is disappearing. As a result, the quality of working life for millions of employees in the United States and in much of Western Europe is improving.

## LEADERSHIP

It is obvious that a major element in the success or failure of any organization, from a small classroom to a large factory, is the nature of the organization's leadership. We know that industry today devotes much time and money to selecting those who are well qualified to be leaders and training them to function with maximum efficiency. Psychologists are very active in selecting and training leaders for the world of work, but their contribution to leadership in industry does not end there. Psychologists are also concerned with the ways in which leaders behave, how their behavior affects the performance of their subordinates, the specific functions or tasks of leaders, and the personality characteristics of effective leaders.

### The Nature of Leadership Behavior

The specific ways in which leaders behave—the ways in which they manage their subordinates—reflect certain basic assumptions about human nature. Although these may not be formally stated, leaders function on the basis of a consciously or unconsciously held theory of human behavior, a view of what their subordinates are like as people. These views or philosophies of management have changed dramatically in the course of the twentieth century.

The philosophy of management that pervaded American industry for many years is called *scientific management*. Developed by an engineer, Frederick W. Taylor, scientific management is concerned solely with increasing production levels by standardizing the production process and by having the machines, and the people who run them, work faster and faster. The workers themselves were believed to be like machines, and no consideration was given to the notion that they might have ordinary human needs, fears, and values.

The leadership style during the scientific management era was authoritarian and dictatorial. In military fashion, managers gave orders and expected them to be carried out immediately, with total loyalty and dedication. Managers had absolute power over all aspects of the workers' lives on the job; the workers had no say and no rights. They worked under the threat of immediate dismissal for disobedience.

Beginning in the 1930s, a new philosophy of management developed, primarily because of research on social and psychological factors affecting job performance. Called the *human relations movement*, this approach focuses more on the workers than on production levels. Workers are recognized as human beings, and industry has become aware of the personal and social needs of its employees and of the importance of interpersonal relationships among all members of the work force. Managers are concerned with ways of satisfying human needs and with enhancing their employees' personal growth and development.

Obviously, the human relations approach to management requires a different form of leadership behavior, one that is much more democratic than the leadership style under scientific management. The more recent evolution of the human relations approach allows for open participation by the workers themselves in management decisions of all types. Although this change from authoritarian to democratic leadership is by no means complete in American industry, progress has been significant and visible.

These two divergent philosophies of management have been formally expressed by psychologist Douglas McGregor in his important and influential work on *Theory X* and *Theory Y*.[1] Many business leaders today are familiar with McGregor's work and have tried, with growing success, to incorporate his ideas in their management practices.

Theory X represents the scientific management philosophy and the autocratic type of leader it spawned. The theory is based on three as-

[1] Douglas McGregor, *The Human Side of Enterprise* (New York: McGraw–Hill, 1960), pp. 33–34, 47–48.

sumptions about human nature: (1) Most people have an innate dislike of work and will avoid it if they can. (2) Most people must be coerced, controlled, or threatened to get them to work hard enough to satisfy the organization's goal. (3) Most people prefer to be led, want to avoid responsibility, have little ambition, and want security more than anything else.

Theory X presents a negative and demeaning image of what people are like. According to this view, people would not work productively at their jobs without a dictating, threatening, and demanding leader. Like unruly children, employees must be scolded and punished because they are basically irresponsible and lazy.

Many managers today still agree with the Theory X viewpoint, although their number is declining. The primary reason for the decreasing influence of Theory X and authoritarian leader behavior may be found in the recent psychological research on the nature of human motivation, particularly the work of Abraham Maslow, who believed that the ultimate human goal is self-actualization, the realization and fulfillment of all of our distinctly human capabilities. Maslow's image of human nature is positive and flattering, and it finds expression in McGregor's Theory Y.

Theory Y is based on the following assumptions about human nature:

(1) Most people do not have an innate dislike of work. The willingness and the motivation to work "is as natural as play or rest." Work can provide a great deal of inner satisfaction. (2) Control, coercion, and punishment are not necessary to get employees to work hard enough to satisfy the organization's goals. Most people will display a great deal of motivation and self-discipline in working for goals to which they are committed. (3) To instill such commitment, the work must be rewarded through opportunities to satisfy self-actualization needs. (4) Most people, if given sufficient opportunity to self-actualize, will actively seek out and accept high levels of responsibility. (5) Most people are able to exercise a "high degree of imagination, ingenuity, and creativity in the solution of organizational problems."

Theory Y presents a radically different picture from Theory X of what people are like. According to Theory Y, people are industrious, creative, and desirous of challenge and responsibility in their work. If given the proper conditions of freedom, responsibility, and autonomy, most people will work hard for the rewards associated with the opportunity to express their self-actualization needs.

These people work best under the democratic style of leadership spawned by the human relations movement, rather than the authoritarian leader of scientific management days. Theory Y workers want a leader who will allow them to participate in making decisions about organizational goals and about the way in which their jobs are to be performed. The Theory Y view of leadership is compatible with modern organization theory, which indeed calls for full worker participation.

Arthur Friedman runs his appliance store in accordance with the Theory Y image of human nature, and he is an example of the kind of democratic leader called for by Theory Y. A democratic form of leadership, whether in a corporation or a country, places a large share of the power directly in the hands of the people, who are then able to influence the issues that affect their well-being. Democratic leaders must be responsive to the needs, longings, and fears of those whom they nominally lead, and must share with them the power and responsibility for running the organization.

The tendency toward a more democratic style of leadership is increasing in modern organizational life. Facilitating worker participation is a major activity of industrial psychologists in their continuing efforts to humanize working conditions and improve the quality of working life.

## The Tasks of Leaders

What do supervisors, managers, and executives do on the job? What functions and tasks are required of them? A broad and simple answer is that they manage the work of other people, but this does not tell us very much about their specific activities.

To determine the daily functions required of managers, we examine psychological studies of leadership behavior. Psychologists who have studied the behavior of leaders for many years have found that their functions can be grouped in two areas: those that deal with people and those that deal with the goals and tasks of the organization. These two dimensions of leadership are known as *consideration* and *initiation of structure*.[2] Consideration deals with people, and initiation of structure deals with organizational tasks and goals.

The leadership functions in the consideration dimension involve the awareness of and sensitivity to the personal feelings of the employees, and the understanding and accepting of them as individuals with unique needs, values, and fears. Leaders must be sympathetic to and considerate of their subordinates while maintaining production levels, a difficult task that sometimes places conflicting demands on the leaders.

The functions in the initiation of structure dimension are those traditionally associated with leadership, that is, organizing, defining, and directing the work of subordinates. To initiate structure (which simply means getting the job done), leaders must assign specific tasks to their employees, direct the manner and speed at which the operations are performed or the tasks accomplished, and oversee the work to make sure that it is completed on time and meets company standards.

The initiation of structure dimension of leadership may require some degree of authoritarian behavior, and organizational goals may sometimes take precedence over employee feelings and needs. There are occasions when the company's survival depends on having the workers produce a certain quantity and quality of output in a given period of time, and this situation can put a strain on leaders who are also trying to meet the demands of the consideration dimension.

Achieving the proper balance between these two dimensions requires a working climate in which employees are able to satisfy their needs and goals in a way that also leads to the satisfaction of the organization's goals. Bringing about this necessary harmony is easier with a democratic leader than with an authoritarian leader.

Within these two broad dimensions of leadership behavior there are a number of specific tasks that effective leaders must accomplish.[3]

*Determining realistic objectives.* Managers must establish goals, covering all aspects of a job, that can realistically be achieved—production

[2] E. Fleishman and E. Harris, "Patterns of Leadership Behavior Related to Employee Grievances and Turnover," *Personnel Psychology*, **15** (1962), 43–56.

[3] After R. C. Miljus, "Effective Leadership and the Motivation of Human Resources," *Personnel Journal*, **49** (1970), 36–40.

levels, safety, maintenance records, and turnover rates, for example. Without the continuous monitoring of such goals, on both a short-term and a long-term basis, there is an inevitable waste of time and energy. Achieving these goals also serves to provide feedback to managers and their subordinates about the quality or competence of the job performance.

*Providing necessary resources.* Managers must arrange for an adequate and continuing supply of tools, equipment, raw materials, and manpower to facilitate the achievement of the organizational goals.

*Establishing expectations.* Through a variety of formal and informal communications, managers must inform subordinates about exactly what is expected of them, if the goals are to be reached. Guidelines, instructions, policies, and procedures must be transmitted to subordinates so that their paths to goal achievement are clearly understood.

*Providing an adequate reward structure.* Both tangible and intangible rewards for achieving organizational goals must be made available to subordinates. Tangible rewards include salary, fringe benefits such as insurance and pension plans, good working conditions, and opportunities for advancement. Intangible rewards include satisfying and challenging work, responsibility, and praise for good job performance. These intangible rewards can satisfy basic human needs such as self-actualization, which, in turn, can increase motivation and job satisfaction.

*Delegating authority and providing for employee participation.* To motivate and challenge subordinates, and to train them for advancement, managers must delegate some of their authority and tasks. As an outgrowth of the human relations movement and the Theory Y approach to leadership, many managers have recognized the workers' need to participate actively in making decisions about the policies and procedures that affect their jobs. Managers must be willing to share their power with subordinates.

*Removing barriers to effective performance.* Managers must be constantly alert for any factor or situation that may impede the satisfaction of organizational or employee goals. Faulty equipment must be replaced, materials delivery speeded up, ineffective workers retrained or dismissed, closed channels of communication opened, and negative attitudes overcome.

*Appraising subordinates.* We know that a vital management task is the fair and objective appraisal of the job performance of employees.

Once the appraisals are made, the results must be communicated to subordinates in an understanding and positive manner so that employees will be motivated to improve their shortcomings.

The tasks of organizational leaders are numerous and complex, and they place many demands on their technical and human relations skills. These skills must be continually refined through periodic retraining programs, and by performance evaluations of the managers by their superiors.

## Personality Characteristics of Leaders

Psychologists have conducted considerable research to try to identify specific traits and characteristics possessed by successful leaders, in order to learn how they differ from leaders who are not successful. Such research is vital to the establishment of selection programs to find those persons who have the potential for being trained to become effective leaders. It is well known that the characteristics of successful leaders vary from one situation to another, and that it is the demands of the specific leadership situation, more than the personality characteristics of leaders, that make for success or failure. For example, the authoritarian structure of a military organization places different demands on leaders than a company that is trying to involve its employees in full participatory democracy.

Nevertheless, within any one situation it is possible to identify specific characteristics that distinguish successful from unsuccessful leaders. Within a traditional American business organization, still more oriented toward the scientific management style of leadership than the human relations approach, psychological research has identified a number of characteristics of successful executives.

One study [4] found that successful managers were motivated to accomplish or achieve as well as by the needs for power, autonomy, and money. In addition, the managers were found to be intelligent, forceful, dominant, and assertive. Another psychologist [5] found that successful managers were characterized by intelligence, initiative, supervisory ability, and self-assurance.

One study of successful executives provides a list of twelve executive characteristics.[6] Although these were compiled some years ago, they are still valid for leaders in many situations.

[4] M. Dunnette, "The Motives of Industrial Managers," *Organizational Behavior and Human Performance,* **2** (1967), 176–182.

[5] E. Ghiselli, "Traits Differentiating Management Personnel," *Personnel Psychology,* **12** (1959), 535–544.

[6] W. Henry, "The Business Executive: The Psychodynamics of a Social Role," *American Journal of Sociology,* **54** (1949), 286–291.

1. A high drive for achievement. Executives are capable of working very hard and their greatest reward and satisfaction may derive from their feeling of accomplishing some task rather than from the actual result or outcome of that task.

2. A strong mobility drive. Executives need to feel that they are constantly striving and moving upward. The ideal way to bring about this continuing sense of upward movement is to provide higher levels of responsibility and challenge.

3. A positive attitude toward superiors. Executives see their superiors not as threatening, but rather as people who can help them satisfy their own drives. They are not resentful or hostile toward superiors but view them positively, as being able to contribute to their own growth.

4. A strong ability to organize. Successful leaders find satisfaction in taking an unstructured or poorly defined situation and organizing it, to give it meaning and structure. They also have the ability to predict the future course of events, based on their organization of present events.

5. The ability to make decisions. Successful executives must be decisive in resolving problems within a short period of time. They have the ability to consider alternative courses of action, choose what appears to be the correct course, and stand by the decision.

6. A positive self-structure. Successful executives possess a strong sense of self-identity. They know who and what they are, have a realistic estimate of their strengths and weaknesses, and are confident about their abilities to reach their goals. Because of this strong self-structure, executives are highly resistant to the influence of other people, maintaining faith in their own decisions even in the face of opposition.

7. A high level of activity and aggressive striving. Successful leaders are striving, driving individuals whose energies are effectively channeled toward the achievement of realistic goals. Their high level of activity is both physical and mental. They are always wound up and find it very difficult to relax.

8. A strong apprehension and fear of failure. Executives are driven to succeed by a continuing, underlying feeling of apprehension and the fear that they will not reach their goals. This apprehension persists, no matter how much success executives have. It is always lurking in the background, goading them to still higher levels of success.

9. A strong orientation toward reality. Executives are practical people oriented more toward the concrete than the abstract or theoretical. As such, they are firmly anchored in the present, not in the past or future.

10. A strong sense of identification with superiors and an aloofness from subordinates. Executives identify with their superiors while re-

maining detached and impersonal with their subordinates. They are not cold or cruel to employees, however; they can often be quite sympathetic to them.

11. Freedom from dependence on parents. Executives are free of parental ties, feel neither guilt nor resentment toward their parents, and are able to proceed with their own lives independently of parental influence or control.

12. A loyalty to the goals of the organization. Executives realize that the achievement of personal goals depends on the organization for which they work. Therefore, they value the organization because it provides the means for fulfilling their own needs.

These characteristics are broad and do not necessarily apply to all executives in all organizations. Different organizations place different demands on their leaders. Consequently, different leadership characteristics are required to satisfy these demands. Thus, in order to understand the nature of leadership, we must first understand the nature of the situation in which the leadership takes place.

The characteristics of leaders, and the styles of leadership behavior they display, exert an enormous influence on the overall efficiency of an organization and the motivations and satisfactions of its employees.

## MOTIVATION AT WORK

A major problem facing virtually all organizations today is that of motivating their employees to work more productively. We as consumers are frequently plagued by shoddy, careless, and imperfect work in the consumer products we buy, in our attempts to have these products serviced, and in errors made by government offices or department stores. Too many employees apparently do not care whether or not they do a good job.

Even substantial pay raises and lavish fringe benefits, once thought to be the surest incentives for better performance, no longer seem to be effective in increasing employee productivity. Money is not the major motivating force it once was. Its value as an incentive has decreased for several reasons. First, we live in relatively prosperous and affluent times. Because well-paying jobs are available to the majority of those who want to work, people do not have to worry about being fired for not doing the best job possible. They know they can almost always get another job, a situation quite different from the disastrous depression of the 1930s.

Second, workers today are better educated than past generations of workers. They want more satisfying, meaningful, and challenging jobs, and will not be content, as their fathers and mothers were, with work that is boring, routine, and unstimulating.

Third, these better-educated workers are more resisting of authority. A high salary alone is not sufficient compensation for working in a situation in which they must follow orders unquestioningly. They want to participate in the determination of those orders.

If the traditional economic incentives no longer work, then new ways of motivating workers must be found. The productivity and satisfaction of all people who work, and the general efficiency of society as well, depend on finding adequate sources of motivation to serve as incentives for more careful and higher quality work. Only in that way will worker productivity and satisfaction increase.

The study of human motivation—whether in basic research conducted in universities or applied research conducted in industry—is one of the most important topics in psychology today. On the basis of this extensive research, psychologists have developed several theories of human motivation, some of which are directly applicable to people at work. Three of these theories are David McClelland's theory of need for achievement, Abraham Maslow's theory of self-actualization, and Frederick Herzberg's motivator-hygiene theory. The need achievement theory of motivation applies primarily, although not exclusively, to the management or executive level; the other two seem to be applicable to all levels and kinds of work.

## The Need-Achievement Theory

The need for achievement [7] is one of the characteristics of successful executives and may be found among nonsupervisory employees as well. This need refers to the desire to do a good job, to be the best, and to accomplish something. People who are high in the need for achievement (also called need achievement, n Ach, or achievement motivation) derive great satisfaction from their accomplishments and are highly motivated to excel in whatever they undertake.

Executives in the United States and other countries (including communistic societies) consistently demonstrate high levels of need achievement. Further, those executives who are more successful show higher levels of need achievement than those who are less successful. Once McClelland demonstrated this, his next step involved research to show what executives who are high in need achievement require from their work in order to satisfy this need.

Organizations that employ executives who are high in achievement motivation do not have to generate the motivation; it is already present.

[7] D. McClelland et al., The Achievement Motive (New York: Appleton–Century–Crofts, 1953).

What organizations must provide, however, are the proper working conditions that will allow for the satisfaction of the need. If the need for achievement cannot be satisfied, these individuals will become unhappy, unfulfilled, and probably unproductive managers.

The research of McClelland and others has shown that persons high in need achievement require the following job characteristics.

1. A working environment in which they can take personal responsibility for solving problems. Persons high in need achievement feel a great sense of achievement by assuming this kind of responsibility, and they are unhappy in situations in which the outcomes depend solely on the decisions of other people or on external factors beyond their control. They are happiest, therefore, in jobs that provide challenge, responsibility, and autonomy.

2. A situation in which they can assume tasks of moderate difficulty. If job-related tasks or goals are too easy, there is little sense of achievement in reaching the goals. Neither is a sense of achievement provided by goals that are so difficult as to be impossible to reach. High-need-achievement persons must always have ahead of them goals of moderate difficulty that require definite effort to reach.

3. Precise and continuing feedback on their progress. Without frequent recognition of their performance, high-need-achievement persons would not know how well they are doing in the pursuit of their goals. With adequate recognition—in the form of production figures, pay raises, promotions, or pats on the back—they have tangible proof of their level of achievement or accomplishment.

Apparently, many people possess the need to achieve. It arises from a unique pattern of parental behaviors that shape the individual so that he or she finds satisfaction, and perhaps emotional security, in doing a good job. Given the proper working environment, these people will become highly productive and hard working members of an organization. A high salary alone will not adequately compensate them for a job that stifles their need to achieve.

## The Self-Actualization Theory

Maslow developed a theory of motivation [8] that has found wide acceptance not only among psychologists but also among business leaders. The theory suggests that all human beings are motivated by five innate needs arranged in a hierarchy from the strongest to the weakest. It is like climbing a ladder; we have to place a foot on the first rung before

[8] Abraham Maslow, *Motivation and Personality* (2nd ed.; New York: Harper & Row, 1970).

trying to reach the second, we must step on the second rung before attempting the third, and so on. In the same way, the lowest (or strongest) need in the hierarchy must be satisfied before the second-level need appears, and so on up the hierarchy until the highest (and weakest) need of all—self-actualization—appears. Therefore, the requisite for achieving self-actualization is the satisfaction of the four needs that are lower in the hierarchy; indeed, it is impossible to achieve self-actualization without first satisfying these lower-level needs.

The needs from lowest to highest are (1) the physiological needs, (2) the safety needs, (3) the belonging and love needs, (4) the esteem needs, and (5) the self-actualization need.

The physiological needs are for food, water, air, sleep, and sex, and they must be satisfied if human beings are to survive. In affluent Western cultures, few people are still concerned about satisfying these survival needs, so they play a minimal role in our lives. A salary sufficient to allow us to satisfy these needs is vital, but once satisfied, they no longer operate as needs. Only if workers become unemployed, or exhaust their savings, do the physiological needs again become paramount.

The safety needs include the needs for security, stability, protection, and freedom from fear and anxiety. Although these needs may be satisfied by activities outside the job, one's work can also contribute greatly to their satisfaction. Salary can provide financial security, as can pension and insurance plans. Competent job performance can help to ensure continued employment by an organization; this also contributes to a feeling of security.

When the safety needs have been satisfied, the belonging and love needs appear. Again, many aspects of a person's life, such as a warm, loving family, can contribute to the satisfaction of these needs. Work can also provide satisfaction when people find a sense of togetherness and belongingness through the relations with coworkers and through a sense of affiliation and identification with the organization or with a labor union.

The esteem needs appear next. They include a sense of esteem and respect from two sources, other people and oneself. Workers can find respect from superiors and coworkers for their personal qualities and for the competence and skill they display on the job. Elements of the esteem needs, such as prestige, success, and self-respect, can be satisfied in part by salary, and by such status indicators as plush carpeting, a corner office, a private secretary, or a reserved parking space. Self-esteem can also be derived from the knowledge that one is doing one's job competently.

All of these lower-order needs may be very well satisfied. We may feel secure physically and emotionally, have a sense of belonging and love, and feel ourselves to be worthy individuals, but unless we are able to satisfy the highest need—the need for self-actualization—we will be frustrated, restless, and discontent. The need for self-actualization may be defined as the supreme development and utilization of all our capabilities, the fulfillment of our unique qualities and capacities.

Maslow insisted that the nature of our work is vital to satisfying the need for self-actualization. He believed that it was impossible to become self-actualizing without an intense dedication to and absorption in work that is meaningful and challenging. In order to satisfy the self-actualization need, we must have work that provides us with opportunities for growth and responsibility, and the chance to exercise and develop ourselves to the utmost. Routine, boring, and nonchallenging work cannot satisfy this need, no matter how high a salary the job pays. Thus, the size of one's salary is an incentive only up to a point. It cannot help to satisfy the highest human need. Only the nature of one's work, and the opportunities and challenges it provides, can do that.

Maslow's theory is popular among managers and executives who have accepted the need for self-actualization as a motivating force to be reckoned with on the job. As a result, efforts are being made to build into jobs elements of responsibility, freedom, and challenge, some of the same factors that Arthur Friedman provided for his employees in the example at the beginning of the chapter.

## The Motivator-Hygiene Theory

The motivator-hygiene theory [9] is a simple theory that has had a major impact on the design of a great many jobs, leading to significant changes in the way in which those jobs are performed. It is similar, in part, to Maslow's self-actualization theory in that it posits a hierarchy of lower-order and higher-order needs. In today's affluent society, Herzberg argued, the lower-level needs are generally well satisfied. If they are not satisfied, however, the result is job dissatisfaction. But the reverse is not true; satisfaction of the lower needs does not automatically result in job satisfaction.

The only way to produce job satisfaction is to satisfy higher-level needs such as self-actualization. But failure to satisfy the higher-level needs does not automatically result in job dissatisfaction.

Therefore, Herzberg proposed two sets of needs: those that produce job satisfaction and those that produce job dissatisfaction. These needs are separate and the presence or absence of one set will not produce the opposite condition. What is required of organizations is to increase the conditions necessary for job satisfaction and to decrease the conditions responsible for job dissatisfaction.

[9] Frederick Herzberg, *Work and the Nature of Man* (Cleveland: World, 1966).

The factors that produce job satisfaction are called *motivator needs*. They are high-level needs that motivate workers to perform at their optimum capacity. The motivator needs are an integral part of the work itself and include such elements as the nature of the work, the worker's sense of achievement and level of responsibility, and opportunities for personal growth and development. You can see the similarity between the motivator needs and Maslow's self-actualization need; both can be satisfied only through stimulating and challenging work.

The factors that produce job dissatisfaction are the *hygiene needs* (or maintenance needs). They do not have the power to produce job satisfaction and they are not concerned with the nature of the work itself. These lower-level needs involve features of the work environment such as company policy and administrative practices, type of leadership, interpersonal relations, fringe benefits, and working conditions. The hygiene needs are closely related to Maslow's lower-level needs (physiological, safety, love, and esteem needs), and they must be satisfied before attention can be paid to the motivator needs. Again, although satisfaction of the hygiene needs can prevent job dissatisfaction, this cannot bring about job satisfaction.

Herzberg suggests that because so much of a worker's satisfaction and motivation derive from the nature of the work, it is possible to redesign most jobs so as to maximize the motivator factors. This process is called *job enlargement* (or job enrichment) and it is being used by many companies with apparent success.

There are several ways of enlarging jobs. (1) Remove some of the controls and restrictions on employees and increase their personal accountability and sense of responsibility for their own work. (2) Provide employees with complete units of work rather than with a single component part of the unit. (3) Give employees greater authority and freedom in their work. (4) Provide reports on production on a regular and frequent basis directly to the workers instead of to their supervisors. (5) Encourage workers to take on new and more difficult tasks. (6) Assign specialized tasks so that workers can become experts in a particular task, operation, or process.

All these techniques for enlarging jobs have the goal of increasing personal growth and advancement, enhancing the workers' sense of achievement and responsibility, and providing recognition and feedback on their performance. In brief, job enlargement facilitates the satisfaction of the motivator needs and thus can lead to job satisfaction.

A large number of organizations have instituted job enlargement programs, including IBM, Maytag, Sears, AT&T, Western Electric, Chrysler, and Polaroid. The programs are reported to be immensely successful in lowering production costs, increasing job satisfaction, and reducing absenteeism, boredom, and monotony.

Let us consider two examples of job enlargement in industry. A telephone company enlarged the mechanical, routine, and boring job of compiling telephone directories. The directories had been compiled in assembly line fashion through a series of twenty-one steps, each operation performed by a different employee. The procedure was very much like an automobile assembly line. With job enlargement, each employee was allowed to construct a complete directory rather than just a small part of one. The responsibility for the correctness of each directory shifted from the supervisor to the individual employee. Both productivity and job satisfaction increased.

Job enlargement was also successfully applied to the job of janitor in a large electronics company. Full responsibility and accountability for the work shifted from the supervisors to the janitors themselves. They decided how the work would be divided and scheduled. Previously, supervisors made these decisions and watched the janitors closely to make sure the work was done. In addition, the janitors were given responsibility for setting and maintaining quality standards. These major changes in the way the work was performed brought about a greatly increased level of job satisfaction, and the facilities were kept cleaner than ever before. Also, turnover, which had been a staggering 100 per cent, decreased to only 10 per cent.

The three theories of motivation discussed here turn out to be not so different after all. The major similarity among the need-achievement, self-actualization, and motivator-hygiene theories is that they all focus on the importance of the work itself and the challenges, responsibilities, and opportunities for personal growth the work provides. They do not focus primarily on salary or other tangible aspects of the job or on the physical environment in which the work is performed. In the following section on job satisfaction, we will show that these same factors of challenge and growth have been found, through psychological research, to be the most rewarding form of compensation in the world of work.

## JOB SATISFACTION

Job satisfaction refers to how people feel about their jobs, the attitudes or psychological dispositions they hold toward their work. As such, job satisfaction is complicated to measure; it is composed of and influenced by such factors as how far the parking lot is from the workplace, the physical working conditions, the behavior of the supervisor, and how much achievement and fulfillment the work itself provides.

Thus, job satisfaction represents a cluster of attitudes, feelings, likes, and dislikes about one's work, and it is affected not only by the job-related factors just noted, but also by personal factors that are not part of the work or working environment. For example, job satisfaction varies as a function of worker age, health, length of time on the job, family relationships, and emotional stability. Also, how well worker needs are satisfied has a strong impact on job satisfaction.

Most organizations today devote considerable effort to the measurement of job satisfaction among their employees, in order to determine those factors that contribute to dissatisfaction on the job so that they may be improved or changed. What many organizations are looking for are the sources of their employees' gripes and complaints so that corrective action can be taken.

The primary methods for measuring job satisfaction are the survey methods (discussed in Chapter 2), which involve, essentially, asking workers how they feel about various aspects of their jobs. The most frequently used approach is to ask employees to fill out questionnaires, usually on an anonymous basis.

Another technique, sometimes used along with questionnaires, is for a supervisor or someone from the personnel department to personally interview employees about their feelings toward their work.

## The Extent of Job Satisfaction

It is not only individual companies that are interested in measuring job satisfaction. Every year, the Gallup poll surveys a large national sample of American workers to ask them how satisfied or dissatisfied they are with their jobs. The overall results indicate that 10 to 13 per cent of the workers surveyed reported that they were dissatisfied with their jobs. However, when workers in different categories, such as by race, age, and education, were questioned, the extent of dissatisfaction ranged from a low of 7 per cent (among workers over age fifty) to a high of 22 per cent (among nonwhite workers).

These figures seem to indicate that the majority of American workers are well satisfied with their jobs. However, as with any survey, the nature of the response varies with the wording of the question. When more specific questions about job satisfaction are asked of workers, the results are not so comforting to the people concerned with the extent of job satisfaction in American organizations.

For example, when workers were asked if they would like to change jobs, large numbers said "yes" even though they had said they were satisfied with their present jobs. What this apparently indicates is that when many people say they are satisfied with their jobs, all they really mean is that they are not dissatisfied. Recall Herzberg's distinction between motivator and hygiene needs; pay and external working conditions (hygiene factors) may be satisfactory, but the work itself (motivator factors) may not be inherently challenging or rewarding. Thus, it is possible that many people define satisfaction as the absence of negative factors rather than the presence of positive factors.

In another survey, a group of workers who had said that they were satisfied with their jobs were questioned in greater detail. They revealed major sources of dissatisfaction, such as the lack of opportunity to grow on the job. Job satisfaction, then, is not the simple or straightforward variable it might have first appeared to be.

One way to probe more deeply into the question of job satisfaction is to ask people what kind of work they would like to do if they had the opportunity to start all over again. It seems reasonable to assume that persons who are satisfied with their present jobs would choose the same jobs again. When white-collar workers were questioned, 43 per cent said they would choose the same jobs again; among blue-collar workers, only 24 per cent said they would stay with the same jobs.

The responses varied with the level of occupation; the higher the level, the greater the reported satisfaction with the present job. Almost twice the number of skilled workers reported that they would choose the same job again as unskilled workers in the same industry.

Another indirect way to question people about job satisfaction is to ask them what they would do with the extra two hours if they had a twenty-six-hour day. Again, the responses varied with the level of occupation. Among college professors, 66 per cent said they would devote the additional hours to their work. Among nonprofessional workers, however, more than 80 per cent said they would use the extra time for activities that had nothing to do with work.

More sophisticated questioning has thus revealed a much higher level of job dissatisfaction than the 10 to 13 per cent reported by the straightforward question: "Are you satisfied with your work?" The reasons for job dissatisfaction uncovered by more specific research focus on aspects of the work itself, primarily the lack of challenge, responsibility and autonomy, the needs proposed by the theories of motivation discussed in the previous section.[10]

## Personal Characteristics and Job Satisfaction

We noted that job satisfaction can vary as a function of level of occupation. It also varies with other personal characteristics of workers, including age, sex, race, intelligence, length of job experience, utilization of skills and abilities, and personality.

[10] *Work in America* (Cambridge, Mass.: MIT Press, 1973); H. Sheppard and N. Herrick, *Where Have All the Robots Gone? Worker Dissatisfaction in the '70s* (New York: Free Press, 1972).

*Age.* Job satisfaction seems to change a great deal as people grow older. In general, job satisfaction is lowest among younger workers and highest among older workers; it gradually increases as we move up the age scale. Among workers twenty-one to twenty-nine years of age, only 25 per cent report that they are satisfied with their jobs. Job satisfaction increases to 43 per cent among workers who are forty-five to sixty-four years of age.

The low reported job satisfaction among younger workers should be particularly significant to you on the threshold of your work career. The high dissatisfaction with work among younger workers has increased over the past several decades and seems to reflect increasing expectations about work held by the young, expectations that are not being fulfilled.

Many young workers begin their jobs expecting to find considerable personal fulfillment. They want challenge, the opportunity for self-expression, and some degree of autonomy in their jobs—the chance to satisfy motivator needs. Past generations of young workers, influenced by the economic depression of the 1930s, were more concerned with the chance to satisfy their hygiene needs—salary, security, and opportunity for promotion. These goals were much easier for business and industry to satisfy than the motivator needs, which involve self-actualization.

This difference in worker goals may explain why older workers report a high rate of satisfaction from their work; their expectations about their jobs were more easily fulfilled. Another explanation is that as workers grow older, they give up any expectation of finding challenge and personal fulfillment in their work (having never found it), and so become less dissatisfied. They may resign themselves to "making the best of a bad situation," persuading themselves that their jobs really aren't so bad after all. Thus, when a researcher asks if they are satisfied, they will say "yes."

There is a third possible explanation for the greater job satisfaction reported among older workers. Perhaps, because of their higher positions and greater responsibilities, some of them do have more opportunities to satisfy the motivator needs. A high-level manager or an experienced skilled worker would have more opportunity for autonomy, challenge, and other personal satisfactions than a young management trainee or an apprentice. Whatever the reasons, the fact remains that job satisfaction increases with age.

*Sex.* As increasing numbers of women join the work force, there have been more studies designed to investigate their levels of job satisfaction. The research to date points consistently to one finding: no one yet knows with certainty the extent of job satisfaction among working women. Some studies report high levels of satisfaction and others report the opposite.

Some evidence suggests that women may be concerned with different aspects of their work than men. A large insurance company found that long-range career objectives were less important to women than to men, and that women were more concerned with comfortable working conditions and the interpersonal relations afforded by a job.

It is useful to distinguish between two kinds of working women: those who are striving for a career in the world of work and those who take a job because they must supplement, or wholly provide, the family income. It is reasonable to expect that these two different groups require different satisfactions from their jobs. The motivations and satisfactions of working career women may resemble more closely those of male executives. Women who work to supplement income may not focus on the work as a major element of personal satisfaction, deriving more fulfillment from home and family.

However, one factor that certainly contributes to job dissatisfaction among women is the obvious discrimination they face in the world of work. Although the situation has improved somewhat since the passage of equal employment opportunity legislation, in general women are still paid less than men for the same work, and they have fewer opportunities for promotion. Also, for many working women, the job opportunities are still limited to traditionally "female" occupations such as clerks, typists, or teachers. Job satisfaction for working women in business cannot be expected to increase until their employment opportunities are equal to those of men.

*Race.* Discrimination also plays an obvious role in the employment of members of minority races. Minority-group workers are twice as likely as white workers to report job dissatisfaction. However, there is a more basic problem for minority-group workers—getting a job in the first place, whether it is satisfying or not. As many as one-third of minority-group members are unemployed or underemployed. If they are working, it is often on a temporary and erratic basis. Another one-third are employed regularly, but in low-level, marginal jobs that offer little opportunity for advancement or for the satisfaction of either hygiene or motivator needs.

Among the remaining one-third of nonwhite workers who hold higher-level jobs that do offer advancement opportunities and higher pay, the rate of job dissatisfaction is, as noted, twice that of their white counterparts. This figure holds no matter what kind of job the nonwhite worker has—blue-collar, white-collar, or management.

Job dissatisfaction remains high until minority-group workers reach their mid-forties, after which dissatisfaction declines considerably, to a level below that for white workers (although their dissatisfaction with life in general remains high). Perhaps, having suffered years of discrimination, older nonwhite workers report more satisfaction simply because they have been employed continuously, rather than because their higher-level needs are being fulfilled by their work.

*Intelligence.* The intelligence of a worker does not seem to have any bearing on the reported degree of job satisfaction. However, when intelligence is considered in relation to the kind of work being performed, it does become significant. The level of intelligence must be appropriate to the demands of the job. If the worker's IQ is too low or too high for a particular kind of work, frustration and dissatisfaction are the inevitable results.

Much research has demonstrated that people who possess a level of intelligence far above that demanded by their job will not be sufficiently challenged. They will become bored and dissatisfied because their motivator needs are not being met. Workers whose jobs require more intelligence than they possess will also be frustrated, because they will be unable to meet the demands of their work. This mismatching of job level and intelligence can be avoided by the use of valid selection techniques.

A factor usually associated with intelligence—level of education—is, in general, positively related to job satisfaction. That is, persons with more education report higher levels of job satisfaction than persons with less education. This may be because those who have more formal education are able to get the jobs that offer more in the way of fulfillment, personal freedom, responsibility, and opportunity for self-actualization.

*Length of job experience.* The relationship between job satisfaction and length of experience parallels that between job satisfaction and age. Indeed, they may be the same phenomenon operating under different labels because the older the worker is, the more years of job experience he or she usually has.

Most new workers tend to be satisfied with their jobs initially, because of its novelty and the stimulation and challenge of a different life-style after so many years of schooling. This satisfaction does not last very long, however, and a sense of dissatisfaction soon sets in when workers begin to feel that they are not advancing as far or as fast as they thought they would. Their high aspiration levels often are not met.

Also, after a few years on the job, it is not uncommon for employees to find out that their salaries are not much higher than what newly hired employees are being paid, certainly a cause for dissatisfaction. (Salary increases for current employees never seem to rise as fast as starting salaries for new employees in the same line of work, especially for white-collar occupations.) Thus, job satisfaction declines from its initial high level. After six to seven years on the job, satisfaction begins to increase, for the reasons discussed in the section on age.

*Utilization of skills and abilities.* Job satisfaction seems to vary directly with the extent to which employees are able to exercise their skills and abilities. This can be seen most easily among college graduates who have majored in subjects that can be directly used on a job—engineering, accounting, or the sciences. The lack of opportunity to use these skills thwarts the self-expression and self-actualization needs and this leads to a decrease in job satisfaction.

*Personality.* Some research suggests that there are workers who are always dissatisfied with their jobs, regardless of the nature or level of the work, or their age, sex, race, intelligence, length of job experience, and degree of utilization of their skills. In these cases, the causes of job discontent lie not so much with the work or anything connected with it as with personal characteristics of the employees.

Chronically dissatisfied workers exhibit symptoms of emotional instability and tend to be dissatisfied with all aspects of their lives. In addition, they may be introverted, not very friendly, and prone to daydreaming. They set unrealistically high standards and goals for themselves. (Trying to achieve at a level beyond your capabilities easily induces frustration and dissatisfaction when you realize that you are unable to reach your goal.)

Thus, there seems to be a clear relationship between chronic job dissatisfaction and poor emotional adjustment. What is less clear is which one causes the other. Does prolonged job dissatisfaction bring about poor emotional adjustment or is it the other way around? Regardless of which is the cause and which is the effect, however, the result is the same: poor job performance and personal frustration.

A growing number of employing organizations have established personal counseling programs, primarily for managerial and executive personnel, to try to deal with long-term emotional disturbances as well as with temporary crises such as marital problems or a death in the family.

## Job Satisfaction and Performance

It seems reasonable to assume that a high level of job satisfaction leads to a high level of job performance. In general, research supports such a relationship, but not consistently. Some studies have shown no relationship between job satisfaction and performance. Therefore, organizational efforts to increase job satisfaction among employees will not always lead to increased production, although they may do so some of the time.

Two psychologists [11] have suggested that instead of considering that job satisfaction leads to improved performance, we should think of improved performance as leading to increased satisfaction. The reasoning behind this provocative hypothesis is as follows. Satisfaction is presumed to derive from the fulfillment of certain needs. If our work has the potential for providing this fulfillment, then we can better satisfy our needs by improving our job performance. For example, if our job satisfies our need for achievement, then by working harder and performing on a higher level we can bring about a greater sense of achievement. This, in turn, increases our satisfaction with the job.

To test this hypothesis, the psychologists studied a large number of managers and found that although high-performing managers were not paid more than low-performing managers, they did report greater satisfaction of such needs as autonomy and self-realization. The high-performing managers also reported higher levels of job satisfaction, supporting the idea that need fulfillment from a job leads to satisfaction, which, in turn, leads to even higher performance levels.

This study supports the theories of motivation discussed previously, which emphasize the importance of fulfilling higher-level needs. Also, it confirms the importance of providing challenging and stimulating jobs that allow for personal growth and self-actualization.

## SUMMARY

Psychologists have conducted a great deal of research on the nature and characteristics of effective employee management, the nature of worker motivation, and the satisfactions people find or fail to find in the world of work. As a result of this research, radical changes are taking place in worker management and motivation philosophies to allow for more employee participation in decision making, and greater autonomy, challenge, and responsibility in the design of jobs.

*Leadership,* a crucial factor in the success or failure of any organization, has been studied extensively by psychologists. They are concerned with the nature of leadership behavior, the functions or tasks of leaders, and the personality characteristics of effective leaders.

The traditional philosophy of management, *scientific management,* required authoritarian and dictatorial leaders. The modern approach, the *human relations movement,* focuses on employee needs and requires more democratic leaders. These philosophies of management are represented in McGregor's Theory X/Theory Y formulations. Theory X pre-

---

[11] E. E. Lawler and L. W. Porter, "The Effect of Performance on Job Satisfaction," *Industrial Relations,* **7** (1967), 20–28; L. W. Porter and E. E. Lawler, "What Job Attitudes Tell About Motivation," *Harvard Business Review,* **46** (January 1968), 118–126.

sents a negative image of human nature and calls for a dictating and commanding leader. Theory Y, with its flattering view of human nature, calls for democratic leadership.

The tasks of leaders can be grouped in two broad areas: the *consideration* function (which focuses on employee needs) and the *initiation of structure* function (which focuses on the goals and needs of the organization). Within these two dimensions of leadership behavior there are a number of specific tasks that effective leaders must carry out: determination of realistic objectives, provision of necessary resources, establishment of expectations, provision of a reward structure, delegation of authority and provision for participation, removal of barriers to effective performance, and periodic appraisal of subordinates.

Much research has been conducted on the personality characteristics of effective leaders. Although these characteristics vary from one situation to another, it is possible to identify those in any one situation. Successful business managers are characterized by the drives for achievement and mobility, a positive attitude toward superiors, the ability to organize and make decisions, a positive self-structure, a high level of activity and aggressive striving, apprehension and fear of failure, orientation toward reality, identification with superiors and aloofness with subordinates, freedom from dependence on parents, and loyalty to the goals of the organization.

*Motivating* employees to work more productively is a problem facing all organizations today. Money alone is no longer a sufficient incentive for greater productivity, and attention has been focused on certain psychological needs and the kind of work that can best satisfy them.

McClelland's *need for achievement theory* involves the need to do a good job and to accomplish something. People high in this need function best in a job that allows them to take personal responsibility and assume tasks of moderate difficulty, and that provides precise and continuing feedback on their progress.

Maslow's *self-actualization theory* argues that people are motivated by the need to self-actualize, that is, to utilize and fulfill all their capabilities. To satisfy the self-actualization need, the four needs lower in Maslow's hierarchy of needs (physiological, safety, belonging and love, and esteem needs) must be satisfied first. The kind of work that can allow for satisfaction of the self-actualization need is that which is challenging, meaningful, and provides responsibility and opportunity for greater personal growth and development.

In Herzberg's *motivator-hygiene theory*, higher needs such as self-actualization must be satisfied in order to increase productivity and job satisfaction. These higher-level needs are called motivator needs and they are satisfied only by inherent aspects of the work. Hygiene needs, which produce job dissatisfaction if they are not satisfied, are concerned with features of the work environment. Satisfaction of hygiene needs can prevent job dissatisfaction but cannot produce job satisfaction. Only satisfaction of motivator needs can bring about job satisfaction.

Herzberg's theory has led to the redesign of many jobs through the process of *job enlargement*. This enlargement of the scope of a job facilitates satisfaction of the motivator needs by increasing personal responsibility, authority, and freedom, by enhancing the sense of achievement, and by providing recognition and feedback.

*Job satisfaction* is a cluster of attitudes, feelings, likes, and dislikes about one's job, and it is measured by surveying workers' feelings through questionnaires and personal interviews. Job satisfaction is difficult to measure precisely because the responses obtained vary with the way in which the questions are phrased. Various surveys reveal that job dissatisfaction ranges from a low of 7 per cent among workers over the age of fifty to a high of 22 per cent among nonwhite workers.

A complicating factor in measuring job satisfaction is that it varies as a function of the following personal characteristics. (1) *Age:* job satisfaction increases as people get older. (2) *Sex:* job satisfaction differences between men and women require more study, but it is evident that women are paid less than men for the same job and have fewer opportunities for promotion. (3) *Race:* minority-group workers are twice as likely to be dissatisfied with their jobs as white workers. Job dissatisfaction among nonwhite workers declines considerably when they reach the mid-forties. (4) *Intelligence:* job dissatisfaction results when an employee's level of intelligence is too high or too low for the job. (5) *Length of job experience:* job satisfaction increases the longer an employee is on the job. This parallels the relationship between job satisfaction and age. (6) *Utilization of skills:* the more employees are able to exercise their skills and abilities, the higher is their job satisfaction. (7) *Personality:* chronically dissatisfied workers exhibit symptoms of emotional instability and introversion, and are prone to daydreaming. There is some question, however, whether the emotional instability causes the job dissatisfaction or the dissatisfaction causes the emotional instability.

In general, there is a positive relationship between job satisfaction and high levels of job performance, although this relationship has not been demonstrated consistently. Also, the question has been raised whether job satisfaction causes high performance or whether improved performance leads to increased satisfaction.

## SUGGESTED READINGS

Argyris, C. *Increasing Leadership Effectiveness.* New York: John Wiley, 1976.
Fiedler, F. E., and M. M. Chemers. *Leadership and Effective Management.* Glenview, Ill.: Scott, Foresman, 1974.

Flowers, Vincent S., and Charles L. Hughes. Choosing a leadership style. *Personnel,* 1978 (January–February), **55,** 48–59.

Foy, N., and H. Gadon. Worker participation: Contrasts in 3 countries. *Harvard Business Review,* 1976 (May–June), **54,** 71–83.

Friend, Kenneth E., and Lawton R. Burns. Sources of variation in job satisfaction: Job size effects in a sample of the U.S. labor force. *Personnel Psychology,* 1977, **30,** 589–605.

Garson, B. *All the Livelong Day: The Meaning and Demeaning of Routine Work.* New York: Doubleday, 1975.

Hackman, J. R., and J. L. Suttle, Eds. *Improving Life in Organizations.* Pacific Palisades, Calif.: Goodyear, 1977.

Hall, J. What makes a manager good, bad or average? *Psychology Today,* 1976 (August), **10,** 52–55.

Kanter, R. M. Power games in the corporation. *Psychology Today,* 1977 (July), **11,** 48–53, 92.

Lawler, E. E. Workers can set their own wages—responsibly. *Psychology Today,* 1977 (February), **10,** 109–112.

Locke, E. The nature and causes of job satisfaction. In M. Dunnette, Ed., *Handbook of Industrial and Organizational Psychology.* Chicago: Rand McNally, 1976. Pp. 1297–1349.

Lopez, Felix E. The anatomy of a manager. *Personnel,* 1976 (March–April), **53,** 47–53.

McClelland, D. C., and D. H. Burnham. Power–driven managers. *Psychology Today,* 1975 (December), **9,** 69–70.

Maccoby, M. *The Gamesman: The New Corporate Leaders.* New York: Simon and Schuster, 1976.

Nord, Walter R. Job satisfaction reconsidered. *American Psychologist,* 1977, **32,** 1026–1035.

Raskin, A. H. The heresy of worker participation. *Psychology Today,* 1977 (February), **10,** 111.

Shapiro, H., and L. Stern. Job satisfaction: Male and female, professional and non–professional workers. *Personnel Journal,* 1975, **54,** 388–389.

Tannenbaum, Arnold S. Rank, clout and worker satisfaction: Pecking order—capitalist and communist style. *Psychology Today,* 1975 (September), **9,** 40–43.

Truell, George F. Core managerial strategies culled from behavioral research. *Supervisory Management,* 1977 (January), **22,** 10–17.

Vroom, V. H. Leadership. In M. Dunnette, Ed., *Handbook of Industrial and Organizational Psychology.* Chicago: Rand McNally, 1976. Pp. 1527–1551.

Vroom, V. H., and P. W. Yetton. *Leadership and Decision–Making.* Pittsburgh: University of Pittsburgh Press, 1973.

Wanous, J. P., and E. E. Lawler. Measurement and meaning of job satisfaction. *Journal of Applied Psychology,* 1972, **56,** 95–105.

Warr, P., Ed. *Personal Goals and Work Design.* New York: John Wiley, 1976.

Weaver, Charles N. What workers want from their jobs. *Personnel,* 1976 (May–June), **53,** 48–54.

# Psychology Applied to the World of Work: IV. The Workplace

**14**

Glostrup is a pleasant little town about 18 miles from Copenhagen in Denmark. The attractive new plant of Sadolins Trykfarver, an ink manufacturer, was built in Glostrup a few years ago and it enjoys a unique reputation in town.* It is considered to be one of the best of all possible places to work. Despite the incredibly dirty work involved in making ink, the company has no trouble finding employees. People like to work for them. One man commutes such a long distance that he has to take a train, two buses, and two long walks each way, and he doesn't want to work anywhere else.

Productivity has more than doubled since Sadolins Trykfarver moved into the new plant. Absenteeism, which in the old plant was as high as 30 per cent, is almost nonexistent, and turnover has been cut from 80 per cent to only 10 per cent. It is rare that anyone quits; of six employees who did quit since the move to the new plant, five have returned.

Why is the Sadolins Trykfarver Company considered such a good place to work? The work is dirty; employees are covered from head to foot with dried ink by the end of the day. The workers are not paid higher salaries than their counterparts in other industries. They don't work fewer hours than anyone else. The answer lies in the exemplary working conditions—both physical and social-psychological—found in the new plant. The physical layout of the entire plant and of individual working areas, and the equipment, machinery, and production processes were designed to be as efficient, safe, comfortable, and attractive as possible and to expedite the work in a rational and sensible way. The employees believe that they have the best and most agreeable working conditions found anywhere. And no wonder—the employees designed the plant themselves!

The employees worked closely with the architect in planning the new facilities and were given the opportunity to contribute to the design of every

* Gerard Tavernier, "The Plant the Workers Planned," *International Management,* **29** (1974), 19–20, 25–26.

aspect of the plant. Only about 15 per cent of their suggestions were not used and, in each case, they were told why their ideas could not be implemented. The rest of their ideas were, as the architect said, "feasible and many of them just perfect."

Most of the employee suggestions contributed directly to the increased production that occurred in the new plant. After all, who should know better how to improve a production process than those who are doing the work? The design problem with which the employees were most concerned related to the location of the work areas and machinery. For example, they wanted the building to be one story so that raw materials would not have to be dragged from one floor to the next, as was the case in the old plant. Employees recommended a system of pipes and hoses to feed the ink-making machines to replace the old method of hand carrying and filling the receptacles for the varnishes and oils. Their arrangement was more efficient and cleaner.

Some of the changes were resisted by the architect and were costlier than the original design. For example, the workers wanted a pit dug so that a large boiler, into which resins had to be poured, would be at a convenient height. In the old factory, the workers had to climb to another level, hauling vats of resins, to carry out this task. The architect complained that the workers would throw cigarette butts and other litter into the boiler if it were only waist high, as the workers wanted. However, the employees won and the pit was dug, at an extra cost of $2500. And the employees kept their promise; in the first year of operation, not a single piece of litter was found in the boiler. In addition, considerable time was saved in carrying out this operation in the ink-making process.

The workers also had many suggestions about how to make the work environment more pleasant. For example, the company wanted to install a large reservoir of water to feed the sprinkler system that was required because of the high risk of fire. The workers thought that if there was going to be a large tank of water anyway, it should be designed to serve as a swimming pool. The architect and the company management agreed that there was no reason why it could not be a swimming pool, and the reservoir design was altered at a cost of $2200.

Because the workers' personal clothing became ink-stained when they changed from their work clothes at the end of the day, they suggested building two changing rooms separated by showers so that they could take off their work clothes in one room, shower, and put on their street clothes in another room. They also requested, and got, a larger number of toilets and a separate smoking room.

Management also participated in improving the conditions of the working environment, and the status of the workers, by instituting some of their own ideas, after due consultation with the workers. For example, management eliminated the separate entrances for workers and managers that existed in the old plant. They built one dining room for everyone instead of separate facilities. At first, the workers resisted the idea of a common dining room because they felt they were too dirty from their work to eat with secretaries and managers. This problem was solved by providing workers with coats to cover their work clothes while they were eating. Those who worked with black inks, which are particularly hard to remove, were given special black chairs in the dining room. To help remove ink dust from their skin, the workers suggested some sort of damp room; management responded by building a sauna for them.

It is not difficult to understand why the employees of this company are so content with their new plant and why production has increased so greatly. As one worker put it, "The new factory is so clean. The work flows more smoothly. There is also the feeling that we are working more closely together." The experience of this Danish company demonstrates vividly the importance to motivation, morale, job satisfaction, and productivity of providing the optimal conditions under which people must work.

The ideal working conditions in this example are both physical and social-psychological. These two sets of factors help to form the ideal working environment. Social-psychological working conditions include factors discussed in Chapter 13—treating employees as mature and responsible human beings and letting them participate in decisions that affect the nature of their work. Social-psychological working conditions also include the nature of leadership, which can create a climate in the working environment that ranges from dictatorial to democratic.

Other aspects of the social-psychological working environment are explored in this chapter. Every organization fosters a unique style in terms of its formal organizational structure. Some companies are rigid, hierarchical bureaucracies (like the military), in which detailed rules and regulations prescribe exactly what employees do and how they do it; no deviation is tolerated. Other companies, like the Danish ink-making plant, offer less rigid and hierarchical structures, in which all employees are treated as integral members of the organization.

Further, within every organization, regardless of its formal style or structure, small, informal, and cohesive groups develop that have tremendous power in shaping employee attitudes, behavior, and, consequently, production levels. Organizational psychologists are conducting much research to determine the nature of these formal and informal structures and their impact on employee satisfaction and productivity.

Psychologists have also been active in the design of the physical aspects of the workplace and the consequent impact on employees.

Although the physical factors of the work environment may not exert as strong an impact on production as the social-psychological factors, they nevertheless influence both the quality and quantity of production. Therefore, psychologists are concerned with such variables as lighting levels, temperatures, noise, color, and music, as well as with the number and arrangement of hours worked.

Industrial psychologists have been influential in designing comfortable, safe, and efficient places and tools of work. Environmental psychologists have been actively involved in the design of the buildings in which we work and of actual work spaces such as offices. Engineering psychologists have been concerned with the design of equipment and machinery used in the performance of work, from simple factory tools to the cockpit of a jet airplane.

Wherever people work, no matter what kind of work they do, psychologists have been involved in all facets of the conditions under which they perform their jobs. This concern and involvement continues to contribute forcefully to the overall quality of our working life, and will have a direct impact on your own career in the world of work.

We will discuss aspects of the physical work environment first, followed by the more subtle and complex social–psychological factors.

## PHYSICAL CONDITIONS OF WORK

You know from your own experience how influential the physical environment is on your work. For example, it is difficult to remain alert and to pay close attention to a lecture if the classroom is hot and stuffy. It is hard to read notes on a blackboard if the lights are dim. In your room at home or in a dormitory it is difficult to study or write a term paper if a neighbor's stereo set is blaring or if your desk is cluttered with your roommate's clothes and books.

So it is in the world of work. The physical work environment includes a wide range of potentially influencing factors, from the location of the parking lot and the physical attractiveness of the building to the number of elevators and the amount of light at an employee's desk or work space. Thus, before workers even get to their work stations, the physical environment can be an irritant that can detract from their job satisfaction and performance. Employees who cannot find a place to park because the company lot is too small may develop a negative and hostile attitude toward their employer and their job before they even get inside the building!

Once inside, there are other potential problems. Is the heating and air conditioning system adequate, are there enough elevators to handle rush hour crowds, are the rest rooms kept clean, is the food in the company cafeteria satisfactory, or even edible? Any of these physical factors may be detrimental to job performance even though they may have nothing directly to do with the actual work an employee performs. Nevertheless, these factors form part of the total physical environment or context in which the work takes place.

In addition to studying these broad aspects of the design of the work environment, industrial psychologists conduct research on specific features such as illumination, noise, color, music, and temperature and humidity levels.

*Illumination.* It seems obvious that the quality of work can be adversely affected by insufficient light. Also, we know from our own experience that trying to read or to perform detailed tasks without adequate illumination over a long period of time can cause eyestrain. Ultimately, such conditions can be permanently harmful to one's eyesight. Despite this awareness, we still find many places of work illuminated at poor levels of brightness.

Of course, the optimum level of lighting intensity or brightness varies for different types of work. Precision assembly such as in watchmaking requires brighter light than retail sales work in a department store. Although there is some disagreement about optimum illumination intensity levels, industrial psychologists and lighting engineers have published guidelines for recommended levels for different kinds of jobs.

In addition to the intensity of lighting, an important factor is how evenly the light is distributed in a room or work area. Prolonged, uneven distribution of light, such as having the specific work area much brighter than its surroundings, can cause eyestrain.

A third factor that contributes to eyestrain is glare, which results from too intense a level of illumination either directly from the light source or from reflective surfaces. Glare not only causes eyestrain and lowers production, but it can also obscure vision; this is what occurs when you approach a car at night that has its headlights on the high beam. These physical aspects of lighting can all be adjusted properly if attention is paid to the illumination requirements for each job and work station.

There is also a psychological component to lighting, which is not so easily corrected once an office or factory has been built. This relates to the question of natural versus artificial lighting, a growing problem in the increasing number of windowless office buildings and factories. Researchers have found that people who work in these buildings are unhappy about the lack of windows, regardless of the adequacy of the artificial illumination. It is not only that people like to see outside, but they also believe that natural light is better for the eyes than artificial light. A number of studies have demonstrated the psychological importance to employees of the natural light that windows provide.

/ *Noise.* Excessive exposure to noise, and the harmful physical and psychological effects that result, is a serious problem in our homes and cities as well as in our places of work. It is well known that prolonged exposure to high loudness levels permanently impairs hearing and causes us to feel irritable, tense, and nervous. In addition, high noise levels produce physiological changes. For example, noise can constrict the blood vessels, change the heart rate, dilate the pupils of the eyes, increase muscle tension, and raise blood pressure. Thus, excessive noise is more than a nuisance, it is a definite threat to our health.

The basic unit for measuring noise is the *decibel*, which measures the subjective or psychological intensity of a sound. Zero decibels represents the lowest sound we can hear. The sound of breathing registers at 10 decibels, and the sound level in an average home is 50 decibels. The federal government has established maximum sound levels to which workers may be exposed: 90 decibels for an eight-hour day, 100 decibels for no more than two hours a day, and 110 decibels for no more than thirty minutes a day.

The loudness levels of various objects and environments are listed in Table 14–1. These figures will give you an idea of how noisy some of our workplaces are. However, as you can see, some everyday noises to which we are exposed may be louder than those found in factories and workshops.

What do these loudness levels mean in terms of health? It is known that daily exposure to levels above 80 decibels causes some hearing loss, exposure for short periods to levels between 120 and 125 decibels causes temporary deafness, and brief exposure to levels above 150 decibels may cause permanent deafness. Also, the physiological changes mentioned previously occur with exposure to noise levels in the 95- to 110-decibel range.

Factors other than loudness may cause noise to be annoying or distracting. Intermittent or irregular noise is much more disturbing than constant or steady noise. Also, intermittent noise that appears regularly is less disturbing than intermittent noise that appears on a random basis. Familiar noises are not as disturbing as unfamiliar ones. High, shrill tones and extremely low tones are much more annoying than tones in the middle range.

Preventing or reducing noise is primarily an engineering and design problem. Most noisy machines (even pneumatic jackhammers) can be designed to operate more quietly, though at great additional expense. Rooms or buildings located near noisy machinery can be lined with

**Table 14–1.** Representative Decibel Levels

| Source of Noise | Decibel Level |
| --- | --- |
| Jet plane at takeoff | 150 |
| Riveting | 130 |
| Hydraulic press | 120 |
| Rock concert | 120 |
| Snowmobile | 115 |
| Thunder | 110 |
| Motorcycle | 100 |
| Power mower | 100 |
| Printing press | 100 |
| Punch press | 100 |
| Woodworking shop | 100 |
| Boiler room | 95 |
| Average factory | 90 |
| Food blender | 90 |
| Machine shop | 90 |
| Dishwasher | 80 |
| Electric typewriter | 70 |
| Normal conversation | 60 |
| Library | 40 |
| Quiet office | 40 |
| Normal breathing | 10 |

sound-absorbing materials, and workers can be supplied with individual protective devices such as earplugs.

*Color.* We have all read articles in popular magazines about how the right color or combination of colors can make us happier, less tense, or reflect our personalities. In our places of work we are often told how color can increase morale and production and reduce errors and accidents. There is only one problem with these claims; they are not supported by empirical evidence.

This does not mean that the use of color has absolutely no effect on the conditions under which we work. Color can provide a more aesthetically pleasing work environment and can also help in matters of safety.

A work area that is drab and dingy can certainly be made more pleasant by a fresh coat of paint, in almost any color. Colors can create different illusions of room size and temperature. Light-colored walls, for example, can give a room a feeling of greater space and openness. It is also thought that some colors, such as red and orange, create the illusion of greater warmth, although little research supports this notion. Color can also prevent eyestrain by cutting down on the amount of light reflected by walls or machinery.

Color is used in many manufacturing plants as a coding device for safety. Fire equipment is usually red, danger areas yellow, and first aid equipment green. Such color coding allows equipment to be more quickly identified.

Thus, color can be used to improve certain aspects of the work environment, but it does not seem to have any direct bearing on job satisfaction or productivity.

*Music.* We are often treated to extravagant claims about the value of music in making employees happier and more productive, but research on the effects of music is meager and contradictory. There is some support for the notion that employees are generally happier when music is available, but little support for the suggestion that productivity increases as a result of having music.

The difficulty with research in this area is that the effects of any music depend in part on the specific nature of the work. It is possible that music increases production on simple repetitive jobs such as on an assembly line. With complex jobs that require the workers' full concentration, however, music could become distracting and interfere with production. The demanding work of an air traffic controller, for example, could easily be impaired by the presence of music in the control tower.

Even on simple jobs where music might contribute to increased production, there is the question of what kind of music to play. Younger employees are likely to prefer a different kind of music than older employees. It has happened that formerly cohesive work units have split into hostile cliques on the basis of different musical preferences.

In brief, then, there is no simple answer to the question about the value of music in terms of worker productivity and satisfaction.

*Temperature and humidity levels.* You know from your own experience how temperature and humidity levels can affect your physical and mental well-being and your ability to work efficiently. Of course, different people are affected in different ways by the weather. Some of us are happier when it is cold, others when it is hot; some are depressed when it rains, others may hardly notice it.

For most work that takes place indoors, the temperature and humidity levels can be controlled to maintain constant conditions the year round. Heating and ventilating engineers report that the most comfortable temperature range is between 73°F and 77°F, and the ideal humidity range is between 25 and 50 per cent.

What about people who work out of doors or in places such as steel mills that are impossible to air condition and heat properly? How are these workers affected by extremes of temperature? Fortunately, the human body is adaptable to weather conditions, and, assuming high levels of motivation, most people are able to maintain somewhat constant rates of production under extremes of both heat and cold. Mental work is usually much less affected than heavy physical labor. Demanding physical work is affected, however, by unusually hot and humid conditions. Production levels can fall under these conditions and the workers need frequent rest pauses. Even should production remain the same under extremely hot and humid conditions, workers must expend considerably more energy to maintain the same output.

## THE MACHINERY AND EQUIPMENT OF WORK: ENGINEERING PSYCHOLOGY

One major component of the physical work environment is the tools, machinery, and equipment people use to perform their jobs. No matter how well employees are selected, trained, and motivated, the finished product is only as good as the tools and equipment they have to work with. This rule applies to everything from hand tools such as hammers and screwdrivers to power tools such as power saws and to elaborate electronic equipment such as that found in the cockpit of a jet airliner.

Equipment must be designed to be compatible with the person who uses it. We can think of a worker using a tool or a machine as a team operation; worker and machine function together to perform some task that could not be accomplished by either working alone. The carpenter with a hammer, the sewing machine operator with a sewing machine, the laborer with a shovel all operate as systems called *man–machine systems*. If the machine and the person are to work effectively together, they must be perfectly matched so that each makes the best use of the strengths and compensates for the weaknesses of the other.

This matching of worker and machine is accomplished by the field of *engineering psychology* (also called human factors engineering), which is a combination of engineering and psychological knowledge. Engineering psychology is the science of designing machinery and equipment for human use. Thus, the work of engineering psychologists exerts a great influence on the conditions under which we work.

This field was created because of the increasing complexity, speed, and precision of newly developing machines, the operation of which exceeded human capacities. For example, airplanes were being built to fly so fast that the reaction times of pilots were being outstripped. The requirements of the machine went beyond the human capability for control. Thus, some decisions and operations that human beings could not carry out had to be given to the machine part of the system so that the total system could function effectively. Small computers were developed to take over some of the functions previously assigned to pilots, in order to compensate for human limitations.

Engineering psychology began with almost an exclusive focus on military weapons systems (such as airplanes, ships, and tanks), but its applications now include the design of equipment and machinery for the workplace as well as for the home (such as automobiles, electric ranges, typewriters, and telephones; the push-button telephone is the result of research by engineering psychologists). Long-haul truckers' heavy-duty rigs are human engineered to provide ease of entrance, excellent visibility for the driver, and optimum climate control for driver and sleeping compartments. Engineering psychologists also design equipment for business, recreational, and medical uses.

Engineering psychologists are usually involved in the earliest stages of equipment design where they influence such important decisions as the most efficient allocation of functions between worker and machine, the kinds of information needed to operate the machine, how best to display or present this information, the kinds of human judgments and decisions required, and the quickest and safest way of communicating these decisions to the machine.

These design decisions require a great deal of knowledge about human strengths and weaknesses, and about the activities for which humans are superior to machines and machines are superior to humans. This information derives from research in many areas of psychology as well as from studies conducted by engineering psychologists on the specific machine being designed. It is imperative that the part of the system (human or machine) that is most efficient at a particular task be given that task so that the worker and machine components are both used to best advantage.

In addition to specific pieces of equipment and machinery, engineering psychologists are involved in the design of larger areas in which work is performed, from a workbench for the assembly of electronic parts to an entire air traffic control center. Guidelines for efficient operation derive from research on the actual work involved as well as from common sense. Some of the empirically derived principles of work space design are the following.

1. All materials, tools, and supplies a worker uses on the job should be located in the order in which they are used. In this way, the path of the worker's hand movements will always be continuous and smooth and the worker will always know exactly where each part or tool may be found.

2. Tools should be positioned so that they can be picked up ready for

use. For example, if a job requires the frequent use of a screwdriver, it could be suspended on a spring just above the work area so that the worker can reach for it without having to waste time looking for it.

3. All parts and tools must be placed within an easy and comfortable distance. The work should be capable of accomplishment without the worker having to change position or stretch beyond the average reaching distance of 28 inches. The greater distance the worker has to reach, the longer each operation will take and the more fatiguing the task will be to the worker.

You can see that considerable common sense is involved in these basic principles of work space design. However, common sense alone is often not a sufficient basis on which to justify the expense of redesigning a work area. When engineering psychologists can demonstrate, through carefully conducted research or observations made on the job, exactly how much time and money can be saved by redesign, management is much more likely to agree to making the suggested changes.

Some people find it hard to believe that making what seems like a simple change could save significant amounts of time and money. The results speak for themselves. In a classic example in 1898, the father of scientific management, Frederick Taylor, changed the size and design of shovels used in handling iron ore. This saved a steel company $78,000 a year. Frank Gilbreth, a pioneer in time-and-motion study (a precursor of engineering psychology concerned with improving work methods), eliminated the wasted hand and arm motions of bricklayers and introduced scaffolding that could be raised or lowered. As a result of his new methods and tools, bricklayers were capable of laying 350 bricks an hour instead of only 120, and they did not become as fatigued in the process.

Gilbreth's work even revolutionized the job of surgeon. Before he analyzed the motions involved in surgery, surgeons had to seek out each tool they wanted to use. Gilbreth redesigned the job so that a nurse stood by the surgeon ready to place the needed tool in the surgeon's hand. As a result, the time required for operations was reduced by as much as two-thirds.

Such changes benefit both employee and employer. Increased efficiency usually results in higher production levels and often in higher-quality production as well. The changes in work space design and in working procedures responsible for greater efficiency also make jobs easier to perform, thus contributing to the quality of working life.

Another important aspect of work space design involves measurement of the physical dimensions of the human body. This research is undertaken by a branch of engineering psychology known as *human anthropometry*. Complete and detailed sets of measurements have been taken from large numbers of people at rest and while performing various activities. These measures include, for example, height (standing and sitting), shoulder breadth, back height, seat height, and foot and hand length. These measurements are of great value in designing work spaces because they are applicable to decisions about normal and maximum reaching distances; optimum height of desks, workbenches, and tools; size and shape of seats; and so on.

We have examined the impact of engineering psychology on the design of individual work spaces. Many jobs require interaction between different machines and workers. One machine may produce a component of a product that must be passed on to another machine for the next step in the total production process. Employees may have to communicate with one another or transmit raw materials or parts. Individual controls on a machine may have to be operated in a specific sequence.

Engineering psychologists are concerned with the nature of such interrelationships because they determine the size of the work area that can be designed for efficient operations. If two workers in a section are required to interact frequently, their work stations should be placed as close together as possible.

To determine the most efficient interactions, engineering psychologists observe the actual work procedures and interview the workers. For complicated systems that involve a large number of interactions, researchers may take motion pictures of the operation, which can then be studied frame by frame to determine the nature and frequency of the interactions.

Another area of application of engineering psychology to the world of work (and to consumer goods as well) involves the presentation of information to the human operator. Many machines require that the person who operates them receive information from the machines on certain aspects of their functioning. This may be in the form of dials, warning lights, or buzzers that sound warning signals.

This is similar to the situation in our automobiles. We receive information on how the car is functioning through visual displays such as the speedometer, temperature indicator, and gas gauge, and through auditory displays such as the buzzer that tells us that our seat belt is not fastened. On an informal basis, we even receive information tactually (through the skin senses), such as the vibrations we feel when the engine is not performing properly.

Machines in the world of work present information to workers through all three of these senses, but the visual sense is the one used most frequently. Therefore, we shall concentrate our discussion on that source of information.

Visual displays must be designed to present information to the worker as quickly as possible and with the least likelihood of mistakes being made in reading them. When engineering psychologists are confronted with the design of a visual display, there are several questions they must consider.

First, is the display necessary? Does the operator of the machine or system really need the information presented in the display? If the system can function without this information, there is no reason to clutter up the instrument panel and possibly confuse the operator. Second, if the information is vital, what is the most effective way of displaying it so that it will be perceived quickly and accurately? Three commonly used types of visual displays are quantitative, qualitative, and check reading.

*Quantitative displays* present information in numerical or quantitative form, that is, by giving a precise number. There are many situations in which an exact numerical reading is required. The speedometer of your car is a quantitative display. It is important that you have a precise indication (rather than an approximation) of your speed so that you know if you are driving within the speed limit. Similarly, pilots must be aware of their exact altitude so they know if they are flying as prescribed by their flight plan.

If a quantitative display is desired, the engineering psychologist must decide on its specific format. Quantitative displays can be circular, semicircular, or rectangular (as in a station selector panel on the radio). If rectangular, the display could be placed horizontally or vertically. Other factors to be determined include the shape and size of the numbers, how far apart they should be placed, and the size of the pointer (Figure 14–1).

The only criterion to keep in mind when making design decisions is: which approach will present the information to the worker as quickly and accurately as possible? There is much research available on the relative effectiveness of different types of quantitative displays. However,

Figure 14–1. Semicircular quantitative display.

for new man–machine systems, it is often necessary to conduct additional research comparing the different approaches in the specific system.

*Qualitative displays* are used in situations in which precise numerical readings are not required. The engine temperature gauge in your car is a qualitative display. Most of us do not need to know the exact engine temperature. All we care about is that the temperature be within the safe operating range, and not overheating or in danger of doing so. There are many situations with industrial machinery where it is necessary to know only within what range the system is functioning and whether it is increasing or decreasing in value.

Figure 14–2 shows a qualitative display of engine temperature. Usually, the operating ranges (cold, normal, hot) are color-coded, with the danger area in red and the safe range in green. This kind of display presents quick and accurate information that is virtually impossible to misread.

The *check reading display* is sometimes called a go/no go display. It indicates whether the system or machine is operating normally or abnormally. The oil pressure indicator in your car is a check reading display. It is not necessary to know what the oil pressure is, in quantitative or qualitative terms. All we need to know is if the oil pressure is sufficient for us to continue to drive the car or if we must stop because there is not enough oil pressure.

The check reading display is the simplest kind of visual display and is usually presented as a warning light. When the light is on, this indicates that something is wrong that must be corrected immediately (a no go condition). When the light is not on, the system is operating satisfactorily (a go condition).

Figure 14–2. Qualitative display.

The applications of the findings and principles of engineering psychology to the world of work are of great importance in enhancing the efficiency of man–machine systems and in improving the quality of working life. We shall discuss the application of engineering psychology to automobile design in Chapter 15.

## HOURS OF WORK

Although the number and arrangement of hours of work are not, strictly speaking, a physical condition of work, they nevertheless comprise a tangible aspect of the work environment. The temporal conditions of work are capable of influencing both job satisfaction and employee productivity. As such, they constitute an area of considerable interest to industrial psychologists.

The number of hours employees are expected to work each week has steadily diminished over the years. Within the memory of many people are six-day workweeks of ten or more hours each day, with no official rest pauses or lunch breaks. The five-day forty-hour workweek is a relatively recent innovation, and shorter workweeks are definitely in our future.

An important caution about prescribed hours of work is that a task will expand to fill the time available for it.[1] What this means is that increasing the number of hours in the workday may not result in increased production; shortening the number of hours may not lead to a decrease in production. Most employees spend as much time as is allowed to complete their daily tasks.

Thus, there is a vast difference between *nominal* working hours (the prescribed number of hours workers must spend at their jobs) and *actual* working hours. In fact, the two rarely coincide. One study of 5000 clerical workers showed this dramatically. Of an average workweek of thirty-seven and one-half hours, no more than twenty hours were spent on actual work. In a very real sense, then, many employers are paying double for the amount of work received.

Some of this time lost from actual work is officially sanctioned in the form of rest breaks, but most of it is unauthorized and beyond the control of the employer. Employees dawdle when they arrive at work and spend (or waste) a lot of time shuffling papers, oiling machines, and sharpening pencils. During the day they socialize with coworkers and talk about yesterday's football game or a television program they watched the previous night. They extend the lunch hour and take several unauthorized rest pauses in the rest room or at the water cooler,

---

[1] This is Parkinson's Law, after the British author and historian C. Northcote Parkinson.

or simply daydream while they pretend to look busy at their desk or work bench.

There is a surprising (and perverse) relationship between nominal and actual working hours. When the nominal working hours are increased, the actual working hours decrease. The longer the workday or workweek, the lower is the actual production per hour. This was demonstrated conclusively during World War II in England when manufacturing plants increased the nominal working hours from fifty-six to sixty-nine and one-half. Production fell by 12 per cent. Some plants went to a seven-day workweek and found that production was no higher than it had been during the normal six-day workweek. One workday out of seven was lost working time.

A similar thing happens with overtime, when employees stay beyond their normal workday for markedly higher rates of pay. Overtime is a poor investment for employers because workers adjust to the longer hours by working at a slower pace during the day.

If production decreases if the workday is lengthened, will production increase if employers shorten the workday or workweek? Although it is not known for certain that this will happen, some studies do suggest this as a possibility. For example, studies of part-time employees working twenty hours a week showed that they actually accomplished more work than colleagues who worked forty hours a week. Perhaps the part-time employees did not take as many unauthorized breaks as the full-time employees. There was a closer correspondence between the nominal and actual working hours for part-time employees than for full-time employees.

In recent years, two innovations in the arrangement of working hours have shown beneficial effects on productivity and satisfaction: the four-day workweek and flexible working hours.

## The Four-Day Workweek

Beginning in the early 1970s, many factories, offices, and government agencies reduced their workweek to four days, either at ten hours a day (a forty-hour week) or at nine hours a day (a thirty-six-hour week with no reduction in workers' pay). These plans were introduced in the hope of increasing productivity and reducing absenteeism, which, in some companies, is extremely high, particularly on Mondays and Fridays.

One of the first plants to switch to a four-day workweek was a small paint company in Massachusetts. The four-day plan, and the reasons for it, were explained in detail to the employees. They were told exactly what it would mean to them: three-day weekends, an extra hour of work each day, the elimination of formal coffee breaks, and the same rate of pay for four fewer hours of work each week.

After a three-month trial period, the company and the union assessed the results. Production had risen by 6 per cent, absenteeism had declined from 3 per cent to less than 1 per cent, worker morale was high, and the company had more job applicants than before.

Other organizations that have switched to the four-day workweek report production increases as high as 15 per cent and a much greater degree of loyalty from their employees. Surveys reveal that more than 90 per cent of the workers who have changed to this schedule want to continue with it.

## Flexible Working Hours

A more radical change in the scheduling of working hours is *flexitime* (or *flextime*), allowing employees to decide for themselves when they will begin and end their workday. This idea was first introduced in West Germany in the late 1960s and it quickly became popular in the United States.

The workday is divided into four parts, two of which are optional and two of which are mandatory. Employees may begin work at any time they choose between 7:30 and 9:00 in the morning and leave any time between 4:00 and 5:30 in the afternoon. The two mandatory periods, during which everyone must be at work, are the morning hours from 9:00 until the half-hour lunch break and the afternoon hours from lunch until 4:00. Everyone must work a minimum of seven and one-half hours each day (Figure 14–3).

Flexible working hours offer a number of advantages at no extra cost to the organization. The morning and afternoon rush hour traffic around the office or plant is eased. Less time is spent commuting and employees are more relaxed when they begin work. Production increases as high as 5 per cent have been reported, and morale and satisfaction improve. Tardiness and absenteeism have been reduced significantly.

Flexible working hours are very well liked by employers and employees. After the arrangement was introduced by the British civil service, a poll of employees showed that 96 per cent approved and would

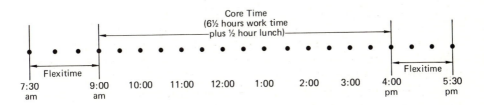

Figure 14–3. Flexitime.

not want to return to the fixed hour system. More than half of the white-collar work force in West Germany works on a flexible hour basis, as do 30 per cent of French workers and 40 per cent of Swiss workers. In the United States, companies such as Scott Paper, Occidental Insurance, and Sun Oil have changed to flexible working hours, as have local governments such as Baltimore, Maryland, and Washington, D.C, and several federal government agencies.

Flexible working hours provide some degree of autonomy and responsibility for employees, who are able to have a say in when and how long they will work each day. This is another example of the trend toward greater worker participation in decisions that affect their jobs, and another step toward full humanization of work and the conditions under which it takes place.

## Shift Work

Another temporal condition of work is shift work. Many companies are in operation around the clock. This means that some employees have to work unusual hours. The traditional shift work arrangement is 7 A.M. to 3 P.M., 3 P.M. to 11 P.M., and 11 P.M. to 7 A.M. In some organizations, employees are assigned to one of these shifts on a permanent basis; in other cases, employees rotate on different shifts, usually changing schedules each week. Those employees who work the evening and all-night shifts receive extra pay to compensate for the inconvenience.

Production is lower on the night shift than on the day shift. In addition, shift work can be harmful to employees, physically and psychologically. When the normal pattern of waking and sleeping is disrupted, there are dramatic physical changes in the activities of certain bodily organs and glands and in the chemical composition of the blood. The most common complaint of night shift workers is an inability to sleep during the day. They are also bothered by headaches, difficulty in concentrating, increased errors at work, and ulcers.

Shift work also disrupts family and social life. If one spouse works during the day and the other at night, they may rarely see each other and have little time together for everyday errands or visiting with friends. The house must be kept quiet during the day while the night shift worker is trying to sleep; this is a hardship for young children and housekeepers.

Rotating workers from one shift to another is much more harmful than keeping them permanently on the same shift. The weekly change from one schedule to another does not allow the body time to adjust to a new sleep–wake cycle. When employees remain on one shift, a better physiological adjustment can be made.

If the rotating shift system must be used, harmful effects can be reduced somewhat by rotating every few weeks instead of every week or by lengthening the time off between shift changes. By whatever arrangement, however, shift work results in a difficult life-style for many people.

## SOCIAL–PSYCHOLOGICAL CONDITIONS OF WORK

A less tangible but no less important aspect of the work environment is the cluster of social-psychological factors that shape the climate or style of the organizations for which we work. Some of these factors are discussed in Chapter 13, such as the importance of proper leadership and of involving employees in decision making. We will discuss here the nature of formal and informal organizational styles and the work of organizational psychologists on the impact of these styles on satisfaction and productivity. We will also consider participatory democracy in greater detail.

Fundamentally, there are two extremes of organizational style and climate, the traditional bureaucratic style, found in most organizations today, and the participatory style, exemplified by the Danish ink-making plant discussed at the beginning of the chapter.

### The Bureaucratic Organization

The word "bureaucracy" conjures up all sorts of negative images, most of which seem to be deserved. Working for bureaucratic organizations, or trying to deal with them in any fashion, we have learned that they are often inefficient, grossly overorganized, rigidly structured, and very successful in stifling original and creative activities.

It is important to remember, however, that when the bureaucratic style of organization was introduced in the 1920s, it was intended to do precisely what the newer participatory style of organization tries to do today: humanize the workplace. Bureaucracy was a revolutionary idea, designed to correct the inequities and cruelties practiced by business owners in the early stages of the industrial revolution. The owners had total control over every aspect of the workplace, and the employees were completely at the mercy of their whims, biases, and prejudices.

The bureaucratic style of organization was supposed to function in an orderly, lawful, machinelike fashion, unaffected by personal prejudice. In its day, the bureaucratic approach accomplished its goal. It greatly improved the working lives of millions of people by breaking down or decentralizing the organization into many separate component parts and operations, each of which was linked to the others in a rigid hierarchy of control.

The decentralizing of the organization resulted in a high degree of

specialization, both in the actual work performed and in the management of that work. Separate work units were established to build different products or different parts of the same product. Thus, a new
concept, *division of labor,* entered the world of work and, as a result,
jobs tended to become simpler and more highly specialized.

The division of labor meant that a new system of managing or coordinating work had to be developed. With ever-increasing specialization, no
single individual was capable of overseeing the entire production process.
Therefore, management, too, had to become specialized and authority
decentralized and *delegated* to different levels of leadership. One person
was made responsible for each set or group of highly specialized jobs.
This leader was responsible solely for his or her work unit, and the
workers in that unit reported only to that leader. Thus, workers were
cut off from contact with other levels of the organization.

These aspects of the bureaucratic style of organization—division of
labor and delegation of authority—can be easily seen in that symbol of
organizational life known as the organization chart (Figure 14–4).

The delegation of authority is represented by the vertical dimension.
The leader in level A has four subordinates, each of whom has five subordinates. Division of labor is represented by the horizontal dimension.
Each unit of five positions in level C is separate (both in terms of its
leadership and its function) from the other units on that level. In other
words, each unit is responsible for a different process or operation.

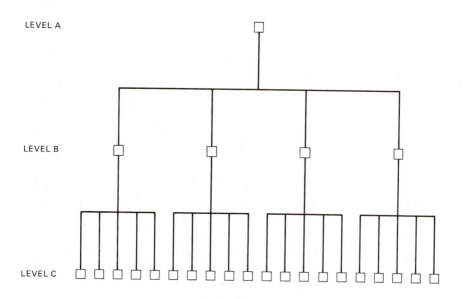

Figure 14–4. Organization chart.

Thus, the total organization is reduced to a number of component parts, each one managed separately. Lines of authority and communication are clear and each person's job and place in the overall structure are well defined.

However, neatly drawn lines and boxes on paper do not always reflect the reality of a work situation. There is an informal organization within the formally structured one, an uncharted complex of informal groups of workers that often undermine the most rigid rules of the most dictatorial organization. These informal groups develop rules, codes, and work procedures, and their own perception of what constitutes an adequate quantity and quality of the work to be performed. The dictates of these informal groups are often at variance with the rules and expectations established by the formal organization. Often it is through these informal groupings that the real work of an organization is done (or undone).

No matter how rationally a bureaucratic organization is designed, how specialized the work, or how well delegated the authority, human beings do not always abide by the formal structure. Therefore, the organization chart may not represent the true nature of the organization.

Employees establish their own structure and organizational style primarily as a defense against the major weakness of bureaucracies, their failure to recognize human values and needs. Bureaucracies view employees as anonymous blocks on an organization chart, as interchangeable as the machines and equipment they operate. By ignoring human values and needs, the bureaucratic organization provides no opportunity for personal growth and self-actualization, which are vital motivating forces.

An employee has no separate or unique identity in a bureaucracy, and no formal control over any aspect of the work or the policies and procedures that influence the quality of working life. The employee is expected to be docile, passive, and dependent, like a child in its relationship with its parents. Decisions are made for the employee because he or she is not believed to be capable of making them alone.

Not only do bureaucracies stifle individual growth and development, but they also thwart their own growth. By fostering stability, rigidity, and permanence, bureaucracies cannot adapt readily or quickly to change. Technological innovations and changing social conditions are perceived as threatening to the orderly structure of the organization, which is more interested in maintaining and preserving itself than in growing and changing. Bureaucracies become choked in the lines and webs of their formal organization charts. Their employees become the passive robots they are intended to be or devote their energies to resisting the trap of rigidity and stagnation rather than to their jobs. Like many revolutions designed to liberate, bureaucracies gave birth to new forms of entrapment. Clearly, the need existed for a new approach to organizational life.

## The Participatory Organization

A major problem with bureaucracies is their emphasis on the total system or organization to the exclusion of the individual human beings who make up the system. The newer approach to organizational style tries to remedy this deficiency by focusing on the individual employees in the belief that any organization is a reflection and a composite of the people who comprise it. Therefore, it is believed that we cannot understand the behavior of the organization as a whole without first understanding the behaviors, attitudes, wants, and needs of the individual members of the organization.

Not only does this organizational style focus on the individual rather than on the system, but it also reflects a different image of what people are like. The contrasting images of human nature held by the bureaucratic and participatory styles of organization are represented by McGregor's Theory X/Theory Y formulation (discussed in Chapter 13).

The Theory X view of human nature is compatible with the rigid requirements of a bureaucracy. Because workers in a bureaucracy are incapable of deciding anything for themselves, they need a controlling and dictatorial leader. In contrast, Theory Y assumes that people are motivated to seek and accept responsibility in their work. Theory Y also assumes a high level of creativity, commitment, and need for personal growth.

Incorporating the Theory Y view, the participatory organization aims to decrease worker dependency, subordination, and submissiveness in order to take full advantage of human potential. Accordingly, jobs must be redesigned to allow opportunities for the employees to determine how best to perform their work. In other words, jobs must be expanded and enriched to increase each worker's sense of challenge and responsibility. Management must become less dictatorial and more responsive to employee participation in decision making. Organizations as a whole must become more flexible, adapting to worker needs and to social, economic, and technological conditions.

Some of these changes are already evident in organizational life today. In Chapter 13 we discuss examples of successful job enlargement programs, which have brought a greater sense of freedom to the workplace, and also the changing nature of leadership (from Theory X to Theory Y) in response to participatory democracy.

This participatory approach to organizational style calls for three major changes in the social-psychological conditions of work: enrichment, enlargement, and expansion of jobs; active worker participation in policy making at all levels; and greater opportunity for individual expression, creativity, and personal fulfillment (this derives from the satisfaction of the first two conditions).

This organizational style, exemplified by the Danish ink-making plant, is a growing and successful movement in American business and industry. Nevertheless, it is still the exception, not the rule, in the world of work today. Participatory democracy promises to be a revolutionary movement, which many people view as a cure for all organizational ills. Whatever its eventual outcome, however, this attempt to humanize the workplace is exciting, and organizational psychologists are deeply committed to it.

## The Organization Within the Organization

As noted previously, within every formal organization informal groups develop that have tremendous power in shaping worker attitudes, behavior, and production. These informal groups do not appear on organization charts, are usually beyond the control of management, and often foster attitudes and behaviors that are antagonistic to management goals.

Every unit, team, or group of people who work closely together over a period of time develop communal norms. In other words, they come to think and to act in similar ways. This encourages and reinforces feelings of closeness or cohesiveness among them. The loyalties of the members of such groups are usually directed toward one another rather than toward the organization as a whole. They may adopt an "us versus them" attitude; "them" refers to members of management.

When new workers join a working unit they are quickly made aware of the group's norms. The group teaches them (in subtle and direct ways) the accepted ways of thinking and behaving, and it demands conformity to the group norms. Thus, the group shapes a new employee's attitudes toward management and toward all other aspects of the work environment.

The classic demonstration of the importance of informal work groups took place in the 1930s as a part of a major series of studies on the nature of work, conducted at the Hawthorne, Illinois, plant of the Western Electric Company.[2] This twelve-year research program, now known as the *Hawthorne studies*, was extremely influential in the development of industrial and organizational psychology. The results revealed the importance of the social-psychological conditions of work.

One study involved the close observation of fourteen men who

[2] F. J. Roethlisberger and W. J. Dickson, *Management and the Worker—An Account of a Research Program Conducted by the Western Electric Company*, Chicago (Cambridge, Mass.: Harvard University Press, 1939).

worked at the same job in the bank wiring room of the Western Electric plant. These workers formed a closely knit group that had many of the characteristics of a family. The workers had common interests, engaged in pranks that were sometimes rough but always friendly, helped one another whenever it was needed, and avoided doing anything that might bring disapproval from the other members of the group.

For our purposes, the most significant observation made of this group was that it determined on its own what constituted a fair and safe level of daily production. The management of the company had stated what was expected of these workers; a standard daily output, with an incentive to be paid for meeting and exceeding that level, had been formally established. Therefore, each worker could make more money by working faster, a reliable means of maximizing production, according to traditional management beliefs. The problem was that the incentive did not work because the informal group's standard of production was lower than the rate set by management.

The workers believed that if they met the company's standard, management would reduce their rate of pay and force them to work harder for the same wages. To avoid that situation, the employees established a more leisurely daily rate of production that they could easily attain, willingly giving up the extra money they could have earned.

All members of the group cooperated in maintaining their own production standard. Some of the men worked harder in the morning and slower in the afternoon; others worked at a slow but steady pace all day. On some days the group produced extra units but saved a number of them for a day when production might be lower. If one of the workers was not feeling well, the others would work harder to make up for his lower production.

The men admitted to the researcher that they could have worked harder and met the company's standard without undue strain, but to do so would be to violate the group's norms. And the group had very effective ways of enforcing those norms. Any man who worked too slowly (unless he was ill), or too rapidly, was subjected to a barrage of name calling and punched on the muscles of the upper arm (a painful blow known as "binging").

Whenever a new worker joined the group, he quickly learned what was expected, which behaviors the group would tolerate and which it would not. Acceptance by the group was much more important than any extra money that could have been earned by working faster.

Incidentally (and this is a common occurrence), the management at Hawthorne was unaware of the existence of these informal groups that had set their own production standards until the researchers told them.

If management is to deal effectively with informal groups, it must recognize their existence and be able to accept, at least to some degree, the group's standards, because management has little power to change them. This is a critical problem for the front-line manager (the foreman or supervisor), who forms the bridge between the informal groups of workers and higher management. The supervisor must balance the needs of the organization with the needs of subordinates in an effort to satisfy both.

Informal groups constitute a powerful and pervasive condition of work serving the needs of the workers. Such groups can, if managed effectively, serve the needs of the organization as well, or can work against them.

Few choices we make in our lives are of greater importance than those involving the kind of work we do. Psychology exerts an enormous impact on our careers, as we have discussed in the last four chapters. From the day we apply for our first job until the time we retire, the applications of industrial and organizational psychologists influence every aspect of the quality of our working lives.

## SUMMARY

The physical and social-psychological conditions under which people work exert a strong influence on their levels of productivity and job satisfaction. Industrial and organizational psychologists, together with engineering and environmental psychologists, are concerned with a variety of physical, social, and psychological factors in their efforts to create working environments that will be efficient, safe, and pleasant, and will satisfy worker needs and motivations.

The *physical conditions of work* include factors such as the location of the parking lot, the design of the plant, environmental variables such as light, heat, and noise, and the number and arrangement of hours worked.

The level and quality of *illumination* has been studied extensively, and recommended levels of intensity have been established for different kinds of work. Other aspects of illumination that influence production are the distribution of light in a work area, glare, and the psychological factors involved in natural versus artificial lighting (a problem in windowless buildings).

Excessive *noise* levels can cause hearing loss and internal physiological changes, both of which are harmful to workers. The federal government has established maximum sound levels to which employees may be exposed, and psychologists and engineers have developed ways of reducing noise. In addition to loudness, the quality or kind of noise (intermittent or irregular noise, and high, shrill tones or very low tones) can annoy and distract people at work.

*Color* can be used to enhance the attractiveness of a work area, to create illusions of room size (and possibly of temperature), and to code safety equipment and safety areas for ease of recognition. Color does not seem to influence productivity.

*Music* may make some people happier at work, but it does not seem capable of increasing production, except possibly for simple repetitive jobs. For complex jobs, music may interfere with production. When music is played at work, there is often conflict among workers as to the kind of music they prefer.

*Temperature and humidity* can be maintained at comfortable levels for most jobs performed indoors. For outdoor work of a physically demanding nature, productivity often declines in very hot and humid conditions.

*Engineering psychology* is concerned with designing the tools, machinery, and equipment that people use to perform their jobs, so as to make them compatible with the workers. The worker and the machine function as a system—a *man–machine system*—which must be matched so that each makes maximum use of the strengths and compensates for the weaknesses of the other.

Engineering psychologists are concerned with all aspects of equipment design such as the most efficient allocation of functions between worker and machine, the kinds of information needed to operate the machine and how best to display that information, the judgments and decisions required to run the machine, and the quickest way of transmitting those decisions to the machine for implementation.

Engineering psychologists are also involved in the design of the total work area, and they have developed basic principles of work space operation to improve the quantity and quality of work. A branch of engineering psychology, *human anthropometry,* is concerned with the measurement of the structure and dimensions of the human body, which measurements are used to determine the optimum size and arrangement of machinery, equipment, and office furniture.

The presentation of information to the human operator of a machine is a major part of equipment design. Engineering psychologists must decide what information is vital to the operation of the system and how it can best be presented. Three commonly used types of visual displays of information are quantitative, qualitative, and check reading.

The *temporal conditions of work* (the number and arrangement of hours to be worked) are an important aspect of the work environment. Psychologists have distinguished between *nominal working hours* (the amount of time workers are supposed to be at their jobs), and *actual working hours.* Studies show that the two rarely coincide. When nominal working hours are increased, actual working hours decrease. Some evidence suggests that the reverse may be true; actual working hours may increase when nominal hours are decreased.

**The Workplace**

Two innovations in the scheduling of work are the *four-day work-week* and *flexible working hours* (in which employees choose when to begin and end the workday). Both plans have been very successful.

*Shift work* presents health, family, and social adjustment problems to those who must work evenings and nights. It also lowers production levels. Keeping workers on one shift permanently is less harmful than rotating them from one shift to another on a weekly basis.

The *social-psychological conditions of work* are studied by organizational psychologists. Two extremes of organizational style are *bureaucracy* and *participatory democracy*. Bureaucracies were originally intended to humanize the workplace by decentralizing authority and dividing the work into separate units. However, in operation, bureaucracies have become trapped in the rigidity of their formal structure. They ignore human values and needs, dehumanize workers, and stifle individual and corporate growth and development.

The newer participatory style of organization focuses on human needs and values; it is compatible with the Theory Y view of human nature. It allows workers to participate in decisions that affect their jobs and thus contributes to personal fulfillment.

Within every formal organization, informal groups of workers develop. These groups have their own loyalties and goals, which are often incompatible with the goals of the organization. These informal groups are beyond the control of management, and often beyond its awareness. If recognized and accepted by management, informal groups can help to serve the needs of both workers and the organization; if not, informal groups will frustrate organizational needs.

## SUGGESTED READINGS

Alluisi, E. A., and B. B. Morgan. Engineering psychology and human performance. *Annual Review of Psychology*, 1976, **27,** 305–330.

Bennett, C., and P. Rey. What's so hot about red? *Human Factors*, 1972, **14,** 149–154.

Brookes, M. Office landscape: Does it work? *Applied Ergonomics*, 1972, **3,** 224–236.

Buisman, B. 4–day, 40–hour workweek: Its effects on management and labor. *Personnel Journal*, 1975, **54,** 565–567.

Chapanis, A. *Man–Machine Engineering.* Belmont, Calif.: Wadsworth, 1965.

Davis, H. L. Human factors in industry. *Human Factors*, 1973, **15,** 103–177; 195–268.

Dempsey, D. Noise. *New York Times Magazine*, 1975 (November 23), 31+.

DuBrin, A. J. *Fundamentals of Organizational Behavior: An Applied Perspective.* Elmsford, N.Y.: Pergamon Press, 1974.

Edwards, R. Shift work: Performance and satisfaction. *Personnel Journal*, 1975, **54,** 578–579.

Elving, A., H. Gadon, and J. Gordon. Flexible working hours: It's about time. *Harvard Business Review,* 1974 (January–February), **52,** 18–28, 33, 154–155.

Goleman, Daniel. Oedipus in the board room. *Psychology Today,* 1977 (December), **11,** 45–51, 124–126.

Grayston, D. Music while you work. *Industrial Management,* 1974, **4,** 38–39.

Hackman, J. R. Group influences on individuals. In M. Dunnette, Ed., *Handbook of Industrial and Organizational Psychology.* Chicago: Rand McNally, 1976. Pp. 1455–1525.

Hackman, J. R., E. E. Lawler, and L. W. Porter. *Perspectives on Behavior in Organizations.* New York: McGraw-Hill, 1977.

McCormick, E. *Human Factors in Engineering and Design,* 4th ed. New York: McGraw–Hill, 1976.

Nemecek, J., and E. Grandjean. Results of an ergonomic investigation of large–space offices. *Human Factors,* 1973, **15,** 111–124.

Nord, W., and R. Costigan. Worker adjustment to the four–day week: A longitudinal study. *Journal of Applied Psychology,* 1973, **58,** 60–66.

Payne, R., and D. Pugh. Organizational structure and climate. In M. Dunnette, Ed., *Handbook of Industrial and Organizational Psychology.* Chicago: Rand McNally, 1976. Pp. 1125–1173.

Poor, R. *4 Days, 40 Hours: Reporting a Revolution in Work and Leisure,* rev. ed. Cambridge, Mass.: Bursk and Poor, 1973.

Porter, L. W., and K. Roberts. Communication in organizations. In M. Dunnette, Ed., *Handbook of Industrial and Organizational Psychology.* Chicago: Rand McNally, 1976. Pp. 1553–1589.

Porter, L. W., E. E. Lawler, and J. R. Hackman. *Behavior in Organizations.* New York: McGraw–Hill, 1975.

Starbuck, W. Organizations and their environments. In M. Dunnette, Ed., *Handbook of Industrial and Organizational Psychology.* Chicago: Rand McNally, 1976. Pp. 1069–1123.

Stein, B., A. Cohen, and H. Gadon. Flextime: Work when you want to. *Psychology Today,* 1976 (June), **10,** 40–43, 80.

Stuart, Gary M., and Arthur Guthrie. Alternative workweek schedules: Which one fits your operation? *Supervisory Management,* 1976 (June), **21,** 2–14.

Zawacki, Robert A., and Jason S. Johnson. Alternative workweek schedules: One company's experience with flextime. *Supervisory Management,* 1976 (June), **21,** 15–19.

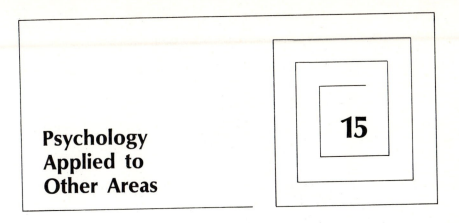

# Psychology Applied to Other Areas

## 15

We have discussed the major and most fully developed areas in which psychology is applied to our everyday lives. There are several other aspects of our lives in which psychology influences us, and we turn to these now. They include psychology applied to sports, behavioral dentistry, traffic safety research, and the behavior of pets and livestock. Either directly or indirectly, we are all affected in some way by the work of psychologists in these areas.

## PSYCHOLOGY APPLIED TO SPORTS

Americans are, in general, a sports-minded people. Sports, games, exercise, and physical fitness are an important part of the daily lives of many of us. Millions jog or run several miles each day. Our tennis courts and golf courses are so crowded on weekends that lines are not unusual.

We flock to the mountains in winter to ski, to the beaches in summer to surf, underwater to scuba dive, and to cliffs for hang gliding. In our public schools and colleges we take courses in physical education in which we learn a variety of games and athletic skills. As children we play in little leagues, and every weekend in our parks we see people of all ages playing touch football, basketball, baseball, volleyball, and soccer.

From childhood to old age we engage in sports. It is not unusual to see people in their seventies running in a long-distance marathon, and in at least one community, St. Petersburg, Florida, there is a baseball team restricted to people over the age of seventy.

Even those of us who do not participate actively in sports may still be affected by them. Watching sports events on prime-time television has become a national pastime, to which people devote many hours

each week. And, as we shall see, we can be influenced by what we are watching.

Thus, sports are not limited to the professional athlete. They are engaged in by millions of other people as well. It should not be surprising, in view of the popularity of sports and exercise, to learn that there is a branch of psychology devoted to the study of sports behavior.

Although the psychology of sport is a relatively new area of psychology, it is growing rapidly and enlisting the enthusiastic support of professionals from other disciplines: physiology, medicine, and physical education. The International Society of Sport Psychology was begun in 1965, and the North American Society of Sport Psychology started a year later. Many journal articles and books have been published, and a growing number of colleges give courses in the area.

Sport psychology covers a broad spectrum of concerns and draws on the findings and techniques of a number of traditional areas of psychology, including learning, motivation, perception, social psychology, personality, mental health, child development, and the treatment of physical and emotional disorders. A typical textbook in sport psychology deals with such diverse areas as the effect of exercise on kidney functioning, physical fitness of the elderly, the effect of feedback on the accuracy of throwing a ball, the effect of stress on athletes, aggression in boxers and wrestlers, athlete–spectator interaction, and the role of exercise in mental health.

The findings of sport psychology are of great importance to coaches and players, providing them with information on how to maximize their performance and minimize the potentially harmful effects of competition and other stresses involved in sport. In addition, the findings are applicable to psychology as a whole because they contribute to psychologists' knowledge of how human beings behave in various situations. Also, the findings are applicable to each of us, professional or amateur, who engages in sports and exercise as a way of making a living or keeping fit, or as a means of reducing the stresses of everyday life.

In our overview of this still young application of psychology, we shall discuss the following areas: the personality and mental health characteristics of athletes, the personality characteristics of coaches, the beneficial effects of sports and exercise, and the effects of sports on spectators.

## Personality and Mental Health Characteristics of Athletes

Knowledge of the personality characteristics of those who engage in a particular sport is of enormous practical value to those who coach and counsel athletes. For example, suppose it were found, through research, that players of a popular college sport were highly dependent individuals who needed constant reassurance about their personal worth and value. Knowing this, coaches could motivate their players by reinforcing them frequently, every time they made a good play or even a good attempt at one.

Let us consider first, however, the mental health of athletes in general and see how it compares with that of nonathletes. It has been found that college varsity athletes experience considerably less anxiety than nonathletes, and are much more dominant as well. Both of these are highly desirable characteristics for athletes to possess. It was also found that women who major in physical education in college are much less neurotic and much more dominant and extraverted than a control group of women who were not majoring in physical education. The women athletes were also high in the needs for achievement, autonomy, and affiliation.

This does not suggest that athletes are totally free of emotional problems; such is not the case. One researcher studied the use of the psychiatric clinic by athletes at Harvard University. Although athletes used the service less than nonathletes, those athletes who did come to the clinic had more problems than the control group of nonathletes. However, most of their problems dealt not with emotional concerns but with worries over their studies. Only about one athlete in four was bothered by anxiety and depression. Many of the athletes in this study were apparently able to handle at least some of their emotional problems through the intense physical activity of the playing field, which is a great benefit of participation in sports and exercise.

An individual sport that has been the subject of a good deal of research is weight lifting, which is very popular among young men in the United States. Weight lifters as a group seem to have more than their share of emotional problems. They are excessively concerned about their feelings of masculinity and tend to be shy people who have little self-confidence. They feel rejected by other people and are extremely dependent, usually on their mother. Perhaps as a result of this mother dependency, they tend toward homosexuality more than heterosexuality, although for the most part, the homosexuality tends to remain latent. In addition, weight lifters are usually hostile to the world at large and have problems coping with their surroundings.

You can readily understand why these people take up weight lifting, and how success in the sport can help them deal with their emotional problems. By developing a highly muscular physique they are attempting to compensate for their feelings of inferiority and masculine inadequacy. By looking extremely virile they can also overcome, or at least deny to themselves, the feelings of femininity that are a source of concern to them.

On the basis of common sense, you may think that boxers and wrestlers are hostile and aggressive people who use their sport as a socially acceptable means of expressing these feelings. This may not be the case, however; once again there is the need to subject commonsense beliefs to experimental test. When boxers and wrestlers were compared with each other and with cross-country runners and nonathletes, the boxers showed the lowest level of aggression. However, the wrestlers showed the highest level of aggression.

One possible explanation for the low level of aggressiveness in boxers is that boxing, certainly the most physically violent of the three sports studied, is an excellent outlet for aggression, allowing a *catharsis* or release of these feelings.

Support for the catharsis explanation was demonstrated in another study of college wrestlers who were tested at three different times: three weeks prior to the beginning of the wrestling season, a few hours before the first match of the season, and the morning after the match. The results showed that although aggressive feelings in wrestlers are high and increased as the match drew closer, they were greatly reduced following the match. This reduction in aggression occurred at the same level whether the match was won or lost, suggesting that it is the sporting activity itself that is cathartic, not necessarily a victory.

Several studies have been conducted on outstanding or champion athletes to see if they differ from athletes of more modest ability. Psychological studies of outstanding performers in other areas of life (for example, in science, business, and the arts), have revealed significant differences in personality between outstanding and average achievers, and so it is in the sports field. For example, champion athletes exhibit high levels of self-confidence (not surprising in view of the recognition they receive for their achievements), high levels of aspiration, and an ability to freely express themselves emotionally; they are not constrained or inhibited. They also demonstrate high levels of anxiety, also not surprising considering the pressure on them to continue to perform at an outstanding level.

Major league baseball players, when compared with players in the minor leagues, are much more ambitious, aggressive, and self-disciplined. However, they also tend to worry more than minor league players.

Another study of the personalities of athletes investigated women athletes who participate in team sports versus those who participate in individual sports. To compete successfully as a member of a group may require different characteristics than competing alone. Also, the choice of participation in a team or an individual sport may reflect certain personality differences and needs; people may choose a team or an individual sport as a way of expressing these needs.

Women who choose individual sports such as diving, riding, and gymnastics are highly independent people who prefer to make their own decisions and who do not need the company of others. They are extremely self-sufficient and dominant, and enjoy (perhaps even need) the attention that is focused on them as individual performers. Women who prefer team sports such as volleyball, relay swimming, or relay running are also self-sufficient, but they are not as self-centered or as introverted as those in individual sports. They are also less dominant and adventurous but tend to be more dependable and reliable.

These examples show clearly that all athletes are not alike in terms of their personality and mental health characteristics. Different sports draw different kinds of participants, and it may follow that they draw different kinds of spectators as well, although the evidence is not yet conclusive. Those of us who watch boxing, for example, may have different personalities from those who watch basketball. You can imagine the impact that definitive findings of this kind would have on designing television advertisements for showing during different sports programs.

## Personality Characteristics of Coaches

Just as the nature of your instructor can make a difference in how well you perform in a college class, so, too, the nature of a coach can influence your performance on the playing field. Coaches, like the players they lead, have unique personality characteristics that distinguish them from people who are not coaches.

First, coaches tend to be highly authoritarian in their leadership roles. In our discussion of business managers in Chapter 13 we noted that many managers are authoritarian but that the organizational climate is shifting to a more democratic leadership style. This is not the case on the playing field. Coaches are, in general, authoritarian, dominant, and aggressive, and they show high levels of organizational and management abilities. The shift toward participatory democracy and the emphasis on sensitivity in human relations that is becoming widespread in business and industry is not taking place in sports. Coaches still lead, direct, even dictate in line with the Theory X rather than the Theory Y approach to leadership.

Male coaches also tend to be very high in the need for achievement, a characteristic also possessed in high degree by business managers. They are competitive, have a strong sense of masculinity, are emotionally stable, and are very sociable. These characteristics support the stereotype of coaches presented on television and in the movies. But there is another set of characteristics that does not agree with that stereotype. Coaches tend not to be very emotionally supportive of others, nor are they high in the need to nurture or take care of their players. They are not very sensitive or sympathetic to others, and they do not favor close interpersonal relationships with others, relationships that would involve dependency and intimacy.

These characteristics give us a picture of coaches as people intent only on achieving and winning, not on supporting, helping, or being personally involved with those they are training. Thus, players may be led and developed as athletes but not as total human beings. Again, this parallels the authoritarian rather than the democratic business manager, and it will be interesting to see if the human relations movement in industrial leadership eventually extends to the world of sport. If so, player performance may well improve, just as worker performance has improved under this system of values in industry.

## Beneficial Effects of Sports and Exercise

Ask any jogger, surfer, skier, or anyone else who participates regularly in some physical activity what it does for them, what they get out of it, and you may be in for a lengthy monologue about how good it makes them feel physically and emotionally. And they are probably not exaggerating because a great deal of research supports these subjective feelings; regular physical exercise is good for you.

We shall discuss the beneficial effects of exercise for the body and the mind. For years, physicians have been urging people to engage in some form of continuing exercise, particularly running, as a way of preventing heart attacks. Indeed, considerable evidence indicates that a sedentary life-style may predispose us to heart disease. Studies show that men whose work is physically active have many fewer heart attacks than those whose work involves no physical activity.

Exercise can improve the body's circulation and respiration and can make us more alert by increasing the oxygen supply to the brain. Exercise can also increase muscle strength and tone, enhance endurance and coordination, and even serve as a relaxant. Regular exercise is an effective means of weight reduction, which is not only healthy physically but mentally as well. Many people who were overweight have reported that their feelings of self-confidence and self-assurance increased dramatically when they lost their excess weight. In short, they felt better about themselves.

Thus, exercise can improve our physical health and prolong our lives. It also has great therapeutic value in treating certain physical disorders. Exercise is a vital part of rehabilitative treatment for persons who have suffered strokes, amputations, nerve injuries, multiple sclerosis, cerebral palsy, and polio. It is valuable for treating less serious disorders, such as lower back pain, hypertension, lumbago, bursitis, and muscle injuries. And, as anyone who has recovered from an operation or a lengthy illness knows, exercise is vital to restoring normal muscle functioning after confinement.

Improvement in or restoration of our physical functioning, as in weight loss or recovery from surgery, also enhances emotional well-being. Our emotional functioning can also be improved more directly through exercise. Studies conducted during World War II demonstrated that increased physical fitness led to a raising of morale, and many studies conducted since then have shown the positive relationship between physical fitness and mental health.

This relationship seems to be especially true for children. Studies show that children with highly developed motor abilities and physical skills are less fearful, shy, withdrawn, and tense than other children, and are socially better adjusted as well. Studies of college students show that those who are higher in physical fitness are better adjusted socially and emotionally.

Success in sports in childhood and adolescence produces a sense of achievement, which, in turn, enhances feelings of self-worth and approval. Such children seem better adjusted emotionally and socially than those who are not successful in sports and other physical activities. Although intense competition at a young age may be harmful to some, it clearly benefits others.

Participation in sports and other physical activities is no guarantee of mental health, of course—it does not render a person immune to emotional problems—but the beneficial effects have been sufficiently documented to conclude that a proper level of physical activity is conducive to improved emotional health.

Exercise and physical activity also have therapeutic value for emotionally disturbed persons, and such programs are often used as a supplement to more traditional therapies. Exercise and physical activity programs have produced noticeable, positive changes in mental patients. For example, patients have shown a reduced level of hyperactivity and aggression, and increased self-confidence, self-esteem, cooperation, emotional control, and contact with reality following such a program.

Exercise programs have been beneficial to psychotics and others whose conditions were so severe that they rarely spoke or took action at all. In one study, these patients were induced to use a punching bag and a basketball, and to engage in other group sports. Afterward, the patients became less aggressive and destructive on the wards, more interested in what was going on around them, and more communicative with each other and with the staff.

The use of dance therapy has also been shown to be beneficial, even with severe psychotics. Many mental patients have great difficulty expressing their emotions verbally but are able to do so through their own spontaneous movements in dance. Whereas social dancing is often used in mental hospitals, modern dance—in which patients express themselves through their own movements instead of following an instructor or a partner in traditional steps—allows for much more freedom and creativity of expression, and thus is more therapeutic. Dance therapy allows patients to express their fears, fantasies, and needs in a symbolic manner which is not as threatening to them as talking about these feelings openly. In addition, through their expressive movements in the company of others, patients receive the recognition and approval that was lacking in their lives. This, in turn, enhances their self-image and improves their ability and willingness to communicate with others.

Swimming is useful in dealing with mental patients. Individual free-style swimming is recommended as well as water games such as volleyball, polo, and racing. The vigorous activity involved in these games apparently serves as a catharsis, by means of which patients can release feelings of aggression and hostility. Swimming therapy also has a calming effect on many patients, reducing the need for tranquilizers and cutting down on the number of disturbances on the wards. Following swimming therapy sessions patients often become less hostile, more alert, and more sociable. In one hospital, outbreaks of violence on the wards were reduced by as much as 75 per cent after the introduction of swimming therapy.

Weight lifting has also been used as a technique of therapy in mental hospitals. We noted earlier that weight lifters tend to be shy people who believe themselves to be inadequate and inferior. Mental patients who suffer from these feelings (especially paranoids) benefit greatly from participation in weight lifting. Their self-image is enhanced as a result of their improved physique, and they experience a genuine sense of achievement and accomplishment. They command not only attention but also admiration from others and become more sociable, particularly with fellow weight lifters. Many patients continue lifting weights long after their release from the hospital, and they attribute much of their improvement to their better appearance and physical fitness.

In the discussion in Chapter 6 of psychology applied to physical health we emphasized the vital interaction between the body and the mind. The studies showing the beneficial effects of sports and exercise on our emotional health reinforce this relationship. Our physical condition definitely affects our mental condition.

## Effects of Sports on Spectators

Watching sports events, whether live or on television or film, has become an American pastime, one that can produce dramatic effects on spectators. Violence among spectators often results from sporting events. Fights have broken out among spectators at high school football games, and in Great Britain and South American countries, full-scale riots frequently follow soccer matches. Apparently, watching violence on the playing field can arouse intense feelings of aggression. Many studies by social psychologists have demonstrated this effect by having subjects watch violence on television and then testing their level of aggression.

In one such study, two groups of college students watched two different films. One film showed a particularly brutal boxing match; the other showed an exciting but nonviolent track meet. Following the films, aggression was determined in the students by measuring their willingness to inflict pain on another person. Those who had watched the box-

ing match showed a considerably higher level of aggression than those who watched the track meet.

It should be noted that late adolescents and young adults are more prone to violence than older people, independent of what they are doing or watching. Nevertheless, in this study, spectators of violence became more violent than spectators of the same age who watched a nonviolent event.

The possibility exists that certain sports, such as boxing, high school football, and soccer, attract people as spectators who already have high levels of aggression; other sports may attract less violent observers. Further, watching certain sports may reduce aggression among spectators. This was demonstrated in a study of spectators at a professional wrestling match. The spectators showed considerably less aggression after the match was over than they had shown before it began. With this sport, and with generally older spectators, watching a violent sport seemed to have the effect of reducing aggressive tendencies.

Sports psychology, although a relatively new branch of psychology, is an important one in terms of its applications to everyday living. Arnold Beisser, a psychiatrist, pointed out that the United States is only the second world power in history to devote such enormous amounts of money and time to organized sport activity. (The first country was ancient Rome, which became fanatically sports conscious during its decline.) "Whether or not the same fate will befall us is a matter of conjecture," wrote Beisser. "Sports are an overwhelming influence in the lives of Americans, and if our society is to progress we must know what we are doing and why." [1]

## PSYCHOLOGY APPLIED TO DENTISTRY

When was the last time you went to the dentist? Did you feel tense and fearful, dreading the visit because of the intense pain you anticipated? If you did, you are like most people in the United States whose instantaneous reaction to the word "dentist" is discomfort and fear. Perhaps you never go to the dentist, or go only when an aching tooth becomes more unbearable than the pain you expect to feel in the dentist's chair. If this is the case, then you are like some 1½ million people in this country, approximately 6 per cent of the population. Dentists seem to have a very negative image, the result of psychological factors and the cause of a great deal of unnecessary tooth and gum disorder.

The sad fact of dental health is that most expensive and painful dental procedures, such as oral surgery, fillings, and tooth replacement, are preventable. We can personally exercise almost total control over our dental health, but only if we have the proper psychological attitude toward dentists and dental care. Thus, the problem of proper dental health is much more emotional than physical in nature.

The most advanced equipment, such as high-speed drills, is worthless if people leave their dental cavities unattended. The simple home techniques for facilitating oral hygiene—regular brushing and the use of dental floss—will prevent no gum disease if people will not take the time to practice them. Changes in attitude are much more important than technological developments.

Thus, you can see the relevance of psychology to dental hygiene. This has been the impetus for the development in recent years of a new area, *behavioral dentistry,* to try to overcome our fear of dentists and to foster more positive attitudes toward dental treatment. Behavioral dentistry combines the talents of dentists and psychologists. Growing numbers of dentists have come to recognize the crucial role of psychological factors and of research and application of psychological findings, and to understand that these can make their work easier. More and more psychologists are finding in behavioral dentistry a new and exciting field in which to apply their research skills, and these efforts can affect the lives of all of us.

Increasing numbers of dental schools are offering courses in psychology and establishing psychological research units, and many articles on

[1] Arnold Beisser, *The Madness of Sport* (New York: Appleton–Century–Crofts, 1967), pp. 13–14.

the applications of psychology are appearing in the dentistry journals. In 1977, the first National Conference on Behavioral Dentistry was held in the United States, evidence of how rapidly the field is growing.

To introduce you to the kinds of work being performed in behavioral dentistry, we shall discuss three areas of application: fear of dentists, pain in the dentist's chair, and techniques to eliminate tooth grinding.

### Fear of Dentists

Most of our fear of dentists derives from our experiences as children in the dental chair. Many of us are conditioned to fear dentists in the same way we learn, as children, to fear other situations and objects. As with other phobias, we carry this fear throughout our lives. Studies of attitudes toward dentists bear this out. Adults who have a strong fear of dentists recall horrible early experiences in the dentist's chair. Adults with no fear of dentists recall their childhood dental visits as being pleasant, or at least not unpleasant.

Obviously, the personality, patience, and behavior of the dentist can be the deciding factor in whether a child grows to adulthood with a passionate fear of dentists and dental procedures. Dentists who take the time and effort to minimize children's anxieties, who are as gentle and painless as possible, can prevent the development of such fears. Children so treated do not learn to dread visits to the dentist and, as

adults, they will be highly likely to undertake the regular checkups so vital to proper oral hygiene.

Psychological techniques of the kind discussed in Chapter 4 on the treatment of mental illness have been used to reduce fear in young children who have not yet been to a dentist. Many children develop such fear prior to their first visit because they have heard horror stories from friends or older brothers and sisters. As a result, the children strongly resist their first dental visit and can become behavior problems even before the dentist looks in their mouth.

*Modeling* (see Chapter 4) is a very successful technique for eliminating fears. By watching another person in the feared situation, either live or on film, and then making progressively closer approaches to the feared object, a person's own fear can be greatly reduced or eliminated completely.

In one study, children were shown a film of a child experiencing a pleasant visit to the dentist. After seeing the film, the children being studied were considerably less afraid of going to a dentist and were much better behaved when they got to the dentist's office.

Thus, fear of dentists can be prevented from developing in children. Can it be cured in adults who have known such fear for most of their lives? Yes. We noted in Chapter 4 that all kinds of phobias in adults have been successfully treated, regardless of their intensity or how long a person has had them.

*Systematic desensitization* has also been used successfully to treat dental fears. In systematic desensitization (again, see Chapter 4), a person is desensitized to fear-producing objects or situations by pairing a state of complete relaxation with the anxiety-producing stimulus. The subject imagines or actually experiences the anxiety-producing situation in small steps, working up a hierarchy from the least feared aspect of the situation to the most feared. The state of relaxation inhibits the anxiety at each step because it is impossible to be both relaxed and anxious at the same time.

In one study, a group of college students who feared dentists were treated by the systematic desensitization technique. First, the desensitization hierarchy was constructed by having each subject rate the fear intensity of each of fourteen items connected with dentists. These items ranged from the sight of the dentist's office to the sound and feel of a dental drill. Next, relaxation training was undertaken in thirty-minute sessions. Then, while relaxed, the subjects were shown the items in the hierarchy successively, until the strongest or most feared item no longer produced any fear.

The ultimate test of this approach was whether or not a subject actually went to a dentist. Of the six subjects studied, four successfully completed their dental treatment and reported that their experiences no longer produced anxiety. The technique was partially successful with a fifth subject, who started but did not complete dental treatment. It was unsuccessful with the sixth subject.

A different technique, designed to *increase pain tolerance*, was then tried on the latter two subjects, both of whom said that their reason for avoiding dental treatment was a low pain threshold. They were treated with progressively stronger electric shocks while in the relaxed state used in the systematic desensitization procedure. The shocks were given in series and were stopped when the subjects said they could not tolerate a stronger one. Each series of shocks started several steps below the maximum shock intensity of the previous series, and in each one the subjects were able to tolerate greater shocks than they had before. After each series, the subjects were given positive reinforcement through praise for having tolerated higher shocks, and they were told that they would probably be able to go even higher the next time. Indeed, their pain tolerance almost tripled. They were told that they could deal with pain in the dentist's chair in the same way they handled it during the experiment, by pairing the relaxation response with the pain. Both subjects were later able to successfully complete their dental treatment.

In sum, our fear of dentists is learned in the same way we learn all fears, and can be eliminated through the use of psychological treatment techniques used to treat other fears.

## Pain in the Dentist's Chair

There is no denying that dental treatment sometimes involves real pain, although pain can be prevented by the use of anesthesia. Although some dental pain is real, there is strong evidence that much of the pain experienced in dental treatment is psychological rather than physical in origin. A lot of the pain is strictly in the mind and exists more in anticipation than in actuality.

In studies of reported pain in the field of dentistry it has been found that younger people expect to feel more pain than they actually experience. People over the age of forty generally anticipate, and experience, considerably less pain. Also, people who have the greatest fear of dentists report feeling the most pain.

Because so much pain in dentistry is psychological in nature and is so strongly associated with fear, it can be alleviated by the techniques discussed in the previous section: modeling, systematic desensitization, and increasing pain tolerance.

We can also minimize such fears on our own, independent of any psychological treatment. Studies of dental patients have found that many invent their own techniques for dealing with the pain, such as consciously constructing elaborate daydreams or concentrating on something else. No doubt you have used this approach yourself in dealing with unpleasant situations. By focusing on something other than the discomfort, you tend to make yourself more relaxed. As noted in the description of the systematic desensitization technique, you cannot be relaxed and anxious at the same time.

## Tooth Grinding

You may be one of the millions of people who grind their teeth, either at night while asleep or during the day while absorbed in other activities. If so, you are suffering from a condition called *bruxism*. Tooth grinding is a serious problem that can lead to a number of difficulties. Grinding can wear away tooth surfaces, crack fillings, and cause pain in the teeth, gums, and face.

Although bruxism can cause extensive dental problems, it cannot be treated by a dentist because the cause is psychological: excessive stress. However, psychologists working in the field of behavioral dentistry can treat and cure tooth grinding by applying the behavior therapy and biofeedback techniques discussed in Chapters 4 and 6.

A portable electromyograph, no larger than a cigarette pack, has been developed which can record the activity of a person's jaw muscles without interfering with normal activities. In this way, the person is made aware of exactly when tooth grinding takes place; we are ordinarily unaware of it. Knowing when tooth grinding occurs can alert the person to the activities or thoughts that precede or trigger it. For example, one person found that he ground his teeth every time he had a meeting with the boss. Knowing the source of the stress can then enable the individual, assisted by a therapist, to learn to deal with the stress-producing situation.

Biofeedback has also been successful in treating bruxism. Through the use of auditory feedback, such as hearing a tone whenever the teeth are being ground, the individual can learn to relax. Through relaxation the patient turns the tone off and soon is able to keep it from coming on. As with the use of biofeedback to treat other stress-induced disorders, in this case the person then learns to sense when tension is mounting without the use of the machine. Thus, tooth grinding can be stopped altogether.

Behavioral dentistry is a new area and there is much yet to be learned about the relationship between psychological factors and dental behavior. The field is growing rapidly and more dentists and psychologists are becoming aware of its importance. The applications to our everyday lives will increase as well.

## PSYCHOLOGY APPLIED TO TRAFFIC SAFETY

Traffic safety affects our lives every day. No one is immune to traffic problems and accidents. Whether we drive a car, ride as a passenger, or try to cross a street on foot, we are all potential victims of accidents. Because traffic safety is so important, it is not surprising that psychologists are deeply involved in it.

The application of psychology to automobile accidents has a long history. Research in the field began in the late 1920s and continues to the present day. In general, psychologists have been involved in three major areas of highway safety—the road, the vehicle, and the driver—and much research has been directed toward the interaction of the human factor (the driver) with the two physical factors.

Recognizing that most automobile accidents (as many as 90 per cent) are caused by human error, a great deal of attention has been focused on the psychological and physical characteristics of drivers, including personality, health, vision, and the effects of drugs, alcohol, and fatigue on driving behavior.

However, traffic safety psychologists also recognize that driver performance is affected by the design of the automobile being driven, the road over which it moves, and the highway signs and signals to which the driver must respond. Thus, the car and driver form a *man–machine system*, discussed in Chapter 14. Driving is a team operation; the driver and the automobile function together. Just as the condition of the driver can affect the performance of the car, so the condition of the car, and the road, can affect the behavior of the driver.

We noted in Chapter 14 that designing man–machine systems to function at maximum effectiveness is the task of engineering psychologists. The principles involved in engineering psychology are essentially the same whether they are applied to an airplane, a computer console, or an automobile. Engineering psychologists have been in the forefront of both research and application in the field of traffic safety and transportation.

Psychologists are also concerned with the study and prevention of accidents in other areas—primarily on the job and in the home. These accidents cause hundreds of thousands of injuries and deaths every year. Psychologists have contributed greatly to the redesign of offices and factories, kitchens and bathrooms, machine tools for industry and power lawn mowers for the home, to give only a few examples, in order to help reduce this staggering accident toll. We discuss here only automobile accidents.

Chapter 2 presented an example of research on highway safety to illustrate the method of systematic or *naturalistic observation*. In that study, driver behavior in response to a stop sign or a blinking red light was compared. The *automobile simulator* was also described. In this technique for studying driver behavior a subject drives a stationary car with the road conditions presented on film under the well-controlled conditions of the experimental laboratory. Both of these methods were employed in the studies described in this section. The *correlational method* is also used extensively in studies of driver safety; usually, personality test results are correlated with driving behavior.

We shall discuss the three major areas of highway safety: the road, the automobile, and the driver.

## The Road

No doubt you already have some idea of how roads can be changed to improve driver behavior. If you have ever driven along one of the older highways in the United States and then on the modern interstate highway system, the differences between them are readily apparent. The newer controlled-access highways are designed to handle the increasing number of cars on the road and the greater speeds at which they are capable of traveling. They are wider, flatter, and straighter than the old highways, which were marked by sharp curves and hills. Modern highways are divided by a median strip to reduce the possibility of a head-on collision.

Because of these improvements, interstate highways have lower accident tolls than other roads and so are safer and easier to drive as well as being less fatiguing and faster. They show clearly how driver behavior can be improved and the accident rate reduced by the design of the road.

Another aspect of road design that affects driver safety is the visibility and legibility of street and highway signs and other traffic control devices. Drivers receive a great deal of vital information from these signs, information that can save our lives if we see the signs in time, interpret the meaning quickly, and respond with the proper action.

A sign informing us of a dangerous curve ahead alerts us to this change in road conditions and tells us that we should slow down to drive safely through the curve. If the sign were not there, if we did not notice it, or if we noticed it but ignored it, we would probably come upon the curve at too high a speed to negotiate it safely.

Psychologists who study human perceptual abilities have provided us with a great deal of useful research results which have been applied to the size, shape, and design of highway signs. This work dates back to the early 1930s, and we can see its impact every time we drive a car.

Factors that affect road sign legibility include the shape and size of the letters on the sign, the contrast between the color of the letters and the color of the background, letter height, the ratio between height and width, the amount of space between the letters, and the amount of space that separates one line of letters from another. By showing people different versions of road signs for a brief period of time (sometimes just a fraction of a second), psychologists have been able to determine how quickly people can understand the information presented on different kinds of signs. Speed of identification is a crucial factor in the design of highway signs because when we are traveling at a high rate of speed, we may have only a second or two to read and understand a sign.

A few of the findings of this research are as follows. Black letters on either a yellow or a white background are the quickest and easiest to read because of the stark contrast. The most readily identifiable letters are those for which letter width is from 15 to 25 per cent of letter height. The distance at which words can be easily read ranges from 50 to 65 feet for each inch of letter height.

Techniques have been developed to calculate the precise letter size needed for roads with different speed limits. Larger letters are needed for a high-speed freeway than for a low-speed city street. Also, signs on high-speed roads have to be placed farther in advance of the condition they are indicating because faster drivers require more time to react to the information being presented.

Some studies have shown that signs located to the side of the road are more readily perceived than those placed above the road, especially when driving at night. When signs are illuminated with floodlights, however, both locations are equally effective.

Traffic signs are coded by shape and color to indicate different functions. Warning signs are diamond-shaped with a yellow background. Regulatory signs, such as those that give speed limits, are rectangular in shape with a white background. Stop signs are octagonal and red in color; yield signs are triangular.

Psychologists also study traffic lights. Almost always, the red light appears above the green light. This is to help drivers who are colorblind; they are able to tell by the position of the light which signal is on. As another aid to colorblind drivers, the red and green lights have other colors mixed with them, blue in the green light and yellow in the red light.

Traffic psychologists have conducted research on the brightness level and size of traffic lights. Partly as a result of their efforts, many cities are switching to a larger lens for traffic signals because studies show that an increase of 4 inches in the diameter of the lens significantly increases driver attention.

Research on the design of roads and traffic indicators is continuing. It is possible that this area of application of psychology may one day save your life.

## The Automobile

Engineering psychologists have been involved in the design of automobiles, primarily to increase safety. Their efforts focus on two major concerns: reducing the chances of collision, and reducing the chances of injury and death once a collision has occurred.

Psychologists have worked to reduce the chances of a collision by striving to increase visibility so that drivers are better able to see what is going on around their vehicle. Psychologists have also worked to improve the design of the instrument panel and driving controls so that information such as speed can be quickly and accurately determined and controls can be operated easily.

To minimize injury and death from a collision, psychologists have been concerned with aspects of car design such as padding and recessing hard or sharp surfaces, providing collapsible steering wheels, and introducing passive restraint systems such as seat belts, shoulder harnesses, and air bags. Psychologists are interested in changing attitudes toward seat belts so that more people will use them. Because relatively few people use seat belts, a warning signal was made to sound when the seat belts were not fastened.

We know that engineering psychologists have long been involved in the design of workplaces so as to maximize the efficiency and safety of the worker. There is a natural carryover of functions from industry to driving because the driver's seat, instrument panel, and controls constitute a workplace. The principles and techniques for designing displays and controls in industry are applicable to the design of cars (see Chapter 14). For example, measurements of the human body, undertaken by the field of human *anthropometry,* are useful in designing the driver's workplace and are applied as the basis for seating and for ensuring that controls are within easy reaching distance and displays within easy viewing distance.

Another aspect of engineering psychology related to the design of the driver's workplace is the way in which information is presented. Modern cars contain buzzers, warning lights, and dials that provide information which must be received and interpreted quickly and accurately. Visual displays of this information may be quantitative (such as the precise numerical reading of a speedometer), qualitative (such as the engine temperature gauge), or of the simple go/no go type (such as the brake warning light).

Warning lights are used frequently in automobiles. Engineering psychologists have determined that warning lights must be bright enough and contrast sufficiently with the background to attract immediate attention. They must be centrally located within the driver's field of vision, not off to one side or hidden behind the steering wheel. Flashing warning lights attract attention more quickly than continuous warning lights.

Psychologists are concerned with the optimum shape and size of numbers and letters used in instrument panel displays, the contrast with the background, and the level of illumination. These involve considerations similar to the problems in the proper design of highway signs.

Another design aspect of the driver's workplace is the various controls by which an automobile is operated: gas pedal, brake, clutch, steering wheel, light switch, heating and air conditioning systems, windshield wiper switch, and so on. These pedals, knobs, levers, switches, and the like must be designed for ease and speed of identification and operation.

Modern automobiles, especially those imported from European countries, use symbols on the controls to indicate their purpose. For example, a tiny headlight is pictured on the light switch and a windshield wiper on the windshield wiper switch. Such coding devices enable us to find the right switch quickly when driving a strange car where the location of the controls may differ from that in our own car. The advantages of coding controls was first demonstrated by engineering psychologists in the design of aircraft instrument panels. Coding is now used in automobiles, farm machinery, heavy construction equipment, and other vehicles that have a number of controls to use.

The specific placement of some controls and the amount of force needed to operate them is also a crucial design consideration, particularly with accelerator and brake pedals. The accelerator or gas pedal must be placed so that the foot and ankle of the driver will not become cramped or stiff when maintaining a steady speed on a highway. Psychological research has shown that the optimum position for the gas pedal keeps the foot resting at a 90-degree angle to the leg. For the most efficient operation, the gas pedal should move through an arc of no more than 20 degrees when depressed all the way to the floor.

The foregoing is intended only as a sample of the highly technical research being conducted by engineering psychologists on automobile design. Their work involves considerable knowledge of human perceptual and motor abilities, and the results are apparent in our cars, which today are easier and safer to drive than ever before.

## The Driver

The majority of accidents are caused by the human element—you, the driver. Although research on highway and automobile design has reduced the likelihood of accidents, and of injury or death once an accident has occurred, highway safety still remains a serious problem. Until drivers are "improved" or "redesigned" as highways and cars have been, the accident toll will remain high.

Psychologists are aware that people change when they get behind the wheel of an automobile. Otherwise decent, considerate, thoughtful people often become hostile, aggressive, and careless when they drive. Why? What causes such drastic changes in behavior?

We do not yet have the complete answer, but two highly promising theories relate to the effects of stress and the driver's personality. Driving today, whether on crowded city streets or fast-moving freeways, is certainly a stressful activity. Studies have shown that commuting to and from work by car is the most stressful part of the day for workers, even for those already in high-pressure, high-stress jobs.

Not everyone reacts to stress in the same way; some people can handle or control it better than others. Some are not visibly affected by stress, whereas others undergo a complete change of behavior as a result of stress. It may be that some personality types are less resistant to stress than others. Put these people behind the wheel of a car and they change under the pressure, giving vent to latent aggression and hostility that they never display in other situations.

Driving a car also gives some personality types a feeling of power over others, causing them to maneuver the vehicle as if it were an extension of themselves. The car comes to be a powerful weapon in their hands, perhaps giving them a feeling of grandeur. The car may also in-

crease their personal space bubble (discussed in Chapter 7). Their personal space now extends beyond the dimensions of the car rather than merely their own body, and any intrusion into this extended personal space—say by another car cutting too close in front—is taken as a personal intrusion or attack.

Thus, the personality of the driver may be crucial, and many studies have been conducted on the relationship between personality and accidents. When the personality characteristics of persons who are involved in a number of accidents are compared with the personality characteristics of persons who have few or no accidents, several findings have been demonstrated. High accident groups tend to be anxious, aggressive, impulsive, socially maladjusted, dependent, egocentric, and poorly tolerant of stress and tension.

At first glance, these seem to be important findings that would enable us to readily identify high-risk drivers. If such people could be identified as being accident-prone, they could be denied driver's licenses or urged to seek counseling to reduce their accident proneness.

However, the situation is not so simple as it initially appears, for two reasons. First, the correlations between personality characteristics and accidents are low, providing suggestive but not conclusive evidence that some people are more prone to have accidents than others. Second, the people who seem to be accident-prone do not have the same frequency of accidents all the time. Thus, neither the personality tests nor a driver's accident history can accurately predict future accidents.

In fact, there may be no such thing as an accident-prone person. Consider the following study. The driving records of nearly 30,000 people were examined for a six-year period, and it was found that fewer than 4 per cent of them were responsible for over 36 per cent of the accidents that occurred. Based on these data, it seems obvious that if that 4 per cent of the drivers were kept off the roads, the accident rate would be reduced by more than one-third. However, when the same statistics were reanalyzed by comparing the accident records for the first three-year period with the second three-year period, a different finding emerged. The same drivers were *not* involved in accidents in both periods. Those who had no more than one accident during the first three-year period had more than 96 per cent of the accidents during the second period. If those who had most of the accidents during the first period did so because they were accident-prone (based on their personality characteristics), then they should have also had the majority of the accidents during the second period; they did not.

Such findings do not mean that personality characteristics play no part in automobile accidents. They are still a factor but apparently only as a function of the temporary state of tension and stress under which a person is operating while driving. One of the personality characteristics, noted earlier, associated with accidents is a low tolerance of stress and tension. Therefore, stress seems to be the major contributing factor in accidents, and some people, because of their personality characteristics, are less able to handle stress than others.

One study that supports the role of stress in automobile accidents involved the use of the Social Readjustment Rating Scale of life stress events described in Chapter 6. Persons who scored high on this scale (those who were subject to more stress) were far more likely to develop a physical illness than those who scored low. Those who score high may also be involved in a greater number of accidents, although the results are suggestive rather than conclusive.

The search to pinpoint the relationship between personality and accidents is continuing, and the difficulties may be less with the hypothesis that personalities are related to accidents than with the complexities of measuring the human personality. Research is complicated and sometimes frustrating, but the outcome in terms of the effect on the lives of all of us is great.

Psychologists have had greater success in demonstrating the relationship between accidents and other personal and physical qualities of drivers. With the factor of age, for example, the evidence seems conclusive that both old and young drivers are more likely to be involved in accidents than those in the middle age range. Also, the types of driving violations differ with age. Speeding is the most frequent violation among young drivers, which makes them the most dangerous group on the road and explains why their insurance premiums are the highest of any group. Old drivers characteristically commit violations involving going through stop signs, passing improperly, and failing to yield the right-of-way.

Despite the stereotype that women are poor drivers, studies show no differences between the sexes in terms of accident rate. There is a relationship between accidents and amount of education; the highest accident rate occurs among those with the least amount of education.

A driver's physical condition also influences driving behavior. Poor eyesight is the most obvious factor. Also, certain diseases are associated with a high accident rate. One study showed that drivers with diabetes, epilepsy, and heart trouble were involved in many more accidents than a control group of people free of these disorders.

It is well known that drinking and driving do not mix. Excessive drinking is associated with one-third to one-half of all accidents. It is also suspected that drug use is a growing cause of accidents. Tranquilizers, antihistamines, pep pills, downers, LSD, and marijuana all seem capable of affecting alertness, reaction time, and general sensory-motor coordination, which, in turn, increases our vulnerability to accidents.

These findings on the relationship between personal and physical characteristics and accidents have been applied to reduce accidents. Virtually every state requires an eye examination in order to get a driver's license. Persons with poor vision have certain restrictions placed on their licenses: for example, forbidding them to drive without wearing corrective lenses or forbidding them to drive at night. Many states test older drivers on vision, knowledge of safe driving practices, and actual driving behavior every few years, and refuse to continue licensing those whose driving skills or vision have deteriorated below a certain level. Level of education is used in at least one state to determine the minimum age at which a person is allowed to drive. Some European countries, notably Sweden, have tough laws against drivers who drink alcoholic beverages. By taking away the licenses of these drivers, these countries have dramatically reduced the number of highway fatalities.

This approach to changing the human element in automobile driving is based on identifying certain characteristics of poor drivers. Another approach to altering driving behavior is driver training, and it is used primarily in two situations: in the public schools to teach driving skills, and as an attempt to rehabilitate people with a record of traffic offenses.

Driver education in the public schools seemed to produce highly positive results at first. Early studies showed that those who took driver education courses had many fewer accidents and traffic violations than those who did not learn to drive by means of these formal training procedures. Later, more sophisticated research that controlled more of the variables in driving behavior has not produced such optimistic results. Indeed, current findings show no differences between graduates of driver education courses and nongraduates. The problem is not with the idea of formally teaching the proper skills and attitudes involved in driving, but in determining precisely what is to be taught and the most efficient means of teaching it. These questions can only be answered by additional research.

The other approach to driver training, rehabilitating people with poor driving records, has had better results. A number of states require attendance at such courses for all those who accumulate a certain number of points for traffic offenses. Both traffic violations and accident rates decline following such training.

Safe driving depends primarily on you, the driver, but the application of psychology also plays a major role in determining your safety behind the wheel of your car.

## PSYCHOLOGY APPLIED TO PETS AND LIVESTOCK

One of the most recent and unusual applications of psychology to everyday living is the use of psychological principles and techniques to change the behavior of problem or "neurotic" pets, and to influence the behavior of farm animals to increase their productive yields.

Psychologists have been studying animals for decades and have learned a great deal about their behavior and physiology, knowledge which has increased our understanding of ourselves. Indeed, the study of animals, from flatworms and rats to chimpanzees, has provided considerable information about human functioning, and large numbers of researchers work in this area of psychology. The physiology and biochemistry of some of the higher animals are similar to our own, and animals can be subjected to experimental procedures which, because of their length and potential danger, cannot be used with human subjects. Animals are used as subjects in basic research on such topics as learning, perception, and motivation, and the white rat learning its way through a maze is a common sight in many psychology laboratories.

Instead of studying animals, the new area of applied psychology attempts to treat or cure their problems by altering their behavior in some way. Although the number of pet and farm psychologists is small, both fields have tremendous potential for growth.

## Pet Psychology

As many as one-third of the people in the United States have a dog or a cat as a pet, and these pets serve an important therapeutic purpose for their owner. Pets can provide companionship and affection for the lonely, ego enhancement for those whose feelings of self-esteem are low (particularly through the ownership of a pedigreed pet), and a feeling of power for those who feel weak. In brief, pets can satisfy many human needs.

But pets can also cause problems, both for owners and for those who must come in contact with the pet. A dog that barks throughout the night interferes with the neighbors' sleep, a dog or cat that fouls a nearby yard violates the neighbors' sense of territoriality, and a dog that has a tendency to bite people is an obvious menace. It is to correct such problem behaviors that pet psychologists have come into practice.

The primary techniques used by pet psychologists are various forms of behavior therapy, of the kinds discussed in Chapter 4 for use with people. Many of these behavior modification techniques derived from research on animals, so it is not surprising that they can be used to treat them.

Two pet psychologists have described some of their problem patients and the techniques they used to eliminate the undesirable behaviors.[2] Consider the case of Higgins, a giant 110-pound sheepdog. Higgins went berserk every time there was a thunderstorm, knocking down anybody

[2] David S. Tuber and David Hothersall, "Behavior Modification Hath Charms to Soothe the Savage Beast," *Psychology Today*, **8** (April 1975), 80–82.

or anything in his path as he tried to get away from the noise. The psychologists desensitized Higgins's fear by playing a tape-recorded thunderstorm at increasing levels of loudness. First the noise was very soft and Higgins was rewarded with candy for lying down and remaining calm. Gradually, the sound was increased, and each time Higgins was rewarded in the same way for remaining calm. Punishment for not remaining calm was never used. After five training sessions Higgins remained calm during a very loud tape-recorded thunderstorm.

It was essential that the dog's owner participate in the training and take over once the sessions with the psychologists had ended. Every time there was a thunderstorm the owner rewarded Higgins in the same way, until finally the dog was no longer upset by these previously disturbing sounds.

Such behavior modification techniques have been used to stop animals from biting, barking excessively, and destroying household objects. They have also been used to teach pets and young children to get along together, in this case modifying the behavior of both pet and child.

## Farm Psychology

Through the use of behavior modification and other psychological techniques, the breeding, eating, and producing habits of farm animals have been changed to increase the profit of the farmers. For example, by speeding up the day and night cycles of sheep, the animals' reproductive cycles were accelerated, vastly increasing mating time. As a result, more lambs were produced in the same period of time.

Another application of psychology to farm animals involved cows, which were induced to give more milk by changing the order in which they were milked. Like many other animals, cows establish a hierarchy of dominance; one cow emerges as the leader of the others. It is the dominant cow that always leads the others into the barn from the pasture. By milking the most dominant cow first, in view of the others, and then milking the rest of the herd in order of dominance, all the cows gave greater amounts of milk. Psychologists are not certain why this technique is so effective, but it does enable dairy farmers to reap higher profits at no additional cost.

Farm psychologists have also helped dairy farmers in selecting cows to purchase. By counting the number of bites a cow takes per day (the average is 36,000) and correlating that with the amount of milk produced, psychologists have determined that cows which bite more produce more. Therefore, farmers should choose rapid biters, for they are the most productive cows.

Farmers often unknowingly reduce the amount of milk their cows give by interfering with the cows' digestion. After grazing, cows like to chew their cud, which helps them digest their food. Proper digestion takes a certain amount of time, and if the cows are disturbed before that time they will give less milk.

There is a great deal yet to be learned about pet and farm psychology, but you can see from these examples the potential importance of this field in our everyday lives.

## SUMMARY

*Sport psychology* is a rapidly growing area of application of psychology which draws upon a number of current areas and has ramifications for players, coaches, and spectators of all kinds of sports, both professional and amateur. Four areas of sport psychology were discussed: personality and mental health characteristics of athletes, personalities of coaches, beneficial effects of sports and exercise, and effects of sports on spectators.

The personality and mental health characteristics of athletes differ from those of nonathletes. Athletes experience less anxiety and are more dominant. Women athletes are less neurotic, more extraverted, and higher on the need for achievement than women who are not athletes. Women athletes in individual sports are independent, self-sufficient, and dominant; those who participate in group sports are less dominant but tend to be more dependable and reliable. Weight lifters show excessive concern about their masculinity and are shy, lacking in self-confidence, and dependent. Their sport helps them compensate for these feelings. Boxers are less aggressive than wrestlers and nonathletes. Wrestlers have a very high level of aggression. This aggression is reduced following a match, suggesting that the sport serves as a catharsis or release for strong emotions. Major league baseball players are more ambitious, aggressive, and self-confident than minor league players.

Studies of the personality characteristics of coaches show that they are highly authoritarian, dominant, aggressive, and have high levels of management and organizational abilities. They are also high in the need for achievement, competitiveness, feelings of masculinity, and emotional stability. However, they are not sensitive or sympathetic to others, nor do they favor close interpersonal relationships.

Beneficial effects of sports and exercise include improvements in circulation, respiration, muscle strength and tone, and weight loss. Exercise programs are valuable in rehabilitating victims of strokes, amputations, nerve injuries, multiple sclerosis, and polio, and in aiding patients recovering from surgery or a long confinement in bed.

Exercise and sports enhance emotional functioning, increasing feelings of self-worth and approval, and are used in the treatment of the mentally ill. Regular exercise, sports and games, and dance and swimming therapies help mental patients express their feelings, gain recognition and approval, and improve their ability to communicate with others.

Some of the effects of sports on spectators include arousing aggression in younger fans of violent sports and reducing aggression in older fans.

*Behavioral dentistry* attempts to overcome our fear of dentists and to develop more positive attitudes toward dentistry. To help overcome the fear of dentists, psychologists have used *modeling,* in which a person watches someone else in the feared situation; *systematic desensitization,* in which a state of complete relaxation is paired with the fear-producing situation; and methods to *increase pain tolerance,* in which a state of relaxation is paired with progressively stronger electric shocks. Pain in the dentist's chair seems to be at least as much psychological as physical, and has been successfully treated by the same techniques. Tooth grinding, which is very harmful to oral hygiene, results from excessive stress and can be cured by the use of behavior therapy and biofeedback.

Psychology applied to *traffic safety* is concerned with the road, the automobile, and the driver. Conditions of the road greatly affect highway safety, and psychologists have been involved in the design of street and highway signs and other traffic control devices. By studying factors that affect sign legibility, psychologists have greatly increased the speed and accuracy of reading highway signs.

Engineering psychologists are involved in the design of the automobile to reduce the chances of collision and of injury or death once a collision has occurred. Through their efforts, visibility has been increased and various safety features, such as padding and recessing sharp surfaces, have been introduced.

The driver's seat and instrument panel constitute a workplace, and many of the same principles used to design industrial workplaces have been applied to the design of the car. Human anthropometry is applied so that seats, controls, and displays can be designed to match human measurements. Displays and controls are designed in accordance with the principles of engineering psychology for ease and speed of reading and operating.

The majority of automobile accidents are caused by the driver, and psychologists have studied the relationship between personality and accidents. Drivers who have accidents have been shown to be anxious, aggressive, impulsive, socially maladjusted, dependent, egocentric, and poorly tolerant of stress. However, the correlations between personality factors and accidents are low. People once thought to be accident-prone do not have the same frequency of accidents all the time. Accidents are more a function of the temporary state of stress the driver is under, and how he or she copes with that stress. Other variables associated with accidents are age (older and younger drivers have more accidents than middle-aged drivers), physical condition (especially poor vision), and alcohol consumption.

Driver education is no more effective in teaching safe driving skills and attitudes to new drivers than less formal procedures, but is effective in rehabilitating people with poor driving records.

Psychology applied to *pets and livestock* is a new area of application that attempts to change the behavior of animals. Pets who misbehave have been cured of their problem behavior through the behavior modification techniques used so successfully with people. Farm animals have been made more productive through the application of various psychological findings and techniques.

## SUGGESTED READINGS

### Sports

Feder, E., and B. Feder. Dance therapy. *Psychology Today*, 1977 (February), **10**, 76–80.

Furlong, W. B. Psychology on the playing fields. *Psychology Today*, 1976 (July), **10**, 40–41.

Kenyon, Gerald S., Ed. *Contemporary Psychology of Sport: Proceedings of the Second International Congress of Sport Psychology, Washington, D.C., 1968*. Chicago: Athletic Institute, 1970.

Morgan, William P., Ed. *Contemporary Readings in Sport Psychology*. Springfield, Ill.: Charles C Thomas, 1970.

Stein, Thomas A., and H. Douglas Sessoms. *Recreation and Special Populations*, 2nd ed. Boston: Holbrook Press, 1977.

Suinn, R. M. Body thinking: Psychology for Olympic champs. *Psychology Today*, 1976 (July), **10**, 38–43.

Whiting, H. T. A., Ed. *Readings in Sports Psychology*. Lafayette, Ind.: Balt, 1972.

### Dentistry

Kleinknecht, Ronald A., Robert K. Klepac, and Douglas A. Bernstein. Psychology and dentistry: Potential benefits from a health care liaison. *Professional Psychology*, 1976, **7**, 585–592.

Klepac, Robert K. Successful treatment of avoidance of dentistry by desensitization or by increasing pain tolerance. *Journal of Behavior Therapy and Experimental Psychiatry*, 1975, **6**, 307–310.

Wroblewski, Phillip F., Theodore Jacob, and Lynn P. Rehm. The contribution of relaxation to symbolic modeling in the modification of dental fears. *Behaviour Research and Therapy*, 1977, **15**, 113–115.

### Traffic Safety

Conley, John A., and Russell Smiley. Driver licensing tests as a predictor of subsequent violations. *Human Factors*, 1976, **18**, 565–573.

Dewar, Robert E., Jerry G. Ellis, and Glen Mundy. Reaction time as an index of traffic sign perception. *Human Factors,* 1976, **18,** 381–391.

Human factors in highway transportation. *Human Factors,* 1976, **18.** [four special issues: June, August, October, and December]

McGuire, Frederick L. Personality factors in highway accidents. *Human Factors,* 1976, **18,** 433–441.

Marek, Julius, and Terje Sten. *Traffic Environment and the Driver: Driver Behavior and Training in International Perspective.* Springfield, Ill.: Charles C Thomas, 1977.

Older, S. John, and Brian R. Spicer. Traffic conflicts—A development in accident research. *Human Factors,* 1976, **18,** 335–349.

Selzer, Melvin L., and Amiram Vinokur. Role of life events in accident causation. *Mental Health and Society,* 1975, **2,** 36–54.

Witt, Harald, and Carl G. Hoyos. Advance information on the road: A simulator study of the effect of road markings. *Human Factors,* 1976, **18,** 521–532.

## Pets and Livestock

Gustavson, Carl R., and John Garcia. Aversive conditioning: Pulling a gag on the wily coyote. *Psychology Today,* 1974 (August), **8,** 68–72.

Tuber, David S., and David Hothersall. Behavior modification hath charms to soothe the savage beast. *Psychology Today,* 1975 (April), **8,** 80–82.

Watson, Peter. Animal behavior and farm profits: Boss cows and sleepy, sexy sheep. *Psychology Today,* 1975 (December), **9,** 93–94.

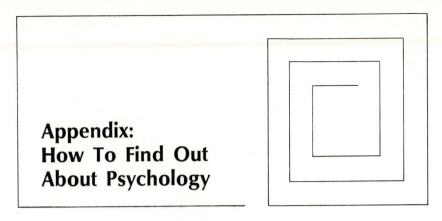

# Appendix:
# How To Find Out
# About Psychology

**Prepared by Sydney Schultz, M.L.S.**

Frank was frantic. The term paper was due in two weeks, and the professor kept asking for his topic. He knew generally what he wanted to write about—something on behavior therapy, which the professor had lectured on. The topic interested him, but he didn't know how to find out anything about it.

He asked a friend who was a psychology major, but the friend shrugged and said, "I don't know. Try *Psych Abstracts,* I guess." Frank had never heard of *Psych Abstracts,* but he didn't want to confess his ignorance. "OK, thanks," he said.

He asked his professor in the psychology department. She told him to search the literature. "What literature?" Frank asked. "The literature," the professor answered brusquely, "in the library. It's all there. Everything you need."

Frank realized that he would have to go to the library and search out this mysterious thing called "the literature."

## WHAT IS THE LITERATURE THE PROFESSOR KEEPS TALKING ABOUT?

Professionals in any field, whether they are conducting research or applying research findings to real-world problems, write up their ideas, activities, results, and conclusions and publish them. In brief, this is *the literature.*

In psychology, much of the literature is published in *journals.* Journals may deal with general or specialized topics, and they contain articles of several types. Journals are issued at various times—some weekly, some monthly, and others only a few times a year. Sometimes they are called "periodicals," "serials," or "magazines."

A journal article reporting *original research* describes the problem being studied, the author's hypothesis, the methods and the subjects used (for example, college students, factory workers, or pigeons), the results of the research (the *data*), and how these data support or fail to support the hypothesis. Sometimes the author offers suggestions for additional research to be undertaken on the problem.

Research reports sponsored by government agencies, private foundations, or university research laboratories may be published in mimeographed form as *technical reports* rather than as journal articles. These reports are distributed to professionals who are interested in the problem being studied; others can obtain copies by writing to the researchers.

Psychologists often write *literature review* articles in which they examine most or all of the journal articles and reports available on a particular topic, comparing the findings and drawing general conclusions. The studies considered are listed at the end of the review in a *bibliography*. Literature reviews are particularly useful for term papers.

Some writers offer *theoretical* articles that try to account for certain research findings or behaviors. They provide a framework of formal propositions that must be tested by conducting new research studies.

There are also *commentaries* or *general* articles on topics of current interest. Sometimes these are published in *newsletters* rather than journals.

Approximately forty thousand articles of all types are published in English-language psychology journals each year. Most of these are written by psychologists who work in the United States.

In addition to this mass of journal articles, psychologists write textbooks, histories, biographies, and monographs (scholarly works on specific topics). They compile books of readings and sourcebooks containing selections from the writings of others, make films and tapes, prepare psychological tests, edit reference books, and hold conferences and meetings, publishing the lectures and papers presented at them. Most graduate students in psychology publish their doctoral dissertations. These are all part of *the literature*.

How is it possible to find what you want out of all these piles of paper? Reference books, which organize the material and give you access to it, and your friendly reference librarian are the keys.

## WHO NEEDS IT?

Who needs the literature and the reference books and the librarian's assistance? Everybody who is interested in psychology! No one can possibly read everything in the published literature, no matter how dedicated they are. To keep up with the psychological literature today, a person would have to read approximately 110 journal articles and books every day of the year.

But anyone interested in any area of psychology needs to be able to uncover the information contained in the published literature. A professor needs access to this information to keep lectures up to date. A researcher needs to be aware of new theories that may suggest additional research studies and must make sure that a planned experiment is not simply a repeat of work someone else has already done satisfactorily. An applied psychologist needs to know about efforts made to apply psychology to similar problems, such as developing a selection program in industry for minority-group employees or treating a patient with symptoms of depression in a clinic.

Students, like Frank in our example, need to search the literature to answer questions, prepare term papers, study for exams, clarify problems presented in class, or read about a topic that interests them whether it is behavior therapy, sports psychology, or the effects of human behavior on houseplants.

It is important to remember, as has been stressed throughout this book, that whatever the problem you are trying to solve, you must consider the results of carefully conducted psychological research and not rely on common sense or speculation, which so often is incorrect and misleading. Therefore, you need to be able to find your way through the psychological literature.

## WHAT DO YOU REALLY WANT TO KNOW?

So you are now ready to search the literature. To find out what reference books you need to use, you must decide what you really want to know. Try to determine, as specifically as possible, what your interests are, then ask a librarian for assistance in locating the materials you will need to use.

Librarians understand your research problems and are sensitive to your need for information. They have a vast and effective collection of tools and skills to help you, but you must meet them halfway. You should have your topic firmly in mind or, if you are still groping for an idea, you should try to be precise so that the librarian can ask you questions to help clarify your thinking. You don't want to be like the legendary student who said, "Just point me toward the psychology books and I'll find what I want," when what the student really wanted was a biography of Sigmund Freud.

Here's an example of an encounter between a librarian and a college freshman that took place at a large university library in Florida. The library has an extensive collection of materials about the state.

Student: Good morning, ma'am. I want everything you have on Florida.

Librarian: Of course. Is there any particular book you have in mind?

Student: Oh no, just bring me everything you have. I can find what I want.

Librarian: It might save time if we knew what field you are interested in—Florida history? Politics? Biography?

Student: No, not exactly.

Librarian: Perhaps some unusual features of Florida—Silver Springs? Alligators? Claude Kirk?

Student: No—what I actually want is a book with lots of pictures in it.

Librarian: Of course! Seminole Indian headdress? Fort San Marco? Bok Tower?

Student: What I want is a picture of a cypress tree.[1]

How do you decide what you really want to know? Consider the following points.

1. Try to express the essence of your topic in one or two sentences. What special terms are associated with the topic? What individuals, by name?

2. Examine all aspects of the problem. Is the topic too broad? Narrow it if necessary. Again, be as specific as possible.

3. Is there a time limit on the material you need? Do you want books and articles published within the last five years or the last fifty years?

4. Is there a limitation by type of experimental subject? Are you interested in research on both humans and animals? If humans, are you interested in children, college students, factory workers, drivers, consumers, mental patients, males, females, elderly people, or everybody?

5. Do you want research performed only in the United States? If you are studying work satisfaction of U. S. employees, for example, you do not want to spend time reading studies conducted on workers in Australia or Sweden.

6. Can you use material published in languages other than English?

7. How thorough are you trying to be? Do you want to find as many books and articles as possible, a few representative studies, a review article or two, a bibliography, or perhaps only a general book?

8. Do you know of any related topics that might also be useful to research?

9. How soon do you need the material? Do you want everything today, in two weeks, or by the end of the term?

To return to Frank for a moment, he now knows that he cannot do a term paper on everything related to behavior therapy. The field is too

[1] Florence Denmark, "Letters: Coping with the 'Clam'," *Library Journal*, November 1, 1972, pp. 3517–3518.

big for him to attempt that. He has to narrow his topic. He looked over the lecture notes from his psychology class on behavior therapy and decided to focus on one behavior therapy technique (systematic desensitization) with one phobia it is used to treat (fear of heights). By clarifying and limiting the topic, the literature search and the amount of material he has to cope with are made much more manageable, and his discussion of the topic in the term paper will be more thorough.

## SO THIS IS THE LIBRARY. WHAT'S IN IT FOR YOU?

Your library probably has guidebooks or pamphlets that tell you about the library's special features, the location and layout of the various areas, the policy on circulation, and the hours of service. Some libraries conduct tours or courses about library use.

The library is organized into several departments. Some of these are concerned with behind-the-scenes work such as selecting the books to purchase, preparing the cards for the catalog, and printing tiny numbers on the spine of each book. The departments important to you as a user of the library are reference, books, periodicals, microforms and media, government documents, and special collections.

### REFERENCE

The reference department—usually a large area or room containing the catalog, sets of books at long tables, and bookshelves full of large, heavy volumes that you are not allowed to take home—is the heart of the library and the place to begin your search of the literature. Once you learn your way around the reference collection and realize what it can do for you, you will have acquired a valuable skill not only for your college career but for your working career and personal life as well.

No matter what topic you are interested in or what question you want to answer, chances are that there is a reference book to point the way for you. There is an encyclopedia of motorcycles, a handbook of rock music, a dictionary of tarot cards, a directory of artists' signatures, and even a bibliography on prostitution. Ask your librarian!

The reference department has four major parts: the reference librarian, the catalog, the classification scheme, and the reference collection.

### The Reference Librarian

There will be several librarians and library aides to assist you in the use of reference works. These people are trained to use reference materials and to make it easier for you to find what you need. In most libraries they will teach you how to use the tools yourself so that you will be able to work independently in the future.

Library staff members are pleasant, supportive, and eager to help you learn your way around the library. Do not hesitate to call on them—that's what they are there for. After all, if you were in a record store looking for an album by your favorite rock group, you would not hesitate to ask the clerk for it. You would assume that the clerk has been trained to know where the different albums are kept.

Furthermore, if you and the librarian discover that there are books, journals, or other materials that seem to be of interest to you but are not in your library's collection, the librarian will arrange to borrow these from another library through the *interlibrary loan* network.

## The Catalog

The *catalog* is a listing of all the library's holdings. It may be in the form of those familiar three-by-five-inch index cards arranged in many drawers and cabinets, it may be a large set of printed books, or it may be stored in a computer that you search on a terminal. Many libraries have separate catalogs for their journals, government documents, audio-visual materials, or special collections, which are often computer print-outs. In general, however, the catalog in the reference area contains information on everything in the library's collections—books, journals, government documents, dissertations, reports, newspapers, phonograph records, microforms, audio cassettes, filmstrips, slides, maps, manuscripts, and music. For convenience we will assume, in our discussion, that the catalog is a card catalog.

The entries in the catalog are arranged alphabetically. In some libraries, the cards are alphabetized in one long sequence that contains entries by the name of the *author*, the *title* of the work, and the *subjects* or topics the work deals with. Thus, each book would be represented by several cards in the catalog. Other libraries maintain three separate sets of cards in the catalog—for author, title, and subject. Still others combine authors and titles in a "name" catalog, with a separate set of cards for subjects.

In any case, you may approach the catalog in three ways: author, title, or subject. For example, if you want to know if your library has the book by Albert Bandura entitled *Principles of Behavior Modification*, you may look in the author cards under "Bandura, Albert," in the title cards under "Principles of Behavior Modification," or in the subject cards under "Behavior modification."

However, you do not have to know all this information to find the book. If you knew only that someone named Bandura wrote a book about behavior modification you could locate it in the author cards. If you remembered the title but forgot the author's name you could locate the book by looking among the title entries. Or if you had no specific book in mind but needed to find books about behavior modification, you could examine the cards in the subject catalog under that subject heading.

In the subject catalog you will also find cards that guide you to headings that may be used instead of or in addition to the one you are using. For example, if you look up "Abnormal psychology" in the subject catalog, you will find a card that says "*See* Psychology, pathological." You must look under this new heading, "Psychology, pathological," to find books about abnormal psychology. If you look up "Educational psychology" you may find a card that says "*See Also* Learning disabilities." This means that you will find additional material of interest to you under this related heading, "Learning disabilities."

If you cannot find any entries in the catalog under the subject headings you have chosen, this does not mean that the library has no material on your topic. What it does mean is that the person who made up the catalog did not guess that you would look under the term you have chosen. It may also be that the headings are out of date. Sometimes the cataloging system is slow to keep up with the changing terminology of all the scholarly disciplines.

Another reason, however, is that perhaps you have not thought carefully about what you are interested in, or are not being specific enough in your search. If you want information on behavior modification, for example, you need not look for it under such broad headings as "therapy" or "adjustment." The librarian will be able to suggest the best words for you to use in searching the catalog if you are having difficulty.

Each card in the catalog contains a code, a combination of letters and numbers, in the upper left corner. This is the *call number.* It tells you where to find the item in the library's collection. You match the number with the proper spot on the bookshelf by following the alphabetical or numerical sequence. You will find a diagram near the catalog showing you where the different call numbers are located in the library building. For example:

Call Numbers A through L—Third Floor
Call Numbers M through P—Fourth Floor
Call Numbers Q through Z—Fifth Floor

A typical call number is HV6080.T6. The first letters stand for the subject field, the numbers indicate a specific topic in that field, and the letters and numbers after the period refer to the author. This book is in the social sciences field (H), specifically criminology (HV6080), and the author's last name begins with T (Toch).

If the call number is preceded by "Ref," this means that the book you want is in the reference area. If the call number is preceded by "Phonorecord," "Cassette," "Govt Doc," or some other designation, the item is not in the general book collection but is in another part of the library. There will be signs telling you where to find these special materials.

## The Classification Scheme

The call numbers are part of the *classification scheme*. Almost all college and university libraries in the United States use the Library of Congress classification. You can visit almost any college library and find that the same books have the same call numbers. There are other classification schemes, for example, the Dewey Decimal System, but these are not widely used in academic libraries. You will find the Dewey system used in city and county public libraries.

Is there some logic or system to the classification scheme? Yes and no. A classification scheme is based on the idea that all knowledge can be organized and that materials about the same or related subjects should be found together on the library's shelves. All psychology books should be kept in the same area, and within that area all books on personality or on educational psychology or on industrial psychology should be grouped.

The Library of Congress classification divides the literature of all fields into 21 categories and designates each by a letter of the alphabet. Each class is subdivided by additional letters and numbers. The major classes are:

A. General works
B. Philosophy, psychology, and religion
C. History (auxiliary sciences)
D. History, general and ancient
E. History, America (general)
F. History, North, Central, and South America (by country)
G. Geography, anthropology, recreation, and folklore
H. Social sciences
J. Political science
K. Law
L. Education
M. Music
N. Fine arts
P. Language and literature
Q. Science
R. Medicine

S. Agriculture

T. Technology

U. Military science

V. Naval science

Z. Bibliography and library science

Psychology is included in Class B (under the broad heading "Philosophy") and is designated "BF," followed by numbers representing the various subfields of psychology. For example, BF683 is used for works on motivation and BF698 covers personality.

Knowing the call numbers for psychology or any field can be a convenience. You could go directly to these shelves in the library and browse for books on the topic you are researching. If you have the call number for one book in your field, you can expect to find other books on the topic next to it on the shelf.

This brings up the "no" part of the answer to the question about the logic of the classification scheme. Many fields, especially psychology, have grown so rapidly in scope and complexity since the 1950s that the classification scheme has not kept pace with the new issues and interests. You may find that books on several topics have been lumped together under a single call number that does not accurately describe any of them, simply because the scheme has not yet made a place for these new developments.

Furthermore, as you have learned from this textbook, many of the applied areas of psychology overlap other disciplines such as education, medicine, and business administration. Therefore, many relevant books will not be shelved at the "BF" class with psychology but rather with works in other fields in different parts of the library's collection. You cannot go to the psychology shelves and assume that all the library's material on psychology is there.

Topics in psychology discussed in this book will also be found in the following classes.

| | |
|---|---|
| Personnel management (Industrial Psychology) | HF (Social Sciences, Business Administration |
| Advertising (Consumer Psychology) | HF (Social Sciences, Commerce) |
| Social psychology | HM (Social Sciences, Sociology) |
| The family, marriage, women | HQ (Social Sciences, Social Groups) |
| Social pathology and criminology (Forensic Psychology—includes addictions, crimes, police, prisons, juvenile delinquency, and rehabilitation) | HV (Social Sciences, Social Pathology and Criminology) |

| | |
|---|---|
| Educational psychology (Includes education of special groups such as gifted and handicapped children) | LB (Education, Theory and Practice) |
| City planning (Environmental Psychology | NA (Fine Arts, Architecture) |
| Animal psychology | QL (Science, Zoology) |
| Physiological psychology | QP (Science, Physiology) |
| Psychosomatics and psychiatry (Medical Psychology—includes psychological aspects of specific diseases) | RC (Medicine, Practice of) |
| Engineering psychology | TA (Technology, Engineering) |
| Environmental pollution (Environmental Psychology) | TD (Technology, Environmental) |
| Construction of specific types of buildings and their protection from burglary (Environmental Psychology | TH (Technology, Building Construction) |
| Motor vehicles (Traffic Safety Psychology | TL (Technology, Motor Vehicles) |
| Consumer psychology | TX (Technology, Home Economics) |

The "BF" class, Psychology, contains general books on psychology and works on experimental psychology, abnormal psychology, counseling psychology, industrial psychology, intelligence, comparative psychology, motivation and personality, developmental psychology (from childhood through old age), and parapsychology.

## The Reference Collection

The reference collection includes many different types of books: bibliographies, abstracts and indexes, encyclopedias and handbooks, directories, dictionaries, series, guides to biographical and professional information, atlases, college catalogs, and even telephone directories of major cities.

Reference books are pathfinders. They guide you to publications in which you will find the information you need. They do not provide the information directly, but they make it easier and quicker for you to find it. For Frank's term paper on a behavior therapy technique, for example, he could look at every issue of every psychology journal in the hope of finding useful articles, or he could examine the index to *Psychological Abstracts* or the monthly issues, which group on a page or two summaries of all current research on the topic.

Why use reference books? Isn't the card catalog good enough? First, journal articles are not listed in the card catalog. In psychology and many other disciplines, the bulk of the current research and applied work is published in journals. Second, there may be many relevant books or other materials that your library doesn't own; of course these would not be listed in the catalog. If you find reference to such materials, your librarian can order them for you. Third, you may need to use reference books to help you limit your search. You may find one hundred books on behavior therapy listed in the card catalog, but a reference book on behavior therapy may recommend only four or five on the use of systematic desensitization with fear of heights (Frank's topic).

What do you find when you look in a reference book? Typically, you find general discussions and lists of books, journal articles, audiovisual materials, organizations, or individuals who are important in the field. The content of each item listed may be summarized in a sentence or two. This description is called an *annotation* or an *abstract*.

The listing or *citation* for a book will give author or editor's name, title, publisher, and place and date of publication. The citation may also include number of pages, size, and special features of the work such as a bibliography, an index, or pictures.

Citations for journal articles include author and title of the article, the name of the journal, the publication date, the volume number and sometimes the issue number, and the inclusive pages. For example: Washburn, S. L., "Human Behavior and the Behavior of Other Animals," *American Psychologist*, 1978, 33(5), 405–418. This citation tells you that the article about human behavior and the behavior of other animals by Washburn was published in the journal entitled *American Psychologist* in 1978. The volume number is 33, the issue number is 5, and the article begins on page 405 and ends on page 418.

Another format may be used, but the information will lead you to the same article. For example: *American Psychologist* 33 (May 1978): 405–418, indicates volume 33, the issue of May 1978, and the same inclusive pages for the Washburn article.

*Bibliographies.* Bibliographies are a good place to begin your library research. They are published separately or included at the end of a journal article, book, or book chapter. Bibliographies provide a convenient list of sources for you to examine, but you must always consider the date of the bibliography. If it was published in 1972, for example, you will have to do some additional searching to make your work current.

*Books in Print* (published by R. R. Bowker of New York) is a listing of books currently available from publishers. It is in several volumes and may be searched by author, by book title, or by subject. It is published annually and supplemented throughout the year. There is also a *Books in Print* volume for paperbound books.

The *Cumulative Book Index*, issued monthly by H. W. Wilson (New York) lists books published in English and can also be approached by author, title, and subject. Back issues are bound in large volumes and are valuable for locating books that are no longer in print. Out of print materials may still be useful for historical research; out of print books are not necessarily out of date.

The *Bibliographic Index*, published twice a year by H. W. Wilson, lists bibliographies alphabetically by topic that have been published separately or as parts of books or articles.

Bibliographies on topics in psychology can be found in textbooks, encyclopedias, handbooks, articles published in the *Annual Review of Psychology* and other series, literature review articles (especially those published in *Psychological Bulletin*), and *Psychological Abstracts* (look for the heading "bibliographies" in the subject index). These sources are all discussed in more detail in the following pages.

How do you know if the books listed in a bibliography are good ones? One way is to locate a professional review. *Contemporary Psychology*, a journal published monthly by the American Psychological Association, is devoted exclusively to reviews of books in psychology and related fields. It also includes some film reviews. Many research journals, such as those listed on the following pages, also publish book reviews in their specialized fields.

*Abstracts and indexes.* Abstracts and indexes are continuing publications that provide access to the most current literature in a field. The difference between an abstract and an index is that an abstract tells you something about the content of the book or journal article whereas an index provides only the citation.

Most abstracting and indexing tools are organized by subject. For example, *Psychological Abstracts* groups material in areas such as "applied psychology," "developmental psychology," and "educational and school psychology," and each of these areas is divided into more specific topics.

Many abstracts and indexes *cumulate* at the end of six months or a year. That is, instead of using six or twelve monthly issues separately, you may use one large volume in which all of the material for those months is presented.

Most of these reference tools include indexes to the material they cite. *Psychological Abstracts*, for example, includes brief subject and author indexes at the back of each monthly issue, more detailed subject and author indexes with every six months of abstracts, and cumulative subject and author indexes every few years.

Instructions for the use of abstracts and indexes are usually contained in the first few pages of each issue. Many university libraries prepare mimeographed instructions for these tools that are easier to understand.

You may also need help in finding the best words to use in searching for material in an abstract or index. The subject headings you used in the card catalog may not be the same ones used by the reference work. For example, one librarian, searching for material about the "military-industrial complex" in the United States, found the following headings in use:

| | |
|---|---|
| Munitions | In the card catalog |
| Defense Contracts | In the card catalog |
| U.S. Defenses | In an index to business journals |
| U.S. Armaments and Defense | In an index to newspaper articles |
| Military-Industrial Complex | In an index to popular magazines |
| Power (Social Sciences) | In an index to social science journals |
| United States—Military Policy | In an index to social science journals |
| Civil Supremacy over the Military | In the subject volume of *Books in Print* [2] |

If you are having trouble finding the correct terms to use in working with an abstracting or indexing tool, ask the librarian for assistance.

Many of these reference works have their information stored in a computer, and these *data bases* are available for *online* searches. Machine-assisted literature searches save a great deal of time, especially when you expect to find a large number of items. Ask if your library has access to any such data bases.

Some of the major abstracting and indexing tools in psychology and allied fields are the following.

*Psychological Abstracts.* Published monthly by the American Psychological Association, Washington, D.C. Provides worldwide coverage of the literature of psychology and related fields. Abstracts books, chapters in books, journal articles, technical reports, and other materials. Arranged by subject categories. You may use this tool by scanning the subject section of interest to you or by looking in the subject index for words that describe your topic; these will direct you to specific abstracts.

*Catalog of Selected Documents in Psychology.* Published quarterly by

[2] John G. Fetros, "Literature search observations," *RQ*, Spring 1971, p. 201. Cited in William A. Katz, *Introduction to Reference Work*, Volume II, 2nd ed. (New York: McGraw–Hill, 1974), pp. 115–116.

**3886. Weinberger, Alex & Engelhart, Roland S.** (U Windsor, Canada) **Three group treatments for reduction of speech anxiety among students.** *Perceptual & Motor Skills,* 1976(Dec), Vol 43(3), 1317–1318. —Administered the State-Trait Anxiety Inventory, Affect Adjective Check List, and Personal Report of Confidence as a Speaker to 19 anxious university students. Conditions of group systematic desensitization, group flooding, and a group discussion/placebo control treatment were employed to reduce Ss' anxiety about public speaking. Three 90-min sessions were provided. Pre- and posttreatment assessments employed self-report and behavioral measures. The desensitization group showed significant pre- to posttreatment change across all self-report measures, whereas the flooding and control groups showed similar improvement on only one such measure. No group showed significant improvement on the behavioral measure. Groups did not exhibit significant intergroup differences in improvement on any measure. —*Journal abstract.*

**3887. Williams, Warwick.** (Northside Clinic, Greenwich, Australia) **A comprehensive behaviour modification programme for the treatment of anorexia nervosa: Results in six cases.** *Australian & New Zealand Journal of Psychiatry,* 1976(Dec), Vol 10(4), 321–324. —Used behavioral analysis and psychodynamic hypotheses to develop a comprehensive behavior modification program for treating primary anorexia nervosa (including desensitization, a points system, self-monitoring, thought stopping, and assertive training). This was applied to 6 female anorectic patients who met all the usual criteria for diagnosis; the results obtained are reported. Overall, the program was a "resounding" failure, and it is suggested that the patients' resistance to behavior change was a secondary gain (covert punishment) from the anorectic symptomatology, which exceeded the disadvantages. —*Journal abstract.*

**3888. Willis, Jerry; Giles, Donna & Bugelski, B. R.** (Eds). **Great experiments in behavior modification.** Indianapolis, IN: Hackett, 1976. xviii, 288 p. —Presents abstracts of 116 experiments on behavior modification, including pioneer experiments, preschool studies, educational applications, behavioral counseling, behavior therapy, institutional programs for behavior change, behavioral approaches to juvenile delinquents and adult offenders, community and organizational applications, and training of behavioral engineers. Target behavior and research design indexes are included.

Behavior Modification [See Also Aversion Therapy, Behavior Therapy, Classroom Behavior Modification, Contingency Management, Implosive Therapy, Reciprocal Inhibition Therapy, Systematic Desensitization Therapy, Token Economy Programs]

behavior modification training, attitudes towared self & child & mother-child interaction, mothers, 7962

behavior modification training, parent attitudes & management skills & child target behavior, parent participants vs nonparticipants, 9963

behavior modification using positive reinforcement & teachers' & parents' & peers' roles, autonomous eating habits, profoundly retarded children in special day school, 1658

behavior modification, abstracts of experiments in educational & treatment settings, book, 3888

behavior modification, application to rehabilitation therapies & problems of physically disabled, book, 1652

behavior modification, changing ethnocentric attitudes, college students, 7520

behavior modification, expansion of social behavior, passive young female with low IQ & character disorder, 3796

behavior modification, language development, autistic children, book, 12110

behavior modification, treatment of obesity, 1653

behavior problems encountered & treated by pediatrician, evaluation of procedures for rapid toilet training & correction of self injurious behavior & shopping behavior problems, 7932

behavioral approaches to treatment of early infantile autism,

Figure 1. Subject index (above) and abstracts (on opposite page) from *Psychological Abstracts.* Copyright 1977 by the American Psychological Association and reprinted by permission. If you want information on the variety of problems to which behavior modification techniques have been applied, scan the subject index under "Behavior Modification" and note the numbers of the works that appear relevant. Then look up the abstracts designated by these numbers. For example, see item number 3888 in the index and the abstracts. Abstracts usually provide sufficient information for you to decide whether or not you need to obtain the article or book described.

the Journal Supplement Abstract Service of the American Psychological Association, Washington, D.C. Contains abstracts of bibliographies and other documents that are not suitable for journal publication, usually because they are too long. You may purchase the complete document in paper copy or microfiche, but you must allow four to six weeks for delivery.

*Readers' Guide to Periodical Literature.* Published semimonthly by H. W. Wilson, New York. An author and subject index to articles in magazines of general interest such as *Psychology Today, Business Week, Consumer Reports, New York Times Magazine, Saturday Review,* and *Scientific American.*

*New York Times Index.* Published semimonthly by the New York Times Company, New York. A subject index to articles in the latest issues of this daily newspaper.

*Dissertation Abstracts International.* Published monthly by University Microfilms, Ann Arbor, Michigan. Contains abstracts of doctoral dissertations from nearly 300 universities. Part A covers work in the humanities and social sciences. Part B covers the sciences and engineering.

*Social Sciences Index.* Published quarterly by H. W. Wilson, New York. An author and subject index to articles in the social sciences (anthropology, area studies, economics, environmental sciences, geography, gerontology, law and criminology, medical sciences, nursing, physical anthropology, political science, psychology, public administration, public health, and sociology). A separate section provides citations to book reviews in these fields.

*Business Periodicals Index.* Published monthly by H. W. Wilson, New York. A subject index to articles on topics in business and industry, for example, advertising, public relations, labor and management, leadership and motivation, interviewing, working hours, and specific types of workers. The terms used to index the material are constantly being revised to keep up with the latest terminology.

*Public Affairs Information Service Bulletin.* Published weekly by the Public Affairs Information Service, New York. A subject index to books, journal articles, government reports, and reports from private agencies about economic and social conditions, public administration, and international relations.

*Education Index.* Published monthly by H. W. Wilson, New York. A subject index to journal articles in education.

*Current Index to Journals in Education.* Published monthly by CCM Information Corporation, New York. Lists approximately 15,000 articles each year from more than 500 journals in education and related disciplines. Part of the ERIC (Educational Resources Information Center) system sponsored by the U. S. Office of Education, which administers a network of clearinghouses that process information in specialized areas of education.

*Research in Education.* Published monthly by the U. S. Government Printing Office, Washington, D.C. Provides abstracts and indexes of documents processed by the ERIC clearinghouses, including reports of government-sponsored research, conference proceedings, and bibliographies.

*Social Sciences Citation Index.* Published three times a year by the Institute for Scientific Information, Philadelphia. Instead of providing citations to the literature, this index tells you who has done the citing. If, for example, you know that a particular psychologist has published a study on systematic desensitization with fear of heights, you may look up the study in the citation index (by the author's name) and find out if anyone has referred to it in a later publication. In this way you may learn if additional work has been done to support or extend the research published in the original study.

Many other disciplines publish abstracting and indexing tools; for example, *Sociological Abstracts, Historical Abstracts, Biological Abstracts, Chemical Abstracts,* and *Index Medicus* (medicine).

*Encyclopedias, handbooks, series, and dictionaries.* Encyclopedias and handbooks are usually prepared by distinguished scholars in the field, and the information they offer is authoritative, readable, and complete. Articles in encyclopedias and handbooks provide you with background material on your topic, an overview of research and theory in the field, and a bibliography of sources for you to follow up. The entries vary in length from brief definitions to chapters of many pages on important concepts, problems, and people in various fields.

As a rule, articles in an encyclopedia are arranged alphabetically, but sometimes the terms "encyclopedia" and "handbook" are used interchangeably.

Books in series provide coverage similar to handbooks and encyclopedias but they usually deal with more current or timely topics. Sometimes they include the papers presented at a convention or symposium. A particularly useful series is the *Annual Review of Psychology*, which contains fifteen to twenty literature review articles with extensive bibliographies. The latest research, theories, and applications are summarized and analyzed. Some of the topics are continued every year. Others change each year as psychologists become interested in new issues.

Specialized dictionaries offer definitions of the terminology characteristic of a particular discipline that may not be found in general dictionaries.

Some standard tools are the following.

*International Encyclopedia of the Social Sciences.* David L. Sills, Ed. New York: Macmillan, 1968. 17 volumes. Contains good general articles on many important concepts in anthropology, economics, geography, history, law, political science, psychiatry, psychology, sociology, statistics, and interdisciplinary subjects. Includes bibliographies. For more historical articles and biographies of persons important in the development of these disciplines, consult the *Encyclopedia of the Social Sciences,* published by Macmillan in 1930 to 1935 (15 volumes).

*International Encyclopedia of Psychiatry, Psychology, Psychoanalysis, and Neurology.* Benjamin B. Wolman, Ed. New York: Van Nostrand Reinhold, 1977. 12 volumes. Contains authoritative articles on important topics in the fields listed in the title.

*Encyclopedia of Careers and Vocational Guidance,* 3rd ed. William Hopke, Ed. Chicago: J. G. Ferguson, 1975. 2 volumes. Provides information on careers of all types and how to prepare for them.

*Encyclopedia of Human Behavior: Psychology, Psychiatry, and Mental Health.* Robert M. Goldenson, Ed. New York: Doubleday, 1970. 2 volumes. Presents more than one thousand articles on concepts, theories, treatments, and important persons in these fields. Includes approximately one hundred fifty case studies of mental disorders.

*Encyclopedia of Psychoanalysis.* Ludwig Eidelberg, Ed. New York: Free Press, 1971. Defines more than six hundred specialized terms and presents articles on topics in the history and theories of psychoanalysis. Contains clinical examples and bibliographies.

*Encyclopedia of Psychology.* H. J. Eysenck, W. Arnold, and R. Meili, Eds. New York: Herder and Herder, 1972. 3 volumes. Provides brief coverage of important concepts in psychology.

The chapters in the following handbooks review current research, theory, and practice in the fields noted by the title. All include good bibliographies.

*American Handbook of Psychiatry,* 2nd ed. Silvano Arieti, Ed. New York: Basic Books, 1974. 6 volumes. Comprehensive coverage of theory, practice, and treatment.

*Handbook of Abnormal Psychology,* 2nd ed. H. J. Eysenck, Ed. San Diego: R. R. Knapp, 1973.

*Handbook of Behavior Modification and Behavior Therapy.* Harold Leitenberg, Ed. Englewood Cliffs, N.J.: Prentice-Hall, 1976.

*Handbook of Clinical Psychology.* Benjamin B. Wolman et al., Eds. New York: McGraw-Hill, 1965.

*Handbook of Gestalt Therapy.* Chris Hatcher and Philip Himelstein, Eds. New York: Aronson, 1976.

*Handbook of Industrial and Organizational Psychology.* Marvin D. Dunnette, Ed. Chicago: Rand McNally, 1976.

*Handbook of Personality Theory and Research.* Edgar F. Borgatta and W.W. Lambert, Eds. Chicago: Rand McNally, 1969.

*Handbook of Small Group Research,* 2nd ed. A. Paul Hare, Ed. New York: Free Press, 1976.

*Handbook of Social Psychology,* 2nd ed. Gardner Lindzey and E. Aronson, Eds. Reading, Mass.: Addison-Wesley, 1968–1969. 5 volumes.

*Handbook of the Psychology of Aging.* James E. Birren and K. Warner Schaie, Eds. New York: Van Nostrand Reinhold, 1977.

*Handbook of Work, Organization, and Society.* Robert Dubin, Ed. Chicago: Rand McNally, 1976.

*Handbook on Contemporary Education.* Steven E. Goodman, Ed. New York: R. R. Bowker, 1976.

*Mental Measurements Yearbook,* 7th ed. O. K. Buros, Ed. Highland Park, N.J.: Gryphon Press, 1972. 2 volumes. The standard information source on tests and the testing literature for psychology, education, and industry.

*Occupational Information: Where To Get It and How To Use It in Career Education, Career Counseling, and Career Development,* 4th ed. Robert Hoppock, Ed. New York: McGraw-Hill, 1976.

*Psychology: A Study of a Science.* Sigmund Koch, Ed. New York: McGraw-Hill, 1959–1963. 6 volumes.

*The Therapist's Handbook: Treatment Methods of Mental Disorders.* Benjamin B. Wolman, Ed. New York: Van Nostrand Reinhold, 1976. Contains chapters on psychopharmacological, behavioral, and psychotherapeutic treatment of mental illnesses. More than 1,800 references.

*Annual Review of Psychology.* Palo Alto, Cal.: Annual Reviews, Inc. Articles on current topics review research, theory, and application. Extensive bibliographies. Typical chapters deal with perception, thinking, motivation, sleep and dreams, environmental psychology, industrial psychology, behavior therapy, psychotherapy, personality, and attitudes and opinions. A good place to begin a literature search.

The volumes in the following selected series are published at irregular intervals (except where noted) and survey the current status of the fields indicated by the title.

*Advances in Child Development and Behavior.* New York: Academic Press. Volume 11 in the series published in 1976.

*Advances in Experimental Social Psychology.* New York: Academic Press. Volume 9 in the series published in 1976.

*Annual Review of Behavior Therapy: Theory and Practice.* New York: Brunner/Mazel. Volume 4 in the series published in 1976.

*Child Personality and Psychopathology: Current Topics.* New York: Wiley-Interscience. Volume 3 in the series published in 1976.

*International Review of Research in Mental Retardation.* New York: Academic Press. Volume 8 in the series published in 1976.

*Minnesota Symposium on Child Psychology.* Minneapolis: University of Minnesota Press. Volume 10 in the series published in 1976.

*Nebraska Symposium On Motivation.* Lincoln: University of Nebraska Press. Annual.

*Progress in Behavior Modification.* New York: Academic Press. Volume 3 in the series published in 1976.

*Stress and Anxiety.* Washington, D.C.: Hemisphere. Volume 4 in the series published in 1977.

Dictionaries of terms in psychology and related fields include the following.

*A Comprehensive Dictionary of Psychological and Psychoanalytical Terms: A Guide To Usage.* By Horace B. English and Ava C. English. New York: Longmans, 1958. A standard reference work discussing approximately 13,000 terms.

*Dictionary of Behavioral Science.* Benjamin B. Wolman, Ed. New York: Van Nostrand Reinhold, 1974. Presents concise and simple definitions in psychology and related fields.

*Handbook of Psychological Terms.* By Philip L. Harriman. Totowa, N.J.: Littlefield, Adams, 1971. Defines approximately 4,000 frequently used terms and concepts in psychology.

*Professional and biographical information.* The American Psychological Association, the organization to which most psychologists belong, publishes journals and books in many areas of psychology. Some of these are devoted to professional concerns.

*American Psychologist.* A monthly journal containing articles on general issues and official papers of the Association.

*APA Monitor.* A monthly newsletter featuring the latest news about psychologists and their interests. Includes editorials and letters.

*Professional Psychology.* A quarterly journal containing articles about the training of psychologists, professional practice, and the applications of psychology in different settings.

*Directory of the American Psychological Association, 1978.* An alphabetical listing of approximately 46,000 members of APA. Includes biographical, geographical, and divisional information. Contains general information about the profession (for example, history of the association, past presidents, ethical standards). Updated every few years.

*Graduate Study in Psychology.* An annual listing of 500 graduate programs in psychology in the United States and Canada. Describes facilities and requirements of each institution and includes much useful general information.

The thirty-five divisions of the American Psychological Association cover various special interests of psychologists. These divisions are listed in Table 2–2 of this textbook (Chapter 2). The current secretaries of the divisions are published in each November issue of the *American Psychologist* journal. If you have questions about study or work in these areas of psychology, write to the appropriate division secretary or to the *American Psychological Association*, 1200 Seventeenth Street, N.W., Washington, D.C. 20036.

Information on the lives and careers of influential psychologists may be found in the following publications.

*A History of Psychology in Autobiography.* An important series of autobiographical sketches of the major figures in the development of psychology. Volumes 1–4 published by Clark University Press (Worcester, Mass.), 1930–36, 1952; Volumes 5 and 6 by Prentice-Hall (Englewood Cliffs, N.J.), 1967, 1974.

*The Psychologists.* Autobiographical sketches of contemporary figures in psychology. Volumes 1 and 2 published by Oxford University Press (New York) in 1972 and 1974, edited by T. S. Krawiec.

*Psychology Today*, a popular monthly magazine about psychology and the behavioral and social sciences, publishes interviews with important people in these fields, covering both personal and professional concerns.

*Biography Index*, published quarterly by H. W. Wilson (New York), is an alphabetical guide to biographical material on Americans in all fields. It lists not only biographies but also biographical material contained in journals, bibliographies, obituaries, diaries, and memoirs.

## THE BOOK COLLECTION

You already know that the book collection in the library is organized on the basis of the classification scheme. If you find books of interest to you in the card catalog, write down the call numbers and locate the books on the shelves.

If the book you want is not on the shelf, ask the librarian about it. Many libraries have a computer-produced *circulation list* in which the books on loan are listed by call number, showing when each book is due. You may leave a "hold" or a "reserve call" for the book, and the library will notify you when it has been returned.

If you are in a hurry, ask the librarian to see if other local libraries have the book. You may then use the book at one of these libraries or borrow it through the interlibrary loan system.

## PERIODICALS

The administrative responsibility for a library's periodicals, journals, and magazines is separate from the responsibility for books. Journals are published in several issues each year and thus continually need more and more shelf space. Therefore, most libraries keep their journals in the periodicals room, a separate area in the library with plenty of seating space and usually with coin-operated photocopy machines so you can make your own copy of the articles you need.

How do you know which journals the library has? First, the journals are listed in the card catalog. You may look under the title of the journal or under its subject. Second, most libraries have a computer-produced *serials* or *periodicals list,* which includes all the journals in the library by title. Both sources tell which issues the library has. For example, the entry "1954—" means that the library has every issue published since 1954.

How are the journals arranged? Some libraries shelve periodicals in alphabetical order by title. Omit the word "The"; for example, *The Journal of Personality and Social Psychology* would be filed under *J* for *Journal.* Other libraries arrange the journals by call number so that those in the same field will be shelved together, although, as noted, this is not always the case for psychology. A few libraries shelve their journals in the book collection by call number.

It is common practice for the library to separate the latest issues of a journal (usually the current year) from the older, bound issues. Be sure to look in both locations.

Journals do not circulate; you may not borrow them from the library. Be prepared to take notes from the articles while you are in the library or to pay for a photocopy. If you can wait a few weeks for your own copy, write to the author of the article for a *reprint;* the address is given on the first page of the article. The researcher may also send you other articles of interest.

If you cannot find the issue you want, ask the librarian. Most likely it is at the bindery. The librarian will be able to tell you when to expect the journal back on the shelf.

What if you don't have a specific journal in mind? Look in the card catalog under your topic. Or check *Psychological Abstracts* under the area you are interested in to see where articles on the topic are being published. The following guide is also useful.

*Serials In Psychology and Allied Fields,* 2nd ed. By Margaret Tompkins and Norma Shirley. Troy, N.Y.: Whitston, 1976. Describes more than eight hundred English-language journals.

Some important journals in psychology include the following.

*American Journal of Psychology.* Urbana: University of Illinois Press. Quarterly.

*American Psychologist.* Washington, D.C.: American Psychological Association. Monthly.

*Behavior Research and Therapy.* Elmsford, N.Y.: Pergamon Press. Bimonthly.

*Contemporary Psychology.* Washington, D.C.: American Psychological Association. Monthly. Devoted to book reviews.

*Criminal Justice and Behavior.* Beverly Hills, Cal.: Sage Publications. Quarterly. Sponsored by the American Association of Correctional Psychologists.

*Developmental Psychology.* Washington, D.C.: American Psychological Association. Bimonthly.

*Environment and Behavior.* Beverly Hills, Cal.: Sage Publications. Quarterly.

*Harvard Business Review.* Cambridge, Mass.: Harvard University Press. Bimonthly.

*Human Factors.* Baltimore: Johns Hopkins University Press. Bimonthly. Sponsored by the Human Factors Society.

*Journal of Abnormal Psychology.* Washington, D.C.: American Psychological Association. Bimonthly.

*Journal of Applied Psychology.* Washington, D.C.: American Psychological Association. Bimonthly. Covers applications of psychology in business, industry, government, and education.

*Journal of Community Psychology.* Brandon, Vt.: Clinical Psychology Publishing Co. Quarterly.

*Journal of Comparative and Physiological Psychology.* Washington, D.C.: American Psychological Association. Bimonthly.

*Journal of Consulting and Clinical Psychology.* Washington, D.C.: American Psychological Association. Bimonthly. Publishes research on all aspects of mental illness, personality, and therapy.

*Journal of Counseling Psychology.* Washington, D.C.: American Psychological Association. Bimonthly. Publishes work on counseling theory and practice.

*Journal of Educational Psychology.* Washington, D.C.: American Psychological Association. Bimonthly.

*Journal of Experimental Psychology.* Washington, D.C.: American Psychological Association. Published in four parts: General (quarterly); Human Learning and Memory (bimonthly); Human Perception and Performance (quarterly); Animal Behavior Process (quarterly).

*Journal of General Psychology.* Provincetown, Mass.: Journal Press. Quarterly.

*Journal of Personality.* Durham, N.C.: Duke University Press. Quarterly.

*Journal of Personality and Social Psychology.* Washington, D.C.: American Psychological Association. Monthly.

*Journal of Psychology.* Provincetown, Mass.: Journal Press. Bimonthly.

*Journal of School Psychology.* New York: Human Sciences Press. Quarterly.

*Journal of Sex and Marital Therapy.* New York: Human Sciences Press. Quarterly.

*Journal of Social Issues.* Ann Arbor, Mich.: Society for the Psychological Study of Social Issues. Quarterly.

*Journal of Social Psychology.* Provincetown, Mass.: Journal Press. Bimonthly.

*Journal of the History of the Behavioral Sciences.* Brandon, Vt.: Clinical Psychology Publishing Co. Quarterly.

*Organizational Behavior and Human Performance.* New York: Academic Press. Bimonthly.

*Personnel.* New York: American Management Associations. Bimonthly.

*Personnel Journal.* Durham, N.C.: Personnel Journal, Inc. Monthly.

*Professional Psychology.* Washington, D.C.: American Psychological Association. Quarterly.

*Psychological Bulletin.* Washington, D.C.: American Psychological Association. Bimonthly. Devoted to literature reviews.

*Psychological Review.* Washington, D.C.: American Psychological Association. Bimonthly. Devoted to theoretical articles.

*Psychology in the Schools.* Brandon, Vt.: Clinical Psychology Publishing Co. Quarterly.

*Psychology of Women Quarterly.* New York: Human Sciences Press. Quarterly.

*Psychology Today.* New York: Ziff-Davis Publishing Co. Monthly.

*Science.* Washington, D.C.: American Association for the Advancement of Science. Weekly.

## MICROFORMS AND MEDIA

Many libraries long ago ran out of space in which to store their bound journals, so they have maintained the journal and newspaper collections on microform—either microfilm, microcard, or microfiche. The card catalog or the serials list will tell you if the journal you want is in microform, and you must ask the librarian in the microforms area to get the journal for you.

The library will have special machines for you to use to read the microforms, and many libraries have reader/printers that make a photocopy of the journal article directly from the microform.

The department of the library that houses journals in microform usually handles other audiovisual aids as well. These may include phonograph records, audio and video tapes, audio and video cassettes, transparencies, slides, filmstrips, motion pictures, photographs, newsreels, computer data bases on machine-readable tape, and recordings of classroom lectures. These items may be listed in the card catalog or in a separate media catalog. When in doubt, ask the librarian.

Most audiovisual materials are described in the media indexes published by the National Information Center for Educational Media (NICEM) at the University of Southern California in Los Angeles. These periodically revised guides list materials separately for each medium. Several guides are devoted to specific disciplines. See their *Index to Psychology—Multimedia*, 3rd edition (1977).

## GOVERNMENT DOCUMENTS

The federal government publishes a vast array of books, pamphlets, reports, and journals. Many major university libraries are *government depository* libraries and have a broad selection of these works. The organization and citation of government materials is sometimes mysterious, and it is best to ask the specially trained government documents librarian for government publications in your area of interest.

If you can wait several weeks for information, try writing to the public information office of the government agency concerned with your problem (for example, federally funded testing programs for preschoolers). Consult the annual *Government Manual*, a directory of all federal agencies, for the address. Agencies working on problems involving the application of psychology include the National Institutes of Health, the Office of Education, the Occupational Safety and Health Administration, the Law Enforcement Assistance Administration, the Food and Drug Administration, and the Employment and Training Administration.

Abstracts of government-sponsored research are published in *Government Reports Announcements and Index* (Springfield, Va.: National Technical Information Service, semimonthly) and organized by subject field. Field 5, "Behavioral and Social Science," includes material on engineering psychology, personnel research and practices, and highway safety.

A useful guide to government publications is *Government Publications and Their Use* by Laurence F. Schmeckebier and Roy B. Eastin (Washington, D.C.: Brookings, 1969).

For state and local government publications, it is best to contact the office or agency directly because these publications do not often find their way into libraries.

## SPECIAL COLLECTIONS

Special collections vary with each library, are usually housed separately from the book collection, and may even have their own catalog and librarian. They represent an exceptional group of materials beyond those provided in the regular library collection. Some types of special collections are recreational reading, rare books, regional collections (for example, material on the Southwest or on a particular state or city), topical collections (such as art history or French literature or butterflies), and personal collections (for example, the papers of a famous writer, political leader, or business person).

A major special collection in psychology is the Archives of the History of American Psychology at the University of Akron in Ohio. The librarians there will answer written requests for information about the development of psychology in the United States.

Ask your librarian if the libraries in your area have special collections related to the topic you are researching.

## NOW WHAT?

Now that you have defined your topic, searched the literature, examined and analyzed the books and journal articles of interest, you write your term paper. Many libraries hold "term paper clinics" each semester to help you learn good study and research habits, procedures for organizing material, and the proper presentation of a paper. Also, there are books to guide you in the preparation of a paper.

Bell, James Edward. *A Guide To Library Research In Psychology.* Dubuque, Iowa: William C. Brown, 1971.

Hoselitz, Bert F. *A Reader's Guide to the Social Sciences,* rev. ed. New York: Free Press, 1972.

Noland, Robert L. *Research and Report Writing in the Behavioral Sciences: Psychiatry, Psychology, Sociology, Educational Psychology, Cultural Anthropology, Managerial Psychology.* Springfield, Ill.: Charles C Thomas, 1970.

Sarbin, Theodore R., and Coe, William C. *The Student Psychologist's Handbook: A Guide to Sources.* Cambridge, Mass.: Schenkman Publishing Co., 1969.

Turabian, Kate L. *Student's Guide For Writing College Papers,* 3rd ed. Chicago: University of Chicago Press, 1976.

For specific information about the format of your paper, especially the typing of the footnotes and the bibliography, see the following works.

*Publication Manual of the American Psychological Association,* 2nd ed. Washington, D.C.: American Psychological Association, 1974.

*A Manual of Style,* 12th ed. Chicago: University of Chicago Press, 1969.

*Form and Style: Theses, Reports, Term Papers,* 5th ed. By William G. Campbell and Stephen V. Ballou. Boston: Houghton Mifflin, 1978.

# Index

# Index

## Index

# AMERICAN ENCOUNTERS WITH ARABS

# AMERICAN ENCOUNTERS WITH ARABS

## THE "SOFT POWER" OF U.S. PUBLIC DIPLOMACY IN THE MIDDLE EAST

William A. Rugh

PRAEGER SECURITY INTERNATIONAL
Westport, Connecticut • London

Library of Congress Cataloging-in-Publication Data

Rugh, William A.
   American encounters with Arabs : the "soft power" of U.S. public diplomacy
in the Middle East / William A. Rugh.
      p.   cm.
   Includes bibliographical references and index.
   ISBN 0–275–98817–1 (alk. paper)
   1. Arab countries—Foreign relations—United States.   2. United States—
Foreign relations—Arab countries.   3. United States—Foreign public opinion,
Arab.   4. Arabs—Public opinion.   5. Civilization, Arab—Study and teaching—
United States.   I. Title.
   DS63.2.U5R84   2006
   327.73056—dc22        2005022472

British Library Cataloguing in Publication Data is available.

Library of Congress Catalog Card Number: 2005022472
ISBN: 0–275–98817–1

First published in 2006

Praeger Security International, 88 Post Road West, Westport, CT 06881
An imprint of Greenwood Publishing Group, Inc.
www.praeger.com

Printed in the United States of America

The paper used in this book complies with the
Permanent Paper Standard issued by the National
Information Standards Organization (Z39.48–1984).

10  9  8  7  6  5  4  3  2  1

To Andrea, David, Douglas, and Nicholas

# Contents

# Tables

# Preface

Since the terrorist attack on 9/11, Americans have focused more attention on the Arab world. All of the terrorists were Arabs and Americans wondered why they did it. Then in the months and years following 9/11, when it was clear that many Arabs were criticizing America, the question became, "Why do they hate us?" Versions of that question were asked, such as "Why is al Jazeera hostile to us?" "Why don't the Iraqis appreciate us for removing Saddam Hussain?" "Why don't they help us fight terrorism?" And some said, "What can be done about this hostility?" or "How can we win over hearts and minds?"

It is true that America's image and reputation among Arabs is lower than it has ever been. A June 2004, Zogby International poll taken in six countries showed overall public attitudes toward the United States were extremely unfavorable, even though the governments in those countries—Saudi Arabia, Jordan, Morocco, Lebanon, Egypt, and the United Arab Emirates (UAE)—have excellent relations with the United States and the first four are among America's oldest Arab friends. Unfavorable ratings in Egypt and Saudi Arabia even reached 98 percent and 94 percent, respectively, while in Morocco, the UAE, Jordan, and Lebanon they reached 88 percent, 73 percent, 78 percent, and 69 percent, respectively.[1]

This book will discuss some of the reasons for those negative attitudes, why they are important to the United States, and what might be done to improve America's image abroad. It reviews how the United States has dealt with Arab public opinion in the past and looks in detail at how it is deal-

ing with it today. It is about ideas, mutual perceptions and exchanges of views between people from two different backgrounds.

A closer look at the reasons for Arab criticisms of the United States reveals that we are not in fact seeing the "clash of civilizations" between Muslims and Christians that Harvard professor Samuel Huntington predicted earlier.[2] Recent opinion polls taken in the Arab world actually show that Arabs tend to have great admiration for American achievements in science, technology and economic developments; they have respect for our society and culture; and they share many of the core values we stand for. What they do object to are aspects of American foreign policy, and many believe we follow a double standard in dealings with other countries.[3]

Arab views about America are not static but have changed over time. Sixty years ago when the U.S. government was just beginning to become involved in the Arab world, America was widely admired while the French and British were strongly criticized for their colonial practices. Today the roles are reversed. As U.S. involvement has grown over the decades, there have been periods of significant tension between Washington and several Arab governments (remember Nasser?), and there have been periods when relations were better. But today we are in a period of tension again, even while many aspects of America are still admired. This book explores the main issues in mutual American–Arab perceptions, past and present.

Why is Arab opinion important at all? Public opinion abroad affects American interests in a number of ways. Foreign public opinion, whether positive or negative, has consequences for American commerce, for the war on terrorism, and for the safety of Americans. Moreover, foreign leaders, even authoritarian rulers, pay attention to the opinions of their citizens in making decisions about whether or not to cooperate with the United States in matters we care about. If their own people are opposed, they hesitate to support us, or their support is limited. American policy makers therefore need to understand foreign public opinion, because as they formulate their policies, they should know in advance how well these policies are likely to succeed. This does not mean that Washington should make policy decisions solely on the basis of what foreigners like or dislike. We must determine what is in our own best interests. But in making policy decisions we need to know how well they are likely to be received by foreign audiences and at least be aware of the costs and benefits of particular courses of action.

As the U.S. Government's Accountability Office (GAO) put it:

> Recent polling data show anti-Americanism is spreading and deepening around the world. Such anti-American sentiments can increase foreign public support for terrorism directed at Americans, impact the cost and effectiveness of military operations, weaken the United States' ability to align with other nations in pursuit of common policy objectives, and dampen foreign publics' enthusiasm for business services and products.[4]

What can be done to improve the situation and serve American interests? Since 9/11 more Americans have focused on the problems in Arab–American relations, and there have been several attempts to answer that question. Some Americans have called for reforming Arab education or bringing democracy to the Arab world. Others have advocated the use of force or economic sticks and carrots. Indeed, education and political reform, and the use of military or economic weapons, all need to be considered in any discussion of remedies. But as Joseph Nye has pointed out, there is another important dimension to international relations that he calls "soft power." Nye distinguishes soft power from economic and military means which are "hard power," and says soft power includes persuasion, the ability to move people by argument, to entice and attract, and to present an ideology and culture that make its power legitimate in the eyes of others. It involves policies at home as well as abroad, since our domestic behavior is even more important today in the global information age.[5]

This book is essentially about how the United States can and should use "soft power" in dealing with the Arab world. The approach is to look at what we are doing today but also to look in some detail at what steps we took in the past that were successful, so that we do not try to reinvent the wheel. There are lessons learned and best practices that professionals who have worked in the Arab world can tell us about from America's half century of experience with engagement in an American–Arab dialogue. What are the differences in perception that each side brings to the table? And what are the communication tools that American professionals have used to make their case and to facilitate mutual understanding? How have Americans over the years, and today, sought to tell our story to the Arabs and improve mutual understanding between our two cultures. Studies of this question that have been published since 9/11 have focused primarily on suggesting remedies for the Washington bureaucracy, and that is important, but this book focuses instead on what happens abroad when Americans engage with Arabs. The story is therefore told primarily from the point of view of American officials working in the Arab world, who are engaged in what they call "public diplomacy." We will define that term in the Introduction, and then present many examples of it in the subsequent chapters.

I am indebted to many people for helping to put this story together, especially current and former Foreign Service Officers (FSOs) who served in the Arab world. I have conducted interviews with nearly two dozen active and retired FSOs, including Barry Ballow, John Berry, Marshall Berg, Jim Bullock, Richard Curtiss, Evelyn Early, Adam Ereli, Alberto Fernandez, Kenton Keith, John Kincannon, Peter Kovach, Duncan MacInnes, Jack McCreary, Haynes Mahoney, Boulos Malik, David Newton, Lea Perez, Martin Quinn, Chris Ross, Elizabeth Thornhill, Katherine Van de Vate, and Marcelle Wahba. I have also used the recorded oral histories of Keith

Adamson, Bob Bauer, Robert Beaudry, Pat Belcher, Jim Halsema, Bob Lincoln, David Nalle, Isa Sabbagh, Tom Sorenson, Howard Simpson, Jim Thurber, Dick Undeland, Dick Viets, and Bill Weathersby. I am very grateful indeed to all of them for their insights, but I alone am responsible for the statements and judgments in this book.

# Abbreviations and Terms

**Al Hurra.** A U.S. government-funded television channel in Arabic under the BBG, started in 2004.

**BBG.** The Broadcasting Board of Governors, an autonomous agency that has the authority to supervise all U.S. government nonmilitary broadcasting including VOA, Radio Sawa, Al Hurra Television and RFI.

**BIB.** The Board for International Broadcasting had some responsibility for U.S. government broadcasting prior to the BBG.

**BPAO.** Branch Public Affairs Officer, who heads the public diplomacy operation in a large provincial capital, such as Alexandria, Egypt.

**CAO.** Cultural Affairs Officer (or Cultural Attaché), the American official who heads the cultural and education section at an embassy, under the PAO.

**Country Team.** Senior management at an American embassy, headed by the ambassador and including the PAO.

**CU.** The Bureau of Educational and Cultural Affairs at the State Department that was responsible for the Washington management of educational exchange and cultural programs between 1953 and 1979, when the function was transferred to USIA.

**ECA.** The Education and Cultural Bureau at the State Department that since 1999 has handled educational exchange and cultural programs.

**FSN.** Foreign Service National, a foreign national who is a full-time employee at an American embassy.

**Fulbrighter.** An American or foreign student or scholar who holds a Fulbright exchange grant from the U.S. government.

**International Visitor Leadership Grantee (formerly International Visitor Grantee).** A prominent foreign visitor to the United States who comes on a grant arranged by the CAO and PAO with input from the ambassador.

**IO.** Information Officer (or Press Attaché), an American official who heads the information section of an embassy, under the PAO.

**MENA.** Middle East and North Africa, the geographic area that includes all Arab States.

**NEA.** The Near East and North Africa Bureau at the State Department.

**OAPEC.** The Organization of Arab Petroleum Exporting Countries, established 1968, includes ten Arab countries.

**OPEC.** The Organization of Petroleum Exporting Countries, established 1961, includes many of the world's oil producers.

**OWI.** The Office of War Information, established in 1943 to carry out information programs abroad, it was the first public diplomacy organization. The State Department assumed its functions in 1945.

**PA.** Public Affairs, the bureau at the State Department in Washington that is responsible for keeping the American public informed about U.S. policy (the term Public Affairs Officer is used abroad for a different purpose).

**PAO.** Public Affairs Officer, the senior American public diplomacy official at an embassy, who reports to the ambassador, and supervises the CAO, IO, and FSNs. Between 1953 and 1999 the PAO also reported to USIA Washington.

**Radio Sawa.** A U.S. government-funded Arabic radio station under the BBG, started in 2002.

**RFI.** Radio Free Iraq, a U.S. government surrogate radio station that existed between 1998 and 2004 to provide news and information to the Iraqi public.

**USAID.** The U.S. Agency for International Development, the Washington agency responsible for foreign economic assistance programs.

**USIA.** The United States Information Agency, established 1953 and abolished in 1999 when its functions were absorbed into the State Department.

**USICA.** The U.S. International Communication Agency, the name that replaced USIA temporarily, 1979–1982.

**USIS.** The United States Information Service is the term used in foreign countries to designate U.S. government information offices. The term USIS started during World War II and has continued to this day, despite the disappearance of the Washington agency USIA in 1999.

**VOA.** The Voice of America, a U.S. government agency established in 1942 to carry

out radio broadcasts to foreign audiences. It was under USIA 1953–1999, then under the Broadcasting Board of Governors.

**Washington File.** A U.S. government daily news bulletin (originally called "Wireless File") prepared in Washington for use by American embassies abroad, now transmitted by Internet.

# Introduction

Public diplomacy is mostly about carrying out information and cultural programs abroad that serve the interests of the United States. Following are ten brief examples of the kinds of programs by public diplomacy professionals that will be discussed in greater detail in this book.[1]

## PRACTICAL EXAMPLES OF PUBLIC DIPLOMACY

1. *Fulbrighters.* An Iraqi Fulbright student said in 2004 of his year-long experience in America: "From what I have observed in American society, in terms of political and social change . . . I think I need to be an evolutionary leader not a revolutionary one. . . . I have a dream to see Iraq and other Middle Eastern leaders advocating change not through bloodshed, violence and hatred, but by advocating peace and love."[2]

2. *Visits to America.* In the 1960s when American–Egyptian relations were becoming tense, Jim Halsema arranged a two-month trip to the United States to observe the American political system for a relatively obscure young politician named Anwar Sadat. Nearly twenty years later, as President of Egypt, Sadat reversed years of official Egyptian hostility to the United States and, with President Carter's encouragement, signed a peace agreement with Israel.[3] And in 2000, in Jordan, Alberto Fernandez cultivated a friendship with a young man from the East Bank who was at first so critical of the United States that he refused to visit Alberto in his office. After Alberto sent him on a Visitor Grant to America, he said he under-

stood America much better. He later became an editorial writer for a leading newspaper, often writing columns helpful to the United States, and although he remained a critic he was much more balanced in his views.

3. *Policy advocacy.* In 2001, in Cairo, Marcelle Wahba called on the managing editor of Egypt's most important newspaper, who immediately launched into a strong criticism of the United States for a recent vote in the UN that gave Israel its only international support. After listening patiently for the editor to get his complaint off his chest, she calmly explained the American rationale for the vote, and said it was clear they had a difference of opinion, but she respected his. He wrote an editorial on the subject but it was milder than it might have been. She continued to stay in touch with him and their regular conversations had a helpful effect.

4. *Facilitating educational exchanges.* After 9/11, the more stringent application of U.S. visa regulations and the additional security checks caused long delays for Arab students and others who wanted to come to the United States. Stories of harassment of Arabs in the United States abounded. As a result, the number of visitors to America declined sharply. In Abu Dhabi, Katherine Van de Vate teamed up with the embassy consular officer to do briefings for students and businessmen to make the visa process understandable and encourage legitimate travel to continue. She also advised Washington on ways the system could be made more efficient so that the valuable exchange of persons programs could continue.

5. *Mediating reconciliation.* In 1997 when Duncan MacInnes was assigned to Jerusalem, he organized a week-long retreat on Cyprus for fifteen Palestinians from the Fatah youth movement and fifteen Israelis from the Likud youth movement, for training sessions in nonviolent political activism led by American instructors from the American Council of Young Political Leaders (ACYPL). On the first day, when they met their counterparts, many of the participants wanted to leave, but they stayed, and by the end of the week, after getting to know each other as human beings, they had become friends. To everyone's surprise they produced a very forward-leaning joint declaration in support of peace. They returned to their respective homes where they were roundly criticized and even threatened by some of their colleagues. But many of the participants then traveled together to the United States on a U.S.-funded program on political organizations. The Fatah youth group organized their own youth political action group modeled on the ACYPL.

6. *Arabic broadcasting.* When Iraq occupied Kuwait in 1990 and Washington needed to mobilize Arab public support to confront Saddam Hussain, Sam Hilmy, as Division Chief of the Voice of America and Mahmoud Zawawi, as Arabic Branch Chief, increased the Arabic program from 9.5 to 15.5 hours daily. They expanded news reports from nine Arab capitals, initiated live simultaneous interpretations of major events including news conferences by President Bush, increased government editorials to

three per day, did thousands of interviews, expanded call-in shows and initiated 24/7 dial-in news service for this "surge" programming during the crisis.[4]

7. *English teaching.* In 1995, John Kincannon arranged for several key young members of Yemen's Islamist "Islah" party, which was rather hostile to the United States, to take English lessons at the Yemen-American Language Institute in Sanaa. Along with English they learned a great deal about the United States from their American instructors, and they became acquainted with some Americans personally for the first time. John also gave the brightest of them grants to visit the United States, and he saw changed perspectives and more sophisticated understanding of America in their attitudes.

8. *American speakers and cultural presentations.* In 2004, when Egyptian–American relations were increasingly tense, Elizabeth Thornhill arranged for an American political science professor to visit Egypt where he gave lectures on the election campaign which was then going on in the United States. At the university in conservative Assiut in Upper Egypt, he spoke to packed halls, and gave them a better understanding of democracy, dispelling many of their myths about America. Thornhill also arranged for a rock-and-roll band to perform in Cairo; this attracted a huge audience of appreciative Egyptian youth who were mostly critical of Washington's foreign policy.

9. *Using local television and books in Arabic.* In 2003, John Berry was assigned to Karbala, Iraq, at a time when the United States was trying to help the Iraqis prepare for their democratic elections. Fluent in Arabic, he appeared on television and in meetings explaining the democratic process. He acquired copies of American books such as the *Federalist Papers*, had them translated into Arabic by a team of Iraqi professors, distributed them widely, and opened a small library. This all helped the Iraqis, who were eager to learn a new system of government.

10. *Providing information to the right people.* In 2004, Jim Bullock provided documentary and background materials on American policy to an Egyptian scholar who was invited to appear on Egyptian television, and who needed up-to-date information on American official thinking. The scholar's observations included some criticism of Washington but they were much more balanced and better informed than most of the other Egyptian commentators, who tended to be critical, and coming from an Egyptian, the observations were more credible than they would have been coming from an American.

These are all examples of different aspects of public diplomacy, and also of "soft power." Joseph Nye, in his insightful discussion of soft power, pointed out that it is based on values, culture and institutions as well as policies. How Americans behave at home and what policies they pursue abroad can contribute to U.S. power in the world, just as military and economic strength can. Information is power and behavior that is admired by

others is a form of power.[5] Public diplomacy is a means of making use of those assets to further national interests.

## DEFINING PUBLIC DIPLOMACY

How has the U.S. government defined "public diplomacy"?

For years, the bronze plaque on the building at 1776 Pennsylvania Avenue in Washington, DC, said: "United States Information Agency: Telling America's Story to the World." American public diplomacy, however, cannot be summarized into the last six words on that plaque. More precisely, over the years it has come to mean a U.S. government information and cultural program for informing, engaging, and influencing foreign public opinion in support of U.S. objectives. It has four distinct components: (1) explaining U.S. foreign policy to foreign publics; (2) presenting them with a fair and balanced picture of American society, culture, and institutions; (3) promoting mutual understanding with those foreign publics; and (4) advising U.S. policy makers on foreign attitudes. Public diplomacy professionals usually refer to these four tasks as policy advocacy, Americana, the "third mandate," and the advisory function. It uses open means and not covert ones, and it is always truthful.

Over the years, the emphasis given to one or another of these four components has shifted back and forth, but professional public diplomacy practitioners usually keep them all in mind. The latest formulation of the goals is:

> to increase understanding of American values, policies and initiatives and to counter anti-American sentiment and misinformation about the United States around the world. This includes reaching beyond foreign governments to promote better appreciation of the United States abroad, greater receptivity to U.S. policies among foreign publics, and sustained access and influence in important sectors of foreign societies.[6]

Public diplomacy is not traditional diplomacy, for two reasons. Traditional diplomacy is the conduct of official business between governments, so traditional diplomats deal primarily if not exclusively with officials of ministries of foreign affairs and some other ministries. On the other hand, public diplomacy professionals deal with the general public and especially with opinion leaders such as media editors, reporters, university faculty, student leaders, and prominent intellectual and cultural personalities. The instruments and techniques are also different. Most traditional diplomacy is conducted in secret, behind closed doors and through classified documents, while public diplomacy is open and unclassified. Diplomacy is thousands of years old; the American government has practiced public diplomacy since World War II and the term was coined in 1965.[7]

The central characters in this book are the Americans serving as Public Affairs Officers (PAOs) who head the public diplomacy sections at embassies in Arab countries, and the Cultural Affairs Officers and Information Officers (CAOs and IOs) who manage the cultural/educational and information sections under the PAOs. (Some tend to be more adept at cultural-educational work while others prefer information work, but they all focus on the same audiences and techniques.) Together with the locally hired Foreign Service Nationals (FSNs) who provide local knowledge, language skills, and continuity, they constitute the team that carries out public diplomacy programs backed by Washington.

Public statements by U.S. officials in Washington are only part of the public diplomacy process. These words can be deliberately distorted, taken out of context, or simply misunderstood by foreign listeners with a different mind-set from ours. The task of public diplomacy officers working at embassies abroad is to facilitate communication between Americans and foreign groups, which they do by engaging in daily discussions with them and helping to bring them together with Americans in various ways.

Those American public diplomacy professionals serving at embassies abroad first worked under the office of War Information during World War II, then the Department of State, 1945–1953, then under the U.S. Information Agency, 1953–1999, and since 1999 again under the State Department. Originally they were called "Foreign Service Reserve Officers" but in 1968, Congress passed a law giving USIA officers career status, integrating them into the regular Foreign Service as FSOs.[8]

When USIA was merged into the State Department in 1999 by the Foreign Affairs Reform and Restructuring Act of 1998 (Public Law 105-277), the FSOs who had been working for USIA came under the State Department. The "United States Information Service (USIS)," which predated USIA, is the name that continues to be used to this day for the information offices in foreign countries that are managed by public diplomacy professionals.

The diplomats who serve as political economic, or consular officers are historically the most likely to become ambassadors. Much has been written about them. This book is about the "other" FSOs who are public diplomacy specialists. They are less well known but they too serve our national interest with great distinction.

Both types of FSO, diplomats and public diplomacy professionals, have the formal responsibility of representing the United States abroad, and at the embassy they both report to the ambassador. But they operate in two different cultures, with different styles and mind-sets. The public diplomacy officer's task is to engage with, listen to, and persuade key people in the general public, while the diplomat's task is to engage and negotiate with foreign government officials. Therefore, a cadre of professionals in public diplomacy was created who were FSOs but who had a

specialty that was distinct from traditional diplomacy. PAOs seek to involve ambassadors and other embassy officers in their programs, but they sometimes resist doing press interviews or other public events out of fear of saying something that would be distorted and create problems. In fact, often traditional diplomats not only hesitate to do public diplomacy but they regard it as a secondary or even frivolous undertaking that is not essential but peripheral to supporting the national interest. This attitude prevailed when the U.S. Information Agency existed. The USIA merger into State in 1999 was intended in part to overcome it, but that did not happen, and it continues to hamper the effective conduct of public diplomacy to this day.

Public diplomacy is not propaganda, which can employ covert means (black propaganda deliberately hides the source), and can be misleading or untruthful. A basic rule in public diplomacy is to tell the truth. As Edward R. Murrow put it, "American traditions and the American ethic require us to be truthful, but the most important reason is that . . . (to) be persuasive we must be believable; to be believable we must be credible; to be credible we must be truthful. It is as simple as that."[9]

Public diplomacy is also not advertising or marketing, which are functions of commercial companies intended to persuade consumers to buy specific products. Nor is public diplomacy to be confused with public relations, a rather uncomplicated activity used to enhance the reputation of a company or political candidate. Nor is public diplomacy merely an American information program as the name "U.S. Information Agency" implies, because it is not a unilateral activity, but rather it involves American understanding of foreign opinion and a dialogue. In the State Department in Washington, DC, the term "public affairs" means the function of U.S. officials to explain and defend American foreign policy to the American public. The public affairs function, performed notably by the spokesman of the department and others who deal with the American press, are not considered to be performing the public diplomacy function because their primary audience is in the United States, although what they say does have an impact on foreign opinion abroad. However, it should be noted that at American embassies abroad, the person acting as a "Public Affairs Officer" (PAO) is the chief of the public diplomacy section, whereas the other two titles used in that section are Cultural Affairs Officer and Information Officer.

Finally, public diplomacy is not psychological warfare (psywar), which is a short-term information and policy advocacy effort conducted by the Pentagon before and during a specific military campaign to increase chances of that campaign's success. In Desert Storm (1991), the Afghan War (2001), and the Iraq War (2003), the Pentagon used information techniques such as leaflet drops and broadcasts from airplanes to persuade the enemy to surrender, but these were narrow, short-term efforts and not public diplo-

macy. Since 1942 the Pentagon has also managed the Armed Forces Network (AFN) radio for DOD personnel, which at times (during the 1991 war) has had an unintended Arab "shadow audience." Pentagon officials have talked about "strategic communication" and allocated funds for information activities in Iraq and Afghanistan since 9/11, but the purpose is different from traditional public diplomacy.

In 2005, the U.S. Agency for International Development (USAID) created the new position of public affairs officer for all of its overseas missions. Prior to that time, the responsibility for publicizing USAID programs and projects at each embassy was in the hands of the embassy's Public Affairs Officer (who reported to USIA while it existed from 1953 to 1999, and now reports to the State Department). The creation of a separate USAID position somewhat diminishes the PAO's scope of responsibility in the embassy.

This book is about how American public diplomacy evolved in the Arab world and what it does today. It covers six decades and nearly two dozen Arab countries, giving the highlights of the chronology and selected examples from specific countries, to illustrate techniques used in the real world of public diplomacy. The men and women who specialize in public diplomacy and who serve in Arab countries, carrying out programs like the ones mentioned at the beginning of this Introduction, are the central actors in this story. They all have management, language, and interpersonal skills, and they work hard at developing a wide circle of personal contacts and bringing Arabs and Americans together. Their story is little known to Americans. The book uses their words, and the words of their Arab interlocutors, as derived from interviews, recorded oral histories, and the personal recollections of the author, who participated in these activities for thirty-one years. It thus attempts to give the reader the flavor of what it was and is like to carry out a public diplomacy program in the Arab world, describing the challenges and activities, successes, and failures in communicating with Arab audiences.

Each Arab country is unique in many ways, so generalizations do not always apply; therefore the stories about specific experiences of the professionals are intended to help illustrate local circumstances as well as useful techniques.

Public statements by U.S. officials in Washington, whether they occur in presidential speeches, State Department or Pentagon spokesman briefings, or on other occasions, are of course a key ingredient of public diplomacy. Public statements by private Americans such as media commentators or public figures also are heard abroad, and in today's world, because of global communications, these statements and comments often have a strong and immediate impact on foreign opinion. But the statements alone are usually not sufficient to constitute public diplomacy, because the person who hears them may not understand what was intended by the speaker. One of the tasks of public diplo-

macy professionals is to help the speaker understand in advance what the impact abroad is likely to be. Another task is to help the foreign audience understand the context and the intention of the speaker.

Readers should keep in mind that while public diplomacy may look like merely the management of programs abroad, in fact the most important element is interpersonal interaction that is the goal of the most effective programs. In the examples listed at the beginning of this Introduction, and in more that appear in the chapters of this book, success required a close knowledge of Arab culture and society, usually based on extensive personal contacts. When he was USIA Director, Edward R. Murrow famously said, "The crucial link in the communication chain is the last three feet—one person talking to another."[10] The "last three feet" dictum has remained the iron rule of public diplomacy professionals ever since. This is especially true in the Arab world where personal contact is so important. An American PAO who takes time to cultivate good personal relations with Arab editors and others and becomes a trusted source is the key to success of the program.

In the following chapters, we will refer frequently to "PAO" and "USIS" since the Public Affairs Officer is the senior embassy official responsible for a public diplomacy program, and who manages the U.S. Information Service staff at the embassy in an Arab country. The focus in this book is on the PAO and other American public diplomacy officers and what they do at embassies in the Arab world. The story of the other Foreign Service Officers who carry out traditional diplomatic functions at those same embassies, as political, economic, or consular officers or ambassadors, has been described in other books and it is not the focus here, but it should be kept in mind throughout this narrative that they are carrying out their functions all the time in parallel to that of the PAO. The PAO's work is less well known and this book seeks to make it better understood.

# 1

# Public Diplomacy Resources and Instruments

American public diplomacy professionals make use of a variety of resources and instruments to carry out their responsibilities in the Arab world. Before we review their work both past and present, we will briefly summarize in this chapter the tools, instruments and other resources they use to carry out their responsibilities.

Some of these instruments have a long history, and many of them have been modified over time to fit changing circumstances; other instruments are relatively new. The main focus in this chapter is on the operations in embassies abroad where most of these instruments are utilized.

A successful public diplomacy operation makes use of short-term "information" instruments such as press releases and radio broadcasts, and also "educational and cultural" programs that have longer-term purposes such as student exchange visits. At embassies abroad, the former are handled by an Information Officer (IO) and staff in an Information Section, and the latter are managed by a Cultural Affairs Officer (CAO) in a Cultural Section, both under the general supervision of a Public Affairs Officer (PAO). The PAO, who is the central figure in this book, reports directly to the ambassador. The PAO is expected to be familiar with both information and educational/cultural matters, unlike the British system where the two functions are separate.[1]

## INFORMATION INSTRUMENTS AND PROGRAMS

### The "Washington File"

The Washington File is a daily bulletin sent to American embassies abroad by the State Department. It contains full texts of the latest U.S. official statements such as speeches by the president or secretary of state, official press releases, excerpts from American media editorials, and special features written by Washington staff. The PAO and staff turn this material into press releases for Arab editors and others. They hope that access to reliable facts and analyses will be helpful in understanding America. They hope also that the media editors will publish at least some of the material, so that it reaches a wider audience. Even if an Arab editor has already seen a wire service report of an official U.S. statement, the full text and the American editorials about it may be useful in providing a more complete picture.

This is the oldest instrument in the American public diplomacy arsenal. It started in 1935, and for many decades it was called the "wireless file," because it used radio-teletype for transmission, and usually it took three or four hours overnight to be transmitted. PAOs in the Arab world have also had an Arabic version since 1977 and PAOs at North African Arab posts had a French version before that. The Arabic edition is about 10,000 words daily, and includes exclusive features to specific editors in the Arab world.[2]

The English versions of File materials are distributed also to all embassy Americans so that they can keep abreast of developments of importance to their work, and help support the PAO's public diplomacy effort.

Most PAOs in the Arab world have considered the File to be their most important instrument because it brings them authoritative official statements and American press excerpts otherwise unavailable to their audiences. In the past it was often the only rapid source of U.S. information besides radio available to Arab media editors. Today, with the spread of the Internet and satellite television, the File is still a valuable PAO tool because it is accurate and authoritative and includes full texts, while many other sources contain only summaries or distorted versions of U.S. official statements. In 1995, the File was shifted from an embassy-only transmission to an Internet product, available to anyone, speeding up the distribution process. Some posts also have set up listserv arrangements with some target audience members who want to have the file sent directly to their individual Web sites.

### Web Sites and Short Text Messaging

For more than a decade now, public diplomacy professionals have made use of the new information technology that has been burgeoning

around the globe. Arab elites and teenagers have been quick to try it and become part of the global discussion. The U.S. Information Agency in the early 1990s was one of the first government entities to introduce Web sites, digital video conferencing, and interactive CD-ROMs, and now, the State Department's international Web site, which is updated every day in several languages including Arabic and French, "is a model of its kind."[3]

By 2005 all U.S. embassies in Arab countries had local Web sites linked to http://usembassy.state.gov. By 2004, approximately 470 other Arabic Web sites had established links to the State Department's main Webpage, and nearly half of the site's users were located in the Arab world. Arabs interested in staying informed on a regular basis on U.S. events and policies can sign up for the daily Washington File in English or Arabic, and in mid-2004 more than 1,200 Arab users were receiving that service in Arabic by e-mail. The Web sites now available to Arabs provide approximately 70,000 page views per day of information about the United States and its policies that only a few years ago were not available, and the amount increases dramatically during periods of crisis or intense focus on U.S.-related international events. For example, when the Abu Ghraib scandal broke in April 2004, activity on the global Web site increased by 14 percent and on the Arabic Web site by 30 percent.[4] Although use of the Internet among the general public in the Arab world is still limited, it is growing, and most Arab journalists depend on it so some of its material finds its way into the newspaper, radio, and television reports that they write.

At a few Mideast embassies, the PAO uses Short Text Messaging to send out notices of important and time-sensitive U.S. official statements to members of his target audience who are interested in the service and who have cell phones capable of receiving the bulletins. This service makes use of new technology to get American materials into the hands of audience members who are already bombarded with large amounts of information from many sources.

### Other Printed Materials

American PAOs in the Arab world make use of other printed materials produced or acquired by the State Department, including books, booklets, pamphlets, posters, and small traveling exhibits on a variety of topics related to American culture, society, history, and policies. Most of these materials are translated into Arabic.

In July 2003, the State Department began to sponsor a new general-interest, 72-page, glossy Arabic-language monthly feature magazine called *Hi* produced by a private firm, with 45,000 copies offered each month for sale in 18 Arab countries; copies are also distributed free by PAOs. The magazine has a Web site in English and Arabic, www.hiinternational.com.

*Hi* also has interactive features that have proven to be effective, including contests and questions about America.[5]

In the past, there were several USIA-produced periodicals in Arabic or English available to PAOs in the Arab world for distribution free of charge to their target audiences, but they all gradually disappeared because of shrinking budgets. The most important one was *Al Majal*, which was written by staff in Washington or contract writers, in a style and format similar to *Life* magazine. It started in 1967 as an Arabic version of a magazine for Africa, then became an independent, Arab-focused magazine in 1971, but it was discontinued as a result of budget cuts in 1994.[6]

Other publications produced by USIA that PAOs in the Arab world found useful were *Dialogue*, a quarterly journal that contained essays and articles on serious topics, reprinted from commercial and intellectual publications and intended for academics and policy makers; *Economic Impact*, a journal intended for economists and business people; *Problems of Communism*, which carried essays and documentation demonstrating the flaws in Communist theory and systems; and *English Teaching Forum*, a professional journal for English teachers. All of these, however, disappeared for budgetary reasons, except for *English Teaching Forum*, which still has a worldwide distribution of 65,000 copies.

PAOs also make use of special pamphlets or brochures that support cultural presentations, special events or English teaching programs, or that convey information and ideas about a particular theme.

### Electronic Journals

Starting in 1996, USIA took advantage of the new Internet technology by developing a series of "electronic journals." They are intended as packages of policy materials from official and nonofficial sources, including statements, analyses, bibliographies, and other referenced sources. The topics are selected at the State Department in Washington, and fall into five categories: foreign policy, economics, democracy and human rights, global issues such as drug trafficking, and U.S. society and values. The materials are all written by Washington staff, commissioned or reprinted from American publications, and are available in Arabic and French as well as English. PAOs in Arab countries have found them very useful, promoting them either in electronic format or printing them out and distributing them in hard copy.[7]

### Radio Broadcasting

The Voice of America is the second oldest of the public diplomacy tools, after the wireless file. It has been an excellent asset for public diplomacy officers in the Arab world. The VOA program was listened to because of its

professionalism, variety of programming, and breadth of audience. VOA began its Arabic broadcasts in 1942, shortly after the English service started, to support the American effort in World War II against German and Japanese propaganda. It led off with the announcement, "daily at this time, we shall speak to you about America and the war. The news may be good or bad. We shall tell you the truth." When the war ended in 1945, VOA discontinued more than half of its language services, including the Arabic Service, although worldwide English continued. The Arabic Service resumed on January 1, 1950, as a result of the Cold War and Washington's desire to reach Arab audiences. Initially, it was only thirty minutes daily, but during the 1950s it grew rapidly as Washington paid attention to crises in the Middle East and the need to do more public diplomacy there. It surged during the Suez Crisis of 1956 to 14.5 hours daily, and by 1958, VOA Arabic had increased to six hours per day, nearly as much as the English Service. VOA established Arabic Program Centers in Cairo in 1951 and in Beirut in 1955. These centers interviewed prominent Arabs in the arts and politics, but they concentrated mostly on nonpolitical programming.[8]

VOA was originally part of the State Department; then when USIA was established in 1953 it fell under USIA's jurisdiction, but it always enjoyed more autonomy from USIA management than the other public diplomacy tools. Over the years, PAOs in the Arab world found the Voice of America, especially its Arabic Service, extremely useful in providing information on American policy, society, and culture to Arab audiences, even though they did not control it directly. Their only complaint was that the VOA signal was not heard in all parts of the Arab world, since Arab listeners increasingly shifted from shortwave to medium wave and VOA's medium wave transmitters were not powerful enough to cover the region.

Voice of America professionals always insisted on protecting the objectivity of their reporting and they have generally been supported, although very occasionally State Department officials have clashed with the VOA.

In 1959, under the Eisenhower administration, VOA director Henry Loomis commissioned a formal statement of principles for VOA and in 1960, USIA director George V. Allen had it issued as a VOA Directive. In 1962, USIA director Edward R. Murrow endorsed it; it was put into law in 1976. On July 12, 1976, Congress gave the VOA a special "charter" that said:

> The long-range interests of the United States are served by communicating directly with the peoples of the world by radio. To be effective, the Voice of America must win the attention and respect of listeners. These principles will govern VOA broadcasts: 1. VOA will serve as a consistently reliable and authoritative source of news. VOA will be accurate, objective and comprehensive; 2. VOA will represent America, not any single seg-

ment of American society, and will therefore present a balanced and comprehensive projection of significant American thought and institutions; 3. VOA will present the policies of the United States clearly and effectively and will also present responsible discussion and opinion on these policies.[9]

When USIA was abolished in 1999, VOA was put under the Broadcasting Board of Governors, an autonomous U.S. government agency whose membership is bipartisan. The secretary of state has a seat on the BBG but in practice, public diplomacy professionals have had little influence over it since 1999. In 2002, the BBG abolished the VOA's Arabic Service and substituted a new radio service for Arab audiences called the Middle East Radio Network or "Radio Sawa," with an initial budget of $22 million that BBG controlled. Unlike the broad and varied VOA Arabic program for all audiences that it replaced, Radio Sawa offered mostly Western and Arab popular music, with periodic brief news bulletins, intended for youth audiences.

In 1998, the Congress established "Radio Free Iraq," an international broadcasting service that was separate from VOA. This was a so-called "surrogate" radio station, as a kind of substitute for Iraq's government-controlled domestic radio, and intended to provide news and information as well as commentary, all in Arabic, that the Iraqi government censors were not allowing the Iraqi people to hear. Radio Free Iraq (RFI) was modeled on the surrogate radio services like Radio Liberty and Radio Free Europe, which were developed during the Cold War for the Soviet Union and East Europe. Ambassador David Newton, a retired Foreign Service Officer with extensive Middle East experience, set up the RFI from an office in Prague in October 1988. He managed it until RFI was abolished in 2004, when Iraqis had access to radio broadcasts other than the ones Saddam Hussein controlled. The mission of Radio Free Iraq, like the Radio Free Europe, Radio Liberty, and other surrogate radio stations, was to promote democratic values and institutions by disseminating factual information and ideas. The content of the RFI program, in Arabic and Kurdish, was news about Iraq and news relevant to Iraqi concerns. Although RFI was not, strictly speaking, a public diplomacy instrument because its mission was not specifically to promote and explain U.S. foreign policy as VOA does, it served some public diplomacy purposes.[10] It operated while the American embassy in Baghdad was closed; it was the only U.S. government broadcasting effort aimed specifically at that country, and it served American interests.

## Television and Film

In the past, PAOs in the Arab world made extensive use of direct projection of documentary films produced by USIA, and acquired Hollywood

feature films. Then they developed extensive video collections for loan. Now both of these are much less useful, because of satellite television.

Information Officers regard the placement of information on Arab television as one of their primary goals and regular activities. Prior to 1990, essentially all Arab television channels were government owned and controlled in countries that were politically friendly to the United States, so television news and commentaries were relatively friendly to the United States and placement was possible. During the 1990s, several new Arab satellite television channels emerged that were seen throughout the region and were not under government control. Some carried news and commentary that put the United States in a bad light, but most were willing to interview American officials and use materials provided by American public diplomacy officers. Many of the new TV channels also carried a great deal of material purchased from American TV networks, and maintained correspondents in the United States who provided daily coverage of events in the United States.

In 1983, the U.S. government set up its own "Worldnet" television service, which sent live and recorded television material via satellite from its Washington headquarters to embassies abroad. Starting in Europe, it was extended to the Arab world in 1987, and soon included transmissions in Arabic.[11] PAOs encouraged local TV stations to access the material directly; they also received it in embassies on TVRO (television receive only) equipment and took it to the local station for placement. Some live interactive programs were arranged between Arab journalists at one or more posts in the Arab world, asking questions of American officials in Washington. But because of the growth of Arab satellite television and the Internet, Worldnet became less useful to PAOs in the Arab world.

In 2004, in the wake of 9/11, the U.S. Broadcasting Board of Governors, with generous funding from Congress, started "al Hurra," a new television channel for Arab audiences. The BBG intended that it would compete with the existing Arab TV channels for Arab viewers, and provide them with American material to which they otherwise would not have access. But it was not initially successful because Arab viewers found that it covered American news less well than the existing Arab channels, was weak in covering Arab news, and seemed like American propaganda, so it did not fulfill its potential.[12] PAOs also had no input into its programs.

## EDUCATIONAL AND CULTURAL RESOURCES

The Cultural Section of an American embassy, managed by an American Cultural Affairs Officer (CAO) under the overall direction of the Public Affairs Officer, has access to a variety of program tools that it can choose from, depending on local circumstances.

## Educational Exchanges

The U.S. government sponsors several types of programs that bring Arab students, scholars, and professionals to America, or send Americans abroad. Public diplomacy professionals in the Arab world regard these programs as among their most effective tools for bridging understanding between the two worlds, because a firsthand experience living in a foreign culture is the best possible way to enhance mutual understanding. Arab students who have attended American universities remember the experience for the rest of their lives. The memory is usually a positive one, and it almost always leads to a more sophisticated understanding of American society and culture, politics, and the basis of American foreign policy. In addition, friendships and connections that develop during a stay in the United States often last for years, so that Arabs who go into business create U.S.–Arab business ties, and Arab academics create scholarly ties, and so on. Foreign students in America also contribute billions of dollars to the U.S. economy, and returnees are more likely than others to buy American products.

An Arab student who spends time in the United States may criticize American policy and society in some respects but the criticism is usually more sophisticated, more nuanced, and based on more accurate information than the criticism of someone who has never been to the United States. American diplomats dealing with Arab officials usually find it much easier to talk with a returnee who knows America firsthand. They often retain an interest good U.S.–Arab relations and are helpful, because their view of the United States is generally positive and they are credible when they help explain America to their compatriots.

Often, Arabs learn to appreciate many aspects of America even while criticizing its foreign policy. For example, an Algerian Fulbright scholar said, in 2001: "I think your government has not lived up to its responsibilities in the Middle East and I condemn it for that, but I have witnessed how this country's democratic institutions work in a small American community and I want that success for my country."[13]

Exchanges also have an impact on Americans. The Arab visitor to America helps educate Americans about the Arab world, and an American going to an Arab country as a U.S. government-sponsored teacher or speaker learns about Arab society, culture, and politics. Each side learns how the other sees the world, deals with problems, and leads a "normal" life. This experience is more powerful for both sides than films or lectures or reading books. Moreover, contacts and friendships made during the visit often are maintained afterwards, leading to productive professional and personal relationships and repeat visits.

Since World War II, the U.S. government has sponsored educational exchange programs for tens of thousands of Arab and American students,

teachers, scholars, mid-level officials, and professionals of various kinds. Many Arabs who have had U.S.-sponsored visits to the United States have risen to important positions in their home countries, playing key roles in politics, the academy, or the arts. Anwar Sadat, for example, was a visitor grantee sponsored by the U.S. government when he was speaker of the parliament, and when he became president of Egypt he showed a good understanding of America and some basic sympathy toward the United States. A large number of Arabs who were Fulbright students in the United States later attained prominence in their home countries or even internationally in various fields. For example, Boutros Boutros Ghali, the former UN Secretary General; Mohammad Benaissa, the Moroccan Foreign Minister; and Abdal Aziz Abdal Ghani, the former Yemeni Prime Minister, were Fulbright students, as were Fatina Shaker, a professor in Saudi Arabia and chief editor of a Saudi magazine, and Laila Takla, chair of Egypt's National Women's Council.[14]

Between 1948 and 2002, approximately 6,600 scholars from the Middle East came to the United States to do graduate work or teach here. Although ten times that number have come from Western and Central Europe, the numbers from the Middle East are significant given the fact that U.S.-sponsored exchanges have often been hampered by political factors, including the breaking of diplomatic relations between the United States and specific Arab countries like Syria, Egypt, Libya, Algeria, and Iraq. Moreover, new security restrictions on visas for Arabs after 9/11, plus Arab concerns about traveling to the United States, have added delays and inconvenience to the visa process, diminishing the flow of Arabs to America. After 9/11, however, the State department increased funding for exchanges with the Arab world, but funding has not reached previous levels.

Reactions from nearly all participants have been very positive. Barry Ballow, who was director of the office of international exchanges at USIA and the State Department for a decade (1994–2004), frequently heard from Arab students, scholars and professionals who spent time in the United States that although they did not agree at all with U.S. foreign policies, they strongly admired American society for its openness, democratic values and its accommodation of the wide diversity of its population. Many stated their determination to replicate the "real America" in their own countries.[15]

There are also survey data showing that a personal experience visiting the United States helps improve opinion about America. A six-nation survey conducted in June 2004 showed that Arab attitudes toward America tended to be more favorable among Arabs who have actually visited the United States (see Table 1).[16]

### Fulbrighters

The Fulbright Program is the best known of the U.S.-sponsored educational exchange programs. Established in 1946 under legislation intro-

Table 1: Influence on Arab Attitudes of a Visit to the United States

| Question: "Have you visited the United States?" | | |
| --- | --- | --- |
| | No | Yes |
| Morocco | | |
| Favorable | 11 | 16 |
| Unfavorable | 88 | 84 |
| Saudi Arabia | | |
| Favorable | 3 | 6 |
| Unfavorable | 94 | 92 |
| Jordan | | |
| Favorable | 14 | 23 |
| Unfavorable | 78 | 73 |
| Lebanon | | |
| Favorable | 17 | 42 |
| Unfavorable | 72 | 45 |
| UAE | | |
| Favorable | 12 | 22 |
| Unfavorable | 72 | 71 |

duced by Senator Fulbright and later updated in the Fulbright-Hays Act of 1961, its purpose is "to increase mutual understanding between the people of the United States and the people of other countries."[17]

Senator Fulbright expressed the program's goals as follows:

> I do not think educational exchange is certain to produce affection between peoples, nor indeed is that one of its essential purposes; it is quite enough if it contributes to the feeling of common humanity, to an emotional awareness that other countries are populated not by doctrines that we fear but by individual people—people with the same capacity for pleasure and pain, for cruelty and kindness as the people we were brought up with in our own countries.[18]

American Fulbrighters going to the Arab world are selected by a peer review process, and Arab Fulbrighters coming to America are selected by binational commissions in Egypt, Morocco and Jordan, and by an embassy committee in the other countries. Morocco is in fact one of the few countries in the world where the host government provides more than half of the funding for the Fulbright program.

Fulbright wanted to ensure that there was no politics in the selection,

and in practice that is so, but the ambassador and country team usually consider policy criteria, that is, what is good for the U.S. national interest. This may mean selecting a person who is currently or potentially influential politically, and in Fulbright Commission countries, local members may push for candidates who are friends or relatives, but that is generally resisted.

### Visitor Grantees

PAOs use "International Visitor Leadership Grants" (formerly called "International Visitor Grants") to send mid-level professionals with leadership potential to the United States for tours of two or three months, so they can see American life firsthand and meet professional counterparts. Half of the grantees travel in small, multinational groups. The embassy makes the selection, and in the United States, there are hundreds of local contract agencies and volunteers who make local arrangements.[19]

### Youth Exchanges

PAOs also arrange exchanges for younger people who have been identified as potential leaders. The shrinking budgets of the 1980s and 1990s forced PAOs to focus on adults, reduce or eliminate youth grants, and to favor graduate students instead of undergraduates because the money would go farther. After 9/11, members of Congress and senior officials in the administration in Washington, seeing that the 9/11 terrorists were all young Arab men, decided that something should be done to reach Arab youth for whom there were no longer specific U.S. government programs. They therefore agreed to initiate new educational exchange grant programs aimed at Arab and Muslim youth.

## American Speakers

The U.S. government sponsors American experts to travel abroad and spend several days speaking directly to local audiences, explaining U.S. policy, society, or culture. Worldwide, about 1,000 speakers are provided to field posts each year. Over the years, USIA has sent many American experts in different fields abroad in this "American Speakers Program" (formerly called "American Participants" or "Amparts"). It is effective because participants are selected for their expertise in subjects of special interest to the particular audience, and they respond directly to concerns and criticisms that are on the minds of the Arab public, thus showing respect for Arab opinion. The experts are usually private citizens and they are not told what to say. In fact, some criticism of the United States usually enhances their credibility and the overall impact is helpful. Some of the most effective Amparts sent to Arab countries have been Muslims, who speak about Islam in America.

The number of speakers sent abroad has declined substantially in recent years, largely due to budget cuts, although there has been some increase recently. In 2003 and 2004, 700 and 872 speakers, respectively, were sent out worldwide. Moreover, only a small percentage of them, 43 in 2004, went to the Arab world and Israel.[20]

Today, when desired speakers are unavailable to travel to field posts, PAOs use new technology to arrange Arab–American dialogues. The simplest format is the "electronic dialogue," which uses an international phone call that brings an expert together with a selected Arab audience. The "Global Exchange" weekly interview program offers American officials in Washington for interviews with Arab journalists at field posts. "Televised Electronic Dialogues" (TEDs) offer one-way television transmissions out of the United States with an audio link both ways, and "video dialogues" offer two-way video exchanges. Benefits are that Arab audiences ask their questions and express their concerns directly to American officials or experts, plus they are easier to arrange and cheaper than travel abroad. The audience abroad usually includes Arab journalists or academics who act as multipliers and disseminate the views of the American to a wider audience. Some of the videoconferences include prepared video footage, setting the stage for the discussion.

## Libraries and Centers

PAOs in most Arab countries maintain some form of "information resource center" (formerly called "library") that maintains databases and some hard copies of books and periodicals, on various aspects of the United States, for use by any interested person in the local community, and also for use by embassy personnel in answering questions from their contacts.

For nearly half a century, the U.S. government has maintained open libraries in the Arab world which have become very popular, especially with Arab students, professionals, and returnees from study in the United States. Public libraries are rare in the Arab world, and these have usually been part of multipurpose American cultural centers, which include also an auditorium or lecture hall for presentations, film or video shows, and conferences; offices of cultural and education staff who provide advice on study in the United States and other subjects; and possibly space for English-language classes. Co-locating all of these services in one center establishes a symbiotic relationship among them, as English students find they need the library and possibly also student counseling services, and they attend lectures or films as well. This was especially effective in the Arab world because it attracted Arab students and others who would not have ventured into an American center that only provided one service. English-language classes have been particularly effective in attracting Arab students.

In recent years, growing security concerns at American embassies in

the Arab world, plus shrinking budgets, have forced the libraries/cultural centers to erect formidable security barriers or shut down completely. For example, the open and very active cultural center in Cairo was closed and replaced by only a small information resource center inside the heavily fortified American embassy compound. The disappearance of the open-access library/cultural center has created significant difficulties for PAOs in the Arab world, because in the Arab world personal contact is extremely important, and there is no longer this convenient venue for interaction with Arab contacts.[21] Many adult Arabs regret the disappearance of the open-access American library/cultural center because they used it to keep up with developments in American society, culture and politics, or to find otherwise unavailable references.

After 9/11 the idea was developed to establish "American corners" in Arab universities or other local institutions, as a way of providing library services while avoiding security risks to Americans, but they are much less useful because they do not provide multiple services under one roof, and especially because they lack an American presence that facilitates contacts.

## English Teaching

The U.S. government has sponsored direct English teaching programs taught by Americans using American materials that can help communicate a great deal about American society and culture. In the past there were USG-operated English-language classes in Morocco, Tunisia, Algeria, Egypt, Saudi Arabia, Bahrain, Iraq, Syria, Jordan, and Yemen. By 2004 only the last two remained and the rest had been privatized or simply closed, for budgetary reasons. Washington also sends English teachers to the Arab world as Regional English Language Officers (RELOs), who advise English-language professionals and local ministries of education on best practices in the teaching of English, and others who go on short-term assignments to teach in colleges and schools abroad. Currently, in the Arab world there are only two RELO positions, one based in Cairo and the other based in Amman, and a very small number of grantee teachers.

## Cultural Presentations

The U.S. government sponsors "cultural presentations" in the Arab world, that is, performances by American musical, theater, and dance groups or individuals intended to bring an understanding and appreciation of American culture to Arab audiences. Some performers give workshops. PAOs in the Arab world select such presentations carefully because not all are useful for all Arab audiences and may seem disturbingly strange or even offensive. For example, a ballet performed by men and women in tights in Riyadh would contravene Saudi conventional behavior and probably would

cause a strong negative reaction, at least from conservative elements in society. An orchestra playing classical music in an Arab city where such music is unknown would probably attract only an American and European audience and therefore be a waste of money. But a small band playing contemporary popular music or a single performer might be the most effective there. Or in countries like Egypt and Lebanon, where interest in American cultural presentations is high, local entrepreneurs have brought in American performers on a commercial basis, and in those cases PAOs need not duplicate what is already being done.

### Book Programs

For nearly half a century, the U.S. government has sponsored translations of American books into Arabic that are intended to make available to Arab audiences books that help explain American history and society and culture, and the U.S. political and economic systems. The small Arabic book program units at the American embassies in Cairo and Amman acquire the rights, hire translators on contract, and arrange publishing by local publishers. Typical print runs are 3,000 copies, of which the publisher sells 2,000 and PAOs in the region distribute the remaining 1,000, giving them as presentation items to their contacts, or making them available to the ambassador and embassy officers to give away. The entire operation, which in 2004 produced twelve new titles, costs only $50,000 annually.[22] The Djerejian Report called this "strikingly reasonable when one considers the benefits of translation" and recommended that the program be expanded to 1,000 titles per year.[23] The selection of titles for translation covers a broad range of topics. For example, recent translations include foreign policy titles such as *Honey and Vinegar*, edited by Richard Haass and Meghan O'Sullivan; a study of Abraham Lincoln by James M. McPherson and one on Mohammed Ali by Walter Dean Myers; de Tocqueville's classic work *Democracy in America;* fiction such as *Cold Mountain* by Charles Frazier; and young adult books like *Sounder* by William Armstrong.[24] PAOs in the Arab world also use the Ladder Editions for Arab audiences who have some limited English. These are American books that have been published by USIA since 1957 in abridged versions with restricted vocabularies of 1,000 to 5,000 words for students of English.[25]

## PROGRAM MANAGEMENT

A typical day for a PAO in an Arab country begins when he or she reads a selection of local newspapers looking for news stories and commentaries relevant to American interests, then meets with the ambassador and other embassy section heads, and confers briefly with staff to discuss plans and projects. The PAO typically devotes time to calls on editors to

discuss issues in the news, university officials to discuss exchange programs, or other discussions. In the evening the PAO may attend a reception and then a dinner where there are more opportunities to deepen friendships, discuss American policies, and learn about local attitudes toward the United States.

Readers should keep in mind that while public diplomacy is in one sense the management of programs abroad, the most important factor in it is the personal element. The job cannot be done by remote control from Washington, although public statements by Washington officials are very important. It also cannot be done from behind a desk at an embassy. The public diplomacy official must be out all the time developing a wide circle of contacts, in order to understand the thinking of the audience, engage them in an ongoing dialogue, and develop appropriate programs for them. Edward R. Murrow's famous "last three feet" dictum has been the byword for PAOs for decades. This is especially true in the Arab world where personal contact is so important. An American PAO who takes time to cultivate good personal relations with Arab editors and others, and becomes a trusted source, is the key to success of the program.

The ambassador and officials at the State Department in Washington monitor the PAO's work and look for ways to measure success. They know, however, that the measurement of effectiveness is very difficult, because there are so many other variables at work. As former USIA director Murrow used to say, "No cash register rings when minds change."[26] Yet it is important to keep trying to assess what impact public diplomacy programs have, or as the Djerejian report says, what is "moving the needle."[27] As a result, most evidence is anecdotal, from close observation on the scene. In the following chapters, anecdotal evidence is presented to illustrate public diplomacy techniques and effectiveness, as witnessed by practitioners.

## 2

# Beginnings in the Arab World, 1940s–1953

America's use of the "soft power" of public diplomacy in the Arab world dates back only to World War II. In fact, the real impetus for it came in the late 1940s with the start of the Cold War, which helped sustain it for decades thereafter. This chapter reviews the tentative start of the U.S. public diplomacy effort in the Arab countries during the presidency of Harry S Truman.

## BEFORE 1945

### America's Initial Low Profile

Before 1945, the U.S. government's involvement in the Arab world was extremely limited. The few American contacts with Arabs were mostly undertaken by private missionaries and oilmen. Some of the missionaries started educational institutions; for example, Daniel Bliss, who was in Beirut in the middle of the nineteenth century, began what later became the American University of Beirut. Other missionaries went to the Arab world in the early twentieth century as medical doctors, like Donald Bosch, who opened the first hospital in Oman, and Patrick Kennedy, who opened the first hospital in the Trucial States (now called United Arab Emirates). Arabs respected and appreciated these men for bringing education and modern medicine to the region, just as they appreciated American petroleum engineers' helping them to find oil. These American

pioneers made a positive contrast with the European colonialists who had dominated much of the region for decades and who had done little to develop local institutions, and whose commercial activities seemed entirely self-serving.

British and French colonial rule began in the middle of the nineteenth century and had spread to nearly the entire Arab world by the 1920s. Britain had special rights over Egypt, Iraq, Palestine, and the small territories on the Persian Gulf (Kuwait, Bahrain, Qatar, the Trucial States, and Oman), while France had special rights over Lebanon, Syria, Algeria, Tunisia, and Morocco. The only Arab lands that remained free of European colonial control were Saudi Arabia and part of Yemen.

President Woodrow Wilson made one brief intervention in 1919 when he sent the King-Crane Commission to study Arab opinion in Palestine, Syria, and Lebanon. Large majorities said they preferred the United States as the mandatory power. The commission expressed fears that the creation of a Jewish national home might be done at the expense of the Arabs, but Washington did not heed its warnings. Neither did the British government, and so the mandatory power withdrew after World War II, allowing the Jewish leaders in Palestine to declare the creation of the State of Israel. Some Arabs still remember the King-Crane Commission's supportive recommendations. They also remember President Wilson's 14 Points of January 1918, which inspired hopes that they could escape from colonialism.[1]

European control of foreign and defense matters, foreign trade, and even some purely domestic matters was widely resented. Arab uprisings, riots, and protests against the colonizers occurred frequently throughout the region during the first half of the twentieth century, and these public manifestations were often suppressed with some brutality. By 1945 there were strong popular mass movements everywhere in the Arab world dedicated to ending colonial rule and achieving national independence. Even when the Europeans relinquished rights in some of these countries in 1945, and later in the rest, bitter memories remained and helped fuel Arab nationalist resentment against foreigners.[2]

Thus, prior to 1945, few Arabs knew anything in detail about the United States, but the American image, such as it existed, was a generally positive one. Washington's effort to communicate with the Arab public was modest, however. During World War II, President Roosevelt created the Office of War Information (OWI), which by 1944 had set up U.S. Information Service (USIS) offices in Beirut, Baghdad, and Cairo. By 1945, OWI was distributing its "wireless file" news service abroad at 100,000 words per day to these posts and nearly sixty others worldwide.[3] The Voice of America had begun in 1942, and it included an Arabic Service, with brief newscasts, partly to counter Hitler's broadcasts.[4]

## THE TRUMAN ADMINISTRATION (APRIL 1945– JANUARY 1953)

Harry S Truman became president in April 1945 when Roosevelt died, just before the end of World War II. As soon as the war ended, 90 percent of OWI's 13,000 employees were fired, VOA programs were cut way back, and VOA's Arabic Service was terminated. President Truman signed an executive order transferring OWI's functions and remaining staff to the State Department and re-designating the program as the Interim International Information Administration (IIIA). The order said the United States would endeavor to conduct an international information program to give foreign audiences a "full and fair picture" of the United States and its policies.[5] The IIIA also included the Cultural Relations Division. At embassies abroad the name "U.S. Information Service" (USIS) was retained, and it has continued to be used to this day.

By 1948, Congress realized that because of the Cold War, a foreign information program was needed, and passed the Smith-Mundt Act. The act was intended "to promote the better understanding of the United States among the peoples of the world and to strengthen cooperative international relations." It called for "the preparation, and dissemination abroad, of information about the United States, its people and its policies, through press, publications, radio, motion pictures, and other information media, and through information centers and instructors abroad."[6] The act prohibited dissemination of these materials inside the United States because Congress feared that the administration would use them for partisan purposes at home. This prohibition remains on the books today, probably because Congress still is concerned not to allow a domestic information ministry, although it is somewhat outdated because of the information revolution. This was the first law endorsing public diplomacy. The first directors of the bureau at the State Department were William Benton, a partner in Benton and Bowles, a leading New York advertising agency, and after 1948 career diplomat George V. Allen, who was able to secure substantial funding from Congress.

### Truman's Worldview

President Truman faced several major international challenges during his presidency. Although World War II had ended, the Cold War was beginning, and the Korean War was on. Moreover, decolonization made India, Pakistan, and many Arab nations independent and led to the creation of Israel, as Arab nationalism began to grow. American public affairs officers in the Arab world found that issues relating to the creation of Israel and Arab nationalism were paramount among the concerns they had

to deal with, while the other events outside the Middle East were of much less importance.

During his first years, Truman became increasingly concerned about the Soviet threat to U.S. interests, as his wartime ally turned into an adversary. He decided that international Communism, backed by the Soviets, was a major threat to American interests, and this became the dominant theme in Washington for the next forty-five years. In a speech on March 12, 1947, Truman announced his determination to confront the Soviet threat and defend democracy against totalitarianism, a policy that came to be called the Truman Doctrine.

President Truman believed that his anticommunist policy required an aggressive overseas information program. As he said in 1950:

> The cause of freedom is being challenged throughout the world today by the forces of imperialistic Communism. This is a struggle, above all else, for the minds of men. Propaganda is one of the most powerful weapons the Communists have in this struggle. Deceit, distortion, and lies are systematically used by them as a matter of deliberate policy. This propaganda can be overcome by truth—plain, simple, unvarnished truth—presented by newspapers, radio, newsreels, and other sources that the people trust. . . . Unless we get the real story across to people in other countries, we will lose the battle for men's minds by pure default. . . . We must make ourselves known as we really are—not as Communist propaganda pictures us. . . . We must make ourselves heard round the world in a great campaign of truth.[7]

For Truman, Europe and the Far East were higher priorities than the Middle East, because of events there: Moscow's domination of Eastern Europe, plus the fall of China in 1949 and the 1950 North Korean invasion of South Korea. Most Arab governments seemed quite friendly and not pro-communist. In fact in some parts of the Arab world, for example in Saudi Arabia, America's anti-Communism warnings were welcomed because Communism was seen first of all as atheistic and therefore reprehensible. In more secular countries the people were not worried about Communism, which they knew little about and which did not seem to be an imminent threat, so the anti-Communism theme was less persuasive.

But the creation of Israel began to focus Truman's attention on the Middle East. In 1948, when Britain's Palestine Mandate ended, the United Nations passed Resolution 181 partitioning Palestinian territory, and Ben Gurion proclaimed the State of Israel, which the United States promptly recognized. But the Arab states rejected the partition as unfair, and on May 15, five neighboring Arab countries (Egypt, Jordan, Lebanon, Syria, and Iraq) joined Palestinian Arab irregulars and attacked the new state. The sporadic fighting that ended on January 7, 1949, left Israel with even more

of Mandated Palestine than Resolution 181 had stipulated (75 percent against 54 percent).

The Arabs accepted the armistice, but their anger grew and became the crux of the Arab grievance against Israel and its Western supporters, including the United States, which has lasted for more than half a century. The main focus of their complaint at first was against Britain and the United Nations for allowing Israel to be created over their objections, although President Truman rushed to make the United States one of the first countries to recognize Israel. Hundreds of thousands of Palestinians became refugees in neighboring Arab countries, fueling this Arab anger.

In responding to the criticism, Public Affairs Officers (PAOs) at American embassies in the Arab countries argued that the partition had been endorsed by the UN and most nations of the world, and that the Arabs had made a mistake to try to resolve the dispute by war, which only led to the loss of more territory. PAOs also privately reminded listeners that the United States itself was a country that had emerged from colonial rule. The Arabs were unconvinced by these arguments, and the issue grew in importance in the Arab–American dialogue in subsequent years, and was a continuing challenge for U.S. public diplomacy.

During the remaining five years of the Truman administration and beyond, Arab–Israeli tension increased and Arab nationalism grew with it. Palestinian irregular fighters conducted border raids into Israel, and several Arab states engaged in military buildups on the grounds that they were in a serious confrontation with Israel. The Arabs came together to form the Arab League and in 1951 it announced a full economic boycott of Israel.

American officials in Washington at first assumed that the Arab–Israeli problem was temporary and manageable. The primary task they assigned to PAOs in the Arab world in the late forties and early fifties therefore was to explain American opposition to international Communism, and to encourage the governments and people of the Arab world to work with the United States in political, commercial, and other fields. PAOs also sought to help present an understanding of American society and culture to the Arab public. In fact, the Arab governments, most of which were emerging from European colonial rule, seemed to be interested in good relations with the United States. In particular, the monarchies in the Arabian Peninsula, plus Iraq, Egypt, and Libya, and also the republics elsewhere, seemed sympathetic to the United States and uninterested in the appeals from Moscow. America began to develop commercial relations with a number of Gulf countries primarily because of new petroleum discoveries that American companies were involved in. Washington expanded its political and diplomatic contacts in most of the Arab world, although not yet in the smaller Gulf states (Kuwait, Bahrain, Qatar, Oman, and the Trucial States) that were still under British tutelage.

PAOs in the Arab countries of North Africa faced special challenges where the influence of France was strong, and not always helpful to American interests. For example, Robert Beaudry was Information Officer in Casablanca from 1948 to 1950, when Morocco was still a French Protectorate. He found that the French were quite hostile to the American information program; they thought USIS officers were intelligence officers and were meddling in Moroccan politics to the detriment of France. The French authorities controlled everything Beaudry did; for example, they allowed him to distribute some printed materials in English and French, but not in Arabic.[8]

The Truman administration moved in the early years to open information offices all over the Arab world, to help deal with what we would now call the "soft power" aspects of the confrontation with the Soviet Union. By the end of the war, Washington (through the OWI) had already set up information offices in Cairo, Beirut, and Baghdad. Then it opened the Thomas Jefferson Library in Alexandria in 1947, a cultural center in Damascus in 1948, a reading room in Port Said and an information center in Algiers in 1949, information centers in Tunisia in 1950, Benghazi and Tripoli Libya and Zahle and Tripoli Lebanon in 1951–1952, and centers in Amman in 1953, Basra and Khartoum in 1957.[9]

In the newly independent countries, centers were often established as soon as the country became independent, but in several cases these centers were established even before Washington assigned an ambassador and opened a full-fledged embassy. This indicated that Washington gave information programs a high priority, as Table 2 shows.[10]

Not all the information programs were lavish. When Lee Dinsmore, former YMCA secretary, was assigned by the State Department in the 1950s to establish a USIS post in Kirkuk, this was the first official pres-

Table 2: Opening Dates of Information Centers and Embassies, 1944–1952

|  | Information center open | Embassy open with ambassador |
|---|---|---|
| Algeria | 1949 Algiers | 1962 |
| Egypt | 1945 Cairo, 1947 Alexandria, 1949 Port Said | 1946 |
| Iraq | 1944 Baghdad | 1947 |
| Jordan | 1952 Amman | 1952 |
| Lebanon | 1944 Beirut, 1951 Zahle, 1952 Tripoli | 1952 |
| Libya | 1951 Tripoli, 1952 Benghazi | 1954 |
| Saudi Arabia | none | 1949 |
| Syria | 1948 Damascus | 1952 |
| Tunisia | 1950 Tunis | 1956 |

ence in the Kurdish area of Iraq, and he set up a small library in his home, arranged to send a few students to the United States on scholarships, and devoted the rest of his time to personal contacts with Iraqis.[11]

Some of the information offices in the Arab world, however, were well staffed and funded. For example, the Cairo office had ten Americans assigned to it: the Public Affairs Officer, Cultural Affairs Officer, Assistant CAO, Librarian, Information Officer, Press Officer, Motion Pictures Officer, Assistant Motion Pictures Officer, and Secretary, plus a large number of Foreign Service National (FSN) Egyptians. It was thought that Egyptians essentially knew nothing about America except that U.S. forces had defeated Rommel in North Africa, so it was important to provide as many Egyptians as possible with basic information about American society, culture, and foreign policy. The Motion Picture Officer produced films about the American economic assistance program of the International Cooperation Administration (predecessor of USAID), and about the work of the Naval Medical Research Unit that was helping Egypt cope with medical problems. He also roamed the country projecting documentary films to thousands of villagers who had never heard of America, and who were even unfamiliar with the cinema. (On one occasion, when he showed a public health film about malaria with close-ups of mosquitoes, the rural audience said the pictures were fake because they had never seen such "big bugs.")[12]

As Washington soon found out, opening information centers also meant setting up convenient targets for those who wanted to show their displeasure with the United States. In 1947, an angry mob invaded the USIS center in Baghdad, doing no serious damage but frightening the entire staff. In 1951, the same building was hit with a bomb that did minor damage and again had a terrorizing impact. Then, in a worse attack on the same building, on November 23, 1952, rioters burned books and equipment to show their anger at the United States. (The Iraqi government did pay for the damage.)

Attacks were also beginning to occur elsewhere. On November 20, 1952, the Lebanese communist youth demonstrated at the USIS center in Beirut, throwing stones and breaking windows. More seriously, on March 28, 1952, the USIS information center in Damascus was bombed, causing considerable damage to the library and killing the radio operator. In October 1954, the PAO in Jordan sent a terse cable to Washington: "USIS library attacked and fired by mob. Heavy damage resulted. Library moved to temporary quarters."[13]

The Voice of America was also important in those early days in reaching Arab audiences. The VOA Arabic Service that had existed 1942–1945 was revived in 1950 for one half hour daily and then it grew steadily. It was one of the first language services to carry English lessons. In 1951 it opened a program center in Cairo and in 1955 it opened another one in Beirut.[14]

Thus, when Truman's presidency ended in January 1953, PAOs in the Arab world were trying to explain U.S. policy toward the Cold War and the Arab–Israeli conflict, and to increase Arab understanding of American society and culture. Those were tasks that they and their successors would continue to struggle with for many years afterward.

# 3

# President Eisenhower and USIA, 1953–1961

## EISENHOWER'S PUBLIC DIPLOMACY

At the beginning of Dwight D. Eisenhower's presidency, his secretary of state, John Foster Dulles, made clear that he disdained the role of public opinion in foreign policy, and he asked Eisenhower to remove the information bureau (IIIA) from the State Department.[1] A Senate investigation, headed by Iowa Republican Bourke Hickenlooper, supported the removal of IIIA from State, but for different reasons, saying in its final report that an effective overseas program "could hardly be met within the outlines of a cautious, tradition-bound, bureaucratic foreign office."[2] (Some people remembered these words 50 years later as prophetic.) In any case, Eisenhower agreed and in 1953 he moved the management of overseas information programs and of the Voice of America into a newly created U.S. Information Agency. He left educational and cultural affairs at State in a new Bureau of Educational and Cultural Affairs (CU), in deference to Senator Fulbright, who thought the scholarships he sponsored would be "tainted" by a government "propaganda" operation if they were managed by USIA. Fulbright did not understand that USIA officers in embassies managed them anyway, but this organizational structure prevailed until the Carter administration.[3]

Eisenhower's first USIA director, from 1953 until 1957, was Theodor Streibert, who came from the advertising business; his second was Arthur Larsen, a Republican labor lawyer, but neither had much impact on the work of PAOs in the Arab world. The third USIA director was George V.

Allen, a veteran State Department diplomat who had headed State's information department a decade earlier. Allen was helpful because he persuaded Congress to provide more money for USIA and that allowed opening of new posts in Asia and Africa.[4]

The Eisenhower administration declared that USIA's purpose was "to submit evidence to peoples of other nations by means of communication techniques that the objectives and policies of the United States are in harmony with and will advance their legitimate aspirations for freedom, progress and peace." It added that this purpose should be carried out primarily

> by explaining and interpreting to foreign peoples the objectives and policies of the United States Government; by depicting imaginatively the correlation between U.S. policies and the legitimate aspirations of other peoples of the world; by unmasking and countering hostile attempts to distort or to frustrate the objectives and policies of the United States; and by delineating those important aspects of life and culture of the people of the United States which facilitate understanding of the policies and objectives of the Government of the United States.[5]

## America's Image

Several major Middle Eastern events took place during the Eisenhower presidency: Iraqis overthrew their monarchy; Lebanon experienced political unrest; the shah of Iran fled his country and then returned; Morocco and Tunisia became independent, but France continued to fight to keep Algeria; and Egypt was attacked by Israel, Britain, and France. The Arab public followed all of these events closely, and the way the United States dealt with them affected the American image. The other major world events that did not directly affect the Middle East, and American domestic developments were of much less interest to the Arab public.

Early in the Eisenhower administration, Washington enjoyed cordial bilateral relations with most Arab countries, and America's image in the Middle East was generally quite positive. PAOs publicized specific examples of bilateral cooperation to demonstrate American friendship with the Arab people. They also devoted time and effort to explaining basic facts about American political, social, and cultural life since these were not well understood.

During the course of the Eisenhower administration, however, Arab nationalism gathered momentum, driven by popular demands for complete independence from foreign rule, frustration over Israel, and disappointment with Arab leadership. This in turn affected Arab–American relations. Governments were overthrown and in several countries military officers came to power, established one-party authoritarian rule, and advocated aggres-

sive Arab nationalist goals that often had anti-Western overtones. The new radical regimes rallied mass support by appealing to Arab interests against colonialism and neocolonialism, and they also criticized the conservative Arab monarchies like the one in Saudi Arabia for not advocating Arab interests strongly enough. The Saudis tried to counter by appealing to the community of Islamic nations. This created new challenges for American diplomacy and public diplomacy. The Arab–Israeli conflict began to loom larger as a problem for PAOs, and this was accelerated especially by events in Egypt. After the overthrow of the Egyptian monarchy in July 1952, Gamal Abdal Nasser gradually emerged as the leader of Egypt and then as the most influential leader in the Arab world. He became the most prominent representative of strident Arab nationalism that in many respects clashed with American policy and therefore became a significant problem for U.S. public diplomacy. Nasser focused increasingly on Israel and this led him to clash with Washington.

Eisenhower's initial concern about the world after he took office in January 1953 was centered not on the Middle East but on Eastern Europe. However, as serious Arab hostility to American foreign policy began to grow, he became more concerned about that region. Arab political movements increasingly attracted Washington's full attention during the 1950s when several key Arab governments, including Egypt, Syria, Iraq, and Algeria began to align themselves internationally with Moscow. The working environment for the PAOs and other American diplomats in those countries became more difficult because Arab officials, prompted by the Soviets, came to regard Americans with suspicion and circumscribed their activities. PAOs in countries with conservative regimes, like Saudi Arabia, on the other hand faced different circumstances. The Saudis were challenged by the radical regimes for lacking Arab nationalist commitment, and they wanted American support, protection, and trade. Their only hesitation about the U.S. relationship was a fear that too close an American embrace by Washington would make them vulnerable to Arab nationalist criticism. Thus, the Saudis wanted U.S. warships nearby but "over the horizon" and therefore invisible to the public, and Saudi media were careful to criticize Washington for supporting Israel, so as not to seem too pro-American.

In the 1950s there was no satellite television, and in nearly every Arab country all the media were controlled directly or indirectly by the government. As a result, the information that was available to the Arab public about the United States or of concern to American interests came to them in a manner that was acceptable to their own government. Insofar as a government was friendly to the United States, the news and commentary was friendly also, but if the government was hostile to the United States the news in their media tended to be slanted against American interests.[6]

Thus, for example, when the Soviet Union downed a U.S. U-2 spy plane, or when civil rights issues heated up in 1954 and Eisenhower used

federal troops in Little Rock, Arab media in countries hostile to the United States played up those stories in a way that made America look bad.

In 1957, when Moscow launched Sputnik, the first man-made object in space, it was a spectacular achievement repeated endlessly by Radio Moscow, and played up in the Arab media friendly to the USSR, which used the version disseminated by the Soviet Union's official news agency TASS instead of the Associated Press or U.S. embassy version. Then in 1958, when the United States sent its first earth satellite into orbit, PAOs and the Voice of America used that story to explain the achievements of the American space program, and friendly Arab media played that up.

The shah of Iran fled his country briefly in 1953, as the result of a power struggle with his nationalist prime minister, Muhammad Mossadegh. President Eisenhower authorized the CIA to help the shah regain his throne, because he feared that Mossadegh was taking Iran into the Soviet orbit. The CIA effort was successful in helping to bring the shah back to power, but CIA's involvement was at first a well-kept secret, so the events in Iran had no particular impact on Arab perceptions of America at that time. Several years later, when the story began to leak out, and then when American participants wrote their memoirs, the CIA's role in helping the shah was a story that became for Arabs (and for Iranians) solid proof that the U.S. government works clandestinely to interfere in the domestic affairs of states in the region.

Another prominent story during the Eisenhower administration was the anticommunist campaign of Senator Joseph McCarthy. This was of concern to PAOs not so much because of the American domestic angle, in which the Arab public had only marginal interest, but because of McCarthy's interest in USIS libraries. In 1953 he investigated USIS library collections and even burned some books, and the State Department panicked, briefly banning books by "Communists, fellow travelers, etc." in its overseas libraries. But not many books were actually removed, and the problem subsided as Congress and the public turned against McCarthy in 1954.[7]

In all cases PAOs worked hard to provide full information on helpful stories, conveying Washington's official interpretation of them, and to put unhelpful stories into context. Because few Arabs watched TV, VOA was especially important, and PAOs found editors quite interested in material that they provided from the wireless file. Then public diplomacy efforts helped shape the Arab discussion because hard information about the United States was in those days relatively scarce.

In any case, Eisenhower and Dulles tended to see the Middle East in the context of the Cold War, not as a region of contending nationalisms. Thus, they developed a concept of a "Northern Tier" of friendly nations as a bulwark against Soviet expansion. This focused their attention primarily on the northern states of the Middle East, due to their proximity to the USSR. They made an effort to improve relations with the Iraqi monar-

chy and in 1954, Washington concluded a military assistance agreement with Baghdad, one of the first of its kind in Arab–American relations. Then in 1955, they encouraged the formation of the Baghdad Pact (later called the Central Treaty Organization) that included Iraq, Iran, Turkey, Pakistan, and Britain. Although the United States did not formally join the Baghdad Pact, Washington strongly supported it because it fit nicely into the "Northern Tier" defense concept.

PAOs were under instructions to promote the Baghdad Pact but many were skeptical about its utility. The director of the Near East Bureau of the United States Information Agency in Washington, G. Huntington Damon, sent one of his brightest young public diplomacy officers, Tom Sorensen (who later became deputy director of USIA) to Baghdad to help promote the pact. Sorensen's task was to help establish a public diplomacy arm of the "Counter-Subversion Office" of the Baghdad Pact, which he did. But as Sorensen said later, the Pact was "a mistaken concept from the start, an alliance of unequals which most Arabs (including most Iraqis) saw as simply the new face of Western imperialism."[8]

The U.S. government was meanwhile watching Nasser closely. After an Israeli retaliatory raid in the Egyptian-controlled Gaza Strip in February 1955, Nasser requested $27 million in arms from Washington but was turned down. Then after another Israeli raid in late summer, Nasser turned to the Soviet bloc for help and bought arms from Czechoslovakia, which was acting on behalf of the Soviet Union. This caused a shock in Washington but Nasser's prestige in the Arab world soared. Egypt's Voice of the Arabs increased its propaganda campaign against the Baghdad Pact and against the pro-Western governments in Jordan and Iraq. Washington extended an offer to help finance part of a loan for Nasser's Aswan High Dam project, and this was well received in the Arab world. But loan negotiations dragged on and in June 1956, after Soviet Foreign Minister Shepilov visited Cairo, Nasser raised new questions about it, and Secretary Dulles, fed up with what he considered to be Nasser's gamesmanship, abruptly withdrew the loan offer. This was widely reported in the Arab world; it came up in many conversations and PAOs had some difficulty explaining it successfully.

But the Israeli-Palestinian question remained a major issue for PAOs everywhere in the region. In Syria, for example, Bob Lincoln, who arrived in Damascus in 1955 as PAO, quickly discovered that the Arab–Israeli conflict was "the first thing that influenced" the Syrians he was trying to communicate with. He found that "it was impossible to carry on any kind of a conversation with a Syrian without the question of Israel coming up."[9] He also found it difficult to broaden the discussion. On June 5, 1956, students in Damascus staged a protest outside the USIS building because they thought that a book in the USIS library contained an Israeli song, and they demanded the interior minister shut USIS down for disseminating "Zionist propaganda." Fortunately, the PAO was able to keep it open.[10]

PAO Lincoln realized that he had to modernize his public diplomacy effort. When he arrived at post he found that every morning at 7:00 A.M. a team of USIS Damascus delivery men, on old Harley-Davidson motorcycles inherited from World War II, fanned out taking USIS press releases to all the newspapers and other media outlets, but that much of the material being sent was not of interest to the recipients. The information minister even told Lincoln that USIS was wasting its time pushing issues that Syrians did not care about, like Eisenhower's "Atoms for Peace" proposal that Washington had instructed PAOs to publicize. Lincoln refocused the program onto issues of interest to Syrians, and devoted much more time to personal contacts, cultivating opinion leaders. As he explained, "We made sure that everything we got in the wireless file of consequence to them was given to them, but quite often we would send it to them with a personal note or something rather than just use a mass mailing or mass delivery." He explained that with editors and reporters he was "working on the possibility that, if you made a small dent in their views, then you would affect, over a longer range, the kinds of things they published or didn't publish."[11]

In Saudi Arabia, the PAO was Isa Sabbagh, who also found himself in regular discussions about Israel, but he had special advantages. Isa Sabbagh was a Palestinian-American, fluent in Arabic, and he was well known and respected among Saudis because of his years as a wartime broadcaster in the Arabic Service of the BBC. In his conversations with Saudi media editors, who strongly criticized American support for Israel, his response was as follows: "I am telling you the truth; I am representing the United States of America [and] the United States policy is as follows: whether you like it or not, the United States is committed to the security of Israel. You can be friendly with Israel and at the same time friendly with somebody who is not enamored with Israel." Isa explained later:

> It was tough, but I said in every dispute, which was the thrust of my daily talking to them: "You can never prove that right is a hundred percent on one side and wrong a hundred percent on the other. Look at the background of Israel, look at what they have done throughout the years . . . they were smashed about by Hitler, whose praises you were singing, who butchered them by the thousands, they have learned how to survive and therefore they designed their approaches to the Western world and certainly to the United States of America and certainly they are still at it. What have you done to prove that you can be not only respected but that they can have confidence in you? The American people do not know much about Saudi Arabia except when they see signs of dollars. What have you done? Your information to the outside world, from my limited knowledge, is not effective."

Isa explained that "the Saudis would take this from me, as a person who had proven to have Arab blood . . . in my veins."[12]

Isa made full use of his fame to establish strong personal contacts with key Saudi individuals, cultivating them purposefully. He personally knew King Saud as well as Crown Prince Faisal, who had heard him on BBC and whom he had interviewed twice in London in the 1940s, and who later became king. He also knew their "gatekeeper" staffs, such as Abdullah Bel Hare, the personal secretary to King Saud. Because one of Bel Hare's tasks was to give the king a daily summary of international news from the BBC, VOA and other sources, Isa provided him with additional information from the wireless file that helped explain the United States and its policies.[13]

Isa did have the advantage being of Arab origin and thus being able to speak frankly, but in fact many PAOs have used his tactic, pointing out the Arab failure to explain their views to Americans and shifting some of the responsibility for resolving the problem to the Arabs themselves. It is also useful to make the point that Americans are generally open to hearing others' points of view, but the Arabs need to make an effort.

Early in his tour as PAO in Saudi Arabia, Isa heard people say they thought he was a CIA officer, and this upset him because he knew it was a stigma and could hurt his contacts. He asked Crown Prince Faisal's office director Ahmad Abdul Sahbar to tell Faisal that he was not CIA and if the talk did not stop he would leave the kingdom. Faisal sent word back, "Tell Isa, my brother, he is living in his second home country and he should let the dogs bark as long as the caravan moves along. Besides, what can anybody spy on us for, our destinies are in the hands of our friends the Americans, they know all about our armed forces and so forth."[14] This was not the first or last time PAOs were suspected of being CIA, since they make an effort to have a wide range of contacts. But Isa's special access allowed him to overcome the stigma.

In Lebanon, conditions were different. Because of Lebanon's variety of Muslim and Christian sects, the PAOs were careful to treat equally all major ones—Sunni and Shia, Maronite, Catholic, and Protestant—since they were all constantly watching U.S. officials for signs of favoritism. If the Cultural Attaché visited a Maronite school he had to visit the others; books were evenly distributed; and if he sent a Sunni to the United States on a leader grant he had to also send a Shia. He called this a "constant balancing act." Also, many Lebanese Christians therefore sought to maintain close contact through USIS, but the post was mindful of the need to show impartiality toward the country's various religious sects.[15]

But it was in Egypt where U.S. public diplomacy faced its most difficult challenge. President Nasser developed a powerful international radio station he called Voice of the Arabs, which carried his speeches and anti-Israeli commentaries all over the region. It became the most popular media

channel in the Arab world, and a major problem for PAOs because it affected Arab opinion negatively.

When Bill Weathersby was PAO in Egypt during the early 1950s, he was confronted with a deteriorating situation caused by several factors. Washington's decision not to support financing of its Aswan High Dam project angered and humiliated Nasser. Nasser had already become upset when Washington had denied his request for military assistance because of American concerns that the arms would be a threat to Israel. Egypt's Voice of the Arabs carried strong criticisms of the United States for failing to support Egypt's national development aspirations and security needs, and described Nasser as standing up for Arab independence and rights. The Voice of America in turn carried American official responses, trying to explain that Secretary Dulles's decision was based purely on financial considerations, but many Arabs were convinced the U.S. position was a deliberate slap in the face of Nasser. Nasser then sought Aswan Dam assistance from Moscow and arms from the Soviet bloc, which increased Washington's concern. The resulting increase in bilateral tension led the Egyptian authorities to begin to restrict exactly the contacts and communication links that PAO Weathersby and his staff were trying to maintain with Egyptian audiences. There was nothing he could do directly about the deteriorating political situation, but he did continue an array of USIS programs, the distribution of an Arabic language periodical, the Fulbright program, and the library, which was well used.[16]

Tom Sorensen, the Information Officer in Egypt at the time, dealt with criticisms of American foreign policy on a daily basis, but he tried to broaden the dialogue to keep it going. He put out a post-produced information bulletin in Arabic, called "al Sadaqa" (Friendship), that was sent to a selected distribution list, limited partly by government regulations. But his main effort was to expand personal contacts. He felt that the Egyptians had a love–hate relationship with the United States. On the one hand they believed that Washington was responsible for Israel, which they saw as an alien intruder in the region, but on the other hand they had special affection for America because of its democracy and its help in Arab development through education and medicine. Sorensen said later: "The role of USIA was to provide sustenance for those who wanted to maintain this American link. They needed to know about us, hear about us. Our explanations about U.S. policy were mostly futile, but the flow of information about the United States, and cultural activities involving the United States, kept the flame alive for the day when relations would be better." He concluded (in 1990), "We are still waiting for that day, but that was the function of USIA. I think it was a valuable one."[17]

PAOs in North Africa had to contend with public diplomacy problems that arose elsewhere in the Arab world, but in addition they faced a troublesome French factor. In the early days after World War II, when the

French still controlled Algeria, Tunisia, and Morocco, the Americans were caught between the Arabs and the French. In Tunisia, for example, there were special constraints before independence in 1957. On June 28, 1955, the PAO reported that the USIS library in Tunis had been bombed, causing damage to the building and equipment. The report does not identify the perpetrators, but they were probably French agents unhappy with American support for Algerian independence. Nine months later the PAO again informed Washington of more violence; he said that on March 9, 1956, "USIS library attacked by French rioters. Heavy damage. Some 1200 books destroyed. . . . Records destroyed." Washington asked Paris to pay for the damage and Paris agreed to do so.[18]

When Dick Viets went to Tunis in 1956 as Assistant PAO, prior to Tunisia's independence, the Tunisians he met with told him they thought that the Eisenhower administration was blindly supporting the French in the region for the sake of preserving NATO unity. The Tunisians were pleased when Senator John Kennedy made a speech in 1954 supporting Arab independence from France, because they hoped that meant Washington's policy was changing. But meanwhile, as Viets later explained, "you had to be creative while still attempting to be loyal to policy" of support for France that he and other embassy officers privately found misguided. He was able to establish excellent contacts quietly with Arab nationalist figures because his senior Tunisian staffer, a Polish woman with considerable language skills, acted as part-time interpreter for Habib Bourguiba before and after he became president, and informally served as an embassy channel to Arab nationalists.[19]

### The Suez War of 1956

The second Arab–Israeli war in October 1956, was another major event affecting Arab–American relations but it proved to be of some temporary help to PAOs by improving somewhat the Arab perception of the United States.

A week after Dulles's announcement in July 1956, withdrawing support for the Aswan Dam, Nasser declared that Egypt had nationalized the Suez Canal, until then owned by Britain and France. The British and French demanded that Egypt allow free shipping in the canal and pull its forces ten miles back from it. Nasser refused, and the British and French military launched a military attack on Egypt. Israel joined the attack, fearing that Nasser's threats, which had made him an Arab hero, were serious.

In October and November 1956, British and French aircraft attacked Egyptian air bases, while Israel occupied the Gaza Strip and the Sinai. President Eisenhower flatly opposed their attack, demanded a cease-fire, full withdrawal, and return to the prewar status quo. The UN agreed with him. The British, French, and Israelis grudgingly gave in to American and in-

ternational pressure, and withdrew from Egypt. Eisenhower did offer the Israelis a guarantee that the Straits of Tiran would be kept open (a key point that they remembered later) but on balance his stance was widely seen at the time as siding with Egypt. The United Nations sent an Emergency Force to monitor the Egyptian–Israeli border in the Sinai, near Sharm al Shaikh.

Arabs throughout the region were favorably impressed with Eisenhower's stance, and that made life easier for PAOs and other American officials in the Arab world trying to explain and defend U.S. policy. Eisenhower's stance is remembered to this day by many Arabs who cite it as an example of an American policy they believe was based on fairness and impartiality. American PAOs in the region said that Eisenhower stood for fairness in the dispute, but they also stressed that it showed he favored a peaceful settlement and opposed not only Israeli but also Arab use of violence.

The VOA Arabic Service was especially helpful to PAOs in disseminating the American version of the story. During the crisis, the VOA Arabic Service surged to 14.5 hours daily, and beamed translations of White House and State Department pronouncements within minutes to Arab audiences. After the crisis the hours were reduced, but by 1958 the regular Arabic program was up to six hours per day. VOA Arabic programs were by then being transmitted on both medium wave and shortwave from a ship, USS *Courier*, anchored off Rhodes, Greece, which facilitated audibility by Arab audiences. (In 1964, the VOA Arabic Service moved onshore to a studio on Rhodes.)[20] Since radio was the main source of news for the Arab public, many Arabs listened to VOA to supplement their local government-controlled radio, which they tended to regard as biased.

Every year VOA did an internal program review of each language service. In 1956 the reviewers who looked at the Arabic Service concluded that it gave too much air time to the Suez crisis and not enough time to the crisis in Hungary. The reviewers thought the story of Hungary should be promoted because it made Moscow look bad, and suspected that the Arabic Service editors had a pro-Arab bias to focus on Suez. But in fact the Arab audience was much more interested in Suez than in Hungary, which the editors felt was sufficiently covered in their broadcasts.[21]

The Suez crisis did not end the Arab–Israeli confrontation. Arab appreciation for Eisenhower's stand in the 1956 Suez crisis was only a temporary help to American public diplomacy professionals in Arab countries, since Arab resentment over American support for Israel continued to grow, causing them problems directly and indirectly.

In the mid-1950s, Moscow's influence in some parts of the Arab world was increasing. The Egyptian government was particularly hostile, and Washington saw this as Soviet-inspired. Nasser in effect controlled all media, with Voice of the Arabs putting out a steady stream of rhetoric on

Egypt's defiance of imperialism and Zionism. Nevertheless, the PAO in Cairo was able to have the Eisenhower Plan for Middle East peace printed as a pamphlet and he put ads in the newspaper, on billboards, and in cinemas offering copies of it free of charge. Egyptians flocked to USIS to get the pamphlet, some taking multiple copies and selling them in the market. The post also increased its book translation program, for example, producing and selling the illustrated book *What Is Communism?* by Arthur Goodfriend, and a book on the Hungarian Revolt against Moscow of 1956, which the post wrote using available documents and pitching the text to the Egyptian reader. Cairo had become the center of Arabic book publishing and USIS-sponsored books published there were distributed throughout the region. Washington also started the "Franklin Book Program" to translate American academic books into Arabic, and hired Datus Smith of the Princeton University Press to manage it in Cairo.[22]

But Nasser continued his strong criticism of U.S. policy and this led to new restrictions on USIS activities in Egypt. Soon Egyptian citizens needed permission to have contact with Americans, so the PAO and other U.S. officials knew that any contacts they happened to make were "authorized" and informants. The American CAO, Bill Lovegrove, tended, however, to have easier access, apparently for two reasons: He brought in American artists and performers people wanted to see, and they learned he was not interested in politics, so this made them more comfortable with him. He was able to have more discussions than others could about American society and culture with important Egyptians, which under the circumstances was very worthwhile.[23]

Other USIS posts also tried to broaden the discussion. For example, in Lebanon in early 1958, the Acting Cultural Affairs Officer arranged for the Minneapolis Symphony Orchestra to visit Beirut, but it was nearly cancelled by the Lebanese authorities when they discovered that about 60 percent of the musicians were Jewish, and they feared they would be criticized for permitting an "Israeli" function. He persuaded the Lebanese to allow the musicians in, and they gave two performances, but audiences were small because many Lebanese feared being out after dark due to the current unrest.[24]

In Syria, too, political relations were strained primarily because of the Arab–Israeli conflict, and USIS was under some restrictions there as well. David Nalle, the Cultural Attaché, believed they were always being watched. For example, when he had a reception for Syrian contacts, always one uninvited person came and stood in the corner watching the other guests. "It put a certain damper on the conversation" he noted. Yet the post carried out programs, mostly on the cultural side, and even though there were only two American officers, they worked hard and managed to make many contacts. USIS maintained a cultural center with a library and published American books in Arabic. It was a time when USIA was send-

ing a fairly large number of American speakers and cultural presentations abroad and USIS Damascus made good use of them. There were also American professors at Damascus University. Because of the difficult atmosphere, Nalle regarded as a "real triumph" the establishment of an American booth at the Damascus International Fair, which included a mock restaurant offering American hot dogs and hamburgers. It also featured a solar energy exhibit with a solar cooker that the CAO's wife used to make chocolate chip cookies, which she handed out while the CAO demonstrated a Polaroid camera. He noted with satisfaction that this exhibit attracted a much larger crowd of Syrians than the more expensive Soviet exhibit with its tractors and Sputnik model.[25]

In Tunisia, the post sought to blunt criticism of American policy by distributing a daily news bulletin in Arabic and French translated from wireless file materials, by showing documentary films and distributing pamphlets in Tunis and around the country, and by bringing Americans and Tunisians together in the cultural center. The post also made good use of visiting speakers and exchanges of persons under the Fulbright and other programs. USIS also took advantage of the fact that Tunisians were increasingly exposed to American culture in the form of Hollywood films and pop music, which they liked. They knew a lot about American music from Willis Conover's VOA program *Jazz USA*, and Conover's visit to Tunisia at this time was very successful in improving the American image. The PAO also used the 1959 visit to Tunisia by President Eisenhower to remind Tunisian media editors and others about Washington's support for President Bourguiba.[26]

These activities were typical of USIS posts throughout the Arab world at that time, where PAOs and their staffs sought to blunt hostility over foreign policy by exposing target audiences to Americans and American society and culture through the use of visiting speakers, the Fulbright and other exchange programs, and at USIS libraries and cultural centers, as well as film programs and publications.

### The 1958 Crises

Several events in 1958 combined to mark a turning point in Arab–American relations that created new challenges for PAOs to deal with.

In February 1958, Nasser persuaded the newly installed Ba'ath regime in Syria to join Egypt in a union, the United Arab Republic. To conservative Arab leaders it was a threatening coalition of radical Arabs. The kings of Jordan and Iraq sought to counter it by promptly signing a mutual cooperation agreement between their two countries.

Turmoil in Lebanon in the spring of 1958 had caused concern in Washington. Lebanon's President Camille Chamoun, a Christian, had welcomed the Eisenhower Doctrine and expressed pro-Western views, but a largely

Muslim insurrection against him broke out that had anti-American overtones. Already attacks had taken place on USIS facilities in Beirut on July 20, 1957, when a dynamite charge was set off at the USIS library, damaging the building. Unrest and violence escalated as opposition elements took over parts of Beirut with Syrian assistance. On May 10, 1958, a mob in Tripoli, Lebanon, attacked, sacked, and burned the USIS library there, destroying almost 5,000 books and forcing closure of the facility. Two days later, another mob sacked and burned the USIS centers in Basta and Ashrafia, destroying many books in each. The PAO in Lebanon tried to continue programming as usual, but the security situation interfered. When he scheduled the "Family of Man" photo exhibit in Beirut, thinking this nonpolitical event would be considered benign and would show the United States was seeking to conduct business as usual, the government shut it down after the opening ceremony (attended by President Chamoun, accompanied by a retinue of armed bodyguards) out of fear that it would become a venue for violence.[27]

Washington's concern increased when on July 14, 1958, a military coup overthrew the monarchy in Iraq, killed Iraq's King Faisal and Prime Minister Nuri Said, and installed a radical republican government under General Abdalkarim Qasim. Qasim withdrew Iraq from the Baghdad pact, and sought closer ties with the Soviet Union. This alarmed officials in Washington. The new Iraqi government ordered the U.S. government to close its information centers in Baghdad, Basra, and Kirkuk. The PAO correctly anticipated that this was going to be a long-term closure so he transferred the library books to other USIS posts nearby.

In Lebanon, President Chamoun requested military assistance from the United States, and President Eisenhower sent the Marines into Beirut, along with a special diplomatic envoy, Ambassador Murphy, to help calm the situation.

Eisenhower saw these events through the optic of his fight against international Communism. In his January 5, 1957, message to Congress he had outlined a policy that became known as the Eisenhower Doctrine. He said that "Russia's rulers have long sought to dominate the Middle East," and that Middle East events were "at times manipulated by international Communism." He said that to counter the USSR, the United States would provide economic and military assistance to nations requesting it "against armed aggression from any nation controlled by international Communism." He also called for new legislation to deal with "the possibility of Communist aggression direct or indirect."[28] When the events of the spring of 1958 unfolded in the Arab world, Eisenhower and Dulles were persuaded to intervene in Lebanon because they saw the region in this context.

USIS Beirut launched an intensive campaign to persuade the Lebanese people that the Americans were there only to restore peace and would leave

as soon as the crisis was over. The USIS staff produced press releases, newspaper articles, and radio texts that they placed in friendly Lebanese media, as well as pamphlets that they distributed and reports and backgrounders that they sent to other posts for their use. Journalists were brought from other countries to see the situation for themselves, and this resulted in some helpful media coverage in the region. The Voice of America tripled its broadcasts to the Middle East, carrying thirty minutes each of Arabic and English every hour on an extended schedule.[29]

The Lebanese reaction to the U.S. intervention was predictably mixed; supporters of Chamoun were very pleased, while his opponents were very angry at Washington. The PAO in Beirut emphasized to his contacts that the intervention would be brief and limited, but some doubted that. Christians welcomed the Marines and one told the American Cultural Attaché that he did not want to see the Americans leave, out of fear that sectarian fighting would break out again when they left. Another said he was pleased to see that the Americans did not stay long and that there was no danger of an American occupation, in contrast to the French and British who would not leave unless forced to do so.[30]

In Syria, where Bob Lincoln was PAO, he and the rest of the embassy apprehensively watched the turmoil in neighboring Lebanon and Iraq. The Syrian government declared a holiday in sympathy with the Lebanese elements opposed to the U.S. intervention. The PAO's contacts told him that if the Marines invaded Syria too, they would be resisted fiercely by the Syrian public. But when the American show of force in Lebanon turned out to be effective in calming the situation there, and when the Marines withdrew in October 1958, PAOs around the region breathed a sigh of relief that the violence had not spread, and that the intervention was limited. Lincoln commented later that Washington had been lucky because he sensed that such a show of American force would not always work so well.[31] He was prophetic.

In discussing the Lebanese crisis, PAOs emphasized that the elected president of Lebanon had asked Eisenhower to send troops, and that they had left after a brief period of time to show they were intended to be helpful and not serve any hidden American purpose.

In countries with radical regimes the media denounced the American intervention as neo-imperialism in support of antiprogressive forces in the region. In countries with conservative regimes the argument that the intervention was against international Communism gained some traction, but elsewhere it did not work because the people were not concerned about a communist threat.

By the end of 1958, the Arab world was increasingly becoming divided into two camps, and the "Arab cold war" had begun.[32] This division was clearly seen in the officially guided media on both sides. A so-called "radical" or Arab nationalist camp had emerged that was led by Egypt, Iraq,

and Syria, and their media were openly critical of governments in the moderate or reactionary camp led essentially by Saudi Arabia. The Arab nationalist commentators were the most strident in their verbal attacks on Israel and support for the Palestinians, and criticized the United States most loudly for its support of Israel and the monarchies, and for intervening militarily in Lebanon. The moderate commentators, on the other hand, were more likely to sympathize with the American concern about Communism and to express milder and pro forma support for the Arab demands that Israel withdraw from the territories it occupied.

The discussion in North Africa was still complicated by the French factor. The PAO in Algeria had a special problem because of the conflict raging at the time between the French and the Arab nationalists. On May 13, 1958, the USIS library was attacked by rioters who destroyed books and damaged equipment. Washington managed to secure restitution from the government, but the center had to remain closed for five months, until October 27. Then on November 11, 1960, rioters attacked the same facility, destroying the book collection of nearly 5,000 volumes. The French government assumed responsibility and paid $11,922 compensation for the damages but the library closed again and did not open until 1961. Then on June 9, 1962, the same facility was bombed and burned again, and nearly 13,000 books were destroyed along with equipment and furniture, a loss costing $22,669. This time the center did not reopen until March 29, 1963.[33] But Washington insisted on keeping these centers going because it was thought that they were helping to reach some key audiences, even if they provoked people to violence.

The decade following 1958 was relatively quiet on the surface. PAOs continued to deal with misconceptions about the United States and misunderstandings of American society. But they were also able to open or expand libraries and cultural centers, and they carried out cultural and educational programs designed to convey a broad and balanced picture of American society and culture. In some countries, such as Egypt and Lebanon, they arranged for American musicians, singers, and even dancers to perform for local audiences. In other countries like Saudi Arabia, most of these programs were impossible because of a very conservative environment. Even in the USIA library in Saudi Arabia the PAO had to be careful what books and magazines he included in the collection because of Saudi censorship that prohibited any material questioning the Saudi interpretation of Islam or the Saudi political system, or strict social codes.

PAOs tried to intensify their personal contacts and engage in a dialogue with a wider circle of opinion leaders. They argued for a peaceful settlement of the dispute with Israel, saying that negotiation was a more sensible course of action than war, but most Arabs disagreed, saying that negotiations would mean concessions and the issue was a matter of victims' rights that Americans ought to recognize and support.

For example, a conversation between an American PAO and an Arab newspaper editor might have sounded like this:

*PAO:* Why are Arab leaders calling for war with Israel? Why don't you negotiate your differences?

*Editor:* Israel took Arab land by force and negotiation would give legitimacy to that illegal act. Arabs have a right to Palestinian land and they should withdraw.

*PAO:* But fighting won't achieve that right, and using violence is wrong.

*Editor:* Wasn't the United States created by fighting for it?

*PAO:* Yes but that was different. You can't beat Israel and it's wrong to try.

*Editor:* We must fight for our principles. That's what the PLO is doing. If negotiation is so good, why don't you negotiate with the PLO?

*PAO:* PLO fighters have killed innocent people so they are terrorists.

*Editor:* Israel has killed innocent Palestinians. That's state terrorism.

*PAO:* That's different. Israel is only defending itself against terrorists.

Conversations like this would be repeated all over the Arab world for many years.

4

# The Kennedy and Johnson Presidencies, 1961–1969

## THE KENNEDY PRESIDENCY (JANUARY 1961–NOVEMBER 1963)

John F. Kennedy took office as president in January 1961, and he appointed the well-known CBS newsman Edward R. Murrow as his USIA director. Murrow set the tone for American public diplomacy, when he told a congressional committee: "American traditions and the American ethic require us to be truthful, but the most important reason is that truth is the best propaganda and lies are the worst. To be persuasive we must be believable; to be believable we must be credible; to be credible we must be truthful. It is as simple as that."[1] As America's most respected journalist, his presence enhanced the reputation of USIA and the morale of PAOs. He also recognized that USIA professionals had talent. He later said, "I could staff any commercial media outfit with people from this agency, and it would be as good or better than any of its competitors."[2]

Kennedy appointed Tom Sorenson, a career USIA officer and brother of his senior political advisor, as deputy director of the agency. Sorensen had had experience as Information Officer at USIS posts in Iraq, Lebanon, and Egypt, so he knew how to conduct public diplomacy in the Arab world better than most senior Washington managers. Sorensen was given the task of drafting a new USIA mission statement, which Kennedy sent to Director Murrow in a 1963 memorandum. Sorensen told Kennedy that USIA's

purpose should be "to persuade, not merely to inform"[3] and Kennedy's mission statement reflected that emphasis.

The Kennedy memo stated: "The mission of the U.S. Information Agency is to help achieve U.S. foreign policy objectives by (a) influencing public attitudes in other nations and (b) advising the president, his representatives abroad, and the various departments and agencies on the implications of foreign opinion for present and contemplated U.S. policies, programs and official statements." It added that "the influencing of attitudes" was to be carried out "by the overt use of various techniques of communication—personal contact, radio broadcasting, libraries, book publication, exhibits, English-language instruction and others." In that memo, Kennedy stated that USIA staffs abroad would be responsible for the conduct of overt public information, public relations, and cultural activities that were intended "to inform or influence public opinion."[4]

Sorensen would have preferred to move the education and culture function from the State Department into USIA, but he knew that Senator Fulbright, the powerful Senate Foreign Relations Committee chairman, was against that. Fulbright had said, "I utterly reject any suggestion that our educational and cultural exchange programs are weapons or instruments with which to do combat . . . there is no room and there must not be any room, for an interpretation of these programs as propaganda, even recognizing that the term covers some very worthwhile and respectable activities."[5] (The move took place later, after Fulbright retired from the Senate.)

Sorensen also stressed the need for planning and measurement of effectiveness of programs, and this affected PAOs in the Arab world and elsewhere because he required them to develop country plans and to do more reporting. PAOs knew that providing "evidence of effectiveness" was difficult, but they did their best, mostly with anecdotes. Director Murrow appreciated the difficulty too. As he once said, "It is very difficult to measure success in our business. No computer clicks, no cash register rings when a man changes his mind."[6]

In 1961 Congress passed the Mutual Educational and Cultural Exchange Act of 1961 (Fulbright-Hays Act) that consolidated earlier public diplomacy legislation. The preamble says it is "an act to provide for the improvement and strengthening of the international relations of the United States by promoting better mutual understanding among the peoples of the world through educational and cultural exchanges." The act states that its purpose is "to strengthen the ties which unite us with other nations by demonstrating the educational and cultural interests, developments and achievements of the people of the United States and other nations . . . to assist in the development of friendly, sympathetic and peaceful relations between the United States and the other countries of the world."[7] The act reflected the longer-term aspects of "soft power" that Kennedy and Sorensen understood.

## America's Image

During the Kennedy presidency, the major domestic events that took place included civil rights demonstrations at home. Internationally, Cuba was the focus of a failed attempt to overthrow Fidel Castro (1961), and a missile crisis with Moscow (1962); civil war that began in Yemen (1962); and a wall was constructed in Berlin, where Kennedy paid a visit. In Arab countries with close ties to the Soviet Union, the media presented the Cuban and Berlin stories from the Soviet point of view, creating special problems for some PAOs. Yet the Arabs did not take much notice of European events, such as President Kennedy's famous "Ich bin ein Berliner" speech in 1963. When USIA headquarters asked PAOs in the Arab world what Arabs thought about the Berlin question, Isa Sabbagh, the PAO in Jidda, replied that they thought about it only as much as the Berliners thought about the Palestinian question, that is, very little.

The Arab public did take note of the U.S.–Soviet space race. The Soviet launch of Sputnik in 1957 had given that country a psychological boost worldwide. In April 1961, Soviet Cosmonaut Yuri Gagarin became the first man to orbit the earth in space. In May, President Kennedy announced that the United States would send a man to the moon before the end of the decade, and that month the United States conducted its first manned space flight. Alan Shepard did not make it into orbit but USIA instructed PAOs to stress that the American flight was conducted entirely in the open, unlike Gagarin's orbital flight which was secret until it had been a success. Emphasizing the openness of American society did help, and Shepard's feat was a big story. Many Arab newspapers published a USIS-distributed article with Shepard's byline. One Egyptian newspaper even claimed (falsely) that it had obtained the Shepard article directly from Shepard himself.[8]

Egypt has always been a key country in the Middle East because of its size, political and military weight, and the influence of its writers and cultural figures. For American diplomacy in the region and for the image of the United States among Arabs, Egypt has always played an important role. Washington watched closely during the 1950s as Nasser became stronger politically at home and in the region, because he was increasingly the leading representative of Arab nationalism that carried with it not only anti-Israeli but also anti-Western and anti-American overtones. When President Kennedy took office, he recognized Egypt's importance and he was interested in finding a way to work with Nasser, but within the limits of America's continuing support for Israel and good relations with Saudi Arabia and other conservative Arab states. Kennedy's approach was symbolized by his appointment of John Badeau as his ambassador to Egypt. Badeau had been at the American University in Cairo from 1936 to 1953, starting as a professor of ethics and then becoming dean and president of the university. He spoke Arabic fluently, he knew Egypt very well, and he was well

liked by Egyptians. He assumed his ambassadorial responsibilities just at the time when the Egyptian government was undergoing a social revolution, sequestering properties of the many wealthy families that had dominated the economy including non-Egyptian longtime residents of Greek or other European origin. Badeau realized that some American diplomats had been dealing only with this wealthy class and he told embassy staff that they should make a special effort to treat Egyptians with respect.[9]

For Marshall Berg, the Branch PAO in Alexandria 1959–1962, this was welcome news, because it seemed Washington was making a strong effort to improve relations with Egypt at a crucial time. Berg conferred with the rector of Alexandria, Dr. Sayid al Sayid, a graduate of Ohio State University, and secured his agreement to accept several Fulbright professors, where there had been none before. Ambassador Badeau enthusiastically endorsed the idea with Washington, and the following year eight Fulbright professors arrived in Alexandria to teach at the university. This was a significant development, a sudden change in U.S.–Egyptian educational cooperation. The American Fulbrighters included deans and highly qualified academics in medicine, economics, history, and other subjects, who quickly improved relations with the Egyptian academic community and opened doors for the USIS operation to undertake new programs. By associating American scholars with the Egyptianization of the system, America gained respect for its educational achievements and this helped blunt the government's growing criticism of American foreign policy.[10]

Yet the efforts of President Kennedy, Ambassador Badeau, and public diplomacy professionals were not enough to prevent a slow deterioration in Egyptian–American bilateral political relations. As a result, during the years when Jim Halsema was PAO in Egypt, 1961–1966, the Egyptian government's restrictions on USIS activities became increasingly onerous, and the secret police (mukhabaraat) surveillance obtrusive. Informers were everywhere, even among his local employees and household staff. But Halsema managed to carry out effective programs primarily in the cultural and education areas. He issued a regular news bulletin with a circulation of about 20,000, and he had some excellent professional media contacts on the level of senior reporter and editor (the media stars such Muhammad Hassanain Haykal and the Amin Brothers were the ambassador's contacts). But his most meaningful work was in cultural programming and personal contacts. For example, he arranged for Robert Lowell, the most noted poet of his generation, to come to Cairo and this attracted Egyptian poets, writers, and intellectuals to his reception. Halsema also invited to Egypt a well-known American ballet dancer whose presence attracted prominent Egyptian cultural personalities. When the architect Buckminster Fuller visited Egypt on his own, Halsema persuaded him to lecture and that attracted prominent architects and engineers. Halsema concluded: "So I felt we were getting our point across despite the problems with the relationship at the government

level." He said, "We were able to maintain a relationship with a lot of very important Egyptians at a time when Egypt was heading more and more into the embrace of the Soviet Union. These were the same people who surfaced again after this relationship [with Moscow] was less warm." The director of the Cairo ballet school told Halsema that although she was pleased the Kirov Ballet had sent instructors to Egypt, the Egyptians did not like the Russians on a personal basis as much as they liked the Americans they knew.[11] Clearly, personal relations counted.

When Washington informed Halsema that he could send several Egyptians to the United States on thirty-day special tours as Visitor Grantees, he knew it would be difficult to find candidates who were prominent enough and also willing to go to America despite the political circumstances. Halsema invited Anwar Sadat, who as speaker of parliament was a relatively unknown personality. At the end of his visit, Sadat told an American official he had been apprehensive about going to America because as a "dark-skinned person" he feared he would face discrimination, but in fact he was very well received. He returned home with a better appreciation of America.[12]

And in Alexandria, USIS also continued to work hard in the cultural and educational arena, despite bilateral political difficulties. An elegant forty-two-room villa was turned into a cultural center, with a library, a film theater, and space for English-language classes. But after Marshall Berg left and Dick Undeland became Alexandria Branch PAO, he found he was increasingly hampered by the political atmosphere, since even in this provincial city, Nasser's stridently anti-American rhetoric and constant criticism of America's support for Israel colored the relationship. An Egyptian intelligence officer assigned to the center made a note of everyone who visited it and interrogated the USIS staff on the center's activities. Yet Undeland found that the people welcomed USIS, and he quietly made some progress. He arranged a trip to the United States for the university president, who visited American campuses where he was impressed at seeing students demonstrating without any police presence. After he returned, the university president became a good contact. The PAO went to him on several occasions, for example, when the police issued orders banning all university students and professors from visiting any foreign cultural centers. The university president admitted the rule was silly and said it would be ignored; in fact students continued to come. "We found ourselves in an antagonistic political atmosphere and yet one in which we developed warm and close personal and professional relationships," Undeland concluded. "Despite official opposition and foully anti-American media, I was eagerly welcomed almost everywhere."[13]

Competition with the Soviet Union played out on several levels in Egypt. When Undeland arranged to bring to Alexandria a team of NBA professional basket ball players for an exhibition game, the game happened

to coincide with a visit to Alexandria by Soviet Prime Minister Nikita Kruschev and the Bolshoi Ballet. The government put Soviet flags all over town, but the Egyptian Sports Federation put up many American flags, supplied by USIS. The game drew a huge crowd, including the governor and other prominent political personalities. Undeland realized: "This was the Egyptian way of saying to the Soviet Union we are friends but don't take us for granted."[14]

The Soviet Union was at the time educating thousands of Egyptians and facilitating tourism but many Egyptians believed their degrees were inferior, and returned to Egypt unimpressed. One Egyptian neurosurgeon who attended Harvard Medical School and also went to the USSR as a tourist, told the PAO when he returned, only half jokingly:

> You Americans are just plain stupid. You're trying to turn us against the Communists by sending us off to the United States, which is OK, but if you really wanted to influence us, you should ship as many as you can off to Russia. I was astounded to find that in comparison with the Soviet Union, Egypt, poor backward Egypt, is miles ahead. The hotels aren't good. The restaurants are awful. You can't buy anything. The people are all badly clothed, downtrodden and unhappy. It's a terrible place. You should show as many of as you can how bad it is.[15]

In North Africa, the Arab–Israeli issue was also of concern to USIS, because the Arabs of that region emotionally shared the resentment of American support for Israel that Arabs farther east felt strongly about. However, issues relating to France and concerns about French colonialism tended to be stronger. Thus, the French factor remained a problem for PAOs.

In Tunisia, for example, after it gained independence from France in 1957, the French kept a military presence at the Bizerte naval base and the airport, which many Tunisians resented, and this indirectly caused a negative view of United States as an ally of France. In addition and paradoxically, many in the Tunisian elite also held negative views of America that they had picked up as students in France. As the PAO said later,

> It seemed so absurd to hear from Tunisians that Americans had taken over the leadership of Western imperialism (despite our support of Bourguiba and his struggle!) and that the U.S. was a country without culture or couth, that Americans were brash and unsophisticated, ill-equipped for [a] world leadership role. . . . The result was we worked closely and usually quite well with Tunisians and Tunisian institutions, but saw very little of these persons outside purely work or official relations.

When Washington did not intervene to stop the French brutal repression of the Tunisian strikes against the French military bases, Tunisians were re-

sentful, and the PAO reported that "An official at the radio station told me he and other Tunisians now felt they could never count on the United States as a completely reliable friend."[16]

The Arab–Israeli issue was not as potent as it was farther East also because Tunisia was farther away, and because President Bourguiba, the dominant political figure, was more moderate than Nasser. The USIS post stressed strengthened bilateral ties with cultural and educational programs, for example, helping to establish, with USAID money, the Bourguiba Institute of Languages, which became the country's leading English-language facility. USIS Tunis also had an active information program, sending out a daily information bulletin in French and Arabic (translated at the post) to government officials, the media, and selected individuals, and going around the country showing documentary films and distributing printed materials in cities and towns.[17]

Yet throughout the region, the USIS cultural and education programs continued to expand and these "nonpolitical" efforts to serve the Arab public were appreciated, enhancing America's image as a leader in education and knowledge. USIS libraries everywhere were packed with students and professionals, who found the resources they offered unique and useful. In Morocco, for example, the USIS library had so many members that the librarian had to issue color-coded membership cards to restrict access somewhat in order to control the numbers.[18]

## THE JOHNSON PRESIDENCY (NOVEMBER 1963–JANUARY 1969)

On November 22, 1963, President Kennedy was assassinated and Lyndon B. Johnson became president. (Johnson was reelected in November 1964, for a full term that ran until January 1969.)

President Kennedy was widely admired in the Arab world and his death attracted sympathetic attention there. The government in Saudi Arabia, for example, declared a day of mourning, a highly unusual gesture for a foreign leader. PAOs in Cairo and Beirut renamed their information centers after Kennedy to capture the positive image the president had created. In Algeria, many people remembered that as a senator, John Kennedy had made a speech on the Senate floor welcoming Algerian independence, and they were pleased when he was elected president. When he died, Senator Ted Kennedy visited Algeria to dedicate John F. Kennedy Square in Algiers, an event to which the Algerians gave wide publicity.[19]

USIA produced a prize-winning documentary film on Kennedy, *Years of Lightning, Day of Drums*, written and directed by Bruce Herschenson, and narrated by Gregory Peck; PAOs in the Arab world used it widely. In Jordan, PAO David Nalle did not wait for *Years of Lightning*, but produced a film locally about Kennedy and Johnson, because there was such

an outpouring of sympathy for America when Kennedy died that he wanted to respond quickly. Nalle mobilized the entire staff to assemble available news clips on Kennedy and Johnson, and prepared a narration that would be appropriate for Jordanians. A USIS officer named George Thompson came from Beirut to help with production. Within a few days the film was ready and Nalle sent it on tour of all major Jordanian cities, where it drew large crowds.[20]

When USIA Director Murrow resigned because of ill health in early 1964 (he died in April 1965), Johnson named Carl Rowan to replace him. Rowan had been a reporter, State Department spokesman, and ambassador to Finland; he was the first African American to head a federal agency. (In July 1965, he resigned and was replaced by Washington lawyer Leonard Marks.) During the Johnson presidency, USIA reached its staffing peak, due partly to the Vietnam War, but posts in the Arab world also benefited. USIA expanded its reach in the area and established several new offices and information centers in some of the less Westernized Arab cities. In April 1964, a USIS post was established in the Yemeni city of Taiz; in June an American Center was opened downtown in the Saudi city of Jidda;[21] and in October a new USIS office was opened in recently independent Kuwait.

### America's Image

During Johnson's presidency, civil rights and the Great Society were major domestic issues, while Vietnam and the Arab–Israeli war of 1967 were his primary foreign policy concerns. In the Middle East, the Arab public paid relatively little attention to American domestic events, and even to Vietnam, but the Arab–Israeli conflict was a preoccupation throughout the region and therefore the number-one challenge for PAOs there.

The Middle East in fact attracted some of Washington's attention from the start of the Johnson administration. First it was because of the Yemeni civil war (1962–1967), where two key Arab states, Egypt and Saudi Arabia, were involved on opposite sides, supporting the republicans and the royalists, respectively. Because of Egypt's considerable influence in Yemen, Yemen suspended formal diplomatic relations with the United States from 1962 to 1967. But the United States maintained a diplomatic presence in Yemen (in April 1966 the embassy moved from Taiz to Sanaa) and USIS continued to operate in the country. After 1967, when Egyptian forces left Yemen as a result of the Arab–Israeli war, operational conditions for USIS improved. By 1974, USIS had opened the Yemen-American Language Institute (YALI) where it offered English lessons in conjunction with USAID and the Peace Corps, a symbiotic collaboration of three U.S. government agencies. YALI was very effective as a venue for public diplomacy programming because it attracted Yemeni students and professionals who were otherwise difficult to reach.

But Washington's main concern in the Middle East was the growing Arab stridency toward Israel. Arab summit conferences in Cairo, Casablanca, and Jerusalem during 1964 and 1965 called for the establishment of the Palestine Liberation Organization (PLO) and the Palestine Liberation Army (PLA), and endorsed a new Palestinian Covenant calling for the destruction of Israel. This raised tensions in the region as Israel feared an Arab attack. PAOs and other U.S. officials continued to argue for a peaceful settlement of the conflict, but their Arab interlocutors rejected the idea. They said that the Arabs were the aggrieved party and Israel should withdraw, and that Israel was intransigent and only understood force. They wanted the United States to put pressure on Israel to withdraw and to recognize the rights of Palestinian refugees to return to their homes, which they said Israel had forced them to leave. PAOs continued to explain that Israel was defending itself against threats and attacks, but to most Arabs Israel looked aggressive.

PAOs and other American officials became increasingly concerned about the mood in the region, as both Arabs and Israelis seemed to be taking hard-line positions toward each other. The cross-border violence remained at a low level but it continued. Egypt's Voice of the Arabs was becoming more strident and gaining more listeners throughout the Arab world, considerably overshadowing the Voice of America and the BBC in popularity. Arabs everywhere listened to the Egyptian radio commentator Ahmad Said elaborate on Nasser's aggressive rhetoric with flourishes designed to rally Arab support. The Voice of the America's moderate tone and reasoned approach was no match for that, and it also had an audibility problem. Most of VOA's transmitter power was in shortwave, which most Arabs had stopped listening to. The only medium wave (AM) signal going into the Arab world came from the Greek island of Rhodes, and it was not audible in many Arab countries. BBC, which had transmitters on the Omani island of Masira, was more widely audible and its commentaries were generally helpful to American policy, but they did not at all convey an understanding of American society or culture.

In Egypt, the USIS post continued to carry out a broad program despite the hostility of the Egyptian government toward the U.S. government. The post had excellent libraries in both Cairo and Alexandria, an English teaching program, an exchange program and an active Fulbright Commission, and a great deal of printed material going out to people on selected-distribution lists. USIS officers noted that President Nasser was "at his worst" and undermining the American image. American support for Israel was a constant Egyptian complaint, but PAOs carried out discussions with Egyptians anyway, on two levels. On the official level there were clear and basically unbridgeable disagreements over Israel, and the USIS staff in this mode had to defend themselves. In private discussions, however, the Egyptians usually showed no passion in arguing about the Israeli occupation of

the Sinai, but usually indicated they simply hoped to avoid another war. What they really wanted to know was how Egypt could obtain more food aid from the United States to help its faltering economy. The USIS officers had many contacts and the CAO, partly because of his "nonpolitical" position, was very active socially; Egyptians willingly came to his dinners and other functions.[22]

In Jordan, where David Nalle was PAO from 1963 to 1965, he found, as he said later, "Our policy towards the Arab-Israeli situation was unacceptable to all Jordanians, so you had to leave that aside. . . . So the cultural activities, and the basic informational, rather than policy, work of the Information officer, Bob Ruggiero, became important. The cultural aspect was the channel through which you could communicate—maybe not always a political message, but communication, in any case." One of Nalle's tasks was to publicize the U.S. assistance to Jordan's economic development. For example, he made a film of the large East Ghor Canal project that brought water to the East bank of the Jordan valley and helped irrigate a large amount of land. His staff also wrote stories for an Arabic-language magazine that was printed in USIA's Beirut printing plant. They also did a series of pamphlets in Arabic written by American officials and Jordanian academics or officials, such as the head of the Jordan Valley Authority, on Jordan's development problems, and sent them to "people who made a difference in the country." In these ways, the post was able to engage Jordanians in a dialogue on mutual interests "once you got past the issue of U.S. Middle East policy."[23]

In Beirut on one occasion the American ambassador gave a speech about the Middle East at a formal luncheon, and in the question period afterward several prominent Lebanese politicians stood up and expressed strong criticisms of American policy in the region, to which the ambassador responded. Some Lebanese media picked up the criticism but ignored the ambassador's response, so the PAO, Boulos Malik, contacted the head of the Lebanese national news agency, gave him the full transcript of the exchange and asked him to use it. The news agency put out the full text to all Lebanese media and many editors used the ambassador's words, which they otherwise would not have known about. The PAO knew that by using the national news agency, which supplied all Lebanese media with news, it was guaranteed that everyone would be aware of the American position, and some of them would use it.[24]

In Algeria in the 1960s, the public continued to see the United States as the inheritor of the French imperialist mantle, because of American involvement in Vietnam and Israel. American officials had no contact with the military or the ruling political party. Information Officer Dick Undeland said later that making contacts was the most difficult of any of the nine Arab countries he served in, because Algerians were suspicious of all foreigners. They often did not give their real names. They explained pri-

vately that their paranoia resulted from the long civil war and struggle for independence from France, saying, "If we cooperated with the French, the Algerians killed us, and vice versa. Families were broken up. Everybody has had a member of their family killed or tortured or both." The USIS staff had good contacts in the media, however, and Undeland put out a daily news bulletin based on the wireless file; he also distributed magazines and pamphlets and had a large film loan program. But Algerian editors flatly disagreed with the PAO on foreign policy matters and the press was stridently anti-American, so they achieved very little placement of American materials in the media. They also occasionally ran afoul of local sensitivities. For example, USIS made a film about President Ben Bella's official visit to Washington, which was useful while he was still in power, but after he was ousted the USIS Center inadvertently loaned it out. The government found out and closed the center. The PAO tried to apologize for the mistake but the government was adamant. The American image, however, benefited from the American assistance program which USIS helped to publicize, and the fact that American companies were developing Algeria's natural gas. The USIS information center was well used, and the post mounted several successful exhibits and a concert. Algerians welcomed the exchange programs.[25]

In Saudi Arabia, a Muslim visitor to the USIS library in downtown Jidda discovered that the latest issue of *Life* magazine had a story on Islam accompanied by a drawing of the Prophet Muhammad. Outraged because Muslims consider rendering the Prophet's likeness in a picture to be blasphemy, he protested to the Saudi authorities and demanded that the library be closed. The PAO, however, explained that it was a mistake and removed the offending issue, which had come into the embassy by diplomatic pouch in order to avoid Saudi censors. *Life* magazine editors heard complaints about the picture from all over the Arab world, so in their next issue they ran a small story about the outcry, and included a reproduction of the offending picture so their readers would see what the fuss was about. As Assistant PAO in Jidda, I caught the new issue in time and kept it out of our library, alerting other posts to the problem.

The growing Arab nationalist sentiment in the region, for which President Nasser was the primary cheerleader, was strengthened by a sense of third-world solidarity against the West. Nasser spoke of causes in Asia and Africa, identifying the Arab struggle with theirs. Patrice Lumumba, the pro-Communist prime minister of the Congo, was murdered in January 1961, two weeks after Kennedy's inauguration, and Moscow blamed the murder on the United States. Lumumba had been supported by Arab radicals who protested against the U.S. role there, and this sentiment resonated with many Arabs, for whom colonialism was such a recent memory. In some places, Arab empathy with such non-Arab causes led to anti-Western violence. Shortly after the murder, pro-Lumumba students in the Sudan smashed the

windows of the USIS offices and library in Khartoum. About the same time, African and Arab students in Egypt who had supported Lumumba broke the windows of the USIS Jefferson Library in Alexandria.[26] Later, on October 22, 1964, as fighting continued in the Congo, a mob attacked the USIS library in Khartoum, doing damage to the building and trying (unsuccessfully) to set it on fire. One month later, on November 26, 1964, a mob of Egyptians and Africans in Egypt expressed their anger at U.S. policy in the Congo by attacking and setting fire to the USIS library in Cairo, completely destroying it along with its 24,000 books plus all of its furniture and equipment. The Cairo police and fire brigade were slow in responding, one sign that led the USIS staff to believe that the government implicitly condoned the act, to punish the Americans for reasons unrelated to the Congo. But when the embassy afterward presented a claim of $423,734 for damages, the Egyptian government agreed to pay it.[27] The government also agreed to provide a substitute building for the USIS library, a well-located villa that it had sequestered from a wealthy owner during the nationalization period. By October 1965, this USIS facility was ready to operate. It was renamed for John F. Kennedy, and Charlton Heston, who was in Egypt on a private trip, was persuaded by the CAO to participate in the opening ceremony by reading Kennedy's inaugural address.[28]

Meanwhile Arab–Israeli tensions continued to rise. Nasser stepped up his rhetoric but some Arabs still criticized him for being all talk and no action, embarrassing him. Syrian gunners periodically shelled Galilee from the Golan Heights. Meanwhile, Egyptian forces were bogged down in Yemen trying to help the republicans against the royalists there.

By early 1967, Nasser was feeling more confident and he decided to challenge Israel. He had received two billion dollars' worth of arms from Moscow since the 1956 Suez War, and he apparently thought that in 1956 he could have beaten Israel militarily if France and Britain had not participated. He had recently (November 1966) signed a mutual defense treaty with Syria, which worried the Israelis and caused concern in Washington. In April 1967, Israel sent troops to the Syrian border, and Nasser declared he would help Syria defend itself. In May, Nasser deployed 100,000 Egyptian troops into Sinai along the Israeli border, a move that bolstered his popularity throughout the Arab world. Arab leaders offered support in case of a new war with Israel. On May 18 he demanded the withdrawal of UN Emergency Force troops from the Sinai, a demand that the Arabs regarded as reasonable since after the 1957 war UN troops had only been deployed on the Egyptian side of the border (Israel had refused them). UN Secretary General U Thant agreed to withdraw them.

Then on May 22, Nasser announced the closure of the Strait of Tiran to Israeli ships and cargos, so they could no longer use their port at Eilat. His speech, carried live by Egypt's Voice of the Arabs, was heard throughout the region, and was widely applauded by the Arab public. But it

shocked Israelis who considered the opening of Tiran their only gain from the 1956 war. President Eisenhower had given Israelis assurances that it would stay open, and they regarded closure as an act of war. Nasser further heightened tension in a May 26 speech to the trade union congress, saying this time Israel would be destroyed. By then Algerian and Kuwaiti soldiers had arrived and there were 250,000 Arab troops on the Israeli border. On May 30, Jordan's King Hussain went to Cairo, concluded a mutual defense pact with Nasser, and placed his forces under Egyptian command. Since Hussain had been critical of Nasser, this was seen as a significant development.

## The June 1967 War

On June 5, 1967, Israel launched a preemptive military strike against Egypt, destroying the Egyptian air force in a few hours, and beginning the third Arab–Israeli war. To bolster morale and encourage other countries to provide support, Egypt's Voice of the Arabs claimed that Egypt was winning the battle. On that basis, Jordan entered the war and Syrian artillery bombarded Galilee. But by June 10, after Egypt had lost Gaza and all of Sinai, Jordan had lost all its air force plus Jerusalem and the West Bank, and Syria had lost the Golan Heights to Israeli occupation. The war changed the map, quadrupling the size of the territory Israel controlled.

When the story of these catastrophic Arab losses came out, the Egyptian authorities tried to explain why their forces had been beaten so badly in a matter of hours, by accusing the United States of having participated directly in the war. The initial air attacks involved very large numbers of Israeli sorties and the Egyptians, who were not aware of the Israelis' short turnaround time, could not believe that the Israeli planes could have done it all alone. They remembered that in 1956, British and French planes had joined Israeli ones. Nasser's accusation of American participation went out to the region over Egypt's Voice of the Arabs radio and the Arab public believed it. The resounding denunciations of America by the Voice of the Arabs' bombastic commentator, Ahmad Said, had a powerful impact on Arab public opinion.

The Voice of America carried the strong denials from the U.S. government, as did BBC and other Western broadcasters. VOA also quoted newspapers in Iran, Turkey, and other Muslim countries, calling Nasser's accusation a lie. Just before the war, the VOA's Arabic Service had gone from six to eleven hours per day on medium wave, so Arab listeners heard Washington's view. But many discounted it.

Most Arab media throughout the region, following the lead of their governments, gave preference to the Egyptian story. All across the Arab world, angry mobs filled the streets of cities denouncing America, and some expressed their outrage by means of violent acts. On June 6, Egyptian mobs

reacting to the broadcast accusation, attacked the USIS centers in Cairo and Alexandria. The Alexandria rioters managed to break into the building and damage it severely, destroying all of the books in the library. In Cairo the USIS staff was able to preserve its 13,118 books, packing them away in hopes that the crisis would quickly be over and they could resume operations. (This was a vain hope; the break lasted seven years and by then nearly all of the books were out of date.)

Based on his accusation, Nasser promptly broke diplomatic relations with the United States and ordered all American official personnel out of the country. Despite the U.S. denials that it had participated, the damage was done. The USIS Americans, along with other officials, were transported by train to Alexandria, and then left the country by a boat that took them to Greece. Spain became the protecting power and the Spanish flag flew over the U.S. embassy compound in Cairo. Nasser made a gesture of resigning because of the war loss but his resignation was brief because a large popular demonstration of support brought him back. All USIA employees and their families were also evacuated from Iraq and Syria, and dependents were flown out of most of the other Arab countries except Saudi Arabia and Kuwait. Nasser called on the other Arab states to break relations with the United States, and four of them did: Syria, Iraq, Algeria, and the Sudan.

In Iraq, a mob of people who heard the same Voice of the Arabs broadcast attacked the USIS Baghdad center, severely damaging the building and its contents. As all American diplomats were being expelled from Iraq, the Belgian embassy, as the protecting power, took custody of the center and what was left of its facilities. The collection of books from the USIS library in Baghdad was shipped to Kuwait, intended for the University of Kuwait.[29]

In Syria, the PAO quickly moved to close his information center, as his cable to Washington tersely explained, "following mob attack during Middle East crisis." Since he and the rest of the embassy staff were being expelled by the Syrian government, and he assumed the break would be a long one because tension had been building for some time between the two governments, he made arrangements to have the 23,350 books in his library sent to nearby USIS posts, Lahore, Riyadh, and Beirut.[30]

Boulos Malik was at the embassy in Jordan in June 1967, when he heard Cairo's Voice of the Arabs broadcasting Nasser's accusation that the United States had participated with Israel in the attack on Egypt. He realized that this was very dangerous because the situation in Jordan was volatile. He immediately went to the director of Jordan's Radio, the official and only station in the country, and gave him the American denial. He told the director that broadcasting the Egyptian accusation was very serious because it might incite violent action against Americans. The director promptly cancelled the story to stop it from being repeated. Only days later, when King Hussain said in a press conference that he believed Egypt's accusation, did Jordan Radio run it again. That time, since the king had en-

dorsed it, there was nothing Boulos could do to stop it.[31] After the king's press conference, the American Center in Amman, which housed a library, offices, and English-language classrooms, was so badly burned by a mob that it was closed and the PAO was forced to find another building.[32]

There was also violence against USIS in other Arab countries that did not break relations. In Libya, the PAO cabled Washington that on June 6 the American Cultural Center was "completely destroyed by mob action over Arab–Israeli war. Center stoned and set on fire. All equipment, furniture and books destroyed." He added that the embassy had submitted a damage claim to the Libyans for $38,283. (Later he was able to restore the center, which reopened in September 1968.) In Tunisia, the PAO cabled USIA that on June 6, "Mob shattered display book cases located outside library. Rock-throwers and club-wielders shattered display windows at USIS center in three demonstrations." He later reported that the estimated cost was paid by the Tunis Municipality but he left the center closed. In some other Arab countries, such as Saudi Arabia, the government kept the public under control and no physical harm came to USIS facilities. But Nasser's accusation was universally believed and the PAOs had to face the task of dealing with what they knew was a lie by a leading Arab head of state.[33]

In Algeria, the government also decided to expel the American diplomats only after Jordan's King Hussain confirmed American participation in the war. Algerians had been skeptical of Nasser's original accusation because Nasser had been so hostile to the United States, but they regarded Jordan as a friend of America's so they assumed he was telling the truth. The PAO in Algiers closed the USIS center there as soon as the war started on June 5, but then a few days later an angry mob appeared at the center and broke into it. A quick-thinking local employee shut off the electricity, plunging the center into darkness, allowing the USIS staff to escape out the back. The mob did some damage in the library and burned some files but they could not see well so they left. The mob then went to the Egyptian cultural center which they trashed because Egypt had stopped the war too quickly, they said. The mob in Algiers caused considerable damage to furniture, windows, books, and equipment.[34]

In the Sudan, there was also a violent public reaction although it was slightly delayed, coming on June 10, when a mob attacked the USIS center and threw two bombs over the back gate, persuading the PAO to close the facility. As soon as Nasser made his accusations, the ambassador to the Sudan, Bill Weathersby (a USIS officer), gave Prime Minister Mahjoub the American official denials and at first Mahjoub did not break relations. But for several days, pro-Egyptian mobs of Sudanese attacked the embassy with stones and burned the USIS library, and Egypt warned Sudan's cabinet members that they would be denounced on Voice of the Arabs if they took a stand against breaking relations. Then when Jordan's King Hussain said

Nasser's accusations were true, this shook Mahjoub's confidence in the American assurances and he broke relations with Washington as Nasser was urging. Yet Mahjoub still had mixed feelings, so he ordered a "soft break," expelling only the U.S. ambassador and military attaché and allowing USIS programs to continue. Because of the break, the mobs stopped demonstrating and the USIS library reopened after a short interval.[35]

In late June 1967, Arab oil producers convened an emergency meeting in Baghdad. Because they believed the United States had participated in the war, they decided to impose an oil embargo on the United States, as well as on the United Kingdom and West Germany. The Arabs had often threatened to employ the "oil weapon" to punish countries that supported Israel, and now they felt compelled to use it.

American diplomatic and public diplomacy efforts and prospects in the Arab world had reached a low point. PAOs and other officials tried hard, with little success at first, to convince their Arab contacts that the United States had not in fact participated in the war that had been so disastrous for the Arab side. Most Arab media refused to publish the American denials, both out of conviction that they were untrue, and also out of fear of contradicting their own government's statements in support of the Egyptian claim. Arab editorials endorsed the breaking of diplomatic relations and the oil embargo as legitimate punishments for the United States and the West. In the countries that expelled U.S. diplomats, PAOs and their American staffs had to leave, so the public diplomacy effort was suspended altogether because the remaining local-hire staffs were unable to carry on any significant information programs. During the months following the war, PAOs and other American officials continued to deny the allegations that America had participated in the attack, and most of the Arab public gradually came to believe that Nasser's allegations were indeed false.

In the long run, many Egyptians and others began to be more skeptical of the reports of Arab government-controlled media. That was of some long-term help to PAOs, in their relations with media editors who were a bit more open to questioning the "facts" put out by their own governments. Yet for some time, the problem for all PAOs in the region was how to convince the public that the Egyptian accusation was untrue. President Nasser had said it, Arab governments accepted it as fact, and many of them had broken diplomatic relations based on the assumption that it was true. Moreover, it seemed logical to the Arab public that it would be true, given the strong and growing American support for Israel. Therefore, even as the Arab public gradually came to realize that the specific accusation was false, a residue of suspicion nevertheless remained in the public mind that the United States somehow had helped Israel, if not by direct intervention then secretly.

The oil producers lifted their embargo by the end of August 1967 but one long-term effect was that in January 1968 they created the Organiza-

tion of Arab Petroleum Exporting Countries (OAPEC), an Arab cartel to coordinate policies better, including prices and possible future oil embargoes. Yet the five governments continued to maintain their break in diplomatic relations throughout the Johnson and Nixon presidencies, and this severely hampered PAO efforts in those countries.

One of the negative consequences for PAOs was that in several Arab countries, the expulsion of American diplomats during the 1967 war took years to be reversed, even though the lie on which expulsions were based had been exposed. Where there were no PAOs, there was no one to work intensely with the media to set the record straight and explain American views, to sponsor exchanges or cultural programs, or otherwise keep the dialogue with target audiences going. Moreover, with many posts in Arab countries closed, the study of the Arabic language became less attractive as a career move. Public diplomacy officers who already had some Arabic became discouraged and moved to other parts of the world, and other FSOs were not encouraged to learn Arabic and make a career of working in the region, since the number of interesting posts was diminished.

As the Arab public absorbed the extent of the defeat and Nasser's lies, his reputation in the Arab world was tarnished, and some Arabs called for a new approach. The defeat led to a rise in activity by militant Palestinian organizations calling themselves "fedayeen," and also an upsurge of fundamentalist Islam, on the grounds that Nasser's secular Arab nationalism had failed. Political Islamists gained a hearing because the defeat was so overwhelming. Muslim zealots said that the Israeli victory must have been due to the deeper religious convictions on the part of the Israelis so their remedy was more fervent adherence to Islam. The slogan "Islam is the answer" became popular. As Islamist groups recruited new converts, this created new problems for PAOs, who often found it difficult to gain access to them because their primary motive was to purify their faith and they wanted little to do with non-Muslims. So for PAOs in the Arab world, the 1967 war made their job much more difficult because it spawned new ideas on how to confront Israel rather than sympathy for peaceful settlement.

Nor did Israel's overwhelming military victory in June 1967, convince Arab leaders to make peace. At their summit conference on September 1, 1967, they issued a declaration that said no to negotiation, no to recognition, and no to peace. The declaration was applauded in the Arab press, but it reinforced Israeli determination to maintain a hard line on the issues. For PAOs and other officials, this made discussions with Arab target audiences more difficult because the gap between American calls for negotiation and recognition and the "three no's" of Khartoum was very difficult to bridge.

In some Arab countries less influenced by Nasser and Arab nationalism, such as Saudi Arabia, USIS was able to continue its programming after the June war with little change. A bomb that exploded in the embassy

perimeter wall at the start of the 1967 war turned out to be the work of a Palestinian, and Ambassador Eilts obtained Saudi assurances and insisted that USIS and all other diplomats stay in the country and continue their work. But Saudi Arabia presented other unique challenges to USIS. The population was relatively isolated and insular and the government did not permit foreign embassies to be located in the capital, Riyadh, which was more conservative. They had to operate out of Jidda, a more open city, accustomed to receiving pilgrims enroute to Mecca. The PAO in Jidda, George Thompson, however, found a way to gain a foothold in Riyadh. In the spring of 1967, he persuaded the Deputy Minister of Education, Hamid Mutawa, to establish an English-language center in Riyadh where USIA-sponsored teachers would provide language instruction to government employees. Thompson hired an English teaching specialist, Bill Royer, to manage the program, and sent me to Riyadh to manage the operation. The June war only delayed the project briefly, and the "English Language Center of the Ministry of Education" opened in the fall of 1967. Partnering with a Saudi ministry made it possible, English study was in great demand, and it was regarded as benign activity that was legitimate for Americans to carry out. The center brought us into contact with Saudi officials in the classroom and the ministry who were otherwise inaccessible to U.S. officials. It opened up excellent opportunities for USIS contacts in the capital city, sixteen years before the embassy was allowed to move there from Jidda. Using the center as a base, USIS undertook programming of speakers and exhibits at Riyadh University and other local institutions, under the radar of the authorities who refused to allow activities of any other embassy in that city. It was therefore an effective public diplomacy operation that made the best of the circumstances.[36]

Meanwhile, the United States pressed for a negotiated Arab–Israeli settlement, and on November 22, 1967, the UN Security Council passed U.S.-sponsored Resolution 242. The Americans thought it represented a fair balance between Arab and Israeli interests. The Israelis were pleased that it called for the recognition of all states in the area (i.e., of Israel), termination of belligerency and threats of force, and freedom of navigation. The Arabs were pleased that it termed the acquisition of territory by force inadmissible and called for "withdrawal of Israeli armed forces from territories occupied in the recent conflict."

But the resolution's "land for peace" formula was not implemented at the time. It became the mantra for PAOs and all American diplomats from then on, and it has survived into the twenty-first century as the essential basis of American policy. The Arab states in 1967 rejected it because they insisted that Israel should make its concessions first, so Resolution 242 was not implemented. In later years, both sides accepted the resolution in principle and it remained the cornerstone of all diplomatic negotiations, but it was never carried out because of disagreements over interpretation. This

became another problem for PAOs and other American officials in the Arab world. Israeli lawyers argued that because the Israeli withdrawal clause said "from territories occupied" and not "from the territories occupied," Israel needed to make only a partial withdrawal, and the American lawyers conceded that this was so. Moreover, Arabs felt that since Israel was the occupying power it should make the first move, but the United States and Israel considered 242 as a total package. PAOs began to engage in discussions with Arab editors and others that went on for at least a decade, and which sounded something like this:

> PAO: Why don't you just go ahead and implement resolution 242, since it would achieve your main goals? It's better than going to war.
>
> Editor: But Israel is already distorting 242 by saying it doesn't mean total withdrawal.
>
> PAO: It doesn't say "total," but we agree that any border modifications would have to be minor.
>
> Editor: But why should there be any modifications at all? That's not fair.
>
> PAO: The perfect is the enemy of the good. Take what you can get.
>
> Editor: We must stick to our principles. Palestinians deserve justice.
>
> PAO: And Israelis deserve security. Threatening violence just makes things worse for everyone.
>
> Editor: We have no choice to be tough because the Israelis are sitting on Arab land. All Arabs agree with this. Why doesn't the U.S. do what Eisenhower did in 1956 and just demand that Israel withdraw from Arab land?
>
> PAO: 1956 was different. The Israelis believe they made a mistake then.
>
> Editor: So the U.S. just does what Israel says?
>
> PAO: No but we favor negotiations and believe that approach is in your interest too.
>
> Editor: The U.S. has refused to negotiate with Castro and others. You're just taking Israel's side. It must be because Zionists control American media.
>
> PAO: That's not true. America is an open society, and you too can make your case there if you try.

Within three weeks of the formal cease-fire in the 1967 war, the PLO began sporadic low-level raids, mostly in the Jordan valley and along the Suez Canal. The Israelis retaliated. This violence continued. From June 1967 until August 1970, as Arab frustrations grew, sporadic fighting took place between Arabs and Israelis that was called the "war of attrition." It was not a declared all-out war but occasional clashes in the air and sporadic PLO raids into Israel. The Arab public and governments supported it because Arab pride required doing something to protest against Israel and it seemed that full-scale war was too risky. The USSR was embarrassed

that the Egyptians and Syrians had done so poorly using Soviet equipment, and in order to bolster their Arab friends they sent them more modern equipment, including some that had not been deployed in the Middle East before. Israel carried out deep-penetration raids into Egypt and built the Bar-Lev defensive line along the Suez Canal on the Sinai side. The United States supported Resolution 242 but it was not self-implementing. The Israelis, who were proud of their military achievements in the 1967 war, grew comfortable with the concept that the occupied territory gave them "strategic depth," and they hoped their overwhelming victory made it the last war they would have to fight. They remembered the prewar period as one in which the UN and foreign assurances offered them little protection so they determined to rely more on themselves.

Therefore, when the Johnson presidency ended, major challenges remained for PAOs serving in the Arab world.

# 5

# The Nixon and Ford Presidencies, 1969–1977

## THE NIXON ADMINISTRATION (JANUARY 1969– AUGUST 1974)

After he was elected in November 1968, Richard Nixon named Frank Shakespeare director of USIA. Shakespeare had been a CBS network executive, and was Nixon's TV advisor in the campaign. He was conservative and strongly anticommunist. Career USIA officers found that Shakespeare's presence tended to elevate the Cold-War rhetoric in the agency's output.[1] He remained director until December 1973 when James Keogh replaced him.

President Nixon was obsessed with the Cold War, and he was preoccupied, as Johnson had been, with Vietnam. Despite the considerable attention he gave to Vietnam, Nixon was also concerned about the expansion of Soviet influence in the Middle East, and he could not ignore the simmering Arab–Israeli dispute which turned into war in October 1973. But Nixon tended to see the Soviet Union as the root cause of Arab hostility to the United States. He wanted to improve relations with the Arab states in order to thwart Soviet ambitions in the Middle East. Iraq, Egypt, Syria, and South Yemen already appeared to have moved into the Soviet sphere of influence. The USSR was supplying them with military equipment, and after the 1967 war Moscow increased that assistance, because it had been embarrassed that the Soviet military equipment used by the Arabs had done so badly against American equipment in Israeli hands. By 1970 as many

as 15,000 Soviet military experts had arrived in Egypt, a development that alarmed American officials. Since 1968 the Soviet navy had been present in the Indian Ocean, adding to Washington's concern. Nixon was committed to the security of Israel and to preventing the Arabs from "driving Israel into the sea." Many in Congress regarded Israel as the only reliable and effective block against Soviet expansion, and therefore a "strategic asset," and Nixon was sympathetic to that view.

## America's Image

PAOs in the region knew that Moscow was not the only problem. Many also failed to see exactly how Israel was much of a strategic asset, since Arab grievances against Israel had become so important that the more America supported Israel, the more Moscow was able to improve its standing among the Arab public. PAOs and other officials had to deal with Arab grievances, and with the impression that Moscow was being more helpful. They stressed Washington's strongly anticommunist policy in places like Saudi Arabia where it had particular resonance, primarily because of the Saudis' strong anti-Communism policy for religious reasons. In other Arab countries where Communism was not considered a threat, and the USSR was seen as a friend, PAOs had a more difficult time making their case.

The Israelis asked for American weapons to respond to the Soviet arms supplies coming into the region, and President Nixon was sympathetic to the request, believing that a weak Israel would invite an Arab attack. When Secretary of State William Rogers wanted to try to energize a peace process, Nixon agreed to hold off on arms to Israel while the "Rogers Plan" of 1969, based on Resolution 242, was tried. The plan went nowhere, however, and in August 1970, Nixon approved the transfer of $7 million worth of arms to Israel.

In these circumstances, the local media in Egypt, Syria, and some other Arab countries were becoming more hostile to the United States and friendlier to the Soviet Union. Editors with a positive view of the USSR had more freedom to express their views, and in editorials they cited Soviet military assistance as evidence of Moscow's positive attitude. Unlike newspapers in Saudi Arabia, that did not hesitate to criticize "godless Communism," newspapers in Egypt and Syria focused on the USSR as a friendly state and not as the center of a global ideology. Thus, Egyptian and Syrian editors felt free to criticize American policy, and those who were friendly to the United States hesitated to praise it.

PAOs also sought to focus attention on other issues. In July 1979, the United States accomplished the first moon landing, and NASA loaned USIA seven moon rocks for tours. The one sent to the Arab world gave PAOs an opportunity to demonstrate American space achievements, and to counter some Arab skepticism that the landing was a hoax. A poll taken

in Morocco, for example, and found that 90 percent had heard of the moon landing but 63 percent thought it was a hoax and 23 percent thought it was a Russian event.[2] In Riyadh, Ambassador Eilts showed it to King Faisal, which generated useful press play. As Branch PAO there, I arranged a public display of the moon rock and I organized a lecture about it by a Saudi scholar; he had recently returned from the United States with a PhD in chemistry and had the credibility to assure a skeptical audience that it was genuine. A Riyadh restaurant owner renamed his place "Apollo 11."

## Black September

PAOs and other officials throughout the region realized that Arab anger and frustration were growing because of the Arab failure to deal with Israeli occupation. New and more radical Palestinian organizations emerged, including the People's Front for the Liberation of Palestine (PFLP), and the Democratic Front for the Liberation of Palestine (DFLP). In the fall of 1970, the PFLP hijacked four Arab airplanes and blew them up in Jordan as a gesture of protest to embarrass Jordan and other governments into helping the Palestinian cause. Some American citizens were killed as a result of the hijackings.

Palestinian militants gained control of a large part of Amman, and in April 1970 they burned the American center there, destroying all of the USIS records. The center had to be abandoned. Three of the four Americans at the USIS post were evacuated, leaving only a PAO, who for security reasons could not risk leaving the fortified embassy.[3]

The Jordanian army moved to put down the Palestinian militants, but Syria sent forces across the border in a move to support them. Israeli forces, with American encouragement, moved into the Golan area and Israel warned Syria to withdraw from Jordan, which it did, and the Jordan army was able to regain control of the situation. President Nixon believed he saw a hidden Soviet hand in the PLO and Syrian moves, and he warned Moscow to stay out. Nixon concluded that the Israeli threat had helped thwart not only Syria but also Soviet plans in Jordan. Many Arabs, however, were not convinced that Moscow had played an important role in the events, and they were puzzled that Washington saw it that way. Some PAOs also failed to see Nixon's logic. But they could at least argue honestly that the situation was complicated and they disputed the Arab assertion that the United States was supporting Israel and conservative Arab monarchies against Arab and Palestinian nationalism. The Palestinians later called the Jordanian episode "Black September," and it increased their resentment of Jordan for not helping them liberate Palestine. The USIS center in Amman reopened in temporary quarters in December 1974. But it was not until 1978 that the post was able to open a new center in adequate space.

The PAO tried to revive the USIS program in Jordan. His main focus

at first was to provide stories to local and USIA media about the economic and military assistance that Washington was giving Jordan, to underline Washington's support for the king. But he also gave the press stories on American humanitarian aid for the Palestinians, to help blunt their anger. For example, he wrote a story on food shipments that the United States provided to a hospital in Ashrafia, the Palestinian quarter of Amman, and quoted Palestinian doctors expressing their gratitude. He made an effort to stay in contact with both Jordanians and Palestinians, and he had access to both groups despite their criticism of American support for Israel. He slowly revived the post's programs, arranging some cultural presentations, educational exchanges, and even got some press placement, although not on American foreign policy.[4]

Washington continued to prohibit all American diplomats including USIS officers from having any contact with the PLO. But this did not prevent USIS from sending Palestinians to the United States on exchange programs. This was particularly easy in Jordan, where Palestinians made up 70 percent of the population and held several cabinet posts. For example, the PAO there deliberately included a Palestinian teenager from a refugee camp in the American Field Service program of 1971–1972. He made a point of personally visiting the huge Bekaa Camp just outside Amman to announce the award, despite the fact that the embassy security officer regarded the camp as unsafe for Americans. When he arrived at the camp he was warmly welcomed by a large delegation including the camp leader. Nobody raised any political issues, even the fact that Washington had provided the weapons that had driven the PLO out of Amman a few months earlier.[5] For the moment they put aside politics in favor of education.

After the crises of 1970, relative calm settled over the region and lasted for three years. When President Nasser died suddenly in September 1970 and was succeeded by Anwar Sadat, Egyptian policy began to change and the task of the PAO in Cairo became somewhat easier. Sadat did not try to emulate Nasser's aggressive nationalist rhetoric. He maintained the cease-fire of 1970 and in July 1972, he suddenly expelled the Soviet military advisors who had been brought in after the 1967 war. He started opening up the socialist-controlled economy to more outside investment (the "infitah" policy), and he seemed to be looking for a way to resolve the conflict with Israel. Washington regarded these moves as signs that perhaps Sadat was more amenable to cooperating with the United States. Several times during this 1970–1973 period he declared that the conflict with Israel would be resolved but he did not say how, and when nothing happened, most people concluded that it was just empty rhetoric. Western media reported that the Egyptian military was in bad shape, and Western and Israeli analysts concluded that Sadat was in no position to wage war. Washington believed its policy of helping Israel to stay as strong as all potential enemies combined was working as a deterrent to war.

PAOs and other officials were therefore hopeful that finally the Egyptians had realized that war was not the answer, and that because Egypt held a natural leadership position, the Arab world might look to a peaceful settlement with Israel. But Arab arguments about Israel did not change, and Arab frustrations remained. PAOs with particularly good contacts warned Washington that the Arab anger was still there and that much of it was directed at the United States, despite the surface calm and the steps in the direction of change that Sadat was taking. They sensed that in fact deep Arab frustrations remained over the continuing Israeli occupation of the West Bank, Gaza, and the Golan Heights.

### The 1973 October War ("Ramadan War," "Yom Kippur War")

Suddenly, on October 6, 1973, Egypt launched an all-out military attack on Israel, crossing the Suez Canal and breaching the Bar Lev line of defense that Israel had been building along the canal's East bank. Syrian forces moved at the same time into the Golan in a secretly coordinated plan. The attack was a complete surprise to Israel and everyone else, who thought Sadat had decided on a more peaceful approach than Nasser's. In the greatest tank battle ever in the Middle East, Israel lost one-third of its tanks in three days, and it also lost 49 aircraft. By October 9 the Israeli leaders realized they would not win the war quickly as they had in 1967, and they were running low on ammunition, so they urgently asked the United States for military resupply. President Nixon agreed, and on October 13 a massive U.S. airlift began to ship 1,000 tons of military equipment per day, supplying more than 33,000 tons by the time the airlift ended on November 15. Nixon asked Congress for $2.2 billion to pay for it.[6]

Bolstered by this support, on October 16, Israel launched a counteroffensive, and crossed the Suez Canal, surrounding and trapping the Egyptian Third Army. Meanwhile the Soviet Union was busy resupplying Egypt and Syria with arms, and Moscow put Soviet forces on alert. Brezhnev warned that the Soviets might intervene; the United States responded by putting its forces on alert and asking Israel not to destroy the Third Army. Diplomats finally arranged a U.S.–Soviet deal that eased the crisis with an Israeli pullback and resulted in the passage of UN Security Council Resolution 338, calling for peace negotiations on the basis of Resolution 242.

Nixon had agreed to the military assistance because he accepted the argument that peace negotiations required Israel to feel secure, and resupply would promote peace negotiations. The war also convinced Nixon that Arab frustrations continued and could erupt into dangerous conflict again. Therefore, during the crisis, the United States promised Egypt that it would actively engage in trying to mediate the conflict with Israel. In the follow-

ing months, during 1974 and 1975, Secretary of State Henry Kissinger's shuttle negotiations resulted in two disengagement agreements between Egypt and Israel and one between Syria and Israel. The United States agreed to participate in monitoring the Sinai disengagements. Kissinger engaged in this mediation to demonstrate to the Arabs that the United States, and not the USSR, was the essential partner in resolving the Arab–Israeli dispute successfully.

The 1973 war also helped confirm Nixon's view that Israel was a strategic asset. In the aftermath of the war, the United States promised Israel that it would not negotiate with the PLO because Washington considered it a terrorist organization committed to the destruction of Israel. The Arabs, however, saw the situation quite differently. They supported Sadat's attack to recover occupied territory and condemned the United States resupply of Israel as unjust interference.

Egypt and Syria were supported by many of the Arab states, several of which had sent troops to the front. Bahrain announced cancellation of the home port arrangement for the U.S. navy that had existed since 1949. (The navy in fact continued to have access to the Bahrain port but had to rename the operation and lower the U.S. profile.) The issue of an American military presence was a sensitive one with Arab public opinion. There were no American military bases in the Arab world because of this sensitivity, although some Arab governments like the ones in Saudi Arabia and Bahrain hoped that they would have American protection in case they were threatened. PAOs and other American officials were aware of this and recommended that an American naval presence "over the horizon" in the Gulf would be the best posture to satisfy local sensitivities and concerns.

On October 9, 1973, the Arab oil-producing states in OAPEC decided to use the oil weapon for a second time, imposing another embargo that lasted into 1974. They called for Israel to withdraw from the territory it occupied in 1967 and the rights of the Palestinians to be restored. Saudi Arabia cut its production by 25 percent (as the world's largest producer at 8 million b/d this made a big difference) but Iran, Iraq, and some others made no cuts, essentially deciding to give economics a priority over politics.

This time the oil embargo had a strong impact on the American economy. Between 1947 and 1970, U.S. oil imports as a percentage of consumption had increased from 8 percent to 30 percent, making this issue more important. Long waiting lines at U.S. gas stations during the 1973–1974 winter brought this home to the American public. PAOs and other officials had a new factor to contend with: American public anger at the Arabs for the embargo that had caused so many to be inconvenienced. It was a problem because it evoked comments in U.S. editorials that were highly negative about Arab price gouging, which Arabs heard and regarded as unfair. But it also created an opportunity for PAOs to point out to Arabs

that the oil weapon was not effective in achieving its intended result with respect to Israel, and that it only made Americans angry.

Washington worked to lift the embargo, making the argument to the Saudis that the boycott weakened the West so it helped the communists. President Nixon also promised King Faisal that the United States would pursue implementation of Resolution 242. Kissinger's active involvement in mediating the disengagement agreements helped persuaded the king that the United States was seriously working for peace. The diplomatic effort succeeded, and the embargo was lifted in April 1974, despite the fact that Israel had not withdrawn and Palestinian rights had not been restored, as the king had demanded.

Although the embargo was lifted, oil prices rose to unprecedented levels and this affected the Arab–American dialogue. At the end of December 1974, the OPEC members meeting in Tehran agreed in effect to increase the price substantially and it later went to $30, because the Arab embargo had made this possible. American policy makers, who until this time had focused on containing the Soviet Union and supporting Israeli security in the region, now also added the goal of access to petroleum at reasonable prices. That goal was made more complicated by the nationalization of the petroleum industry that took place in several Arab countries in the 1972–1976 period.

It later became clear that Sadat had not intended his surprise military move in October 1973 to "drive Israel into the sea," which he knew was impossible, but rather to lead to peace by recovering enough Arab pride through bold military action so that he could take the political risk of making peace. This plan was not obvious at the time and it required a considerable effort on Sadat's part over several years to make it work, but eventually it succeeded.

The impact of the 1973 war, and the task of PAOs in dealing with it, varied by country. In places where diplomatic relations were not broken, PAOs nevertheless faced new challenges.

In Jordan, for example, the 1973 war caused an immediate and total halt to most USIS activities, even though the Jordanian role in the war itself was minor (it sent two elite units to the front line in Syria). The post could only distribute the wireless file bulletin to an expanded list of recipients in the media and government, but it had to shut down all public events. The PAO's contacts, both Jordanian and Palestinian, quietly suggested a temporary low profile during the war, and they assured him that things could return to normal after the war. The PAO and the FSNs maintained their contacts throughout, and the PAO wrote a daily memo to the ambassador on what people were thinking, much of which went into embassy reporting cables. In conversations with both Jordanians and Palestinians, the PAO often found that when one of them started to castigate the Americans, another would interrupt and say "There's no reason for us

to get into this again. We differ, and a big argument isn't going to serve any useful purpose for any of us." Often the PAO's contacts would indicate that they admired most things American and they sought USIS out to learn more about the American approaches to such various matters as education or its social security system, and they liked Americans personally. This gave them mixed feelings; one said, "I wish you were different, so it would be easier for us to hate you."[7]

At the time of the 1973 war, the chairman of the political science department at the university in Jordan, Dr. Anabtawi, broke off all contacts with USIS, to protest American support for Israel. After a few months he asked to be put back on the distribution list for the USIS bulletin but he still refused to see the PAO. The PAO offered him a trip to the United States on an International Visitor Grant, and he accepted it but he said before he left that he wanted to be clear that in accepting it he was "not approving in any way your one-sided policy in the Middle East, which I wholeheartedly oppose." The PAO, said in response, "If we only dealt with people in Arab countries who supported U.S. Mideast policy, we would have very little to do with anybody." That broke the tension, and after the professor returned from America, he surprised his students and colleagues with the positive comments he made about most things American.[8]

During the October 1973 war, as President Nixon promised active diplomacy in the Arab–Israeli conflict, he agreed to support an international conference in Geneva to that end. Washington instructed American embassies to promote the Geneva conference. At the embassy in Beirut, Boulos Malik convinced the prominent Lebanese publishing house al Nahar to publish a book called *Road to Geneva*, which was a collection of statements he put together about the Arab–Israeli peace process. Boulos always preferred if possible to find local people to make the American case because they are more credible. The book did not reveal that the USIS was the source of the material (it was all in the public domain), and it did include some Soviet statements for balance, but the selection was heavily weighted to favor the American side of the story.[9]

Elsewhere there were serious obstacles to promoting American policy. In four of the five Arab countries that had broken diplomatic relations with the United States in 1967, USIS programs had been stopped completely. In 1974, Egypt, Syria, and Algeria restored diplomatic relations with Washington. (In the Sudan, where diplomatic relations were suspended from 1967 until 1972, the USIS library was able to reopen in September 1967 and function quietly during the diplomatic hiatus. Iraq continued for another decade to refuse to mend relations with Washington.) As soon as relations were restored in Cairo, Damascus, and Algiers, USIA moved to reconstitute USIS posts in these countries and try to recover ground lost during the break. In Egypt, for example, Cairo's American Center reopened in December 1974, but an entirely new book collection had to be purchased

for the library because during the seven-year closure the old collection had become badly outdated. A Branch PAO was assigned to Alexandria in 1976, and by March 1977 the refurbished center there was reopened.

In Damascus, Syria, Kenton Keith reopened the USIS post in 1974. It was clear that Syrian government officials wanted to resume relations for several reasons, including the fact that Kissinger was pushing disengagement talks that Syria wanted to succeed, and also that its economy had suffered from being cut off from the West and was depending only on commerce with the Soviet bloc. But the Syrian public had been subject to seven years of anti-American government propaganda, and there was no embassy or USIS presence to try to mitigate the hostility. Moreover, there were some elements in Syria who opposed the reconciliation. The PAO decided that the best way to give the public confidence that it was all right to have contacts with Americans was to organize a big public event, something he otherwise would not have done. He hoped it would publicize the return of America, stress nonpolitical aspects of the relationship, and demonstrate Syrian government approval for the American presence. With the help of USIA Washington, plus the State and Commerce Departments, he arranged for a major exhibit at the July 1974 Damascus Fair that included a moon rock, a space lab, and the Florida State Marching Band, complete with majorettes. He also scheduled concerts by small ensembles of band members around Damascus. Syrians opposed to the American return placed a bomb at the American pavilion and wrote editorials in Tishreen and Ba'ath newspapers, but thousands flocked to the exhibit, ignoring the East German exhibit next to it which only displayed tractors. The event opened opportunities for USIS at the university and elsewhere, previously closed to Americans. The Fair manager was so pleased that he helped the PAO gain access to several ministries. Syrians knew it was all right to have contact with Americans, so the PAO was able to expand USIS activities and he pursued a big program agenda in his first year.[10]

One priority target was the university. A U.S.-trained Syrian told the PAO that East European–trained academics were embedded in the Syrian universities and that U.S. degrees were regarded there as inferior. The PAO negotiated with the government and persuaded officials to give U.S. degrees parity. The equivalency issue was important because it made study in the United States attractive. The PAO also used USAID money to send Syrians to the United States to study and that led to an increase in educational exchange with America. He persuaded the USAID regional officer in Beirut to give him six scholarships for Syrians to study at the American University of Beirut, which helped him achieve his objectives. He also established strong relations with the Ministry of Culture and within two years negotiated a cultural agreement that opened the way for a large educational exchange program of the kind the Soviets had unsuccessfully sought for years.[11]

By 1977, the American Center in Damascus finally reopened, after Syrian president Assad signed a formal decree authorizing it. The PAO found initial use of the center disappointing, however, because some public suspicions remained. So he used a creative approach that gradually made it possible to reach a priority target audience. He set up a controlled system of memberships for invited members, actively recruited from his primary audience lists by personal contact or written invitation, and gave them exclusive use of the library. The approach built a high-priority membership of about 500, half professionals and half university students. They all received book alerts and article availability lists on the 240 periodicals to which the post subscribed. They used and appreciated the book collection of 2,000 volumes because it was strong in American literature keyed to the needs of the English Department of Damascus University, and it offered sources unique in Syria. The USIA inspectors recommended the approach as a "model" for the kind of library PAOs who faced such difficult conditions.[12]

Moreover, in North Africa, conditions were unique for public diplomacy programming. For example, America's relations with Algeria were still broken and Switzerland was the protecting power, so the Swiss flag flew over the American embassy. Howard Simpson, who was PAO in Algeria from 1972 to 1974, found he was hampered by limited access to Algerians and by surveillance from intelligence personnel who watched him and his staff constantly. He was able to arrange for some Algerians to travel to the United States on visitor and student grants. But his media contacts were limited and most editors and reporters were loyal government employees anyway. Occasionally, editors requested an official text of a U.S. government statement, but they preferred to have it delivered by messenger, in order to avoid having a discussion with the PAO. Simpson was therefore unable to establish any close personal relations, because that was what the Algerians wished to avoid. At times when he was able to engage Algerians in conversation at social functions, he found that they were not very forthcoming. They would make only pro forma criticisms of American support for Israel, for example, but they did not waste much time on it. "It wasn't something you would find yourself in an argument about," he noted, because Algerians were very "diplomatic;" they raised contentious issues only at formal office meetings. It was difficult to know their true feelings. Another problem was that there was considerable Soviet influence on Algerian thinking, especially in the military, because Moscow was providing supplies of military equipment. The PAO, however, found it relatively easy to have contact with resident Soviet and Chinese officials including generals. As he concluded, "Our operation was mainly sort of a holding operation until diplomatic relations returned."[13]

Diplomatic relations were restored with Algeria in 1974 but the USIS post did not reopen until 1976. Even then the PAO had no information

center and the staff had to work out of the embassy which restricted public access. Later they were able to move to a small, renovated prefabricated building nearby, where they established a small collection of reference books. The USIS branch offices in the provincial Algerian cities of Constantine and Oran, which had been closed in 1967, never reopened.

As for East Jerusalem, it was a special case. It had been part of Jordan until 1967. In the 1967 war, it was occupied by Israel, so the United States established a Consulate General there that reported directly to Washington, and its constituents were the Palestinian Arabs in the Israeli-occupied West Bank and Gaza. There was no USIS presence there at first, but finally in 1977, USIA established a new post there, assigning a PAO to it. The small USIS staff operated out of the Consulate General facility, had no library or information center, and reported directly to USIA Washington, not to the embassy in Tel Aviv. The PAO tried to establish contacts with Palestinians, but it was not easy because of the occupation.

### Persian Gulf

President Nixon's main concern in the Persian Gulf was to prevent Soviet encroachment into the area. For him this meant a sustained effort to cultivate relations with Iran and Saudi Arabia, since he regarded the smaller Arab states of the Gulf as under a British sphere of influence. But then in 1968 the British government announced that it would leave its commitments east of Suez within two years, meaning the British would no longer control the foreign and defense policies of Bahrain, Qatar, the Trucial States (which became the United Arab Emirates), and Oman. In March 1968, the Soviet navy appeared in the Indian Ocean for the first time. Nixon was convinced Moscow was seeking Arab oil, warm water ports, and the overthrow of conservative regimes like Saudi Arabia that were anticommunist. Following the overthrow of the monarchy in Iraq in 1958, that country's leaders had developed a close relationship with the Soviet Union, and by the time Nixon came to office, Moscow had become Iraq's primary arms supplier. Iraq was in effect in the Soviet sphere of influence, and the Iraqi leadership and media were increasingly critical of the United States. (In 1972, Moscow and Baghdad signed a treaty of friendship and cooperation.)

Because of this concern and because U.S. forces were tied up in Vietnam, the president, in January 1970, declared what came to be known as the "Nixon Doctrine," which in essence meant that the United States would not replace Britain but would work actively through its allies in the region to defend its interests. In his January 22, 1970, State of the Union Address, President Nixon said: "Neither the defense nor the development of other nations can be exclusively or primarily an American undertaking. The nations of each part of the world should assume the primary responsibility

for their own well-being, and they themselves should determine the terms of that well-being. We shall be faithful to our treaty commitments but we shall reduce our involvement and our presence in other nations' affairs."

Nixon called Iran and Saudi Arabia the "twin pillars" of America's policy of support for Gulf stability and independence, and he supported the sale of weapons to both countries to protect mutual interests. It was obvious that because of its size and geography, Iran had far more capability of playing the role of strategic partner than Saudi Arabia, but Nixon sought to appeal to the Saudis as a key friendly Arab state by giving them prominence.

When the British left Bahrain, Qatar, the United Arab Emirates, and Oman in 1971, the United States promptly recognized and established diplomatic relations with all of them. At first the American ambassador in Kuwait, Bill Stoltzfus, was given the responsibility of handling diplomatic representation in the five new embassies, but when the host governments complained that they each deserved "their own" American ambassador, Washington named separate ambassadors for each one. The new PAOs found the media and public opinion environments in all four countries hospitable, since the newspapers, although privately owned, tended to support the policies of their governments and the governments were well disposed to the United States except when the Arab–Israeli question arose.

American overt support of Iran with very substantial military sales and political backing of the shah was received with mixed feelings by Saudi Arabia and other conservative Arab states, however. They liked the idea that Iran was a conservative monarchy, Muslim and anticommunist, but they were concerned simply because a large and powerful non-Arab state was interested in supporting Shiite minorities in places like Bahrain and eastern Saudi Arabia.

USIS operations, for example, in Kuwait, where the post opened shortly after independence in 1961, were limited by local conditions. The post in Kuwait had a small budget, mainly because USIA Washington assumed that the Kuwaitis could pay for anything they wanted, such as visits to the United States. In fact, many Kuwaitis would turn down a ticket provided by USIS because it would be economy class and not first class; but USIS was able to arrange some visits. For example, the PAO sent mid-level Kuwaitis in social service professions to the United States under the Cleveland International Program, which arranged for them to see American social services organizations and which gave them useful information as well as a positive view of the United States. There was no USIS library or information center in Kuwait. The government-controlled radio and TV, always hungry for material, accepted some USIS placements as long as they were nonpolitical. Palestinians made up nearly one-third of the resident population and they staffed most of the working-level positions in the media, as well as in other professions, which meant that many of the PAO's

discussions with contacts concerned the Arab–Israeli conflict. The university was accessible to some extent because a number of faculty members were Kuwaitis with American PhDs, and the PAO arranged programs there, including a successful book exhibit.[14]

Public diplomacy programs elsewhere in the Persian Gulf were similarly modest in these early years. But later, USIS programs in Kuwait and other Gulf Arab states were to expand as Washington increasingly paid attention to that region.

## THE FORD ADMINISTRATION (AUGUST 1974–JANUARY 1977)

Gerald Ford became president when Nixon resigned in August 1974. During his twenty-nine months in office, he made few important changes in policy or public diplomacy strategy toward the Arab world. He did make one attempt to move the Arab–Israeli peace process forward, by announcing a "reassessment" of policy in May 1975 when Israel requested new military assistance, but members of Congress objected strongly, and Ford acceded to their pressure. Thereafter he reverted to the Nixon policy of generous support for Israel. The Arabs were appalled that Ford had caved in to Congress, and they said so. In discussion with them about this event, PAOs and other officials tried to use the opportunity to explain the American democratic process and the important role of the Congress in making foreign policy. Some Arabs understood the lesson, but others failed to see how an American president could appear to be so weak in the face of Israeli and domestic pressure.

One significant improvement in broadcasting to the Arab world did take place during the Ford administration. PAOs knew that the VOA Arabic Service was a very useful public diplomacy tool wherever its signal could be heard, since it had an excellent and varied program. But it was not audible everywhere in the region because the VOA transmitter at Rhodes in the early 1970s was still limited by international agreement to a low-power signal that was weak at night and inaudible to most Arabs in the daytime. Also, the British were trying to help BBC by cutting VOA out with their more powerful signal. One American official therefore negotiated a deal with the Greek government, by which the Greeks let VOA Rhodes use the Greeks' better frequency at very high power, and in return Greece used the VOA transmitter one hour a day for their Greek program so Greeks all over the Middle East could hear it. This helped give Arab listeners access to the VOA Arabic Service, and they listened to it.[15]

During the Ford administration, USIA also stepped up its reporting on foreign opinion. In 1974, posts in the Arab world and elsewhere sent in media reaction cables from time to time and the media reaction staff at USIA headquarters compiled these into a report three times a week that

was sent around to other offices. But policy makers at State and the White House paid little attention to it. Jim Thurber, the chief of USIA's Media Reaction unit, who later became Near East bureau director, upgraded the reporting effort by changing it into a daily report that went out at 8:00 A.M. each morning to senior policy makers not only in USIA but also at State and the National Security Council, and he also began computerizing the process. He found that policy makers then read it because it was timely and useful in their deliberations.[16] This served them, and it was also helpful in making them more aware of one important aspect of the public diplomacy process, namely, the assessment of foreign opinion. The reporting function was to prove valuable later in times of crisis.

# 6

# The Carter Presidency, 1977–1981

President Carter, who took office in January 1977, was forced by circumstances in the Middle East to pay more attention to that region of the world than his predecessors had. In fact, during his presidency, the most important international events and developments took place in the Middle East or nearby: Camp David and Egyptian–Israeli peace agreements (1978–1979), the Iranian revolution and subsequent hostage crisis (1979–1981), the Soviet invasion of Afghanistan (1979), and the start of the Iraq–Iran war (1980).

In April 1978, President Carter ordered that USIA be renamed "International Communication Agency" ("ICA"), but this change was not generally welcomed by PAOs in the Arab world because many people confused it with the CIA. Field offices kept the well-known designation USIS in order to avoid confusion. In 1979, President Carter moved educational and cultural affairs from the State Department to USIA. This change was welcomed by PAOs because it consolidated their Washington support into one agency, but it had little effect on field posts because PAOs were already handling these matters. (The USIA name change did not stick and President Reagan changed it back to USIA in 1982.) PAOs were also pleased that Carter appointed John Reinhardt as director of the agency because he was the first Foreign Service Officer to hold that position in nearly two decades.

President Carter also redefined the mission of public diplomacy. Whereas Kennedy's mission statement had emphasized policy advocacy and persuasion, Carter's emphasized mutual understanding, reflecting Carter's

approach. On March 13, 1978, he sent a memo to the director of ICA say-ing that the "principal function of the agency should be to reduce the de-gree to which misperceptions and misunderstandings complicate relations between the United States and other nations." The three main tasks that he spelled out were: "(1) To encourage, aid and sponsor the broadest pos-sible exchange of people and ideas between our country and other nations; (2) To give foreign peoples the best possible understanding of our policies and intentions, and sufficient information about American society and cul-ture to comprehend why we have chosen certain policies over others; and (3) To help ensure that our government adequately understands foreign public opinion and culture for policymaking purposes, and to assist indi-vidual Americans and institutions in learning about other nations and their cultures." This third point made explicit for the first time the function of educating Americans about the world, but it was unclear how it was to be done other than through exchange programs. He also directed that "the Agency will undertake no activities which are covert, manipulative or pro-pagandistic," meaning USIA would not be a cover for CIA officers.[1]

The VOA Arabic Service expanded to 7.5 hours per day in 1977. By then the VOA signal from the United States had improved so much, be-cause of the use of satellites, that the program center was shifted from Rhodes back to Washington.[2]

## America's Image

As before, the Arab–Israeli conflict remained the most troublesome issue for America's image in the Arab world, and PAOs had to deal with it constantly.

By the beginning of the Carter presidency, Israel had reached its high water mark of territorial control as a result of four Arab–Israeli wars. We know now that there have been no more such wars in over thirty years, but at the time the fear of another war was real. Moreover, the hard-line Likud leader Menachem Begin had become prime minister in Israel in 1977 after decades of Labour governments. Increasing Arab resentment against the United States as Israel's benefactor had resulted from a succession of Arab military defeats and continued Israeli occupation. President Sadat had helped restore some measure of Arab pride in launching the 1973 war and recovering half of the Sinai in the Sinai disengagement agreements, but there was still no peace. PAOs and other U.S. officials continued to argue for a negotiated settlement but the parties seemed to be stuck, and criti-cism of American policy continued. Criticism was especially strong in the media in Iraq, Egypt, Syria, Algeria, and part of the press in Lebanon, and privately throughout the region. But the situation appeared to be stable and Washington did not give it high priority.

American efforts to persuade the Arab governments to engage in ne-

gotiation to settle the conflict seemed to fall on deaf ears. PAOs tried to make the case with Arab editors, academics, and others, just as ambassadors and other embassy officials did with Arab officials, but they all met with rejection. Then in 1977, Egyptian president Anwar Sadat suddenly announced that he would be willing to travel to Jerusalem and speak before the Israeli Knesset to explain directly to the Israeli people that Egypt wanted peace. His announcement surprised everyone, and his trip to Jerusalem in November 1977 was a sensational event. The Arab public watched it with intense interest, astonished to see a major Arab leader in Israel for the first time and shaking hands with the enemy. The only Arab journalists accompanying Sadat were Egyptian, because other Arab countries did not allow their citizens to visit Israel so the Arab public followed the drama on Egyptian and non-Arab media, including VOA and the BBC. On his return to Cairo, Sadat was cheered by large welcoming crowds, and the Egyptian press dutifully applauded his initiative. But elsewhere in the Arab world, the move was strongly criticized. He had not consulted in advance with other Arab leaders and they did not endorse his move. At a hastily called high-level Arab meeting in December 1977, in Tripoli, Libya, five countries—Syria, Iraq, Libya, Algeria, and Yemen—plus the PLO, strongly condemned Sadat's trip to Jerusalem. Jordan and the Gulf states remained neutral but expressed disapproval through their official media. Sadat responded robustly by breaking diplomatic relations with these five states before they could do the same to him.

For PAOs and others, the game had changed. American PAOs throughout the Arab world now had helpful talking points because the leader of the most powerful country in the Arab world was publicly and dramatically opting for a negotiated peace. American officials had been advocating a negotiated settlement for decades with no tangible result and suddenly, unexpectedly, they had a prominent Arab example to cite in their arguments. They hoped that Sadat, who was obviously acting alone and taking a huge risk, could pull off his gamble. The Israelis were pleased by Sadat's trip but they did not reciprocate with a gesture of their own, as Sadat hoped. For nearly a year after the trip, Egypt and Israel conducted negotiations without result, and then finally, President Carter called Sadat and Menachem Begin to a meeting at Camp David in September 1978 that led to the Camp David Accords, calling for a bilateral peace agreement. On November 5, 1978, the Arab states met and condemned the Accord, but Sadat pursued further negotiations that led finally to an Egyptian–Israeli peace agreement on March 26, 1979. Arab media widely reported the ceremony on the White House lawn, but (except in Egypt) they also widely condemned it.

The peace agreement represented a turning point in America's longstanding public diplomacy effort to urge Arabs to agree to a peaceful settlement of the most troublesome issue affecting U.S.–Arab relations. PAOs

could now argue forcefully that direct Arab–Israeli negotiations would bring positive results for the Arabs. They said Sadat was proof of that. PAOs urged their interlocutors that the other Arab states should follow Sadat's example, but many regarded Sadat as a traitor to the Arab cause.

The peace agreement created both opportunities and problems for PAOs. All of the other Arab states flatly rejected Sadat's initiative. At their summit conference in Baghdad on March 31, 1979, they declared that he had signed a separate peace that broke ranks, undermined Arab unity, and made a comprehensive peace much more difficult because there was no linkage between the Egyptian agreement and the rest of the problem. They said that Sadat was a traitor to the Arab cause because he had abandoned the Palestinians, as well as Jordan, Syria, and Lebanon, states that were all directly affected by the dispute with Israel and that got nothing from Egypt's deal. Even Sadat's foreign ministers Fahmy and Kamal resigned, and Egypt's most prominent columnist Muhammad Hassanain Haykal expressed criticism in print. The Baghdad summit passed a resolution suspending Egypt from the Arab League, moving the Arab League headquarters from Cairo to Tunis, and calling for an Arab boycott of Egypt. Most of the Arab governments—all but Oman, Sudan, and Somalia—broke diplomatic relations with Egypt in protest, and severed other ties as well.

Arabs everywhere realized that when Sadat signed a peace agreement he effectively removed war as an option from the Arab side, but this did not make them less adamant in their refusal to negotiate with Israel. They continued to feel that the Arabs were the aggrieved party, and that justice was not being done. Their increased sense of weakness did not translate into a willingness to follow Sadat's example and make new concessions. The non-Egyptian Arab media continued to attack Israel as the enemy and the United States as its patron, and now added Egypt as its third target. They pointed out that despite the Egyptian–Israeli peace, Israeli Prime Minister Begin allowed settlements in the occupied West Bank to continue to grow, and they applauded Palestinians who carried out sporadic raids into Israeli territory. And when Sadat opened the Egyptian economy to Western investment, Arab critics saw an Egyptian–American–Israeli conspiracy.

Egypt was a special case for public diplomacy. For one thing, Sadat's peace agreement led to a very large American economic and military assistance for Egypt for the first time ever, and USIS made an effort to publicize that. Egyptian radio and television were directly controlled by Sadat's government, and the large-circulation daily newspapers were strongly influenced by him, so they not only applauded his peace agreement with Israel but they also were supportive of the United States in their editorials and headlines. Some of the smaller-circulation papers that were less influenced by the government were more critical of the United States. But the Egyptian leftist intellectuals who had been among our sharpest critics in print during part of the Nasser era were not being allowed to write. As

PAO in Cairo from 1976 to 1981, I had regular contact with the leftist journalists and heard their strong complaints about American support for Israel and other perceived American sins. Some Islamist publications were also hostile. My efforts to reach the Islamists met with little success because they were reluctant to meet with embassy officials. The government watched us closely but not obtrusively and its surveillance did not intimidate Egyptians as it had during the Nasser era. On one occasion I attended a meeting of political opposition figures and the next day the foreign minister phoned Ambassador Atherton to ask why I was doing that, implying that it was improper for an embassy officer to consort with the opposition. The ambassador told the foreign minister that I was just doing my job and he approved of what I had done. We heard nothing more and I continued to seek out people with many different views. When Egyptians asked me why I was in contact with communists, I told him my approach was to engage in dialogue with people of any persuasion, including critics of America.

But even in Egypt, it was very important to carry out a broad-based program that was not confined to political issues, but strengthened social and cultural connections between America and Arab countries. When Lea Perez was a young USIS officer in Cairo, she discovered that the renowned local architect Hassan Fathi had inspired many Egyptians by espousing the values and benefits of traditional Egyptian architecture that involved inexpensive adobe walls, natural cooling systems, and traditional crafts. She realized that the architectural heritage of the American Southwest shared many of these same features, so she organized a small comparative exhibit of southwest American and Egyptian adobe architecture and construction techniques. She used magazine articles and photographs and put the exhibit together at minimal cost. The Egyptian public response was extremely positive. It was the first time anyone could remember seeing a long line of Egyptian students snaking out the front door of the American cultural center, through the garden and into the street. It helped make a cultural and emotional connection for them between America and Egypt.[3]

Elsewhere in the Arab world, however, PAOs found that essentially all their contacts were very critical of both Egypt and the United States. PAOs told them about the financial "peace dividend" that Sadat had received from Washington for his agreement with Israel, but this was not enough to change their minds. Since all the other Arab governments opposed Sadat's move, it was difficult or impossible for the media to endorse it.

In countries where the government was especially hostile to the United States, the problem for PAOs was compounded because of barriers that existed to our communication with the public. For example, in Syria in the late 1970s and early 1980s, the official government attitude toward the United States was highly negative, and as a result there was no access to the military (which had close relations with the Soviets), or to the Ba'ath

Party, whose members were under instructions to have no contact with the Americans. For Dick Undeland, who was PAO there from 1979 to 1983, USIS relations with the press were almost nonexistent. He saw the chief editors of the newspapers only once a year because they were not receptive to his efforts. The three dailies were tightly controlled by the regime and almost identical to each other, and although the editors were polite, they all spoke from the same script so there was little point in trying harder. But the PAO sent out USIS press bulletins and some reporters were pleased to receive them, as were some officials such as the interpreter for the president. Syrian intelligence services regularly interrogated USIS local employees to monitor their activities.[4]

In these circumstances the PAO found that his best public diplomacy tool was the International Visitor Grant program, which sent about seventeen Syrians to America every year. Since the Syrian government insisted on making the original nominations, he had to manage the process carefully to avoid being stuck with unqualified candidates. He conducted private discussions with contacts to identify the best people and then drafted the invitation narrowly to fit the targeted candidate, and this worked. For example, in his discussions with the vice president of Damascus University, he identified and nominated an engineering professor who had a PhD from the Soviet Union and was also a campus Ba'ath Party leader. The professor returned from the United States a changed person, strongly defending American education and scholarship, and opening the two engineering departments to USIS that had previously been fiefdoms for Soviet graduates. The PAO sent more academics to the United States and assigned an American Fulbright professor to one engineering department. Soviet-trained Syrian professors at Aleppo University went to the United States with similar results. The PAO concluded: "These people carried the message of America in ways and to places we never could have on our own."[5]

In Tunisia, when the PAO dealt with the press, he found that editors were always very cordial, and they liked to receive USIA press releases. But they used the USIS press materials essentially for background information and they rarely drew on them directly in their newspapers. Criticism of U.S. support for Israel was common but it appeared to the PAO to be automatic and routine rather than intensely felt. There were occasional digs at the United States on other matters but they were not a major problem. The PAO realized that Tunisians felt somewhat removed from the Arab–Israeli conflict but they needed to express their pan-Arabism from time to time. Ben Ali, who replaced Bourguiba as president in November 1987, adopted a more pan-Arab stance than Bourguiba, yet he did not want to go too far in criticizing America, and since he controlled the media, the editors followed that line.[6]

The PAO in Algeria also operated under political constraints that forced him to concentrate on educational and cultural programs. And be-

cause of very high rents in Algiers he could not afford to open a cultural center, but by 1978 he had created a small resource center, which included reference, student counseling, and English teaching collections plus a small collection in American literature and civilization. In 1979 he arranged for an American Fulbright professor who specialized in curriculum materials for teaching English as a Foreign Language (TEFL), to spend a year as a consultant to major Algerian institutions. The professor organized English teaching and American studies seminars, and initiated a program of direct teaching. He made books available to a university audience in English teaching and American studies and gave books on English teaching, linguistics, methodology, and semantics to the University of Algiers English Department.[7]

The Arab public in some closed societies like Iraq had access to outside information and opinion only via the Voice of America and other radio broadcasts. But in some border areas the public had access to diverse sources of news and commentary via terrestrial television (satellite TV did not yet exist). For example, Jordanians in the 1980s could watch four different terrestrial channels: They could watch the news on Jordanian, Israeli, Lebanese, and Syrian television sequentially at different times. This affected the public diplomacy program because much of the audience was well informed about different views including the Israeli one, and USIS personnel could build on that base.[8]

In the newly independent Arab states on the Persian Gulf, the constraints on our public diplomacy were of a different order. In Bahrain, in early 1977, a public diplomacy mission post was established, but it had no center or library, because the PAO had limited resources and the Bahrainis had their own facilities. They also had independent access to American materials if they wished. In October 1977, for example, the PAO in Bahrain sent copies of the Arabic translation of the book *Oil and World Power*, by Peter Odell, to the development minister and others interested in petroleum issues, with a personal letter recommending it. The minister wrote back that he had already read the book in English, knew Odell's ideas well, but disagreed with them and felt Odell's advice to the West contributed "in no small degree to the debacle since 1973." The PAO reported this to USIA Washington with the comment that it seemed the Bahraini target audience was quite sophisticated in some areas and aware of the latest Western American publications, so that if USIS was to be taken seriously, it would be better to focus on distributing the USIS article alert service, the Arabic wireless file al Majal, and recently published English texts.[9]

Meanwhile, President Sadat held firm on his position, and Arab sanctions against Egypt were slowly weakening. After he was assassinated on October 6, 1981, his successor, Husni Mubarak, quietly reduced the Egyptian media's propaganda attacks against the other Arab states without formally changing Sadat's go-it-alone policy. Eventually, during the 1980s the

other Arab governments restored diplomatic relations with Cairo, in effect conceding their failure to block Sadat's peace with Israel. This helped relieve at least part of the stress in U.S.–Arab relations that PAOs had to contend with.

### The Gulf Crises of 1979–1980

In 1979, amid dramatic events relating to the Arab–Israeli conflict, a series of crises began in the Gulf. They affected the work of American PAOs throughout the Arab world, although more intensely in the Gulf countries that felt directly threatened by new problems.

In the first weeks of 1979, a revolution in Iran led to the shah's flight out of the country and brought Ayatollah Khomeini back from exile in Najaf, Iraq. The Iranian revolution shocked Washington. President Nixon had depended heavily on the shah as a pillar of support for U.S. interests in the Gulf, and President Carter had also praised the shah, calling Iran "an island of stability in one of the more troubled areas of the world." Now suddenly the shah was out. PAOs noticed that Khomeini had cleverly used some simple communication technology: audio tapes of his exhortations that were smuggled into Iran and helped win him popular support.

What impressed many Arabs was the fact that although the CIA had helped restore the shah to the throne in 1953, Washington did nothing to save him from abdication this time. Many had assumed that American policy of support for conservative monarchies in the region meant that the United States would use its great capabilities to prevent such revolutions from overthrowing them, but in this case that did not happen. Moreover, the radical Islamic nature of the new Khomeini regime, which appeared to have the support of the Iranians, surprised many people in the region, especially Sunni Muslims, who wondered if this was the start of a wave of Islamic fundamentalist takeovers that would sweep the area. Islamist political leaders throughout the region were encouraged to think that their time to gain political power was coming, while the elites were apprehensive. And everyone wanted to know what the United States would do under the circumstances.

At first Washington was hopeful that the United States could work with the new Iranian regime. But when President Carter let the shah come to the United States for treatment, that awoke Iranian suspicions of a new U.S. plot like the one in 1953 to restore the shah to the throne, and it led to a takeover of the American embassy in November 1979. The Iranian regime tolerated (and probably encouraged) the takeover. PAOs and other U.S. officials throughout the region argued strongly that taking diplomats hostage was a clear violation of diplomatic rules that was unprecedented in the Middle East. Washington protested strongly through diplomatic channels, banned Iranian oil imports, and froze $12 billion in Iranian de-

posits in U.S. banks, but the hostages were not released. They continued to be held, eventually for 444 days. This began a policy of U.S.–Iranian confrontation that has continued into the twenty-first century.

Meanwhile, in February 1979, as Soviet influence was increasing in Afghanistan, a mob of Afghans attacked the U.S. embassy in Kabul and murdered U.S. ambassador Spike Dubs. A new Afghan president invited Soviet "advisors" into the country, and by December 1979 more than 120,000 Soviet troops had entered Afghanistan. This was the first time since 1946 that Soviet troops had moved outside their country anywhere except Eastern Europe, and Washington regarded it as an ominous move toward the Gulf.

Reacting to these threats, President Carter, in his January 23, 1980, State of the Union address, enunciated what came to be known as the Carter Doctrine. It said, "An attempt by any outside force to gain control of the Persian Gulf region will be regarded as an assault on the vital interests of the United States of America and will be repelled by any means necessary, including force." He followed these words by moving more naval forces into the Gulf and Indian Ocean, and in March 1980 establishing the "Rapid Deployment Force" with a mission to be ready to respond to developments in the Gulf.[10] Later this Force was transformed into the Central Command, parallel to other U.S. military commands abroad, but unlike the others, Centcom had to maintain its headquarters in Tampa, Florida, because of the Arab public's opposition to foreign bases on Arab soil.

Many Arab editors and others asked PAOs what the Carter Doctrine meant. Although Carter did not specifically name the Soviet Union in his statement, it was clearly intended as a warning to Moscow, and they said so. But was this also a warning to Iran? And what was the United States going to do about the fifty-five American diplomats being held hostage, against the rules and norms of international law? PAOs had little guidance on the questions about Iran, except to say that Washington was protesting the holding of Americans hostages and that many nations had supported the protest. The situation left many in the Arab world confused. President Carter was taking a tough line that seemed to be directed against the Soviet Union but he was focused on Iran and on Afghanistan where America had minimal interests. He seemed not to be doing anything specific to deal with Iran, whose regime was overtly hostile and potentially represented a wider threat if other governments in the region were taken over by militant Islamists. PAOs simply had to refer to the illegality of the Iranian actions. Many Arabs were surprised that the United States, as one of the world's two superpowers, seemed to be stymied by a previously obscure Shiite cleric.

American prestige in the Arab world was further weakened by the failed American hostage rescue attempt in Iran in April 1980, which was widely reported in Arab media.

As it became known that the United States was giving support to the anti-Soviet forces in Afghanistan, and that Saudi Arabia was also doing so, America's Afghanistan policy was applauded by the conservative Arab governments in the Gulf and by their media. The media in those countries were critical of the USSR for intervening in Afghanistan and supportive of the efforts of the mujahideen fighters and of the United States to oppose Soviet efforts. The story was, however, not of major interest to Arabs outside the Gulf because they were further removed geographically from Afghanistan, and they had other priority concerns. Yet PAOs throughout the Arab world pointed out that the Soviet Union was occupying a Muslim country.

On September 22, 1980, Iraq attacked Iran, and a war began that was to last for eight years. The Iraqis expected a quick victory to seize some territory, because Iran appeared to be weak, and it was clear the United States would not defend Iran now that the shah was gone. The United States announced a policy of neutrality, said that it would not supply weapons to either side, and called for an end to the violence. Washington was at odds with both countries and did not want either to win a decisive victory. The United States was concerned about the security of the Gulf, the war's impact on the flow of oil from the region, and the danger that Moscow would exploit an unstable situation. President Carter, in September 1980, said, "It is imperative that there be no infringement of . . . freedom of passage of ships to and from the region." When he did so, he explained that suspension of oil shipments from the Gulf would be a "threat to the economic health of all nations." The Arabs, however, clearly supported Iraq, and wanted the United States to do so as well. American officials stressed that it was in everyone's interest to end the fighting quickly, because Iran, Iraq, and other states on the Gulf depended on oil exports that were threatened by hostilities, and consumers around the world depended on importing this oil. But this war was not the outside threat that the Carter Doctrine addressed. It was an unanticipated threat coming from conflicts among Gulf states themselves, and that aroused more interest and passion in the Arab world, where the public was entirely on the side of Iraq.

Because of the crises, the Omani government in 1980 accepted a U.S. military agreement providing for pre-positioning of U.S. equipment. But the other Arab Gulf states still refused to do so because their publics continued to oppose open alliance with Washington.

Events in the Persian Gulf forced President Carter to focus more on Middle East issues and relatively less on America's global anticommunist posture, which had dominated Washington's thinking for many years. To most Arabs, this shift made U.S. policy more understandable and welcome, since they had always been less concerned about Communism and the USSR than they were about local issues.

U.S.–Iranian negotiations led finally to an agreement for the release of the American hostages, but by then President Reagan had been elected. The

Iranians delayed implementation of the agreement until inauguration day, January 20, 1981, to spite Carter. Relations between Washington and Tehran were still strained as the Iranian government continued to be critical of many aspects of U.S. policy, including U.S. support for Israel. The Arabs were gratified that Washington was in confrontation with Iran but they still wished the United States would tilt more in Iraq's favor as the Iran–Iraq war continued.

# The Reagan Era, 1981–1989

## REAGAN'S PUBLIC DIPLOMACY

Shortly after Ronald Reagan became president in 1981, he named his close friend Charles Z. Wick as director of USIA. In 1982, Director Wick initiated Project Truth, to counter and expose Soviet propaganda themes and techniques.[1]

President Reagan defined the public diplomacy mission as follows:

1. Strengthen foreign understanding and support for the United States policies and actions; 2. Advise the president, the secretary of State, members of the NSC and other key officials on the implications of foreign opinion for present and contemplated United States policies; 3. Promote and administer educational and cultural exchange programs for the purpose of facilitating international understanding and the national interest of the United States; 4. Unmask and counter disinformation attempts to distort or frustrate the objectives and policies of the United States; 5. Cooperate with private American institutions and interests to increase the quality and reach of United States public diplomacy; 6. Assist in the development of a comprehensive policy on the free flow of information and international communication; 7. Conduct negotiations on information and educational and cultural exchanges with other governments.[2]

During the Reagan presidency, much of his focus was on the American relationship with the Soviet Union, and he had four summit meetings

with Gorbachev (1985–1988). But several Middle East crises also required his attention: the Israeli invasion of Lebanon and the American intervention there (1982–1983); several kidnappings and killings of individual private Americans in the Middle East, the bombing of Libya in retaliation for a Berlin terrorist incident (1986); the Iran–Contra affair (1986–1987); and the Iran–Iraq War (1980–1988). Therefore, President Reagan had to deal with problems both in the Arab–Israeli arena and in the Persian Gulf, and these problems defined the context for public diplomacy in the Reagan presidency.

## America's Image

The Reagan administration took steps that Arabs regarded as tilting against them and in favor of Israel. President Reagan believed Israel was a "strategic asset" against the Soviet Union and assured Prime Minister Begin of qualitative superiority against any threat, that is, all Arabs combined. American aid to Israel had been generous since the Johnson administration, and it grew under President Nixon, but it grew more under President Reagan.[3] In November 1981, the United States signed a Strategic Cooperation Agreement with Israel that facilitated the provision of increased military assistance. Washington seemed to be tilting more in favor of Israel.

When Reagan came to office in January 1981, he knew little about the Middle East and he understood almost nothing about the dynamics of the Arab world. Where Carter had a regional focus and appreciated the importance of American direct involvement as an honest broker in the peace process, Reagan had a global outlook and tended to see the region strictly in Cold War terms. When his first secretary of state, General Al Haig, learned that Sadat had expelled the Soviet military advisors and signed a peace agreement with Israel, he thought that it would be possible to form a "strategic consensus" alliance between Israel and the moderate Arab states (like Saudi Arabia) against the Soviet Union. PAOs and other American diplomats in the region knew that the governments and peoples of the region would not accept that idea, that they did not regard the Soviet Union as a real threat, and that they had pressing concerns other than the Cold War. One PAO later expressed the view of many when he said he was relieved when Haig left office because he no longer had to try to defend his idea of an Israeli–Saudi anticommunist pact, which was a very difficult concept to explain.[4]

PAOs in the Arab world did their best to defend Reagan's Middle East policy. In Qatar, for example, brand new PAO Jim Bullock cultivated personal contacts in the local media, both with the chief editors who were usually wealthy Qataris, and with the reporters who were non-Qataris from Palestine, Jordan, and elsewhere. He called on them often. For example, when President Reagan announced his Middle East peace initiative on Sep-

tember 1, 1982, Jim took the Arabic wireless file translation in person to the chief editors, late at night when the editors were most likely to be found in their newspaper offices. He had a well-written Arabic translation and taking it in person resulted in getting the text published in its entirety. He was providing a useful service because the Internet did not yet exist and the media had no other source of the full official text, and the reporters trusted the messenger. The USIS office in Qatar was in a small villa which Bullock turned into a modest information and cultural center. In those days he did not need to deal with a lot of bureaucracy. Rather than formally negotiating with the Qataris for permission to open a cultural center, he just had a sign painted saying "American Cultural Center" and started providing friendly service, mainly educational advising and answering basic reference library questions. It was successful in attracting Qataris who came by for information on the United States. They would drink coffee with him, try out their ideas about the state of the world, and ask his opinion on many subjects.[5]

The June 1982, Israeli invasion of Lebanon ("Operation Peace for Gallilee") created problems for PAOs. The Israelis intended to destroy the PLO and help the Maronite Christian president Bashir Gemayel, but the nine-week siege of Beirut cost 19,000 lives, mostly Lebanese civilians, and angered most of the Arab world. The Arabs thought the U.S. official reaction favored Israel because it was mild, and because the United States vetoed a UN Security Council resolution of condemnation as one-sided. Then on September 29, 1982, after a Lebanese Christian militia had massacred several hundred Palestinians in the Sabra and Shatilla camps, the United States sent 1,800 Marines into Lebanon to help end the conflict.[6] Reagan explained his rationale: "The marines will help prevent the Middle East from joining the Soviet Bloc." PAOs were puzzled at how he came to that conclusion, and they only surmised that he saw a Soviet hand because the Lebanese Druze and Shia were being supported by Syria which in turn was receiving Soviet arms aid. It was true that Druze artillery hit U.S. positions, and that the U.S. battleship fired back into Lebanon to help the [Christian] Lebanese Forces recapture territory from Druze. In any case, the United States appeared to have become a combatant on the Christian side.

But car bombs destroyed the American embassy in Beirut on April 18, 1983, killing sixteen Americans; and the U.S. Marine barracks there on October 23, 1983, killing 241 Americans; and in February 1984, President Reagan had decided to cut American losses and withdraw the Marines. The United States did help mediate an Israeli–Lebanese cease-fire, and when Arafat and 7,000 PLO militants were trapped in north Lebanon, the Marines helped them evacuate from there to Tunisia. This was a minor event but one the PAOs could use with their Arab interlocutors to help blunt their broad criticism of the American intervention in the Lebanese crisis. However, on balance the intervention hurt the American image.

The PAO in Damascus had his hands full. During the Israeli incursion into Lebanon in 1982, Israeli forces destroyed Syrian surface-to-air missile sites in eastern Lebanon and a number of Syrian planes. This affected Syrian public opinion toward the United States in two contradictory ways. On the one hand, Syrians told the PAO privately that when they saw the Russian-made SAMs and planes destroyed easily by U.S.-made Israeli planes, they concluded that Moscow was giving Syria inferior equipment and "old models" while America was giving Israel the best. The PAO regarded this as a plus. On the other hand, the Syrians blamed the United States for "allowing" the Israelis to intervene in Lebanon, and most Syrians shared that view; for them the proof was that Israel used American weapons in the incursion. The PAO insisted in his conversations with Syrians that the United States had opposed the invasion but they tended not to believe him. They typically said: "Can't you finally see how bad the Israelis really are?" They asked how Washington could continue to support Israel "so blindly." They told the PAO that if the United States had wanted to, it could have prevented the massacre of Palestinians at Sabra and Shatilla camps while Israeli forces were present. The PAO told them they were expecting too much from the United States, but they continued to believe in American omnipotence. And when an American battleship approached the Lebanese coast and fired 16-inch rounds into the Lebanese villages, a dean at Damascus University asked the PAO, "How can you do this? How can you make it impossible for any Arab to be a friend of the United States? What do you think you are accomplishing?"[7]

The Syrians, like many Arabs, preferred to distinguish between American policy, which they disliked, and everything else about America. In 1983, in a conversation with the PAO, the Syrian Minister of Culture praised the USIS-managed educational exchange and cultural programs and the information center, and commented, "We don't have anything against the American people, but only against your government." The PAO responded by thanking her for her nice words but pointing out that all the programs she had just praised were sponsored by the U.S. government; she responded: "Oh, we don't look on you and what you are doing in that way at all," implying that PAOs were benign in contrast to embassy political officers who were considered to be spies.[8]

In December 1983, while Israeli forces were in Lebanon, Syria shot down two American planes over Lebanon and incarcerated the one pilot who survived, Lt. Goodman. Syria released Goodman only after Jesse Jackson traveled to Damascus to plead with President Assad. During this period, demonstrations took place regularly at the American embassy in Damascus protesting U.S. policy. Usually they were small crowds of disciplined Syrians sent by the regime to provide Syrian TV with footage for the evening news. On one occasion, however, armed Palestinians appeared, tried to enter the embassy, and then climbed on the roof, forcing Ameri-

can diplomats to take shelter in the vault. Syrian security personnel did nothing to protect the embassy but the Palestinians failed to gain entry and retreated. Fortunately, they failed to notice the PAO, whose unprotected office was across the street.

Secretary of State George Schultz, who had taken office in the summer of 1982, negotiated a peace agreement that was signed on May 17, 1983, between Israel and Lebanon. Washington thought this would begin a new Arab–Israeli peace process. But when Schultz traveled to Syria to ask President Assad to sign on to it, he discovered that Assad was not at all ready to do so, and by May 1984, Lebanon had cancelled the deal with Israel. Schultz believed the Arabs had "squandered an opportunity."

PAOs and other American diplomats in the Arab world were not very surprised at Assad's refusal to make peace, and the subsequent collapse of the Lebanon–Israel agreement. Many had been hearing criticism of American policy on a daily basis and they knew that most Arabs regarded the Reagan approach as tilting unfairly in Israel's direction. Reagan's apparent acquiescence in the Israeli invasion, the failure of the Marines' intervention, and of Schultz's attempt at brokering peace, were seen by Arabs as symptoms of a biased policy. They thought that Lebanon was too weak to resist it but Syria was not. In retrospect, some Arabs admitted privately that President Carter had been much more of an honest broker, who was sincerely trying to bring about an agreement that was fair to both sides. They were disappointed that Reagan seemed to lack Carter's sensitivity to Arab concerns and interests.

After the collapse of Schultz's negotiations, officials in Washington seemed to lose interest in further direct involvement. For the next five years, the United States played no important political role in the Arab–Israeli conflict, but Washington did continue as a major arms supplier for Israel and Egypt.

Circumstances for Americans varied a great deal throughout the Arab world. Lebanon, for example, remained very dangerous, even for Americans. The Lebanese government was friendly to the United States, but it was weak and unable to provide sufficient security for its own people or anyone else. Between 1984 and 1986 a number of private Americans were kidnapped and some were killed. In 1984, Malcolm Kerr, the president of the American University in Beirut, was assassinated. In March 1985, journalist Terry Anderson was kidnapped; he was held for seven years and only released in December 1991. In March 1984, the Islamic Jihad kidnapped CIA station chief Bill Buckley; they later killed him. Some of the hostile acts were carried out by Hizbullah, a Lebanese organization with strong ties to Iran, and their animosity to Americans was partly due to Tehran's confrontation with Washington.

In Syria, USIS officers in the mid-1980s found their task frustrating. They had no success at all with the media which were all government-controlled and hostile. They were nevertheless able to carry out some cul-

tural activities. For example, USIA sent a break-dance group that the post programmed in Damascus, Aleppo, Latakia, and Homs, and that Syrian youth in all places welcomed enthusiastically. However, the Hindawi incident in the fall of 1986 caused a worsening of relations. A Syrian agent named Hindawi tried to blow up an El Al plane by placing a bomb on it at Heathrow, but he was caught and the British government publicly condemned Syria and closed its embassy in Damascus. Washington followed suit, withdrawing Ambassador Eagleton and all USIS Americans except the PAO. The PAO started English-language classes, which were an immediate success, but day-to-day personal contacts were limited because the USIS staff found it difficult to meet people they wanted to meet. Students and professionals came to the American center but they were reluctant to accept invitations to American homes because Syrian intelligence (mukhabaraat) were usually posted outside taking names. A visit to the university or a ministry required a letter to the Foreign Ministry requesting permission, and the Syrians would not meet with the Americans without advance approval. Syrians were very guarded in what they said to Americans, and they spoke frankly about any political matters only when they were certain that they were not being overheard. They felt they were under constant surveillance.[9]

In Egypt, circumstances were different. The Egyptian government had made peace with Israel, and the United States was providing massive amounts of economic and military assistance to Egypt as a "peace dividend," so the atmosphere for USIS was quite favorable. It was the largest USIS post in the Middle East, with information centers in Cairo and Alexandria, staffed by nine American officers and more than eighty FSNs. The post offered English teaching and an International Visitor Program that sent about eighty Egyptians to the United States every year. A busy press section provided wireless file and other materials to the media. Although the media were beginning to have access to more material from the improving international wire and television services, and sometimes the USIS press releases were too late to be used, the Egyptian editors nevertheless liked the USIS summaries of American media editorials and the full texts of U.S. official statements. The post received new Worldnet television service several hours each day, placed some of the features on Egyptian television, and used it to conduct some interactive interviews at the embassy between Egyptian journalists and American officials. The post made a special effort to publicize the USAID program, for example, by helping Egyptian reporters do stories on the new phone system, clean water for Cairo, new generators for the Aswan Dam, and scholarships. Visiting American speakers such as former Assistant Secretary of State Hal Saunders were very effective in explaining the complexities of the peace process and breaking down stereotypes about American policy.[10]

As PAO in Egypt in the late 1980s, Kenton Keith worked closely with Ambassador Wisner to raise private funds to increase the number and qual-

ity of American cultural presentations in the country The purpose was to show a positive American face and to demonstrate that the United States sought a broad bilateral relationship, not one based only on security and political considerations. They also wanted to show Egyptians that they should not fear American private enterprise. The ambassador brought American businessmen together over breakfast and had the PAO make a pitch for money, which resulted in large donations allowing three major American cultural events that would have been too expensive for the U.S. government to pay for: the Houston Grand Opera, the Paul Taylor Dance Company, and the Dance Theater of Harlem.[11]

As Information Officer in Egypt, Marcelle Wahba began to make connections with hitherto unreachable audiences because as a bilingual Arab-American she could reach out to some of the more hostile journalists. For example, the outspoken chief editor of one important newspaper, who had been a communist and then an Islamist, regularly wrote anti-American editorials, but she called on him and found he had never met with an American official. She developed a personal relationship with him, and when he met with Ambassador Wisner at her home, he heard explanations of American policy firsthand, without any filters. He did not cease his criticisms but his articles became more helpful than they had been.[12]

In Saudi Arabia, the circumstances for USIS were difficult because most Saudis knew little about the United States, except for those who had been students in America. The government allowed no tourism, all business visitors required a Saudi sponsor, and until 1983 foreign embassies were not permitted in the capital, Riyadh. Personal contacts were consequently difficult, despite the government's strong and cordial official relations with Washington. No USIS programs that brought men and women together were possible, and male embassy officers generally had no contact with Saudi women. Cinemas were banned, and strict local social customs plus the unfamiliarity of most Saudis with American culture precluded much American cultural programming.

When Dick Undeland was PAO in Riyadh, from 1983 to 1985, he tried an Ansel Adams photography exhibit, but nobody came to the opening, and then the authorities closed it because they feared it would set a precedent for Western art exhibits. His personal contacts with Saudis were mostly on weekends at the farms and roadside restaurants outside Riyadh, and at dinner parties he hosted for men only. He did meet with media editors who welcomed the daily wireless file bulletins. They used some of its material because of the government's good relations with Washington, but the press rarely published the pieces on America's Middle East policy. There was no USIA educational exchange program because Saudis were wealthy enough go to the United States on their own, and go first class. But USIS did a great deal of student counseling to help students find the right American university. The PAO's best contacts were returnees from study in the

United States, because they wanted to keep up their American connections. USIS had maintained small libraries in Jidda and Riyadh, but they were not used by Saudis, who could buy any book they wanted, so in the early 1980s the PAO reduced the libraries to small reference collections. In discussions with him, Saudis often complained about the support that America gave Israel, saying it was not only morally wrong but it was strategically detrimental to America's interests in the region. These discussions were cordial, and the PAO always politely agreed to disagree with his interlocutors. The Saudis did not dwell on this issue because they were interested in cordial relations with the United States in order to do business with Americans and send their children to American universities.[13]

In Morocco in the 1980s, French influence was still very strong, and one of the USIS goals was simply to raise the visibility of the United States and increase Moroccan familiarity with American culture. USIS made use of American cultural programs that were provided by USIA, or were improvised locally. For example, on one occasion, the post arranged for a U.S. Navy band from the Sixth Fleet to visit Casablanca and play an open concert in a park that gave Moroccan teenagers a unique experience with live American popular music. USIS also imaginatively publicized the work of USAID programs and the Peace Corps, two of its largest programs in the world. For example, the post took Moroccan journalists to inaugurations of USAID projects presided over by the U.S. ambassador and arranged for them to interview local people whose lives were directly and positively influenced by the projects. The resulting coverage on TV, radio, and in print told a human story rather than merely documenting another ribbon cutting.[14] Also during the 1980s, USIS arranged for many Moroccan Inspectors of English to travel to the United States to attend annual seminars in English teaching, and when they returned home they undertook substantial changes in the Ministry of Education's required English teaching curriculum and textbooks that reflected American thinking.[15]

One PAO in Morocco, Boulos Malik, always made sure that when an American official or visitor made a speech, he would provide the text or a summary of it to the local press. This helped prevent inadvertent distortions or errors in reporting by the local media, and even reduced the chances of deliberate misreporting. The press did not always get the full text. For example, when a U.S. cabinet member visited Morocco and held a press conference, at one point he misunderstood the question and in response made a misstatement of U.S. policy. Boulos had made a recording of the session and released a transcript labeled "excerpts" with the misstatement deleted, so the error was corrected.[16]

In Yemen, during the mid-1980s when I was ambassador there, we had cordial bilateral relations and USIS was active, but the government's intelligence officers maintained such tight surveillance on all embassy personnel that it often hampered our activities. Any Yemeni coming to the embassy

compound was interrogated at our gate by a plainclothes officer who made a note of his visit. On one occasion when I hosted a lunch with the PAO and the Commercial Officer at a local hotel, intelligence officers in the hotel lobby stopped each of our guests and turned them away. The one Yemeni guest who insisted on coming to our lunch despite the harassment was taken away afterwards and interrogated for ten hours. But the PAO was able to establish very useful contacts through the Yemeni-American Language Institute (YALI), where he had his office and where his English-language classes, taught by Americans, were very popular and attracted a variety of types of Yemeni who were of interest to USIS. The PAO also used YALI as a program venue for films and student counseling as well. In fact, it was clear that the PAO had much better access to the Yemenis than other embassy officers did. In contrast, Jack McCreary, the embassy Political Officer, had great difficulty in meeting Yemenis in spite of his fluent Arabic, because they were reluctant to have contact with a political officer. When his tour was up in 1985, he stayed on for another tour by switching his jobs to PAO, and suddenly many contacts of all kinds opened up for him because as "Attache for Education and Culture" the Yemenis regarded him as nonthreatening. Jack decided to make a career change and move from State to USIA because of that experience.

When Duncan MacInnes was PAO in Yemen, 1987–1991, he made full use of the speakers' program and he insisted on bringing the same speakers back each year to make them more effective. His State Department colleagues asked why he didn't bring new people ("That one's already been here before"), but the PAO knew that a familiar face had more impact, just as repeated contacts by the PAO paid dividends. He also arranged cultural programs, even though American culture is unknown to most Yemenis. For example, he brought an American graphic artist to Yemen who stayed for a month, conducted workshops for Yemeni artists, lived with them, and at the end held a large joint exhibition with them. This drew extensive press coverage that was very positive. It served the purpose of demonstrating that the United States is interested in more than just strategic and political relations; that the American government cares about other aspects of the relationship, and that it wants an intellectual dialogue. It showed respect for Yemenis and helped validate the rest of the relationship.[17]

As a public diplomacy officer in Yemen, Peter Kovach sought out some of the Muslim Brotherhood intellectuals, befriended the conservative editor of *Al Islah* and immediately succeeded in placing wireless file material and some materials translated at USIS on American life and politics.[18]

In Palestine, in December 1987, the Intifada began. It was a popular uprising that started with strikes by Gaza merchants and workers, and expanded with rock throwing by teenagers at Israeli soldiers. It added a new challenge to the task of PAOs throughout the region. PAOs continued to argue for peaceful settlement of disputes, but their Arab interlocutors sym-

pathized with the Palestinians, who were deeply frustrated and some were taking matters into their own hands, using violence against the Israeli occupation. The Americans said it was wrong for Palestinians to attack Israeli civilians, and it was also counterproductive because the violence would simply escalate and Israel was able to defend itself. The Arabs responded that the Israeli government used violence against Palestinians and Palestinian civilians were being killed, so for the Americans to condemn only one side revealed a double standard. The Americans said there was a distinction between Israeli actions which were defensive and by a legitimate government, and the acts of Palestinian individuals, but the Arabs said they failed to see that distinction.

In 1988, at the end of Reagan's second term, Secretary Schultz tried again to propose a comprehensive Arab–Israeli peace. But by then the two sides were farther apart, and Prime Minister Yitzak Shamir, the Likud leader and prime minister since December 1986, rejected the American peace proposal. But in November 1988, the 450-member Palestinian National Council met in Algiers and passed resolutions implying recognition of Israel's right to exist. The United States wanted the Palestinians to be more explicit, and in December 1988, Secretary Schultz stated that the United States would meet with PLO representatives only if it accepted UN Resolutions 242 and 338, recognized Israel's right to exist, and renounced terrorism. Arafat accepted all three, and as a result, Ambassador Robert Pelletreau in Tunis began to meet with PLO representatives. This signaled a tactical change in U.S. policy after fifteen years of refusing to meet with PLO representatives. It was of help to PAOs in dealing with Arabs, who had been urging this step for years. Nevertheless, the Arabs believed the Reagan administration was insensitive to their concerns, and the Reagan presidency ended with Arab–Israeli peace no closer than when it had begun eight years earlier.

The Reagan administration, however, also had to deal with the crises in the Persian Gulf, which in turn exacerbated the American position in Lebanon as the new Iranian regime encouraged the Hizbullah to attack American interests.

### The Gulf

In the Persian Gulf, support for the independence of Saudi Arabia remained a central tenet of Reagan's policy. His commitment was based on oil and Saudi stability. In October 1981, at a press conference, he said, "There is no way . . . that we could stand by and see [Saudi Arabia] taken over by anyone who would shut off the oil."[19] Later, after years of the Iran–Iraq War, he recalled the 1973 oil embargo "that shook the economy to its foundations," adding:

I'm determined that our economy will never again be held captive, that we will not return to the days of gas lines, shortages, economic dislocation and international humiliation. Mark this point well: the use of the sea lanes of the Persian Gulf will not be dictated by the Iranians. These lanes will not be allowed to come under the control of the Soviet Union. The Persian Gulf will remain open to navigation by the nations of the world.[20]

Reagan was thus reiterating the Carter Doctrine warning to the Soviet Union, but expanding it to include a warning to Iran, with a justification based on access to oil. To the Arabs, what was important was the tough U.S. stance on Iran. The United States continued to insist that it was neutral in the Iran–Iraq War, and Washington did not supply arms to either side. But it seemed that the United States was definitely tilting in Iraq's favor.

One sign of that tilt was that the United States and Iraq reestablished diplomatic relations in November 1984, in the middle of the war, ending a seventeen-year break. USIA sent Jim Bullock to Baghdad to reopen the USIS post. He had to start from scratch: He rented space for a small center, furnished it, and made a major effort to bring equipment and supplies from Kuwait. He knew educational advising would be his biggest draw. Some came to him for advice on studying in America, while others wanted to have their American academic degrees certified, services that attracted several hundred Iraqis each month. He had a small International Visitor program, and a small American speaker program. For example, he arranged for the dean of Cornell's school of architecture to lecture at Baghdad University, a novelty at that time.[21]

Bullock's greatest obstacle in Iraq was the total lack of any social contact with Iraqis outside of the office. He tried to invite Iraqis to his home but none came, and the only one who ever invited him was his landlord. All the others were still fearful of government reprisals for contact with Americans. Even Bullock's wife Carole, who taught French at the French Cultural Center, had no social contact with her students except once a year when they accepted her invitation; they made clear that was a unique event, and they never discussed politics. Conversations with Iraqis were always about the Iran–Iraq War or bilateral relations, never about the Arab–Israeli conflict. Bullock befriended an Iraqi who worked at the embassy, whom he knew was an intelligence officer, and made sure the man was informed on what he was doing. This was the most tightly controlled society in the Arab world, so the PAO had to tread carefully.[22]

The next PAO in Iraq (1987–1989), Jack McCreary, had to deal with the Arab government that was still more hostile to the U.S. government than any other, despite the fact that relations had been restored. Under Sad-

dam Hussein, the Iraqi authorities continued to limit access of all foreign diplomats to a handful of designated mid-level Iraqi officials. The secret police monitored and punished private Iraqi citizens who attempted to make contact with foreigners. Jack's key public diplomacy objective was therefore the most basic: finding a way to reach the Iraqi public, who obviously would not risk the political dangers of visiting an embassy office. He decided to open an American-language center several miles distant from the embassy. He faced high startup costs with a limited budget, but he exploited the artificially inflated official currency exchange rate of the Iraqi dinar of ten dollars each when the fair market rate made one dinar worth less than one dollar. He charged his Iraqi students modest fees, as measured by the real market value of the dinar, and then "sold" these dinars back to the embassy at the required legal exchange rate, making enormous dollar credits which were used for rent, salaries for American teachers, and so on. Once open, the American Language Center in Baghdad provided a unique environment, where Iraqis and Americans for the first time had a venue to meet and exchange ideas. The center advanced U.S. policy at a time when Washington sought to engage the Iraqis and break down mistrust and decades-old hostility. Unfortunately, this opening for improved relations had a very short life. The policy of engagement was discarded in the wake of Saddam's invasion of Kuwait in 1990 and the subsequent Gulf War (see below).[23]

When John Berry was Information Officer in Saudi Arabia during this period, he found that professional contacts were fairly easy to make, but it was difficult to become acquainted with Saudis on a personal basis, even though he was fluent in Arabic. Saudi social life revolved almost entirely around the extended family. Saudis who had studied in the United States were more accessible because they wanted to maintain their American connections, but in all cases the Saudis preferred to move slowly to develop personal relationships. Saudis tend to spend most of their time with close family and other relatives, and their homes typically are surrounded by high walls, symbolizing their concern for privacy. Only after calling on Saudis in their offices several times might they be willing then to visit him at home. In conversations, the Arab–Israeli conflict was rarely uppermost in their minds as it was in some other Arab countries. They focused instead on local concerns. Saudis who had studied in America expressed admiration for many things American, but they often criticized American materialism, lack of religiosity, and what they saw as lax moral standards that they felt inappropriately influenced American children. One Saudi physician who had studied in the United States complained about the prevalence of violence in America, and said that even Tom and Jerry cartoons promoted violence, which he said Saudis abhor.[24]

In his professional contacts with the Saudi media, Information Officer Berry found that editors were reluctant to use material supplied by the U.S.

government, assuming that it was probably slanted. One technique he used was to arrange for the chief editor of a major Saudi newspaper to have an exclusive interview with a prominent American; his only caveat was that the editor had to promise to print the full text of the interview, but he could write any editorial on it that he wished. He did this successfully, for example, with Ambassador Richard Murphy, the former assistant secretary of state who was visiting the kingdom. This succeeded in getting an informed American view of our policy into print.[25]

As PAO in Bahrain from 1982 to 1985, Peter Kovach developed contacts among the Shia population by attending their soccer and basketball games and their funerals and feasts. He brought an American university basketball team to play against two of the major Shia clubs, and the goodwill generated by this sports exchange helped soften the attitudes of the younger generation toward the United States.[26]

In Kuwait, American officials had an advantage in making contacts because of the local custom of "diwaniya," the weekly open-house social gathering hosted by prominent families that were a kind of pseudo-political meeting where they could take the local pulse. When Alberto Fernandez was PAO in Kuwait, he regularly attended diwaniyas, where he used his Arabic to good advantage. For example, he became acquainted with one leftist, and arranged a visit for him to the United States, after which he was more inclined to defend America in discussion with his colleagues. Fernandez also sought out areas of common interest with Kuwaitis; for example, he arranged Worldnet interactive interviews on such diverse subjects as Afghanistan and highway safety, both of which were of concern to Kuwaitis. When Dr. Zalmay Khalilzad, an Afghan-American academic (who later was appointed ambassador to Afghanistan and then Iraq), visited Kuwait, Fernandez arranged an interview for him with a publication of the Muslim Brotherhood. And when the U.S. Navy ship *LaSalle*, the flagship of the Fifth Fleet in the Persian Gulf, visited Kuwait, Fernandez took aboard a group of journalists from two Kuwaiti newspapers for a briefing. Both papers did full-page stories that were positive, implying the U.S. Navy's presence in the Gulf was benign. The papers, however, omitted the fact that the *LaSalle* had visited Kuwait, because of Kuwaiti and Gulf sensitivity at the time to the presence of American land bases. (Gulf Arabs had for years preferred the U.S. Navy to remain "over the horizon," available in an emergency but not too close.)[27]

As the Gulf War escalated, Iraq fired missiles into Iranian cities and ships, and Iran attacked neutral shipping and laid mines in the so-called "tanker war." Kuwait felt vulnerable because it was supporting Iraq financially and Iran was attacking its merchant ships. So in December 1984, the Kuwaitis asked the U.S. Navy to escort those ships through the Gulf. The United States agreed to put eleven of them under an American flag and escort them. Then when Iranian missiles hit a U.S.-flagged Kuwaiti tanker

(October 1987), and a U.S. frigate hit an Iranian mine (April 1988), American planes retaliated by striking Iranian oil platforms. The United States had become a temporary combatant on Iraq's side. During 1987 the U.S. Navy's Middle East Force, home-ported in Bahrain, was increased from seven to thirteen ships, and the navy arranged to keep about thirty ships in the Gulf including minesweepers. PAOs in the Gulf and elsewhere in the Arab world pointed out that the United States was helping the Arab states in several ways, while remaining basically neutral in the war.

The November 1986 revelation of Washington's secret initiative to improve relations with Iran reinforced Arab fears that the United States secretly wanted to take sides against Iraq in the war. Some Arab commentators expressed deep concern that Reagan had gone soft on the mullahs in Tehran; this revived Arab paranoia about shifting American alliances. At the same time, the Arabs felt relieved that the "Iran–Contra" attempt had failed. PAOs could only reassure their audiences that the incident was over.

Meanwhile, American relations with Iraq continued to improve, despite American neutrality in the war. By August 1987, the United States and Iraq had signed a trade agreement, and two months later the United States banned imports from Iran. The United States was also secretly providing intelligence information to Iraq to help it defend itself in the war, although Washington still refused to supply arms to either side. The improvement in U.S.–Iraqi relations, plus the reflagging, and the attacks on Iranian oil platforms, convinced everyone that Washington was taking Iraq's side despite U.S. claims of neutrality, and this was welcomed by the public and governments in the Arab states of the region.

An inadvertent American act brought the war to an end. On July 3, 1988, a U.S. Navy ship, the USS *Vincennes*, accidentally shot down an Iranian civil airliner over the Gulf, killing all 290 people on board. Washington apologized for the mistake, but the Iranians thought it was deliberate, and this misunderstanding persuaded Ayatollah Khomeini to accept the cease-fire two weeks later (which he had previously rejected). On July 18, 1988, Iran accepted UN Resolution 598, effectively ending the war. It was over because Khomeini thought the United States had entered it on Iraq's side.

PAOs ironically faced an ambiguous situation because a positive result had come out of a misunderstanding. They tried to explain that the downing of the Iranian plane was an accident, but like the Iranians, most Arabs refused to believe that because they could not imagine that the U.S. Navy would make such a mistake. They therefore assumed that the U.S. had taken a major step in support of the Arab side in the war, and that step had persuaded Khomeini to end the war. That pleased them. PAOs did not reinforce the misunderstanding, which would have been dishonest, but neither did they feel obligated to make a major issue of insisting on the true story.

During this period, the United States became more involved in Afghanistan, steadily increasing its aid to the Afghan mujahideen in their fight against Soviet occupation. Saudi Arabia and Egypt also helped the mujahideen. PAOs in the Arab world encountered only modest interest in Afghanistan, but they did make efforts to publicize what information was made available because it demonstrated American–Arab cooperation in a common cause.

At the conclusion of the Reagan presidency, therefore, U.S. officials saw an improvement in the Gulf situation. The war had ended in a stalemate, Iran appeared to be contained, and relations with Iraq seemed to be getting better. The United States had replaced Britain as the dominant outside power in the Gulf, and the Arabs there increasingly sought U.S. security support, as long as the American presence remained offshore. However, the apparent calm was to last little more than one year.

8

# The Presidency of George H. W. Bush, 1989–1993

## BUSH'S PUBLIC DIPLOMACY

When President George H.W. Bush took office in January 1989, he appointed Bruce S. Gelb, a businessman and vice chairman of Bristol-Meyers, as director of the U.S. Information Agency. Gelb presided over the agency during one of public diplomacy's greatest tests, the Iraqi occupation of Kuwait and the U.S.-led war in the Gulf. In 1991, after the war, Gelb went to Belgium as U.S. ambassador, and President Bush appointed Henry E. Catto Jr. as USIA director. Catto had been ambassador in El Salvador and Britain, and assistant secretary of defense and chief of protocol; he remained director through the remainder of the Bush presidency, when Washington turned to promotion of Arab–Israeli peace.

### America's Image

Several major international developments took place during the Bush presidency that involved the United States one way or another. The Soviet Union and Yugoslavia broke apart, the Berlin wall opened and Germany was reunited; the United States invaded Panama and arrested Noriega; the Chinese crushed a demonstration in Tiananmen Square; Iraq invaded Kuwait and the United States led a war to liberate Kuwait; and historic Arab–Israeli peace talks were held in Madrid. Only the last two events had any real impact on American–Arab relations and the image of the United

States in the Arab world, however, since the Arab public was not very interested in the events outside the region.

For different reasons, President Bush was very much involved in both the Arab–Israeli peace process and the Gulf crisis. In the Arab–Israeli arena, the United States was the leading outside power when he took office, because it had brokered the Israeli–Egyptian peace agreement and continued to maintain its strong financial and political support of Israel. But it was Saddam Hussain's invasion and occupation of Kuwait in 1990 that presented Bush with the biggest and most urgent crisis of his presidency. The United States had replaced Britain as the dominant outside power in the Gulf, and had maintained an enhanced military presence there for a decade. Washington was already in direct confrontation with both Iran and Iraq, and had fully established its relations with the six smaller Arab states in that region. Any change in the situation there would affect U.S. interests.

When President Bush took office, the trends in the Persian Gulf seemed to be very positive for American interests. The Iran–Iraq War had just ended with neither side winning, and the smaller Arab states were protected. Soviet forces left Afghanistan in February 1989, ending a ten-year occupation of that country. American policy makers tended to assume (wrongly as it turned out), that the Afghan problem had been resolved, and Washington quickly lost interest in the country.

The collapse of the Soviet Union was welcome to Americans because it diminished the international Soviet threat and also the threat of Moscow's intervention in the Arab world. But it caused mixed reactions among Arabs. Those Arab countries that had maintained especially good relations with Moscow and benefited in terms of financial or military assistance, such as Iraq, Syria, and South Yemen, were concerned that this support would disappear. Elsewhere it was of less concern, although some Arabs were apprehensive that with the United States emerging as the world's only superpower, the Arab states would be weaker on the international stage because superpower competition would disappear.

In fact, even the Iraqi government seemed to be sending signals that it wished to improve relations with the United States. The American embassy in Baghdad had reopened in 1984, and the PAO was offering English lessons at his cultural center that were very popular with Iraqi students. Baghdad had lifted its ban on travel abroad for Iraqi citizens, so the PAO was able to begin to help Iraqi students apply for study in the United States, which many wanted to do. The embassy regarded these as promising signs that Baghdad sought to reverse the hostility toward America. High-level meetings were positive gestures and symbolized Washington's hopes. In February 1990, Assistant Secretary of State John Kelly visited Baghdad and met with senior officials, and in April 1990 a congressional delegation led by Senator Bob Dole went to Iraq and met with President Saddam Hussain. Washington was trying to nurture a better relationship with Iraq, and

when VOA broadcast an editorial on February 15, 1990, naming seven dictatorships and saying, "the tide of history is against such rulers,"[1] the State Department objected to the inclusion of Iraq among the seven. But it was clear to the PAO in Baghdad that there was a great deal of work to do to overcome the years of Iraqi adverse propaganda. When he tried to have conversations during the break with the students taking English classes at his center, he found them very reticent and cautious, unwilling to discuss any political subjects, because they feared they would be reported by the government's intelligence moles in the classes.[2]

Meanwhile, Saddam Hussain was rattling his saber. He made territorial demands on Kuwait and economic demands on other Arab states, and on April 1, he threatened that he might "burn half" of Israel. On May 28, he hosted a summit meeting of Arab states and accused his Arab neighbors in the Gulf of conducting economic warfare against Iraq. American officials and Arab leaders discounted this as overheated bombast. Even the Kuwaitis thought he was simply seeking to make gains through empty threats. On July 25, Saddam summoned the American ambassador, April Glaspie, to a meeting, and she told him that the United States wanted Iraq to settle its differences with the other Arab states by peaceful means, but that the United States did not take sides in local territorial disputes. She believed he would do so, as did everyone.

### The Iraqi Invasion

On August 2, 1990, Saddam invaded and occupied Kuwait. This was the first time in memory that one Arab state had invaded and occupied another. The move was a great surprise to Washington and to all the governments in the Middle East, including Kuwait. Even when Iraqi forces had moved up to the Kuwaiti border just before the invasion, the most pessimistic analysis was that Saddam might send forces a few kilometers across the border but would go no further.

The Arabs were stunned by Saddam's move, and at first they did not know how to react. In Qatar, for example, the people had been confidently assuring PAO John Berry and other U.S. officials that Saddam was bluffing, and that he would never invade Kuwait. For twenty-four hours after the invasion, Qatari media, at the time heavily influenced by the Qatari government, reflected Qatari confusion about how to react. Only one Qatari daily paper appeared at all on the first day; the others were timid because they lacked guidance on how to report or comment on the news; then they slowly and cautiously reported on the story. During the first week, media editors and other Qataris told Berry they were very concerned that Iraqi forces might continue their march and invade their country next, and the press reflected extreme caution in its comments.[3]

President Bush had to decide how to respond to this major new crisis.

Saddam Hussain calculated that the United States would not do anything to reverse his annexation of Kuwait. Saddam remembered that in 1979, Washington did nothing to save the shah, and in 1983 the United States had intervened in Lebanon briefly but withdrew after a small number of Americans were killed. Saddam also calculated that the Arab states would not come to Kuwait's rescue either. President Bush decided that it was important to stand firmly against Saddam's action in order to oppose the annexation of a sovereign state that was friendly to the United States, and to deter Saddam from any further move into Saudi Arabia. He acted promptly. He consulted with his advisors and allies, and within two days he made a firm decision that the United States would assist in the liberation of Kuwait. On August 5 he told the press: "I view very seriously our determination to reverse this awful aggression. . . . This will not stand, this aggression against Kuwait." That set the American goal for the next six months.

The Kuwaitis asked for American help but President Bush knew that it would be crucial politically to have support also from the Saudis and other Arabs, so he sent Defense Secretary Dick Cheney on a quick trip to the Gulf to mobilize a coalition. Cheney met with King Fahd on August 6 and secured a formal request from Saudi Arabia for American intervention. That was very important for the American image, to avoid the stigma of unilateralism.

During Secretary Cheney's tour, the Arab states there joined in declaring they would support Washington's confrontation of Saddam. In Qatar, for example, where apprehension over the crisis was high, the news of U.S.–Arab cooperation against Iraq and that the first group of American F-16s had landed in Qatar helped to generate a sense of relief among the Qatari public, and sent a signal to the media that they could take a stand against Saddam. But the media were still cautious, and their story on the F-16s simply said, "A force from a friendly power has landed in Qatar." PAO John Berry asked the editor at Qatari television to identify them as American planes and he did, after securing clearance from his government. The press became generally supportive of U.S. policy, but with occasional lapses. During the following six months' standoff between the United States and Iraq, some Qatari editorials began to express the suspicion that Washington had created the crisis for its own ends, and tricked Saddam. Some also said that Iraq should leave Kuwait but it would be better if the United States was not involved, and they commented when Ambassador Glaspie met Saddam that perhaps she was colluding with him. As each issue arose, the PAO had to explain the American view.[4]

When Saddam refused to withdraw, an intense six-month period of diplomacy and public diplomacy ensued. On the diplomatic front, urgent American contacts in many places produced declarations of support from many countries for the American-led effort to liberate Kuwait. It was especially significant that Egypt and Syria signed declarations because Egypt

was always a key player. The fact that Syria joined in and offered to send troops, if necessary, was also important because Syria had been at odds with Washington on many other issues. A few Arab states, including Jordan and Yemen, refused to stand up to Saddam, and this made the PAO's task in those countries more difficult. But most Arab states did join Bush's coalition, giving him local cover. It was also significant and helpful to PAOs that Washington persuaded Moscow to condemn the invasion, since Moscow had been a consistent and strong supporter of Saddam for many years. Washington also persuaded the United Nations to pass a series of resolutions condemning Iraq and demanding its withdrawal, adding to the legitimacy of Bush's position. But still Saddam refused to budge, and American public diplomacy went into high gear.

### Prewar Public Diplomacy

Iraq's invasion and occupation of Kuwait, Bush's demand that Iraq withdraw, and Saddam's defiance of that demand, presented public diplomacy with a major new challenge. Saddam still assumed that neither the Arab world nor the United States and the West would force his withdrawal or even put up serious opposition to his occupation of Kuwait. His calculations turned out to be wrong, but for six months, between August 1990 and January 1991, that was not clear. This was a period of an unusual battle of ideas between Baghdad and Washington, with intense involvement of American public diplomacy professionals in the Arab world.[5]

Immediately after he invaded and occupied Kuwait, Saddam mounted a major propaganda campaign, consisting of several key themes designed to weaken any opposition to his move. First, he stressed that any disagreement over the occupation was strictly a local Arab affair, that non-Arabs should stay out of because it was none of their business. He intended this to build on the sense of Arab nationalism that abhorred any foreign interference. Second, Iraq claimed that Kuwait was legally part of Iraq, an assertion designed to interpret recent history in Iraq's favor. Third, he tried to focus attention on Israel, the "real enemy" of the Arabs that he said he was fighting, in order to unite Arab opinion behind him. Fourth, as soon as American military forces began arriving in Saudi Arabia, Iraq sought to mobilize Muslim opinion against them by charging (falsely) that non-Muslim Americans had entered the holy city of Mecca and were "violating" its sanctity. Finally, Iraq portrayed its occupation of Kuwait as a poor country claiming its rights in a rich country, trying to evoke an Islamic sense of social justice and also to arouse the resentment against Kuwaitis that existed in some Arab quarters.

To counter Saddam's propaganda and support the American position, Washington began a comprehensive public diplomacy campaign, led by USIA with involvement of PAOs and other embassy officers throughout the

world, especially in the Arab countries. The lead office at USIA headquarters was the Near East/North Africa/South Asia Bureau that had half a dozen Foreign Service Officers with public diplomacy experience in various Arab countries serving as desk officers, and in addition another half dozen who had been evacuated from Arab countries close to Kuwait because of the crisis and were pressed into service in Washington. USIA and State agreed to set up an interagency Policy Coordinating Committee for public diplomacy to bring together all of the relevant U.S. government agencies, including also the National Security Council, several bureaus of the Defense Department, the CIA, and the Commerce Department. Ambassador April Glaspie (who happened to be out of Iraq when the crisis began, and could not return) was a key member of the group. As the director of USIA's Near East/North Africa bureau, I co-chaired this committee with a senior State Department officer, Ambassador Jerry Hellman. We met twice each week to discuss public diplomacy strategy and enlist various Washington elements in the production of public diplomacy tools. I also met daily with a small subcommittee of five people, including Ambassador Glaspie, to discuss urgent tactical matters.

American public diplomacy with regard to Iraq during the summer and fall of 1990 had several goals and themes. First, it was aimed at Saddam to help persuade him to withdraw from Kuwait peacefully by demonstrating to him that he was facing overwhelming political opposition from several quarters including from the Arab world, where he hoped to draw his major support or at least acquiescence. Second, it was intended to persuade Saddam that if he did not withdraw voluntarily he would be forced out of Kuwait by a war that he would lose. Finally, the public diplomacy strategy also sought to rally enough public support from the Arab governments and people, and from the rest of the world, to demonstrate that Washington's confrontation of Saddam had solid backing.

At USIA's Near East Bureau we set up a 24/7 monitoring system by which PAOs in all Arab countries submitted time-sensitive material on media news and opinion coverage, and conversations with opinion leaders, by telegram and telephone. Other regional bureaus at USIA tracked public opinion in their areas on the crisis and coordinated with us. We closely followed Saddam's propaganda and disinformation effort, and tracked where it was being picked up regionally and globally. We wrote analyses of problem issues and recommended themes that we believed would be helpful for U.S. officials to use, including denials of Saddam's false accusations. We sent our media monitoring reports and suggested talking points to senior officials at State, DOD, CIA, and the NSC and the White House. These were well received and often they were passed to the secretary of state and even the president. They helped secure USIA a "place at the table" with policy makers at State and elsewhere in Washington.

Starting in late August, we at USIA pressed hard for senior officials in

Washington and abroad to do interviews with VOA, Worldnet, and foreign media, to explain our policy and refute Iraqi propaganda. State and NSC agreed to allow Washington officials to do interviews, and in September, for example, Worldnet television interviewed Undersecretary of State Robert Kimmitt, UN Ambassador Thomas Pickering, the NSC's Richard Haass, and DOD Undersecretary Paul Wolfowitz. USIA also arranged telephonic press conferences with foreign audiences, some in Arabic, for several State Department officials. But State and the NSC authorized only three of our ambassadors to give press interviews on the record with local Arab media, because of the delicacy of the ongoing worldwide negotiations focused on keeping the anti-Saddam coalition together.[6]

President Bush himself played a key role in the public diplomacy campaign. He was very interested in following Arab reaction to developments, and four of us were summoned to the Oval Office twice before the war to brief him on Arab opinion. In August, USIA proposed that he should make a televised statement directed at the Iraqi people. He agreed in principle and we helped prepare the text, which emphasized his determination to liberate Kuwait and the worldwide support he had for that objective. In the drafting process, CIA informed us that they had found an old statement by Saddam that "An Arab country does not have the right to occupy another Arab country. God forbid, if Iraq should deviate from the right path, we would want Arabs to send their armies to put things right." When the president, on September 12, 1990, made a video recording of his statement, he used the quote. But we made sure that the voice-over for the Arabic version used the original Arabic text of the quote, taken from a copy of the November 29, 1988, issue of Iraq's *al Jumhuriya* newspaper.

Meanwhile, State had discussed the president's statement with the Iraqi ambassador in Washington, who said that it could be broadcast on Iraqi television. The American networks got wind of the statement and asked for a copy but it was embargoed pending Iraq's use of it. The video recording was rushed to Baghdad by courier, and handed over to the Iraqi authorities. To our surprise, Iraqi television aired it in its entirety in prime time the next day, although they followed it with a twenty-minute official rebuttal of all of Bush's points. We lifted the embargo, Worldnet distributed it by satellite worldwide, and PAOs placed it on TV channels all over the Arab world.

The public diplomacy effort was helped by several developments during the five months of prewar confrontation, August 1990 to January 1991. The United Nations Security Council passed a series of resolutions condemning Iraq and demanding that it withdraw; the Soviet Union agreed; most of the Arab states also agreed and said so; key Arab states like Egypt and Syria sent troops to the front; and several of them coordinated their public diplomacy with Washington. However, our effort was hampered by several factors. A few Arab states, including Jordan and Yemen, refused to

join in the opposition to Iraq; Saddam's focus on Israel had an impact on Arab opinion generally, and persuaded the PLO to support him; some of Iraq's lies were widely disseminated in the Arab press and believed by many; and Saddam did not show any sign that he was having second thoughts about annexing Kuwait and facing war.

PAOs around the world went into high gear and participated actively in advocating American policy, seeking coordination with friendly governments, and reporting intensively on relevant local opinion. In the Arab world PAOs were extremely busy, working around the clock, and some had to operate with reduced staffs because of the personnel draw-downs for security reasons. In Kuwait, where Iraqi forces had taken over the entire country and surrounded the American embassy, however, the ambassador and the rest of the embassy staff were locked in the embassy compound, unable to conduct normal business.

At USIA headquarters in Washington, we developed a series of major themes that we stressed in Washington and at all our posts in the Arab world and elsewhere during the five-month war of words. They were:

1. Most of the world has condemned the occupation of Kuwait and termed it illegal, as evidenced by all the UN resolutions, and by governmental declarations. Even the Soviet Union, which had been closely allied with Iraq for many years, joined the demands for Iraq to withdraw.
2. Kuwait and Saudi Arabia invited the United States to send troops.
3. Most of the Arab world supported Kuwait and demanded that Iraq withdraw. Syria, a country that for years had been at loggerheads with the United States, not only demanded Iraqi withdrawal but agreed to send troops to the Gulf to enforce the demand.
4. Iraq's brutal treatment of the Kuwaiti population violated their human rights, and Iraq's looting of the country proved that the annexation was not benign but hostile to Kuwait and served only Iraqi interests.
5. Iraq should withdraw peacefully but if it failed to do so, it would face a war that it would certainly lose and would cost Iraq dearly; a massive U.S. military force was already deploying in the Gulf region to be ready.
6. The Arab–Israeli issue was unrelated and should be dealt with separately.

The public diplomacy effort generated several unique projects, all designed to support these themes and achieve the goal of peaceful Iraqi withdrawal from Kuwait. Following are some of the projects implemented:

First, the wireless file in English, Arabic, and (for North Africa) in French expanded its service, disseminating official texts, backgrounders,

American press summaries, and other materials. Second, USIA persuaded U.S. officials at the State Department and elsewhere to do interviews for VOA and Worldnet to explain and advocate U.S. policy, and to debunk Iraqi lies. Third, USIA arranged for a special filmed message by President Bush to Saddam Hussain and the Iraqi people that was placed on Arab and other television stations, and interviews for the president with selected Arab editors. Fourth, PAOs helped persuade Arab governments to step up their media criticisms of Iraq and to stress themes that were most effective coming from Arab countries, such as reporting on the deployment of Arab military forces to the Gulf region in support of Kuwait. Fifth, USIA helped disseminate the views of the Kuwaiti government in exile, describing the atrocities Iraqis were committing in their country, and USIA media carried additional material on this subject.

The most complicated public diplomacy project was a thirteen-minute documentary film that USIA produced, demonstrating American military capabilities that would be brought to bear against Iraq in a war, which would assure Iraq's quick defeat. The public diplomacy Policy Coordinating Committee approved it in late September as an interagency effort. A USIA–State team developed a narrative, footage was supplied by the Pentagon graphically showing U.S. military resources, and USIA film professionals produced the film. Because it evoked such great interest in Washington, it was reviewed by the highest levels of the U.S. government. The USIA director selected its title, *Nations of the World Draw a Line in the Sand*, and the final version was screened for senior officials at State and the NSC. They insisted that President Bush himself should see it, and that was finally done by December 17, as the clock was ticking on the ultimatum for war. The delay in production turned out not to be a problem in the end, as it was given to Worldnet on December 18 for worldwide dissemination via satellite. PAOs in Arab countries arranged for placement on local TV stations and most used it. (After the war, Saudi TV repeatedly reran the video because they had little else to show related to the conflict.)

The VOA role was especially important because Saddam controlled all Iraqi media and his propaganda output was trying to turn the Arab world against the U.S.-led coalition. VOA increased its Arabic Service broadcasts from 7.5 hours per day to 15.5, and focused heavily on Iraq. Most broadcasts were all-news and live. VOA Arabic aired full texts of U.S. and coalition official statements, broadcasted government editorials three times daily, and cancelled all music programs during hostilities. VOA Arabic expanded its round-the clock automated call-in service that received more than 70,000 calls from August 1990 through February 1991. The editors were especially careful about their program. As Arabic Branch Chief Mahmoud Zawawi explained: "During the Gulf War we exercised great caution because for the first time this conflict involved the United States against

an Arab country, and it also divided the Arabs among themselves. So we had to be as objective in our coverage as possible in order to maintain our credibility."[7]

Despite this care, VOA received some complaints during the crisis, in the American press, from foreign governments, and even from the State Department. Some Arab governments complained to Washington that the VOA was insufficiently hostile to Iraq. Saudi Arabia and Egypt, for example, said that they found VOA Arabic was soft on Saddam, and suggested it was because many of the VOA Arabic staff were Palestinians who had personal reasons to be biased. They also complained that VOA had a stringer in Baghdad who was reporting Iraqi official statements without adding context or negative comment. VOA and USIA rejected the general criticism of bias but VOA did terminate the services of its stringer in Baghdad, realizing that he was unable to report objectively under the circumstances. However, independent analyses commissioned by VOA in 1991 found that VOA broadcasts in the crisis were "effective and responsible." Saddam jammed the VOA broadcasts so his people could not hear them, but he listened himself. (In the spring of 1990, ABC's Peter Jennings interviewed Saddam and afterwards, when he asked Saddam's interpreter how the president kept so well informed, he was told that Saddam had just come from listening to VOA Arabic.)[8]

VOA listenership increased substantially during the crisis in many Arab countries, but we were concerned that the VOA signal was not carrying well into Iraq and the Gulf. We knew that the British used a powerful transmitter on Masira Island off Oman that allowed BBC broadcasts to cover the Gulf and Iraq, so we asked the British government to allow VOA to use that transmitter for a few hours each day. After lengthy diplomatic discussions in London and Washington, it became clear by late September that the British would not give VOA access to the transmitter, so we focused on Saudi Arabia and Bahrain. Special transmitters were set up in Saudi Arabia, and USIA Director Gelb negotiated with Bahraini Information Minister Tarek al Moayyed to arrange VOA broadcasts out of his country. Later, after Kuwait was liberated, the Kuwaitis allowed VOA to broadcast from their soil into Iraq.

### Public Diplomacy in the Field

In the majority of the Arab countries, the government supported the American military intervention to confront Saddam, and there the task for PAOs and their staffs was to help sustain public support, and to assist the media in refuting Saddam's propaganda.

Saudi Arabia was one of the strongest supporters of American intervention, but there were special challenges for the public diplomacy staff in that country because it was at the center of the crisis from start to finish, from August 1990 through February 1991.

Shortly after the invasion of Kuwait, the United States began sending tens of thousands of American military personnel into Saudi Arabia. This presented USIS and the other American officials with several challenges because of cultural and other differences that American officials feared would cause friction between Americans and Saudis. The Americans took some steps to mitigate the problems caused by cultural differences, and the Saudis also proved accommodating, at least for the duration of the crisis. Because alcohol was illegal, General Schwartzkopf ordered American troops not to bring it into the kingdom, and prohibited its consumption. (Some soldiers heard that long-time American residents at Aramco were making alcoholic drinks at home and they tried to do the same but they failed because they did not have the right recipe.) Avoiding alcohol helped avoid problems. Saudi Arabia also had strict rules for Saudi women, who were completely veiled in public, so the appearance on Saudi streets of many American female soldiers dressed in army fatigues was shocking to many Saudis, but the Saudi government sent out word to the mutaween (religious police) to leave the American women alone, and by and large they did. The Armed Forces Radio and Television System (AFRTS) also brought in and set up radio transmitters that broadcast programs to the troops, including music and other American content that Saudis could also hear (the "shadow audience" effect). Some conservative Saudis complained about the programs to their government, which in turn asked the United States to censor AFRTS broadcasts to delete material never heard on Saudi radio, such as Christmas music. The USIS staff managed to avoid censorship by helping to persuade AFRTS to encode the broadcast signal. This resolved the problem, although U.S.-educated Saudis who had liked the programs then complained they could no longer hear them. (In fact, the encoding was not entirely effective so the programs could still be heard in some places.)[9]

The American and other foreign journalists seeking to cover the Desert Storm story in Saudi Arabia presented a special challenge to USIS. It had always been very difficult for foreign journalists to obtain visas to enter Saudi Arabia, but with the encouragement of the Press Attaché at the American embassy in Riyadh, John Kincannon, and others in the embassy, visas for American and other journalists were approved. By the end of August 1990, the Saudis had already approved 300 visas for journalists, 80 percent of whom were American, and by the time the war started, there were over 3,000 foreign journalists in the kingdom. In fact, generally speaking, the Saudi government's decision-making process was significantly streamlined and decentralized, which was a major change because usually decisions took a great deal of time as even the smallest issues were passed to the top for decision. During the crisis, senior officials delegated and expedited requests, making American tasks much easier. (Six months after the crisis was over, the old system was back in place.)[10]

In the Arab countries where the public was in sympathy with Saddam,

the PAO's task was even more difficult. In Yemen, for example, the government refused to cooperate with the United States in confronting Iraq. The Yemeni and Iraqi governments had been close in the past (Yemen sent military personnel to Iraq during the Iran–Iraq War for example), and President Salih made the decision to stick with Saddam. The Yemeni people who knew Americans or had lived in the United States generally regarded America favorably; they did not admire Saddam but they were supportive of the Iraqi people. In the Kuwait crisis the government signaled its clear support of Saddam, and the press followed that lead, so the highest priority issue for Duncan MacInnes as PAO was dealing with a hostile press. He kept in touch with editors, and when there was an egregiously unfair article in a newspaper he would call on the editor and complain. But when he did, his approach was to begin the conversation in a listening mode, letting the editor get criticism of the United States off his chest, since he knew that this was the only way he would be listened to. Then he would say, "I hear you but I was surprised because I respect you and you were so unfair in your article," and bring up his own complaints about Yemeni support for Saddam. He believed this was usually the best way to handle a contentious conversation in Yemen (and in the Arab world generally), by first listening carefully and then making his pitch on a personal basis. He would point out errors in the Yemeni press and say he was personally disappointed because it did not meet the standard of good journalism. "As a friend, I know you can do better. I expect you to be more professional." He knew he would not be able to change the editor's opinion completely, but after such discussions the articles would be better for some time. Then when another distorted article came along and he would make the approach again, in person. This required vigilance and staying in touch constantly.[11]

In Morocco, USIS officers also faced a problem over Iraq. Much of the Moroccan public supported the Iraqi invasion of Kuwait because of their image of Kuwaitis as rich and spoiled playboys who deserved what they got. USIS staff and other Americans therefore started by explaining how the Iraqi occupiers were brutally treating innocent Kuwaitis. They also stressed that not only Kuwait but also Saudi Arabia and other Arab neighbors of Iraq had requested assistance in ending the Iraqi occupation. As the buildup of forces in the Gulf took place and other Arab states joined in the confrontation with Saddam, the Moroccan criticism became more muted. In any case, because of their distance from the Gulf, Moroccans tended not to regard the Iraq–Kuwait crisis as a priority issue, so it ended up being somewhat less intense than elsewhere.[12]

In Tunisia, prior to the Kuwait crisis the PAO had had considerable success in all respects including with the media, but as soon as Saddam invaded Kuwait and the United States opposed him, the atmosphere turned negative. The Tunisian government of Zine al Abdine Ben Ali had been friendly to the United States, but it now condemned the Bush administra-

tion for sending troops to the Gulf, and asserted that the Iraqi invasion of Kuwait was an intra-Arab matter and the United States should stay out of it. Tunisian media, which Ben Ali strongly influenced, tended to take Saddam's side against the United States. The PAO protested to the editors and made the case against Saddam, but they told him that Saddam deserved support because he was standing up to Israel and America, and they also criticized the Kuwaitis and Saudis. Clearly, part of the problem was that their view of American support for Israel colored their perception of the situation. The Tunisian media printed lies coming out of Baghdad, and text and photos distributed by the Iraqi embassy in Tunis. The PAO gave media editors excellent materials supplied by USIA Washington but he could not get them published locally. He protested to the Information Minister but the problem continued. He consulted his Tunisian friends privately about how to handle the situation and they told him there was little he could do with the press because Ben Ali in effect controlled it. They told him that Ben Ali's public position was designed to prevent the Tunisian Islamists from attacking him on the issue. The Tunisian government did provide excellent security to USIS and other Americans during the crisis, but even the security measures proved to be a problem. When two armored personnel carriers appeared at the entrance of the USIS center to protect it against demonstrators, the PAO had to close it to the public. He did increase his distribution of news bulletins, sending staff out with them by taxi instead of embassy vehicle to reduce their visibility and therefore their risk. Then, as soon as the Desert Storm fighting stopped, Tunisian criticism of the United States also stopped, on orders of the president, and USIS quickly reverted to its prewar situation.[13]

### The Gulf War

Despite the intense diplomatic campaign led by the president and Secretary Baker, backed up by a strenuous public diplomacy campaign from Washington and at field posts, the summer and fall months of 1990 went by without any sign that Saddam was inclined to back down. The U.S.-led military buildup in the Gulf continued, and the United States gave it considerable publicity. U.S. diplomatic activity continued also, and on November 29, 1990, the UN Security Council, with Washington's support, passed Resolution 678 demanding that Saddam withdraw and saying that unless he fully implemented UN resolutions by January 15, 1991, the UN member states could "use all necessary means" to "restore international peace and security in the area." President Bush made one last try to avoid war, sending Secretary of State James Baker to Geneva on January 9 to meet with Iraqi Foreign Minister Tariq Aziz. Meanwhile, Saddam tried to draw Israel into the war and appeal for Arab support by firing Scud missiles into Israel in January; however, American diplomats persuaded Israel to stay out

of the war in order to avoid the pressure this would have put on Arab states to leave the coalition.

On January 8, only one week before the start of the war, President Bush made one last public diplomacy effort to avert hostilities. He gave a speech on VOA and USIA's Worldnet television in which he reviewed the American attempts to resolve the crisis peacefully, and his determination to liberate Kuwait. This helped to bolster the allies in the coalition arrayed against Iraq but it did not persuade Saddam.

Because Saddam did not withdraw, and ignored the UN ultimatum, on January 16, 1991, the U.S.-led attack began. It was clear that the start of hostilities meant that the public diplomacy campaign had failed in its first task of helping to persuade Saddam to withdraw without war. However, it succeeded in its task of supporting the diplomatic effort to build and maintain a broad coalition against Saddam that in the eyes of the Arab public legitimized and spread responsibility for the use of force.

The Desert Storm war started with forty-three days of air strikes, followed by a ground war on February 24, 1991, that lasted only 100 hours. During the war, Saddam continued his propaganda against the United States. The Iraqis falsely accused the United States of deliberately killing innocent civilians and destroying mosques. USIA worked to monitor every charge and mobilize U.S. officials to refute the disinformation that was picked up by media in the Arab world and elsewhere. Iraqis arranged scenes for the foreign journalists who were in the country to make it look as if the United States was deliberately killing Iraqi civilians. In one widely reported incident, when American planes destroyed a fortified bunker at Amriya, the Iraqis claimed it was only a civilian air raid shelter, and displayed bodies of dead women and children. Washington insisted the target was a military one, and that Iraq had faked the evidence, but the Iraqi claim was carried on CNN and other international media, and many Arabs believed it. Only later did investigations confirm that the target did have a military purpose and that the Iraqis had placed civilians there as hostages.

In Qatar, for example, PAO John Berry met with the Deputy Information Minister, who scolded him for the "American atrocity." Berry denied the charge but the official believed it because he had seen it on CNN. Berry realized that the Qatari failure to believe Washington and Arab anger at the United States derived more from an emotional attachment to Saddam as a fellow Muslim, and an assumption that a Muslim would not behave as Washington claimed Saddam was behaving, unless he had been tricked by Washington. An interpretation that was complex and included hidden motives and a conspiracy seemed more believable to the Qataris, who refused to accept at face value the official statements coming out of Washington.[14]

American reporters, including Peter Arnett of CNN, who were in Baghdad during the war were sometimes misled by clever Iraqi officials.

On one occasion Ambassador Glaspie spotted an Iraqi Information Ministry official she knew well, who was posing as a poor Iraqi victim of U.S. bombing in a CNN report, telling a made-up story to the innocent American reporter.

But the war was brief and President Bush declared the cease-fire on February 27. He said: "Kuwait is liberated. Iraq's army is defeated. Our military objectives are met. Kuwait is once more in the hands of Kuwaitis, in control of their own destiny."[15] USIA media and PAOs gave wide dissemination to that statement and others by U.S. officials, as well as to the Iraqi formal surrender on March 3 at Safwan.

American public diplomacy still had work to do, but the PAOs had some useful new themes they could use. They emphasized that the United States had led a broad coalition which successfully achieved the liberation of Kuwait, and that the United States did so with minimal loss of life, since President Bush called for a cease-fire in order to avoid unnecessary Iraqi casualties. They also stressed that the United States withdrew its forces after the war showing that America did not covet Arab territory.

In the months after the end of the war, some in the Arab world asked why the United States had not continued the war and marched to Baghdad, to topple Saddam's regime. PAOs responded with several reasons. The UN mandates legitimizing the war only called for the liberation of Kuwait, not Iraqi regime change. Likewise, Arab support for the war was only based on liberating Kuwait, and while Arab armed forces entered Kuwait at the end of Desert Storm, they did not even enter southern Iraq when American and other Western forces did. Moreover, the general assumption, shared in Washington and in the region, was that Saddam had been so humiliated by losing another war, he would probably not survive politically.

President Bush himself answered the criticism in his book, saying:

> Trying to eliminate Saddam, extending the ground war into an occupation of Iraq, would have violated our guideline about not changing objectives in midstream, engaging in "mission creep," and would have incurred incalculable human and political costs. Apprehending him was probably impossible. We had been unable to find Noriega in Panama, which we knew intimately. We would have been forced to occupy Baghdad, and, in effect, rule Iraq. The coalition would instantly have collapsed, the Arabs deserting it in anger and other allies pulling out as well. . . . Furthermore, we had been self-consciously trying to set a pattern for handling aggression in the post-Cold-War world. Going in and occupying Iraq, thus unilaterally exceeding the United Nations mandate, would have destroyed the precedent of international response to aggression that we hoped to establish. Had we gone the invasion route, the United States could conceivably still be an occupying power in a bitterly hostile land.[16]

This statement was very useful to PAOs, to convey the idea that the United States is a reliable friend, despite its overwhelming power, because it shows restraint and respects the sovereignty of other nations.

After Desert Storm, on April 3, 1991, the UN Security Council passed Resolution 687, which imposed unprecedented conditions on Iraq including a permanent ban on weapons of mass destruction, an embargo, and inspections to monitor compliance. The United States and its allies also imposed a no-fly zone called "Northern Comfort" in Iraq north of the 36th parallel, to support the Kurds, who had established an autonomous region out of Saddam's reach. To demonstrate that these restrictions should not harm the Iraqi people, the United States and the United Nations, in September 1991, approved a humanitarian oil-for-food program that would have allowed Iraq a controlled sale of some of its petroleum.

Saddam Hussain, however, put obstacles in the way of arms inspections, and he initially rejected the arms-for-food program. During the remaining time of the Bush administration, Washington led the international community in enforcing the restrictions on Iraq and assumed they would eventually work. The Bush administration also sought to consolidate its relations with the smaller Arab states of the Persian Gulf by concluding military agreements with them that would allow for prepositioning of military equipment and protections for U.S. military personnel while in the country. Bases were still politically impossible, but the American role in Desert Storm had somewhat reduced local opposition to an American military presence, and the Bush administration began to negotiate "status of forces agreements" (SOFAs) with Kuwait, Bahrain, Qatar, and the United Arab Emirates.

One criticism of Bush was raised in the United States after Desert Storm and during the 1992 presidential campaign, primarily by congressional critics of President Bush, that the American ambassador to Iraq, April Glaspie, had triggered the invasion of Kuwait by giving Saddam the "green light" in her July 25 meeting with him, because she had told him that the United States did "not take sides" in Arab territorial disputes. Foreign Service Officers, and President Bush, knew that this was an unfair accusation.[17] In fact, it gained little resonance in the Arab world.

## The Arab–Israeli Conflict

President Bush also faced problems elsewhere in the Middle East during his administration. The 1989 Taif agreement settled the Lebanese civil war, and in 1991, American journalist Terry Anderson was released, marking the end of the kidnapping of Americans in Lebanon. But the perennial problem of the Arab–Israeli conflict continued. In fact, the way he dealt with it turned out to be very helpful to American public diplomacy professionals.

Saddam Hussain had tried to generate Arab support for his occupation of Kuwait by tying it to the Israeli issue and loudly advocating support for the Palestinians. His focus on Palestinian concerns succeeded in persuading Yassir Arafat to support him, and Washington was worried that Saddam's ploy would undermine the coalition opposed to the Kuwait occupation, because support for the Palestinians was an emotionally potent issue for most Arabs. When Saddam, during the prewar confrontation, proposed a conference to discuss both Kuwait and Palestine, President Bush refused, saying Kuwait and Palestine were two entirely separate issues, but he promised to deal with the Arab–Israeli issue after the Kuwait issue was resolved. Some Arabs were skeptical, believing he was trying to avoid the Palestinian issue by putting it off.

In fact, Bush was true to his word, and after Desert Storm, his administration undertook a serious diplomatic initiative on the Arab–Israeli issue. By October 1991, Washington had arranged an unprecedented international conference in Madrid that included Israel and all the major Arab parties. Israeli Prime Minister Yitzhak Shamir, PLO leader Yassir Arafat, and representatives of Syria, Jordan, Egypt, and other key Arab governments met in Madrid with U.S. Secretary of State Baker and other outside representatives. The conference set the stage for further negotiations that developed into the "Oslo" peace process that made significant progress in subsequent years. PAOs welcomed Bush's effort, and the Madrid Conference gave them an excellent talking point for months and years afterwards.[18]

When the Bush presidency ended, American prestige was high in the view of most Arabs, because the United States reversed the Iraqi occupation of Kuwait and then withdrew its forces; moreover, President Bush had given the Arab–Israeli peace process new momentum at the Madrid Conference. This relatively positive Arab perception of the United States remained for a while into the Clinton presidency, but it did not last indefinitely.

9

# The Clinton Era, 1993–2001

## PUBLIC DIPLOMACY POLICY

Shortly after taking office in January 1993, President Clinton appointed Joseph Duffey as director of the U.S. Information Agency. Duffey was president of American University and before that he had been president of the University of Massachusetts and he had served as chairman of the National Endowment for the Humanities. Duffey remained director until USIA was abolished in 1999.

During the Clinton presidency, several major events occurred in the Middle East. Israel made peace agreements with the Palestinians and Jordan (1993–1994); Yassir Arafat was elected president of the new Palestinian Authority (1996); and Ehud Barak, who became prime minister of Israel in 1999, negotiated with Arafat under American auspices up until the end of Clinton's second term, and the start of the Second Intifada in September 2000. Mideast-related terrorist incidents against Americans occurred in New York (1993), Saudi Arabia (1995–1996), East Africa (1998), and Yemen (2000). The Arab public followed all of these events with great interest, and they gave much less attention to other events during his presidency, such as the split of Czechoslovakia, the fighting in Bosnia and Kosovo after the dissolution of Yugoslavia, the conclusion of NAFTA, and the impeachment of President Clinton.

## America's Image

Throughout his administration, President Clinton built on policies in the Middle East set by his predecessor. In the Persian Gulf, Washington regarded Iraq and Iran as continuing threats, and worked to strengthen cooperation with the six smaller Arab states on the Persian Gulf.[1]

The Clinton administration coined the slogan "dual containment" for its policy toward the Gulf. This extended to Iran and Iraq the policy of containment which had for years been applied to the Soviet Union. But PAOs did not find this label helpful in explaining our policy. It was not like containment of the Soviet Union since we had always maintained diplomatic and trade relations with Moscow, while we had neither with Iran or Iraq. Moreover, although we were in confrontation with both countries, there were differences between them that the label obscured. The Arabs were confused by our combining the two countries in a single policy. Most of them remained fundamentally wary of Iran, the most powerful state in the region and led by proactive Shiite mullahs, while they were much more sympathetic to Iraq, a Sunni-ruled Arab country, and despite their dislike of Saddam Hussain, they knew he was very weak after Desert Storm. Yet President Clinton continued to seek closer military and political cooperation with the smaller Arab states of the Gulf, solidifying the military agreements and selling them significant amounts of military equipment.

## Iraq

The United States continued to take the lead in managing the UN-imposed sanctions on Iraq. The U.S. Navy undertook most of the task of monitoring Iraqi compliance with the embargo, detaining commercial ships in the Persian Gulf that carried contraband goods to or from Iraq. The U.S. Air Force made regular surveillance flights over Iraq to enforce the no-fly zones in the north and south. The Clinton administration took aggressive action to reinforce the restrictions on Iraq, and even on occasion fired cruise missiles into Baghdad. Washington also supported Iraqi exiles, and Congress appropriated some funds for their use in opposing Saddam.

But the U.S.-led policy toward Iraq was not bringing about the hoped-for Iraqi full compliance with UN resolutions. During the 1990s, Iraq's Arab neighbors became increasingly uncomfortable with the confrontation as Saddam stayed in power and continued to defy the United States and the international community, because the Iraqi people were suffering and Saddam was not. Saddam eventually allowed the oil-for-food program but he restricted the UN weapons inspectors; it was clear that he was diverting much of the country's wealth to a privileged few and that the Iraqi people were suffering more and more. PAOs and other U.S. officials in the Arab world found that many Arabs were beginning to say that the re-

strictions on Iraq should be lifted because they were not making Saddam change his ways. Many Arabs even believed that the United States was deliberately denying the Iraqi people needed food and medicine to keep the country weak. PAOs argued in response that the suffering of the Iraqi people was entirely Saddam's fault, not a result of the embargo, because Iraq was permitted to import all the food and medicines that it needed, and Saddam was artificially creating shortages to gain Arab sympathy and force an end to the embargo. PAOs added that the United States and the allies showed more compassion for the Iraqi people than Saddam did because the oil-for-food program was intended to provide direct assistance to the Iraqi people.

PAOs used the argument made by Washington that because Saddam was not allowing weapons inspections he must be hiding a program that was developing weapons of mass destruction, and that he would be willing to use them or give them to terrorists. Everyone assumed Saddam had some WMD capability, but the question was what he would do with them. Arabs responded that they did not really consider Saddam a threat, and they were surprised that Americans did. PAOs argued that Saddam was not only a threat to others but that he was also doing great harm to his own country. They pointed out that because Saddam rejected UN conditions on weapons of mass destruction, the sanctions continued, costing Iraq tens of billions of dollars in oil revenues.

The Arab states on the Persian Gulf—Saudi Arabia, Kuwait, Bahrain, Qatar, the UAE, and Oman—were all supportive of the American Desert Storm intervention of 1990–1991, and the environment for American public diplomacy there during the Clinton administration was initially quite favorable. Radio and television in all of these countries were government owned and the newspapers were private but uniformly loyal to their governments, so all the media in these countries were on balance helpful to the United States.[2] These countries were also open to other types of public diplomacy programming. For example, in the United Arab Emirates where I was ambassador, PAO Magda Siekert was able to carry out programs with very little difficulty, providing advising services for the many students who wanted to study in America, and bringing American speakers to the UAE on a variety of subjects.

During the 1990s, however, the Arab public increasingly sympathized with the Iraqi people and began to say that the restrictions should be lifted because they had gone on long enough. The September 1996, U.S. military strike on Iraq was supported only by Saudi Arabia and the United Arab Emirates, and the U.S. military strikes in the winter of 1998–1999 received even less Arab support. PAOs increasingly heard their contacts saying that the United States was following a double standard in the region because it was imposing a stiff punishment on Iraq for noncompliance with UN resolutions, while condoning Israeli noncompliance on other UN resolutions.

PAOs rejected this comparison between Iraq and Israel, saying the cases were entirely different, but Arabs did not agree.

It did not help PAOs' arguments that European governments that had been part of the 1991 war coalition against Saddam were developing "sanctions fatigue." France and Russia sought business opportunities in Iraq that were denied because of the continuing sanctions rules, while the Clinton administration remained steadfast in support of the original policy.

By the end of the 1990s, Arab media in much of the region were critical of the United States for carrying out military strikes on Iraq, but some PAOs were able to make Washington's case. For example, Ambassador David Newton, a career FSO, went to Syria in the winter of 1998–1999 to talk to officials about Iraq, where he had served. The PAO, Evelyn A. Early, decided to try to arrange an interview for him on Syrian television to explain U.S. policy. It was a long shot, because ordinarily Syrian TV did not give air time to an American official, but Newton was favorably known to the Syrians because he had earlier served there as Deputy Chief of Mission at the embassy. The PAO called on the host of a weekly talk show and suggested he invite Newton for an interview, and she also contacted the journalist's boss, a long-standing acquaintance of hers, to reinforce the importance of treating Newton well. The journalist, who was usually in the habit of making negative comments about America, did the interview, and was polite to Ambassador Newton, allowing him to explain American policy at length, and mostly in Arabic. The PAO feared it would be heavily edited, but in fact the entire session was broadcast uncut, and with accurate subtitles for the English portion, providing the Syrian public with an unusual opportunity to hear about American policy unfiltered. She concluded that personal relations made the difference.[3]

In the later years of the Clinton administration it seemed to some PAOs that Washington was losing interest in making the strongest possible case against Saddam, perhaps out of frustration that sanctions had not forced Saddam to change, and coalition partners were tiring of the confrontation. Whether the administration hoped the problem would just go away or cool off if they ignored it, PAOs did not receive much proactive policy guidance from Washington. Some PAOs felt that Washington was missing opportunities to be more aggressive in countering Arab criticism and pointing out that the suffering of the Iraqi people was due to Saddam's brutal treatment of them, not to the U.S.-led sanctions. Officials made occasional statements on Iraq and some public diplomacy materials were produced, but the effort was diminished.

For example, when Jim Bullock was PAO in Tunis in the mid-1990s the Tunisian government restricted the press, and editors were afraid to criticize the president or fundamental official policy, but he nevertheless engaged them in lengthy political discussions, usually in French. Some editors used the wireless file material he gave them but most did not, and he

found that printed material was not as effective as face-to-face dialogue in persuading them to listen to his point of view. They regularly complained that the U.S.-led confrontation with Iraq and the embargo were unnecessary and inhuman. In dealing with misconceptions, he found there were two types of journalists. Editors and reporters at the privately owned newspapers were reasonable people but they could only function within government restrictions, and he succeeded with them through ongoing discussions. But he had little impact on the official newspapers, where the editors resisted his arguments and the only materials they would print were his cultural center announcements.[4]

Bullock moved to Morocco as PAO in 1996, and he found that his Moroccan contacts also were increasingly critical of the American policy of confrontation toward Iraq. They argued that the U.S.-led embargo was causing innocent Iraqi babies to die. Bullock had served as PAO in Iraq earlier and could respond with specific evidence that Saddam treated his own people very badly. He also pointed out that the United States supported the UN oil-for-food program out of a concern for the Iraqi people that Saddam himself did not have. His experience in Iraq helped with some Moroccans, although others had their minds made up and did not listen to his arguments.[5]

The post in Morocco sought to broaden its contacts and in the process it arranged a trip to the United States for the editor of the pro-communist newspaper *Bayan*, who had never been to the United States. Although State Department officers at the embassy were at first opposed to the idea, because they did not see why the United States should "reward" a communist journalist with a trip, the PAO prevailed and sent him; when the editor returned he wrote a very positive series of articles about the United States, based on his firsthand experience.[6]

### Iran

Although Iran had kept out of the 1990–1991 confrontation with Iraq, Washington still considered Iran a threat to its interests. The Clinton administration was concerned with Iran's continuing hostility to Israel, and support for the Hizbullah in Lebanon, as well as Iran's possible development of weapons of mass destruction, noting with alarm its test of the new "shihab" missile. In 1995 the administration tightened restrictions on commerce with Iran, and in 1996 Congress passed the Iran–Libya Sanctions Act ("ILSA"), which imposed penalties on any American company doing more than $40 million in business with Iran. Muhammad Khatemi's election as president of Iran in 1997 brought a brief period of hope that he would be less hostile to Washington, but a thaw in relations did not materialize. The hard-line mullahs who were opposed to reconciliation with "the Great Satan" still had considerable influence in Tehran.

PAOs in the Arab world at first had little difficulty in defending America's tough policy on Iran. The smaller Arab states on the Persian Gulf had been apprehensive about Iran ever since the Khomeini revolution of 1979 had brought mullahs to power, because they seemed intent on exporting radical Shiite fundamentalism throughout the region. The intensity of concern varied; the United Arab Emirates, which had an ongoing territorial dispute with Iran, encouraged Washington to be tougher on Tehran, while others tended to be somewhat more conciliatory.[7] Then after Khatami came to power, the smaller Arab states, even the UAE, softened their position somewhat on relations with Iran. They continued to do so during the late 1990s, but by then Washington was moving in the opposite direction, again intensifying its confrontation with Tehran. Saudi Arabia made gestures toward Tehran and other Arab states did the same. PAOs in the Arab world had to try to justify the continuing American hard line at a time when the Arabs were seeking reconciliation.

## Arab–Israel

During his first term, President Clinton was less engaged in trying to resolve the Arab–Israeli conflict than President Bush had been. Yet this was a period of great hope in the region because of the Oslo peace process. The Israelis and Palestinians made some progress on their own, in direct negotiations, without American involvement. Secret talks in Oslo involving only Israelis and Palestinians led to the August 1993 "Declaration of Principles" and the first Oslo agreement on September 13, 1993, which called for a final status agreement to be negotiated by 1999. In May and August 1994, Israel and the Palestinians signed agreements that transferred authority to the Palestinian leadership in parts of the West Bank and Gaza, and in July, Yassir Arafat returned to Gaza, ending his long exile. By October 1994, Jordan had also signed a peace agreement with Israel. On September 28, 1995, a second Oslo agreement was signed in Washington between Arafat and Israeli Prime Minister Rabin. Some other Arab states also became involved in the peace process, and several annual multinational conferences representing "track two diplomacy" (i.e., Israeli meetings with several Arab states, supplementing the Israeli bilaterals) were held between 1994 and 1997 that brought businessmen from Israel and some Arab countries together to discuss common projects. A few Arab countries such as Morocco, Oman, and Qatar allowed Israelis to open offices, and discontinued the secondary and tertiary Arab boycott.

The American role was mostly quiet diplomacy behind the scenes, but PAOs throughout the Arab world found all these developments very helpful. They were able to argue that other states should join the process, stressing the importance of supporting the direct negotiations and track two diplomacy as beneficial to all Arabs.

In Syria, where diplomatic relations were downgraded in 1986 (see Chapter 7), they warmed up a bit after the Syrians participated in the U.S.-led confrontation of Iraq, 1990–1991, and the atmosphere for public diplomacy work there improved. Americans who served at USIS in Damascus in that period found the Syrians were less fearful of being seen with American officials than they had been. They organized discussions with Syrians at the American Center that turned out to be candid and open. They brought American academics from the United States to lecture and that had an impact on Syrian society, which had for years been closed to outside ideas. Syrians even talked about the possibility that an Israeli flag might one day wave over Damascus. USIS officers developed contacts with Ba'ath Party officials, starting with the party's officer responsible for education. This was an unprecedented breakthrough since party officials had previously been prohibited from meeting with any Americans.[8]

As PAO in Damascus from 1993 to 1996, Alberto Fernandez sought out one sector of society that had been neglected by the embassy, the leftist, formerly pro-Moscow secularists. They were mainly writers and intellectuals, whom the collapse of the Soviet Union had made ideologically "homeless." They were very suspicious of Americans, but Fernandez reached them using a mix of programs, energetic efforts at personal contact, and judicious use of travel grants to the United States. For example, he arranged a visit to America for a leading Syrian television news director, an ex-communist who had been a student in Russia, who went with his wife, who was also a TV director. The PAO found that some of his State Department embassy colleagues objected to his giving a U.S. government grant to leftist media people because they preferred to reward friends of America with such trips. But the grantees returned with a much better appreciation of the United States; they said they admired aspects of American society such as self-criticism, and they saw its complexity. Fernandez continued to work with them and people like them during his three years in the country. His view was that the personal experience trumps the hypothetical concept that "Americans are all devils."[9]

Progress in the peace process during the 1990s was especially helpful to the PAOs who served at the Consulate General in East Jerusalem, who were responsible for West Bank Palestinians, and the PAOs at the embassy in Tel Aviv who were responsible for the Gaza Palestinians.

In the years 1993–1996, when Lea Perez was PAO in Jerusalem, with responsibility for the West Bank, she met an Imam who served as the Friday preacher in the most prominent mosque in a significant West Bank city; he also edited an influential weekly newspaper. When she first met him, he was quite hostile to the United States, and she knew he had always resisted previous attempts by American officials to engage in more than minimal pleasantries. Her first courtesy call began somewhat awkwardly, but she decided to tell him that she was the daughter of an American minister and

she asked him to speak about the meaning of being a Muslim, for him and for his community. What ensued was the first of many long discussions, in Arabic, about his mosque, his role in the spiritual life of the community, their aspirations and fears. Ultimately, he agreed to travel to the United States on an International Visitor Program for Middle Eastern religious leaders. He was so impressed by his visit that when he returned he decided to write a series of front-page articles in his newspaper, and to dedicate an entire series of Friday sermons to his firsthand observations of tolerance and diversity in the United States. Sustained personal contact had brought results.[10]

By the time Duncan MacInnes went to Jerusalem as PAO in Jerusalem in the mid-1990s, he found that because of the Oslo peace process, the mood among the Palestinians had become upbeat, and that Washington was ready to be extremely generous with funds to carry out a variety of programs to support the peace process. He had the second-largest Fulbright program in the Middle East. It provided a budget of $1 million to send West Bank Palestinians to the United States as students and researchers. His well-funded International Visitor Program and a constant stream of other short-term exchanges allowed him to send up to sixty Palestinians annually to America. On rule-of-law issues alone, he had more than a dozen programs, including workshops and exchanges on alternative dispute resolution, court case management, legal education, and revitalizing the Palestinian Bar Association. He put forward a $2 million proposal to USAID to set up two fully equipped journalism centers, one in the West Bank and another in Gaza, to support Palestinian journalists, who had few resources and little sense of professionalism. He provided U.S. trainers on writing, photojournalism, Internet research, and editing. This project demonstrated U.S. interest in Palestinian development despite our history of political differences, and it also gave him excellent contacts in the Palestinian media: He often visited the media centers where they hung out. USAID was eager to work with USIS because they knew that the PAO and his staff understood Palestinian society and institutions well and could open doors with small projects that could be followed later with much larger ones that USAID would manage.[11]

MacInnes also carried out many people-to-people projects to bring Israelis and Palestinians together, paid for from both U.S. government and private funds. He conceived and implemented three or four dozen imaginative projects that focused on areas of mutual concern, such as environmental, health, and education issues. He knew the Palestinians had been deeply traumatized by years of occupation, and in conversations with them he often started by acknowledging their suffering and said the United States wanted to help them build a strong civil society. He worked with journalists, educators, writers, and professionals such as lawyers, the natural USIS target audience, and talked about cooperation in professional and institu-

tional development. He had funds that helped them meet their needs so his dialogues with them were constructive. Palestinians continued to criticize America's Middle East policy but they did not dwell on it exclusively at that time because they were more focused on internal Palestinian development than on confrontation with Israel.[12]

During this period, USIA programs for Palestinians in Gaza were handled by Martin Quinn, the Cultural Affairs Officer in Israel, based in Tel Aviv. At first, he visited Gaza three or four times each year but after the Oslo agreement accelerated the peace process, Washington's funding for Palestinian programming increased very substantially and he spent up to 60 percent of his time in Gaza. During his last four months at post, in 1995, he traveled to Gaza every day. He felt that Gazans were regaining their pride and identity; Israeli contacts told him that they saw in Gaza Palestinians what they themselves had gone through in 1948 with the creation of Israel. In 1994, Washington started a new Israeli–Palestinian Co-existence Program which provided up to $50 million annually, managed by USIS and intended to bring Israelis and Palestinians together on a variety of projects. Israeli and Palestinian groups made proposals for projects; Quinn felt that created a great deal of mutual good will. He also arranged for meetings between Israelis and Palestinians in Cyprus and Turkey, and at the USIA-sponsored Salzburg Seminar in Austria, because outside the region the atmosphere was more relaxed and the Palestinians were on a more equal footing. At these meetings, both Israelis and Palestinians tended to avoid political arguments and instead concentrated on other issues of mutual interest.[13]

On one occasion in the fall of 1994, Quinn brought a group of American judges and law professors to Gaza where they met with the Palestinian Minister of Justice, and with Palestinian judges and lawyers at the Gaza Bar. Because of Israeli security measures restricting travel, he had difficulties at the border checkpoints, but once in Gaza, the meetings went well, with several hundred Palestinian jurists participating in discussions and in workshops led by the American legal specialist acting as facilitator. They discussed presentation of evidence, cross-examination, alternative dispute resolution, and other matters. On another occasion, Quinn arranged for a group of ten American businessmen to travel to Gaza to discuss investment opportunities, and they also met with Chairman Arafat.[14]

In Jordan at this time, discussion topic number one was also the peace process. But the discussions in Jordan that the PAO, Marcelle Wahba, had about Israel were different from the discussions she had had as IO in Egypt: Palestinian families in Jordan were in touch with Israelis regularly, many crossing the border on weekends to see relatives. The peace process was not a conflict in the abstract as it was elsewhere. It was intensely personal, and the PAO saw the conflict as a human tragedy on both sides. She felt the Jordanians and Palestinians humanized the Israelis much more than

other Arabs did; even if they had bad experiences with some Israelis, they had good experiences with others. Jordanians knew firsthand about the relationship, and knew firsthand there were some Israelis they could live with, some they couldn't, and that the Israelis were there to stay. In contrast, most other Arabs saw the issue as a regional and international level political one and not in human terms. In discussions with Jordanians about the peace process, many times the PAO had to explain the U.S. position, but because the Oslo process was under way, there were many positive things to point to, and the discussion was about details and how the latest negotiation had progressed.[15]

PAOs also focused on other issues. Peter Kovach, another PAO in Amman in this period, worked to support democracy, among other issues. He brought Harry Valentino, an American expert in the creation of "public service announcements" (PSAs) to Jordan to help the government promote participation in the upcoming national election. Valentino trained Jordanian TV directors to make brief TV spots encouraging voter registration as well as traffic safety and earthquake damage prevention. The PSAs ran on Jordanian television and were at least partly responsible for the fact that voter participation increased by hundreds of thousands of Jordanians who had returned home from the Persian Gulf. The election results showed an increase in moderates and a decline in the percentage of Islamists. The PAO also supported the visit of President Clinton to Jordan on the occasion of the signing of the Jordanian–Israeli peace treaty, by providing talking points for the president's speech before the Jordanian parliament, an historic event.[16]

In Qatar in the early 1990s, both the PAO and Ambassador Kenton Keith, a career public diplomacy officer, focused on the fact that the Qataris had no effective intellectual property laws, and this was a problem for the United States. The Qataris were open to the idea of passing such a law but they did not know how to structure it. The PAO sent an official from the Qatari Commerce Ministry on an International Visitor Grant to the United States, where he met with U.S. experts in intellectual property protection. When he returned home, he wrote an intellectual property law modeled on American laws that had enforcement provisions. The visit helped both Qatar and the United States.[17]

In the second half of the 1990s, the peace process was faltering, as extremists on both sides opposed it and the governments were unable to move forward. In October 1995, Prime Minister Rabin was assassinated by an Israeli fanatic. As a result of the February–March 1996 Palestinian attacks in Jerusalem and Tel Aviv and the April 1996 Israel incursion into Lebanon, civilian casualties on both sides increased, raising the anger level on both sides. In May 1996, a new government came to power in Israel under Benjamin Netanyahu, who was less inclined to make any concessions to the

Palestinians. In November 1997, when the fourth "track two" conference was convened, most Arab states boycotted it in protest.

By 1998 it was clear that the Oslo process had stalled, and the type of Palestinian–Israeli contacts that USIS officers in Jerusalem and Tel Aviv had brokered just two or three years earlier declined significantly. Israel tightened travel restrictions for Palestinians, and border crossings became more difficult, severely hampering meetings and USIS programming. And the pessimistic atmosphere that descended on the peace process made Palestinians and Israelis less willing to meet together.[18]

PAOs in the Arab world argued that the peace process had been going well and bringing benefits to the Arabs, and should be revived. Their Arab interlocutors, however, generally disagreed, saying that Israel had reaped the benefits in terms of recognition of the status quo. They pointed out that Palestinian demands for an independent state were far from being realized, and Israelis were still building and expanding settlements all over the West Bank and Gaza, precluding achievement of Palestinian goals. PAOs could only urge that the Arabs eschew violence and return to negotiations as the only way to make progress. Arabs were skeptical, saying Americans failed to understand Palestinian frustrations.

In his seventh year in office, President Clinton decided to become more active in promoting the peace process. He hosted a meeting between Yassir Arafat and Israeli Prime Minister Netanyahu in October 1998 at the Wye Plantation in the United States. In September 1999, when Ehud Barak was prime minister, several other meetings took place including one at Camp David in July 2000 and others at Sharm al Shaikh and Taba. Prime Minister Barak made an offer to withdraw from part of the West Bank, but Arafat did not respond and talks were then suspended pending the Israeli elections. As a result of the elections, Barak was replaced by Sharon, who rejected the deal, but President Clinton blamed Arafat for not having accepted it earlier. By then President Clinton's term was over. He had also tried to bring Syria into the negotiations, hosting Syrian–Israeli negotiations between Barak and Syrian Foreign Minister Sharaa in January 2000 at Shepardstown, but these talks also were without result.

Therefore, at the end of the 1990s, PAOs all over the Arab world faced increasing difficulty arguing for a peaceful settlement because the peace process was breaking down. Violence was increasing. On September 29, 2000, Palestinians rioted at the al Aqsa Mosque/Temple Mount in Jerusalem in protest against the visit there of Ariel Sharon. This began what the Palestinians called the "al Aqsa Intifada," which lasted well into the next administration, and signaled the end of Oslo peace negotiations. In October 2000 the UN Security Council passed Resolution 1322, which condemned Sharon for provoking the violence but the United States abstained on the vote. PAOs faced considerable criticism for the American policy.

Arab critics said the United States revealed its unfair bias in favor of Israel by blaming only Arafat for the collapse of the peace negotiations, when, they said, Barak's offer had been woefully insufficient. They also criticized the United States for not supporting the UN's condemnation of Sharon. (This UN vote was one instance among many in which the United States sided with Israel against large UN majorities, and which Arabs always cited as evidence of American bias.) The PAOs countered that Palestinian violence was indefensible and did not serve Arab interests, but the Arabs responded that the Palestinians were only expressing their extreme frustration and sense of helplessness that the Israeli occupation had continued for a quarter century with no prospect of relief in sight.

The problem was compounded by the fact that in the United States, the Palestinians continued to have a reputation for violence and for being unreasonable, and they did not make much effort to improve their image. When a U.S. official suggested to Yassir Arafat that part of his problem was negative congressional opinion of the PLO and asked if he planned to lobby Congress to improve it, Arafat said that was not necessary because he knew President Clinton personally and that was enough.[19]

Even in Egypt, which had a peace treaty and diplomatic relations with Israel, the PAO had to deal with the Arab–Israeli issue. It became somewhat heated when an Egyptian newspaper editor decided to make a personal attack on the new American ambassador to Egypt just because he was an Orthodox Jew. The editor, who had not even met the ambassador, wrote a piece linking him negatively with Israel, to which the ambassador responded in a letter to the press defending himself. Unfortunately, this only made the editor angry and his attacks became worse. The PAO realized that the editor regarded an open letter as a public humiliation, so she worked to mitigate the problem in private discussions with leading journalists, and she arranged monthly meetings over coffee for the ambassador with key editors. After the editors became acquainted with the ambassador personally, the matter eventually died down, and he developed a very good press.[20]

Meanwhile, PAOs throughout the region worked hard to improve American–Arab relations and mutual understanding in other areas. In Egypt, for example, PAO Marcelle Wahba made use of several available assets, including English teaching and a large economic assistance program. Because the embassy's economic assistance program was huge, the USAID director asked the PAO to handle several small grants of $10,000 to $50,000 each that the USAID staff simply had no time to deal with. The PAO agreed to manage them and they added up to more than $1 million a year that USIS used effectively. The USIS staff had much better knowledge of various groups in Egyptian society than any other part of the embassy, and they had extensive local contacts that enabled them to make projects successful. USIS at that time also had its own administrative staff (since the USIA–State merger, it no longer does) which made it efficient in

programming. One example of effective USIS–USAID collaboration was that USIS conducted training in civil society for Egyptians using USAID funds. Another was that USIS gave small grants to Egyptian nongovernmental organizations working in the area of social affairs. The PAO selected groups of fifteen female social workers to send to the United States to observe how American social welfare organizations function. When they returned, these women successfully set up their own organizations based on American models, even in rural Egypt where they were badly needed.[21]

The PAO also benefited from the presence in Cairo of USIA's Regional English Teaching Officer, Richard Boyum. Although some State Department officers at the embassy regarded English teaching as trivial, the PAO knew that Boyum had developed strong professional relationships with all of the English-language inspectors and curriculum developers in the Egyptian Ministry of Education, giving him the only real access the embassy had to that important ministry. Boyum was the key person in a series of USAID-funded projects to strengthen Egyptian civil society and democracy. Democracy was a politically sensitive subject for the Egyptian authorities but Boyum conducted a series of English-language teaching workshops that deliberately included substantive content on conflict resolution and other issues that were designed to help promote democracy. This was ostensibly an academic exercise but in fact had a political purpose, and it worked.[22]

In Yemen, PAOs regarded the Yemen American Language Institute (YALI) as their greatest asset because everyone wanted to study English. In the late 1990s, more than 1,000 Yemenis were studying there, and many of them did so despite attempts by Islamists to enroll them in their schools. Many professionals from the Ministry of Petroleum studied there and this helped them work with the American company Hunt Oil. Officials from the Planning Ministry, including the deputy minister himself, studied at YALI and this was helpful to the USAID mission. The embassy security officer was worried that YALI might be a terrorist target but the PAO insisted on keeping it open and it was in fact protected by the presence of important Yemenis.[23]

In Yemen also, the PAOs usually spent time attending social sessions in private homes with Yemenis, where they had discussions that sometimes lasted for many hours, chewing "qat" and smoking a water-pipe. For example, one PAO met often in such sessions with a Yemeni judge who came from a long line of judges, and they discussed Yemeni and American legal systems. The PAO explained Western legal systems to him at length, and then arranged for the judge to visit the United States to see our judicial system, accompanied by an escort-interpreter. The judge returned to Yemen with a deep understanding and appreciation of our legal system. A decade later, after 9/11, the judge challenged Yemeni al Qaida supporters to public debates in which he said he would demonstrate that al Qaida violated basic tenets of Islam. It is likely that the PAO's efforts years earlier helped

the judge to decide to speak out against al Qaida. This is important because the most powerful antidote to al Qaida comes from recognized Muslim scholars rather than from American officials.[24]

Throughout the Clinton administration, personal contact remained extremely important to USIS personnel in the Arab world. Effective officers used every opportunity to meet people helpful to their work. For example, a Public Affairs Officer in Doha, Qatar, arranged for a male member of the ruling family to visit the United States to observe American private organizations. Prior to his trip he had been critical of American materialism and consumerism, but when he returned he said he now appreciated American generosity and volunteerism, which he wanted to emulate. He started a series of science clubs based on an American model. Another PAO in Qatar developed other useful contacts, some of which happened fortuitously. She met an important female academic close to the Qatari ruling family, because they both had daughters in the same first grade class. Although Qataris tend to be very reserved with strangers, the PAO showed sincere interest in Qatar, a friendship developed, and they often discussed American education, which helped to clarify and reinforce the academic's interest in American education. The woman later became prominent in the country's leadership and was instrumental in introducing American models into the country's education reform efforts.[25]

In one unique instance, the PAO in Yemen, Haynes Mahoney, had to use his interpersonal skills to mitigate a dangerous situation. Tribes in Yemen sometimes kidnapped foreigners and held them in return for some material compensation, not for political purposes as elsewhere. On November 25, 1993, Mahoney was kidnapped in the middle of Yemen's capital city Sanaa, after he left an evening reception. He was forced into a jeep by three tribal men and taken to a Bedouin camp in the Marib area of the country. In the antiterrorism course he had taken at the State Department prior to his assignment in Yemen, his trainers had told him that if kidnapped his chances of surviving would increase the more he talked to his captors in the first minutes and hours of being abducted, in order to try to establish rapport. An Arabic speaker, Haynes immediately engaged them in conversation as they drove through the alleys of Sanaa and then out into the desert. They had a wide-ranging conversation, talking about the merits of Saddam Hussain (his captors liked Saddam) and the usefulness of shooting the rabbits who scampered in front of their headlights. By the time they reached the abductors' camp, they were "on reasonably amicable terms given the circumstances." He was held for six days, and they told him they had abducted him because they were having a dispute with the Yemeni government and because he was a Westerner he had been selected as a hostage to help them bargain with the government over their grievances (they wanted better roads and schools, and more jobs guarding the oil pipeline). The embassy reported him missing, the Yemeni government

searched for him, and meanwhile Haynes kept up discussions with his captors and listened to their complaints about the government. He was well treated and after six days he was released when his captors struck a bargain involving a pledge by the Yemeni government of two Landcruisers and some guns. The lesson he took from the experience was that the techniques employed by a successful PAO in doing public diplomacy also work in hostage situations: Engage your adversaries in an ongoing discussion, listen carefully to their grievances, and speak Arabic if you can even if it isn't perfect. He continues to use that technique in more normal public diplomacy work, making a broad range of contacts of all kinds and keeping the conversation going.[26]

### Terrorism Issues

The Clinton administration also became concerned during the 1990s about Mideast-related terrorism. In November 1995, a bomb at the National Guard headquarters in Riyadh killed five Americans, and in June 1996 a bomb at the Khobar Towers apartment house in eastern Saudi Arabia killed nineteen Americans. Washington was disappointed at the extent of Saudi cooperation in the investigation. In August 1998, the American embassies in Kenya and Tanzania were bombed, killing more Americans, and Washington was certain that Usama bin Ladin, from his base in Afghanistan, had been behind it. In reaction, the Clinton administration launched missile strikes against targets in Afghanistan and Sudan that it said were bin Ladin sites, and made diplomatic moves to pressure Afghanistan to cease harboring bin Ladin. On October 12, 2000, the USS *Cole* was bombed in Aden harbor, killing seventeen Americans; again Washington suspected bin Ladin, and the Clinton administration supported additional sanctions on Afghanistan.[27] Washington was not entirely satisfied with the extent of Yemen's cooperation. PAOs in the region tried to argue for more American–Arab cooperation in fighting terrorism, but many Arabs indicated that they saw terrorism as a domestic political problem that should not be discussed with foreigners.

The increased terrorist threats against Americans had the effect of hampering the efforts of public diplomacy professionals in making and maintaining essential personal contacts. New security barriers erected at embassies and cultural centers, and strict access procedures, strongly discouraged people from coming to USIS offices and facilities. For example, in Qatar, a bomb threat at the embassy in 1999 led to a decision to move the embassy from a building that was adjacent to a street to another building set way back and therefore out of reach of car bombs. Mandatory security procedures requiring prior searches even of ministerial vehicles alienated senior Qatari officials, so most Qataris stopped visiting the embassy and the USIS office located there.[28]

When the Clinton administration ended, therefore, Washington's belated effort to promote the Arab–Israeli peace process had failed, the sanctions regime against Iraq was losing support throughout the Arab world, Afghanistan was unbending in harboring bin Ladin, and Washington had failed to be helpful in the brief Yemeni conflict. There was little for PAOs to point to with pride.

## Demise of USIA

Near the end of his second term, President Clinton undertook a major reorganization of the U.S. government's public diplomacy structure. Members of Congress, in particular North Carolina Senator Jesse Helms, the chairman of the Senate Foreign Relations Committee, demanded that USIA be absorbed into the State Department. Proponents of the merger argued that the change would improve efficiency and bring public diplomacy closer to policy. Critics of the merger feared that State would simply swallow USIA's resources and the public diplomacy function would be burdened and made less efficient by being part of a many-layered bureaucracy, so USIA's flexibility and professionalism would be lost. USIA director Joe Duffey opposed the merger but Secretary of State Madeleine Albright finally accepted Helms's proposal, hoping he would in return approve the Chemical Test Ban Treaty, which he did. Negotiations between USIA and State on the working level took place in 1997. USIA negotiators insisted on protecting educational exchange budgets behind a "firewall" to prevent State from taking it for nonprogram items like building new embassies.[29]

The merger was made law in the 1998 Foreign Affairs Reform and Restructuring Act and implemented in 1999. The function of the USIA director was in effect converted into the new position of Undersecretary of State for Public Diplomacy and Public Affairs, but without the same budgetary or personnel control over the public diplomacy staff. Personnel from USIA were transferred into State not as a unit but scattered throughout the Department, assigned to various existing bureaus. Personnel from the five USIA "area offices," organized according to five geographic areas of the world, were assigned to the public affairs offices in the State Department's regional bureaus. Most public diplomacy professionals seem to agree that after the merger the flexibility and autonomy that existed under USIA was lost, as the opponents of the merger had feared, and that the hoped-for increase of influence over policy by public diplomacy professionals was minimal.[30]

One factor behind some of the difficulties in the merger is that the practices of public diplomacy and traditional diplomacy are different roles. Proponents of the merger hoped it would eliminate the gulf between them, but in large measure the gulf remains. The political officer who is carrying out traditional diplomatic functions abroad works primarily with host govern-

ment officials and deals mostly with policy matters and classified materials. The public diplomacy officer, in contrast, has the task of reaching the general public and dealing with a greater variety of people, and working mainly in an unclassified and open mode. Both need sensitivity to the foreign culture in which they are operating, but the public diplomacy officer must have an ability to communicate with different types of people and an interest in a broad range of contacts, as well as language skills that are not so necessary for a political officer, whose contacts usually speak English. The two types of Foreign Service Officer therefore focus on rather different tasks and they are rewarded for different accomplishments. The political officer typically sees little benefit to his performance evaluations in giving press interviews or public speeches, while the PAO works hard to make an impact in the public sphere. PAOs are sometimes frustrated with the lack of interest (or even unspoken disrespect) that some political officers show for public diplomacy programs.

This difference in roles carried over to some extent after the USIA–State merger. Some State Department officials argue that the merger did bring policy and public diplomacy closer together as the merger was intended to do, because both types of FSO now work in the same building and cooperation is easier. But many public diplomacy specialists feel that at least in Washington, their involvement in policy making has not improved as it was intended to, nor have policy officers increased their interest in public diplomacy. Many officials who have policy responsibilities still lack interest in doing interviews with Arab or other foreign media, or other public diplomacy chores. They see only a risk in speaking openly to the press when they work primarily with sensitive classified information.[31]

At embassies abroad, many public diplomacy professionals also believe that the merger has created new practical obstacles to their effective performance. In the past, the PAO had a USIS executive staff familiar with program rules, vehicles, independence in personnel and operational matters, and above all a separate budget, but that is now gone. The PAO also reported directly to USIA Washington and could usually evoke a prompt response to urgent requests. But since the merger the PAO must clear messages with the ambassador and often with the Political Officer as well, and this slows or distorts communication. Since the merger, the PAO's performance has been skewed more in the direction of traditional diplomacy and short-term information work, and away from the equally important long-term aspects of public diplomacy. Some PAOs also now complain that their ambassador gives them assignments that are not properly public diplomacy functions, and it is difficult to avoid them because it is awkward to appeal to Washington for relief from such problems. In Washington, public diplomacy professionals in the regional bureaus have been able to provide some support to PAOs but they cannot do so as quickly or as efficiently as they used to because they must contend with many more levels of bureaucracy

and clearances than they used to have at USIA. Even the senior State Department official responsible for public diplomacy, at the undersecretary level, does not communicate easily with PAOs in embassies abroad because of the new structure. The larger bureaucracy has proved to be slower and more cumbersome than USIA was, and skillful officers seek ways to work around it.[32]

Changes also took place in the structure of international broadcasting during the Clinton administration. The act abolishing USIA transferred all of the U.S. government's international broadcasting institutions, including VOA, to the Broadcasting Board of Governors as an independent agency. This made VOA much more independent of the State Department than it had been before. The secretary of state has a seat on the BBG but this gave him little influence over VOA in practice. In the summer of 1998, Congress established Radio Free Iraq as a surrogate radio station and put it under the BBG also. It was intended to be an Iraqi station, to be truthful but also to promote democracy, human rights, and freedom of expression. Unlike VOA, it has no mission to explain the United States or U.S. policy, so it is only partially a public diplomacy instrument. The tone of RFI was similar to NPR, but it competed well with the BBC because of its focus on Iraq. David Newton, a retired Foreign Service Officer, was selected to head RFI, and in October 1998 he set up the RFI office in Prague. RFI went on the air first with only one-half hour each day, gradually expanded to three hours, always broadcast in the evening with a repeat in the morning, in Arabic and Kurdish.[33]

Meanwhile, major changes took place during the 1990s in Arab broadcasting, as several new Arab-owned satellite television channels emerged to challenge the government-controlled channels for Arab viewers throughout the region. When al Jazeera started in 1996, it broke many taboos, covering events inside Israel, arranging talk shows that dealt with political and social subjects that had been considered too sensitive before, and making other innovations. Washington did not pay much attention to this development at the time, although PAOs in the Arab world realized that Arab satellite TV was beginning to provide a source of information that was different. This phenomenon was to grow in popularity among Arab audiences in subsequent years, and cause Washington to take notice of it as a problem.

Nevertheless, PAOs in the Arab world took these organizational changes in stride. They continued many of the programs and projects that they had always undertaken, despite the new bureaucratic obstacles. They continued quiet work in a variety of ways to improve communication and understanding between Americans and Arabs, despite changes in Washington and political developments in the region, including the breakdown of the Arab–Israeli peace process and the erosion of support for the American confrontation with Iraq. These political issues were to heat up in the following years, however.

# President George W. Bush's First Two Years, 2001–2002

## GEORGE W. BUSH'S PUBLIC DIPLOMACY CHALLENGES

This chapter discusses the Arab–American relationship during the first two years of the administration of President George W. Bush, 2001–2002, and analyzes how American public affairs officers (PAOs) and their staffs in the Arab countries dealt with the challenges they faced during that period.

In October 2001, President Bush appointed Charlotte Beers, a Madison Avenue advertising executive, as Undersecretary of State for Public Diplomacy and Public Affairs, the senior public diplomacy position in the U.S. government. In March 2003 she resigned, and in October the post was filled by Margaret Tutwiler, who was ambassador to Morocco and who had previously served as State Department spokesperson and in the White House. Margaret Tutwiler, however, remained less than one year in the job, leaving in June 2004 to take a position on Wall Street. In 2005, President Bush appointed Karen Hughes, his longtime political advisor, to the undersecretary position, and Dina Habib Powell, an Arab-American who had served as his director of personnel, as Hughes's deputy. Patricia Harrison, the Assistant Secretary of State for Educational and Cultural Affairs, served as acting undersecretary in the interim periods.

## America's Image

Throughout the Arab world, the election of George W. Bush as the forty-third president of the United States in December 2000 was widely welcomed. When "Bush 43" was inaugurated in January 2001, most Arabs assumed that his foreign policies relating to the Middle East would closely resemble those of his father, the forty-first president, George H. W. Bush. They regarded "Bush 41" as having followed a more even-handed policy toward the Arab world, by working with Arab countries to expel Iraq from Kuwait and by showing concern for the interests of Arabs in their dispute with Israel. They recognized that Washington would always be supportive of Israel but they believed that President Clinton had tilted far more in Israel's direction than had Bush 41. They expected Bush 43 to correct that tilt and listen more to their interests because his father had done so. In Arab society sons tend to heed their fathers' advice.

For the first eight months after his inauguration, President Bush took no steps that dispelled these Arab expectations. It is true that the Arabs wished for a more proactive effort by Washington to revive the peace process, believing that American intervention was necessary for any progress to be made, and they began to be concerned about the president's lack of engagement in the issue. But they hoped he would take it up in due course as his father had done in sponsoring the Madrid Conference of 1991 to promote peace in an even-handed manner (see Chapter 8). American PAOs in the Arab world remained optimistic that this presidency would give them opportunities to make progress in achieving their public diplomacy objectives with their audiences.

## 9/11

The September 11, 2001, terrorist attacks on the United States evoked a mixture of emotions in the Arab world. A very small number of Arabs expressed pleasure that America had been attacked because they thought Americans deserved to be punished for supporting Israel. But the dominant emotion of the overwhelming majority of Arabs was sympathy for the American victims. Images of the collapse of the New York towers and of part of the Pentagon were shown repeatedly on Arab television, and Arabs all over the region expressed genuine sorrow to their American friends or to U.S. officials. Arabs also felt a sense of embarrassment as the perpetrators were identified as young Arab men. Many shared the initial apprehension expressed by an Arab student watching the event on television, who later remembered, "my first thought was, I hope to God it's not one of us, it wasn't an Arab."[1] His fears were based on knowing there was an undercurrent of Arab anger at the United States for its policies in the Middle East.

At the same time, partly because of wishful thinking, false rumors began

to circulate that discounted the American version of the 9/11 story, and doubt was expressed that Arabs were involved. Some even said that Arabs did not have the capability to do such a thing.[2] Some feared all Arabs would be blamed for the actions of a few. Conspiracy theories sprang up, some saying that the "real" perpetrators must have been Israelis who wanted to blacken the reputation of the Arabs by faking an Arab attack on the United States. Rumors circulated in the Arab world that Jews who had offices in the twin towers had stayed home on September 11 and survived because they had been warned by Israel. Another version of the story was that the Arabs identified by Washington as the hijackers had in fact only been passengers on the planes and the crime had been committed by other passengers whose identity was being covered up for some reason.

As soon as Washington identified the perpetrators and Usama bin Ladin as the mastermind, U.S. official statements to that effect were disseminated widely, and PAOs used them to try to knock down rumors to the contrary. Washington, however, did not provide much in the way of hard evidence implicating al Qaida, but rather simply reiterated the accusation. For Americans, a simple accusation was sufficient. But for Arab audiences, who fervently hoped that reports of Arab culpability would turn out to be incorrect, the simple statements were not enough, and for a while doubts remained.

## Afghanistan

Immediately after 9/11, Washington led an international effort that issued ultimatums giving Afghanistan's Taliban government a few weeks to expel Usama bin Ladin.[3] The Taliban ignored them, and after waiting twenty-seven days, the United States led a military assault on Afghanistan starting on October 7, 2001, that ultimately brought down the Taliban regime. During the fighting in Afghanistan, rumors circulated in the Arab world about mistreatment of the Afghan people. For example, Egypt's *al Ahram* newspaper reported that American planes were dropping booby-trapped toys that were killing Afghan children. This was a special problem. It was possible the *al Ahram* report was sloppy journalism, since the editor did not bother to check its accuracy with the American embassy. But the PAO had to deal with it promptly because *al Ahram* is one of Egypt's oldest, most respected and largest-circulation newspapers, and many readers likely believed that the United States was deliberately killing Afghan children. The PAO had to deny the report before it went any further. The denial had to be unequivocal and straightforward, since an explanation in detail involving a discussion of American bombing strikes and the possibility of accidental collateral damage could have been regarded as validation of the original report. In any case, such denials never erase completely the impact of the original reports. PAOs in the Arab world worked to ex-

plain and justify the U.S. military campaign and refute false accusations such as these.

Nevertheless, for the most part, the Arab public understood the American war in Afghanistan, and accepted it. For many Arabs, the war was simple revenge against the perpetrators of the 9/11 attacks and against Usama's Taliban protectors. Some were uneasy that America was attacking a Muslim country, but the Taliban's extreme interpretation of Islam did not have many avid supporters in the region, so this was not a major consideration. PAOs were able to stress that the military action in Afghanistan was being undertaken with the direct support of Pakistan, a key Muslim country, and also with the endorsement of the United Nations.

(The Department of Defense also conducted information programs during the Afghan war. The Pentagon dropped leaflets over Afghanistan and beamed radio broadcasts into that country.[4] In February 2002, the American press revealed that the Pentagon had set up an Office of Strategic Influence, reportedly to include disinformation, feeding false reports to the U.S. and foreign press, but public outcry forced DOD to cancel this unit.[5] These were psywar operations to support military objectives, which the Pentagon also used in the 2003 war in Iraq. They were not public diplomacy.)

The Taliban ambassador in Islamabad, Pakistan, was particularly troublesome because he held daily briefings of reporters from the Arab and international press, in which he strongly criticized the American military intervention and liberally used lies and distortions to cast a negative light on American policy. He put out false information that the Taliban was shooting down American planes and killing large numbers of American troops, and said that the U.S. war was against Islam, not the Taliban and bin Ladin. These stories were being published by media in the Arab countries and elsewhere. Washington responded by establishing a Coalition Information Center in Islamabad, and a special information office in London, to provide the American side of the story to Arab journalists and others. Washington assigned as director of the Islamabad center Ambassador Kenton Keith, a retired Foreign Service Officer with extensive experience in the Arab world, and he was joined by an Egyptian press specialist from USIS Cairo. He opened the center in November 2001 and he invited representatives of the United Kingdom and other nations that were supporting the war to join him. Both the Islamabad and London centers received daily guidance by conference call from senior officials in Washington. Briefings at the Islamabad center were attended by reporters from Arab newspapers, radio and television channels including al Jazeera, Abu Dhabi TV, and Egyptian TV, and they all used material explaining the American side of the issue. It also was helpful in the Arab world that the Pakistani media, which had been hostile as late as October, became much more supportive after that, because the Arab reporters covered the Pakistan story as well.[6] The Islamabad center shut down in February 2002, but State Department

Middle East specialists remained in London to continue to work with UK-based Arab media.

Meanwhile, the U.S. government began to notice the importance of Arab media because Qatar-based al Jazeera television carried statements by Usama bin Ladin, which were picked up and rebroadcast by American commercial networks. American anger at al Qaida for the 9/11 attacks was high, and there was a tendency to blame the messenger, al Jazeera, for carrying Usama's messages. In October 2001, when the Ruler of Qatar, Hamad bin Khalifa, was in Washington, Secretary Powell complained about al Jazeera, saying the TV station was helping Usama bin Ladin by uncritically broadcasting his messages. The ruler rejected the complaint, saying he had no responsibility for al Jazeera program content because it was a private station. (This was technically accurate but al Jazeera depended on his financial subsidy.) This exchange was the first revelation of a new dilemma that Washington faced; some critics said the United States should not ask Qatar to censor al Jazeera because freedom of the press is an important tenet of American democracy.[7]

### Globalizing the War on Terror

Although the Arab public basically understood President Bush's decision to go after Usama and the Taliban, they began to have doubts when he developed a broader global strategy that targeted other organizations worldwide. The Pentagon quickly coined a new acronym, "GWOT" for the "Global War on Terror," and the Bush administration gave the Defense Department the lead role in it. President Bush consistently used the term "war," apparently to help mobilize the American public to support it, but many Arabs were puzzled by the term since the effort against terrorism was not a traditional war. They saw terrorism as a technique used by disparate groups and individuals for many different reasons, and believed terrorists could not be confronted on the battlefield by military means like conventional states.

President Bush demanded cooperation from other governments. Shortly after 9/11, he declared, "Every nation, in every region, now has a decision to make. Either you are with us, or you are with the terrorists. From this day forward, any nation that continues to harbor or support terrorism will be regarded by the United States as a hostile regime."[8] He did not publicly acknowledge that some Arab governments, notably Egypt and Saudi Arabia, had been fighting terrorism for years, more aggressively and seriously than the United States had done, and they noticed this omission. They believed it was unfair for Americans, in our newspapers, on our television, and in Congress, to criticize them for condoning or even encouraging terrorism. When American newspaper editorials accused Saudi Arabia of providing funds to terrorists, allowing anti-Western textbooks in their schools, and providing an atmosphere that nurtured terrorists, Saudi leaders won-

dered why the Bush administration did not recognize the earlier Saudi role in fighting terrorism. The PAO and other embassy officers in Saudi Arabia tried to explain that the American comments had been generated because most of the hijackers on 9/11 were Saudis, and they also stressed that the harsh criticisms were coming from private Americans and not from U.S. officials. Yet embassy officials watched with growing dismay as an unprecedented Saudi–American feud developed, to a large extent in the newspapers and on TV in both countries.

On November 8, 2001, President Bush declared, "We will wage a war to save civilization itself. We did not seek it but we must fight it."[9] This clearly signaled a geographic expansion of the war on terrorism beyond Afghanistan to other countries. The State Department reissued its list of terrorist organizations that had many more than just al Qaida on it. Arabs, however, immediately noticed that it included only Middle Eastern groups, not Latin American or Asian ones. Several on the list were of special concern to Arabs, including Hizbullah, a legal political party in Lebanon, where several of its leaders were elected members of the Lebanese parliament. Lebanese prime minister Hariri, a friend of the United States, made clear he would not restrict Hizbullah, saying it was "fighting Israeli aggression." In fact, Hizbullah had won the respect of much of the Lebanese population for compelling Israel to withdraw its forces from southern Lebanon. The Bush administration did not punish Lebanon for tolerating the presence of Hizbullah, and PAOs in the Arab world were sometimes asked about this apparent contradiction, but Washington did not explain it.

Within six months of 9/11, the Arab public was starting to have misgivings about the U.S. policy of globalizing the war on terrorism. A poll taken in April 2002 in three key Arab countries, for example, showed that public opinion regarded U.S. policy toward terrorism unfavorably. The favorable/unfavorable ratings in Saudi Arabia were 30:57, in Lebanon they were 30:65, and in the UAE they were 37:48. By June 2004 the favorable views had declined even further, to 2 percent, 10 percent, and 9 percent, respectively.[10] In Jordan and Morocco, two countries with a history of friendly relations with America, polls conducted in May 2003 found only 2 percent of Jordanians and 9 percent of Moroccans favored the U.S. war on terrorism. By March 2004 the numbers had improved but only slightly, with 12 percent of Jordanians and 28 percent of Moroccans approving. Three-quarters of the people in both countries said the United States was overreacting to terrorism, and very few (11 percent in Jordan, 17 percent in Morocco) believed the United States was sincere about it.[11]

## Homeland Security

A related issue that affected America's image in the Arab world was security in the United States. Shortly after 9/11, the U.S. government im-

posed new regulations on visa applications from people of twenty-five Arab and Muslim countries. The rationale was that since the nineteen hijackers were Arabs, who had come to the United States on visas issued legally to them, preventing another such attack required more careful screening of Arab visa applicants. To Arabs, it looked as if the United States was unfairly targeting an entire group for the crimes of a few. In addition, incidents of harassment of Arabs and Muslims took place in the United States in the weeks and months after 9/11, and reports quickly spread around the Arab world, giving Arabs the impression that America had become an unfriendly place for them. When it became known that Arab visitors would be fingerprinted and possibly subjected to lengthy interrogations at entry points, or even detained by the FBI once they were in the United States, many Arab students and businessmen decided they did not want to travel to the United States any more, or at least not until the new restrictions were eased. Before 9/11 Arab students had tended to regard attendance at U.S. universities as a high priority goal, but afterward, when they heard about the new security regulations, and about harassment, many decided to cancel or postpone travel plans. Requests for visas by Arabs and Arab attendance at American universities declined.

PAOs in the Arab world, as well as their ambassadors and embassy consular officers, found they had to devote a great deal of time to the visa and "harassment" issues. They tried to explain the new visa rules, which continued to change, and the delays caused by close scrutiny by the Department of Justice (later by Homeland Security). This hampered the exchange of persons between the United States and the Arab world, which is a vital public diplomacy tool. It also raised doubts in Arab minds about the nature of American society and its treatment of Arabs and Muslims, which PAOs and other U.S. officials had to try to deal with. Stories about bad experiences at airports or with the FBI, including exaggerations and distortions, continued to circulate and made the task of PAOs difficult. One of America's "soft power" assets, a reputation for hospitality to foreigners, was being eroded.

### The Arab–Israeli Issue

When President Bush came into office in January 2001, the effort by President Clinton to broker an Arab–Israeli peace had just collapsed. Prospects for an early revival of the peace process seemed slim, since hardline Likud leader Ariel Sharon had replaced Labour leader Ehud Barak as Israeli prime minister. In any case, it appeared that the Bush team was disinclined to follow Clinton's approach on anything. President Bush took no initiatives prior to 9/11 on the Arab–Israeli issue.

After 9/11, President Bush continued to ignore the Arab–Israeli issue because he focused almost exclusively on the war on terror, but the Arab

public was preoccupied with other issues, predominantly the continuing Israeli–Palestinian violence. For most Americans, 9/11 was a defining event. But for most Arabs (and other foreigners), 9/11 scarcely changed their lives or altered their main priorities: Palestinians struggled daily with the Israeli occupation that involved roadblocks, violence, and economic hardships; and other Arabs who saw news reports of Palestinian–Israeli clashes every day on their television screens were moved by Palestinian suffering. By contrast, Americans watching their own television saw little of the Palestinian scenes but they were reminded every day of the tragic events of 9/11. Professor Shibley Telhami has described the disconnect, saying the "prism of pain" for Americans is 9/11 but for Arabs it is the Palestinian–Israeli conflict. These contrasting experiences helped widen the gap between American and Arab perceptions of the world.

The Palestinian–Israeli issue remained the most troublesome one that American public diplomacy professionals faced in the Arab world. A public opinion survey taken in March 2001, in five Arab countries—Egypt, Saudi Arabia, Lebanon, Kuwait, and the UAE—found that more than 60 percent of the public said that Palestine was the most important issue for them.[12] A poll taken in April 2002, in three key Arab countries, showed that public opinion regarded U.S. policy toward Palestinians very unfavorably. The unfavorable/favorable ratio in Saudi Arabia was 90:5 percent, in Lebanon it was 89:6 percent, and in the United Arab Emirates it was 83:10 percent.[13]

In early 2002 the Arab public began to become alarmed that President Bush seemed to adopt the Israeli view. When Israel sent military forces into the West Bank to try to prevent Palestinian terrorist attacks, President Bush expressed understanding of the Israeli move. He asked Prime Minister Sharon to withdraw, but Sharon ignored the request and tightened Israel's occupation of the West Bank, so many Arabs believed that Bush secretly had given Sharon a green light to use harsh measures. They could not imagine that Israel would blatantly ignore the public request of the President of the United States. When Bush referred to Sharon as a "man of peace," the Arabs were astonished. They regarded Sharon's military strikes on Palestinians and incursion into the West Bank, which resulted in the deaths of innocent civilians, as "state terrorism." Many condemned Palestinian suicide bombing but they also believed the United States should condemn Sharon. They remembered Sharon's role in the 1982 Sabra and Shatilla massacre in Lebanon (for which he was censured by an Israeli investigation), and believed he was unrestrained in using force against Palestinians. Sharon portrayed his moves against Palestinians as part of Bush's global war on terrorism, but Arabs failed to see any connection between 9/11 and Palestine. It was a common view among Arabs that Sharon had "hijacked" Bush's war on terrorism for his own purposes.

These developments added further challenges to the task of PAOs

throughout the Arab world. Arabs asked PAOs how the president could praise Sharon and ignore legitimate Palestinian grievances. They said this was evidence of a double standard and an anti-Arab and anti-Muslim attitude. PAOs could only respond by quoting the president's statements that he was not condemning a whole people and that he respected Islam. For Arabs who focused on the daily Israeli–Palestinian clashes, this was not very convincing because they believed the United States had the ability to dissuade Israel from using force.

President Bush endorsed the establishment of a Palestinian state, and PAOs pointed out that this supported Palestinian goals. But for most Arabs, his qualifiers and his obvious support for Israel gave them an overall negative impression of his policy on the issue.

The Bush administration decided that Yasir Arafat was a major obstacle to peace because he failed to prevent Palestinian suicide bombers from killing Israelis, and failed to condemn them clearly. Bush therefore banned any official contact with Arafat, reversing the policy of President Clinton, who had himself maintained regular contact with Arafat as the elected and recognized leader of the Palestinians.

The general Arab view was that Arafat was in fact unable to prevent the suicide bombers. Arabs pointed out that Israeli forces were deployed all over the West Bank and Gaza but they too had not prevented the Palestinian attacks. Many Arabs including Palestinians privately criticized Arafat for his corruption and other failures, and most were appalled that Palestinians would kill innocent Israelis. But they hesitated to condemn the suicidal acts too loudly because they understood and empathized with the Palestinian people for their deeply felt grievances against their Israeli occupiers. Arabs considered the American blacklisting of Arafat, whom they considered a symbol of Palestinian resistance, as evidence of American hostility to the Palestinian people. PAOs throughout the region found it difficult to convince their Arab contacts that the U.S. government refused to deal with Arafat because he was responsible for the violence. Washington gave PAOs very little hard evidence of Arafat's alleged support for terrorism, so they had to fall back on a repetition of simple statements produced by Washington that Arafat was not helping the peace process and not preventing terrorism.

On June 24, 2002, President Bush gave a speech on the Arab–Israeli conflict that introduced two new elements that the Arabs believed were unfairly biased against them. He made Palestinian democracy a condition for progress toward peace, and he put the onus on the Palestinians to take the first steps (before the Israelis were required to do anything) by insisting first on internal political reform and stopping terrorism. Many Arabs saw this as giving Sharon excuses to stall, because he could claim that he was waiting for the Palestinians to comply fully. Then the United States began promoting a "road map" intended to show the way to peace between the Arabs

and the Israelis, containing these provisions. When the details leaked, even some American experts pointed out that the road map contained serious flaws that had prevented the achievement of peace in the past, so it would fail. The formal issuance of the road map was delayed, but in April 2003, the UN, the European Union, and Russia joined the United States in putting it forward.[14]

### Targeting Muslims?

In addition, the Arab public increasingly gained the impression that the United States was deliberately targeting Muslims. A few days after 9/11, President Bush referred to the war on terrorism as a "crusade," not realizing that for Arabs and Muslims the word had a very specific negative connotation. Although in the past Americans had used the word for other campaigns, such as the crusade against poverty or drugs, this time it resonated badly in the Middle East because to Arabs it meant the Christian crusade against Islam. One American ambassador told the president privately that his use of the word had been counterproductive in Arab ears, and the President never used it again.[15] Bush also appeared a few days after the remark at the Islamic Center in Washington, where he pointedly said, "The face of terror is not the true faith of Islam. That's not what Islam is all about."[16] But the damage was done. Arabs repeatedly quoted the crusade remark and remembered it, since it reinforced their fears about American policy. PAOs throughout the region dealt with this issue simply by explaining that in American parlance, the term "crusade" meant only an aggressive effort, and had no anti-Muslim connotations or intent.

In his January 2002, State of the Union address, President Bush said Iran, Iraq, and North Korea constituted "an axis of evil" that "pose a grave and growing danger." He said these states could provide arms to terrorists, giving them the means to match their hatred, and enabling them to "attack our allies, or attempt to blackmail the United States. In any of these cases, the price of indifference would be catastrophic."[17] To Arab ears, this formulation was further evidence (beyond his statements on the Arab–Israeli issue) that President Bush had become hostile not only to Arabs but to Muslims, since he singled out two key Muslim states as "evil." America's differences with Iran were well known, but they had been kept within the bounds of a policy dispute. The Arabs were puzzled by this escalation because they saw no immediate cause for it. In fact, Arab moves in the opposite direction, toward rapprochement with Iran, had been under way for some time, for example, by the governments of Saudi Arabia and even the United Arab Emirates. PAOs found that only a few hard-liners in the region welcomed Bush's designating Iran as "evil." To most Arabs, Bush's claim that America's allies were in grave danger from Iraq and Iran was puzzling, since even the Arab neighbors of these two states did not consider that they were so dangerous.

### War on Terror Cooperation

President Bush's strong messages demanding international support against terrorism did in fact help to galvanize some Arab governments to cooperate with teams of experts from the U.S. Treasury Department, the FBI, and other agencies, to help track down al Qaida agents. Arab leaders realized that the war on terrorism was President Bush's highest priority, and that their bilateral relations with Washington would be significantly affected by the way they responded to Bush's calls for cooperation. For example, when the terrorist attacks on Americans took place in Dhahran in 1996 and in Aden in 2000, Saudi Arabia and Yemen did not cooperate with the United States as much as American officials had wanted in investigating incidents and pursuing the perpetrators.[18] After 9/11, these countries and others such as Syria were much more forthcoming and helpful in the pursuit of terrorists, giving the U.S. government unprecedented access to bank records and to police and intelligence files on known terrorist suspects. But these Arab governments gave little or no publicity to their newfound positive attitude toward Washington's requests, because of the view among the public throughout the Arab world that the United States under President Bush was acting against the interests of the Arabs, with respect to Palestine and other issues. To maintain good relations with Washington these governments cooperated more on terrorism because they knew how much President Bush cared about it, but they kept the cooperation quiet because they knew their own publics would have criticized them for it.

In discussing the war on terrorism with the Arab public, it would have been helpful to PAOs to be able to talk openly about this cooperation, but much of it was classified so the PAOs could not provide concrete evidence of it. They were hampered in making a strong case for the war on terrorism because of other issues that at the time clouded the U.S.–Arab relationship.

Arab dissatisfaction with American policy on terrorism and on Arab–Israel had therefore increased by the spring of 2002. A poll conducted in five Arab countries in the spring of 2002 showed majorities in all five had an unfavorable opinion of the United States. In contrast, majorities in all five had a favorable opinion of France, and in three out of five, of Russia (see Table 3).[19] The positive Saudi view of Russia is especially noteworthy in view of the kingdom's long history of hostility to the USSR.

### The State Department's Role

When the Bush administration first took office, senior officials did not seem to have much interest in public diplomacy. The position of Undersecretary for Public Diplomacy at the State Department, the highest-level U.S. official responsible for it, remained vacant for nine months. Then after the 9/11 terrorist attacks, the president appointed Charlotte Beers to that

Table 3: Arab Opinions of the United States, France, and Russia, Early 2002

|  | United States | France | Russia |
|---|---|---|---|
| Lebanon |  |  |  |
| Favorable | 26 | 69 | 62 |
| Unfavorable | 70 | 17 | 38 |
| Jordan |  |  |  |
| Favorable | 34 | 56 | 44 |
| Unfavorable | 61 | 33 | 38 |
| Kuwait |  |  |  |
| Favorable | 41 | 63 | 33 |
| Unfavorable | 48 | 35 | 61 |
| Saudi Arabia |  |  |  |
| Favorable | 12 | 50 | 51 |
| Unfavorable | 87 | 46 | 43 |
| UAE |  |  |  |
| Favorable | 11 | 53 | 13 |
| Unfavorable | 87 | 39 | 69 |

position. She had been an unusually successful professional in the advertising business, and Secretary of State Powell was impressed with her intelligence and skills in the American business world, so he brought her to the State Department. However, she had no experience in government or in international affairs.

Charlotte Beers took up her responsibilities shortly after 9/11, and she therefore faced a challenge of major proportions, which only increased as time passed, because foreign opinion of the United States became more negative. When she began her tenure, she spoke about "branding" America, a concept then in vogue in American advertising circles, but never before used in public diplomacy. She assumed that if the right slogan or brief description of America could be found and communicated to audiences abroad, it would help improve the American image. She revealed her Madison Avenue approach to the task when she said, "I consider the marketing capacity of the United States to be our greatest unlisted asset." She said, "It is almost as if we have to define what America is. This is the most sophisticated brand assignment I ever had." When Colin Powell heard criticism of that approach he defended it and her, saying, "There is nothing wrong with getting someone who knows how to sell something. We are selling a product. We need someone who can rebrand U.S. foreign policy, rebrand diplomacy . . . Besides, she got me to buy Uncle Ben's rice."[20] Powell seemed to assume that public diplomacy was the same as marketing.

Because of her advertising background, Charlotte Beers valued audience research to know the market and craft the message to respond. She commissioned a number of polls in Arab and Muslim countries, sought anecdotes from PAOs, held a conference for all PAOs worldwide, and convened focus groups. PAOs welcomed that approach. She learned that Muslims thought the United States was anti-Muslim, so in response to that she decided to show that America is a tolerant society. She did not want to give initial priority to the Arab–Israeli issue or Afghanistan because she wanted first to establish a dialogue on the basis of religious tolerance. So she ordered a "Muslims in America" campaign using television (including paid time on foreign TV), speakers, and print materials.[21] It was conceived shortly after 9/11 when reports were circulating abroad about incidents of maltreatment of Muslim Americans and Muslim visitors to the United States that had taken place. The documentaries were intended to counteract that negative publicity by demonstrating that the overwhelming majority of Muslims in America are well treated. She gave the project to the New York advertising firm McCann-Erikson for a reported $10 million. However, the materials could not be placed in the media in the Arab world and in most Muslim countries; these governments did not want to appear to their own publics that they were presenting a positive image of the United States because there was so much criticism of America. Also the documentaries took much too long to produce, because they were done by a private contractor and had to be cleared by several levels at State. By the time they were ready the audience had moved beyond that issue and focused on Afghanistan, the Arab–Israeli conflict, and Iraq. The effort was criticized as misdirected and the project was quietly dropped.[22]

Some PAOs in the Arab world were privately rather skeptical of a Madison Avenue approach and branding. They believed that effective public diplomacy required a long-term effort, a sustained dialogue, and nuanced presentations, not unilateral slogans or clever use of words in declarations.

Another Beers initiative was to launch a new Arabic-language magazine for the Arab world, called *Hi*. It was somewhat like the earlier magazine *al Majal*, but produced by a contractor. PAOs regarded the magazine as marginally useful, but attempts to sell it, like attempts to sell *al Majal* in the past, were not very successful, so most copies were given away free. Also, some Arab governments blocked its distribution, for various political or cultural reasons.[23]

Many PAOs at embassies in the Arab world found that in dealing with the post-9/11 crisis after the USIA–State merger, they no longer had a strong and cohesive agency in Washington to back them up, to respond promptly to their requests, and to promote their interests in requesting funding. The public diplomacy professionals at the State Department were scattered around in many different offices, under bureaucratic layers of people who

did not understand much about what they were doing and did not form an integrated unit, so they could not act quickly to respond to the daily challenges and opportunities presented by the new situation. In the 1990–1991 Gulf crisis, USIA's more tightly organized staff, wholly dedicated to meeting the public diplomacy challenge of that time, had reacted with flexibility and effectiveness as a unit, and it also coordinated closely with the State Department on all policy questions. Moreover, VOA in 1990 had gone into "surge" mode in that crisis. But after 9/11, the VOA, now under the Broadcasting Board of Governors, and in effect independent of State policy makers, did not alter its programming very much. Thus, the public diplomacy instruments that had been mobilized during the 1990–1991 crisis under USIA were less able to do so after 9/11.

It is true that after 9/11, State Department officials, with the support of key members of Congress, did obtain some increased funding for educational exchanges for Arabs and Muslims, with particular emphasis on youth, underprivileged groups, and women. It was recognized that Arab youth had been neglected and it was important to try to influence them because attitudes are formed in high school and college. Increasingly over the years, funding had shrunk and the remaining resources were given to adults, so this needed to be rectified.

Congress also became active in trying to increase funding for U.S. public diplomacy. Senator Edward Kennedy of Massachusetts for example proposed a Cultural Bridges Act that would provide funding to make possible an increase in exchanges of students with the Muslim world, including teenagers.[24]

Between 2000 and 2003, exchanges with the Near East and South Asia sponsored by State doubled, from 1,152 to 2,358. In early 2003, Congress stipulated that 24 percent of State's exchange funding must go to the Middle East and South Asia programs. Between 2002 and 2004, State devoted $40 million to its new "Partnerships for Learning" education programs related to the Muslim world, and then requested even more money for that purpose.[25] The State Department initiated a new Youth Exchange and Study (YES) program for Arab and other Muslim teenagers, and a Partnerships for Learning Undergraduate Study (PLUS) program for Arab undergraduate college students. In 2004, the YES program brought 170 Muslim teenagers to America, most of them Arab, and by 2006–2007, State hopes to have 1,000 YES program students in the United States. In 2004, 170 PLUS grantees from 12 Arab countries came to America. These had a good, if limited, effect. One PLUS student said in 2004: "While I was preparing to come here, some of my friends told me that Americans are very hostile and they are very anti-Arab and anti-Muslim. So, along with the two heavy suitcases I brought with me, I brought a lot of wrong notions and ideas about this country. That was the first adjustment I had to go through."[26]

## Changes in International Broadcasting

Norman Pattiz, a member of the Broadcasting Board of Governors (BBG), proposed that the U.S. government establish a new radio station to broadcast to the Arab world in Arabic. Pattiz, the head of Westwood One, a large chain of American commercial radio stations, argued that the new station should use an American-style format, consisting largely of American and Arab popular music, with a limited amount of news, to appeal primarily to youth. He promoted his idea with Congress and it quickly found supporters there; they passed legislation creating "Radio Sawa," a new Arabic-language station with an initial funding of $135 million. The BBG decided that the new station would replace the existing Voice of America Arabic Service so that it could take over its transmitter time and some of its personnel. Radio Sawa went on the air in June 2002.[27] It specifically targeted Arab youth, as did several of State's new educational exchange programs. Congress and some at State apparently focused on youth because youth were seen as having been neglected in the past. American academics who pointed out that 70 percent of the MENA population is under age 30 and 50 percent under age 20 seemed to reinforce this thinking.[28]

Many PAOs in the Arab world lamented the demise of VOA's Arabic Service because Radio Sawa does not have the breadth and variety of programming that VOA Arabic had. They tend to regard Radio Sawa as being of marginal utility. They were pleased that young audiences were considered important as they had been in the past, but concerned that an exclusive focus on youth by Radio Sawa diverted resources away from policy makers and other adults who are still essential target audience members. Radio Sawa is reaching some Arab youth, but adults, including policy makers, tend not to find it interesting because it is not serious, so the demise of VOA Arabic led to the loss of an important audience. As the veteran international broadcaster Alan Heil put it, after 9/11, "there was a renewed strategic need for the Voice of America to offer in-depth news and analysis of the terrorist threat in the Arabic language, for serious reporting and discussion of this new plague. Instead, six months after 9/11, undreamed of new resources were obtained and invested in Radio Sawa, largely entertainment-driven and completely divorced from VOA."[29] In short, the public diplomacy effort was seriously diminished on two counts. Radio Sawa targeted youth but gave them only pop music when it could also have given them serious content, and the cancellation of VOA Arabic caused the unfortunate and unnecessary loss of adult listeners.

Radio Free Iraq, meanwhile, continued to broadcast and was very effective. It was staffed by highly regarded professionals and as a nongovernmental organization funded by Congress, it had some managerial flexibility.[30] Its great strength was that its programming was tailored specif-

ically for Iraqis, but because of that it did not serve public diplomacy purposes throughout the region.

## Challenges for Public Diplomacy Field Officers

Therefore, during the first two years of the presidency of George W. Bush, American public diplomacy professionals faced a number of new challenges in the Arab world. First they had to contend with the false rumors about 9/11. Then, although the Arab public generally was understanding of the war in Afghanistan against the Taliban, they were increasingly critical of Washington's subsequent steps in the Middle East, including the Global War on Terror, the president's embrace of Prime Minister Sharon, the "axis of evil," and new security measures, both at home and with respect to visa issuance. In addition, comments after 9/11 by private Americans who were critical of Arabs and Muslims, and stories of harassment in the United States, reinforced the Arab public's negative impression of American society.

In dealing with the new post-9/11 challenges, PAOs in U.S. embassies all over the Arab world used many tools at their disposal. Most of the issues that they dealt with were related to U.S. policy, and PAOs were forced by circumstances to devote more attention to short-term information tools than to long-term ones. The exchange programs ran into serious visa delay problems which PAOs tried to alleviate without much success, especially in the first eighteen months after 9/11, when the security measures were new and the slow process seriously disrupted the incoming flow of Arabs into the United States.

Throughout the region, PAOs also focused on distribution of official statements and analyses on foreign policy from Washington File materials, and they brought documents on the State Department and embassy Web sites to the attention of their audiences. They arranged meetings for official visitors with media editors in which intense discussions were held on American policy. They sent out American speakers on lecture tours, even including Middle East specialists who criticized some aspects of American policy, making the point that private Americans can and do criticize their own government. These speakers helped correct errors in the audience's negative view of America and they explained how and why a large portion of the American public was supportive of Bush's policies.

In Jordan, when Alberto Fernandez was PAO there from 1999 to 2002, he deliberately sought out journalists working in the weekly newspapers and magazines who had previously been ignored by the embassy. For example, when he first called on the chief editor of *al Bilad*, the next issue carried a front-page story, "Our argument with the American counselor." It was mostly what the editor said but it gained the PAO access to the paper

and its dynamic young reporters who were anti-American but had never been to the United States or met an American. Fernandez cultivated them and they gradually became more balanced in their reporting. Another important contact was in the Jordanian National Movement, a political organization for people in the East Bank who were badly misinformed about the United States. The PAO sent some of them to the United States on International Visitor Grants, which helped them see America in a better light. He also met often with the chief editor of an Islamist publication, who was known to be bombastic and full of misinformation about the United States, broadly insisting, for example, that America was anti-Muslim. Over time, the man increasingly saw the world more the way the PAO did, and he wrote more positive editorials about America. From time to time he reverted to unfounded attacks on the United States, but Fernandez kept in touch with him and pointed out his errors, because he realized the relationship needed constant engagement and regular tending. All of these new media contacts proved to be especially valuable after 9/11 when criticism of the United States and its policies markedly increased.[31]

There were other problems. One was that PAOs in the Arab world all worked to restore and maintain levels of student and professional exchanges despite the new security restrictions. For example, before 9/11 the United Arab Emirates had been sending most of its students studying abroad to the United States. But America's new post-9/11 visa rules severely reduced the numbers, especially in 2002 when the procedures entailed delays of up to nine months, causing many to give up waiting. The governments of Britain, Australia, and other countries lobbied to divert UAE students to their educational institutions. Katherine Van de Vate, the PAO, worked with her local employee educational advisors and her consular colleagues to reverse the downward trend. They gave media interviews to explain the new visa regulations and also to refute false stories about the mistreatment of Arabs and Muslims at airports and on U.S. campuses, arguing that U.S. education was still the best in the world and that America still welcomed Arab students. They gave briefings at all major academic institutions and at the government agencies that sponsored students for scholarships to study in America, explaining the new process to demystify it and encourage continued travel to the United States. They explained that despite visa delays and some instances of bigotry against Arabs and Muslims, American universities did want foreign students to come, and the vast majority of American citizens were still welcoming to foreign visitors and treated them well. Together with the ambassador, the PAO urged senior UAE officials to continue to send students to the United States, and they had success in that effort. They also urged Washington to pay more attention to the negative impact the new visa rules were having on educational exchanges, and to make the new process more efficient. They followed up

on some specific cases of extended delays that seemed unreasonable. This effort helped stem the decline in student visa applications, although pre-9/11 levels were not reached.[32] PAOs elsewhere undertook similar measures.

A few PAOs were able to take advantage of some special post-9/11 funding. Congress allocated millions of dollars to USAID for democracy-building projects abroad, in small grants programs, but USAID had difficulty in administering small grants because it was accustomed to managing larger sums and did not have the staff to oversee many small ones. USAID asked PAOs at embassies abroad to undertake the management of this new money, and they did so. For example, in Morocco, where bilateral relations were excellent and the atmosphere for programming was felicitous, Jack McCreary, who was PAO there from 1999 to 2002, made use of well over $200,000 per year, in small grants of up to $24,000 each to Moroccan civil society organizations. He sponsored creative projects such as a touring women's theater group that raised human rights awareness among rural women, a training program that brought civic activists and municipal employees together to design and implement joint projects, and the creation of short radio spots urging citizens to participate in elections.[33] These activities in support of democracy and human rights by PAOs and funded by USAID predated the high-level emphasis and high visibility on such matters that came later, during the second term of President George W. Bush (see Chapter 12).

The PAO in Qatar faced a unique situation because the Qatari government was doing almost everything that a public diplomacy program would want to do. At great expense, the Qataris brought several American university programs and an American education consulting firm to Qatar to revamp the education system along American lines. The government wrote a new constitution and held elections, with limited outside assistance. It maintained cordial relations with Israel, and it hosted a huge American military base on Qatari soil. And the government also welcomed American businesses to develop its enormous gas reserves. The PAO's only problem was with al Jazeera, and she had to complain regularly to the Qatari government, on instructions from Washington, about the TV station's programs. At her level and higher, the United States made clear that al Jazeera was negatively affecting bilateral relations, and this problem continued.[34]

American public diplomacy professionals all over the Arab world therefore struggled to carry out their programs to deal with these new challenges. But it was to get worse. In the next chapter, we will discuss the unfolding of Washington's Iraq policy, from confrontation to war to occupation, and the consequences that had for American public diplomacy in the Arab world.

# 11

# The Bush Presidency and Iraq

## IRAQ AND PUBLIC DIPLOMACY

The U.S.-led confrontation, invasion, and occupation of Iraq had an enormous impact on U.S.–Arab relations. But during the war and occupation (March 2003–June 2004), the Pentagon and the White House controlled information dissemination with respect to Iraq. No normal public diplomacy program for that country was established until after Iraqi independence and the reopening of the American embassy in June 2004.

### The Confrontation

By the summer of 2002 everyone knew that President Bush was seriously considering an American-led war to topple Saddam Hussain, although he said no decision had been made. He declared Iraq part of the axis of evil in January 2002, and he made several other statements raising the level of confrontation with Iraq. At West Point on June 1, 2002, he outlined a new foreign policy doctrine of preemption, based on his judgment that deterrence and containment no longer would work. He said, "The war on terror will not be won on the defensive. We must take the battle to the enemy. . . . In the world we have entered the only path to safety is the world of action. And this nation will act."[1] The United States also began to increase the deployment of its military forces in the Persian Gulf region.

Reacting to Bush's rhetoric and deployment of forces, strong objections

were raised in almost every Arab country. Arab governments warned against taking military action in Iraq. Egypt's president Husni Mubarak said it was the wrong way to fight terrorism, and going to war would help lead to the recruitment of more terrorists. Only in Kuwait, where the government and public were very anxious to see Saddam Hussain removed from power, was there strong support for a war. Other Arabs advanced many reasons not to use force against Iraq. They despised Saddam but they did not regard him as a threat to others. They believed containment had worked, and if Saddam tried again to expand his borders, there was plenty of time for the United States to respond. They pointed out that Saddam was at odds with Usama bin Ladin and argued that he would not give weapons of mass destruction (WMDs) to terrorists, since that would bring American retaliation. They wanted to give the UN inspectors time to complete their work in Iraq, to settle the WMD question. They did not perceive Iraq to be as high a priority as the Arab–Israeli conflict, which was costing Arab lives every week.

American PAOs in the Arab world tried to respond to these concerns by explaining the American position as best they could, but it was difficult. As far as they knew, President Bush had not made a decision to go to war. American forces in the Persian Gulf were steadily being augmented, but PAOs could only deflect questions about whether the United States was going to attack Iraq and reiterated the president's arguments about Saddam's transgressions. They insisted that diplomacy still remained an option, and said little about the deployment of U.S. forces.

In September 2002, in a speech at the United Nations, President Bush indicated the United States would act alone if necessary, because "Iraq is expanding and improving facilities that were used for the production of biological weapons." He said: "The history, the logic and the facts lead to one conclusion. Saddam Hussain's regime is a grave and gathering danger."[2] That same month, his administration issued a comprehensive policy statement underlining the unilateralism theme: "While the United States will constantly strive to enlist the support of the international community we will not hesitate to act alone, if necessary, to exercise our right of self-defense by acting preemptively."[3]

Congress passed a joint resolution on October 2, 2002, that authorized President Bush to "use the armed forces of the United States as he determines to be necessary and appropriate in order to (1) defend the security of the United States against the continuing threat posed by Iraq; and (2) enforce all relevant United Nations Security Council Resolutions against Iraq." Encouraged by the congressional vote, President Bush then gave a radio address on October 5, 2002, in which he said, "The danger to America from the Iraqi regime is grave and growing. . . . Iraq has stockpiled biological and chemical weapons, and is rebuilding the facilities used to make more of these weapons. . . . We cannot leave the future of peace and the

security of America in the hands of this man. . . . Iraq has longstanding tries to terrorist groups, which are capable of and willing to deliver weapons of mass destruction."[4] On December 7, Iraq gave the UN a report denying it had weapons of mass destruction. The United States said Iraq was lying.

Friendly Arab governments realized that Bush was preparing for war and they did not want to seem unhelpful, but they continued to warn against it. The Bush administration tried to mobilize support among them for the war, and Vice President Cheney made a special trip to the region for that purpose, but that effort failed. Arab media, encouraged by Arab official opposition to war, continued to publish strong criticism of U.S. policy toward Iraq. Every day PAOs tried to counter this and answer difficult questions. They cited the frequent statements by President Bush and other administration officials regarding Iraq's defiance of UN resolutions. But in most cases the Arab audiences continued to reject the American assessment that Iraq was an immediate danger that needed to be dealt with urgently. Arabs expressed puzzlement that the United States, thousands of miles away from Iraq, was so concerned about an Iraqi threat that those sitting in the same neighborhood did not feel. They regarded Saddam Hussain as a problem that could be contained as he had been for over a decade. They believed bin Ladin could only be dealt with by international cooperation in intelligence and police work, and by political means of patiently removing the grievances that al Qaida exploited. Thus, they disagreed fundamentally with President Bush. For the president, everything had suddenly changed because of 9/11, but for them little had changed.

Throughout the year 2002, as Washington escalated its confrontation in the Gulf, the Arab public showed much less concern about Iraq than about the Arab–Israeli conflict which they believed was much more urgent. Arab media carried daily reports of Israeli actions in the West Bank and Gaza, some of which led to the death or injury of Palestinian women and children, and this kept alive Arab anger and frustration with Israel and its American ally. The "road map" was not being implemented and there was little visible effort on the part of the U.S. government to push it along, as senior U.S. officials spoke only about the war on terror and Iraq. When PAOs were pressed by their Arab contacts on the Arab–Israeli issue, they could only point out that President Bush had been the first president to call clearly for a Palestinian state, and this proved that he was in fact also concerned about the Palestinians. The Arab response was that such a declaration was not enough; the United States should be actively engaged in trying to bring about an end to the violence. As one senior Arab official said to an American in January 2003, "Tell him that 'It's Palestine, stupid,'" a rephrasing of the advice of President Clinton's staff during an election campaign.[5]

When PAOs presented the case against Saddam based on his defiance of the UN, the Arab response was that Israel too had ignored UN resolu-

tions. PAOs asserted that the two cases were entirely different. A wide gap between the Bush administration and Arab opinion on priorities had become the biggest problem for PAOs.

Officials in Washington tried to help PAOs at our embassies deal with the continuing criticism of the U.S. policy. The public diplomacy staff in State's Near East Bureau drafted a one-page talking paper each week on a specific current issue related to Iraq and Saddam. These papers presented arguments about Saddam and weapons of mass destruction, Saddam and the environment (he had drained the marshes), his treatment of women, and so forth. They were cleared and sent as a weekly telegrams to PAOs abroad to use with their contacts, and to provide material for ambassadorial speeches, and so on. That system evolved into a more generic "One-pager" that was later expanded to cover various global issues. The experienced public diplomacy staff at State knew PAOs faced hostile questions every day and needed support, but instead of flooding them with lengthy messages, as State had done during the Afghanistan war, they sent brief and timely papers that PAOs could use in talking to the media and to other contacts. These bulleted papers included citations and Web sites for more background if required, but for most busy PAOs, less was more, and they usually needed only one page. The State Department and White House continued to issue longer pieces, and pamphlets, which were a favorite in Washington but of little use in a fast-changing situation requiring engagement in dialogue. A clear set of timely talking points was the best support material for this oral Arab society.[6]

In January 2003, President Bush created an Office of Global Communications (OGC) in the White House, to facilitate interagency efforts to communicate with foreign audiences, and build support for and among coalition members. But it had little practical impact on PAOs at embassies.

In his January 2003, State of the Union speech, Bush made clear that he had no intention of waiting very long for the UN to act against Iraq, saying, "If Saddam Hussein does not fully disarm for the safety of our people, and for the peace of the world, we will lead a coalition to disarm him."[7] Arab governments and editorial writers continued to argue against taking military action in Iraq, and PAOs tried to explain the U.S. position, using the president's words. Most Arab audiences remained unconvinced. On March 9, in a press conference, Bush gave a strong hint that he would soon start military action, saying, "The price of doing nothing exceeds the price of taking action, if we have to." He stated his rationale clearly: "I believe Saddam Hussein is a threat to the American people. I believe he's a threat to the neighborhood in which he lives. And I've got a good evidence to believe that. He has weapons of mass destruction."[8]

The Arab public was skeptical. A poll taken just before the Iraq war in February and March of 2003 asked what the Arab public thought war with Iraq would bring. Large majorities of Egyptians, Lebanese, Jordani-

Table 4: Attitudes Toward the United States on the
Eve of War

|  | Favorable | Unfavorable |
|---|---|---|
| Morocco | 6% | 91% |
| Saudi Arabia | 4 | 95 |
| Jordan | 6 | 80 |
| Lebanon | 32 | 59 |
| UAE | 10 | 86 |
| Egypt | 13 | 79 |

ans, and Moroccans thought it would: (a) bring less peace and less democracy to the Middle East, (b) worsen the chances of an Arab–Israeli settlement, and (c) lead to more terrorism. Majorities in these countries believed that the real motives for Bush's confrontation with Iraq were to gain access to oil and to help Israel. The same poll showed that public opinion toward the United States had become unfavorable to an unprecedented degree, largely because of U.S. Middle East policies (see Table 4).[9]

All of these views were directly contrary to President Bush's assertions, but he was undeterred. On March 17, after failing to get a new resolution passed by the UN threatening war unless Saddam gave up banned weapons, he issued a unilateral ultimatum: "Saddam Hussein and his sons must leave Iraq within 48 hours. Their refusal to do so will result in military conflict, commenced at a time of our choosing. For their own safety, all foreign nationals—including journalists and inspectors—should leave Iraq immediately."[10] On March 18, the Iraqis rejected Bush's ultimatum, and on March 19, 2003, the United States began its attack with a targeted strike on Baghdad.

## The Invasion and Occupation

The invasion and military takeover of Iraq went quickly, as the Iraqi forces retreated and then melted away. On May 1, President Bush declared that major combat was over. The Arab public had mixed emotions. They were pleased to see Saddam's regime toppled but they empathized with the Iraqi people, seeing scenes of Iraqi civilian dead and wounded on their television screens. They regarded the rapid collapse of the defense of Baghdad, one of the most famous cities in Arab and Muslim history, as an embarrassment. Americans saw the war from the point of view of the American military as reported by American journalists "embedded" with U.S. military

units, and American television carried pictures of American heroics and American suffering. Arab television, however, showed the other side, since Arab reporters were prepositioned in Iraq, and they showed scenes of many Iraqis being killed or wounded. Because of customary Arab journalistic practice, many of the scenes were more graphic and shocking than is usual on post-Vietnam American television, and this added to the impact.

American civilian teams under General Garner moved into Iraq behind the advancing military forces, in order to set up an occupation government that they called the "Coalition Provisional Authority" (CPA). The Defense Department allowed a small number of State Department experts to join the CPA but the Pentagon remained in charge.

Washington policy makers thought the transition would go smoothly and peacefully, and at the beginning of the occupation some Americans involved were told privately to expect that the number of American forces required could be reduced more than 80 percent by summer.[11] They soon learned, however, that security was a major problem. Looting of cultural treasures, businesses, and government establishments was widespread. Violence became rampant, threatening ordinary Iraqi civilians, and as the Americans tried to protect them, they too came under attack. Ambassador L. Paul Bremer replaced General Garner and he decided to dismiss most of the Iraqi military and police, on the grounds that they had been implicated in Saddam's regime. This made the security problem worse because now thousands of former military personnel were out of work, and desperate to care for their families. They retained their weapons; some of them turned to looting, others joined the insurgency to vent their anger on the Americans and Iraqis in the CPA. Very quickly, living conditions in Iraq deteriorated because of the lack of security, shortages of electricity and water, and the slow pace of reconstruction of damaged infrastructure.

As soon as the occupation began, the United States faced a highly unusual situation with respect to public diplomacy. First, this was a huge worldwide story that affected America's image and reputation everywhere but especially among Arabs, most of whom had opposed the war. How should the United States handle the story? Second, how should the CPA help the Iraqi authorities gain credibility, since both shared responsibility for improving conditions in the country? Third, how should the occupiers treat Iraqi media? The CPA now could control the Iraqi media directly, and this could help disseminate the American story, but should not the United States support freedom of the press in Iraq? Moreover, what should be done with Iraq's Information Ministry, one of Saddam's instruments of authoritarian control? As a practical matter, the Pentagon and the White House answered these questions with almost no involvement by the public diplomacy professionals in the State Department, most of whom were excluded from the occupation along with other State Department officials, even those who had expertise in the Middle East.[12]

The CPA abolished the Iraqi Information Ministry, and sent all of its 4,000 employees home as unreliable. Some of the Americans in the CPA's information task force thought that most of them could have been retrained and co-opted into the new system, although some were irredeemable hard-core Ba'athis who had to be removed. With the ministry gone, the CPA lost access to many Iraqis who had extensive knowledge and experience in Iraq's information system.[13]

Iraqi public criticism of the government and of the United States and United Kingdom as occupiers began to mount. The public was surprised that the world's only superpower could allow conditions in Iraq to deteriorate; some Arab commentators expressed suspicion that Washington must have an ulterior motive in allowing that to happen. Americans and others at the ministries were so busy and overworked that they had no time to speak to the Iraqi press to explain what progress was being made to solve problems, so the CPA assigned young army reservists to the ministries as spokespersons. Although they had no prior training for this task, they took to it with gusto and generally performed it well.[14]

### CPA Media

The Coalition Provisional Authority adopted a policy of controlling some of the Iraqi media for CPA purposes. On April 10, 2003, after the U.S. military had taken control of Baghdad, American officials took over the Iraqi television facilities and immediately changed the programming from Saddam Hussein's to their own. They broadcast recorded messages from President Bush and British Prime Minister Blair, aimed at the Iraqi people. President Bush, in his statement, said, "The nightmare that Saddam Hussein has brought to your nation will soon be over."[15]

The CPA took steps to create its own communication channels. Before the war, the Pentagon gave a contract to the U.S.-owned Scientific Applications International Corporation (SAIC) to manage its media in Iraq. SAIC is a San Diego–based company that specializes in advanced technologies for the Pentagon, but had no experience in the media field. SAIC took over some existing Iraqi facilities, created an FM radio station and a TV station and began publishing a newspaper called *al Sabah*.

The CPA's "Iraq Media Network" (IMN) television channel at first faced difficulties because the existing facilities were in bad repair, to some extent because of American bombing. When it finally went on the air with four hours in the evening on May 13, 2003, its programs were regarded as uninteresting by the Iraqi public, who had eagerly anticipated a significant improvement in television now that Saddam was gone and the Americans had taken over. IMN's Iraqi TV Director Ahmad Rikabi resigned, criticizing the American managers, and a newsreader also quit over CPA editorial policy, saying the Iraqi people were "not as simple-minded as they

believe." The CPA's own surveys showed that Iraqis preferred to watch Arab satellite channels such as al Jazeera or al Arabiya. Iraqis also watched the Iranian TV channel al Alam coming from outside Iraq, which carried considerable material critical of the United States. It broadcast in Arabic twenty-four hours a day, with interesting news and commentary, on a signal that was clearly received by both terrestrial and satellite transmission. Iraqis preferred it to the CPA's TV channel which they said was too "stodgy" in style and too much like a government-owned station. One report said it was considered the Pentagon's Pravda.[16]

In January 2004, the Pentagon switched contractors to the Harris Corporation of Florida to manage its media operations. Harris subcontracted with the Lebanese Broadcasting Corporation (LBC) to manage IMN television, which had by then been renamed "al Iraqiyya." Some Iraqis criticized al Iraqiyya's programs as being Lebanese rather than Iraqi in tone and content.[17] The dean of media studies at Baghdad University said, "Everyone is watching al Jazeera and other Arab TV stations. There is a war of information going on and the Americans have not been able to fill the gap. Al Jazeera is not intentionally distorting the facts—it's just rushing into exciting news and making quick conclusions. But at the same time, Americans want to hide things."[18] A U.S. government–sponsored viewer survey, in October 2003, found that fewer than one-third of the Iraqi public with satellite TV said they depended on IMN television for news, while 37 percent preferred al Arabiya and 26 percent al Jazeera. Of those Iraqis with no satellite capabilities, a slight majority (59 percent) preferred IMN TV while many watched the Iranian Arabic-language station.[19]

One public diplomacy professional concluded that al Iraqiyya was a failure because it started with the burden of being a CPA-owned channel that Iraqis expected to be of high quality, but it turned out to be not very good because the contractors had no experience, and the subcontractor provided poor program material.[20]

At the Coalition Provisional Authority, it was recognized that for their newspaper *al Sabah* to have credibility, it had to include some criticism of the CPA and report at least some bad news such as electricity shortages, so that it would not seem to be a typical Arab government propaganda organ. At the same time, there was a need to encourage Iraqis to believe that things would improve, so there was a fine line between being credible and encouraging. Some people in the CPA thought the CPA-sponsored media should present happy news, stress that democracy and prosperity were coming, and ignore stories about long lines of cars at the gas pumps. Others wanted the press to be free. The *al Sabah* editor, Ismail Zahir, eventually quarreled with the CPA leadership; he resigned and founded his own newspaper, *al Sabah al Jadid*.[21] As one participant said later, direct control of some Iraqi media was badly mismanaged and there was some tension

between two goals of doing an information program and creating an in-dependent Iraqi media.[22]

## Stratcom

The CPA established a special media Strategic Communications (Strat-com) Unit to monitor the reporting and commentary in all media relating to the occupation of Iraq. In some ways this resembled an American pub-lic diplomacy operation because one of its purposes was to enable the U.S. government to provide information on U.S. Iraq policy to the world. But it was different because it was a short-term measure during the occupation, and its primary task was to take care of the Western press corps and pro-mote U.S. media coverage that was supportive of the president's mission. Its work was 90 percent focused on the U.S. media and only 10 percent on others.[23] Stratcom compiled a "truth matrix" showing fact versus Arab media allegation, and drafted guidance for the briefers whenever they spot-ted an error or lie. Stratcom also put out information that the CPA wanted disseminated, such as development and humanitarian assistance being pro-vided to the Iraqi people, and successes on the military front, but its tar-get audience for this was primarily the American media and public.[24] PAOs outside of Iraq had to depend on what Defense Department officials were putting out in Washington and Baghdad about Iraq and American policy related to Iraq.

Stratcom supported the American briefers, who normally met with the press on a daily basis. The usual briefers were a senior U.S. military offi-cer, Brigadier Mark Kimmitt, and a civilian spokesman, Dan Senor, former spokesman for Energy Secretary Spencer Abraham. They answered ques-tions from Arab as well as non-Arab reporters, and frequently made state-ments based on Stratcom monitoring reports to correct errors and distortions in the media. They occasionally invited an Iraqi briefer to join them, but as one American observer commented, it would have been more effective and given the Coalition an Iraqi face to have Iraqi representatives of the Interim Government regularly participate in the briefings rather than confine the exercise usually to two Americans.[25]

One experienced public diplomacy officer concluded that the informa-tion program was being very badly done because it was in the hands of ideologues assigned by DOD and the White House whose only purpose was to present a rosy picture of Iraq to the American media. Moreover, many of them had only contempt for Iraqis, who knew it and they there-fore reacted negatively to American arrogance by resisting everything the Americans tried to do. In private conversations among Iraqis, even senior Iraqi officials who had a vested interest in the United States often spoke in pejorative terms about Americans they had to deal with, calling them by

the common epithet "donkeys" (hameer). On the other hand, they did not want the Americans to leave just now because they were concerned about security.[26]

## Iraqi Media

From the start of the occupation, the CPA allowed locally controlled media to emerge, which also provided competition to the CPA-controlled media. Shortly after Saddam was toppled, Iraqi merchants began selling satellite dishes, many of which they had fashioned out of local materials plus small components which they imported. This was the biggest growth market in the first days of occupation, so that within only a few months many people had access to Arab satellite television including al Jazeera. Satellite dishes, which had been illegal under Saddam, suddenly flooded into the market and were bought by many people eager to have access to the world unfiltered by Saddam's controls. By March 2004, an estimated one-third of all Iraqi households had satellite access. During the first 12 months of occupation, reportedly more than 200 newspapers, 20 (small) television stations, and many radio stations appeared.[27]

Despite more than thirty years of strict controls over the media by Saddam Hussein, and the pervading police state mentality, the Iraqi journalists very quickly showed they knew what a free press was supposed to do. A few Ba'athi loyalists wrote nasty things in their newspapers about the Americans, but many were reasonable. To maintain access to American sources, they had to cope with very annoying security checks, including body searches, but they came to the Green Zone where the CPA was located to attend press conferences, and asked fair questions.[28]

The CPA also took steps to restrict some Iraqi media that it believed were inciting violence. For example, in September 2003, it closed al Mustaqilla newspaper, and in March 2004 it suspended al Hawza newspaper for sixty days. These American actions against the media angered some Iraqis. The action against al Hawza brought thousands of supporters of the cleric Muqtada al Sadr into the streets in protest, since the paper was one of his channels of communication.[29]

## Normalizing Public Diplomacy in Iraq

Media in the Arab world reported in detail on the Iraq situation as it unfolded, and Arab commentators increasingly criticized the Americans for mishandling the occupation of Iraq. PAOs in the various Arab countries tried to stress the positive aspects of the Iraq invasion, arguing that the removal of Saddam Hussein from power was a significant benefit that the United States had brought to the Iraqi people and the world. The Arabs acknowledged that Saddam's removal was a benefit, but they pointed out

that it had cost a large number of Iraqi lives, and that the occupation was not bringing stability and prosperity. (The CPA and the Pentagon refused to give out numbers of Iraqis killed or wounded.)

Washington sought to portray the opposition as mostly foreign elements but it soon became clear that the majority of its participants were Iraqis, motivated to a degree by nationalist feeling against foreign occupation. Arab media had plenty of material from American and international press sources to use to portray the suffering of the Iraqi people under the American-led occupation. When the story of mistreatment of Iraqi detainees at Abu Ghraib prison broke in the United States in the spring of 2004, the photos of their humiliating treatment at the hands of Americans were carried by Arab media repeatedly. The U.S.-led major military moves into Falluja in 2004, and into the area of the Holy City of Najaf, plus the daily skirmishes, were reported in graphic detail by Arab media as they happened. One incident in Falluja in November 2004, for example, involving an American soldier killing a wounded Iraqi, that was filmed and broadcast worldwide, enraged many Iraqis and led to a new wave of hostile Arab media editorials.[30]

The very few State Department public diplomacy officers assigned to Iraq during the occupation faced extraordinary difficulties. Their biggest obstacle was the continuing violence in Baghdad and other areas, directed mostly at the American occupiers and at Iraqis helping the occupiers. Security in Baghdad confined the American staff essentially to the Green Zone, which had tight security, and they mostly had to meet Iraqis there. American security officers refused to allow them to visit some university campuses, including Baghdad University's liberal arts college and Iraq's second most important university, because they were close to where much of the insurgency was taking place.[31] They were able to carry out a modest educational exchanges effort, sending a few Iraqi students and professionals to America. An Iraqi Fulbright student said, in 2004, of his experience in America: "From what I have observed in American society, in terms of political and social change . . . I think I need to be an evolutionary leader not a revolutionary one. . . . I have a dream to see Iraq and other Middle Eastern leaders advocating change not through bloodshed, violence and hatred, but by advocating peace and love."[32]

Because of security problems, it was also difficult to contribute to understanding or analyzing Iraqi public opinion, except through some summary reports on the daily Iraqi press prepared by a Foreign Service National working in the Green Zone. What was known otherwise about public opinion came from a series of polls conducted separately by CPA contractors.[33]

Despite security problems, one young public diplomacy officer who knew some Arabic worked with local Iraqi staff and reached out to newly emerged newspapers, managing to establish rapport with the press quite effectively. Another public diplomacy professional, a fluent Arabic speaker,

gave interviews to the media in Arabic. For example, he briefed the press on meetings with leaders of the Muslim Ulama Council, an organization of Sunni clerics who control 3,000 mosques, and stressed that the embassy encouraged their participation in the political process. He also arranged to send carefully selected Iraqi religious leaders to the United States on International Visitor Grants, and although some embassy officers wanted to send only moderate leaders, he insisted that the group include some hardliners who were more of a problem for the United States.[34]

Some public diplomacy officers worked in the Iraqi provinces. For example, Hugh Geogehagan, assigned to al Anbar Province to work on civilian affairs developing democracy, could only leave the heavily guarded American compound to do his job carrying a weapon, wearing protective armor, and traveling in a military convoy. He nevertheless managed to undertake some local democracy-building programs and organize local elections.[35]

And John Berry, who worked in Shia-dominated Karbala Province, also had to devote most of his time to dealing with the issue of democracy. No one brought up Israel and Palestine or any of the issues PAOs had to deal with in other Arab countries, because Iraqis were totally focused inward on their own problems. He met and talked with hundreds of Iraqis of all types, including Muslim zealots. Since he had done extensive graduate research on Shiite Islam, and was fluent in classical Arabic, he could hold his own in a discussion where Koranic references were used, and he knew when they were being misused. In discussing democracy, he stressed several points relevant to the situation. Because Iraq had been highly centralized for decades, he stressed that citizens everywhere should be proactive and exercise their rights. But since the Shia would be a majority in the future national parliament, he also explained that democracy means respect for the minority. He told the men and women that Iraqi women could organize themselves politically, and he quoted the Koran in support of women's rights. Berry organized town hall meetings, and he appeared on Iraqi television discussing democracy in Arabic. He hired thirty university professors to translate into Arabic a set of American books relevant to Iraq's interests, like the *Federalist Papers* or Plato's *Republic*, and he set up Karbala's first public library. Most of the Iraqis responded favorably.[36]

Several experienced public diplomacy professionals serving in Iraq found that the occupation badly tarnished America's image. One of them realized that some Americans unintentionally evoked considerable hostility from the Iraqi population by their insensitivity to the local culture. Young American soldiers in Iraq often manhandled Iraqis and generally treated them with contempt. They used insults and profanity in English that they assumed Iraqis didn't understand, but many did, and most understood the negative body language. The few military personnel who took the trouble and had the opportunity to befriend Iraqis found it paid off. With so few

culturally sensitive, Arabic-speaking officers, our public diplomacy efforts in Iraq have been handicapped.[37]

## Broadcasting

The absence of the VOA Arabic Service, replaced by Radio Sawa, hurt the public diplomacy effort in Iraq, since Arabic-speaking listeners no longer had the extensive and serious news and public affairs programming that VOA Arabic had provided. Before and during the war, Radio Free Iraq provided excellent and comprehensive news and public affairs programs, that provided accurate information about Iraq and the world, but RFI was intended only for Iraqis. RFI continued during the occupation to provide trusted and professional news service. It was, however, discontinued after the occupation, apparently on the grounds that the surrogate function was no longer needed. Its annual budget of $2.6 million was first reduced to $1 million in 2003 and then in 2004 it was cancelled altogether.[38] Some of RFI's staff went over to Radio Sawa.

In 2004, the Broadcasting Board of Governors launched al Hurra, a new U.S. government–sponsored television channel in Arabic, intended to compete with al Jazeera and the other new Arab satellite TV channels. Al Hurra started with previously used material that was subtitled or dubbed into Arabic. It included many cultural programs such as fashion and cooking shows, that were irrelevant to audience interests, but it also had thirty-five correspondents and stringers in Iraq during the occupation.[39]

The Broadcasting Board of Governors boasts that al Hurra and Radio Sawa have been successful, but most Arab observers and specialists in Middle Eastern affairs disagree, saying the efforts are not at all competitive against the existing electronic media that are controlled and managed by and for Arabs, and that instead more should be done to get American voices on the latter.[40] According to one public diplomacy professional, al Hurra has yet to find its vocation in the crowded world of Arab satellite television broadcasting. In his view, al Hurra's mission should not be to duplicate the news coverage of other stations, but to become the platform for advocates of reform, democratization, the rights of women and minorities, and similar issues both in the region and in the United States.[41] One Arabic-speaking American scholar who looked closely at actual programs demonstrated that al Jazeera does that better than al Hurra on these issues, and even covers American news better.[42]

Many Arab viewers of al Hurra regard it as a Lebanese channel because so many of its personnel are Lebanese and the program sounds Lebanese. Also, oversight is weak because there is no mechanism for independent review of programs by Arabic speakers as VOA had had. The Arabs expected an up-to-date, modern TV station that was objective but they were disappointed, and polls show al Hurra considerably behind other Arabic channels such as al Jazeera.

## The Al Jazeera Issue

During the war in Afghanistan in the winter of 2001–2002, when al Jazeera television carried statements by Usama bin Ladin, Washington became concerned about its impact on the Arab public. In the spring of 2004, Washington officials again became concerned because of its coverage of the U.S. invasion and occupation of Iraq. On April 27, 2004, when Qatari Foreign Minister Shaikh Hamid bin Jassim bin Jabir was in Washington, Secretary of State Colin Powell complained to him that al Jazeera was inciting Arab audiences to violence against U.S. troops and their allies in the Iraqi government, and this hampered cordial U.S.–Qatari relations. State Department spokesman Richard Boucher said, "We have very deep concerns about al Jazeera's broadcasts because again and again we find inaccurate, false, wrong reports that are, we think, designed to be inflammatory." Secretary of Defense Rumsfeld publicly accused al Jazeera of "vicious, inaccurate and inexcusable" reporting, and other U.S. officials in Iraq said that al Jazeera falsely accused U.S. forces of deliberately attacking Iraqi civilians.[43]

The Iraqi Governing Council complained that al Jazeera and al Arabiya gave publicity to the insurgents and Saddam. The council punished both channels on several occasions, temporarily denying them access to the council, or use of the satellite uplink, or by closing their offices.[44] Al Jazeera and al Arabiya were periodically restricted in one way or another by the Iraqi authorities even after the end of occupation, but both found ways to continue to cover the news inside Iraq, even when their reporters were banned, by the use of stringers and cooperative agreements with other news channels. Al Jazeera in particular remained a thorn in the side of the Iraqi authorities, as it was for most Arab regimes. Many Arabs who liked the news coverage of al Jazeera and al Arabiya regarded these actions as American-inspired because they saw the council as a puppet of the United States.

By the time of the Iraq War, television in Arabic had become a very important communication channel. An opinion survey conducted in March and June 2004 in five Arab countries found that television was the most important news source in all of them, and that satellite television was widely available in most of them (see Table 5).[45]

Yet the same survey did "not find compelling evidence that al-Jazeera and the other Arab satellite channels dictate how Arabs think and feel. Rather, individuals glean information from a variety of sources and assess them in conjunction with their own values, beliefs and interests to form attitudes. . . . Unfavorable attitudes toward U.S. foreign policy, for instance, are not produced by specific media coverage."[46]

American officials therefore faced the challenge of deciding how far to go to permit and support free speech in Arab media, and how much to protest and act against what it regarded as specific media transgressions.

Table 5: Television Is the Most Important Arab News Source

|  | TV is the most important news source | Satellite TV is available at home |
|---|---|---|
| Jordan | 81 | 58 |
| Syria | 78 | NA |
| Lebanon | 72 | 85 |
| Palestine | 75 | 84 |
| Egypt | 70 | 26 |

Clearly, the media situation in Iraq was entirely different under American occupation from what it was under Saddam Hussain. But some Arabs were surprised that when Americans were in charge, they did not allow the complete freedom of the press that they espouse at home. They were also surprised that the media controlled by the U.S. government were unimpressive.

## Independent Iraq

On June 8, 2004, the UN Security Council passed a resolution endorsing Iraq's return to sovereignty. It called for an interim Iraqi regime to govern between July and December 2005, a new constitution, and then a full-fledged elected government taking over on January 1, 2006.

The U.S.-led occupation of Iraq ended formally on June 28, 2004. The United States reopened its embassy in Baghdad, with a public diplomacy section staffed by the State Department, a more normal arrangement. But the United States also maintained a huge military presence of nearly 150,000 troops in Iraq, and some DOD personnel from Stratcom remained to work on information dissemination. The Americans continued to control al Iraqiyya television until April 1, 2005, when it became an independent Iraqi station. Because of this presence, and the fact that the United States had appointed the interim government, most Arabs saw the arrangement as a façade for continued American control. State did assign experienced public diplomacy officers to the embassy but they faced considerable challenges.

American policy in Iraq continued to generate significant criticism from the Arab public in the region. A poll taken in Jordan and Morocco by the University of Jordan in February and March 2004 found that the public in both countries thought the Iraqi people were worse off than before the invasion (Jordan 61:8, Morocco 70:25). Large majorities in both countries (69:22 in Jordan, 48:22 in Morocco) said the United States was not just misinformed about weapons of mass destruction but had deliberately lied

about them.[47] (This view was reinforced in May 2005 when the *Sunday Times of London* reported the "Downing Street Memo," a previously secret British document that said Bush had decided by July 2002 to go to war and was fixing the intelligence and facts to fit the policy.)[48] Another opinion poll conducted in five Arab countries in March and June 2004 revealed substantial disagreement with official U.S. claims about Iraq. Majorities in all five (Egypt, Jordan, Saudi Arabia, Lebanon, and the Palestinian territories) said the U.S. intervention in Iraq would not provide the Iraqis with a better standard of living than they had under Saddam Hussain, and would not turn Iraq into a model for democracy in the region. Majorities in all five also said that the U.S.-led war would enhance Israel's security, which was not from the Arab point of view a valid reason for war.[49]

And a June 2004, Zogby International poll taken in five Arab countries revealed that approval of America's policy in Iraq was almost nil. The unfavorable/favorable ratings were 97:1 in Saudi Arabia, 98:1 in Morocco, 91:4 in the UAE, 93:4 in Lebanon, and 78:2 in Jordan. When asked what America could do to improve its image in the Arab world, the second or third most common reply in all five countries was to get out of Iraq (the first was related to Israel or justice).[50]

Public diplomacy professionals throughout the Arab world therefore had to deal with criticism of America's Iraq policy and they did so in various ways. To cite one example, in Kuwait the Information Officer gave an interview on June 21, 2004, to two of Kuwait's principal daily newspapers, *al Ra'i al Aam* and *al Siyaasa*. The reporters challenged him with sensitive questions regarding extremism in the Gulf, and asserted that the American intervention in Iraq had been the cause of recent terrorist attacks in Saudi Arabia against Saudi citizens. The IO responded that it was in fact the growth of extremist ideologies and groups in the region, not the situation in Iraq, that was the cause of these attacks, and he indicated that the Arabs themselves had some responsibility in dealing with the problem.[51]

Meanwhile, U.S. public diplomacy faced other challenges and the next chapter will examine some of them.

# 12

# Democratic Reform and Other Issues

## PUBLIC DIPLOMACY AFTER THE IRAQ WAR

The invasion and occupation of Iraq in 2003 had a profound impact on U.S.–Arab relations and on America's image among Arabs. But that image was also affected by other issues as well, the most important one being President Bush's call for democracy in the Arab world.

### Calls for Arab Democracy

During the occupation of Iraq, Washington shifted its rationale for the war after the United States failed to find any weapons of mass destruction (WMDs) in the country. The Bush administration had argued before the war that Saddam had them and that they posed a "grave and growing danger." But when the inspectors sent in by the United States found none, Washington began emphasizing other reasons for the war. American officials stressed that the United States had done Iraq and the world a favor by removing Saddam. They also stressed the importance of bringing democracy to Iraq, and said it would spread democracy throughout the Middle East region. The Arabs were puzzled by this shift. They had assumed that the United States, with all of its sophisticated technology and its huge intelligence agency capability, surely would have known the truth about Saddam's WMDs. When they did not materialize, this reinforced the Arab conviction that Bush's ulterior motive all along was to seize Iraqi oil and help Israel.

President Bush had only hinted at the democracy theme before the war, in his West Point speech in June 2002 and his UN address in September 2002. On the eve of the war he talked about democracy in Iraq and Palestine. He said: "We'll help that nation [Iraq] to build a just government, after decades of brutal dictatorship. The form and leadership of that government is for the Iraqi people to choose. Anything they choose will be better than the misery and torture and murder they have known under Saddam Hussein."[1] He said, "Success in Iraq could also begin a new stage for Middle Eastern peace, and set in motion progress towards a truly democratic Palestinian state. Old patterns of conflict in the Middle East can be broken. . . . America will seize every opportunity in pursuit of peace. And the end of the present regime in Iraq would create such an opportunity."[2] But the democracy goal was clearly secondary to the primary one of getting rid of Iraq's WMDs.

Then in November 2003, when the occupation of Iraq was going badly, President Bush greatly expanded on the freedom theme and enunciated a broad policy when he said: "The establishment of a free Iraq at the heart of the Middle East will be a watershed event in the global democratic revolution. . . . Therefore, the United States has adopted a new policy, a forward strategy of freedom in the Middle East. . . . We believe that liberty is the design of nature; we believe that liberty is the direction of history." He pointedly mentioned specific Arab countries, praising Morocco, Bahrain, Oman, Kuwait, and Jordan, but criticizing leaders in Palestine and Egypt, saying: "Governments across the Middle East and North Africa are beginning to see the need for change" and "democracy is . . . the only path to national success and dignity."[3]

This was new. No previous president had given the spread of democracy such high priority and made such specific criticisms of domestic practices of friendly governments. By the end of 2003, President Bush had clearly endorsed a theory that domestic Middle East political change was in the U.S. national interest, and moreover that American values were universal and should be promoted by Arabs. Then after his reelection to a second term, he made democracy a priority in his inaugural address and his 2005 State of the Union speech. Talk of the WMD threat and even of terrorism was being replaced by this new theme. President Bush's "Greater Middle East Initiative" of 2004, renamed "Broader Middle East and North Africa Initiative," intended to support political, economic, and social reform in the Arab world, became a priority for Washington.

## Other Issues

Meanwhile, other developments also affected the American image in the Arab world. The U.S. presidential election campaign that was in the news during most of 2004 was covered regularly by Arab media, includ-

ing the debates and the party conventions. This display of America's democratic process tended to enhance America's reputation, despite the fact that all candidates expressed support for Israel and few mentioned the Palestinians. The growing dissatisfaction among the Arab public with their own governments for various failures and lack of transparency contrasted sharply with news coming out of America. As one American diplomat commented privately, disseminating information about the U.S. election was a better way to promote democracy than using force in Iraq.[4]

The revelations in the spring of 2004 about American abuses of Iraqi prisoners in Abu Ghraib, and later news of abuses of prisoners at Guantanamo, followed in 2005 by American news reports of American military personnel mishandling the Koran, all reinforced negative images of American behavior. But in May 2004, when congressional committees subjected Secretary of Defense Donald Rumsfeld and other senior officials to harsh questioning about these abuses, Arab media including Arab television gave full coverage to the internal debate and self-criticism in the United States. This public display of congressional criticism of the administration mitigated the negative impact of prison abuses somewhat by showing the role of the free press in the United States and demonstrating that the American system has ways of holding officials accountable.

## Arab Political Developments

In January 2005, elections took place in Iraq. Also in early 2005, elections took place in Palestine following the death of Yassir Arafat, and in Saudi Arabia. In Lebanon, when former Prime Minister Rafiq Hariri was killed, huge popular demonstrations against Syria and for democracy took place. Many Lebanese had for years resented the presence of Syrian military and intelligence personnel on their soil, but the Hariri assassination catalyzed it and led to such a huge popular outburst that Syria was compelled to withdraw. Pro-democracy demonstrations also broke out in Egypt and Kuwait, that led to some changes in electoral rules in both countries. President Bush welcomed these events. In March he said: "The chances of democratic progress in the broader Middle East have seemed frozen for decades. Yet, at last, clearly and suddenly, the thaw has begun." He claimed some credit for the changes and said the democratic movement spreading in the Middle East was essential to defeating terrorism. "It should be clear that the best antidote to radicalism and terror is the tolerance kindled in free societies." He warned Syria and Iran against thwarting the "momentum of freedom." He said Egypt should allow "freedom of assembly, multiple candidates, free access by those candidates to the media and the right to form political parties."[5]

Support for democracy was potentially a good theme for PAOs in the Arab world, given the fact that in many countries there was discontent with

Arab leadership and Arabs generally admired American democracy. PAOs sought to link the events in Iraq and elsewhere in the region to Bush's policy agenda, but the Arab reaction to his new initiative in support of democracy was mixed. The president's statements had helped give the issue more public prominence in the Arab world, but it was unclear whether they would lead to genuine reform. Arab governments that had been friendly with the United States were uncomfortable at being singled out for criticism, and resented this interference in their internal affairs. Egypt's President Mubarak and Kuwait's prime minister said so publicly. But because they wanted to maintain good relations with Washington they felt they could not oppose Bush's new democracy initiative too directly. The Arab leaders met and issued a declaration that claimed they supported reform, but the specifics were sufficiently qualified so that they were not obligated to do anything new.[6]

Even Arab opposition leaders and reformer groups had mixed feelings. They were, on the one hand, pleased that the American president was now calling for democracy but on the other hand, embarrassed to have President Bush as an ally, because they were very critical of his policies toward Palestine, Iraq, and other issues. Some reformers pointed out that they had been working for change for decades, and had made some progress slowly, and Bush's focus on it was welcome but he had only belatedly discovered the issue.[7] Others said that the popular uprisings in Georgia in 2003 and in the Ukraine in 2004 had been more of an inspiration to the Arab public than Bush had been, and the Arab events had local causes (the Palestinian election because of Arafat's death, the Lebanese uprising because of Hariri's assassination). Reformers were also unsure that Bush's pronouncements meant a real change or that the United States would impose it. For example, polls taken in Morocco in February and March 2004 showed that 51 percent of the public in Morocco believed that democracy was a Western way of doing things that could not work well in Iraq, while only 39 percent believed it could work there.[8]

When President Bush appointed Condoleezza Rice as the new secretary of state, she expanded on the reform theme in the Arab world, saying that the Middle East was not stable and would not be stable so change was imperative, adding: "And when you know that the status quo is no longer defensible, then you have to be willing to move in another direction." She admitted she did not know what the outcome would be. This alarmed some Arabs, who warned of anarchy; one liberal democrat Arab said the United States seems to be supporting chaos and instability as a pretext for democracy "But people would rather live under undemocratic rule than in the chaotic atmosphere of Iraq for example which the Americans tout as a model." Another one said that Arab societies are too fragile for the kind of rapid and unchecked change Rice seems to favor. Extremists could come to power or societies could collapse. He said it appeared to have links with

a trend in right-wing Israeli thinking that favors destabilizing Arab societies.[9]

## Arab Public Opinion

Despite the Bush administration's shift from using force to talking about democracy, Arab overall opinion of the United States continued to deteriorate. Between April 2002 and June 2004, opinion polls taken by Zogby International in six Arab countries showed declines in overall public approval ratings for the United States, even though the governments in those countries—Saudi Arabia, Jordan, Morocco, Lebanon, Egypt, and the UAE—have excellent relations with the United States and the first four were among America's oldest Arab friends. Favorable ratings in Egypt and Saudi Arabia fell to 4 percent and 2 percent, respectively, while in Morocco, the UAE, Jordan, and Lebanon they were 11 percent, 14 percent, 15 percent, and 20 percent, respectively (see Table 6).[10]

By 2005, American prestige in the Arab world had reached an all-time low point, with overall favorable ratings approaching zero in many countries.[11]

But a closer look at the Zogby polling data for 2004 shows that these negative attitudes were driven by what Zogby called "Arab anger and frustration with American policy, especially toward what was seen as its 'unbalanced policy in the Israeli–Palestinian conflict'." Zogby concluded that "what ultimately determined how Arabs viewed America was how they saw America treating Arab people." This poll asked Arabs in the six Arab countries, "What is your first thought when you hear 'America'?" In four of the six (Egypt, Morocco, Saudi Arabia, and the UAE) the most common answer by very large majorities was "unfair foreign policy." In the other two countries that was the second most common answer behind "imperialistic" (in Jordan) and "oil interest" (in Lebanon). Asked what was the worst thing about America, the most common answer in Egypt, Lebanon,

Table 6: Favorable Approval of the United States, 2002–2004

| Country | 2004 favorable/ unfavorable | | 2002 favorable/ unfavorable | |
|---|---|---|---|---|
| Morocco | 11 | 88 | 38 | 61 |
| Saudi Arabia | 4 | 94 | 12 | 87 |
| Jordan | 15 | 78 | 34 | 61 |
| Lebanon | 20 | 69 | 26 | 70 |
| UAE | 14 | 73 | 11 | 87 |
| Egypt | 2 | 98 | 15 | 76 |

Table 7: Attitudes on American Products and Policies, June 2004

|  | Morocco | | Jordan | | UAE | |
|---|---|---|---|---|---|---|
|  | fav | unfav | fav | unfav | fav | unfav |
| Science and technology | 90 | 8 | 83 | 13 | 84 | 12 |
| Products | 73 | 24 | 61 | 35 | 63 | 34 |
| Education | 61 | 16 | 59 | 29 | 63 | 23 |
| Movies and television | 60 | 37 | 56 | 41 | 52 | 44 |
| Freedom and democracy | 53 | 41 | 57 | 40 | 39 | 53 |
| People | 59 | 29 | 52 | 39 | 46 | 35 |
| Policy toward Arabs | 4 | 90 | 8 | 89 | 7 | 87 |
| Policy toward Palestinians | 3 | 93 | 7 | 89 | 5 | 90 |
| Policy on terrorism | 13 | 82 | 21 | 75 | 9 | 84 |
| Policy toward Iraq | 1 | 98 | 2 | 78 | 4 | 91 |

and the UAE was that Washington follows an unfair Middle East policy, and in Morocco and Jordan it was that the United States murders Arabs (foreign policy was the second most common answer).[12]

It is important to note that majorities in the Arab world in fact have positive opinions about most things American except our foreign policy. For example, a poll taken in June 2004 showed that public opinion in Morocco, Jordan, and the United Arab Emirates, three Arab countries whose governments have had excellent relations with the United States, was very positive about many aspects of America except our foreign policy (see Table 7).[13]

Public opinion surveys conducted by the University of Jordan in March and June of 2004 in Jordan, Egypt, Syria, Lebanon, and the Palestinian Authority, further showed that anti-American attitudes in those countries are driven by perceptions of American foreign policies in the region, not by religious or cultural factors, and not by a clash of civilizations or the "al Jazeera factor." It said: "This study finds that Arabs do not 'hate' the US and UK for 'who they are' or for the cultural values they hold. Negative sentiments are being fueled, rather, buy 'what they do'—that is, for specific policies and the impact these policies have upon the Arab world. . . . this study finds that the Arab public disagrees profoundly with the foreign policies of the US . . . and that this disagreement is at the root of anti-American, and by extension, anti-Western sentiments that permeate the region." On specific foreign policy issues, majorities of respondents expressed views that were directly contradictory to those espoused by the U.S. government. The percentages of people polled who said yes to the specific statements about U.S. policy are shown in Table 8 (in which American officials would say

Table 8: Arab Perceptions of U.S. Policies, 2004

---

Question: "Do you agree with the following statement?"

A. The United States aims to dominate countries by offering them aid.
B. The United States always violates human rights in the world.
C. Force was not at all justified in Iraq.
D. The U.S. handling of the Arab–Israeli conflict is satisfactory.
E. The "Road Map" is a just solution to the Arab–Israeli conflict.
F. The United States always supports the practice of democracy.

| | A | B | C | D | E | F |
|---|---|---|---|---|---|---|
| Jordan | 98 | 80 | 81 | 5 | 8 | 25 |
| Syria | 95 | 78 | 80 | 1 | 6 | 2 |
| Lebanon | 60 | 50 | 48 | 5 | 12 | 35 |
| Palestine | 96 | 70 | 80 | 1 | 6 | 10 |
| Egypt | 95 | 72 | 70 | 2 | 36 | 18 |

---

no to the first three and yes to the last three statements).[14] These conclusions conform generally with conclusions reached by opinion research experts in the U.S. government.[15]

One reason for America's low prestige is that Arabs are suspicious that Washington has ulterior motives. A Zogby International poll in February and March 2004, which asked about America's true motives in the world, found that 71 percent of the public in Jordan believed they were to control Middle Eastern oil, 70 percent said they were to protect Israel, 61 percent said to dominate the world, and 53 percent said to target Muslim governments. The same question in Morocco revealed similar numbers: 63 percent, 54 percent, 60 percent, and 46 percent.[16]

## Recommendations for Public Diplomacy Reform

Since the first days after the 9/11 attacks, there has been a great deal of talk by members of Congress and by private organizations about the need to improve America's public diplomacy. In Congress, Representative Henry Hyde, the Republican Chairman of the House of Representatives Committee on International Affairs, and Representative Tom Lantos of California, its ranking Democrat, proposed a Freedom Promotion Act that was intended to mandate changes that would improve the State Department's public diplomacy structure. Republican Senators Chuck Hegel and Richard Lugar as well as Democrat Senator Joe Biden have repeatedly urged the administration to do more in public diplomacy.

Several government agencies have made studies and issued reports on public diplomacy. In October 2001, within weeks of the 9/11 attack, the Defense Science Board issued a report on interagency coordination, and in September 2004 its Task Force on Strategic Communication issued another report. In 2002, the U.S. Advisory Commission on Public Diplomacy issued a report on structural reform. In June 2003, Congress created an Advisory Group on Public Diplomacy for the Arab and Muslim World, headed by a distinguished retired Foreign Service Officer, Edward Djerejian. Their October 2003 report advocated substantially increased funding and measures to revive programs that had been successful in the past. The July 2004 report of the "9/11 Commission" called on the government to increase efforts in broadcasting, exchanges, and library programs; and in April 2005, the U.S. government's Accountability Office presented a report to the Congress that criticized the lack of a national communication strategy. Private organizations also joined the discussion. The Council on Foreign Relations issued reports in June 2002 and June 2003, calling for reform. In April and May 2003, the Heritage Foundation issued reports; in July the Center for the Study of the Presidency published one on U.S.–Muslim Communications, and in January 2004 the Brookings Institution published its report on communicating with the Arab world. The Public Diplomacy Council issued one report on public diplomacy in December 2004 and another in January 2005.[17]

All of these reports called for increased funding and most stressed that public diplomacy requires listening to foreign opinion and conducting a dialogue rather than a monologue. PAOs in the Arab world applauded those suggestions. A few reports recommended some form of privatization for public diplomacy, but that is based on a misunderstanding of public diplomacy since it is by definition a government function, although it has enlisted private individuals for the effort.

Several government agencies also began to focus more on foreign information programs after 9/11. The Defense Department became very active in Iraq with an information program (see Chapter 11), and the U.S. Agency for International Development decided, in September 2004, to establish a new position of "Development Outreach and Communication Officer" to help publicize U.S. assistance efforts abroad, with one at each of its eighty-four missions abroad.[18] But State remained the only agency formally responsible for public diplomacy. The position of undersecretary for that function was filled, after Charlotte Beers's resignation, by Ambassador Margaret Tutwiler, but she remained in it for less than one year and resigned in the summer of 2004. In early 2005, President Bush appointed his longtime advisor Karen Hughes to the position, and his White House personnel director Dina Powell as her deputy.[19] Public diplomacy professionals hoped their appointments would reinvigorate the effort.

## Quiet Public Diplomacy Continues

However, these many studies and reports had little significant practical effect on the work of PAOs in the Arab world. They continued their quiet work with a variety of programs designed to further the interests of the United States by the employment of "soft power," to help reverse the decline in America's prestige among the Arab public. Some of their programs were enhanced by modest funding increases, but most Americans were unaware of their efforts. Following are some examples of the work that PAOs and their staffs in the Arab world continued to undertake during the 2003–2005 period.

First, on a daily basis, they had to devote time to explaining American foreign policy, including on Iraq and the Arab–Israeli conflict, as well as President Bush's calls for democracy. They did that in many ways. For example, in the spring of 2004, two public diplomacy officers in Jordan, one of whom had recently returned from a short-term assignment in Iraq, engaged a group of political science faculty members and students from the university in a heated discussion in which the Jordanians vigorously criticized American policy toward Israel, Iraq, and the Greater Middle East Initiative, Bush's proposal to support reform in the region. The Jordanians expressed deep fears that U.S. policies were encroaching on Arab and Islamic culture and Arab self-determination. The Americans did their best to assure the Jordanians that American intentions were benign. A month later, the American officers invited some of the most outspoken students from that discussion to a workshop at the embassy on the U.S. political system, information resources, and Internet communication, and the Jordanians eagerly participated in it.[20]

In Cairo, Information Officer John Berry discovered that despite the Egyptian–Israeli peace treaty of 1979 and the existence of an Israeli embassy in Cairo, many Egyptian journalists still refused to visit Israel or have any contact with Israelis pending a final peace settlement. John told them that this was unprofessional and self-defeating, because they will never know what is going on in Israel or have a full understanding of the Arab–Israeli problem until they talk with Israelis. But they still refused. They pointed out that the Journalism Syndicate is opposed to contact with Israelis and even if they went to Israel and wrote about it their editors would not print it. Some of them said also that the United States used a boycott of Arafat so criticizing the Egyptian private boycott of Israelis was following a double standard.[21]

In Jordan, in June 2004, USIS held its third annual conference for women journalists. An Arab-American speaker stressed the need for Arab media to reach out to American audiences, to convey an accurate picture of Arab culture and society, and to improve networking and professional

standards. The participants included nearly sixty women from thirteen Arab countries. The PAO included Israelis as well, so the conference also served the purpose of bringing Israelis and Arabs together.[22]

But foreign policy was not the only item on PAOs' agendas. There were many other issues that they focused on, to help build long-term relationships and understanding.

PAOs reported to Washington that they missed the American centers and libraries that had been closed for financial or security reasons because an important instrument of access had been lost. They wanted to find a way to revive it without weakening security. Washington responded by approving the establishment of "American Corners," collections of American books and periodicals placed in local institutions such as universities, where the materials would be available to Arab students and professionals. In 2004, six were opened in five Arab countries: Oman, the UAE, Kuwait, Syria, and Iraq. The problem, however, was that the "American Corners" lacked the vital element of an American presence that had made the American libraries so valuable in the past.[23]

PAOs also asked for more support for English teaching because English lessons were in demand and could be an effective public diplomacy instrument. When Ambassador Margaret Tutwiler was the Undersecretary for Public Diplomacy she approved a large program that she called "Microscholarships" of $1,000 each to "nonelite" young Arabs from disadvantaged sectors of the society to enable them to study English in local institutions. In the first half of 2004, $1.8 million was allocated for this purpose in twelve Arab countries from Morocco to Saudi Arabia, and it affected the lives of more than 1,500 youngsters.[24] This project avoided the post-9/11 visa problems and allowed posts to reach more people because it was much less expensive per person than the usual exchange program.

In Cairo, the USIS staff worked hard to bring classic American theater to Egyptian audiences. They first arranged for American theater director Seth Gordon, of the Cleveland Playhouse, to visit Egypt; then they had Thornton Wilder's classic play *Our Town* translated into classical Arabic by the book translation program, and then into colloquial Arabic for the stage. They raised funds from private Egyptian and American corporate sponsors, auditioned and cast Egyptian actors, had sets and costumes produced locally, and put on the play in Cairo, Ismailia, Minya, and Fayoum. The press section arranged extensive publicity. Despite initial public skepticism as to the embassy's motives, the performances were very well received by the public and the critics.[25]

In 2004, the USIS staff in Cairo offered professional training to Egyptian journalists in several ways. They brought a number of them into their Information Resource Center for "electronic classroom" workshops on use of the Internet to obtain accurate and timely information about the United States, especially from State Department Web sites. They gave grants to

provide English lessons to individual journalists at a local school. And they gave a grant to Georgia State University for a week-long seminar for journalists on how to report on civil society activities.[26]

In Tunisia, the PAO stressed nonpolitical programs. In the spring of 2004, an American professor sponsored by USIS addressed 500 students in a university auditorium on American architecture. They gave him a friendly reception, and when a heckler tried to shout denunciations of American foreign policy, the students persuaded him to leave because they wanted to hear the lecture. In Morocco, the CAO held a workshop for women nongovernmental organization leaders in Oujda, one of Morocco's most marginalized and politically sensitive regions where students are well known for their extremism and hard-line positions. Afterwards there was a meeting with twenty graduate students, members of the Islamic Party of Justice and Development (PJD) in the residence of a PJD parliamentarian. This was the first time that an American officer had spoken to students affiliated with that party, but they were very receptive to hearing presentations by American officials, and it established a productive relationship.[27]

PAOs worked harder to expand their contacts. In the United Arab Emirates, PAO Katherine Van de Vate and Ambassador Marcelle Wahba, both career public diplomacy officers, knew that despite strong government-to-government relations, local public opinion was very critical of U.S. foreign policy. They both made an effort to attend UAE cultural events such as art shows, exhibits, or education conferences, to demonstrate American interest in aspects of UAE other than oil and politics. Arab friends told the ambassador they were pleasantly surprised she would show up at these events when the people are so unhappy with American policy, and the gesture was appreciated. This also illustrates the fact that women public diplomacy officers can achieve successes in the Arab world and overcome gender issues. Both had excellent access to journalists and others who were especially open to both of them as women. Marcelle found that UAE nationals went out of their way to welcome her, and "they let me know it did not matter." She also had access to UAE women, which male American officials never had. In fact, after 9/11 when Arab–American relations deteriorated, being of Arab origin was also an advantage to her because the Arabs believed she understood what they were going through.[28]

In Egypt, PAO Jim Bullock worked to counter hostile or misinformed editors by spending time with them one-on-one, and making sure that his FSNs were fully informed since they were in constant contact with important Egyptians. Also, Jim's Information Officer and his senior FSN met weekly at a coffee house in downtown Cairo with a cross section of intellectuals and journalists, which enabled them to keep abreast of Egyptian thinking and try out their arguments. Jim remained alert to harmful press stories and protested when appropriate. For example, in February 2005, Egypt's largest-circulation daily paper ran a story reporting on *Time*'s Man

of the Year accompanied by photos of President Bush and Adolph Hitler, saying Hitler had earlier been Man of the Year. Jim called on the paper's editor in chief, and said that the juxtaposed photos hurt cordial relations with the United States because readers do not understand that *Time* selects its Man of the Year on the basis of importance, not approval. The editor had visited America on a USIS grant, and he accepted Jim's point. On another occasion Bullock was contacted by an Egyptian professor who had been invited to participate in a TV roundtable on the impact of U.S. military presence in the Middle East. The professor was not a military affairs expert, and she asked the PAO for help in preparing for the roundtable, so he briefed her and showed her appropriate documents. At the roundtable, she presented our policy positions accurately, although she did not always agree with them. Her presentation was much more balanced and better informed than most of the other Egyptian commentators, who tended to be flatly critical of the United States. This is an example of how PAOs often do better using "third-party validators" instead of engaging in direct advocacy.[29]

The CAO in Cairo, Elizabeth Thornhill, was also effective. For example, she provided funding for the American University in Cairo to undertake a Model Arab League program. During the exercise students criticized American policy and some of the CAO's embassy colleagues said the program was a waste of money, but in fact she knew this was a way of expanding USIS contacts with Egyptian students and laying a basis for further dialogue on issues related to the United States and to its policies. Like other public diplomacy professionals, she knew that cultural programs opened doors to target audiences that were otherwise difficult to reach.[30]

All over the Arab world, PAOs and many others recognized the central importance of educational exchange programs in helping to repair Arab–American relations and to restore the American image.

When the State Department's Director of Academic Exchange Programs visited Damascus in 2003, many Syrian officials and academics told him how valuable the exchange program was in maintaining connections between the United States and Syria in a time of continuing political stress. For example, the president of the University of Damascus said, "We Syrians are very anxious to have more American students in this country and more of our students in your country. This is the best way possible of overcoming some of the political disagreements that exist between our nations."[31]

In Riyadh, the PAO secured the cooperation of the Education Ministry and sent more than fifty Saudi religious educators to the United States in groups of eight to ten for periods of three weeks during 2004–2005, where they examined religious education as practiced in the United States. The project was very successful. In Kuwait, the PAO worked with the American nonprofit organization AMIDEAST to arrange for ten Kuwaiti boys

from conservative, poorer, nonelite families to spend four weeks at the Chevron Texaco 2004 English Language Summer Camp in the United States. Parents of several of the boys effusively expressed gratitude for the opportunity their sons had. The event was reported positively in four of five Arabic daily newspapers and two of three English dailies in Kuwait.[32]

In Jordan, the USIS post arranged for Jordanian judges to visit the United States where they learned about American methods of alternative dispute resolution and case management, which they applied when they went back home, resulting in greatly reduced waiting time for the resolution of cases. Also several program alumni wrote books about American case management that have been incorporated into the curricula of Jordanian law schools. The director of Jordan's Judicial Institute told an American official the program has "had benefits on every level—social, economic and investment. People now see that the judiciary is not a closed system; it is a branch of government, which can be improved [and this] leads to greater protection of citizens' rights."[33]

In Tunisia, USIS arranged for a series of visits to the United States by Tunisian business women, who met with American counterparts. One group of fifteen visited Iowa and shadowed American women entrepreneurs; another group of twenty-five worked on business plans, and a third group of sixty exchanged ideas with Americans on such topics as small business loans and binational collaboration.[34]

In Egypt, USIS arranged a series of exchange visits for Egyptian parliamentary staff to do internships in Congress, and return visits to Egypt by congressional staffers. The post also arranged exchange visits for Egyptian educators to learn about civil society institutions in the United States to help them develop training programs for other Egyptians in community service, volunteerism, and conflict resolution. In Damascus the PAO arranged for a group of Syrians to participate in a one-year conflict resolution project managed by Columbia University, which included study of American political, civic, and academic practices, and was designed to promote ongoing communication between Americans and Syrians interested in the subject. And in the Gulf, USIS posts arranged for a group that included Kuwaitis, Omanis, and UAE nationals to visit the University of Michigan's Center for Political Studies to learn about American methods of opinion research, and to develop standardized American-style procedures for use in their countries.[35]

Finally, despite the stagnation of the Arab–Israeli peace process, public diplomacy officers continued to work to bring Arabs and Israelis together under American auspices.

For example, the PAO in Jerusalem arranged for Palestinian media professionals to visit the United States to study American journalism. The Palestinians were part of a group that also included Israeli journalists so they had opportunities to discuss Middle East issues in presenting the news. And a

regional project involving Jordanians, Syrians, Palestinians, Algerians, and UAE nationals provided training in the United States in teaching English as a foreign language, plus curriculum design for civic education. The purpose of this project was not only to improve the quality of English teaching but also to strengthen democratic political practices and to help build networks of educators who were interested in those purposes.[36]

Another public diplomacy project arranged for a group of forty-seven Palestinians, Israelis, Jordanians, and Americans to meet in Aqaba, Jordan, in January 2004, for an advanced workshop on communication and media skills. The seven U.S. participants were Arab-Americans and Jewish Americans. The Middle Eastern participants returned home with improved skills that they used as educators and facilitators in their communities, and they also agreed as a group to pursue several joint projects, including the strengthening of support for tolerance in school textbooks and curricula.[37]

Clearly, most of these programs were not directly related to President Bush's "forward strategy of freedom in the Middle East." But they indirectly helped promote that strategy and other goals by building on the positive Arab view of American democracy that exists as an important element in America's soft power. His forward strategy, however, will also require a strong diplomatic effort, and success will depend heavily on how the Arab governments and people respond. Public diplomacy can play an important role, but as always it is a supporting one.

## 13

# Conclusion

The history and examples presented in this book should have demonstrated that public diplomacy is not simply a matter of providing information to a foreign audience or marketing a product. It is also much more than finding the right words for Washington officials to use in explaining today's foreign policy, although that is important. It is, rather, a complex process that depends not only on Washington officials but also on public diplomacy professionals who live abroad and work out of our embassies, engaging daily with a wide range of people, and managing a variety of programs. They facilitate communication across cultures on American foreign policy and other aspects of our society, to enhance mutual understanding.

This book describes the work of professionals who have been laboring on this mission in Arab countries over the years. Their work is largely unknown to the American public even though they play a vital role in advancing American national interests. Working side by side with traditional diplomat FSOs who focus on government-to-government relations, these public diplomacy officers develop contacts with local editors, academics, and other opinion leaders, to understand their thinking on matters of importance to the United States, and engage them in an ongoing dialogue—listening as well as talking. Based on these encounters, they develop programs that bring Arabs and Americans together in ways that are effective in the local culture, to expand that dialogue. And they help policy makers in Washington understand foreign perceptions that are relevant to American policies and actions.

The revolution in communication technology has resulted in a proliferation of sources of information about America available to Arabs. Today they have access to a large volume of news and comment on the United States through Arab newspapers, radio, television, and the Internet. Arab television has reporters in the United States, and also carries American programs including CNN and Fox News. Some of the information about America is inaccurate, whether because of deliberate distortions, media simplification, simple misunderstanding, or cultural filters. A PAO at an American embassy must therefore compete against many other sources of information about America.

In addition, PAOs today must deal with an unusually high level of Arab criticism directed at U.S. policy, as discussed in this book. PAOs do not make policy, but they can help address misperceptions of our policies, and explain how the U.S. government sees the world. They can provide background and context by explaining the American political process and domestic influences on policy making. They can convey Arab views to Washington policy makers so these views can be taken into account in policy formulation.

The task of public diplomacy professionals, however, extends far beyond foreign policy advocacy. They undertake programs that include exchanges of students and professionals, conferences and workshops, library services, musical and theatrical performances, English teaching, lectures by visiting American experts, videoconferences, and media interviews, on many subjects of mutual interest. Nonpolitical programs broaden the dialogue and help the two societies withstand temporary differences over short-term policy issues. We know through opinion polling that the Arab public admires most aspects of America, and that Arab criticism focuses primarily on foreign policy. The reinforcement of ties in other areas can make an important contribution to American national interests. The American–Arab relationship can weather policy disputes as long as it is based on broader interests. Those interests must be continually reinforced.

The Bush administration has taken some tentative steps to try to address the tensions in American–Arab relations since 9/11, but much more could be done. First, it is vitally important to increase the exchanges of persons in both directions. Firsthand experience is the most effective way to increase understanding across cultures. The U.S. government should make a point of welcoming Arab students and others to the United States. We should send more Americans to Arab countries to learn the Arabic language and to learn about their culture and society. If more American English teachers were sent to the Arab world, for example, it would help reverse the decline in levels of English capability, help prepare Arab students for study in the United States, and give them tools to read American books and periodicals. The American teachers would in turn learn about Arab society. We should also expand the use of videoconferencing between

Arabs and Americans, official and unofficial, to enhance the cross-cultural dialogue using technology now available.

Second, security measures taken in the wake of 9/11 have not been adequately balanced by an effort to protect vital public diplomacy programs that are undermined by those measures. The implementation of much tougher visa regulations has dissuaded many Arab students and professionals from coming to the United States. The great mutual benefit derived from exchanges of persons has diminished. Barriers and security screening procedures erected around embassies and USIS offices and libraries have severely hampered contacts with Arabs. While it is important to implement necessary security measures, ways should be found to make them less onerous so they do not prevent the personal contacts that are the most essential ingredient of a successful public diplomacy program. Visa procedures should be streamlined more and explained better, and the libraries/cultural centers that in the past have been so effective in bringing Americans and Arabs together should be reopened with user-friendly security in place.[1]

Third, we should make better use of the power of broadcasting. The Voice of America Arabic Service should be restored and supported. Television funded by the U.S. government should be made effective through better programming and oversight. We should encourage Americans to participate in discussions on the existing Arab television channels that today are the most effective means of reaching the broad Arab public. Instead of just criticizing al Jazeera and other channels we should make use of their programs to get our message across.

Fourth, the State Department could more efficiently support public diplomacy by recognizing public diplomacy as an important specialty. That should attract the best and the brightest young officers. PAOs in the Arab world find that since the State–USIA merger they are regularly distracted with tasks unrelated to their primary function. Also, the public diplomacy officers at the State Department in Washington, who support the PAOs, have been submerged under layers of bureaucracy that hamper efficiency. This did not exist under USIA.[2] State should become more streamlined, nimble, and responsive to the needs of PAOs at our embassies abroad.

Fifth, all of these measures require a strong cadre of officers devoted to the tasks of public diplomacy: people who have the special skills required: cultural sensitivity, empathy, languages, plus the ability to listen as well as communicate effectively across cultures. Ed Murrow's dictum about "the last three feet" is still valid, despite the advances in communication technology that have taken place since he said it. If we focus on supporting the public diplomacy professionals who do this job 24/7 on the "front lines" in the Arab world, expand their numbers, and give them the resources they need to carry it out, we will improve our effectiveness. This will help dispel the malaise that is currently plaguing Arab–American relations and harming our national interests.

Table 9: The Public Diplomacy Budget and Staff, 2000–2006 (budget in $millions)

|            | PD programs | Exchanges | Total PD budget | PD staff total |
|------------|-------------|-----------|-----------------|----------------|
| FY 00      | 234         | 204       | 484             | 2,843          |
| FY 01      | 246         | 232       | 529             | 2,861          |
| FY 02      | 280         | 280       | 585             | 2,930          |
| FY 03      | 299         | 299       | 611             | 3,954          |
| FY 04      | 300         | 300       | 682             | 3,002          |
| FY 05 est. | 316         | 316       | 761             | 3,002          |
| FY 06 req. | 328         | 328       | 862             | 3,008          |

Finally, these measures require more financial resources. When the Cold War ended, public diplomacy funding was cut, staffing and programs were significantly reduced, facilities abroad were closed, and the United States was left with a severely weakened ability to cope with the problems that arose after 9/11. There have been modest increases in funding since 9/11 (see Table 9),[3] but these have not reflected the sense of urgency that the issue deserves. Current funding remains woefully inadequate for the present situation. It is equivalent to approximately 0.4 percent of our military budget, and half of that is for broadcasting. Funding should be substantially increased.

In short, although public diplomacy is not a panacea for all of our present problems, it is a potentially valuable asset that has been underutilized and should be reinvigorated to deal with the problems we face in the twenty-first century. Soft power has been neglected for too long.

# Notes

**PREFACE**

1. Zogby International, *Impressions of America 2004*, 3.
2. Samuel P. Huntington, "The Clash of Civilizations?" *Foreign Affairs* 72, no. 3 (summer 1993): 22–49.
3. Polls reported by James J. Zogby, *What Arabs Think* (Washington, DC: Zogby International, 2002); and Shibley Telhami, *The Stakes* (Boulder, CO: Westview, 2002), 46–49.
4. U.S. Government Accountability Office, *U.S. Public Diplomacy: Interagency Coordination Efforts Hampered by the Lack of a National Communication Strategy*, Report GAO-05-323 (Washington, DC, April 2005), 1.
5. Joseph S. Nye Jr., *Soft Power: The Means to Success in World Politics* (New York: Public Affairs Press, 2004), especially 99–125; and *The Paradox of American Power* (New York: Oxford University Press, 2002), 8–10, 73, 141–143.


**INTRODUCTION**

1. The examples are from interviews and oral histories (further identified below) with the people named, unless otherwise indicated.
2. Barry Ballow, "Academic and Professional Exchanges in the Islamic World: An Undervalued Tool," in William A. Rugh, ed., *Engaging the Arab and Islamic Worlds through Public Diplomacy* (Washington, DC: Public Diplomacy Council, 2004), 119.
3. James Halsema, oral history interview, in the oral history project of the Association for Diplomatic Studies and Training, Washington, DC (in subsequent footnotes, "oral history interview" refers to this collection).

4. Alan Heil, "A History of VOA Arabic: A Half-Century of Service to the Nation and to the Arab World," in W. A. Rugh, ed., *Engaging the Arab and Islamic Worlds through Public Diplomacy* (Washington, DC: Public Diplomacy Council, 2004), 59–60.

5. Nye, *Soft Power.*

6. U.S. Government Accountability Office, Report GAO-05-323, 4.

7. Retired diplomat Edmund Gullion, Dean of Tufts Fletcher School of Law and Diplomacy, first used the term in the 1960s.

8. Wilson P. Dizard Jr., *Inventing Public Diplomacy: The Story of the U.S. Information Agency* (Boulder, CO: Lynne Rienner, 2004), 98–99.

9. Murrow statement in congressional testimony in 1953, quoted in Allen C. Hansen, *USIA: Public Diplomacy in the Computer Age* (Westport, CT: Praeger, 1989), 2.

10. Kenton Keith, "The Last Three Feet: Making the Personal Connection," in Rugh, *Engaging,* 12.

**CHAPTER 1**

1. Some professionals prefer one or the other side of the program. Interview with Richard Curtiss, April 2005.

2. Howard Cincotta, "Wireless File to Web: State Department's Print and Electronic Media in the Arab World," in W. A. Rugh, ed., *Engaging the Arab and Islamic Worlds through Public Diplomacy* (Washington, DC: Public Diplomacy Council, 2004), 141.

3. Barry Fulton, "The Uses of Modern Technology in Public Diplomacy," in Rugh, *Engaging,* 30.

4. Cincotta, 142–143; the embassy Web sites are not, however, linked to the main State Department Web site, http://state.gov, because of the Smith-Mundt Act of 1948 that prohibits dissemination of information intended for foreign audiences within the United States.

5. Ibid., 148–150.

6. Ibid., 146–147.

7. Ibid., 147–148.

8. In 1945, VOA was cut from 43 to 20 language services and from 167 hours per week to 46; Alan Heil, "A History of VOA Arabic," in Rugh, *Engaging,* 50–52; also see Allen C. Hansen, *USIA: Public Diplomacy in the Computer Age* (Westport, CT: Praeger, 1989), 117.

9. Quoted in Hansen, 122–123. The VOA Charter was promulgated in PL 94-350, signed July 12, 1976, by President Gerald R. Ford.

10. Interview with David Newton, Washington, DC, March 2005; and see http://www.refrl.org, and the 1973 International Broadcasting Act, quoted in Hansen, 17.

11. Hansen, 110.

12. Marc Lynch, "America and the Arab Media Environment," in Rugh, *Engaging,* 100–108.

13. Barry Ballow, "Academic and Professional Changes in the Islamic World," in Rugh, *Engaging,* 112.

14. Information from Barry Ballow.

15. Communication from Barry Ballow.

16. Zogby International, *Impressions of America 2004*, 14.

17. Hans N. Tuch, *Communicating with the World* (New York: St. Martin's Press, 1990), 75.

18. Fulbright statement published in March 1967, in USIA/IPS Byliner F-67-73, quoted in Tuch, 75.

19. Hansen, 152–153.

20. Ballow, in Rugh, *Engaging*, 112.

21. See, for example, James Bullock, "The Role of the Embassy Public Affairs Officer After 9/11," in Rugh, *Engaging*, 44.

22. Cincotta, 145–146.

23. Report of the Advisory Commission on Public Diplomacy for the Muslim World, Edward P. Djerejian, Chair, *Changing Minds, Winning Peace: A New Strategic Direction for U.S. Public Diplomacy in the Arab World* (Washington, DC: 2003), 40.

24. Cincotta, 145.

25. Hansen, 146.

26. Wilson P. Dizard Jr., *Inventing Public Diplomacy* (Boulder, CO: Lynne Rienner, 2004), 5.

27. Djerejian, 66.

## CHAPTER 2

1. Rashid Khalidi, *Resurrecting Empire: Western Footprints and America's Perilous Path in the Middle East* (Boston: Beacon Press, 2004), 120–121, 154.

2. See Khalidi, 9–34 for details.

3. Wilson P. Dizard Jr., *Inventing Public Diplomacy* (Boulder, CO: Lynne Rienner, 2004), 26.

4. Alan Heil, "A History of VOA Arabic," in W. A. Rugh, ed., *Engaging the Islamic Worlds* (Washington, DC: Public Diplomacy Council, 2004), 50–51; and Dizard, 23–25.

5. Heil, 51; Keith Adamson oral history interview; and Dizard, 37–40.

6. Public Law 584, 79th Congress (chapter 723, 2nd session) S.1636, cited in Hans N. Tuch, *Communicating with the World* (New York: St. Martin's Press, 1990), 17–18.

7. President Truman's campaign of truth speech, at a luncheon of the American Society of Newspaper Editors, April 20, 1950, Public Papers of the Presidents—Harry S Truman 1950, 260–264, quoted in Tuch, 15.

8. Beaudry oral history interview, in the collection of the Association for Diplomatic History and Training, Washington, DC (oral history interviews cited below are all from this collection).

9. Information from USIA files, in the State Department historical office.

10. Information from State Department archives. During the Eisenhower administration, U.S. embassies opened in Morocco and Sudan in 1956, and an information center opened in Sudan in 1957; in Lebanon, information centers opened in Ashrafia and Basta in 1957 and in Nasra in 1959.

11. Dizard, 158, citing Lee Dinsmore, "Communications: Kirkuk," *Foreign Service Journal* (January 1994): 60.

12. Adamson oral history interview.
13. State Department archives.
14. Heil, 51.

**CHAPTER 3**

1. Wilson P. Dizard Jr., *Inventing Public Diplomacy* (Boulder, CO: Lynne Rienner, 2004), 54–55.
2. Ibid., 55.
3. Hans N. Tuch, *Communicating with the World* (New York: St. Martin's Press, 1990), 18–20.
4. Dizard, 76–77.
5. 1953 Mission Statement for USIA, quoted in Allen C. Hansen, *USIA* (Westport, CT: Praeger, 1989), 25.
6. William A. Rugh, *Arab Mass Media* (Westport, CT: Praeger, 2004).
7. Dizard, 56–58, 180.
8. Sorensen oral history interview.
9. Lincoln oral history interview.
10. State Department archives.
11. Lincoln oral history interview.
12. Sabbagh oral history interview.
13. Ibid.
14. Ibid.
15. Undeland and Sorenson oral history interviews.
16. Weathersby oral history interview.
17. Sorensen oral history interview.
18. State Department archives.
19. Viets oral history interview.
20. Alan Heil, "A History of VOA Arabic," in W. A. Rugh, ed., *Engaging the Arab and Islamic Worlds* (Washington, DC: Public Diplomacy Council, 2004), 53.
21. Interview with a former broadcasting professional.
22. Stephen Paterson (Pat) Belcher, oral history interview.
23. Sorensen oral history interview.
24. Undeland oral history interview.
25. Nalle oral history interview.
26. Undeland oral history interview.
27. Undeland oral history interview, and State Department archives.
28. *The Eisenhower Doctrine*: The March 5, 1957 joint resolution of the U.S. House and Senate stated: "The United States regards as vital to the national interest and world peace the preservation of the independence and integrity of the nations of the Middle East. To this end, if the President determines the necessity thereof, the United States is prepared to use armed forces to assist any such nation or group of such nations requesting assistance against armed aggression from any country controlled by international communism."
29. Thomas C. Sorensen, *The Word War* (New York: Harper and Row, 1968), 109–110.
30. Undeland oral history interview.
31. Lincoln oral history interview.

32. Malcolm Kerr coined this term and used it as the title of his landmark study of the Arab world.

33. State Department archives.

## CHAPTER 4

1. Statement by Edward R. Murrow in 1953, in hearings before the Subcommittee on International Organizations and Movements of the House Committee on Foreign Affairs, chaired by Rep. Dante Fascell (D-Fla.), quoted in Allen C. Hansen, *USIA* (Westport, CT: Praegar, 1989), 9.

2. Thomas C. Sorensen, *The Word War* (New York: Harper and Row, 1968), 134.

3. Sorensen, *The Word War*, 122; Sorensen was given the post partly because his brother Ted was Kennedy's senior policy advisor; Sorensen oral history interview.

4. President Kennedy's memorandum of January 25, 1963, to the director of USIA, Hansen, 10–11, 27.

5. Sorensen oral history interview; and Hansen, 27.

6. Sorensen, *The Word War*, 144–145.

7. Quoted in Hansen, 26.

8. Sorensen, *The Word War*, 180–181.

9. Communication from Marshall Berg.

10. Ibid.

11. Halsema oral history interview.

12. Personal communication.

13. Undeland oral history interview.

14. Ibid.

15. Ibid.

16. Undeland oral history interview; the Tunisians were also less hostile because Bourguiba was more moderate and not an acolyte of Nasser.

17. Undeland oral history interview.

18. Sorensen, *The Word War*, 168.

19. Undeland oral history interview.

20. Nalle oral history interview.

21. I was director of the Jidda Center, 1966–1967.

22. Robert Bauer oral history interview, printed copy at Georgetown University Library, 62–64.

23. Nalle oral history interview.

24. Interview with Boulos Malik.

25. Undeland oral history interview.

26. USIA archives at the State Department.

27. Ibid.

28. Robert Bauer oral history interview, printed copy at Georgetown University Library, 68–70.

29. The collection was so large that it went overland in a 16-wheeled trailer truck, and in order to avoid a Kuwait customs inspection it was sent as diplomatic cargo, and the PAO had the entire truck wrapped in canvas, with dozens of wax seals, to resemble a huge diplomatic pouch; Undeland oral history interview.

30. State Department archives.

31. Interview with Boulos Malik.

32. State Department archives.

33. Ibid.

34. Undeland oral history interview, and State Department archives.

35. Weathersby oral history interview.

36. Royer later managed the large English-language program in Tehran until 1979 when he was held hostage for 444 days along with other embassy officials.

## CHAPTER 5

1. Weathersby and Nalle oral history interviews.

2. Wilson P. Dizard Jr., *Inventing Public Diplomacy* (Boulder, CO: Lynne Rienner, 2004), 113.

3. Only ambassador Brown was able to leave the embassy, and he did so in a heavily guarded Jordanian APC. Undeland oral history interview, and State Department's archives.

4. Undeland arrived in Amman 9/26/70 and stayed until 1974; Undeland oral history interview.

5. Undeland oral history interview.

6. Between then and June 1974, the United States provided unprecedented assistance to Israel, and since 1973, Israel has become America's largest aid recipient.

7. Undeland oral history interview.

8. Ibid.

9. Interview with Boulos Malik.

10. Kenton Keith interview, Washington, DC, 4/8/2005.

11. Ibid.

12. Report of the post's inspection of February–March 1979, State Department archives.

13. Howard Simpson oral history interview.

14. Undeland oral history interview.

15. Interview with an official who was involved.

16. Thurber oral history interview.

## CHAPTER 6

1. Quoted in Allen C. Hansen, *USIA* (Westport, CT: Praeger, 1989), 11, 29–30.

2. Alan Heil, "A History of VOA Arabic," in W. A. Rugh, ed., *Engaging the Arab and Islamic Worlds* (Washington, DC: Public Diplomacy Council, 2004), 55–56.

3. Communication from Lea Perez.

4. Undeland oral history interview.

5. Ibid.

6. Ibid.

7. Algiers Field Message #6, 7/26/78; Algiers Country Plan for Fiscal Year 1980–81; and PAO cable # 0299 of 1/27/80, in State Department archives.

8. Interview with John Kincannon, Washington, DC, 3/18/05.

9. Bahrain Field Message #6, 10/1/77; and Bahrain Country Plan for Fiscal Year 1979–80, May 1978, in State Department archives.

10. By January 1980 there were twenty-five U.S. Navy ships, including three carrier groups, in the Indian Ocean.

## CHAPTER 7

1. Quoted in Allen C. Hansen, *USIA* (Westport, CT: Praeger, 1989), 9.

2. Fact sheet issued by USIA's Office of Public Liaison stated USIA's mission, quoted in Hansen, 32.

3. In the period from 1949 to 1985 the United States provided $28.1 billion ($14.6 billion in grants), and between 1979 and 1983 the average was $2.7 billion/year; and after 1986 it was $3 billion/year.

4. Undeland oral history interview.

5. Interview with Jim Bullock, Cairo, February 2005.

6. In February 1983 the Israeli Kahan Commission found Sharon responsible.

7. Undeland oral history interview; he was PAO in Damascus, 1979–1983.

8. Undeland oral history interview.

9. Interview with Martin Quinn, Washington, DC, 3/18/05.

10. Undeland oral history interview; he was PAO in Cairo, 1985–1988.

11. Keith interview.

12. Interview with Marcelle Wahba, Washington, DC, 3/23/05.

13. Undeland oral history interview.

14. Bullock interview and information provided by Peter Kovach.

15. Communication from Barry Ballow.

16. Interview with Boulos Malik.

17. Interview with Duncan MacInnes, Washington, DC, 3/29/05.

18. Information provided by Peter Kovach.

19. State Department, *Current Documents*, 1981, #405.

20. State Department, *Current Documents*, 1987, #262, 5/29/87, quoting Reagan statement of May 1987.

21. Newton and Bullock interviews.

22. Ibid.

23. Communication from Jack McCreary, 4/29/05.

24. Interview with John Berry, Cairo, February 2005.

25. Berry interview.

26. Information provided by Peter Kovach.

27. Interview with Alberto Fernandez, Washington, DC, 3/18/05.

## CHAPTER 8

1. *New York Times* (March 30, 1990), A31; and (September 10, 1990), A23; and FBIS-NES-90–074 (April 17, 1990).

2. I visited this Center on March 31, 1990, and had the same experience trying to converse with Iraqi students.

3. Berry interview.

4. Ibid.

5. For examples of Iraqi propaganda, see USIA Fact Sheet, 2/4/1991 (http://intellit.muskingum.edu/othercountries_folder/iraq_dis.htm); and "Apparatus of Lies" (http://www.whitehouse.gov/ogc/apparatus).

6. Ambassadors Chas. Freeman in Riyadh, Frank Wisner in Cairo, and Chris Ross in Algiers were authorized for this task.

7. Alan Heil, "A History of VOA Arabic," in W. A. Rugh, ed., *Engaging the Arab and Islamic Worlds* (Washington, DC: Public Diplomacy Council, 2004), 59.

8. Ibid., 60–63.

9. Interview with U.S. officials and personal observation.

10. Ibid.

11. MacInnes interview.

12. Interview with Elizabeth Thornhill, Cairo, February 2005.

13. Undeland oral history interview.

14. Berry interview.

15. President Bush television address to the nation, February 27, 1991.

16. George H. W. Bush and Brent Scowcroft, *A World Transformed* (New York: Alfred A. Knopf, 1998), 489.

17. Bush and Scowcroft, 311, exonerated April Glaspie.

18. Bush also sought to persuade Israel to end its building of settlements in the occupied territories by holding up American assistance, but Congress strongly protested and the effort did not last.

**CHAPTER 9**

1. Namely: Saudi Arabia, Kuwait, Bahrain, Qatar, the United Arab Emirates, and Oman.

2. William A. Rugh, *Arab Mass Media* (Westport, CT: Praeger, 2004).

3. Communication from Evelyn A. Early.

4. Bullock interview.

5. Ibid.

6. Interview with a U.S. official, February 2005.

7. The UAE's dispute over the three islands, Abu Musa and the Tumbs, went back to 1971, but heated up in 1992 when Iran sought to assert total control over Abu Musa.

8. Interview with U.S. official, April 2005.

9. Fernandez interview.

10. Communication from Lea Perez.

11. The institutions that USIS helped build, such as the journalists centers, were smashed by the Israelis when they entered the West Bank in the spring of 2002; MacInnes interview.

12. MacInnes interview.

13. Quinn interview.

14. Ibid.

15. Interview with Marcelle Wahba, Washington, DC, 3/23/05.

16. Information provided by Peter Kovach.

17. Keith interview.

18. Quinn and MacInnes interviews.

19. Private communication from an official.

20. Wahba interview.

21. Ibid.

22. Ibid.

23. Interview with Adam Ereli, April 2005.

24. Interview with a U.S. official; see *Christian Science Monitor* article by James Brandon, 2/4/05.

25. Interview with U.S. official.

26. Haynes Mahoney communications, 4/18/05.

27. In November 1999, Afghan Air flights were banned and Taliban foreign assets were frozen; additional sanctions were imposed on Afghanistan as a result of UN Security Council Resolutions 1267 of January 2000 and 1333 of December 2000.

28. Ereli interview.

29. Keith interview.

30. Interviews with numerous public diplomacy professionals.

31. Interviews with experienced FSOs.

32. Interviews with experienced FSOs; and James Bullock, "The Role of the Embassy Public Affairs Officer," in W. A. Rugh, ed., *Engaging the Arab and Islamic Worlds* (Washington, DC: Public Diplomacy Council, 2004), 40–47.

33. Newton interview.

## CHAPTER 10

1. AMIDEAST and the Anwar Sadat Chair for Peace and Development, University of Maryland, *Colloquium on U.S.–Arab relations: an American-Arab Student Dialogue*, Amy Pate, ed. (Washington, DC, 2002), 2.

2. For example, many highly educated Arabs from different countries who gathered at the University of Maryland for a colloquium in October 2001, expressed doubt that Osama was behind 9/11; ibid., 22.

3. UN Security Council Resolutions 1368 and 1373 of September and October 2001, sponsored by the United States, included these demands.

4. Wilson P. Dizard Jr., *Inventing Public Diplomacy* (Boulder, CO: Lynne Rienner, 2004), 221.

5. Ibid., 139.

6. Keith interview.

7. William A. Rugh, *Arab Mass Media* (Westport, CT: Praeger, 2004), 233–234.

8. President's speech to a joint session of Congress, 9/20/2001.

9. Address to the nation, 11/8/01, and state of the union address, 1/29/02.

10. Zogby International, *Impressions of America 2004*, 4.

11. The Pew Research Center for the People and the Press, *A Year After Iraq War, Mistrust of America in Europe Ever, Muslim Anger Persists*, http://people. press.org/reports/pdf/206.pdf; Zogby International, *Impressions of America 2004*, 4.

12. Shibley Telhami, *The Stakes* (Boulder, CO: Westview, 2002), 98–99.

13. Zogby International, *Impressions of America 2004*, 4.

14. The road map text is available at http://state.gov; for a critique of its ap-

proach, see Robert Malley and Hussein Agha, "The Last Negotiation," *Foreign Affairs* (May/June 2002).

15. Information made available confidentially to the author.

16. White House press release, 9/19/01, www.whitehouse.gov/releases.

17. State of the Union address, 1/29/02.

18. The bombing of a facility in Khobar, eastern Saudi Arabia in June 1996, left nineteen American airmen dead, and the bombing of the USS Cole in Yemen's Aden Harbor in October 2000, left seventeen American sailors dead, but Washington was not satisfied with either investigation.

19. James J. Zogby, *What Arabs Think* (Washington, DC: Zogby International, 2002), 61, 64.

20. Dizard, 220.

21. Ambassador Christopher Ross interview, Washington, DC, 4/13/05.

22. Dizard, 221.

23. For details on *Hi*, see Howard Cincotta, "From Wireless File to Web," in W. A. Rugh, ed., *Engaging the Arab and Islamic Worlds* (Washington, DC: Public Diplomacy Council, 2004), 148–150.

24. Dizard, 223–224.

25. Barry Ballow, "Academic and Professional Exchanges," in Rugh, *Engaging*, 114–117.

26. Ibid., 118.

27. Dizard, 223–225; see also Heil, in Rugh, *Engaging*.

28. Anthony H. Cordesman, "The Strategic Meaning of U.S. Intervention in Iraq: Four Wars and Counting," *CSIS Report*, 12/1/03, 2.

29. Heil, in Rugh, *Engaging*; see also Marc Lynch, "America and the Arab Media Environment," in Rugh, *Engaging*, 68, 90–108.

30. Newton interview.

31. Fernandez interview.

32. Interview with Katherine Van de Vate, May 2005.

33. Communication from Jack McCreary.

34. Ereli interview.

## CHAPTER 11

1. Speech at the West Point graduation, 6/1/02.

2. Address to the UN, 9/12/02.

3. "The National Security Strategy of the United States of America," http://whitehouse.gov/nscnss.html.

4. Radio address, 10/5/02.

5. Comment by a UAE official to the author, Abu Dhabi, January 2003.

6. MacInnes interview; pamphlets included "Duty to the Future," "Iraq's Voices for Freedom," "Iraq: A Population Silenced," "Iraq from Fear to Freedom," and "Iraq Liberated"; see http://www.usinfo.state.gov.

7. State of the Union, 1/28/03.

8. Press conference, 3/6/03.

9. Shibley Telhami, "Arab Public Opinion on the United States and Iraq," *The Brookings Review* 72, no. 3 (Summer 2003): 24–27.

10. Speech, 3/17/03.

11. Information from a participant.

12. For further analysis of Iraq during occupation, see William A. Rugh, "How Washington Confronts Arab Media," *Global Media Journal* 3, no. 5 (Fall 2004).

13. Interview with U.S. official.

14. Ibid.

15. *Washington Post*, 4/11/04, A-1, B-1.

16. Anne Alexander, MEIonline, 2/6/04; *The Economist*, 12/11/03; Katrin Dauenhauer and Jim Lobe, *Inter-Press Services*, 8/13/2003; Sabrina Tavernise in the *New York Times*, 4/29/04.

17. Stephen Schwartz, *Tech Central Station*, 5/3/04 (www.techcentralstation.com); and Nicholas Pelham in *Financial Times*, 5/4/04.

18. Dr. Hamida Smaysam, quoted in the *Los Angeles Times*, 4/27/04.

19. Catherine A. Fitzpatrick, Radio Free Europe/Radio Liberty, report 3/29/04 (www.rferl.org.reports).

20. Interview with a U.S. official.

21. Ibid.

22. Ross interview.

23. Interview with Ambassador Christopher Ross and others.

24. Christopher Marquis, *New York Times*, 4/29/04; Jim Krane, *Capital Hill Blue*, 4/5/04; and Mark Schapiro, Stratcom officer, lecture at the University of Maryland, 3/8/04.

25. Max Boot, in the *Los Angeles Times*, 4/27/04.

26. Interview with a U.S. official.

27. Edmund Sanders, *Los Angeles Times*, 3/25/04; Alistair Lyon, *Reuters*, 3/27/04; and interview with a U.S. official.

28. Interview with a U.S. official.

29. *New York Times*, 3/29/04, *Federal News Service*, 3/30/04.

30. www.juancole.org.

31. Interview with a U.S. official.

32. Barry Ballow, "Academic and Professional Exchanges," in W. A. Rugh, ed., *Engaging the Arab and Islamic Worlds* (Washington, DC: Public Diplomacy Council, 2004), 119.

33. Ross interview.

34. Interviews with U.S. officials.

35. Personal communication.

36. Berry interview.

37. Interview with a U.S. Arabic-speaking official who served in Iraq during the occupation.

38. Newton interview.

39. Ibid.

40. See Norman J. Pattiz, "Radio Sawa and al Hurra TV: Opening Channels of Mass Communication in the Middle East," and Marc Lynch, "America and the Arab Media Environment," in Rugh, *Engaging*, 69–108; plus testimony by William A. Rugh, Shibley Telhami, and Edmund Ghareeb before the Senate Foreign Relations Committee on 4/29/04.

41. Ross interview, Washington, DC.

42. Lynch, 95–98, 102–104.

43. Paul Richter in *Los Angeles Times*, 4/28/04, and Rowan Scarborough in the *Washington Times*, 4/28/04.

44. *Daily Telegraph*, 3/4/04; *The Guardian*, 4/21/04 and 4/23/04; *Washington Post*, Talabani oped, 12/4/03.

45. Center for Strategic Studies, University of Jordan, "Revisiting the Arab Street: Research from Within," February 2005 (http://www.css-jordan.org), 65.

46. Ibid.

47. The Pew Research Center for the People and the Press, *A Year After Iraq War, Mistrust of America in Europe Ever, Muslim Anger Persists*, http://people.press.org/reports/pdf/206.pdf.

48. *Washington Post*, 5/13/05, A-18.

49. Center for Strategic Studies, "Revisiting the Arab Street," 2005, 70.

50. Zogby International, *Impressions of America 2004*, 3, 8.

51. State/NEA unclassified paper, "(7/2/04) PD Anecdotes."

## CHAPTER 12

1. Press conference, 3/6/03.

2. Speech at the Washington Hilton, 2/26/03.

3. Speech at the National Endowment for Democracy, 11/6/03.

4. Personal communication.

5. *Washington Post*, 3/9/05, reporting Bush speech of 3/8/05 at the National Defense University.

6. Arab summit declaration, Tunis, 5/23/04 (www.arabsummit.tn/en/summit.htm).

7. Saad al Din Ibrahim, for example, made this point.

8. The Pew Research Center for the People and the Press, *A Year After Iraq War, Mistrust of America in Europe Ever, Muslim Anger Persists*, http://people.press.org/reports/pdf/206.pdf.

9. *Washington Post*, 3/29/05.

10. Zogby International, *Impressions of America 2004*, 3.

11. Information from a U.S. official.

12. Zogby International, *Impressions of America 2004*, 2, 5, 7.

13. Ibid., 3.

14. Center for Strategic Studies, University of Jordan, "Revisiting the Arab Street," 2005, 5, 61, 67, 69.

15. Information from a U.S. official.

16. The Pew Research Center for the People and the Press, *A Year After Iraq War*; Zogby International, *Impressions of America 2004*, 4.

17. Complete references to these reports are in the bibliography.

18. U.S. Government Accountability Office, *U.S. Public Diplomacy: Interagency Coordination Efforts Hampered by the Lack of a National Communication Strategy*," Report GAO-05-323, Washington, DC, April 2005, 16.

19. *Washington Post*, 4/18/05, 2.

20. State/NEA unclassified paper, "(7/2/04) PD Anecdotes."

21. Berry interview.

22. State/NEA unclassified paper, "(7/2/04) PD Anecdotes."

23. Ibid.

24. Ibid.

25. Information from State/NEA/PD.

26. Ibid.

27. State/NEA unclassified paper, "(7/2/04) PD Anecdotes."

28. Wahba interview.

29. Bullock interview.

30. Thornhill interview.

31. Communication from Barry Ballow.

32. State/NEA unclassified paper, "(7/2/04) PD Anecdotes."

33. Information from the State Department's Education and Culture Bureau (State/ECA).

34. State/ECA memo.

35. State/ECA memo, "Current Citizen Exchanges Grants in NEA 2/8/05."

36. Ibid.

37. State/ECA memo, dated 2/24/04.

## CHAPTER 13

1. See Cresencio Arcos, "Reasonable and Proportional Security Measures in International Academic Exchange Programs," in W. A. Rugh, ed., *Engaging the Arab and Islamic Worlds* (Washington, DC: Public Diplomacy Council, 2004).

2. James Bullock, in Rugh, *Engaging*; and conversations with a number of FSOs.

3. The "PD programs" line includes regional bureaus, the International Information Programs Bureau, and the functional bureaus at State, plus budgets for PAOs in the field. The "exchanges" line includes the budget for the Education and Culture Bureau at State. (Figures courtesy of Stan Silverman, former USIA Comptroller.)

# Selected Bibliography

Advisory Commission on Public Diplomacy for the Muslim World, Edward P. Djere-
    jian, Chair. *Changing Minds, Winning Peace: A New Strategic Direction for
    the U.S. Public Diplomacy in the Arab World.* Report submitted to the U.S.
    House Appropriations Committee. Washington, DC, October 2003.
Amr, Hady. *The Need to Communicate: How to Improve U.S. Public Diplomacy
    with the Arab World.* Washington, DC: Brookings Institution, January 2004.
Center for the Study of the Presidency. *Strengthening U.S.–Muslim Communica-
    tions.* Washington, DC, April 2003.
Council on Foreign Relations. *Public Diplomacy: Strategy for Reform.* New York,
    2002.
———. *Finding America's Voice: A Strategy for Reinvigorating U.S. Public Diplo-
    macy.* New York, 2003.
Dizard, Wilson P., Jr. *Inventing Public Diplomacy: The Story of the U.S. Informa-
    tion Agency.* Boulder, CO: Lynne Rienner, 2004.
Hansen, Allen C. *USIA: Public Diplomacy in the Computer Age.* Westport, CT:
    Praeger, 1989.
Heritage Foundation. *How to Reinvigorate U.S. Public Diplomacy.* Washington,
    DC, April 2003.
———. *Reclaiming America's Voice Overseas.* Washington, DC, May 2003.
Nye, Joseph S., Jr. *The Paradox of American Power: Why the World's Only Su-
    perpower Can't Go It Alone.* New York: Oxford University Press, 2002.
———. *Soft Power: The Means to Success in World Politics.* New York: Public
    Affairs Press, 2004.
Public Diplomacy Council. *A Call for Action on Public Diplomacy.* Washington,
    DC, 2005.

Rugh, William A. *Arab Mass Media*. Westport, CT: Praeger, 2004.

Rugh, William A., ed. *Engaging the Arab and Islamic Worlds through Public Diplomacy*. Washington, DC: Public Diplomacy Council, 2004.

Sorensen, Thomas C. *The Word War: The Story of American Propaganda*. New York: Harper and Row, 1968.

Telhami, Shibley. *The Stakes: America and the Middle East*. Boulder, CO: Westview, 2002.

Tuch, Hans N. *Communicating with the World: U.S. Public Diplomacy Overseas*. New York: St. Martin's Press, 1990.

U.S. Advisory Commission on Public Diplomacy. *Rebuilding Public Diplomacy through a Reformed Structure and Additional Resources*. Washington, DC, 2002.

U.S. Government Accountability Office. *U.S. Public Diplomacy: State Department Expands Efforts but Faces Significant Challenges*. Report to the House of Representatives, September 2003.

———. *U.S. Public Diplomacy: Interagency Coordination Efforts Hampered by the Lack of National Communication Strategy*. Report GAO-05-323. Washington, DC, April 2005.

U.S. Government, Office of the Secretary of Defense. *Report of the Defense Science Board Task Force on Managed Information Dissemination*. Washington, DC, October 2001.

———. Defense Science Board. *Report of the Task Force on Strategic Communication*. Washington, DC, September 2004.

Zogby International. *Impressions of America 2004*.

Zogby, James J. *What Arabs Think*. Washington, DC: Zogby International, 2002.

# Index

## About the Author

WILLIAM A. RUGH was a career Foreign Service officer with the U.S. Information Agency (1964–1995). He served as U.S. ambasssador to Yemen and to the United Arab Emirates. He is the author of *Arab Mass Media* (Praeger, 2004) and the editor of *Engaging the Arab and Islamic Worlds through Public Diplomacy* (Public Diplomacy Council, 2004). He is a Trustee of the American University in Cairo, a Board Member and past President of AMIDEAST, an Associate of Georgetown's Institute for the Study of Diplomacy, an Adjunct Scholar of the Middle East Institute, and an Executive Committee member of the Public Diplomacy Council.